D1199120

CONCISE
NAMES OF
CHRIST

CONCISE
names of
CHRIST

JAMES **LARGE**

CONCISE NAMES OF CHRIST
Copyright © 2009 by AMG Publishers
Published by AMG Publishers
6815 Shallowford Road
Chattanooga, TN 37421

All Rights Reserved.

Originally published by Hodder & Stoughton in 1888.
Previously published by AMG as *Two Hundred and Eighty Titles and Symbols of Christ.*

ISBN 13: 978-0-89957-641-1
ISBN 10: 0-89957-641-9

First printing—January 2009

Cover designed by Bright Boy Design, Chattanooga, Tennessee
Interior design and typesetting by Warren Baker
Edited and proofread by Christine St. Jacques and Warren Baker

Printed in Canada
14 13 12 11 10 09 –T– 8 7 6 5 4 3 2 1

Contents

Foreword

Concise Names of Christ is an exceptional collection and exposition of thoughtfully selected types and symbols of Jesus Christ. In this comprehensive analysis, which was originally published in 1888 by Hodder and Stoughton in London, James Large gives concise yet thorough explanations of approximately 283 titles and symbols of our Lord found throughout Scripture.

In producing *Concise Names of Christ*, we at AMG Publishers have made some minor changes to the original work to help make its content more clear to modern readers: We have updated some archaic terms, and we have updated spelling in accordance with how our language has changed over the years; in some cases, unusual forms of punctuation have been simplified to eliminate confusion. Apart from these minor modifications, however, we have remained true to Large's original work in every way.

Additionally, readers should note that the points of current history mentioned by Large are from the latter half of the nineteenth century.

Preface

PERHAPS it is too much to expect that no critical eye will scan the following pages, and therefore the writer may be excused for offering a few words in explanation of his purpose and his plan. As to the latter, its alphabetical character may be open to objection; yet the writer deems it the best he could have adopted for his purpose. Although a theological or topical arrangement might seem at first sight, to have much to recommend it, practically it would be found to bring with it more disadvantages. While a haphazard or casual arrangement, (if such a thing can be), would be worse still.

Then, as to the List of Subjects the author does not regard his summary as a perfect enumeration, however carefully he has endeavored to render it so. But it scarcely admits of a doubt, that if one were to select any dozen Bible students, and ask them to prepare from the sacred pages a catalog of Titles and Symbols of our Lord, no two of them would arrive at precisely the same results. On this point, therefore, perhaps the writer may reasonably expect the indulgence of his readers. If he has collated too many, such as are deemed unwarranted can be rejected; if he has unwittingly omitted any, the fault may be as easily remedied. It will be seen that while some of the subjects are more fully elucidated, others are merely touched upon. This became necessary in order to avoid undue repetition and extension; but the Titles and Similitudes, thus cursorily noticed, are more fully explained under some analogous head.

It will be obvious that the book is not written for persons of great reading and education; but that it has an aspect rather towards another class. In preparing these pages, he has endeavored to imagine himself with a senior Sunday-school Bible class; or with such a gathering as is usual at a mothers' meeting, or town missionary's cottage service. Or, again, he has supposed himself addressing such an assemblage as very often constitutes a household. Indeed it was with an eye to this last that he fixed on that part of the title—"A Year's Sunday Readings."

Suppose then a household gathered together on a Sabbath evening for the purpose of holding a domestic service. There would be the children, elder and younger. These demand, if the subject be not wholly appropriated to them, that, at least, they should not be repelled by what is altogether above their comprehension. They should rather be attracted by an admixture of what is entertaining and pictorial. There are the servants, who have been indulged with but few advantages of education, and possess but little time for reading. These require something, which, while it is instinctive, shall be both simple and direct. Then there are also the two or three older persons at the head of the family—the parent, the grandmother, the aunt; who, for the sake of the rest, will not resent an occasional excess of the colloquial and the familiar.

Without professing to divide a portion equally to each of these, the author has endeavored so to write, that the younger ones should not have to complain that the reading is heavy and dry, nor the elder ones that, with its lessons and inferences, it is too trivial to benefit them. In exploring such subjects, there may be found many a shallow place through which the young and tender may be led, where "the water is to the ankles." But there must be also, in the nature of the case, many a deeper plunge—"waters to swim in, a river that cannot be passed over."

Having done his best in following out the plan selected, the writer must commit his work to that special Providence which extends to books as well as to their writers and readers, with the prayer, that if not very extensively appropriated to the purposes indicated, it may be made useful wherever it has an errand. In the days wherein the Person, Mission, and character of our Lord—and it may be added, more particularly His Atonement—are very irreverently, not to say profanely handled by many, he trusts this contribution of "Sunday Readings" on the great subject, may inform some, fortify others, and benefit all who become acquainted with its contents.

Part of the work was published several years ago, in a somewhat different form and under a different title, and has been through two editions. And part of it has never seen the light, although the manuscript has been in existence a considerable time.

The writer has not altogether followed his own impulse in sending this work to the press, but has been repeatedly urged to do so by those who have made a considerable use of the part already published—in Sunday schools—in families—and in cottage readings and lending libraries amongst the poor—and who bear encouraging testimony to its usefulness.

The whole has been revised, and much of it rewritten and rearranged. In its completed form it is now sent forth with the author's prayers, and the prayers of many others, for the Divine blessing on its circulation. May He who distinguished the voluntary offerer of a box of precious ointment with the kind commendation, "She hath done what she could," in like manner graciously own this "labor of love," and make use of it to render His Name pleasant and attractive, "like ointment poured forth."

Thus far the preface to the former edition. That being exhausted, a new edition, revised and extended, is sent forth upon its travels. It is printed in type two sizes larger than the last, and on larger paper. More than forty fresh pages have been incorporated with the work; and twenty or thirty additional Titles or Symbols introduced; (the enlargement having been effected without increase of price). Touching a few of these, (and some others before included), the writer ventures to add a word or two. He does not claim to be a theologian. He therefore asks the forbearance of the critical reader, (his forgiveness indeed), if he has seemed to transgress the more rigid axioms of theological exegesis. But there is a certain latitude into which it is hardly possible not occasionally to glide, induced by the peculiar position of Christ in the Trinity, and His compound nature. Especially since in theology (as in other sciences) there have not yet been discovered those hard and fast lines of exact definition of which all are in quest.

Jesus Christ is the Representative of the Father, and of the Godhead. Some expressions, therefore, which are supposed to be peculiar to the Father, are in the Scriptures appropriated to the Son—thus He is The Everlasting Father. Characteristics regarded as applicable alone to the entire Godhead are used in describing Him—thus He is called The Only Wise God. Again, He is at once The Image of the Invisible God, and, as to the inscrutableness of His Deity, Himself is Invisible also. If then the writer has seemed to err in the direction indicated, perhaps he may be allowed to shelter such instances under the more comprehensive term, Symbols.

As to the three compound Titles, Jehovah-jireh, Jehovah-nissi, Jehovah-shalom, two out of the three, it must be remembered, are connected with One Who personates God, speaks in the first person, and in other respects comports Himself as only Jehovah could be supposed to do. The highest angel, Gabriel himself, (if he it is who occupies that lofty preeminence) is infinitely too insignificant to be the Representative of God in any such way. Only He is equal to it Who is at once Jehovah and Jehovah's Messenger. It is not therefore on the footing of inference or argument merely, but on the foundation of fact, that the appropriation of the Titles, Jehovah-jireh and Jehovah-shalom, to the Lord Jesus Christ, is claimed to rest.

The writer has added a few personal Types of our Lord. Not all that are claimed. He would not have known where to stop. For it is difficult to draw a line, and say positively what is, or what is not, typical, in histories which are, as Dr. Dykes expresses it, "Saturated throughout with gospel meanings."

For instance, both the nativity of Isaac, and that of Samson, were fore-announced to their parents by an Angel. This of itself suffices to lift them both into significant prominence. And while the former, in his miraculous birth of a mother 90 years old, seems to foreshadow the Divine Son, miraculously born of a virgin (as also in some other points of his history), it is hard to deny that the latter, in his supernatural might and extraordinary feats, was intended to pre-figure the prowess of Him "Who is able to subdue all things to Himself." Indeed, was not every anointed king, and every consecrated priest, among the Hebrews, a type of Christ? But of alleged personal historical types, eleven only are intro-duced in the following pages. (See *Classified List* at the end of the volume.)

One point which seems to demand apology is the unequal length of the Readings. The writer set out with the intention to restrict each to seven or eight pages, and never to exceed nine. He did try to observe that rule. But being lim-ited to 52 sections, with their 288 sub-divisions of varied lengths, he found it hardly practicable in some instances. But it will be easy for such as use the book for social reading, to curtail or omit just that will bring the offending lesson within the proper dimensions. To others he trusts it will be no inconvenience.

Right thoughts of the Lord Jesus Christ lie at the very root of all Christian religion. If, through the blessing of the Holy Spirit, the attainment of these should be in any degree promoted by the republication of this volume, or if the perusal of it should prove half as useful and refreshing to the reader, as the preparation of it has been to the author, his reward will be most abundant.

1

Introduction. Alpha and Omega. Adam. Anointed. Anointed with the Holy Ghost. Aaron. Altar.

IT is a trite saying, that God instructs mankind by means of three books. The book of *Creation*, which tells us of His power, wisdom, and goodness; the book of *Providence*, which also displays *His* justice and His patience; and the book of *Revelation*. The last, we find, is intended to supply what the others omit. It proclaims the whole character of God. It speaks of His forgiving mercy, His wonderful love, His faithfulness, and His truth. This volume is therefore the key to the two first. It informs us who is their Author, "what is His name, and what is His Son's name." It apprises us that the way to know God is through Christ: and, as it goes on to unfold to us what Christ is, in parables and prophecies, it is wonderful to what an extent it refers us to Creation and Providence, for symbols whereby to describe His work and illustrate His worth. It says, Jesus Christ is like this beautiful tree, or that pure fountain, or yonder innocent lamb. Thus the first two volumes, which teach us nothing about Christ as a Savior, when we use the Bible as the key to unlock their treasures, furnish us with the most precious instruction concerning Him.

We cannot read David's psalms without observing how he was accustomed to view every scene in creation, as well as every event in Providence, in connection with God. The "great mountains" reminded him of God's immutable righteousness; and their awful precipices of the "great deep of His judgments." The lofty firmament led him to dwell sweetly on the thought that "God's mercy to them that fear Him is as high as the heavens are above the earth." The brimming river, glistening in the sunshine, spake to him of God's exuberant goodness, which "preserveth man and beast."

If David in those early times thus read and compared these three open volumes, surely we, with our greater advantage, should do so much more. Many of the secrets of nature, which were hidden then, are open now; and many mysteries of revelation, not known to him are unfolded to us. We should not only set our affections on "things above," but make a ladder of "things below," by

1

which to climb upwards. Then the heavens will declare to us the glory of Christ, and the earth will show forth His redeeming work. Our opened eyes will read mystic lessons of evangelic wisdom in every object we see; our unclosed ears will hear mystic voices sounding from every side, effectually instructing us in the things that pertain to salvation.

But our purpose in these Sunday readings is not to wander at random through the world in quest of comparisons wherewith to illustrate revealed truth; but rather to confine our attention to those Names and Emblems which the Scriptures have themselves specially consecrated, as symbols of the Lord Jesus Christ. They are culled from the earth, and from the air, and from the waters—from past history, and from things that come under daily observation—from things the most familiar that can be, and from such as are far beyond our ken. Many of them were adopted by our Lord Himself, who, when He taught the people, "used similitudes," and dealt largely in parables.

Thus, when He would have them to know that there was no way to heaven, but through Him, He said, "I am the Door." And when He would teach them how kind He was to them that follow Him, He said, "I am the Good Shepherd." When He would impress on their minds how weak and worthless they were without Him, He spake of Himself as the Vine, and His disciples as the branches. If we follow His counsels, then, He says, we build on a rock; and if not, then we are like the foolish man who built his house on the sand. And all this a child can easily understand, much more a wayfaring man, though a fool. None can err therein, except those who wish to go astray. Our Lord's object was to preach *Himself*, to call all the world to the love and worship of *Himself*. And as a picture of some part of a temple could not give the mind a full idea of its magnificence, so our Lord, finding no *one* thing worthy to compare Himself to, brings forward the most beautiful and endearing things in the universe, to shadow forth His glory, And in the same manner do the prophets witness to His worth. They exhaust all the powers of words and things in describing Him, heap one figure on another, and end by telling us we can never by searching find Him out in perfection.

> Join all the names of love and power,
> That ever men or angels bore:
> All are too mean to speak His worth,
> Or set Immanuel glory forth.
>
> Nor earth, nor seas, nor sun, nor stars
> Nor heaven, His FULL resemblance bears;
> His beauties we can never trace
> Till we behold Him face to face.

We will begin with one of our Lord's highest Titles—a description of Him as sublime as it is simple—

ALPHA AND OMEGA.—Revelation 1:8. Four times this remarkable Title occurs in the Book of Revelation. On one occasion it was announced with a clear and penetrating voice, "a great voice as of a trumpet"; and the Speaker was "One like unto the Son of Man,"—like Him whom John had formerly known, at whose feet he had sat, in whose bosom he had lain—like Him, but how changed! Invested now with glory insufferably dazzling, when the Apostle saw Him, he fell at His feet as dead. "I am Alpha and Omega," said the voice, "the First and the Last."

This Symbol appeals alike to the child and to the man, to the ignorant and to the learned. Every one knows that Alpha and Omega are the first and last letters of the Greek Alphabet; so that, translated, it would read—I am A and Z. And as A is the first letter, so Christ is the first, the oldest of all beings. He lived before the world was. He *always* lived, and in all other respects Christ stands before all. He is the greatest and best, the strongest and kindest of all; the First in His claim to our love and obedience; with whom none can be compared. And as Z is the last letter in the Alphabet, so Christ will be the same when this world will be put away as a worn-out garment, and the skies be rolled up like a scroll of parchment. He is "from everlasting to everlasting." "He only hath immortality"; known to Him are all things that shall be, as perfectly as the things that have been. He is the Last. There is nothing beyond Him, nor can His resources ever be exhausted.

Again, Alpha and Omega are not only the first letter and the last, but may be accounted by us to represent them all. With the twenty-six letters of the alphabet, we can make thousands of words—whatever word we want to spell. Just so, when we have rightly learned to know Christ, we shall never be at a loss; for all we want is treasured up in Him. We are complete in Him, for "in Him are hid all the treasures of wisdom and knowledge." If the children are to read the Bible, they must learn their ABC's, first; and, till they have learned that, they cannot read one word; for that is the key which unlocks the sense of it. So, if ever any of us spiritually *understand* the Scriptures, it must be by learning first this *Divine alphabet*; Christ, the Alpha and Omega, is the true key to the whole; the door to all saving knowledge, the beginning of all sacred lore, the "key of knowledge," which some would take away, but which we must grasp as that which is dearer to us than life.

The Jews have the Bible, and they read it in their Synagogues; but they do not understand it. And why? Because they refuse the "key of knowledge," the Alpha and Omega. Therefore is the Bible a sealed book to them; the veil is on their hearts; they cannot unlock its treasures, nor make out its meaning. Nor will they, "till they turn to the Lord," the ALPHA AND OMEGA, and "then the veil shall be taken away."

But is there a veil on *thine* heart too? Are the words of that blessed book "unto thee as the words of a book that is sealed?" You can read it, and repeat it; but, "seeing, you see not, and hearing, you understand not." You have not yet "so learned Christ," as to be able to read the hidden meaning of the word. But remember, "if the gospel be hid, it is hid to them that are lost." Wherefore, bethink yourselves of the sin and danger of ignorance, and seek to know Christ. So shall you understand the Scriptures, and be able to unravel their hidden meaning; "crooked things shall be made straight, and rough places plain," before you wondering eyes. And there is another book, too, which you shall be able to read, when you shall know Christ truly. You shall "read your title clear" to the heavenly mansions, and rejoice that your names are written in the Lamb's book of life.

"I am ALPHA." Does He not here assert His pre-eminence in *all things?* And thus claim the first place in our thoughts, our affections, our plans? Whom do *we* put first? Christ or self? Christ or friends? Christ or the world? Christ's teachings or man's opinions? Where do you place Him? First? Or only second? Or lower down still? Ah, let me tell you, you cannot have Christ on these terms. If He may not occupy the first place, then know, He disdains any other.

This symbol suggests, if it does not sanction, our *plan.* For we propose to range from Alpha to Omega—through all the alphabet from A to Z—in a brief examination of every Title and similitude which the sacred volume appropriates to the Savior.

There was a tree reported to exist somewhere in Tartary, which, instead of fruit, produced precious stones. Its branches glittered with huge clusters of pearls and diamonds. Certainly a very wonderful tree, and very attractive; if it could be discovered, it would not long retain its treasures. But perhaps this was only a dreamy version of a certain fact in natural history. There is a little creature called the diamond beetle, whose elytra, or wingcases, are marvelously brilliant, and, when seen in the sunshine, seem to sparkle with emerald and gold. These insects sometimes congregate on the acacia tree in such multitudes, that its branches seem as if loaded with a profusion of gems, while the sun invests them with unearthly splendor. But, however that may be, let this fabled tree of Tartary be to us an illustration of the Bible. For among its leaves we behold clusters of well-chosen words descriptive of Christ, "the lovely chief of all our joys"; words which, for variety and beauty, may well be said to resemble precious stones and sparkling diamonds, all reflecting, to those who can steadily look thereon, the glory of the Sun of Righteousness. We will search this tree narrowly, and shake its branches again and again. We will be like "the merchant man seeking goodly pearls"; and we shall find among its folded leaves many a radiant gem, in comparison with which "no mention shall be made of coral or of pearls; nor shall the topaz of Ethiopia equal them; they cannot be valued with gold of Ophir, nor the precious onyx, nor the sapphire." Or, to change the simile, shall I compare our Alphabet of Christ's Symbols to a beautiful garden full of choice trees, loaded with delicious fruit? Then would I invite my readers to accompany me through this "orchard of pomegranates," that they may delight themselves with refreshing clusters, richer than the grapes of Eschol. Come with me; "I will go up to the palm tree, I will take hold of the boughs thereof," I will pluck the fruit and spread it before you, and you shall sit down under His shadow, and eat and drink, and own that the fruit is sweet to your taste. Who will go with me? We shall find all manner of pleasant fruits, "camphor with spikenard, saffron and cinnamon, with all trees of frankincense, myrrh, and aloes." And let us devoutly address the Holy Spirit, in the words of the ancient Church, and say, "Awake, O north wind, and come, thou south; blow upon this garden, that the spices thereof may flow out."—Our next Title shall be "THE LAST ADAM."

ADAM. In Romans 5:14, we read that the first Adam is the figure of Him that was to come; and, in another place, Christ is expressly called the LAST ADAM. You are well acquainted with the sad story of the first Adam, in which we are all so deeply concerned. God put him into a beautiful garden, and gave it to him for himself and his children, with permission to make use of everything except one tree; and He charged him not to taste the fruit of that, on pain of death. But the serpent tempted Eve to eat the forbidden fruit, by telling her "that it would make her wise, and that God did not speak the truth when He said, Thou shalt die." And alas! Eve believed Satan rather than God, and plucked the fruit, and persuaded Adam also to eat of it.

Now this garden was a most delightful place, for God had shut death and sorrow and pain out of it. And Adam might have kept them out. Instead of which, he opened the door and let them all in. God did not, it is true, say to Adam, "I will put it out of your power to sin; I will lock you in, and take the key of the gate away with me, so that you shall not be able to let your enemies in." This would not have been treating him as a reasonable being. But He closed the door against death and sorrow, and, as it were, gave the key of the gate to him to take care of, and strictly charged him not to open it; warning him of what would follow if he did. The garden was fenced in as with the strongest walls; and there was but one door at which misery and death could enter; and this door Adam might have kept fast bolted, if he had liked. But he chose to disobey God; and, by this one act, he let a host of enemies into his leafy bower, and all its pleasant things were laid waste. And instead of securing his Paradise as a portion for his children, he lost it all, and has left us, instead, the sad inheritance of sin and death and woe.

But, how then, you say, could Adam be a "figure of Christ"? Why in this—
that Adam acted for others as well as himself, and through his disobedience millions were undone. So also Christ did what He did for others, and through His
obedience millions are saved. Adam opened the door through which sin and
death entered and seized us all. And the SECOND ADAM opens a door too, but it
is the door of mercy. He opens the kingdom of heaven to all believers. And now,
though you cannot go back to Eden, you may all come in at this open gate, and
enter a far better Paradise than that which Adam forfeited. Let us see what the
Bible says of the First Adam and the Last. Read Romans 5:19: "As by one man's
disobedience (*i.e.* Adam's) many were made sinners, so by the obedience of One
(*i.e.* Christ) shall many be made righteous." Again, 1 Corinthians 15:21, 22, "For
since by man came death, by Man came also the resurrection of the dead. For
as in Adam all die, even so in Christ shall all be made alive." (See also vv. 47–49.)
So you see Adam brought ruin; and Christ brings salvation. Adam was the first
of his kind, and gave a name and nature to us all. Christ also is the first of His
family, and gives His name and His nature to all that belong to Him. Adam set
us a wicked example, which we have been eager to follow; but Christ, by example too, teaches us to resist the devil, that he may flee from us.

The history of Adam has many lessons. You blame him for what he did; and
very justly. And you think that if you had been in his place you would not have
been so wicked. But why do you do the very same things yourself? Why believe
anybody's word rather than God's? Why think unkind and hard thoughts of
God, like Adam? Does not your own conscience condemn you? Do you not often
covet some forbidden thing, and feel discontented because you have not all you
want? And, when you have done wrong, do you not "cover your sins as Adam"?
Surely we cannot but feel that we are indeed all of us his children; for we are
like him; and, in his place, would doubtless have done as he did. But will you
bear the image of the earthly always? Oh, aspire to be like the SECOND ADAM!
Pray for the Holy Spirit, that you may be *born again*, that

> Prevenient grace descending, may remove
> The stony from your heart, and make new flesh,
> Regenerate, grow instead.

The next Title is the English word for Christ (which is Greek); and also for
Messiah (which is Hebrew), viz., "ANOINTED."

ANOINTED. Psalms 2:2; 45:7; Acts 10:38. The expression indicates His designation to His high office; and the pre-eminent gifts and graces whereby He was
qualified for the discharge of all its functions. In all ages, kings and queens have
been anointed with oil, when crowned or set over a people. This oil, being composed of rare balms and spices, typifies the extraordinary qualities required for
the due discharge of the office. Thus Samuel anointed Saul to be king over Is-

rael; and also David. And you may read of Solomon's anointing and coronation in 1 Kings 1:32–40. So Christ, being the King whom God has "set on His holy hill," is said to be ANOINTED. In Psalm 45, it is said, "All His garments smell of myrrh, aloes, and cassia," as He comes forth "out of His ivory palaces." When He came down from the courts of heaven, though clothed with mean garments— for He put on our nature—yet His excellent worth betrayed itself through this disguise. It could not be hid. Nicodemus perceived this fragrance, when he called Him a "Teacher sent from God"; and *they* found it out, who, being sent to take Him, came back without Him, saying, "Never man spake like this man." It was the "savor of his ointments,"—in other words, His great worth and goodness, His wisdom, love, and power—which thus allured people to Him, and made them admire Him.

But more definitely we read that He was

ANOINTED WITH THE HOLY GHOST and with power (Acts 10:38), in order to qualify Him for the work which GOD had given Him to do. This special anointing was promised beforehand (see Isa. 11:1–3; 41:1; 42:1), and the promise was richly fulfilled at His baptism. Previously pure and undefiled, He then received a new and vast accession of spiritual power, the outcome of which filled men with astonishment (Luke 4:22). And this measureless impartation of the Spirit (John 3:34) accompanied Him to the end. We see it in His death; for it was "through the Eternal Spirit He offered Himself without spot to God" (Heb. 9:14). And again, immediately after His death, He was "quickened by the Spirit" (1 Pet. 3:18).

But it may occur to some to ask, "Since Christ was truly God, possessed of infinite powers, in what possible sense could the grace and Anointing of the Spirit be needed by Him?" Be it remembered that He assumed our entire nature. In all things He was made like to His brethren. Whatever laws we are under, He came under the same, sin excepted. One great law of human nature is its entire dependence on the Holy Spirit in all that belongs to God's service. We cannot think, nor pray, nor watch, nor serve God aright, only "in the Spirit." The perfect human nature of Christ under the same law must be equally beholden to the Holy Spirit. Would it be human nature if it were otherwise? Further, God is not used to give gifts where they are not required; must we not therefore conclude that our Lord needed the power of the Holy Spirit for the work He had to do, or that it would not have been imparted? But forget not, we ourselves must all be conformed to this model. Did Christ need all this to fulfill His commission? And can any hope to realize the end for which they were born, unaided and alone? Nay. Each in his measure must have precisely the same anointing, or his life will turn out a failure; and for it each must ask, it may be, with "strong crying and tears."

Priests also were Anointed with sacred oil. In Exodus 29:7 we read that Moses consecrated Aaron thus by God's express command. "For no man taketh this honor to himself, but he that was called of God, as was Aaron."

AARON. Hebrews 5:4–6. We cannot dwell on the instructive particulars noted concerning the first Jewish high priest. His holy garments for glory and beauty; his golden mitre inscribed with "Holiness to the Lord"; his jeweled breastplate bearing the names of the twelve tribes. But it is said of him, "he was made *without* an oath," leaving it to be inferred that there was no perpetuity in his office. But Jesus Christ was consecrated *with* an oath. "The Lord sware, Thou art a Priest forever." He will continue to exercise His priesthood in the sanctuary above, until the number of the elect shall be accomplished, and the last soul be saved.

And as to the anointing oil, it was to be compounded of most precious spices, according to Divine prescription. Nor might any among the Jews prepare oil like unto it for common use. He who should presume to do so was to be "cut off." The sacredness of the office could not be more emphatically taught. This anointing oil was very costly. A spoonful was worth several pounds. And its perfume was most fragrant, pointing to the Lord Jesus, who is "Anointed with the oil of joy above His fellows."

But now, having placed Aaron in his proper place in the series as an eminent official type of Christ, the reader is referred for further particular to the lesson for the twenty-third Sunday—HIGH PRIEST. Observe, however, before we pass on, that while ordinary priests were only sprinkled with the oil, upon the high priest it was literally poured, so that it "went down to the skirts of his garments" (Ps. 133:2). Here we come upon a practical lesson. Was the aromatic unction thus lavished upon AARON, covering him entirely with its rich perfume? So the Anointing Spirit, which was poured without measure on Christ, comes down upon the meanest of His followers; and it cannot be hid—it will surely betray itself. Out of the fullness of the heart the mouth speaks, and the actions speak, and the Christian will carry with him the "savor of Christ" wherever he goes. General Burn, when a young man, was ordered to a new station among strange companions, whom he found to be lovers of sin. But, the very first day, he observed one among them very unlike the rest, and on watching him, the "savor of Christ" was soon made manifest in him, both by words and actions; for he also was a Christian. And so the hearts of those two were drawn to each other by the same Anointing, which both had received from Christ; and by that they found each other out, almost as soon as they met. For it cannot be concealed. Like Solomon's "ointment of the right hand," it betrays itself in one way or other. It may be by the lips; or by the behavior; or even by the aspect. Madame de Krudener sought all her happiness in worldly pleasures, till a profound melancholy seized her, which nothing could relieve. One day a shoemaker waited on her in compliance with her orders. A single glance at his countenance, as he took her measure, showed her that he was as happy as she was miserable. She could not forbear saying, "My friend, are you happy?" To which he replied, with a face on which peace sat enthroned, "Madame, I am indeed the happiest of men." His looks and his words deeply impressed her; nor could she rest until she had sought him out, and learned from his lips the secret of his joy. He was a devout Moravian, and gladly seized the opportunity of preaching Christ to her. She also received the "Anointing," and to the close of her life served the Lord with gladness, diffusing in her turn the same saving aroma to others—the rich and the titled, among whom she associated.

Oh seek for this anointing! It will be the "oil of joy, whereby thou shalt be made glad." It will be the "unction of the Holy One," whereby thou shalt know all things, for "this anointing teacheth us all things." It will bring thee health and beauty, and make fat thy bones. It will make you both useful and pleasant; others will take knowledge of you, that you have been with Jesus, and will desire to acquaint themselves with Him who hath "anointed thee with oil, and made thy cup run over." Finally, this Anointing will entitle you to sit with Christ on His throne, as a *King* forever. And in the meantime, while you live here on earth, it will fit you to be a *Priest*, to offer up "spiritual sacrifices, acceptable to God through Jesus Christ." For He is the "ALTAR which sanctifieth both the gift and the giver."

ALTAR. Hebrews 13:10. An Altar was that whereon all offerings to God were to be laid. There were two Altars in the temple. The brazen Altar for sacrifices in the outer court; and the golden Altar for incense in the Holy Place before the veil. Both were Types of Christ; the one of His dying for us on earth, the other of His praying for us in heaven. Revelation 8:3. But now those two Altars are overturned; Solomon's temple is no more; the sacrifices are done away; the priests no longer minister. But there is an ALTAR still; for the apostle says, "We *have* an ALTAR." Hebrews 13:10. This ALTAR is Christ. But an Altar must have priests to minister at it, and sacrifices offered on it. And the Bible tells us of a *Holy Priesthood*, anointed "to offer up *spiritual sacrifices* acceptable to God through Jesus Christ."

And who are the *Priests*? Every Christian is "made a priest unto God." This honor is not confined to ministers. They are not priests in any other sense than their hearers. Yea, the youngest child may have this privilege. "Out of the mouth of babes and sucklings Thou hast perfected praise." When our Lord rode into Jerusalem, He was accompanied by children of all ages, who rent the air with their hosannas; and their service of song was accepted, however rude and unpolished. And still He loves the prayers and praises presented by youthful priests, whose hearts are tender, and who seek Him early.

> When you devote your youth to God,
> 'Tis pleasing in His eyes;
> A flower when offered in the bud
> Is no vain sacrifice.

And just as there were sacrifices, "according to the pattern" prescribed, offered under the Jewish dispensation, so there are sacrifices commanded and specified in our New Testament directory. What are these?

1. *Prayer.* David asked God that his prayer might be "set before Him as incense, and the lifting *up* of his hands as the evening sacrifice." And we are commanded to "pray always with all prayer"; prayer for daily bread and all temporal blessings; much more for the Holy Spirit, the pardon of sin, and grace to help in time of need. "If any be afflicted, let him pray."

2. *Praise* is a sacrifice. And this we are to offer continually, "even the fruit of our lips, giving thanks to His name." We should praise Him for everything, and always in the name of Christ. What a delightful sight is a whole assembly, joining together with one accord, to offer this sacrifice! "'Tis like a little heaven below." If all are spiritual priests, worshiping at the true ALTAR, the incense of their praise, "like pillars of smoke perfumed with myrrh," goes straight up to heaven, and is most acceptable to God.

3. *Good Works* are sacrifices. Psalm 4:5, "To do good and to communicate, forget not; for with such sacrifices God is well pleased." They are "an odor of a sweet smell to God." A life, "holy in all manner of conversation," is an incense most acceptable; while a wicked, idle, quarrelsome life is a noisome vapor—no incense at all, but an abomination to God. Isaiah 1:13.

4. We must offer *ourselves* on the ALTAR, *body and soul.* Our *bodies* are to be "living sacrifices." We read of some who say, "Our lips are our own; who is Lord over us?" But God's priest thinks otherwise. He says,

> My hands, my eyes, my ears, my tongue,
> Have Satan's servants been too long,
> But now they shall be Thine.

And God says, "My son, give me thine *heart.*" This must never be wanting. God abhors the sacrifice, if the heart be left behind. But the contrite heart is a sacrifice, which He will not despise.

And now what inferences should we draw from these our first subjects? From among many, we will name the following—

1. That Jesus Christ must be God. The title ALPHA AND OMEGA so sublime in its simplicity, leads back our thoughts to the awful recesses of eternity, and onward to the hidden abysses of immortality, "In the beginning was the Word, and the Word was God,"—the FIRST and CHIEF of beings. How impossible that such

titles as these could ever, by the most extravagant fancy, be appropriated to any but the Living God! We are required therefore to adore the Lord Jesus as the "True God and Eternal Life"; and to yield Him our best affections, our most entire confidence, and our devoted obedience.

2. That sin should be avoided as the most atrocious and destructive evil. The second Title—ADAM, "the figure of Him that was to come"—refers us also to a "beginning"; for Adam too was an ALPHA, the first of our race. But what a disastrous commencement he made! How appalling the consequences of a single act of sin! What a destructive ocean of sorrow rushed in at one narrow breach! Ever be afraid of sin; nor dare to say, when you are tempted, "It is but *once*, and only a *little* sin"; for all sin is hateful to God, and hurtful to His creatures and must be inevitably followed by punishment. Resolutely refuse to touch the forbidden fruit, however inviting it may look.

3. That we should pray much for the Holy Spirit, and cherish His benign influences. What an honor to be made "kings and priests unto God!" And how precious that "anointing of the Holy One," which alone can qualify us for so great a vocation! Servants, with this "holy anointing," will "adorn the doctrine of God our Savior in all things"; "not answering again, not purloining, but showing all good fidelity." Children, thus distinguished, will be obedient, modest, and docile. Masters and parents will be kind and considerate, and concerned for the best interests of those committed to their charge. And all will "do good," not only by deliberate efforts, but also by involuntary and unconscious influence. They will diffuse a "savor of Christ" wherever they are, just as the subtle perfume of some rare spice betrays where it is deposited.

4. That our worship can be accepted only through Christ. Be careful, therefore, when you worship God, to come in the right way. God formerly told His people that the Altar was the spot where He could meet with His worshipers; nor would He look at those who pretended to worship Him in ways of their own devising. If you wish that your prayers and praise and offerings should be received, offer them through Christ. "Bind the sacrifice with cords" of love, "even to the horns of the ALTAR."

2

Ark. Amen. Author of Eternal Salvation. Author and Finisher of Our Faith.

WHEN the Patriarch Noah was about five hundred years old, he began to build an enormous vessel "for the saving of his house." He seems to have had one hundred and twenty years allowed him for its preparation (Gen. 4:3). This vast work could not go on without observation; it would necessarily attract the notice of his neighbors, and they would of course inquire, "What can it be for?" The venerable builder was quite willing to explain the matter, and to "give a reason for the hope that was in him." They listened with incredulity to his statement, laughed at the earnest expostulations with which it was accompanied, and pronounced the whole thing to be the freak of a madman. And as the huge pile grew from year to year, shouts of laughter at the good man's expense would often echo along the highways in the neighborhood; and scoffs would be heard, mingled with the sound of axes and hammers, among the carpenters and shipwrights employed at the works. "*Noah's Folly*" would be a byword through all the region round about, and he himself "the song of the drunkard," during all the long period occupied in its construction. But the steadfast man of faith and prayer was not to be turned aside. It was by command of God he had commenced the work; and by the help of God he was enabled to persevere, till at length it was finished within the allotted time, pitched inside and out, and fitted up for its perilous voyage.

This extraordinary fabric is calculated to have been half as large as St. Paul's Cathedral, and equal in capacity to eighteen first-rate ships of the line. There was room enough, within the compass of its enormous ribs, for twenty thousand men, together with provisions and all needful stores for six months. So that it was abundantly capable of carrying all the passengers God intended it for.

But now the hundred and twenty years are over and gone; and portentous signs of coming changes begin to appear. Wonderful processions of animals of all kinds present themselves at the building ground, conducted by some secret influence. These, forgetting their vile habits and mutual antipathies, sociably enter the Ark, and are quickly disposed of in various pens by the busy "eight" with whom they are destined for a season to share the strange home. All this being accomplished, God said to Noah, "Come thou and all thy house into the Ark." So these eight persons entered, and the door was closed after them, for "the Lord shut them in" (Gen. 7:1, 16). Whether these wonderful transactions were witnessed by a tumultuous assemblage, filled with amazement or transported with rage, the record does not state. But it seems probable; and God's "shutting them in" sounds very like snatching them from the murderous intentions of their fellow townsmen; just as the angel delivered Lot from those who threatened his life in Sodom on the last night before its overthrow. The Lord knoweth how to deliver the godly out of temptation, and to reserve the unjust unto the day of judgment, to be punished.

It is the seventeenth day of the second month, which answers to our third of November. On that fatal day, while men are buying and selling, singing and carousing, suddenly darkness overspreads the earth; the voice of the Lord is upon the waters; the God of glory thundereth. From the open windows of heaven a cataract pours heavily down; and at the same time "the fountains of the great deep are broken up." Seas, rivers, lakes, forget their boundaries, and every living thing is speedily involved in one fearful overthrow. Deep calleth unto deep at the noise of God's waterspouts. There is the rush of waves and the roar of the elements, mingled with wild shrieks of despair from drowning men and women, till all His waves and billows swallow them up, and their cries are smothered in death. Thus the world that then was, being overflowed with water, perished. Only Noah and his family survived to tell the tale; while those disobedient spirits to whom Christ had preached in vain by His servant Noah, were consigned to the prison prepared for them (1 Pet. 3:19, 20). This fearful event prefigured the still more awful destruction which awaits the world at the end of time; and the overthrow of those ungodly rebels is a melancholy picture of the tribulation and wrath in which all will be involved who obey not the gospel; while the

ARK is an instructive type of the Lord Jesus Christ. See 1 Peter 3:20. It was so, inasmuch as—

1. *It was the ONLY place of safety.* This was evident to Noah's more immediate neighbors who knew the purpose for which it had been built. When the flood came, perchance some of them succeeded in gaining the higher ground, which the waters did not immediately reach; and if, during that short interval, they were able amidst the gloom to distinguish the huge vessel as it drifted past, almost within hail, how agonizing must have been their reflections at the sight— "Yonder goes the only refuge under heaven from this pitiless storm. Yesterday, woe unto us! we despised it; today we would give the world to be in it. But this wide waste of waters prevents all approach and nothing remains but that we

perish miserably!" So the name of Christ is "the *only* name under heaven given among men, whereby they can be saved." He is the one refuge from the storm. And the Christian man is described as "a man in Christ," while all others are lost men.

2. *The Ark was of God's appointment,* and being planned by Him, was exactly adapted for its purpose. So God contrived the plan of salvation, and appointed Jesus Christ to be the Savior. Whence He is just such a Savior as we require.

3. *It was perfectly secure.* The rain which beat upon it could not sink it, nor were the wild waves which tossed it about able to dash it in pieces. So Jesus Christ shields His people from temptation, or saves them in all the assaults of Satan.

Many more points of *resemblance* might be traced, but we must not fail to take notice of one special point of *difference.* The Ark seems to have been intended for Noah alone, and no others. At least, there is no proof that he was at liberty to invite any to enter, except his own family. But however that might be, all without exception, are alike invited, warranted, yea *commanded* to come to Christ. It is not said—All, save murderers, blasphemers, and the very aged in rebellion, may come to Christ. The gospel invitation is not couched in these terms, "Come thou, and thy house, thou upright moral man!" But, "Come, thou hypocrite, thou swearer, thou self-righteous, thou polluted one—Come each one of you, and thou *shalt* be saved." For "*all manner of sin* and blasphemy shall be forgiven unto men." There is no restriction as to the *amount* of criminality. Christ is able to save to the uttermost. The only sin that is unpardonable is an obstinate refusal to come. This is the sin against the Holy Ghost, which can never be forgiven.

Neither are the servants of God restricted as to the number of persons on whom they are to press the gospel call. To every one whose ear they can gain, they are to say, Come *thou*—and come *thou*—into this Divine Ark. Their orders are to preach the gospel *to every creature.* They are to cry "Ho!" to every one that thirsteth; and to assure him that "*whosoever* shall call on the name of the Lord SHALL BE SAVED." Unlike Noah's Ark, there is room for all the world *here.* Millions are already housed in this Divine Asylum, and yet there is room for millions of millions more—

> Room for the feeble and the faint,
> The helpless and the poor,
> Who wait, and hope, and watch, and cry
> At mercy's open door.

> There's room for Gentiles, room for Jews,
> There's room for bond and free,

There's room for every precious soul
Christ died for on the tree.

But though all *may* come, how many hear the pressing invitation and come not! A few years ago, a noble ship, with hundreds of people on board, left England to go to a far country. And as they sailed swiftly on, they entertained themselves with thoughts of the new home they were going to, and planned what they would do when they should get there. But, in the midst of their dreams, a fearful cry arose—the ship was on fire!—the flames had caught the spirit casks! In an instant water was poured down, but in vain; the flames roared, and the timbers cracked, and the smoke poured out its stifling clouds, till they could get near no longer.

Dreadful condition! All around there was nothing but the deep sea. And, between fire within and water without, what hope was there of escape? Then the sailors, who had just before blasphemed God, prayed: and women and children, with frantic cries, sought their husbands and parents. And there were children there, too, who had been taught to know the Savior, and in that fearful moment they were seen praying to Him; and all on board expected to sleep that night in eternity. They let the sea into the ports, to check the flames, and then awaited their fate. But God, in His great mercy, sent them deliverance. Another vessel almost immediately came in sight, and all who were willing made their escape though with difficulty, from the burning ship. Yet strange to tell, *some* were NOT WILLING! They saw others get away safely, but nothing could arouse *them*. They obstinately refused to move. You say, naturally enough, "What infatuated men they must have been!" Indeed, but for the suspicion that fright had stupefied them, you would say, "They richly *deserved to perish*." But, pause for a moment. In condemning their conduct, do you not pass sentence on yourself? Is it *certain* you will outlive this night? Is there not a more dreadful fire waiting to devour the ungodly? and a far more dreadful flood fast rising to overwhelm the unbelieving? "Because there is wrath, beware lest He take thee away with His stroke." You are in danger, and you are warned of it. You are a sinner, and you know it. You are unhappy, because insecure, and you feel it. And yet when God provides an ARK for your salvation, even Christ, you will not come unto Him that you might have life. This, then, is your condemnation, that God has provided a Savior, and you will not be saved. Take care, that that which overwhelmed the scoffers in the days of Noah, does not come upon you.

Think of the fright and dismay, which everywhere prevailed within an hour after God had shut Noah into the Ark. In the market place, where the sellers and the buyers were busy, wrangling as usual over their bargains—how their faces gathered blackness, and their knees smote against each other, as the dreadful tidings spread, that Noah's despised flood was come! In the joyous festival, where the reveling guests were saying "that tomorrow should be as this day, and more abundant,"—in taverns and gardens, in palaces and prisons—what wild disorder! what sudden fright! what dreadful despair!

Were there ever any who hardened themselves against God and prospered? Oh! take heed, lest there be in any of you an evil heart of unbelief; lest God say to you hereafter, "Behold, ye despisers! and wonder and perish; because, when I called, ye refused, now, when your fear cometh, I will laugh at your calamity." Come with me into the ARK. Let us knock at the door of mercy, and enter before the storm breaks, that we may be housed "when it shall hail, coming down on the ungodly." Now the long-suffering of God waits on *thee*, as it did on the disobedient in the days of Noah. Oh despise it not, but let it lead thee to repentance. Now the tempest of God's wrath is held back; oh, fear it, and hide yourselves in time. For one hundred and twenty years those evil men waxed worse and worse, saying, "Where is the promise of His coming?" They laughed at the threatening. Not so Noah. He was moved with fear. And for one hundred and twenty years did he also wait the promised salvation. He waited and wrought at his Ark, and thus "worked out his own salvation." Nor did he wait in vain, for blessed are all that wait for God. Learn, then, that *promises and threatenings* will be both fulfilled by the Lord, for he is "the AMEN, the Faithful and True Witness."

AMEN (Rev. 3:14). The meaning of the word, Amen, is *true* and *certain*. You must have been often struck with our Lord's frequent use of the word *Verily* in His sermons. This is the same word as Amen, and calls us to mark the *certainty* of all He says. You know nothing is more common than for men to make promises to each other and to forget them. You remember the story of Joseph in the Egyptian prison. Pharaoh's butler was in the same prison with him, and dreamed a dream. And when Joseph went to him in the morning, seeing him to be sad, he asked what ailed him: "Oh," said he, "I have had such a strange dream." So he related the dream; and Joseph told him what it meant, that in three days he should be led out of prison, and should wait on Pharaoh as before; and added, "But think on me, when it shall be well with thee, and mention me to Pharaoh, and bring me out of this house; for indeed, I was stolen away, and have done nothing that they should put me in this dungeon"; and no doubt the butler promised to do so. But though it came to pass, as Joseph had said, that in three days the man again handed wine to Pharaoh, "*yet did not the chief butler remember Joseph, but forgat him.*" And if the king had not dreamed a dream, two years afterwards, that wanted interpretation too, the unfaithful man might never again have thought of the poor captive he had left behind him in the dungeon.

Suppose someone were to make you a promise that he would promote your interest in the world. He might be a kind man, and mean what he said; but still you would be afraid *fully* to reckon on it. And why? Because something might happen to prevent your receiving the benefit. He might *forget*, or *change* his mind, or he might *die*, before he could fulfill his promise. So another might threaten to do you harm; but for the same reasons you would hope to escape his anger. But you see at once, it cannot be so with Christ. He has said "it shall be well with the righteous and ill with the wicked." And though the sky over our heads, and the ground under our feet, shall pass away, not a jot of anything He has said, shall pass unfulfilled. He is the AMEN, the Faithful and True Witness. Think not, then, that He can forget His threatenings; neither suspect His promises, but take Him at His word; follow His directions; do just what He tells you to do: so shall you experience Him to be "the AUTHOR OF ETERNAL SALVATION."

AUTHOR OF ETERNAL SALVATION unto all them that obey Him. This is another of our Lord's many Titles. See Hebrews 5:9. Now, to *obey* Him, is to *believe* on Him with your heart: for He commands us to believe; and he that believeth hath *everlasting* life, and shall not come into condemnation. He is saved with an "*eternal* salvation." After the ark had carried Noah and his family about for a few months it landed them again on the earth; and left them still sinners, and liable to sickness and death; while that ARK, of which Noah's was an image, will surely carry all that are in it to that land, "where the inhabitant shall no more say, I am sick," and shall be forgiven his iniquity, and sin no more.

Why is it called *eternal* salvation? Because it is *from* everlasting—"I have loved thee with an everlasting love, therefore with lovingkindness have I drawn thee." And because it is to everlasting—"This is the promise that He hath promised us, even eternal life." Think not, however, that because it is called *eternal* salvation, we do not enjoy it here on earth. It is indeed made perfect in heaven, but it *begins* here. Thus the Apostle speaks of our *now* "receiving the end of our faith, even the salvation of our souls." He means receiving the sure beginnings of it— the earnest of all the rest—receiving it by confident anticipation. Nor should any Christian rest till he can say, "I know Whom I have believed, and am persuaded that He is able to keep that which I have committed to Him."

But what is salvation? To be released from condemnation, to receive forgiveness of sins, and to be justified in the sight of God for the sake of Christ— *this is Salvation*. To be lifted up out of the horrible pit of our unregenerate condition, to be cleansed with the "washing of regeneration," and to take rank among those who are kings and priests unto God—*this is Salvation*. To be adopted into the family of God, and made a member of His royal household to be invested with the dignity of a son, and enriched with the wealth of an heir, of God—*this is Salvation*. To be rescued from the power of evil passions, to be delivered from the turmoil of evil tempers, and saved from the fangs of evil spirits; to be adorned with all beautiful graces and divine virtues, so as to be like Christ— *this is Salvation*. But this salvation includes everything; and time would fail to go over it all—peace, and joy, and holiness and wisdom. Get this—and earth will be yours; affliction shall be yours; death shall be yours; heaven shall be yours; and there you shall wear a crown of glory, and white robes, and walk the golden streets of the heavenly city, and drink of the river of God's pleasures. There you will have no more pain, no more sorrow, for Christ's own soft hands shall wipe away all tears from your eyes. And God will smile on you, angels will greet you and rejoice over you with singing. The spirits of the just will embrace you lovingly, and your joy will last *forever*. And who is the AUTHOR of all this? The Lord Jesus. Oh let us love Him and try to please Him. And if this prospect delights us, shall we think much of the troubles we meet with in getting there? Nay: but "let us lay aside every weight, under the sin that easily besets us, and run the race set before us, looking unto Jesus" as the "AUTHOR AND FINISHER OF OUR FAITH."

AUTHOR AND FINISHER OF OUR FAITH. Hebrews12:2. Do we ask, how came Noah to prepare an ark for the saving of his house? The answer is, he did it "by faith"; and faith is "the substance of things hoped for, the evidence of things not seen." Just now I told you about a ship taking fire, and the danger the people were in of a dreadful death. And they *believed* the danger; but then, it was because they *saw* it. *That* belief could not be called *faith*. But we read that Noah believed things "*not seen* as yet." This was faith. God said that He would drown the world. And though it was contrary to all Noah had ever seen or heard of, and seemed very unlikely, yet, because God had said so, therefore he believed it. So Abraham believed things not seen as yet. So Moses believed just what God told him. And so *we* believe—though not seen as yet—that

> There is a land of pure delight,
>   Where saints immortal reign;
> Infinite day excludes the night,
>   And pleasures banish pain.

And, though not seen as yet—and God grant that none of us may ever see it!—we believe that there is a place of punishment prepared for them that obey not the gospel. If we steadfastly believe these things, then we are moved with fear, and we say "what shall we do to be saved? how shall we escape the one, and gain the other?" Then the Holy Spirit shows us the way, and leads us to Christ, the ARK of our refuge; and by *faith* we enter into Him, and continue in Him, and are carried safely to heaven. But how is Christ the AUTHOR of our faith?

(1.) He is the AUTHOR of the Bible. It contains "the faith once delivered to the saints" by His Spirit, and is our sole authority as to *what* we are to believe. (2.) He is the AUTHOR of all our advantages. It is His contrivance which placed us in a Christian land, or a pious family, where we are brought to *hear* the gospel; and "faith cometh by hearing." Then (3.) it is He who removes our ignorance, convinces us of sin, casts down high thoughts, and prepares us for faith. And (4.)

He works this very faith in us by His Spirit, who persuades and enables us to give full credit to His word, and so draws us to Himself. "To you it is given, on the behalf of Christ, to believe on Him."

And then He is the FINISHER OF FAITH. He prays for us, that our faith fail not; and daily "fulfills in us the work of faith with power"; and helps us to keep up a lively impression of the things that are to be believed all along, till we come

> Where faith is sweetly lost in sight,
> And hope in full, supreme delight,
>   And everlasting love.

Thus "by grace are ye saved, through faith, and that not of yourselves, it is the gift of God."

Let me sum up what has been said, and direct you to a few of the lessons to be learned from the whole. You have seen an emblem of the deluge of wrath, which is surely coming upon the wicked. And if, moved with fear, you cry out "What shall we do?" the answer is, "Believe on the Lord Jesus"; fly to Him who is the appointed Refuge! get within that

ARK of Salvation, and all shall be well. Do not be afraid to venture. Do not rashly conclude that you are too sinful for admittance. But listen to the kind invitations, the solemn promises of Him who cannot lie; for He is the

AMEN. What saith He? "Come unto Me, and I will give you rest." "To him that knocketh it shall be opened." You are to come, then, with full confidence, and just as you are, without waiting till you are better prepared; for it is He who is the

AUTHOR OF YOUR FAITH. He will help your unbelief; He will prepare your heart, and give you that "precious faith" which is like "gold tried in the fire," and repentance, and every grace. It is folly to stay away from Him, under pretense of waiting for qualifications that He alone can give. Take Him at His word, follow His directions, do just as He says; for, consider further, He is the

AUTHOR OF ETERNAL SALVATION only to them that *obey* Him. The fearful and unbelieving shall have their part with liars, in the lake that burneth with fire and brimstone. If you will be saved, you must resolve to take pains, and work out your salvation with fear and trembling. Noah thought little of the labor and expense of building the Ark. Nor must you expect to obtain eternal salvation, although it is a free gift, without much labor, and diligence, and fervent prayer. And you must make up your mind to brave the sneers and ridicule of the wicked. If Noah had consulted his credit instead of his safety, he would have been drowned with the rest. And what think you? Is it not better to be laughed at with a few who are saved, than to perish with the multitude? "For whosoever shall be ashamed of Me, and of My words, of him shall the Son of man be ashamed when He shall come in His own glory, and in His Father's, and of the holy Angels."

> Fearless defy all human blame,
>   And boldly own thy Lord;
> Endure the cross despise the shame,
>   And reap the rich reward.

3

Apple (or Citron Tree) among the Trees.
Altogether Lovely.

"THERE are many who say, 'Who will show us any good?'" But those who agree in this inquiry are not agreed as to the kind of good they so eagerly covet. One prizes pleasure most, another fame. But perhaps a majority regard gold and silver as the principal good; and multitudes resolve to pursue wealth at all hazards. Often they succeed, and what then? Are they satisfied? Was the rich baron, who died not long ago, leaving behind him the astounding sum of forty-four millions, satisfied? Nay, not he. An inspired writer says, "He that loveth silver, shall not be satisfied with silver." The richest man upon earth, if he have no better portion, finds himself as far as ever from rest and satisfaction. Put what you will, of created things, into the aching, hungry, craving void of the human heart; it still cries out insatiably, "Give! give!"

But suppose silver and gold *did* satisfy people. Suppose twenty shillings would always buy a certain amount of happiness; so that a man's joy increased just as fast as his riches were multiplied. And suppose that the man who had a hundred pounds was happy; and he that had a thousand pounds was more happy still; and he that had many thousands was happiest of all. What then? Why, just as the man might begin to think he had got enough, (if ever, indeed, such a time should come, and say to his soul, "Soul, thou hast much goods laid up for many years; eat, drink, and be merry"—just then might death strike him with his dart, and God would pronounce him a fool, because he had not laid up his treasure in heaven. Where, then, would be the glory, even if riches could purchase happiness, seeing that we must so soon be stripped of all, and go out of the world naked as we came into it? But riches *cannot give* us *contentment*, nor buy an hour's real pleasure. But here is something that can! Here is that which will be a full and satisfactory answer to, this most interesting question—"Who will show us any good?" "As the APPLE TREE among the trees of the wood, so is my Beloved among the sons."

APPLE TREE among the trees of the wood (Song 2:3). By the apple tree, to which Jesus Christ is here compared, is most likely meant the *citron apple tree,* which, in the East, is a very beautiful tree, and grows to a great size. Its height and comeliness render it the choicest "among the trees of the wood." A powerful reviving scent comes forth from the tree, perfuming the air, refreshing the weary traveler as he passes by, and inviting him to repose under its cool shadow. The leaves are of a deep green, and always continue on the tree; and its boughs are laden with fruit of a rich golden color, and of a most delicious taste. And so reviving is even the smell of these delicious apples, that the people use them just as we use scent—bottles, to restore the fainting, and revive the drooping; and the women of the country carry them about, or lay them up, for that purpose.

At one season of the year the golden apples and the snow-white blossoms hang both together on the tree. This may explain that passage—"A word fitly spoken is like *apples of gold in pictures* (or lattice-work) *of silver*" (Prov. 25:11). Words, you know, are in the Bible called "the fruit of the lips." And oh, how fit, how reviving, how delicious are the fruits of Christ's lips! His promises, His precepts, His invitations. "The words of the Lord are pure, enlightening the eyes, rejoicing the heart, converting the soul, making wise the simple. More to be desired are they than gold, yea, than much fine gold, sweeter also than honey and the honeycomb" (Ps. 19:7–10). What precious words are these, "Come unto Me, and I will give you rest"; and "If any man thirst, let him come unto Me and drink." No other tree but the Lord Jesus can bear such fruits as these, fruits which revive the fainting spirit. And well may they, who have tried their virtue, say still, "Comfort me with apples" (Song 2:6). "As the APPLE TREE among the trees of the wood, so is my Beloved among the sons."

Suppose yourself in a great forest, where you had taken refuge from the scorching heat of the sun. You have wandered about all day in want of food, and are fainting with thirst. Would you not be delighted to see before you a great apple tree, loaded with rich, ripe, golden fruit? Nothing could induce you to pass it by. It would be too tempting. "Oh," you would say, "this is just what I want! This is the best tree I have seen yet." And you would hasten to get under its shadow, and eagerly pluck the tempting fruit.

Now here you have a picture of the Lord Jesus. As this "*Apple tree among the trees of the wood, so is my Beloved among the sons,*"—so is Christ among all created objects. No other tree is to be compared with this. Some are poisonous trees, which Satan has planted. And some are prickly, and wound the hands of those that touch them. Only this Tree of trees can furnish the soul with food and medicine, shelter and support, and satisfy all its wants. Those that have tasted that the Lord is gracious, can witness to this. Each of them is ready to say,

"I sat down under His shadow with great delight, and His fruit was sweet to my taste."

You have often thought what a beautiful place the garden of Eden must have been, when Adam and Eve walked through its groves, before their sin brought a curse upon it, and uprooted it all. "Out of the ground made the Lord God to grow every tree that is pleasant to the sight, and good for food." But amidst all the trees, there were two there which no other garden or orchard on earth ever had. There was "the Tree of Knowledge of good and evil"; and *that* was a *forbidden tree*. And therefore, however good it might be in itself, it was evil for those who offended God by touching it. Then there was "the Tree of Life," the fruit of which they were not forbidden to touch.

You would listen with great interest if I could show you what sort of trees they were, and what kind of fruit they bore. But though I cannot satisfy you curiosity; I cannot show you boughs plucked from those trees, nor set before you pictures of them; yet, blessed be God! I can show you *a better Tree than either of them*. "What! better than the Tree of Knowledge?" Yes, better than the Tree of Knowledge, for that turned out to them that ate of it, the Tree of Death. And better than the Tree of Life too. Behold it! Come and look at this TREE of trees, the true TREE OF KNOWLEDGE, of which you may eat and grow wise, and *not* die—the true TREE OF LIFE, of which, if you eat, you shall live forever. Oh, taste its fruit, "taste and see that the Lord is good"; and tell me if you think there is such another tree in all the world. Its wide-spreading branches stretch far away over the whole earth, laden with the blessings of salvation. Its *shadow* gives safety and defense. Those that dwell under it shall "revive as the corn and grow as the vine." Its *leaves* are for the healing of the nations; and its *fruit*—no tongue can describe it. Angels and men, to all eternity, will feed and feast on it; and drink in from its wondrous virtue, immortality and eternal life, fullness of joy, and pleasures forevermore. But in vain we discourse of its excellence. You must taste it, or you can know nothing of it. Ho! ye wanderers! ye discontented ones! ye who feed on husks, and say, "Who will show us any good?" Bend your steps hither. Come and sit down under the shadow of this Tree. Yea, *dwell* here and live on the fruit that continually drops from its branches. "Eat abundantly, O friends, and drink, O beloved; eat ye that which is good, and let your souls delight themselves in fatness." So, when you have *tasted* and *handled* for yourselves, shall you be ready to speak of Him to others, and joyfully witness, with all true Christians, that He is the

ALTOGETHER LOVELY (Song 5:16). We often speak of a lovely face or a lovely character. But neither is the person nor character of any man or woman on earth "*Altogether lovely.*" You can scarcely name one who has not some visible fault or prominent failing. One is good-tempered, but slothful. Another may be learned, but selfish. He may be versed in all sciences; but, as dead flies spoil the savor of the richest ointment, "so doth a little folly him that is in reputation for wisdom and honor" (Eccl. 10:1). We read in the Bible of a great field marshal who had fame and fortune—BUT he was a leper. Absalom was exceedingly handsome in face and figure—BUT he was a monster of wickedness. Solomon was wise above all that ever lived, BUT he was foolish enough to bow to false gods. Peter was a man of great boldness and courage, BUT once a serving maid jeered him out of his religion. And suppose you could find one who was free from all the faults just mentioned; still, whoever he is, he is a *sinner;* and this is ever a most serious deformity.

We must go to the higher world to find one who answers to "Altogether Lovely." Come, let us search among the angels. But, "Behold, He put no trust in His servants, and His angels He charged with folly"(Job 4:18). At the best their loveliness is but a little stream flowing from the Great Fountain of Uncreated Beauty. Lo! yonder, in the midst of the throne, is He of whom we are in quest. Fasten your eyes on the Lord Jesus. He is the ALTOGETHER LOVELY. You cannot name a single good quality that He does not possess in all its perfection. He is "the brightest, sweetest, fairest one, whom eyes have seen or angels known." A Lamb truly without spot or blemish.

> All over LOVELY is my Lord,
> Must be beloved and yet adored;
> His worth, if all the nations knew,
> Sure the whole earth would love Him too.

Oh that I could worthily set Him forth! Oh that I had the tongue of that man of God, which was like the "pen of a ready writer," when his "heart was indicting a good matter" concerning the King! "Thou art Fairer than the children of men," said he. "Thou art the Chiefest among ten thousand," said Solomon. "As the APPLE TREE among the trees of the wood, so is my Beloved among the sons." Isaiah's lips are on fire when he talks of Christ. He calls Him the "BRANCH beautiful and glorious," the "FRUIT comely and excellent." And again he describes Him as a Mighty Conqueror arrayed in "glorious apparel, traveling in the greatness of His strength." Ezekiel paints Him as a tender SHEPHERD, going forth on the "mountains, where His sheep have been scattered in the cloudy and dark day," and gathering the poor wanderers into His fold. And the apostles, who were "eye-witnesses of His majesty," and saw how *full* He was of grace and truth, could not speak or write of Him without wonder and praise. If we talk of wisdom, does He not know everything? If we speak of mercy, is He not Love itself? If of glory, O how glorious must He be who made the bright sun and built the lofty sky! He is a complete universe of unimaginable beauty and multifarious excellence which eternity will not unravel; an unsearchable shoreless ocean of ineffable loveliness. ALTOGETHER LOVELY! Lavish all your love upon Him, Christian! Expend on Him all the reverential admiration, and exulting praise, and adoring delight, of which your nature is capable. Do this now, do it always, do it through all eternity, and all will fall infinitely short of His transcendent beauty. He is Fairer than all the children of men, and Brighter than all the angels of light, and infinitely more glorious than the maturest conceptions even of Cherubim and Seraphim. Alas! how deplorable that blindness which does not see His beauty so as to be in love with it! You pity the condition of the blind man, who never has aught before him but a dismal blank, while you can see the green fields, the lovely sky, and all the fair objects of which the world is so full. And you say, when you contrast your own favored lot with his, "Truly, the light is sweet, and a pleasant thing it is for the eyes to behold the sun." But yet that blind man may have his inward eye open, and be entertained with such sights of the glory of Christ; as may cause him to sing for joy.

But here is a blindness that shuts the soul quite out from the light of God's love: one who is thus blinded, "*cannot see* the kingdom of God"; cannot at all "*see* the good of His chosen." Satan blindfolds him, lest the light of the glory of the Sun of Righteousness should shine into his mind. Poor benighted soul! Oh, awake out of sleep, and hasten to Him who counsels *thee* to anoint thine eyes with eye-salve of His own providing, that thou mayest see. "Rise, He calleth thee," and is waiting to perform that wondrous cure on the eyes of thy mind, which He performed on the bodily eyes of those who cried to Him, "Thou Son of David, have mercy on us." Then you will (by that faith which is the evidence of things not seen) "behold the beauty of the Lord," while you "inquire in His temple"; and hereafter, in the land that is very far off, you shall, without a veil, "see the King in His beauty," and be "satisfied when you awake in His likeness."

> Millions of years you wond'ring eyes
>   Shall o'er His beauties rove;
> And endless ages you'll adore
>   The glories of His love.

ALL AND IN ALL (Col. 3:11). "Christ is ALL AND IN ALL." He is ALL in creation, providence, redemption, grace, and glory. He is IN ALL. He is IN ALL events, making all to work together for good to His people. He is IN ALL places. "He compasses our path, and our lying down. If we ascend up into heaven, He is there; if we make our bed in hell, behold, He is there!" and whither can we flee from His presence? He is in the sunless depths of the sea, and keeps the great whale alive, and watches over the scattered bones of those who have sunk in the mighty waters, till He shall bid them rise. He is at the top of the frozen mountain, where none can stand before His cold; and there, where there is no eye but His, "He giveth snow like wool, and scattereth the hoar frost like ashes." He is alike in the waste howling wilderness, which "no man passeth through," and in the crowded city; He is equally in the hovel of the beggar and the palace of the prince. But in a higher sense, He is IN ALL the assemblies of His people, for he has *appointed* to meet them, and "that to bless them." And in a higher sense still, He is IN ALL their hearts, "formed in them the hope of glory."

Now, is Christ thus in you? If He is, He is your ALL, and for you to live is Christ. That which men love best, is their *all*. The covetous man loves gold best. He worships it; he gives his time, and sells his soul for it. This is his *Apple tree among the trees*. He admires it above all the trees of the wood, and he seeks to protect himself under its shadow, and solace himself with its fruits—but in vain. He finds out that peace and joy do not grow on this tree; the apples he gathers from its branches do but mock his hunger, and provoke his thirst. And so, miserable and dissatisfied, he "pines away in his iniquity." In the same manner does the proud man seek for praise and honor. *His* All is to shine in the world, no matter by what means; so that he can but climb to a higher and still a higher pinnacle, and look down on his neighbors, he thinks he shall be satisfied. While she that liveth in pleasure, makes that her All, and is dead while she lives.

I could take you to a mean lodging in London, where there lives a poor woman nearly eighty, whose income is but two and sixpence per week. Yet, this is her language, "Though in the depths of poverty, I am contented and happy, for Christ is my ALL and having Him, I am rich. I have known Him from my youth, and He has 'carried me to hoar hairs.' I am solitary, but not alone; Christ is my Friend and Companion. And even if death find me without a friend near, I still have him by my side; and what can I want else? Who can do so much for me as He?" She feels she is "complete in Him." And who can be more than complete? Happy saint! destitute, but rolling in riches—poor, yet possessing all things. Having found one Pearl of great price, she has seized on this as her sole treasure, and thus possesses all things in one. She can say,

> I've found the Pearl of greatest price,
>   My heart doth sing for joy!
> And sing I must—a Christ I have,
>   All gold without alloy.
>
> Christ is my meat, Christ is my Drink,
>   My Med'cine and my Health—
> My Peace, my Strength, my Joy, my Crown,
>   My Glory, and my Wealth.
>
> My Savior is the Heaven of Heaven—
>   And what shall I Him call?

> My Christ if First—my Christ is Last—
> My Christ is ALL IN ALL.

Now all, whether young or old, who come to their right mind, are led thus to make Christ their ALL. For Him they live and labor; they love to speak of Him and to praise Him. To serve Him in their meat and drink, and to promote His cause is their business. Is He thus your ALL? Very soon you will be laid in the grave. All your worldly plans will fail; and that part of you which thinks, and enjoys, and grieves, will go into another world. Do you think it will give you any pleasure *there*, reflect on fine clothes, riches, or earthly pleasures? Will it matter to you *there*, whether you have been poor or rich? Whether admired or unknown? Not at all. Life will have passed away "as a dream when one awaketh." Christ will be ALL, and these things nothing. The most obstinate lover of money, the most devoted follower of pleasure, will then own it to be so. The only question with us in eternity will be, "Did we love Christ in time?"

A few years ago there lived in London a celebrated sculptor, who was often commissioned to set up costly statues and monuments, in cathedrals and other public places. This sculptor possessed both skill and genius, and by his labors he acquired more money and fame than at first he had aspired to. But he had a better portion than these, for Christ was his ALL; and so his life was useful and his death happy; as they shall be indeed with every one who thus chooses the good part. This man not only made magnificent and costly tombs for other people, but he made one for himself. It was a very modest one, and this was the inscription—"*What I was as an artist, seemed of some importance while I lived; but what I really was as a believer in Christ Jesus, is the only thing of importance to me now.*" At his death, it was placed in Tottenham Court Road Chapel; where, by it, he, being dead, yet speaketh, and by that silent monument impressively remindeth every beholder that *a man's glory and riches cannot go with him to the other world.*

But what *does* go with him into the other world? The dying man takes *something* away, which he did not bring with him. What is it? What does that man carry away with him, who makes Christ his ALL? He takes away with him "holiness, without which no man can see the Lord." And this Christ gives him, for He is made unto him sanctification. And then the man who made riches and pleasure his *all*—ah! what does *he* take with him? Nothing of that he has toiled for all his life? Must others gather *all* the riches he has heaped up? I remember reading an account of a most dreadful storm at sea, which overtook a vessel on her way from India. There was one on board who had spent his whole life in getting money, and who now was returning home, as he thought, to live at his ease and enjoy his fortune. And in that awful moment, when death stared him in the face, he "cursed his God and looked upward"; and bitterly complained that the treasures he had labored for so earnestly, were now about to sink in the ocean. Well may the poet say—

> How shocking must thy summons be, O death!
> To him that is at ease in his possessions;
> Who, counting on long years of pleasure here
> Is quite unfurnished for the world to come.

But does the wicked man take nothing away with him when he goes into eternity? He takes that away with him, which he would give the world to shake off. But he *cannot get rid of it*. It cleaves to him, and will not leave him. What is it? He *takes all* HIS SIN *with him*. And the fearful burden will sink him into hell. "Ye shall die in your sins; and where I am, thither ye cannot come."

And now, you are about to go your ways into the world once more. You daily walk in the midst of tempters. And one says, "Lo here!" and another, "Lo there!" Go not after them, but remember that you have had set before you, today, that which is *really good*; viz., Jesus Christ as a TREE, bearing all manner of fruit, fruit that makes rich, fruit that gives life, fruit that quenches the soul's thirst, fruit that enlightens the eyes, and abundantly satisfies all who eat of it.

Also, that same Jesus, as the ALTOGETHER LOVELY. He has no spot, nor defect, nor blemish whatever. He is in every way worthy of your highest love. He is ALL AND IN ALL; and having Him, you will want nothing. If, in this life, God should give you outward comforts, then you will enjoy Him IN ALL. And, if you be destitute of them, then you shall enjoy ALL in God; and be able to say with Habakkuk, " 'Although the fig-tree shall not blossom, neither shall fruit be in the vines, the labor of the olive shall fail, and the fields shall yield no meat,' yet, since no mildew can ever taint the fruit which grows on Christ the TREE OF LIFE, I shall still partake of that, and be able to 'rejoice in the Lord, and joy in the God of my salvation.' " Oh come, all of you, "TASTE and SEE that the Lord is good."

> Dear Savior, let Thy Beauties be
> My soul's eternal FOOD;
> And grace command my heart away
> From all created good.

4

Anchor. Advocate. Almighty. Ancient of Days.

WHAT is a patron? A friend, but with special qualities. A friend may be poor and dependent, like ourselves; whereas a patron is higher than we; more influential, or richer, stronger, wiser, and therefore able to do much more for us than one in our own station. Now I know of One, who more than answers to this description, and is willing to befriend *you*. His friendship I earnestly recommend you to make sure of this day. He can plead your cause on earth, and speak a good word for you, at the same time, in heaven. In the day of judgment, that tremendous day, He can sustain you, and, before angels and men, pronounce you free from condemnation, and own you as His. Listen, then, to what I have to say of Him; and then tell me if you will not choose Him for your Patron. And first, take this Scripture image of Him. He is an "ANCHOR of the soul, both sure and steadfast."

ANCHOR. Hebrews 6:18, 19. " 'Hope,' in these two verses, cannot well mean the grace of hope that is in us, for it is said to be a hope set before us, and a hope which we fly to, and take fast hold upon. Hope, therefore, includes, and in this verse directly signifies, the Object of hope, or that which is hoped in, as it often does in other places; and this object of it most directly means Christ."

The anchor is attached to the ship, to keep it steady, and hold it fast in one place. In the dark night, on a dangerous coast, when the sailor cannot see his way, he throws out his anchor; which, hid amongst the rocks under water, keeps the vessel from drifting about. Anciently, they used to have as many as eight anchors, besides a principal one, which was called the sheet anchor. When Paul was on that voyage, in which he and the crew were shipwrecked, they found themselves, one night, running into great danger; and so, wishing to keep still till morning, "they cast four anchors out of the stern, and wished for the day." If it had not been for those anchors, the ship would have been driven ashore and dashed to pieces in that dark and stormy night.

And do we not here see an instructive Image of Him who is called our Hope and our Confidence? The anchor is not seen; and one might wonder why the buoyant ship is so steady amidst the boisterous waves; and why the wind, that bloweth where it listeth, doth not drive her to destruction. So Christ is not seen. He has entered within the veil, and only faith can reach Him there. But then this faith, like the cable, which connects the vessel with the anchor, so joins Christ and the soul together, that, while she holds fast without wavering, she cannot perish, nor be cast away; but shall outride every storm.

Look at the ships in yonder harbor, heaving up and down on the unsteady wave. Last night you watched them, while the heavens gathered blackness, and the wind rose, and the waves lifted themselves up, and rushing onward with wild disorder, threatened to carry everything along with them. All night the wind howled over the roof, and roared in the chimneys, and you thought, surely nothing but a strong house, built on the firm earth, could be safe at such a time. And you remembered the ships, and were not without fears that they must be all swept away, or dashed in pieces against each other. But when the night had passed, and the commotion had ceased, you looked for them, and they were all there; not one was missing. Even the little boats had not moved away. How was this? What enabled them to weather the storm? They were all made fast to their anchors, and these were sure and steadfast. And that which kept the people in the ships from fear, was the confidence they felt in their anchors. So the Christian's heart is fixed on his Savior, and he can sing and give thanks in a storm; as it is written, "Thou wilt keep him in perfect peace, whose mind is stayed on Thee; because he trusteth in Thee."

> Amidst the roaring of the sea,
> My soul still stays her hope on Thee;
> Thy constant love, Thy faithful care,
> Is all that saves me from despair.

Oft has the world wondered, while fire, and sword, and torture have been applied to drive Christians to deny their Savior. Cruel persecutors have kindled a fire, and, summoning before them some victim of their spite, have bidden him prepare for a frightful death! But, while they would have turned pale at the bare thought of holding one of their fingers in the flames for half a minute, they have looked at the martyr, and, lo! he stood before them with undaunted countenance, prepared for the worst they could do. And what was the secret of his steadfastness? Was it obstinacy? Was it hardness of heart? Not so. The holy man had fastened his faith on an unseen Savior, and that Savior supported him in his hour of trial. The world saw the threatening waves; it marked the frailty of the little bark exposed to their rage, and said, "It will certainly founder!" But it saw not the STRONG CABLE—FAITH, nor the STEADFAST ANCHOR—CHRIST WITHIN THE VEIL.

There lived at Carthage, two hundred years after the crucifixion of our Lord, a Christian lady named Perpetua. She loved the Lord Jesus, and, not being ashamed to own Him, she was seized, and together with her dear little infant, cast into prison. Her father, who loved her tenderly, knowing that there was nothing but a dreadful death before her if she did not recant, went to see her in the prison, and tried to persuade her to deny Christ. First he sought to move her by tears and entreaties; and then he tried reproaches; and then he set before her the grief of her mother, and the helplessness of her babes. But all in vain; she would not deny Christ. The judge also urged her to consider her own life, and her father's tears; but she loved her Savior better than all, and she would not forsake Him. At last the day of execution came, and this lovely and innocent woman suffered herself to be thrown to the beasts in the amphitheatre, rather than deny Christ. Her faith had taken a fast hold on her unseen Savior as the AN-CHOR of her soul, and this hold on Him kept her unmoved amidst the fierceness of the storm. She was faithful unto death, and received a crown of life.

In all tempests of trouble, this divine ANCHOR it is which saves the good man from shipwreck. "I had fainted," said David, "unless I had believed." In the storm of temptation, Peter was sorely tossed on the billows, and well-nigh wrecked. But this ANCHOR saved him from drifting quite out to sea; and he lived to write, years afterwards, of the Lord, "who knoweth how to deliver the godly out of temptation"; while Judas had no hold on this ANCHOR, and was dashed in pieces against the rocks. Woe! woe to that ship that loseth her anchor! She must be driven to sea, or be broken on the shoals. Wherefore, "let us hold fast the beginning of our confidence steadfast to the end." For Christ is "as an An-chor of the soul, both sure and steadfast; which entereth into that within the veil," where He appears as our "ADVOCATE WITH THE FATHER."

ADVOCATE. 1 John 2:1. And what is an Advocate? Amongst us it signifies one who pleads for another in a court of justice. Two travelers agree to pursue their journey in company. They have not been many days together, before one of them misses his purse, and accuses the other of having robbed him, which he stoutly denies. Notwithstanding, he is cast into prison, there to await the As-sizes. Immediately, he sends for one, whose business it is to plead before the judges, and puts his case into his hands. The time of trial draws near; the arrival of the judge is proclaimed by sonorous trumpets, heard by the outside world without emotion, but awakening the utmost excitement within the prison walls. By-and-by, the accused one is placed at the bar, his indictment is read, witnesses are examined, and the case against him fully argued. He listens anxiously, his restless eye ofttimes wandering towards the place where sits his only friend in the crowded court—the Advocate; while his ear eagerly catches every question ad-dressed by him to the witnesses in their cross-examinations. Presently his Advocate rises amidst the hushed court, and makes a touching and eloquent speech, carefully dissecting the adverse testimony, and, in the end, overturning all the evidence. He concludes with an appeal, not to the *clemency* of the court, but to its, *justice,* and boldly claims the acquittal of his client. Meanwhile look at the prisoner! His eye is lit up with exultation, and his countenance flushed with conscious victory. Well—but what say the jury? "NOT GUILTY." And so he goes forth with a character clear and unsullied, and "receives beauty for ashes, and the garment of praise for the spirit of heaviness." Would this man ever forget his Advocate?

Now thus it is written in the New Testament concerning Christ Jesus, "If any man sin, we have an ADVOCATE with the Father, Jesus Christ the Righteous" (1 John 2:1). And thus it is written in the Old Testament, concerning the same gracious Patron, "He shall stand at the right hand of the poor, to save him from them that would condemn his soul" (Psalm 109:31). And who are those who would condemn the soul of the believer? There are several that accuse and condemn him; and alas! there is too much reason.

First, there is Apollyon. He is called the "Accuser of the brethren." He accused Job, before God, of being a hypocrite. And in Zechariah 3:1, we read that when "Joshua stood before the Lord, Satan stood at his right hand to resist him." And the Lord rebuked the accuser, pleaded Joshua's cause, and told those who stood by to "take away his filthy garments." So his polluted "prison dress" was taken away, and he was clothed with change of raiment. And still Satan accuses the brethren. Then if Conscience is tender, *that* accuses. For "what man is he which liveth and sinneth not?" And that is not a Christian conscience, which takes no notice of sins and miscarriages. And God, who is greater than the heart, and knoweth all things—He by His Spirit convicts, and by His Law condemns. And the World accuses the Christian; sometimes falsely; and sometimes it calls those things crimes which are his glory.

What, then, would the Christian do, if it were not for his Advocate? And, oh! what an Advocate! Think, for a moment, who He is that "pleads the causes of his soul." Do we look for worth and dignity in our Advocate? "He is lifted up in the heavenly places, far above principality, and power, and might, and dominion, and every name that is named." But does this, His excellence, make us afraid? Are we unwilling to tell our troubles to One so great, so high? Do we suspect He is too lordly to plead for our unworthy names? Behold, it is written, "The Lord will maintain the cause of the afflicted, and the right of the poor" (Psalm 111:12). And "though the Lord be high, yet He hath respect to the lowly." Or do we ask for eloquence in an advocate? Never man spake this Man, for grace is poured into His lips. And "Him the Father heareth always." Who then shall lay anything to the charge of those for whom Christ pleadeth? It is God that justifieth. Who is he that shall condemn? Give Him, then, your cause to plead, nor fear the result.

But still you object—you say, "Indeed, if I were innocent—if I could say, 'They lay to my charge things which I know not,' I would expect him to notice me. But it is not so. My case differs from that just mentioned; *I am verily guilty.* Alas! whither shall I go? *I have done the things whereof I am accused.*" Well, Jesus Christ knows all that ever you did. And yet He is still willing to undertake your cause! What if Satan accuse, and the Law arraign, and Conscience condemn, and all justly? Labor not to contradict or satisfy them! Tarry not to argue it out with them! Away with all your excuses and apologies! Throw yourself on Christ, the ADVOCATE, who "maketh intercession for the transgressors"; who is also your Judge; and who, after all, will have the last word, when Satan, and the World, and Sin, and Conscience, and Law, shall have said their worst. Lift up your heads,

> Your Advocate appears
> For your defense on high;
> His plea the Father hears,
> And lays His thunder by;
> Not all that hell or sin can say,
> Shall turn His heart, His love away.

"If any man sin, we have an ADVOCATE with the Father, Jesus Christ the righteous; and He is the propitiation for our sins." This word "propitiation" means a *Covering.* And Christ covers our sins with His most precious blood. The crimson stream flows over them, and conceals them from view. Here, then, we see the reason why His advocacy prevails. You know an Advocate must have something to show on behalf of his clients. Christ cannot show our righteousness; we have none. He cannot say to the Judge, "These accused ones are innocent." No; we have dishonored the law, insulted the Majesty of heaven, and done what we could to overturn the government of God. And the penalty, which we have thus incurred, if borne by ourselves, will crush us forever. What then was to be done? What way of escape could be devised?

> Blest be the Lord that sent His Son
> To take our flesh and blood!
> He for our lives gave up His own,
> To make our peace with God.
> He honored all His Father's laws,
> Which we have disobeyed;
> He bore our sins upon the cross,
> And our full ransom paid.

This, then, is what the Advocate shows—*Himself* as our ATONEMENT. His blood is the price of our ransom. And He says, "Let these go their way, for I have borne their sins in my own body. I received their chastisement. I was bruised for their iniquities." The Father allows the plea; and thus "with His stripes we are healed." Not one of all the angels in heaven could have done or suffered thus for us, and, therefore, no angel could be our Advocate; not having any means of reconciling us to God. But the Lord Jesus could suffer and die in our stead, and so plead effectually on our behalf. Yea, in all things He is able to save to the uttermost; for He is "the ALMIGHTY."

ALMIGHTY. Revelation 1:8. While some profanely blaspheme the worthy name of Christ by denying His Deity, we rejoice to cry, Hallelujah! for the Lord Omnipotent reigneth! Who but the ALMIGHTY could create yonder sun, and those stars of light, and this world, and you and me? And yet the Scriptures say, "all things were made by Him," viz., Christ. Who but the ALMIGHTY can hold up the great planets in their places, and urge them in their courses round the sun, without deviation from year to year? But the Scriptures affirm that by Jesus Christ "all things consist." Who but the ALMIGHTY could by one effort take away the sins of the world? Who but the ALMIGHTY can save your soul, Christian? Could a creature do it? Would you trust Gabriel? Could you commit the keeping of your soul to the eldest, the strongest, the greatest of all the Angels, or to hundreds of them together? No! "Salvation belongs only to the Lord." Only the ALMIGHTY can be trusted with souls. Therefore, we are exhorted to "commit the keeping of our souls unto Him as unto a Faithful Creator."

And when He was on earth, and to the outward eye seemed nothing more than a man, miracles attended Him wherever He went; and virtue went from Him to all around. At His word devils gave up their captives, and death surrendered his prey. One day he entered a house in Judea; and found a young girl smitten, like a blighted rose, by the hand of death; and the mourners stood around, bewailing her untimely end. But He who is the ALMIGHTY bade them stay their wailings; and then by a word, He brought her back from the realms of death. Once as He journeyed He met a mournful train at the gates of a city; a widow following her only son to the grave. He felt for that poor widow; and stopping the procession He said, "young man, I say unto thee, Arise"; the young man heard the command of the ALMIGHTY and straightway "he that had been dead sat up." Two sisters wept for the loss of their brother. "In their affliction He was afflicted"; for He "wept" with them. But He said, "Thy brother shall rise again." So He led them forth to the place of the dead; and there, at the mouth of that dreary and silent chamber He stood and called with a loud voice, "Lazarus, come forth!" And the sound of His words had not died away among the hollow caverns ere the dead man, aroused by the voice of the ALMIGHTY, rent the grave clothes with which he was bound, and stood before them alive!

By-and-by He who gave life to others was hanged on a tree, and yielding up His Spirit, was numbered with the dead. But at the appointed hour this ALMIGHTY Captive of the grave, who could see no corruption nor be held in the bands of death, burst the fetters and *raised Himself* from the dead. And at the last day, He will call to the dead who are hidden underground, and in charnel houses and churchyards, and under the lofty pyramids; and at His command the sea will give up the dead that are in its dark caves; and all will come to life, and stand up an "exceeding great army." Then will His Angels gather them together from the four winds, and rise with them to meet the Lord in the air; while He who is ALMIGHTY will set the whole world on fire, and melt it with fervent heat, as in a furnace. But while heaven and earth shall be thus passing away with a great noise, and all the nations of the earth, in one vast crowd, will be waiting mute with wonder and amazement, the wheels of His chariot will be heard rolling in heaven. And "every eye shall see Him" coming in the clouds with power and great glory. And thus, when all other thrones are forever cast down, Jesus, the ALMIGHTY, will ascend His great white throne and sit in judgment; for He is that ANCIENT OF DAYS, of whom we read in Daniel 7:9–11.

ANCIENT OF DAYS. "His garment is white as snow, and the hair of His head like the pure wool; His throne is like the fiery flame, and His wheels as burning fire. A fiery stream issues and comes forth from before Him; thousand thousands minister unto Him, and ten thousand times ten thousand stand before Him." And now "the judgment is set, and the books are opened." But who can paint that awful scene? And where shall the impenitent hide their heads? What rocks can conceal them? How will they answer those who accuse them? The ANCIENT OF DAYS has been the Witness of all their doings. He stood by when Cain slew his brother; and in the book of His remembrance are written all the sins of mankind, from the creation of the world to its burning. And now this book is opened, and "God requireth that which is past" (Eccl. 3:15). Thrice happy they who see in the Person of this awful Judge their prevailing ADVOCATE! who have made a Friend of Him before this "evil day came upon them," and have "put on the Lord Jesus" as the Lord their Righteousness. They, and only they, can now lift up their heads with joy, for their full salvation draws nigh. On every side see the wicked dragged unwillingly from their graves! Hear them cry affrighted, "Ye mountains! fall on us, and hide us from the face of the Judge; for the great day of His wrath is come, and who shall be able to stand?" But behold the believer in Christ! He springs joyfully from his open tomb, and raising his happy eyes to the great white throne, confidently claims Him who sits thereon as "The Lord his Righteousness," "his Glory and the Lifter-up of his head."

> Jesus, Thy blood and righteousness.
> My beauty are, my GLORIOUS DRESS:

'Midst flaming worlds, in these arrayed,
With joy shall I lift up my head.
Behold shall I stand in that great day,
For who aught to my charge shall lay?
Fully absolved through Thee I am,
From sin's tremendous curse and shame.

And now let me ask you—Will you have this glorious Being for your *Friend* and *Patron*? I will tell you once more what He is, and what He will do for you who trust in Him.

1. As an ANCHOR to your souls, He will keep you quiet in the dark night of sorrow, and peaceful in the midst of storms and troubles.

2. As your ADVOCATE, He will plead for you in heaven all the while you live on earth; and *such* a Friend at *such* a court is surely beyond all estimation.

3. As the ALMIGHTY, He will do all for you in the best manner, and without fail; He will befriend you till you die, and raise you up from the ruins of the grave.

4. After He shall have done all this, He it is, and not another, who will sit as the ANCIENT OF DAYS and judge you. And oh! who would you have for a Judge, if not One who has known you thoroughly, and loved you sincerely all your life long; who has said all He can say in your behalf; who, as your ATONEMENT, has spilt His heart's blood for you; and who conceals all your shame, by giving you His own most perfect righteousness for your glorious apparel?

I ask again, WILL YOU HAVE THE LORD CHRIST FOR YOUR FRIEND AND PATRON?

5

Angel. Apostle. Arm of the Lord.

THE tabernacle lamp was still burning, for the sun had not yet risen, when the child Samuel was aroused from his soft chambers by a voice pronouncing his name. Thinking it was the aged Eli who called him, he rose hastily and ran to know what he required. However, it was not the High Priest, but the Lord who had spoken. God had something to say to him. And so, when the voice came the third time, the awestruck boy timidly whispered, "Speak, Lord, for Thy servant heareth." And God calls each one of you. Not, it is true, with audible voice, mysteriously sounding in your chamber, at midnight or early dawn: but He calls you by His Son. The parent, the minister who admonishes you from the Scriptures, is the echo of *His* voice who is God's Messenger to a lost world, the "ANGEL OF THE COVENANT."

ANGEL, or "Messenger of the Covenant" (Mal. 3:1). See also Genesis 48:16, where He is called the "Angel of God's presence"; also Isaiah 63:9. There are several reasons why He is called an Angel, which perhaps we shall discover if we first inquire What Angels are—What they were made for—and How they are employed.

Kings have their favorite cities where they dwell in state. All Judea was under King Solomon, and all the Jews were his subjects. But there was one place above all others, where his greatness was seen, and where he held his court. That was Jerusalem. And there he built a sumptuous house of costly stones and cedar. And he set up on lofty steps his famous ivory throne, overlaid with pure gold and adorned with carved figures of lions. And around it stood his officers and servants in gorgeous apparel. When the queen of Sheba visited King Solomon, and saw his palaces and gardens, his cupbearers and officers, the silver, the gold, and the ivory—and when she heard his wisdom—for he was wise above all princes—she almost envied his servants, and exclaimed, "Happy are these thy men, and happy are these thy servants, which stand continually before thee and hear thy wisdom."

But do we not know of a greater King than Solomon, and happier servants than his, and a much more glorious palace, and a far loftier throne; where, robed in splendor, and clothed with majesty, and shrouded in dazzling brightness, sits the Almighty Lord of Angels and King of Kings? All creation was built for a temple to show His glory; all creatures are His servants and do His pleasure. But in that splendid house He is *most seen* and *best served*. We here beneath see but the "beams of His chambers" which He hath laid in the firmament, and on which He hath reared His stories in the heavens. And the stars we gaze at in the clear night, are but as the distant glimmering of the ten thousand lamps that encircle the throne of the Eternal. But there, in the third heaven, the Almighty has His "throne, high and lifted up," whence He issues His commands. And though He needeth not their help, there, continually, ten thousand times ten thousand bright Angels surround Him to wait on Him and do His commandments.

And surely if the queen of Sheba was overcome with admiration when she saw Solomon's glory, and called his servants "happy!" much more must we say of the Angels which "stand continually" before God. "Happy are they!" And their happiness you shall share if you give yourself up to Him, for He will take you by the hand, before long, and lead you into that holy company; and you shall be "like unto the Angels."

But more about the Angels. They are called "Thrones, Dominions, Principalities, and Powers." Some of them "do always behold the face of the Father," abide by His throne and cry one to another, "Holy, holy, holy, is the Lord of Hosts! Heaven and earth are filled with the majesty of His glory!" Some fly hither and thither, swift as the lightning, to do His errands; and coming again at the appointed times give account of their embassies (1 Kgs. 22:19; Job 1:6; 2:1). Some fight the battles of the Lord against the Prince of the power of the air. Michael and *his* Angels "contend with the Devil and *his* Angels" (Jude 1:9; Rev. 12:7). Sometimes they come to earth with orders to kill and to destroy. An Angel, one night, killed one hundred and eighty-five thousand soldiers who were come up to fight against God's People (Isa. 37:36). At evening when the sun went down, there they lay encamped in the field like grasshoppers for multitude. But when the king arose early in the morning, "behold they were all dead corpses!"

> For the Angel of death spread his wings on the blast,
> And breathed in the face of the foe as he passed;
> And the eyes of the sleepers waxed deadly and chill,
> And their hearts but once heaved, and forever grew still.
>
> And there lay the warrior distorted and pale,
> With the dew on his brow, and the rust on his mail;

And the tents were all silent, the banners alone,
The lances unlifted, the trumpet unblown.

That was the errand of justice; but how often, since the foundation of the world, they have winged their way to it on errands of love. And still they encamp around the good at night, and bear them up in their hands by day, and wait on them continually. "Millions of spiritual beings walk the earth" and throng the air. And all are invisible as the wind, and swift and silent as the sunbeams. But if you ask me how those ethereal spirits live, and how they move so swiftly, I cannot tell you. Perhaps the ease with which your *thought* moves about may best explain it. You know we can send our *thought* to the most distant part of the world. Our *thought* can travel about like an Angel. It can go a thousand miles in an instant. It can sail across seas and oceans without fear of shipwreck. It can fly over deserts and forests where the foot of man cannot read. Stone walls offer no impediment to its progress; it can get into palaces and prisons, and climb up the steep mountainside without danger.

Let us try. Let our *thought* take a flight or two. We will imagine ourselves, hundreds of years ago, in Canaan. Before us lies a plain with clusters of palm trees. On this plain there are flocks and herds and camels, and many servants busied in tending them. In the midst are tents; and within the door of one of them, to shade himself from the heat of the day, sits a mild and venerable man, called Abraham. While we admire this lovely scene, behold three men draw near; and Abraham makes haste, and bows himself to the ground, and invites them to eat with him. And soon Abraham finds out that in entertaining these strangers, he has "entertained Angels unawares." One of the three is the Lord Jesus, the Uncreated ANGEL. And after their repast, the Lord, giving the two Angels, His attendants, their orders, and telling them to go forward to Sodom, stays behind with Abraham and talks with him.

But what can the good Angels be sent to that riotous and wicked town for? Let us go after them, and see what their business is. It is evening when they get to Sodom, and going in at the gate they are seen by Lot, who hastens to salute them and entreats them to tarry all night at his house. They appear to be strangers, but they know more of the town than Lot does, and they tell him more than he knew before—That the cry of the wicked people had gone up to God; and that they were sent to deliver him, and burn the place and the people. So they urge him to arise and call all his sons and daughters, and get ready to desert. And at the early dawn those kind Angels hasten him; and while he lingers they lay hold on him, and bring him forth, and his wife and his daughters. And they say, "Escape for thy life! Make haste! for we cannot do anything till thou art safe." And so Lot hurried away, and as the sun arose he entered Zoar. And when

Lot was safe, a horrible tempest of fire and brimstone came down on the guilty place he had left behind, and burned it up.

But now let our *thought* go elsewhere. Let it go to Babylon, that far-famed city with its hundred gates of brass, and its walls whose broad tops were like wide streets. We stand by the palace of the king. The shadows of night are just breaking away. The gate of the palace suddenly opens and forth issues Darius the king. Let us follow him. He quickens his steps. He makes his way to the place of execution. And now he stops close beside the dens where the lions are kept which devour the condemned. Listen! He calls with a lamentable voice, as to someone at the bottom of the den among the beasts. "O Daniel! Servant of the living God! Is thy God, whom thou servest continually, able to deliver thee from the lions?" At once a cheerful voice from within answers, "O king, live forever! *My God hath sent His Angel, and he hath shut the lions' mouths*, and they have not hurt me."

If you are not tired we will take another journey. We will fly over deserts and mountains, and scale the walls of the prison at Jerusalem. Within a gloomy dungeon, chained up, is a captive. Beside him sit two grim-looking Roman soldiers. Observe the prisoner! How peaceful are his slumbers! A smile lights up his countenance as though he were dreaming about heaven. But suddenly the dark cell is filled with a dazzling light! An angel stands over him, and causing his chains to fall off, tells him to "gird himself, put on his garments, and follow him." Like one in a trance he follows his shining leader; while the iron gates of the prison one after the other fly open before them of their own accord. They reach the street, and then the Angel disappears, leaving Peter to himself and says, "Now I know of a surety that the Lord hath sent His Angel and hath delivered me out of the hands of Herod."

But we must return.—You see what Angels are and what they do. They are the guards and guides of God's people, and minister to them as long as they live. And when the good man lies on the bed of death, there, in the sick chamber, unseen, unheard,

> Angels, joyful to attend,
> Hovering, round his pillow bend;
> Wait to catch the signal given,
> And escort him quick to heaven.

But now it is high time to ask, Why is our blessed Savior called an Angel? Is He of the same nature as the Angels? That cannot be. For it is written, "He took not on Him the nature of Angels." In what way then does He resemble them?

1. *Christ is like the Angels in His appearances.* Long before He took on Him the seed of Abraham He used often to appear in the world. And when He did so, He chose to come in the form in which Angels appeared, which seems to have been that of beautiful and dignified men. Thus He visited Abraham in company

with two created Angels. Again, one night, "there wrestled a Man with Jacob, and he held Him till morning." And then this Unknown Traveler said, "Let me go, for the day breaketh." But Jacob held Him fast and clung yet more closely to Him. He dared not let Him go; for he found it was his Savior who thus stopped to try the strength of his faith. And Jacob "wept and made supplication to Him" till he obtained the blessing. In after years the Lord, the Uncreated ANGEL, came to Gideon as he was thrashing wheat; and sitting down in a friendly manner He saluted him, saying, "The Lord be with thee, thou mighty man of valor." Again, He appeared to Manoah and his wife, in the garb of a prophet or man of God; only with a countenance so glorious that the woman at once saw He was more than man; and when they asked after His name He told them it was Wonderful, or Secret. Thus in His appearances He was an ANGEL.

2. *Christ is like the Angels in His disposition.* The Angels take great delight in the affairs of this world. When it was first built, those "morning stars sang together, and the sons of God shouted for joy." And when sinners repent and begin to pray, Angels carry the news to heaven; and there is joy and singing among them in the presence of God. Yes, Gabriel the highest Angel, rejoices over a penitent boy or a little girl who loves her Bible and her Savior. So the great ARCHANGEL, the Lord Christ, when the foundations of the earth were laid, "rejoiced in the habitable parts of it, and His delights were with the children of men." On earth He was a Man of Sorrows. But what was that which once made Him rejoice in spirit and break out in a song of praise? Hear Him! "I thank Thee, O Father! Lord of heaven and earth! that Thou hast hid these things from the wise and prudent, and hast revealed them unto babes!"

3. *Christ is like the Angels in His ministrations.* As Angels are ministering spirits sent forth to minister to the heirs of salvation, so Christ "came not to be ministered unto but to minister." He stooped to wait on us, to carry our burdens, and guard and guide us through life; and in death He will come again and receive us to Himself. He is the "Angel who redeems us from all evil"; the "ANGEL of God's presence who saves us." In all our afflictions He is afflicted; and in His love and pity He redeems us, and carries us in His everlasting arms, as He did His people all the days of old. "Call upon Me," He says, "when you are in trouble, and I will deliver you." We may not pray to Angels, nor worship them, for they are creatures. But we must pray to this Uncreated ANGEL—this Lord of Angels. As did the Patriarch Jacob when Joseph's two boys stood at his bedside, waiting for his last dying blessing. Laying his hands on their heads, the venerable old saint said, "God, the God that fed me all my life long unto this day, the ANGEL which redeemed me from all evil, *bless the lads.*"

You remember the Angel coming to shut the lions' mouths while Daniel was among them? Just so does our blessed Savior restrain that "roaring lion" who desires to have us, to devour and to sift us. Glory be to Him! He will take the prey from the mighty. He will bruise Satan under our feet. Fear not, Christian, to walk in the path of duty! The lions may roar, but they are chained. You may have to walk through the very midst of them; but the Angel of the Covenant is by. Keep the strait and narrow path of duty; for "no lion shall be there, neither shall any ravenous beast go up thereon."

You remember the Angel leading Peter forth from the prison? Oh, what a delightful emblem of Christ's work in this world! He comes to deliver the lawful captive out of his dungeon. He comes to take off his chains! He comes with kind aspect to bid us "follow Him," that He may lead us where no frowning walls of despair shall enclose us, no chains of darkness gall our bruised limbs. Hast thou learned to rejoice in the ANGEL who comes to preach deliverance to captives—to proclaim the jubilee, the year of release? Only those who know what it is to groan under their spiritual fetters, know how to prize the liberty He brings. But, "If the Son shall make you free, you shall be free indeed."

> Long my imprisoned spirit lay,
> Fast bound in sin and nature's night;
> Thine eye diffused a quick'ning ray—
> I work—the dungeon flamed with light;
> My chains fell off, my heart was free,
> I rose, went forth, and followed Thee.

You remember the Angels delivering Lot? Thus does Christ come to snatch us from a fiery doom—a far worse tempest than that which buried the five wicked cities of the plain. And He holds back the tempest till "all that the Father hath given Him shall come to Him." And not till the last of His servants is safe, will He pour out the vials of His wrath on the world. But what the Angels said to Lot, that Jesus Christ says to you as you loiter, "Escape for thy life! Tarry not in all the plain." "Remember Lot's wife!" "Strive to enter in at the strait gate." Oh, listen to His counsels, linger no more, give not slumber to your eyelids! The night of respite is far spent! The day is at hand!—"the day of His fierce wrath which will burn as an oven." If the word spoken by the Angels to Lot was steadfast, and everything came to pass as they had said, oh, what will become of you if you neglect the warnings of this Lord and Maker of Angels?

4. *Christ is like the Angels in His errands.* As angels are messengers so Christ is SENT with tidings. And that must needs be an important message, which could not come by the hands of a *servant*, but must be brought by the *Son*. But this more properly belongs to the next Title in the series—

APOSTLE of our Profession (Heb. 3:1). The word "Apostle" signifies an AMBASSADOR, one sent with tidings, or on important business, or entrusted with power to make proposals. You know the Lord Jesus chose from among His disciples twelve to be Apostles, And He said to them, "As My Father hath SENT Me even so send I you" (John 20:21). An Apostle, then, is a minister of the gospel. But, just as an Archangel is great among Angels, so an Apostle is chief among preachers. God had sent many with great tidings to the Jews from age to age. "Last of all He sent His Son." How richly has God kept that promise to the Church, "I will give to Jerusalem one that bringeth good tidings." And when Christ went up into the mountain, and His disciples came unto Him, and He preached unto the assembled multitudes as they sat or stood scattered about on the hillside—surely some of them must have remembered the words of Isaiah, which they had often heard read in the Synagogue—"How beautiful upon the mountains are the feet of Him that bringeth good tidings, that publisheth peace!" Well might the children surround Him with palm branches, and shout as they followed Him into Jerusalem, "Hosanna to the Son of David!"

Angels are not sent to *preach the Gospel*; it is not their business. When an Angel came to Cornelius, it was not to show him the way of salvation, but to tell him to send for an *Apostle*, and to ask of him what he should do. Angels delivered the law on Sinai, as we read in Acts 7:53. But it was reserved for the Un-created ANGEL, the Prince of Angels, to be also the great APOSTLE, to bring the joyful tidings of salvation and to *preach the Gospel*. To this He was anointed. "Therefore we ought to give the more earnest heed to the things which we have heard, lest at any time we should let them slip. For if the word spoken by Angels was steadfast, and every transgression and disobedience received a just recompense of reward; how shall we escape if we neglect so great salvation; which at the first began to be spoken by the Lord and was confirmed unto us by them that heard Him?" (Heb. 2:1–4).

But what is the message that this GREAT APOSTLE brings from Him that sent Him? This is the substance of it. "Poor sinner, thou hast destroyed thyself body and soul! But I have good news for thee. I am willing to save thee. I have one Only-Begotten Beloved Son. He is the Bearer of these tidings. I have sent Him to die for thee, and to bless thee in turning thee away from thy iniquities. Yield thyself up to Him and thou shalt be saved. Thou art poor, but return to Me through Him, and I will enrich thee. Thou art vile, but I will cleanse thee. Thou art starving, but there is bread enough and to spare in My house. There is room in My heart for you all, and room in My house, too. Come then: I have spread My table, I have killed the fatted calf, I have made ready the feast; come to the banquet! Let not shame exclude thee! I will clothe thee in fine linen, clean and white, which is the righteousness of saints. I will lift up thy head so that thou shalt appear with honor before My holy Angels. I will enrich thee and exalt thee. I know thou art unworthy of all this; thou hast greatly sinned against Me. I know it all. But how can I give thee up, Ephraim? How shall I deliver thee to destruction? My heart is turned within Me, and My repentings are kindled together. I will not destroy thee, for I am God and not man. I have seen thy ways, and will heal thee and restore comfort to thee. I can speak peace to him that is near and to him that is far off. Wherefore look unto Me and be ye saved all ye ends of the earth." This is the message. And He who brings it is appointed to carry out all its provisions. He is "THE ARM OF THE LORD."

ARM OF THE LORD (Isa. 53:1). ALMIGHTY He is by virtue of His divine nature, so that no *physical* obstacles can stand against Him. But ALMIGHTY also by virtue of His appointment, so that no *legal* obstacles can stand against Him. Think of this, ye who pray; and hear Him say, "If ye ask anything in my name, I 'the ARM OF THE LORD' will do it." Think of this, trembling penitent. No guilt is too great for Him to deal with. The ARM OF THE LORD will take it away from off your shoulders, and plunge it into the depths of the sea. Think of it, perplexed afflicted Christian. The ARM OF THE LORD can "make a way in the sea, and a path in the mighty waters." Think of it and be encouraged, drooping soldier of the cross, as you contend with fierce temptations. He can overmaster all the strength of thy proud or sensual nature, and mold thee to His will. The Emperor Caesar once said to an attendant who treated his words with indifference, "Know, young man, he who says these things can *do* them." If Caesar can undertake to make good his words by his power, how much more Jesus Christ! How surely will He help thee, if thou invoke the ARM OF THE LORD, and "take hold of His strength."

> Christian! dost thou feel them, working still within,
> Striving, tempting, luring, goading into sin?
> Christian! never tremble! never yield to fear!
> Smite them by the virtue of almighty prayer!

6

Babe. Blessed and Only Potentate. Bright and Morning Star. Breaker.

THE city of Lystra was once thrown into great commotion through a miracle that was wrought by Paul and Barnabas. The people were running about shouting that "the gods had come down in the likeness of men!" The cry reached the ears of the priests of Jupiter; and straightway they brought oxen adorned with garlands and flowers, and prepared to offer them up in the streets as sacrifices to the two strangers, whom they mistook for gods in human shape. But when the Apostles heard this uproar, and saw the mistake which the people had made, they ran in amongst them and said, "Sirs, why do ye these things? Turn from these vanities to the living God!" But scarcely could they keep the people from paying them divine honors. Paul and Barnabas informed those idolaters that they themselves were only men; but that there had been a real visit of this kind to earth. They told them that the One True God, the God that made heaven and earth, had not only come down in the likeness of a Man, but that He had actually become a Man! and have lived a life of poverty, and was crucified, and rose again from the dead. But those pagans cared not to hear of this; it was foolishness to them. The visit of Christ was not to their minds. They saw no glory in His humble life and shameful death; so they stoned those who told them the strange history, though just before they had been ready to worship them. Now this wondrous visit of our Lord to earth we are about to contemplate today. And I trust we shall not be like Lystrians, but be all led to *admire* this "great mystery of godliness, God manifest in the flesh!" Let us consider our Lord as "the BABE OF BETHLEHEM."

BABE of Bethlehem (Luke 2:12–16). One day, about 1,800 years ago, the pathways leading to the little town of Bethlehem in Judea were unusually thronged with passengers, all drawn together for the same object. They were going to have their names enrolled in the records of the city in order that they might be taxed. From all parts little groups and companies of travelers were seen making their way to this ancient city of David. Some were toiling along on foot, carrying their little stores of provision; while others were mounted on camels and asses, and were better furnished with such conveniences as were required in that country. For there were no such inns for accommodation as there are in our own land. An eastern inn, or caravansera, is a large square court surrounded by buildings containing a great many apartments. But there are no provisions supplied in them; they are only places for shelter. And just such a building as this is supposed to have been "the inn" at Bethlehem, at the time of which we speak.

The travelers to Bethlehem on that day made their way to this great inn, or caravansera, in the center of the town. They continued to arrive till the inn was full; and those who came afterwards and had no acquaintances in the town, to whose houses they might go, were obliged to lodge in stables and outhouses. Amongst them was a poor couple meanly clad and very weary. They had traveled all the way from Nazareth, a distance of eighty miles, and stood in special need of repose and accommodation. Yet no one was found willing to give up his apartment for their use. So into the stable were our two travelers, Joseph the carpenter, and Mary his espoused wife, compelled to betake themselves. And there it was that Mary "brought forth her firstborn SON, and wrapped Him in swaddling clothes, and laid Him in a manger." But though thus meanly lodged and poorly accommodated, this little family was visited and attended by angels; who, unseen and unheard, filled the lowly place, and worshiped their INFANT LORD.

Let us go in imagination to Bethlehem, and "see this great thing which is come to pass, and which the Lord hath made known unto us." Let us pay a visit to the stable. And let our thoughts dwell on this most interesting scene, till our hearts are filled with wonder and praise. That smiling BABE who lies in yonder manger, is not just what He seems to be. It is true, He is what you and I and all of us once were, a BABE; but He is also the LORD OF GLORY and the KING OF KINGS. Well, but if He be a Prince, why is He not the Child of some King's daughter? And why not born in a palace surrounded with the state and splendor suited to His high rank? Or, at least, why is He not born in a decent dwelling? Why in this poor outhouse? Ah! that is indeed a mystery. Angels who hovered round Him wondered, just as we do. But none of the princes of this world knew Him, else they had crowded round Him, and been forward to pay their homage to One from whom they had received their crowns and kingdoms.

This Prince of the kings of the earth, and Lord of all worlds, was more meanly lodged than any of you were, when brought into this world. There is not one here, whose parents were so destitute at the time of his birth, as to be compelled to put up with the inconveniences of a stable. There is not one who was cradled in a manger when an infant. But the Son of God, when He began His life here, "had not where" else "to lay His head!" Wonder, O heaven! and be astonished, O earths!—And you, if you live in lowly huts or mean cottages, and if your fare and your work be hard and you are but coarsely clad, murmur not! But think, I beseech you, of the poverty of Christ's parents and the lowliness of His birth.

But let us look again. There, on yonder hard bed, lies this mysterious Infant; and over Him bends Mary (highly favored indeed among women!) gazing with the fond yearning affection of a mother at her firstborn. She beholds in Him One who is at the same time her CHILD and her LORD! Her OFFSPRING and her CREATOR! But oh! how completely has He laid aside all His majesty! How has He veiled His glory! It must indeed have been a strong faith that could recognize in this helpless BABE, thus attended and thus lodged, the PRINCE OF GLORY. But while, in the stillness of the night, we stand gazing and wondering at the BABE, what is that noise on the outside? It comes nearer. Hark! there is the trampling of feet! It is a crowd of rude countrymen from the fields with lanterns and staves. They come in haste! What can they want at this unseasonable hour of the night? Fear not, they come on no hostile errand. They do not mean to disturb the mother and her Infant. They want just to see this wonderful BABE! They are eager to feast their eyes on this great sight. Yet, they draw near with gentleness, and their unruly haste is checked as they approach the stable. And now they crowd within the walls, and stand around the manger, and look on the lovely and interesting object of their search.

But how came these shepherds to know anything about Him? Who informed them that at such a place, and at such a time, this BABE was to be born? I will tell you. The Angels knew of it in heaven; and they could not contain their joy, but longed to come and tell of it on earth. And so they got permission and came trooping down, whole armies of them, with songs and music. And whither did they wing their way? Surely they would go straight to the palace of Herod, and cause its lofty roof to ring with their songs. But no; they would rather go to Rome to the imperial halls of Caesar, the greatest potentate of the earth, and tell him of the event; that with all his court he might hasten to Judea, and do homage to his Lord and King. Or would they not rather go to the temple at Jerusalem, where priests and Levites watched by night around the altars of God, and tell them that the REAL SACRIFICE, the TRUE ALTAR, the GREAT HIGH PRIEST Himself, was now come, and that their work was soon to cease? No; they passed by gorgeous palaces and lordly castles. The marble walls of the temple echoed not to their heavenly music. They did not call the wise men after the flesh, the mighty and the noble, to hear their message; but they chose the foolish things of the world instead of the wise, and the weak things instead of the thing which are highly esteemed.

On that night, there were abiding in the fields near Bethlehem a company of shepherds, watching over their flocks. To them the angelic messengers winged their way; and, in their untutored ears alone, they poured forth their unearthly music. Those simple men are at work, when, all at once, in the dark still night, they are surprised with a blaze of light above the brightness of the sun. While they stand amazed, the Angel of the Lord comes upon them! They are frightened and would fain hide themselves. But the Angel speaks. And soon their disturbed minds are quieted; their fears are dispersed. "Fear not," says this kind messenger, "for behold, I bring you good tidings of great joy which shall be to all people; for unto you is born this day, in the city of David, a Savior which is Christ the Lord! And this shall be a sign unto you—Ye shall find the BABE wrapped in swaddling clothes, lying in a manger." No sooner do these words reach the astonished ears of the shepherds, then suddenly there is seen in the heavens a multitude of the heavenly host surrounding the Angel. And they praise God and say, "Glory to God in the highest, on earth peace, goodwill towards men." For a little time the heavenly music rings in their ears and ravishes their hearts. And then the glorious army, mounting on high, is once more lost in the obscurity of night; while the last sound of their triumphant song dies away in the clouds.

Then said these shepherds one to another, "Let us go now even unto Bethlehem and see this thing which is come to pass, which the Lord hath made known unto us." And they arose with haste to search for the stable and the wondrous BABE. They were not offended at the "sign" by which they were to know this Prince of Glory. It was as if the Angel had said, *Inquire for the Babe that is most meanly lodged in all Bethlehem*—THAT IS HE. This sign they kept in view, and no sooner did they commence their search, than, as we have seen, they found the stable and the manger and the BABE. How perplexed and astonished were they to see Him whose birthday song a host of Angels had just been singing, lying in such a place! And how eagerly did they tell His delighted mother the strange tale of the bright and glorious light that shone upon them, and the message, and the heavenly music, and the Angel band! With what wonder and rapture did they gaze on Him! One moment, though fearful to disturb His lumbers, they were eager to embrace Him, and the next they were ready, with solemn awe, to prostrate themselves before Him and to hail Him as the promised Messiah. So when they had worshiped Him, and had looked around, marveling at the meanness of the place, and the poverty of the parents, and all the strange circumstances which attended the birth of this truly Great One, they went forth again, spreading the news abroad, and with loud voices glorifying God who had thus visited His people.

And some, when they heard, wondered; and some laughed at the shepherds, and reckoned all they said a fable. But, believed or not believed, the report was all true. The Lord of Glory, the Ancient of Days, the Great I AM, had laid aside the brightness wherewith He shone in heaven—shone so, that the Angels covered their faces with their wings, they were so dazzled—He had laid aside all that glory and majesty, and had come down to be a little BABE. And wherefore did He thus come? For your salvation and mine. Let us, then, with the shepherds, praise God. "For unto us a SON is born—unto us a CHILD is given. And the government shall be upon His shoulders; and His name shall be called Wonderful, Counselor, the Mighty God, the Everlasting Father, the Prince of Peace." And well might His name be called WONDERFUL! To the eye of sense He was only a feeble BABE, brought forth in a stable, and cradled in a manger, and nursed in poverty; the helpless Offspring of lowly parents; yet was He, at the same time, "the BLESSED AND ONLY POTENTATE."

BLESSED AND ONLY POTENTATE, the "King of kings and Lord of lords, Who only hath immortality" (1 Tim. 6:15). He is the ONLY POTENTATE of men, angels, and all other beings. One with the Father. BLESSED forever, and the Fountain of blessedness to the universe. The kingdom of this BLESSED AND ONLY POTENTATE is one of peace and love; and to this end was He born, that He might establish the reign of peace throughout this unhappy world. It is a remarkable fact that at the time of His birth, all the nations of the world were at peace one with another. War had ceased and all the earth was still. And that was the time significantly chosen for this BLESSED POTENTATE to enter on His peaceful reign.

> No war, or battle's sound
> Was heard the world around.
> The idle spear and shield were high up hung;
> The hooked chariot stood
> Unstained with mortal blood;
> The trumpet spake not to the armed throng;
> And kings sat still with awful eye,
> As if they surely knew their Sovereign Lord was nigh.
> And peaceful was the night!
> Wherein the Prince of Light
> His reign of Peace upon the earth began.

The BLESSED POTENTATE shall reign till all His enemies shall become His footstool; till all kings shall own Him for their only Sovereign Lord from whom they receive their crowns; and till all nations shall partake of the blessedness of His peaceful rule. Then, in a higher sense will peace be universal. And then will the angels, who sang "Peace on earth" at the beginning of His reign, again be heard harping with their harps. And the song shall be "Hallelujah! for the Lord God Omnipotent reigneth! The BLESSED AND ONLY POTENTATE rules! The Prince of Peace governs! The kingdoms of this world are become the kingdoms of our Lord and of His Christ!" The zeal of the Lord of Hosts will perform this. The sure word of prophecy began to be fulfilled when Jesus "the DAY STAR," the STAR OF BETHLEHEM, arose on the earth as the earnest and pledge of the coming day. He says, "I am the BRIGHT AND MORNING STAR."

BRIGHT AND MORNING STAR (Rev. 22:16). What a cheering sight to the traveler or the mariner, who has lost himself in the long dark night, is the Bright Morning Star! *Bright*, in that it shows him where he is. And the *Morning Star*, in that it ushers in the light of day, and puts an end to his fears. And what a joyful hour was that when Jesus the BRIGHT AND MORNING STAR, first rose on this wretched dark world! Long had those who looked for His coming, waited for His salvation. Throughout the dark night of types and shadows, they had looked for this MORNING STAR, and longed for the brightness of His rising, "more than they that watched for the morning." But He whose "goings forth are prepared as the morning" tarried not beyond the appointed hour. When the angels appeared to the shepherds, the MORNING STAR, earnest of approaching day, was just above the horizon. And they who looked for consolation in Israel, when they saw this STAR, rejoiced with great joy. And, blessed be God, the gospel-day thus ushered in is still advancing, and shortly the glory of the Lord shall cover the whole earth.

You have read of the "Star in the east" which guided the wise men from their own country until it stood over where the young Child was. And when they saw the wondrous Star hovering over the city of David, it is said, "They rejoiced with exceeding joy." And what was the cause of their joy? Not that blazing meteor, however much they might have admired it; but the BRIGHT AND MORNING STAR—the Lord Jesus—to whom this had but led them, in whose light all the nations of the earth were to be blessed. This is the STAR that brings promise of relief to the poor, convicted sinner, who mourns over his dark and bewildered state. When he sees this STAR hope springs up in his bosom, and he begins to rejoice though with trembling. But it lights him on his way, it raises his courage, and, as he gazes, "his path shineth more and more unto the perfect day."

But now, allow me to ask how you have received the tidings of Christ's coming into the world. Are you any better for it? You have again and again heard the history of the BLESSED AND ONLY POTENTATE becoming a BABE "for us men, and for our salvation." You have often been told of Jesus rising on a dark world as the BRIGHT AND MORNING STAR to guide our feet into the way of peace. Does this afford you no matter for praise? Did the angels sing, and will not you? Do they still desire to look into these things, and will you, whose eternal interests are bound up with them—will you turn away with carelessness and indifference? What did the people of Bethlehem say to the strange things the shepherds told them? It is written, they "wondered." It does not say they believed. And still most people are satisfied with *wondering* at what the Bible tells them. They think it an interesting story, but that is all. There they stop. They are at no pains to inquire what *they* themselves have to do with all these things. Oh, how will they repent of their folly hereafter. *Now*, they wonder with feelings of idle curiosity. *Then*, when there shall be no place for repentance, they will wonder how they could possibly throw away such blessings. *Here*, they wonder why Christians make so much stir, and talk so much of the excellence of Christ. But *there*, when they stand before His great white throne, their wonder will be that men did not love Him more, and worship Him better, and obey Him with greater zeal. Ah, if your wonder does not now lead you to embrace Him and rejoice in His salvation, then you will wonder with far different feelings, when God shall say, "Behold, ye despisers! and WONDER and PERISH!"—But before we conclude this reading, let us glance at a descriptive Title of Christ, which occurs in the prophecy of Micah.

BREAKER (Mic. 2:13). Before the eye of the seer there passes a dim vision of One conducting a multitude of captives through great obstructions. But gates of brass and bars of iron are broken up, and the captives are free. And Him who is at the "head of them" the seer terms Jehovah. Yet the interpretations of this passage are various. It means John the Baptist, or Cyrus, or some Assyrian commander; while Dr. Gill and others refer it to Christ. Yet here again the interpretations are as diverse as the fancies of the expositors. While one connects it with the release from Babylon, others identify it with national and political deliverances yet to come. But as all inferior deliverances are eclipsed by the great work of Redemption, which Christ is carrying on in the world, or are quite absorbed into it, we shall not err if we regard it as applicable to that.

Christ is a great BREAKER and DESTROYER. He always has been and always will be, "till He hath put all enemies under His feet." He was manifested on purpose to destroy the works of the devil. That is His business. He has been breaking them up, and breaking them down, and breaking His way through them, for ages. And the end is not yet.

If we apply it to conversion, that process by which the individual soul is rescued from spiritual thralldom, we can trace the hand of a Breaker in it from first to last. What will not bend must break. The heart is broken, and the iron sinew of the will. Self dies before another Self, even Christ. Fascinating habits, and loved companionships, and idolized worldly schemes—everything gives way. For the Breaker does not spare till the soul has learned to say—

> To do or not to do, to have
> Or not to have, I leave to Thee;
> To be or not to be I leave,
> Thy only will be done in me.
> All my requests are lost in one;
> Father, Thine only will be done.

Again, if we refer the prediction to the triumph of the Church over the world, the BREAKER says to her foes, "Associate yourselves and ye shall be broken in pieces." Yes, the power of the oppressor, the contempt of the scorner, the ravings of the infidel, and the delusions of the idolater, will all be broken. Happy they who yield to the Great Conqueror without further conflict.

Soon after Messrs. Moody and Sankey began their meetings at Liverpool, a comic singer conceived the idea of writing a burlesque about them, to be put upon the stage. Feeling that he could not make his work complete without some more "points" or "hits" to give it zest, he determined to attend a meeting himself, and hear the men whom he intended to lampoon. He went. But the power of God arrested him, and held him a reverent listener. He became an earnest inquirer, nor was it long before he accepted the Lord Jesus as His Master; and from that time the tenor of his life was totally changed. Oh, come, all of you, submit yourselves to Him who was once the BABE of Bethlehem, and who now sitteth as the BLESSED AND ONLY POTENTATE at the right hand of the Father. Be wise now. Be entreated. "Kiss the Son, lest He be angry, and ye perish from the way when His wrath is kindled but a little."

7

Beginning of the Creation of God. Beginning and the End. Brightness of the Father's Glory. Brother. Bridegroom. Beloved.

GOD is a Spirit, and therefore we cannot see Him. But when the world was about 4000 years old, the Word (who was God) put on a created nature and made Himself visible to His creatures. This wonderful event we talked of last Sunday. We then spoke of the Ancient of Days becoming the Babe of Bethlehem; the Creator and the Creature, in the Person of Christ, being joined in one. There is a remarkable Title appropriated to Him in Revelation 3:14, which seems to have this twofold meaning—the

BEGINNING OF THE CREATION OF GOD. In the eighth chapter of Proverbs, Christ speaks thus of Himself (vv. 22–31), "The Lord possessed me in the beginning of His way, I was set up from everlasting." Again we read, "In the beginning was the Word, and the Word was God." Thus, then, He who was from eternity, whose "goings forth were from of old, even from everlasting," as to *one* of His natures—as to *the other* had a beginning. This is the fundamental fact and doctrine of Christianity; which whosoever rejects, virtually rejects Christianity itself, for nothing remains of it worthy of the name. If, therefore, we would think of Christ as God has revealed Him, we must conceive of Him as at once the BEGINNER OF THE CREATION OF GOD; for He made all things, and is therefore TRULY GOD. Also the BEGINNING OF THE CREATION, (not in order of time, but of supremacy), the First and Chief of all creatures; for he is TRULY MAN, and the Glory of the whole Creation. "I am Alpha and Omega," saith He, the

BEGINNING AND THE END (Rev. 21:6). Are you among those who are seeking salvation? Then consider, do you really make Him the BEGINNING? Or do you set something else first—feelings, prayers, sincere endeavors—with the secret hope that somehow they will be a passport to His favor? "Why not," you ask, "when we are sometimes told that 'the promises are made to *character*'?" There is a sense in which that is true. But there is also a sense in which it would be most dangerous to apply it. Many anxious inquirers go wrong just here. They fully intend to go to Christ whenever better feelings shall encourage them to do so. A little more penitence and humility, will, they hope, impart to them a "character" which will entitle them to consideration. This is not to "obey the truth," but to "frustrate the grace of God." As well might men say, "We will not venture into the water till we have learned to swim." The law of the kingdom of grace is, you must come to Christ *first of all*. Make Him what He claims to be, The Beginning. All other things will then be added, right feelings, godly sorrow, progress in sanctification, acceptable works. But not one breath of real life will there ever be, until you shall become united to Him by a living faith.

And as He is The Beginning, so is He The End (Rev. 21:6). Not a stepping-stone to some further End. Himself is The End. You cannot have pardon and strength and holiness apart from Him. He does not send down saving gifts as from a distance. It is Himself you are to appropriate. "He that hath the Son hath life." And remember He is the Beginning and End of sanctification as well as of justification. With an unintermittent faith the believer must abide in Christ to the last. And at the end of half a century of experience and service he will still have to say, in common with the youngest pilgrim,

> Weaker than a bruised reed,
> Help I every moment need.

BRIGHTNESS OF THE FATHER'S GLORY (Heb. 1:3). God, the great Spirit, dwelleth in light, which no man can approach unto. His habitation is "dark with excessive bright." But Christ is God come down to be a Brother, to set Himself before us in a form on which we can look without fear. The eye that dares to look *at* the sun, aches and is distressed. But our eyes can bear that milder light which beams *from* the sun. It is refreshing and sweet and pleasant. So we cannot see God. He is veiled in "terrible brightness." But we are made acquainted with God, by means of Him who is the Brightness of the Father's Glory—His Softened Radiance. For Christ says, "He that hath seen Me, hath seen the Father also." All the glory of the divine character is seen in the Lord Jesus. And we can gaze on His countenance and His form.—"His *dread* does not fall upon us, His excellency does not *make us afraid*."

The Holy of Holies was a most sacred place. No footsteps ever trod its unpolluted floor save those of the high priest. But even he could not go in without incense, because of the blaze of the Divine Glory, which shone forth from the ark of the testimony. But when the cloud of incense arose and moderated the dazzling luster, then he could enter without being destroyed by it. And Jesus Christ is like that incense; He is the medium through which the rays of the Godhead come to us in a way in which we can bear them. So we view the insupportable glory of God shining through the veil of our own nature. The Lord

Jesus was found in fashion as a Man, and humbled Himself that we might become familiar with Him. He was lowly and meek and self-denying. And yet what luster was there in His wisdom and knowledge! What glory beamed from Him when He cast out devils! What bright proofs of His Deity betrayed themselves from time to time to the confusion of His enemies! Ascended now into heaven, the brightness of His glorified Person none can conceive of. He fills all heaven with light; for "the city has no need of the sun, neither of the moon to shine in it; for the glory of God lightens it, and the LAMB is the LIGHT thereof."

> Oh the delights, the heavenly joys,
> > The glories of the place.
> Where Jesus sheds the brightest beams
> > Of His o'erflowing grace!

How bright is the fierce lightning that plays around the dark clouds in the summer night! And how bright is the sun at noonday! But what is the brightness of the lightning or the sun, compared with that celestial Light which beamed on Saul of Tarsus, and struck him to the ground! It was the brightness above that of the midday sun, the BRIGHTNESS OF THE FATHER'S GLORY, which appeared to him. And Saul, unused to such distressing brightness, became blind for many days. Our eyes could not bear *this* glory of Christ now. When we shall see Him as He is, our eyes and our minds will be fitted for the dazzling vision. But those who are enlightened by the Spirit, already see a little of His spiritual glory here on earth. And the sight of it rejoices the heart.

We connect brightness with gladness; it excites the mind and fills the heart with joy. How refreshing is the morning hour! How cheering are the bright beams of the sun after darkness! They awaken you, and invite you to walk abroad in the meadows and wander beside the streams. And how lovely everything looks bathed in the glory of the sunbeams! The fields seem to laugh, and the little hills to leap for very joy! The sparkling brook dances and exults in the sun's bright ray! There is life and joy spread through all nature. And the inanimate things—the little murmuring rills and the rustling trees—seem almost endued with voices wherewith to utter their delight. "The little hills break forth before you into singing. The valleys shout for joy and all the trees of the field clap their hands." What a contrast is all this to the dismal gloom which hung over everything during the absence of the sun! And so when the BRIGHTNESS OF THE FATHER'S GLORY penetrates the darkness of our minds and shines into our hearts—what unspeakable delight fills our expanded souls! How do we exclaim, "My soul doth magnify the Lord! My spirit hath rejoiced in God my Savior!" The light is felt to be "marvelous light," and we glory in Him who is GOD with us—God come down out of heaven to take part of our flesh and blood, and thus to become our BROTHER.

BROTHER (Heb. 2:11, 12). What a wonderful thing for us to be permitted to call Christ our BROTHER! Let us see how He is our BROTHER.

1. *Brothers are children of the same parents and members of the same family.* All who receive the gospel are the children of God. They are born of God. God has a great family, some of whom are in heaven and some on earth, and all are named after Himself; and God's Dear Son is the Elder BROTHER of this great family, "the FIRST-BORN among many brethren." When about to leave the world, He acknowledged the relationship in the following affectionate message— "Go to my BRETHREN, and say unto them, I ascend to MY FATHER AND YOUR FATHER."

2. *Brothers are partakers of the same nature and likeness.* Angels are not called the brethren of Christ. Of them it is not said, "They are members of His body, of His flesh, and of His bones." But this is said of believers, so close is the fellowship. There is a oneness of nature in them; and therefore He is not ashamed to call them Brethren. He takes their nature on Himself; and then He makes them "partakers of the divine nature," and changes them into His own image.

3. *Brothers share in the same privileges and are joint-heirs of the same inheritance.* The father commonly lays up for his children, and by-and-by, when they grow up, his children succeed to his wealth and share it amongst them. And Christians are "heirs of God, joint-heirs with Christ." All things are theirs through their union to Him.

4. *Brothers receive the same education, discipline, and training.* Christians must enter heaven through much tribulation; "for what son is he whom the father chasteneth not?" So Christ was "made perfect through sufferings," and "learned obedience by the things which He suffered." And that because He would in all points be made like unto His brethren, and share the common portion of the family. In all these respects Jesus Christ is a BROTHER. Be not afraid to approach Him in the hour of thy sorrow and temptation. He is thy KINSMAN, the NEAREST RELATIVE! He will not disown thee nor turn away from thy complaint. He who says to us, "Hide not thyself from thine own flesh," will not do this Himself; He who says, "Thou shalt not despise thy poor brother," will not despise us though we are poor and needy. No! He cannot—

> His heart is made of tenderness,
> His bowels melt with love.

> He, who in days of feeble flesh,
> Poured out His cries and tears,
> Still in His measure feels afresh
> What every brother bears.

Touched with a sympathy within,
He knows their feeble frame;
He knows what sore temptations mean,
For He has felt the same.

Brothers often dwell together, and their interests are one. If one brother should come to the possession of great honor and riches, he would naturally share them with the rest of his family. Now the Lord Christ has gone up into heaven; but He does not mean to live there alone in His grandeur. When He has made the place ready for them, and has made them ready for the place, He will come again and receive them to Himself, that they may behold His glory. He has left it on record, that He will not be satisfied till He has every one of His brothers and sisters sitting down with Him at His Father's table and all dwelling beside Him in His "Father's house where there are many mansions." But He owns those only for His brothers and sisters who do the will of His Father. If you belong to this number, you may each of you boldly say, "The Lord is my Helper, my Shepherd, my Friend, my Brother; I shall not want seasonable, suitable, and sufficient supplies, all my life long—

And when I'm to die, Receive me, I'll cry,
For Jesus hath loved me, I cannot tell why;
But this I do find, we two so are joined,
He'll not live in heaven, and leave me behind.

There is a beautiful story in the Bible about the devotion of Judah (one of Jacob's sons), to Benjamin, his youngest brother. When Jacob's sons were returning from Egypt the second time with the corn they had bought, they had not gone far before they heard a messenger calling them to stop. When he came up with them he accused them of having stolen his master's silver cup. They denied it. But he would search all their sacks. So they all set down their sacks to be searched, beginning at the eldest. The first opened his sack, and the man looked into it, but there was no cup there. And then the second showed his sack, but neither was the cup there; and so on, till the youngest brother's sack was opened. And there, sure enough, hidden amongst the corn in Benjamin's sack, was the lost silver cup! Then they all rent their clothes, and loaded every one his ass, and returned to the city. And the lord of the country seemed to be very angry with them, and said, "The man in whose hand the cup is found, he shall be my slave." And that was poor Benjamin, his father's darling, whom they had promised to bring back to him in safety!

Then came Judah near to the ruler, pleading the cause of his younger brother. And, oh! how affectionately did he plead! You can read his touching speech in Genesis 44:18–34. And he finished his eloquent appeal with these words—"Now then, I pray thee, let me, thy servant, abide instead of the lad, a bondsman to my lord, and let the lad go up with his brethren." Was not this a most wonderful act of kindness? Well might dying Jacob say, "Judah, thou art he whom thy brethren shall praise!" But why does Judah thus undertake his younger brother's cause? Why is he so anxious for his safety? He was not only Benjamin's Brother, but Benjamin's Bondsman. He had said to his father, "I will be SURETY for him. Of my hand shalt thou require him. If I do not bring him to thee and set him before thee, then let me bear the blame forever." And so his honor and his truth were engaged as well as his affection. He had *made himself answerable* for Benjamin, and rather than break his word, he would suffer loss of liberty or life. You can apply this story yourselves. I think I need not tell you how Judah in all this resembles Christ, our Elder BROTHER. He, too, offered to become our BONDSMAN, and has solemnly undertaken to save to the uttermost them that come unto God through Him—all that the Father giveth Him. And think you that He can break His word, His oath? Shall Judah feel himself bound by his promise, and will not Christ abide by His? Most assuredly.

> His honor is engaged to save
> The meanest of His sheep;
> All that His Heavenly Father gave,
> His hands securely keep.

According to this agreement, this bond, He pays their mighty debt to the law, answers all its demands, and bears the punishment due to them. He knew beforehand "what it would come to at the worst to save." So He set His face as a flint, and was not discouraged till He had finished the work His Father gave Him to do. But, as if the term BROTHER were not sufficiently endearing to express the great love wherewith He loves His people, He condescends to use that of BRIDEGROOM.

BRIDEGROOM (Matt. 9:15). The term implies the highest degree of affection and tenderness, and the most complete identification of interest known among human relationships. But who shall set forth the fathomless meaning of it here? When He, whose whole Nature is defined by one word LOVE, uses this sacred Title to illustrate the affection which He bears, and the relation which He sustains to His Church, we can scarcely do more than silently adore. God only knows the love of God.

In the sacred story there occur many beautiful instances of devoted love. Who has not admired Jonathan's love to David? It is said, "The soul of Jonathan was knit with the soul of David, and he loved him as his own soul." The beautiful story of their friendship you may read at length in 1 Samuel 20. And in 2 Samuel 1 you may also see the affecting lamentation, which David made over his friend when he died. "How are the mighty fallen in the midst of the battle! O Jonathan, thou wast slain in thine high places! I am distressed for thee, my brother Jonathan; very pleasant hast thou been to me; thy love to me was wonderful, passing the love of women! how are the mighty fallen, and the weapons of war perished!"

How tenderly also did David love his unworthy son, Absalom! When tidings were brought that he was dead, David covered his face and cried, "O my son, Absalom! O Absalom, my son, my son!" He refused to be comforted, and went up into his chamber and wept. And as he went still he said in the hearing of the people, "O my son, Absalom, my son, my son! Would to God I had died for thee! O Absalom! My son, my son!" And how Jacob loved Rachel! He served her father, Laban, seven years for her. And those seven years "seemed to him but a few days for the love he had to her." But neither the love of Jonathan to David, though it was so generous; nor the love of David to Absalom, though it was so passionate; nor the love of Jacob to Rachel, though it was so devoted—can set forth the love of Christ to His people. It is but as a drop compared with the ocean. David's heart yearned over his lost Absalom because he was his own child. Jonathan loved David because his virtues attracted his regard. Jacob loved Rachel for her beauty and for her goodness. But Christ set His affections on His people while they were yet sinners and ungodly. He loved the Church while as yet she was poor and worthless, and at enmity with Him. The "Church," you know, signifies the redeemed in all ages, from Adam till doomsday. And Jesus Christ loves them all alike. The promises He makes to one belong to all. He views them all in one unbroken fellowship, "the Church"; and in order to exalt our thoughts of His tender love to this Church, He calls her by the endearing name—"the Bride, the Lamb's Wife." That "Song of Songs, which is Solomon's," and the forty-fifth Psalm, describe, in mystic terms, the love of the Royal BRIDEGROOM to His Church.

And what does He propose to do for His Church? Having betrothed her to Himself in righteousness, He clothes her in a wedding garment in which she will shine without spot or blemish. He endows her with all His riches, even to a share of His very throne. He will provide for her beyond her utmost thoughts, and study, by all means, to make her happy and holy, honorable and glorious, throughout eternity.

How precious must she be in His sight! Think of the price at which He redeemed her! It was "not with corruptible things such as silver and gold." The ransom was not a whole world, nor 20 worlds! He gave HIMSELF for her, and thus made her His "purchased possession." And "He rests in His love," and says to her, "Yea, I have loved thee with an everlasting love, and therefore with lovingkindness have I drawn thee." And what does He require of her in return? LOVE! What less can He ask than an undivided heart? "Hearken, O daughter, and consider and incline thine ear. Forget also thine own people and thy father's house. So shall the King greatly desire thy beauty; for He is thy Lord; and worship thou Him." Thus the Lord Jesus is the Church's BELOVED.

BELOVED (Song 2:16). He wins her love, and gains her consent, and she becomes His, and loves Him with a pure heart fervently. The highest love the human heart is capable of is joyfully rendered. But let us come to the individual question. Do we love Christ? Is He our BELOVED? Then these things follow— We often think of Him; we often converse with Him; we love all that belongs to Him; we are above all things concerned to please Him. But leaving you to revolve these points within your own hearts, I will name two or three more particulars of this love. That ointment of spikenard, very precious, which Mary poured on the sacred person of her Lord, was not only a *proof* of her love but an *emblem* thereof—and it may serve also to symbolize that of all Christians. And just as several sorts of spices are compounded together in the preparation of costly ointments, so the believer's affection is made up of many ingredients. There is the sweet spice of *Gratitude*, the rich frankincense of adoring *Admiration* or *Delight*, and the essential oil of close *Relationship*. There is the generous balm of intimate personal *Friendship*; and lastly, the aromatic perfume of the "*Love of Espousals*." These several sorts of love (if I may use such an expression), enter into the composition of that sacred affection which the disciple cherishes for his BELOVED, and which is the most acceptable offering he can present.

First. There is in this divine passion the love of *Gratitude*. The believer loves his Lord because He first loved him, and because He hath done, and hath promised to do, such great things for him. But that is not all. What would be thought of a bride who loved her husband solely, or even principally, because of the jewels that he had given to her, or the pleasant home, which he had prepared for her? If that were all, it would be a very mercenary sort of affection, far from being satisfactory to her husband. The Christian's love hath in it, then, something more than Gratitude.

Second. There is in it the love of *Admiration* or complacency. The Christian delights and glories in his Lord because of His surpassing worth. He is fairer than the children of men; kinder than the best of fathers; more tender than the fondest of mothers; more faithful than the most devoted of friends—

> All human beauties, all divine
> In his BELOVED meet and shine.

"Oh," said Rutherford, "O angels, who stand before Him; O blessed spirits who now see His face! Set Him on high! For when you have worn out your harps in His praises, all is too little to disperse the sweetness of the praise of that Fair Flower, that Fragrant Rose of Sharon, through many worlds."

Third. There is in it the love of *Relationship*. What a strong tie is that of kindred! The affection of the brother to the sister, the mother to the child, the son to the father! Where no evil passion interferes with its action, it is one of the mightiest of the impulses that sway the human heart, and depraved indeed must they be who are wholly dead to its power. Now this ingredient enters into the composition of our love to Christ. If we are born of God, His Father is our Father, His God is our God. We are partakers of the Divine Nature. He is the First-born of the whole family, our Elder Brother. Hence, in the renewed heart, there vibrates instinctively (more or less) this fraternal chord.

Fourth. This is the love of *Friendship*—a pure unselfish love. There may be, alas! there is, very little of it in the best. But what there is of genuine love is of this character. It might seem incongruous to talk of *benevolence* or *disinterested love* to Christ! We can render Him nothing that we have not first received from Himself. If we could we certainly would. But our *all* is surrendered. Nothing is kept back. Every chamber of the heart is thrown open to Him, and we hail Him as our One Lord and Proprietor, the intimate Friend of our heart, and the trusted Confidant of all our secrets.

Fifth. There is in it the "*Love of Espousals*." "I remember thee, the kindness of thy youth," saith He to the Israelite Church, "the *love of thine espousals*." It is a pledged, plighted love, a sacred, covenanted, conjugal affection, which the Church cherishes for her Glorious Bridegroom—a love which, having chosen its object, adheres to it with jealous fidelity, defies every change—yea, denies the possibility of change, and says, "My Beloved is mine, and I am His. Who shall separate me from the love of Christ?"

Now, there are various degrees of this holy love to Christ among His sincere worshipers. A few may be able, like the venerable author of the "Sinner's Friend," to say, "I feel that my soul is actually glazing with love to my Savior." But there are many who dare not speak thus strongly. Yet, though sensitively alive to the danger of self-deception and deeply conscious of a thousand deficiencies, they are able to say, "Thou knowest all things; Thou knowest that I love Thee." But there are multitudes more, the language of whose hearts, if we might put it into words, would be, "Ah, I wish I could say I truly loved Christ. I think sometimes I do love Him. I know I long to love Him. But at other times I feel another mind within me that seems to turn away from Him. At one time, when I read and hear of Him, my heart is softened and feels the strong attraction of His love. At other times, it is like a stone, and I could weep because I cannot weep; and I say to my Lord—

> To hear the sorrows Thou hast felt,
> Dear Lord, an adamant would melt;
> But I can read each moving line,

And nothing moves this heart of mine.
The rocks can rend, the earth can quake,
The sea can roar, the mountains shake,
All things of feeling show some sign,
Save this unfeeling heart of mine.

Well, poor mourner, it is something to know that your heart is hard. It is one step towards a cure to be brought to acknowledge the disease. But do not rest here. Take your heart to Christ. He will soften it. Remember His gracious promise, and ask Him to fulfill it in you: "I will take the stony heart out of your flesh, and give you a heart of flesh."

Oh! Love divine, how sweet thou art!
When shall I find my willing heart
   All taken up with thee?
My only care, delight, and bliss,
My joy, my heaven on earth be this—
   To hear the BRIDEGROOM'S voice.

8

Brazen Serpent. Branch. Bread.

THERE is a great deal about FAITH in the Bible—its mighty force and wonderful exploits. But there is only one *definition* of it, and that is a very concise one. "Faith is the evidence of things not seen, the substance of things hoped for." Faith cannot make a thing real, which does not exist; but whatever hath a real existence, faith makes it *real to us*. And if it is anything we have a personal interest in, faith brings it home to our feelings and convictions. If someone were to place 100 pounds in the bank in your name, that would be a real fact. But you would not feel yourself at all the richer unless you believed it. It is your believing which gives you a conscious interest in it. In other words, your faith gives substance to your friend's act and witnesses within you, without your *seeing* the entry, that the money he has placed there for your use is really your own. And it is only by faith, acting thus, that you can become acquainted with Christ. Faith, as it were, gives substance to Him, that is makes Him *real to you*. Your eyes do not see Him. You cannot hear His voice. You cannot touch Him with your hands nor walk to Him with your feet. But yet we are said to see Him, to hear Him, to go to Him. He speaks, and faith is the ear that listens; He calls us to approach, and faith is the foot that moves toward Him; He tells us to look to Him, and faith is the eye that sees. Faith is the mouth that feeds on Him and the hand that takes hold on Him. Faith is *all that* to the soul which every separate sense is to the body—the hand and the mouth, the eye and the ear. This we shall see exemplified while we contemplate Christ under three Similitudes. We are to *look* to Christ as the BRAZEN SERPENT; to *feed* on Him as the BREAD OF LIFE; to *lay hold* on Him as the BRANCH, and to pluck from Him such fruits as shall refresh and replenish our souls. Consider then—

I. Faith is to the soul what the EYE is to the body.

The *Eye* enables us to see the worth and beauty of things. Choice paintings, valuable jewels, chests of gold might be placed before a blind man, but he would not observe them. So we may set before men who have not faith the most excellent blessings, but they cannot perceive their worth. "The natural man discerneth not the things of the Spirit of God, for they are foolishness to him; neither can he know them because they are spiritually discerned." Again, the *Eye* enables us to discover danger. And if there be a way of escape, it is by the *Eye* that we are directed to it. A blind man may be just on the brink of a deep river, but unless someone speak to him of danger he doth not suspect any. Or he may be in imminent peril from wild beasts, and there may be a covert at hand, yet can he not flee to it because he seeth it not. So without faith we should be lost, because it is by faith that we discover danger. And by faith we discern the salvation that there is in Christ. We see also His worth, His fitness, and His all-sufficiency. And thus we are persuaded to embrace Him as our Savior. May this faith be in exercise now, while we direct your attention to the Lord Christ, under the type of the "BRAZEN SERPENT."

BRAZEN SERPENT (Num. 21:9; John 3:14). The occasion of the setting up of this Serpent of brass by Moses was the sin of the people of Israel, and the punishment wherewith God visited their sin. Though God was so bountiful to them they murmured against Him, and complained that the manna was not good enough for them though it came down from heaven. So God was sorely displeased, and sent among them a host of fierce fiery serpents, which stung them, so that many people died. There was no charming them, and it was hard to escape from them, for they came in great numbers. So that whithersoever the miserable people turned, there were deadly serpents waiting to torment them. Their venomous fangs inflicted wounds that poisoned the springs of life, and filled them with burning fever. Ah! If you wish to see what dreadful consequences sin brings with it, survey the scene of desolation in the camp of Israel! But God will not always chide, neither will He keep His anger forever. He told His servant to set up a Serpent of brass on a pole in the midst of the camp where all might see it. And whoever should look on that was to be healed. "So Moses made a Serpent of brass and put it upon a pole, and it came to pass that if a serpent had bitten any man, when he beheld the Serpent of brass he lived." What a movement there must have been amongst the wounded the moment the joyful news spread through the camp that the pole was set up! How would the poor fainting men and women strain their dying eyes just to get one glimpse of it! And those who were so exhausted that they could not stir, how would they implore their relatives to carry them to some spot whence they might, by one glance at the remedy, be redeemed from death. See that mother! Her darling child is bitten. She takes him into her arms and holds him up, and with her gentle fingers lifts up the heavy eyelids, almost closed in death, and cries, "Look, look at yon shining serpent!" He strives to look and though just now the fiery poison drank up his spirits and swelled all his bursting veins, yet one look quite cures him!

Now what if one of those bitten people had refused to look at that brass serpent? Imagine him dying of his wounds, and his brother comes to him and says, "Let me carry you to the tent door. *One* look at yon pole will cure you. *I* was bitten, and I looked, and now I am quite well: look, brother, look!" "No," says the dying man, "I am sure that cannot cure me—I am too far gone—it is too late. Oh, I shall die!" "Nay," cries the other, "but you need not die; while you have strength to look there is hope." But the wretched man turns his face the other way. He refuses God's own medicine, and nothing can save him. And thus it is that "wise men after the flesh" despise God's way of salvation, and refuse to "behold the Lamb of God" who alone can take away their sin. For such there remaineth no further sacrifice, no other way of deliverance, nothing but a certain fearful looking-for of judgment and fiery indignation.

Hear the words of our Savior—"As Moses lifted up the Serpent in the wilderness, so must the Son of Man be lifted up, that whosoever believeth on Him should not perish, but have everlasting life"; thus Jesus Christ illustrates His own elevation on the Cross and the effects of faith in Himself, by the lifting up of the Serpent and the results which followed the Israelites' sight of it.

1. As the lifting up of the Serpent was by the appointment of God, so Christ crucified is God's own remedy for those who are wounded by sin. Moses, you see, was not told to invite the people to bring their brass ornaments, and so to contribute something towards the casting of this Serpent. He was to do it all himself. The sufferers had no more to do with its preparation than with its contrivance. All they had to do was just to look at it and appropriate its healing virtue. So in the wonderful method of redemption, man's reason is not consulted, nor his opinion asked, nor his approval conciliated.

> Done is the work that saves,
> One and forever done;
> Finished the righteousness
> That clothes the righteous one.

Man's reason is forever scanning it, as with an eyeglass, critically, even sometimes contemptuously; and he often ends by totally rejecting it. But,

2. As there was not other cure for the Israelites but the one prescribed, so there is no name given under heaven, whereby men can be saved, but the name of Christ.

3. It was a certain, infallible remedy. So the blood of Christ CLEANSETH FROM ALL SIN.

4. The Serpent of brass was lifted up in the sight of all; so Christ is set up for all the world to look at. His salvation is called "the common salvation," because it is for all who are willing to have it.

All mankind are ruined by sin. This fatal poison has spread itself through their whole nature and corrupted all its streams. It has not the same effects in all. Some are excited by it, and evil passions and deeds of violence are the modes in which it displays it malignity. Some are filled with anguish, by which their lives are made bitter unto them. Others are lulled to sleep and cannot be awakened, or persuaded that there is anything the matter with them. Nevertheless, all are badly, fatally wounded, and from the sole of the foot to the head there is no soundness, but wounds and bruises and putrefying sores. But whoever, of all the children of men (let him be ever so far gone), looks to Christ with the eye of faith, receives immediate benefit and begins to feel in himself an effectual cure. It is true that while men are in the wilderness they are liable to get fresh wounds in the fight with sin and Satan. But here is God's grand remedy, Christ crucified. On Him let them fix their gaze; and they shall find the tide of health gushing into their souls and springing up into everlasting life. "They looked unto Him and were lightened, and their faces were not ashamed."

Come, then, thou poor serpent-stung sinner, who feelest thy misery, and are dying of thy wounds! Be of good cheer; rise, He calleth *thee*. Thou hast not strength to go to Him. Then *look* to Him. Cast thy burdens of sin on Him, for indeed He careth for thee. Come all of you and gaze on this Savior lifted up. You who have looked before, come and look again. You cannot look at Him too much or too often. God hath set Him up on high in the view of an expiring world on purpose that all may look to Him. And that not *once* but *often*. We are to run the race set before us *looking unto Jesus*. We are to do this daily, hourly. So shall the wounds the old serpent hath given to us be cured. "Iniquity shall not be our ruin." The poison shall be drawn forth, and we shall be healed. But if we will not look we must inevitably die of our wounds.

And do you ask how you are to know that you have looked aright? I answer, You will have spiritual life; just as the dying Israelite, on looking to the Brazen Serpent, found himself restored. You will have peace; the pain arising from a guilty conscience and fear of God's anger will be eased. And you will also have a dread of sin, which "is as the gall of asps within" (Job 20:14). Though sin may be ever so sweet or pleasant, they who trifle with it find out that, like those serpents, it has a most fatal sting; for the wages of sin is death. But we must proceed. We have seen that Faith is as the *Eye* of the Soul; for by it we look unto Christ and are saved.

II. Faith is to the soul what the HAND is to the body.

The beggar who stops you in the street asking for relief holds out his empty *hand* to receive your bounty. Now Christ has alms to bestow, and faith is the empty hand stretched out to take what He gives. If you wished to get possession of the fruit which hangs on yonder tree you would put forth your *hand* to pluck it; thus faith procures spiritual blessings; it is the hand by which we pluck fruit from the BRANCH of the Lord, the Tree of Life. If a man had fallen into a pit, and someone were to let down a rope to him, how would he avail himself of the offered help? He would take hold of the rope with his *hands*, and cling to it till he was drawn out of danger. And thus it is said concerning the act of faith, "Let him *take hold* of My strength." And we read in the Bible of our faith *laying hold* on "the hope set before us." Now then let us consider Christ as the "BRANCH."

BRANCH of the Lord, "Beautiful and Glorious" (Isa. 4:2; Zech. 3:8). Suppose we were walking by the side of a deep river, when suddenly we hear a splash like something falling into the water. We look towards the quarter from whence the sound proceeded, and there on the other side we see someone struggling in the flood! Ah! he is gone and the gurgling wave closes over him! No! there is his head just above the swelling tide close by yonder overhanging trees, and he cries for help. Tell him to seize the Branch that dips into the stream. See! he has got fast hold of the bough, and now he is climbing up and will soon be out of danger. Was not that a Beautiful Branch that saved him from destruction when no other help was near? Take that Branch for a figure of Christ; and the hand by which the drowning boy laid hold on it and clung to it, let it be an emblem of that faith by which the perishing sinner cleaves to the Savior.

We shall all know what it is to suffer. Man is *born* to troubles. These are compared to deep waters, and the tide seems sometimes as though it would carry us away; and we "sink in deep waters where there is no standing." David was heard once complaining to God—"Deep calleth unto deep, at the noise of Thy waterspouts. All Thy waves and billows have gone over me." And we may be almost ready at times to say the same thing. But blessed be God, this Divine BRANCH from the Root of Jesse overhangs the deep dark waters. And if we seize hold of it by the hand of faith, it keeps us up that we sink not. "*In that day*," the day of affliction, "the BRANCH of the Lord shall be BEAUTIFUL AND GLORIOUS." Therefore remember, all of you, when in trouble or when ready to be swallowed up by temptation, to keep fast hold of this "Beautiful BRANCH." Never fear it will break. It is the BRANCH that God made strong for Himself. It holds up millions of people, for God holds it in His right hand and stretches it forth that we may be saved. Therefore "take fast hold of it; let it not go; keep it, for it is thy life."

But let me name two or three particulars in which Christ is more obviously symbolized by a Branch. A Branch is first a tender slip, and its present form gives no clue to its future appearance. But who, looking at the little oak sapling which springs from a buried acorn, would imagine that it could ever become a tall tree, producing multitudes of boughs and heaps of acorns?—the little one becoming a thousand. So those who saw Christ in His low estate, turned away from Him, saying, "This cannot be the Messiah." They judged by their carnal reason. What was He? A little helpless babe, cradled in a manger and nurtured in poverty; His anxious parents fleeing hither and thither to screen Him from the murderous hands of bad men. Is this He of whom it was prophesied, "The government shall be upon His shoulder?" What was He? An interesting boy, dutiful to His parents and gentle in all His behavior, seeking instruction from the Jewish doctors in the temple, and surprising them by His answers and remarks. But did He then look like the Savior of the World? What was He? A benevolent man, scattering to all around, wherever He came, life and health, happiness and peace. But still a poor man, and therefore despised and rejected by almost all. What was He next? In the eyes of the nation a malefactor, scourged, spit upon, buffeted, hanged on the cross, the scorn of all save a few poor timid followers. "If He *be* the Son of God," said His revelers, "let Him prove it." But instead of coming down from the cross He gave up the ghost; and all that remained of Him was a mangled corpse, which weeping, disappointed friends took down from the cross and laid in a tomb. "Alas!" said they, "we thought it had been He which should have redeemed Israel." And so it was. For, "who hath despised the day of small things?" This Root out of a dry ground, so destitute of form and comeliness in their eyes, was all the while the "BRANCH of the Lord, Beautiful and Glorious," whose fruit was destined to be "Comely and Excellent," throughout the whole earth.

And what is He now? The tongue of angels cannot worthily describe the majesty and transcendent glory to which He is exalted. All power is in His hands. All riches are His right. All worlds depend on His care. He is the Lord of all power and might; and to Him every knee shall bow, every tongue confess. Already this BRANCH is beginning to fill the whole world with its blessings. And some of all nations sit down under its shadow; and by faith they pluck the fruit which grows so plentifully upon it, and it administers to them life and health. And it is *your* privilege to sit under the shadow of this BEAUTIFUL BRANCH. Every time you hear the Gospel you sit under its shadow. And it is loaded with fruits pleasant to the eye, and worthy to be desired to make you wise. Be not satisfied with the bare sight of them, but put forth the hand of faith and pluck them and make them your own.

III. Faith is to the soul what the MOUTH is to the body. So we read, "*Eat* ye that which is good" (Isa. 55:2). "If so be ye have *tasted* that the Lord is gracious" (1 Pet. 2:3). The use of the mouth is to feed on that which nourishes the frame; and so the soul, by the mouth of faith, feeds on the Lord Jesus and finds strength; for "His flesh is meat indeed and His blood is drink indeed." Let us now contemplate our Lord as the BREAD OF GOD.

BREAD of God that came down from heaven, and giveth life to the world (John 6:51–58). Bread is called the staff of life, because it is the principal thing on which we subsist. And just as food is necessary to the life of the body, so Christ is needful to our spiritual life. The human spirit is poor, hungry, and famished. Whatever of this world—honor, money, lands, pleasure—it strives to satisfy itself with, it is still starved and craving. "Give, give!" is its constant cry; and ever will be as long as it attempts to live apart from God; for only He can satisfy its insatiable want. Now the Lord Jesus comes to put us into communion with the only and all-satisfying Food, to reveal God to our knowledge and to our hearts. Yea, He Himself is the very BREAD, the nourishment we want, without which we must forever remain hunger-bitten, starved, dead. His taking on Himself our nature and dying for us is that by which we live. His death becomes our life. "If any man eat of this BREAD he shall live forever; and the BREAD which I will give is my flesh, which I will give for the life of the world." The men who first heard this language from the lips of our Lord were offended, and said, "How can this man give us his flesh to eat?" And in the present day multitudes attach a carnal meaning to it, as if they were to eat Christ's veritable body with their mouths! Monstrous! See you not that the language is plainly figurative? In like manner a tree may be said to "eat" the elements that surround its roots; and to feed upon the air and the light, which play around its branches; and to drink the dew and the rain, which drench it from the clouds. Not *literally*, but by appropriating and absorbing the virtues of the earth, the rain, and the atmosphere, whereby it lives and thrives. So we are said to eat of the Divine BREAD, when we believe in Christ, appropriate Him, and make use of Him. And just as the body requires frequent supplies of food, so must we continually feed on Christ.

The Israelites in the wilderness were sustained upon Manna. That was their Bread. But, it is written, they loathed that "angels' food" and demanded a change. Just so it is with this BREAD OF LIFE. "Why do you speak so much of Christ?" say some. "Whatever you begin with you are sure to get to Christ directly. We are tired of this same thing over and over again." Alas! they do not really know the forlorn emptiness, the utter destitution of their spirits without Him; nor have they ever tasted of the BREAD OF LIFE, or they would not speak thus. May you have awakened within you a relish, an appetite, for this heavenly BREAD! For except you eat it you must remain dead in trespasses and sins. But be advised: starve no longer. "Eat ye that which is good, and let your soul delight itself in fatness." For "this is the BREAD which cometh down from heaven, that a man"— any man, any child—"may eat thereof and not die."

And now remember the importance of Faith as that by which alone we can receive any good from Christ. As we cannot see without eyes, nor handle without hands, nor support life without eating and drinking; so no more can we be saved without faith. Wherefore have faith in God.

Look unto Christ if you would be saved, as the Israelites looked to the BRAZEN SERPENT.

Lay hold on Him as your only Hope. "He is the BRANCH which God made strong for Himself."

Feed on Him as the Source of Life and Health, the "BREAD which came down from heaven."

9

Creator. Child. Carpenter. Christ.

AN atheist being disposed to sport with one whom he knew to be religious, asked him, "Is your God a great God or a little God?" The poor man silenced the caviler with this answer: "My God is so great that the heaven of heavens cannot contain Him, and so little that He can dwell in my heart." That peasant had a more sublime idea of God than the scoffer, because he had read the Bible with a teachable mind, and seen it written there, that "the High and Lofty One that inhabiteth eternity dwells also with him that is of a contrite and humble spirit."

Our attention is now to be directed to Four Titles of our Lord that combine the most wonderful extremes the mind can conceive of, as meeting in one person. We are to contemplate Him as the CREATOR, "without Whom nothing was made that is made"; the "CHILD born unto us"; the CARPENTER of Nazareth, and the CHRIST, the Son of the Living God, on whose shoulders is the government of the world.—And first, behold in Him the

CREATOR. He calls Himself the "CREATOR of Israel" in Isaiah 43:15. In Hebrews 1:10, God the Father speaking to the Son saith, "And Thou, Lord, hast laid the foundations of the earth, and the heavens are the work of Thy hands." In Colossians 1:16, we read that "by Him all things were *created*, that are in Heaven, and that are in earth, visible and invisible, whether they be thrones, or dominions, or principalities, or powers; all things were *created* by Him and for Him."

When we survey the works of our fellowmen we justly wonder at the skill and contrivance displayed in them. We cannot read of Thebes, or Babylon, or Nineveh, without astonishment at the might and ingenuity of the men who built those vast cities. Or if we visit some ancient cathedral in our own country, we admire the beauty of its cloisters, the elegance of its towers, or the massy strength of its walls; nor do we forget to praise those who set them up. Every house is built by some man, and the builder hath more honor than the house. Now He that built all things is God. But how is He robbed of His glory! How many are there who, while they admire the works of creation, refuse to converse with the CREATOR, and banish all thoughts of Him from their minds. But there is no excuse for this forgetfulness. Whenever we go we are surrounded with proofs of His skill and power. If we walk in the flower garden, His exhaustless ingenuity displays itself before our eyes at every step, in an inconceivable variety of lovely forms and beautiful colors. There the stately lily lifts it head, and the blushing rose fills the air with its fragrance; while the passion flower, the honeysuckle, the hyacinth, the anemone, all present themselves to us with some fresh peculiarity, either of scent or color or form; and each proclaims silently though plainly, "The hand that made me is divine." How wonderful must be the mind of Him who contrived them all! How beautiful His conceptions! See them in all their endless variety, their amazing minuteness and richness:

> Admire their color, fragrance, gentle shape,
> And thence admire the God who made them so,
> So simple, complex, and so beautiful.

It is the Lord Jesus Christ, without Whom nothing is made, who thus clothes the lily and paints the violet. It is our Savior who lavishes so much contrivance and care on these little fading things, and invests them with such beauty. Let this thought endear them all to us, and let every flower in the garden henceforth become a remembrance of Him.

If we wander into the forest we are struck not only with the beauty of the Divine ideas, but the grandeur of them. The stately cedar, the majestic oak, the lofty fir, lift up their heads towering towards the sky, and cover the ground with their dark shadows. The solemn gloom invites to thoughtfulness of God. And as the wind rustles among the trees, they wave their branches, and with hoarse murmur seem to acknowledge the presence and power of their great CREATOR. If we walk on the shore of the vast ocean, how does the mighty mass of water fill us with wonder at the stupendous power of Him "who measures the waters in the hollow of His hand, and layeth up the depth in storehouses." If we roam abroad by night and survey the sky, bespangled with countless worlds, there is still more to amaze us, and we shrink into nothing before that mighty CREATOR, who "telleth the number of the stars, and calleth them all by their names."

Yonder sun which warms and enlightens us, is ninety-five millions of miles distant; and the nearest star is so far off that we are confounded when we think upon the amazing distance. Suppose you could travel like an angel from world to world, and were to fly at the rate of ten miles every minute, how long do you think it would take you to reach the sun? Twenty-five years! And how long to reach the nearest fixed star at the same rate. *Fourteen hundred thousand years!* If an angel had set out from earth to one of those stars, on the day Adam was driven out of Paradise, and had traveled two thousand miles every minute till now, he would not have arrived there yet! So vast are the spaces between the heavenly bodies. And there are millions of those worlds thus divided from each other. Blessed Lord Jesus! and are the "heavens the work of Thine hands" (Heb. 1:10)? And didst Thou create those great worlds, and hang them upon nothing in yonder fields of space? And dost Thou sustain them from day to day? Lord, what is man, poor, degraded, insignificant man, that Thou shouldest take upon Thyself his nature, and suffer and die for him?

But amongst all His wondrous works, which we see, the creature *Man* is the most wonderful. At his formation there is a consultation by the Father, the Word, and the Holy Ghost, "Let Us make man in OUR image, after OUR likeness." So man was made in the image of God. Fearfully and wonderfully was he made. And God gave him a reasonable soul, and thus fitted him for an exalted state of friendship with his Maker. But alas! Man being in honor continued not. He sinned and fell, and lost the image of God. And there must be a new creation, he must be made over again, or he can never hold converse with God. And Jesus Christ is the "CREATOR of Israel." "This people," He says, "have I formed for Myself." They are His workmanship. He calls and quickens them, and takes great delight in this new creation; and over His Israel He rejoices with singing and rests in His love.

The first creation was most beautiful. But sin hath marred it and introduced death. This outward frame is therefore destined to pass away. The flowers flourish for a day, and then fade and droop and die. The trees arise, and year after year flourish and grow; but the axe levels them to the ground, or they are weakened by decay till the wind casts them down. Even man, the lord of the earth, comes up like a flower, lives a few years, and then like the flowers bows his head and passes away. Thus generation after generation is swept from the earth. And at last the fire shall devour all which death has spared. All is destined to perish.

> The cloud-capped towers, the gorgeous palaces,
> The solemn temples, the great globe itself,
> Yea, all which it inhabit, shall dissolve—
> And like the baseless fabric of a vision,
> Leave not a wreck behind.

But in the midst of this universal ruin the voice of the great CREATOR shall be heard, saying, "Behold I make all things new; I create new heavens and a new earth." And in them "there shall be no more death, neither sorrow nor crying nor pain; for the former things are passed away." But only such as are created anew by Christ Jesus, will find a place in the new heavens and earth. You have heard that you must be *born again* before you can see the kingdom of God. This is that *new creation* of which Jesus Christ is the Author. Cry to Him, then, for a new creation. Take with you words, and say, "Create in me a clean heart, O God, and renew a right spirit within me." Thank Him that you are in being. Thank Him that He has placed you where you are in the scale of creatures—"made you wiser than the beasts and caused you to know more than the fowls." Beg of Him that you, the creature of His power, may be the subject of His grace. Then you shall have part in the new heavens and the new earth, which are to take the place of former things when they shall have passed away. You shall join those millions of glorious beings who cast their crowns at His feet, and say, "Thou are worthy, O Lord, to receive glory and honor and power; for *Thou hast* CREATED *all things*, and for Thy pleasure they are and were created."—But this glorious Being was also a CHILD.

CHILD, "The HOLY CHILD JESUS" (Acts 4:27). Let us not lose sight of the one grand distinction there was between this CHILD and all other children. It is true that, like others, He was born into the world helpless and liable to death. Nor did He become a perfect Man at once; He had to grow in stature like others; yea, even to acquire ideas and to grow in wisdom also like others. In all these respects He was really and truly a CHILD. But yet there was a marked superiority; He was the Son of the Holy One of Israel, and therefore was the HOLY CHILD JESUS. You and I were born *unholy*. And all children are unholy; they go astray from their birth; every imagination of their heart from childhood is only vanity; foolishness is bound in their hearts, and they have within the seeds of every vice. But the HOLY CHILD Jesus stands alone amongst all others. He was perfect without any taint of sin.

Behold this HOLY CHILD mingling with other children in their education and pastimes. When they were angry and spiteful there were no rebukes in His mouth, no quarrelsome words, no railing for railing, but contrariwise blessing. He was obedient to His parents. He loved and honored His mother, Mary, and till He was required to be "about His Father's business," He attended to her wishes and sought to please her in all things. In His behavior to others there was nothing forward or unbecoming; He was modest and retiring. As he grew up such rare virtues attracted the notice and regard of everyone. It was such a new thing to see a HOLY CHILD. There never had been such a sight on earth before, so that He was in high favor with God and men.

It would be interesting to us to know a little of His domestic history, and how He spent the years of His childhood and youth. But the Scriptures say nothing to satisfy our curiosity. We may suppose, since both Joseph and Mary were descended from the royal line of David, that, at least, between the two they were able to muster a complete collection of the sacred writings. A most rare piece of furniture, no doubt, in those days for a carpenter's house, but a possession very likely to have been handed down from remote ancestors; a sacred heirloom to be treasured up from generation to generation as a boon more precious than gems of priceless worth. We can scarcely imagine that Providence had omitted to secure this. As soon, therefore, as the HOLY CHILD had learned to read, the Scriptures became His constant delight. There, in the Law, and the Psalms, and the Prophets, He would read with eagerness of all the wonderful things, which were prophesied and expected of Him—the works He was to perform and the sufferings He was to bear. And often we may imagine Him rising from their perusal and saying, "The Lord God hath opened Mine ear. I will not be rebellious nor turn back" (Isa. 1:5). "In the volume of this book I find it thus and thus written of Me. O righteous Father! here I am, Thy willing Servant. Lo, I come to do Thy will. Thou hast prepared Me a body. In that body I will fulfill Thy law and suffer for the sins of the people. The Lord God will help Me, therefore shall I not be confounded." And as He became older and more able to understand the difficulties of His work, doubtless He spent whole nights in strong crying and tears unto Him who was able to save. Many parts of Isaiah and the Psalms are written in His Person, and detail the workings of His mind, His anxiety or His confidence in prospect of His mighty work.

Now in some of these things the youngest of you are able to imitate Him. He has passed through childhood, and has set before you a pattern of holiness. Walk in His steps;

> Let love through all your actions run,
> And all your words be mild;
> Live like the blessed Virgin's Son,
> That sweet and lovely CHILD.

Think what snares and dangers you would escape if you were to begin, like the HOLY CHILD, to love prayer and the Bible. God requires duties from you as well as from Him, and He gives you full directions about them. Of yourself you cannot perform them, but must cry to Him for strength. Make His book then your constant study. Learn its sacred portions till you can say, "Thy word have I hid in my heart that I might not sin; by the words of Thy mouth I have kept myself from the paths of the destroyer."

When He was twelve years of age He went up to the temple with His parents to celebrate the Passover in the month of April. It was the practice of the Jews to go up to Jerusalem to their holy festivals in large companies. Almost all the people of a town used to go and return together; and they traveled forward by short stages, beguiling the toils of the way with the sons of Zion. Psalms 122, and 84, and others, seem to have been intended to express the feelings of the pious Jews in their journeys to the city of their solemnities. Thus they went on from strength to strength, till each one of them appeared before God in Zion. And we may imagine the shout of rapture which would burst from their lips when the white marble walls of their glorious temple, rising like a mountain of snow above the hills, first appeared in view—"How amiable are Thy tabernacles, O Lord of Hosts! Our feet shall stand within thy walls, O Jerusalem!"

It was on an occasion of this kind that our blessed Lord accompanied His parents to Jerusalem. The feast is ended and they prepare to return. The parents of Christ, knowing His social disposition, and that He is a favorite amongst their acquaintance, and very likely occupied with other cares, have proceeded a long way before they discover that they have left Him behind. How sorrowfully do they retrace their steps, reproaching themselves all the way for their carelessness of so choice a treasure! They arrive in Jerusalem, and commence a search in all directions after their missing CHILD. On the third day they find Him; not in the streets and broadways of the city, but in the temple, sitting at the feet of the doctors of the law, asking questions, and astonishing everyone by His wonderful knowledge. To His mother's inquiry, why He had thus dealt with them, He answered that He was "about His Father's business." This was a joyful meeting and a satisfactory explanation; so they all three returned to Nazareth where this HOLY CHILD, as it is written, was still "subject to them."

From this time we have no further account of Him till He entered on His ministry. During this interval of 18 years, He labored with His hands and earned His own livelihood. The early Christian writers tell us that He learned the trade of His reputed father Joseph, and levied with him in his employment as a CARPENTER; and that He made ploughs and yokes for oxen. And Jesus is called a "CARPENTER" in Mark 6:3.

CARPENTER. The further we go the more astonishing the subject grows. The Lord of Glory is a Carpenter! We have regarded Him as the Creator of this lovely world we live in, and everything in it; also as the Child of poor parents, dwelling in obscurity in His own world, which He had created. Let us now with reverence and admiration think of Him as a Carpenter!

Many years since there was to be seen in the dockyard at Woolwich a foreign-looking man working as a common carpenter at the ship's side. He kept the same hours as the rest of the workmen, wore the same sort of dress, and worked as hard as any of them. There was little externally to distinguish him. And yet there was a great difference between him and his fellow workmen. For though he labored thus, he was owner of several palaces and millions of acres of land. He had under him dukes and lords, generals and captains. Whole towns and cities were subject to him, so numerous that only to mention them would occupy an hour; for this ship's carpenter was Peter the Great, Emperor of Russia.

Now that was called condescension, for he undertook those labors for his country's good. But what was that compared with the condescension of our Savior? This is indeed a wonder of wonders! Though heaven and earth were filled with the majesty of His glory, and legions of angels waited to do His commandments, yet was He found in fashion as a man, a poor man! And in this condition He would not be idly dependent on others, He would not sit still and command the stones to be made bread, but wrought with His own hands at a common trade in order to earn His livelihood.

> In vain the loftiest princes try
>> Such condescension to perform.
> For worms were never raised so high
>> Above their meanest fellow worm.

Is not this the Carpenter?—not the builder, the architect, but the CARPEN-TER. We all know what sort of work this would involve. It did not consist in preparing plans and specifications, but in real hard work. Now if He who created "Arcturus with his sons" was content to fulfill the duties of this lowly calling, should they who deem themselves His followers shrink from manual labor as though it were degrading? Degrading! Can anything be otherwise than honorable in which such a One as He chose to be occupied? Let us all learn of Him, who was thus meek and lowly in heart! And let the brother of low degree rejoice in that he is exalted: exalted by being made a companion of so illustrious a Laborer. Doubtless those shipwrights who worked with the Emperor were proud of their comrade, and thought themselves and their trade very highly honored by his being engaged with them. How much rather has our Lord put an honor on industrious labor, by engaging in it Himself! And may we not be quite sure, that if there ever went forth from Joseph's workshop at Nazareth any careless carpentry, it was none of His doing? Whatever He had to do He would finish in a workman-like way. It was not slighted because it was wrought for some poor person, or because it was not meant to last long. His human work would be as perfect in its way, as all His divine work is. And there is as much exquisite skill lavished upon the organs of a tiny insect whose life only lasts a day, as upon the huge planet which is built for countless ages. Let us avoid doing work carelessly as if we thought *anything* would do. What is worth doing, in any department, is worth doing as well as we can, "as unto the Lord." We are quite sure that Jesus, the CARPENTER of Nazareth, wrought in this spirit.

In due time, the illustrious CARPENTER of Nazareth laid aside His labors, and entered on the great duties of His ministry. He began to be about 30 years of age when, by His miracles and discourses, He drew upon Himself the eyes of his countrymen and compelled many of them to exclaim—"Is not this THE CHRIST?"

CHRIST (John 7:41). In other words, Is not this that ANOINTED ONE whom God hath promised to send, and whom we and our forefathers have waited for so long? At this period, as you have often heard, there were great expectations of the promised Messiah among the Jews. And not without ground. The prophets had predicted that about this time He would come to sway the scepter of the whole world. The Jews interpreted this *literally*, so that when they saw the Savior in His lowliness, they rejected Him with disdain.

Soon after He began His ministry He went to Nazareth where He had been living. He entered their synagogue one Sabbath morning and stood up to address them. After reading as His text a most beautiful prophecy by Isaiah concerning the CHRIST, He began His sermon by saying, "This day is this Scripture fulfilled in your ears." As He went on, for a time they were struck with wonder and admiration at His gracious words. But towards the close of His discourse, being offended at His faithfulness, they cast Him out, saying, "This is only a CARPENTER; we will not receive Him, nor acknowledge Him to be the CHRIST."

He then went about preaching everywhere the Gospel of the kingdom, and working miracles to prove the divine origin of His mission. But though the devils whom He cast out of such as were possessed, knew Him, and cried aloud, "Thou art the CHRIST!" yet those obstinate Jews believed not. Some, indeed astonished at His miracles, and yet still in doubt whether to receive Him or no, asked timidly whether CHRIST when He should come, would do mightier things than these? and the prejudices of a few at once gave way to conviction; as in the case of the woman of Samaria, with whom He conversed so closely and convincingly as He sat on a well by the wayside, that she straightway left her water-pot and ran into the city, saying, "Come see a Man who told me all that ever I did. Is not this the CHRIST?"

Whilst men wondered, John the Baptist sent his disciples to our Lord with this question, "Art Thou the CHRIST, He that should come, or look we for another?" Jesus answered not a word; but turning to the crowd of suppliants who surrounded Him, healed their various maladies. He then said to the messengers, "Go, tell John what things ye have seen and heard; how that the blind see, the lame walk, the lepers are cleansed, the deaf hear, the dead are raised. Blessed is he who is not offended in Me." After a time, the Lord asked His disciples who had been witnesses of all these things, "Whom do men say that I am?" They answered that some said one thing and some another. "But whom say *ye* that I am?" Then Peter in the name of the rest said, "THOU ART THE CHRIST, the Son of the Living God." Happy Peter! Happy all they likewise who thus call Jesus Lord and CHRIST, by the Holy Ghost. And what think you of CHRIST? You have as much to do with this question as the Jews, for you need Him as much as they. "He is a Light to lighten the Gentiles" as well as "the Glory of His people Israel." Have you thought of this?

The Jews were without excuse from first to last. At His birth all Bethlehem was in commotion through the report of the shepherds; and all Jerusalem was troubled at the inquiries of Herod and the wise men of the East. The very doctors of the temple were made to point out Bethlehem as the place of the Savior's birth; and the event was *burned* into men's memories, by Herod's cruel destruction of the young children of that city. The same men were afterwards astonished witnesses of the wisdom of Jesus, when at 12 years of age, He visited Jerusalem. Why did they not inquire further? Throughout His whole ministry, also, one miracle followed another in quick succession. They saw those whom they knew to have been blind walking about without anyone to lead them. They saw those who a little while before could scarce crawl from one door to another, leaping and walking. The dumb were made to sing His praise. While some who had died were brought again from the dead, and were the living witnesses that He was certainly the CHRIST. But all in vain—the Jews despised and rejected Him. And finally, "against the HOLY CHILD Jesus whom God had anointed, both Herod and Pontius Pilate, with the Gentiles and people of Israel, were gathered together to do whatsoever God's counsel determined before to be done." They wickedly rejected the Christ, God's Anointed, and the insulted Jehovah hath poured upon them the vials of His wrath.

But if the Jews were without excuse in rejecting Him, so are you. I ask again, What think ye of Christ? Do you ask for signs from heaven or wonders on earth? They are all here. The New Testament is full of the miraculous story, and every page of history combines to prove that the HOLY CHILD Jesus, the CARPENTER of Nazareth, was indeed the Christ, the Anointed Savior of the world. Must we not infer from what has been said—

1. That men should trust their souls in the hands of Jesus, seeing He made them at first, and can therefore form them anew and save them to the uttermost. "Let us therefore commit the keeping of our souls to Him as unto a faithful CREATOR."

2. That convinced sinners should not fear to approach God and converse with Him, seeing that He presents Himself as a lovely artless CHILD, inviting our confidence in His sympathy and tenderness. "Unto us a CHILD is born."

3. That we should honor the industrious poor, and work industriously ourselves, seeing that Jesus hath set us an example of lowly diligence. "Is not this the CARPENTER?"

4. That all should hasten to acknowledge Him as their Savior, and say with Peter, "Thou art the CHRIST, the Son of the Living God." Blessed are all such; but if any are offended in Him it is at their peril, for other Foundation can no man lay. "On this Rock will I build my Church, and the gates of hell shall not prevail against it."

10

Commander. Captain of the Lord's Host. Captain of Salvation. Chief among Ten Thousand.

EVERY one has heard of Alexander the Great. He conquered all the world, and therefore to this day the world rings with his fame. Every country and every period has its renowned generals and commanders. None make so much noise in the world as the successful warrior. The poet composes songs in honor of his exploits; the sculptor is commissioned to hew a monument to his memory out of the marble block; and the painter to hand down pictures of him and his deeds to children's children. Who has not heard of Washington, Nelson, and Napoleon? The events of their lives are a favorite theme with the historian, and every schoolboy is familiar with their names. The fields where they fought, and the places where they won their victories, are still pointed out to the traveler. And when they die, their arms and even their clothes are laid up with care, and looked at with reverence; and the places of their burial are regarded as sacred. And all this without inquiry whether they were good men and holy, or whether they fought on the side of right and virtue.

But, there is one Mighty Man of War who exceeds all others in valor, and who always draws the sword on the side of righteousness, of whom, however, comparatively few care to speak. Every one has heard of His wonderful doings among the children of men, and yet only one here and there cares to sing His praise or speak well of His works. Who is this great Conqueror? What is His name? In Exodus 15:3, we read, "The Lord is a Man of War. JEHOVAH is His name." In Revelation 19:11, He is called "FAITHFUL AND TRUE." And in verse 13, "His name is called THE WORD OF GOD." We hear many talking with rapture of the skill of one general and the bravery of another; but what are they all compared with Him? Yet if we mention to them the triumphant wars of IMMANUEL, His trophies, His victories, His "chosen and faithful" armies, it is with difficulty they can be brought to enter into the subject at all. Let us not be like them. Let it be our delight to "declare His mighty acts and to talk of the glorious honor of His majesty."

Come! Behold your Redeemer under a new aspect today, namely, a "MAN OF WAR." And first consider Him as "given to be a LEADER and COMMANDER to the people."

COMMANDER (Isa. 60:4). God has set His people a great work to do. It is thus described; *warring* a good warfare, *fighting* the fight of faith, *wrestling* with principalities and powers, *keeping under* the body and *bringing* it into subjection. The truth is, they are all called to glory and honor. But the road to the palace of their King runs through the heart of the enemy's country. And an arduous thing it is to fight their way on from day to day. Of themselves they know not what to do. They need much instruction and direction. So God gives them a COMMANDER, and says to them, "This is my beloved Son, hear Him." And indeed He has the most wonderful qualifications for this office. Let me enumerate a few of them.

1. *He has almighty power.* He commandeth the sun and it ariseth. He commandeth the devils and they obey Him. He commandeth the stormy wind and it fulfills His word. He toucheth the mountains and they smoke. He uttereth His voice and the earth melteth. With a word He can create legions of servants, and with a word He can destroy armies of foes.

2. *He has wonderful skill and knowledge.* He knows what Satan is plotting in the very depths of hell. Earthly commanders may lay their plans with great wisdom, but some counterplot of the enemy may frustrate it all. But this can never happen with our Omniscient COMMANDER. He can never be taken by surprise, for He knows every movement of the enemy in the most distant part of the field. He knows also all His officers and soldiers thoroughly. Earthly commanders are frequently deceived. They often set men in places of trust who have not wisdom or honesty enough to fill them. Not so the COMMANDER of God's host. He knoweth what is in man and needeth not that any should testify of him.

3. *He is full of compassion and love.* Thus there is everything to Him to win the confidence of His servants. It is said of the armies of Napoleon, that they worshiped their leader and would obey his orders at all hazards. They would venture on almost certain death rather than disobey him. But what love ought all the soldiers of Christ to have for *their* COMMANDER! How should they take delight in the most hazardous services! And thousands of thousands have thus labored for Him. They loved not their lives to the death; and if each had had a hundred lives, all would have been at His service. He is their beloved COMMANDER.

And what commands has He issued? "Watch and pray—Endure hardness as good soldiers—Be sober—Be vigilant—Put on the whole armor of God—Fight the good fight of faith—Lay hold on eternal life—Be thou faithful unto death, and I will give thee a crown of life." These are some of them, and there are many more, which we cannot now speak of. You may find them in the Book of His wars, which is in the hands of every one of His soldiers.

But not only is He their COMMANDER, He is more. Commanders may sit at home in their stronghold and issue their orders, declining to share in the toils of the camp. But Jesus Christ leaves His palace and takes the field Himself against the foe. He asks His soldiers to submit to no drudgery, nor toil, nor labor, which He has not tried and taken part of in His own Person. He has been set in the thickest of the fight, and has set us an example of courage and constancy as "CAPTAIN OF THE LORD'S HOST."

CAPTAIN OF THE LORD'S HOST (Josh. 5:14, 15). And though we see Him not, He is always and everywhere present throughout His whole camp, amongst all the thousands of Israel. On some occasions, however, He has made Himself visible to His servants for their encouragement. The children of Israel were encamped around Jericho, straightly besieging it. Joshua their general was in the fields beside the town, busy, most likely, in devising the plan of attack. Suddenly he looked up and saw over against him a Man with a drawn sword in His hand. Joshua was at once struck with His noble appearance, and went up to Him, saying, "Art thou for us or for our adversaries?" To this the Warrior replied, "Nay, but as CAPTAIN OF THE LORD'S HOST am I come." Then Joshua fell on his face to the earth and did worship Him saying, "What saith my Lord unto His servant?" And the Lord talked with him.

Without doubt all Immanuel's soldiers would greatly delight in an occasional visit like this. We should very much like to see our Great CAPTAIN with out bodily eyes. *We* think it would be a great encouragement to us, and would wonderfully help the cause in which we are engaged. But *His* thoughts are not as our thoughts. We are not to *see* Him here. Our fight is the *"fight of faith."* But though we cannot hope to see Him, we have the testimony of those who have seen Him "glorious in His apparel." And more than that, He has left us His portrait drawn by the unerring hand of the Holy Ghost. Survey this majestic picture. "Behold a white horse! And He that sits on him is Faithful and True. His eyes are as a flame of fire and on His head are many crowns: and He has a name written that no man knows but He Himself. And He is clothed with a vesture dipped in blood. And His name is called the Word of God. And out of His mouth goeth a sharp sword, that with it He should smite the nations. And He hath on his vesture and on His thigh a name, written, KING OF KINGS AND LORD OF LORDS."

Lo, this is the CAPTAIN of the LORD'S HOST! Who would not enlist under such a COMMANDER? Who would not feel honored in being allowed to fight under His banners? Well, you have the opportunity. Now is the accepted time. He is willing to receive you, one and all, and put down your names as His soldiers. He sends forth His servants to beat up for recruits. He will have all men to turn unto Him, and He has issued a proclamation to that effect. He would fain have some from amongst you, and I am therefore commissioned by Him this very day to inquire, "Who is on the Lord's side?" Let me read to you the substance of the proclamation.

"*To all that dwell on the earth, of every nation, and kindred, and people, and tongue; to all, both small and great, rich and poor, young and old, bond and free—Ho! every one!* The Majesty on high, the King of Kings, is enlisting for the camp of the saints, a number which no man can number of faithful and valiant warriors. He requires them in the wars now carried on by 'Michael and his angels,' against the 'Dragon and his angels.' The fight is arduous, but the victory is certain, and the reward glorious. The wages are eternal life. Invincible weapons of war are provided without money and without price, and every want supplied at the expense of the CAPTAIN OF THE LORD'S HOST. The Spirit and the bride say Come! And let Him that heareth say Come! And whosoever will let him come. But cursed are all they who come not to the help of the Lord against the mighty."

This is, for substance, the King's proclamation. And there is no time to be lost. If you will come at all, you must come *now*. The Lord will be offended if you trifle with His summons. How long then halt ye between two opinions? If the Lord be God, follow Him. Need I say a word to recommend His service? I can well assure you that He is a good Master. His commands are not grievous. His service is perfect freedom. And though He is so exalted a Being, He does not disdain to eat and drink, and walk and talk, with the meanest of His followers.

I have one thing to tell you. Whether you know it or not, you are all either fighting *against* this CAPTAIN or else fighting *with* Him. You cannot stand on *neutral* ground. There is none. You cannot be merely *spectators* of the battle. Either you are on the side of the old Dragon, or else on the side of Immanuel. Which is it? Conscience will decide. Do you speak lies and falsehood? Do you take God's name in vain? Do you despise God's Sabbaths, and live without prayer? *You* are the person! The seal of Satan is on your forehead. *He* is your Captain, and his commands you are obeying. Unhappy being! Let me solemnly warn you that it is a horrible thing, and most disgraceful, to be on the side of Satan, that old Serpent, the Father of lies; and it is most dangerous to be found fighting against such a Warrior as this CAPTAIN OF THE LORD'S HOST. Indeed it is a *ruinous* battle, which you fight. It is dreadful to rush on "the thick bosses of the Almighty's buckler." "Every battle of the warrior is with confused noise, and garments rolled in blood; but this shall be with burning and fuel of fire." Oh, "it is a fearful thing to fall into the hands of the living God!"

But now I can imagine that some of you are almost persuaded, but want just to ask a question or two before you set your names down. You say, Why are we required to fight? Why does not God destroy our enemies by one stroke of His power? I will answer your questions. First, it is the will of God that you fight, and there is no appeal against that. Second, you are to be "conformed to the image of His Son." *He* was a "Man of war." You must therefore learn to handle spiritual weapons. Third, you are to be trained in difficult service, and thus prepared for the places you are to fill hereafter in the future state. God will have no cowards in heaven. They are all "good soldiers" that get there. The "fearful and unbelieving" must be cast into hell, along with the vilest of rebels. Heaven is no place for *them*.

> The fearful soul that tires and faints,
>   And walks the ways of God no more,
> Is but esteemed almost a saint
>   And makes his own destruction sure.

For such, I say, there is no room in heaven. Those who will wear the crown of glory must first bear the cross. A certain renowned English general wanted to raise for himself a regiment of valiant soldiers. So he enlisted a number of those who offered themselves. They all professed to be very courageous. But he thought within himself, "How shall I know whether these fair-speaking men are all brave men or no? What if some run away just when I want them to face the foe?" So he would try them before he would trust them. On a certain day he appointed that they should be ready on their horses to go with him on a journey. Now they were to pass through a wood where, unknown to his recruits, he had stationed a party of soldiers, hidden among the trees. These were instructed to rush out when he should pass, and fall upon his little regiment. So when they arrived at the wood, the concealed soldiers started up and made a great show of opposition. Now was the time for this Captain to see what his men were. The faint-hearted straightway turned their backs and fled, but the valiant stood their ground. Thus did he rid himself of all the timid and fearful. And his little army, after being thus tried and sifted, were never known to flee from an enemy, and were never beaten in the obstinate wars which followed. Wherever they went they conquered, and thus earned for themselves the title of "Ironsides." In a somewhat similar way God told Gideon to prove his army. He appointed a test by which they were all to be tried, and thus he discovered who among them were bold, and who were timid. The army was in this way reduced from 32,000 men to 300! But with that little remnant of tried and chosen men Gideon wrought wonders. You will find the story in Judges 7.

Now do not be discouraged when I tell you that the CAPTAIN OF THE LORD'S HOST proves every one of His followers also. And the ordeal is sometimes very severe: insomuch that many fall away in the trial and are never more heard of. But those who are with the Lamb are "called and chosen and faithful." He prepares them here on earth for the places they are designed for hereafter in heaven. If they are faithful over a few things He made them rulers over many. He gives them according to their deeds. To one He will say, "Be thou ruler over five cities," and to another, "Be thou over ten." Let us therefore (like Moses) have respect to the recompense of the reward, and patiently endure the cross, despising the shame.

Thus I have answered your inquiries, and now I ask again. Who is on the Lord's side? Who among you has determined to write his name down in the muster roll of Christ's army? Must I go back to Him that sent me and say, "Lord, it is done as Thou didst command; I read the proclamation, and explained the matter, but they would not hear." Or may I say, "Lord, I had no sooner delivered my message, than many came forward and offered themselves. And one said, 'I am the Lord's,' and another subscribed with his hand unto the Lord, and another surnamed himself by the name of Israel." Oh, it will be a happy day when you are thus brought to make this surrender of yourselves.

Let me address a few counsels and cautions to those who have already set their names down, or who mean to do so. Your enemies are lively and strong. You have to withstand the world, the flesh, and the devil. The world will either flatter and ensnare you, or else ridicule and frown on you. But your chief foes are those of your own household; I mean sinful desires and propensities. Against these you have need to be doubly watchful. Tremble at the dreadful threatenings, which He has caused to be proclaimed, as with sound of trumpet, against the *Apostate*, the *Turnaway*, and the *Deserter*. "If any man draw back, my soul hath no pleasure in him." There remaineth nothing for him but the same "fiery indignation which shall devour the adversary." Look to your armor and keep it bright. Seek to adorn your profession and to walk worthy of the Lord. You go not to this warfare at your own charges. Your great CAPTAIN has supplied you with all things necessary for life and godliness. He teaches your hands to war and your fingers to fight, and provides you with a coat of mail from head to foot. Furnish yourselves at His expense; "put on the whole armor of God."

Let me show you where you are to obtain your weapons. You must go to the "tower of David, which was built for an armory, where there hang a thousand bucklers, all shields of mighty men." The Bible is that armory. There you can examine Samson's shield and Gideon's sword. There also you may see the weapons wherewith David slew the giant. And there you may learn how the mighty men of old "waxed valiant in fight, subdued kingdoms, and turned to flight the armies of the aliens." They overcame by their faith and by the sword of the Spirit, "by the blood of the Lamb and the word of their testimony." There also you may see the very arms which were worn by our great CHAMPION when, after forty days of fasting and prayer, He entered the lists against Satan and overcame him (Matt. 4:1). Often pay a visit to this armory, for there those same weapons are still laid up for us against *our* time of need. Fix your eyes ever on the prize of your high calling. There are mansions of glory, diadems of beauty, palms of victory, golden harps, and white robes. He that overcometh shall inherit all these things and many more. And lastly—although I would not advise him who putteth on his harness to boast as he who putteth it off—yet settle it in your minds that none can harm you if ye be followers of Christ; and that the *victory is certain.*

> The promises are on your side,
> And safe to glory, lo! you ride,
> By countless deaths surrounded.

The very name of our CAPTAIN imports this, for He is called the "CAPTAIN OF SALVATION."

CAPTAIN OF SALVATION (Heb. 2:10). He leads to *certain* victory. He never yet lost a battle. He *must* reign till He hath put all His enemies under His feet. Some generals have been thought by their soldiers to possess charmed lives, so that bullets and swords had no power to wound them. Under leaders thus invested with unconquerable qualities, the soldiers have fought with wonderful energy and untiring zeal. But in this case, not only is the CAPTAIN Himself unconquerable, but all His soldiers are destined to overcome. He not only never lost a battle, but He never yet lost a *true* follower. Those whom God gives to Him He keeps, and not one of them is lost. They are all like Mount Zion, which can never be moved. Though a thousand fall at their right hand, and ten thousand on their left, destruction cannot come nigh them. Wherefore, soldier of Christ! gird up your loins and hope to the end for the reward that is to be brought to you at the coming of Christ. "Watch ye; stand fast in the faith; quit you like men; be strong!"

> Now let your soul arise,
> And tread the tempter down;
> Your Captain leads you forth
> To conquest and a crown;
> A feeble saint shall win the day,
> Though death and hell obstruct the way.

Having offered these few counsels to the soldiers of Christ, I will close by just mentioning one more Title under which He is known on the field of battle. It is this—

CHIEF, (or rather **STANDARD BEARER**), **AMONG TEN THOUSAND** (Song 5:10). We are exhorted to exert ourselves in our conflict, "looking to Jesus." Now lest we should be deceived by the enemy saying, Lo, here is Christ! or lo there! it is well for us to know where to look for Him, and by what signs to know

Him. For if the standard be hidden or the trumpet give an uncertain sound, who shall prepare himself for the battle? But Christ is CHIEF AMONG TEN THOUSAND. You may tell His Standard from every other in the world. King Saul attracted attention because he was taller, by head and shoulders, than his fellows. So Christ draws all eyes upon Him, being declared to be the Son of God with power. He is the most extraordinary Being in the world; there is none like Him; He is both God and Man in One Person! His name is WONDERFUL, and He is ALTOGETHER LOVELY.

Among the Israelites, during their journeys in the wilderness, standards were borne by the princes or chiefs of each tribe round which the whole tribe was gathered. They were used also by the Romans and other nations in their wars. Their commanders all had standards which were of various colors. Mottoes also were inscribed on them, such as "Victorious," "Thunderer." Thus they were distinguished from each other. These standards were lifted up on high, and being seen from afar served for direction where to go; also for union, to draw those together who would otherwise be separated, and as a point to which to retreat in time of danger. A standard lifted up served also for encouragement during the battle and triumph afterwards.

Various passages of the Bible refer to Christ and His truth as a STANDARD. "There shall be a Root of Jesse which shall stand for an *Ensign* of the people; to it shall the Gentiles seek" (Isa. 11:10). "Thou hast given a Banner to them that fear Thee, that it may be displayed because of Thy truth" (Ps. 60:4). "When the enemy shall come in like a flood, the Spirit of the Lord shall lift up a *Standard* against him" (Isa. 59:19). And "His *Banner* over me was Love" (Song 2:4). Yes, "LOVE!" This is the inscription on our STANDARD BEARER'S banner, and this is the watchword, which should unite every soldier to his fellow. But there are many imperfections in Immanuel's armies which hinder their success. One is a sad propensity to divide themselves into parties and fight under separate banners, and to assert the superiority of one division of the army over another. They do not obey to the letter the directions of their great CAPTAIN, who would have them all to unite and arrange themselves under His ONE BANNER. *His* Banner over us is LOVE. "By this shall all men know that ye are My followers, if ye have love one to another." Instead of this affectionate union, Satan hath sown many divisions in the camp. One party lifts up a banner with some watchword inscribed on it, asserting that all should arrange themselves under it. The rest remonstrate against this, and dividing into parties lift up standards of their own, while each accuses the other of beginning the strife.

But in the midst of so many divisions and distinctions is there no danger of confounding friends with foes? Indeed there would be were it not that the glorious Banner of our great STANDARD BEARER waves among them, and towering far above all, is seen from afar as the CHIEF AMONG TEN THOUSAND. Yet scarcely can they be kept together. At times they all rally round it in pursuit of the "common salvation," and in opposition to the common foe. It is often thus when the Man of Sin makes some sudden onslaught, or threatens to come in like a flood. Then they call each other brethren. But when the danger, which called them together, is past they again fall out by the way, and stand aloof each from the other. Thus is their strength weakened. And for want of union, that victory which will eventually crown the efforts of Christ's followers is deferred from age to age. There is a time coming, however, when these divisions will be healed. Judah will no longer vex Ephraim, nor shall Ephraim envy Judah. Then shall the Church of God, purged for her errors, go forth with her Lord to the conquest of their mutual foes, "clear as the sun, fair as the moon, and terrible as an army with many banners."

11

Covert from the Tempest. City of Refuge. Confidence.

SIN and danger go together. If there had never been sin in the world there had been no dangers. Eden was a safe place so long as its bowers remained unpolluted. Adam lived there undisturbed by the thought of danger because his conscience was free from guilt. But sin changed the whole state of things. *Now*, dangers "stand thick through all the ground." The mariner cannot sail to the distant shore without danger of shipwreck. The traveler cannot pass through the desert without danger from beasts of prey. The rich man is in danger from robbers. The poor man is in danger of starving. Dangers are everywhere, and we are constantly exposed to sickness and death.

Not that men are always mindful of this state of things. They go about their daily labors without thinking of danger. But when some dire disease or plague is raging around, and one after another is carried to the grave, then they see their danger and hasten to escape from the scene of contagion.

When a hurricane stews the streets with fragments of roofs and chimneys, and there is danger abroad, then how do men prize a safe hiding place from the violence of the storm! Or when the sailor, tossed up and down on the yawning ocean, is delivered from danger, how he enjoys the first moments of peace and tranquility! "Then they are glad because they are quiet; so He bringeth them to their desired haven."

One night there were some fishermen in a little ship in the middle of a lake. All at once the waves began to roar and a dreadful storm came on. The ship creaked as though it would go to pieces, and heaved up and down on the unsteady billow as if it had been a nutshell. Suddenly a flash of lightning ran along the heavens. And all with one accord shrieked aloud with fear; for they saw in the momentary glare a figure moving along the foaming waves just as upon dry land! Another flash! There was the same figure again! and it came nearer and nearer. There could be no mistake, for they all saw it. What should they do?

Their knees smote together and the hair of their heads stood up. "It is a spirit!" they cried. But the next moment they heard a voice rising above all the din of the tempest, "Be of good cheer, it is I; be not afraid!" The well-known voice of their Master in a moment quieted their fears; and then He hushed the tempest and made the waves smooth as oil. Thus their sorrow was suddenly turned into joy. Oh! who can tell save those who have experienced it, how refreshing is the consciousness of safety immediately succeeding to fright and alarm?

Now thus it often is with the children of God. They are overtaken with storms of affliction. The floods of sorrow lift up their waves and they feel the boisterous winds of temptation, so that their hearts are overwhelmed within them. But Jesus Christ knoweth the way which they take. And He comes after them walking on the billows. His encouraging voice is heard rising above the noise of many waters. And what does He say? "Come, My people, here in My bosom is a Hiding-place from the storm. Enter into thy chambers and shut the doors about thee, and hide thyself for a little moment till these calamities are overpast." Oh, how precious is this safe Hiding-place from threatening danger!

Let us proceed to contemplate the Lord Jesus in several particulars, as a sure and safe Retreat from danger. And first let me direct you to Isaiah 32:2, where He is called a

COVERT FROM THE TEMPEST. Also, Isaiah 4:6. We have accounts of several tempests in the Bible. That was a most memorable tempest which laid waste the earth in the time of Noah. The fountains of the great deep were broken up, and meeting the floods descending from the heavens, speedy ruin swallowed up the earth and all living creatures. And was there a Covert from that fearful tempest? None, save the Ark in which Noah and his family found refuge. And that was a "very grievous" storm which laid waste the land of Egypt in the time of Pharaoh. Fire mingled with hail ravaged the fields and smote all the beasts which were abroad. And was there any Covert for God's people? Yes. The Scriptures say, "In the land of Goshen there was no hail." But there are tempests of the mind and conscience, and storms of sorrow and wrath. There is no retreat from these nor Covert provided in all the universe except *Christ*. I will speak of five tempests, and we shall see how precious Christ is as a Covert from them.

1. *There is the Tempest of Conviction.* All men and children *know* that they are sinners. But to *feel* it is another thing. That is conviction when one is made to *feel* that he is a sinner, and that sin is a monstrous evil. When Peter preached on the day of Pentecost, there were 3,000 thus moved and *pricked in their hearts*, and all crying out, "What shall we do?" And he showed them the Covert, and they all went in and were saved, and "walked in the comforts of the Holy Ghost." Now if any of you are distressed and feel that it is a bitter thing to sin against God, here is the Covert from the Tempest! Enter by faith and you will straight-

way feel calm and secure; for "we which have believed do enter into rest." Happy are all they who are overtaken with this tempest if it do but drive them to Christ for shelter!

2. *There is the Tempest of Temptation.* Jesus Christ knows full well our danger when we are in this Tempest, and therefore He hath taught us to put up this prayer, which we should never forget when we go forth in the morning, "Lead us not into *temptation*, but deliver us from evil." For many have been shipwrecked in this storm. What was Peter's temptation? Fear that he would be laughed at if it should be known that he was one of Christ's followers. And the devil tempted him to deny with oaths and curses all knowledge of Christ, that thereby the people might be led to believe that he was not one of Christ's friends. And Peter yielded to the temptation. Oh, what a storm must the good man have felt in his bosom before he could thus lose himself! And if such a man as he was overcome, ought we not to fear? Now Christ knows how to deliver the godly out of temptation, and to rescue them from its entanglements. For even if you have been overcome, Christ is still a Covert. You must not keep away from Him. Peter found Him the same compassionate Savior after his sin as before. Affrighted at what he had done he first ran away from Christ; but he was glad to get back again. And, oh, how refreshing was it to find himself once more safe in the arms of Christ's love!

3. *There is the Tempest of Inbred Sin.* We read of the wicked that they cannot rest; they are like the sea casting up mire and dirt. Their bosoms are the seat of frequent tempests, which are sometimes pent up within till they drive them mad; and sometimes they break forth without, to the great dismay of those around. Sin, wherever it is, is more or less of this nature. Now the Christian is only in part made holy, and the remainders of sin within cause much sorrow and pain; and many violent tempests he passes through on account of the sin that dwelleth in him. David was a man after God's own heart. But being left to himself, how was he filled with terror through the struggles of his own inbred sin! Whenever we feel such temptations rising within us, whether pride, anger, envy, or discontent, we must betake ourselves to our divinely provided Covert; for there is safety nowhere else. "When my spirit is overwhelmed within me, lead me to the Rock that is higher than I."

4. *There is the Tempest of Affliction.* Most people know something of this. But we read of one who had to encounter storms of extraordinary violence in quick succession. One day a man ran and told him that a band of robbers had killed his laborers and driven away 500 yoke of oxen. And while he was speaking there came another and said, "The lightning has burned up 7,000 sheep and all the shepherds, and only I have escaped." Directly afterwards there came another messenger and said, "The robbers have just driven off 3,000 camels, and

slain those who had the care of them." And he had but just told the sad news when another came in out of breath, saying, "Your seven sons and three daughters were all feasting together in their brother's house, when a great wind blew the house down and smothered them all." What frightful tempests breaking all at once on the head of the poor sufferer! But alas! black as the clouds were, they grew heavier still. For Satan smote his poor body with sore boils from head to foot. And being desolate—his property, his health, his children, all gone—he sat him down on the ashes seven days and uttered not a word. But Satan's spiteful malice was not satisfied yet; he filled his mind with dreadful thoughts of God, so that, almost desperate, he opened his mouth and cursed the day of his birth. And last of all his three friends who came to comfort him spoke unkindly and exasperated his grief.

Here were all the tempests we have spoken of, bursting on him at once. And his inward troubles were even greater than his outward. But was not Christ a Covert? Yes, indeed He was. For though it was so dark and the clouds were so thick that the poor afflicted man could not *see* Him, yet he was enabled to say, "I know that my Redeemer liveth." Thus was he supported till the skies again cleared. And after he had suffered as much as was good for him, God made it all up; and his last days were better than his first. Perhaps it may be the lot of some of us to be afflicted in mind, body, and estate, all at the same time. And if in this condition we are driven from our Covert, or cannot find our way to it, all will be over. But all will yet be well if we are able to say,

> Amidst temptations sharp and long,
> My soul to this dear Covert flies!
> My hold on Christ is firm and strong,
> While tempests rage and billows rise.

5. *There is another Tempest, even the Tempest of the Everlasting Wrath of Almighty God.* Oh, who can describe that? What burning and dreadful words can we choose, which shall suitably set forth that most awful storm which will forever beat upon the wretched heads of the impenitent? "Upon the wicked God will rain snares, fire and brimstone, and a *horrible tempest!*" (Ps. 11:6). And observe, whereas there is a Covert from the first four tempests, even in the midst of them, while as yet they are coming down, unless you are housed before it comes, there is none from the last! Those who feel one drop of it must bear it all. Every way of escape will be closed. There will be neither shelter nor hiding-place provided from the pitiless storm through eternity. "Now, therefore, be ye not mockers, lest your hands be made strong; for I have heard from the Lord of Hosts a consumption, even determined on the whole earth." Do you not see when a thunder storm is approaching and its distant peals begin to sound, how the cattle, perplexed and affrighted, betake themselves to a Covert?—how the lit-

tle birds fly hither and thither, and try first one shelter and then another, and still flit to and fro dissatisfied till they attain to some Covert which promises to hide them quite from the violence of the tempest? Now, do you imitate them, for indeed there is a storm coming! Oh rest not till you are safe! Hide yourselves in time; and then, secured and enclosed within this divine COVERT, "the tempest shall not come nigh *thee*; only with thine eyes shalt thou see the reward of the wicked." And "when it shall hail, coming down on the ungodly, *thou* shalt be in a quiet resting-place and a sure habitation (Isa. 32:19).

But let us proceed to consider another emblem of Christ as a Retreat from danger, namely,

CITY OF REFUGE. In Numbers 35, we have an account of this institution. God directed the Jews to appoint six Cities of Refuge for the manslayer. If a man had killed his fellow without meaning to do so, he might flee to one of these and be safe from the avenger of blood. The ancient City of Refuge was a very beautiful Type of Christ. There are six points of resemblance which commentators acquainted with Jewish writings have noted. (1) *Everything was done to render the city easy of access.* It was not to be built in a valley, but set on a hill that it might be seen from afar. So "Christ is *exalted* to be a Prince and a Savior." (2) *The roads leading to it were very wide.* Once every year the magistrates sent workmen to put them into complete repair. So the way to Christ is plain, and it is the work of ministers to keep it clear. God says to them, "Cast up the highway, take up the stumbling-block, gather out the stones, prepare the way of my people." (3) *A stone was set up on the roadside at every cross way*, for fear the fugitive should go astray. The word REFUGE! was written on the stone in large letters, so that one might read as he ran. Thus do faithful preachers and teachers direct sinners to the Savior, and point to the REFUGE! crying, "Flee from the wrath to come!" (4) *The gates were never shut day nor night*, so that at any hour the manslayer could enter. Christ says, "Him that cometh to Me I will in no wise cast out." (5) *The people of the city were to receive the fugitive* and provide him with food and lodging and everything he needed. So does Christ receive with open arms those who flee to Him, and he that believeth shall never hunger nor thirst. There is no want to them that fear Him (6) *The city was for strangers as well as for Jews.* So Christ is offered alike to all, of every kindred and people and nation and tongue. Thus was the City of Refuge a Type of the Savior as our Retreat from danger.

Suppose you had dwelt in the land of Judea some hundreds of years ago; you are walking along the street and suddenly you hear angry words passing between two men. From words they proceed to blows; and now they grappled with each other, and fall together to the ground. One of the combatants is badly wounded and presently ceases to breathe. Bystanders instantly urge the wretched man who had struck him this mortal blow to make haste to the City of Refuge. "Fly!" they say to him as he lingers, scarcely believing the mischief he has done, "fly! before his relatives hear of it. They will certainly avenge him. Get upon the high road instantly as you value your life!" Would you not be greatly surprised if the man were to answer, "True, but it is a long journey, and I may be absent a great while. I have just bought some oxen and I must first fetch them from the field; I am building a house and I must tell the laborers how to proceed; a certain man owes me money and I must go and receive it." "Fool!" they would exclaim, "if you trifle thus, in less than an hour you will be a dead man! then whose will be the money and oxen you speak of? and of what use will your house be to you?" With these words the man is scarcely persuaded, but at last he slowly turns his face towards the City of Refuge. You follow him a little way on the road, and lo! the first person he meets he turns aside to gossip with, and by-and-by he stops to pick up some flowers that grow by the wayside; and presently, seeing a pleasant arbor, he seats himself in it. You run up to him and you say, "My heedless friend! you must indeed make haste; your life is at stake." "Oh, but," says he, "I can hide myself behind this wall; I shall fare well enough; do you mind your business and I will mind mine!" "Alas!" you say, "for the man's reckless folly!" And you return to the town, concluding that he will surely be overtaken and slain by the avenger who will soon be on his track.

Ah, you say, no man in his senses would throw away his chance of escape in this foolish way. He must be a madman who would act thus in a matter of life and death. You condemn such folly at once; and you turn to me and tell me that it is a very foolish story, this which I have related; for such a thing never could have happened. Perhaps not. But who are they that are risking the precious life of their souls in a way still more absurd? Are there none here who are thus trifling, and throwing away their fair opportunity of escape for foolish vanities like those which occupied the attention of the man in this parable? We tell you the life of your soul is threatened! there is instant danger! You are urged to flee at once to Christ! God urges you! conscience urges you! ministers urge you! death among your neighbors urges you! everything conspires to urge instant flight. But you loiter away week after week, and despise all warning. Once more I implore you to hear instruction. The gospel gates are open. The CITY OF REFUGE waits to enclose you within its friendly precincts. Be persuaded. "Do this now, my son; give not sleep to thine eyes nor slumber to thine eyelids—deliver thyself as a roe from the hands of the hunter, and as a bird from the snare of the fowler!" Escape for thy life! Tarry not in all the plain! Flee instantly! lest ye be overtaken and destroyed!

Happy! thrice happy are those who have already entered the CITY—who have fled for refuge to Christ! If you are of that number I congratulate you.

There is "strong consolation" for you. We have a strong CITY. Salvation has God appointed for walls and bulwarks. "Blessed be God, who has showed us His marvelous kindness in a strong CITY." Survey your goodly heritage. Walk about the Place of your Refuge, tell all its towers and battlements; examine its security. Study the great and precious promises of God, those immutable barriers which shut you in on every side. "Mark ye well her bulwarks and consider her palaces. For this God is your God forever and ever. He will be your Guard even unto death." For it is written, "The Lord shall be thy CONFIDENCE, and shall keep thy foot from being taken."

CONFIDENCE (Prov. 3:26). And you may look forth on your pursuers with triumph, just as people in a strong city, with lofty walls and solid bulwarks and plenty of stores for many a day, would be disposed to look forth on their besiegers and laugh at their threats. So may the people of God say to their foes, "The virgin, the daughter of Zion, hath despised thee and laughed thee to scorn! The daughter of Jerusalem hath shaken her head at thee! The Lord of hosts is with us, the God of Jacob is our Refuge." But always remember one thing. If the avenger of blood ever found the manslayer outside the walls of the City he was at liberty to slay him. So we must *abide* in Christ. For Satan has full power over everyone whom he finds in his own grounds. And he will show them no mercy, as it is written in Numbers 35:28, "Because he should have remained in the CITY OF HIS REFUGE." Wherefore cleave to the Lord with full purpose of heart.

In conclusion, I call upon you to admire the grace of God in providing, of His own accord, this Divine COVERT. But if you are not yet within its safe enclosure, do not content yourselves with good thoughts about it. The fugitive manslayer when he arrived at the City, would not pause without the gate while he examined the strength of his retreat, the height of its walls, or the beauty of its architecture. He would hasten to get within, and would admire it afterwards at his leisure.

So we counsel you to come into your Divine HIDING-PLACE while you may. Your convictions and tears and prayers all go for nothing till you come to Christ! Salvation is not connected with mourning or praying or feeling your burden, but with *flying to Christ!* Vain would all the tears and entreaties of the manslayer be if overtaken by the avenger; and all in vain his regret and shame, his sorrow and grief, on account of what he had done. There was only one path of safety, and that was to *get within the City*. Wherefore fly at once to Christ!"

12

Chosen of God. Called. Consecrated. Covenant to the People. Corner Stone. Crown of Glory and Diadem of Beauty.

GOD has given us many gifts. He gave us life at first; and He gives us all things by which that life is sustained. He gives us food to eat and raiment to put on. The bed on which we recline our weary limbs at night is His gift. The health and cheerfulness which make our lives pleasant to us, and the friends who take care of us, are all alike God's gifts. But there is One Gift which, by way of eminence, is called God's Unspeakable Gift. It is Christ. "Thanks be to God for His Unspeakable Gift." In this reading, I shall first bring before you some particulars regarding the PREPARATION of this Gift, and afterwards consider the BESTOWAL of it.—First, God *prepared* the Gift, for He speaks of Christ as CHOSEN, CALLED, CONSECRATED. When a master has some very difficult errand he looks about amongst his servants, and considers who would perform it best. And he *chooses* that servant who is most fit for it. When he has thus fixed on a proper person he next calls him. And lastly, he empowers him to act. Thus God *chose* the Lord Jesus, and *called* and *consecrated* Him to be His "Servant, to bring Jacob again to Him." Let us then consider Christ as the "CHOSEN."

CHOSEN OF GOD (Ps. 89:19; Luke 23:35). God foresaw that Adam would fall into sin, and bring his children into the same state. But He determined to disappoint the enemy of souls by bringing many from among this fallen race to heaven. There were very great obstacles in the way. Their sins must be atoned for, and the outrage done to God and His government must be repaired. God's righteous law must not be made void by the way in which they are screened from punishment.

Imagine a large family of young persons, happy in each other's love and in the approbation of their father. They are allowed to follow their sports everywhere throughout their father's grounds, excepting on one particular spot, which he chose to reserve for his private retreat. One day, some of these indulged, and till then happy children disregarded the injunction, and were found within the sacred enclosure. Now, do you not see that if these offenders were to be treated with the same kindness as before, how the authority of the parent would be undermined, and this indulgence have an evil influence on the rest of the family? Might they not begin to think that they could occasionally transgress without much risk? And thus this once happy family would become as notorious for confusion, as it was before remarkable for order. If the offenders were banished, then the rest might fear, and the father's authority would be kept up. But suppose he loved his children very much, and could not bear to part with them; would it not require great wisdom so to bestow his forgiveness as not to sap the foundations of his authority, and make them all think lightly of it?

Keep this familiar illustration in your minds when you consider the state of fallen man. Sin must be followed by punishment. And yet God, having determined to redeem a remnant according to the election of grace, their redemption must be so planned, that He shall be more honored in receiving these rebels back again to His favor, than in destroying them. But who could resolve this great question, *How man could be just with God—or how God could continue to be righteous and yet justify the ungodly?* Who was able to unfold this secret, and loose the seals thereof? None in heaven, nor on earth, none except Christ the CHOSEN Servant of Jehovah. Milton represents God calling a council in heaven and setting before the assembled principalities His purpose to save man; and asking of them what was to be done and who was able to undertake it?

> Man, with his whole posterity, must die—
> Die, he or justice must—unless for him
> Some other able, and as willing, pay
> The rigid satisfaction—death for death.
>
> .   .   .   .   .   .
>
> He asked; but all the heavenly quires stood mute!
> And silence was in heaven; on man's behalf,
> Patron or intercessor, none appeared.

The angels were all unequal to the mighty undertaking. None of them could by any means redeem his fellow-creature man, or give to God a ransom for him. But God says, "I have *found* David my Servant; I have exalted One CHOSEN out of the people. He shall perform the work, and my hand shall be with Him." He was CHOSEN to this work because He was the only being fit for it, and equal to the difficulty. He alone could provide a proper ransom for man. And being CHOSEN, He is also

CALLED (Isa. 49:1; Heb. 5:10). "CALLED of God, a High Priest forever, after the order of Melchizedek." Aaron the Priest did not minister at God's altar of his own accord, but was *called* of God to the work. So also Christ did not take the office of His own will merely, but was "CALLED of God as was Aaron." He speaks of Himself in Isaiah 49:1, 2, as God's CALLED Servant. And when He lived on earth He often told the Jews that they must attend to Him because He was CALLED of God, and appointed to do what He did by His express warrant. He came into the world and offered up His life on the cross, in obedience to this call. He was not *constrained*, but CALLED. "Lo, I come to do Thy will." "I lay down my life of Myself." And He is also

CONSECRATED forevermore (Heb. 7:28). You know the meaning of this word, *Consecrated*. It was applied to the anointing and setting apart of kings and priests. Of this we have spoken before. Christ was CONSECRATED to His great work by the solemn "word of the oath" of God—"Thou art a Priest forever, after the order of Melchizedek." And "Him hath God the Father sealed." He was CON-SECRATED by the special anointing of the Holy Spirit, and thus endowed with all the gifts required for His undertaking. At His baptism the Holy Dove descended on Him and pointed Him out to all as the CONSECRATED ONE, separated for the service of God and man. And the office to which He is set apart doth never pass away. Aaron died, with all his sons, and his priesthood is abolished. "But this Man hath an *unchangeable* priesthood."—Thus have we seen how God hath *prepared* for us this unspeakable gift. Now let us consider,

Secondly, *Its Bestowment*. And here are three particulars. First, "I will give Him for a COVENANT." Second, "I lay Him in Zion for a CORNER STONE." Third, "He shall be for a Crown of Glory and a DIADEM OF BEAUTY." First, God says, "I will give Him for a

COVENANT TO THE PEOPLE" (Isa. 42:6). A Covenant is a mutual agreement entered into between two or more parties, each engaging to perform certain conditions. Not in this sense can Christ be a Covenant. Again, a Covenant is a sign, token, or pledge of such agreement; usually a paper or parchment duly signed and sealed on which the agreement is written. This is the earnest or pledge of the things which are to be made over from one party to another, the bond or title-deed. And the man who owns the title-deed claims the estate. And even if he do not immediately take possession, he has that by him which will ensure it at last. Now this is the sense in which Christ is a COVENANT. He is the Pledge and Security of God's Covenant promises. "All the promises of God are in Christ," and "He that hath the Son hath life," and every good thing.

When God promised Noah that He would no more drown the earth, He appointed the rainbow as a token or sign of the Covenant. He said to Noah, "This bow shall be in the clouds, and I will look on it and remember my Covenant." Noah looked on it also, and assured himself of God's protection. And we look on it still as the sign of a Covenant made with all the earth, and rest satisfied that God will keep His promise. But wherever we see that beautiful bow in the heavens with its seven lovely colors glistening in the sun, and remember what it is placed there for—namely, to be a sign of God's promise that the waters shall not return to destroy the earth—we should also remember Christ as the Pledge of a more important, even an eternal Covenant. "For this is as the waters of Noah unto me. For as I have sworn that the waters of Noah shall no more return to destroy the earth, so have I sworn that I will no more be wroth with thee nor rebuke thee."

We read in the Bible of several Covenants. One was made in eternity between God the Father and Christ the Everlasting Son of the Father. In this Covenant God commits a work to Christ, which He undertakes; and God promises a reward. "He shall see of the travail of His soul and be satisfied." But this is not the Covenant we have to speak of today, although it is the foundation of it. Again, there was a Covenant with Adam, the terms of which are these—"Obey my commands and thou and thy see shall be blessed; but if thou disobey thou shalt die." This Covenant has been long since void; so that this is not the one we inquire for. Then there was a Covenant with the Jews, that if, as a nation, they would obey God's laws they should live and prosper, but if not, they should become a byword everywhere. It is written, "God sware and entered into Covenant with them, but they despised the oath and brake the Covenant." Therefore, neither is this the Covenant we are in quest of.

But the same Book, which informs us of those ancient Covenants, tells us also of another called the New Covenant. In this God undertakes to give grace and glory and all good things. And on the other part, there is nothing required in exchange and nothing to be done—nothing, but that those entering into Covenant with Him do agree to these terms, and take the blessing so freely offered. This is, as you see, totally unlike all the other Covenants. One party is to give the most precious gifts; the other party is to give nothing, only to receive. This Covenant is for substance as follows—That God will freely save all who "take hold of" it. That He will work in them faith and repentance and take away their stony hearts. That He will write His laws in their hearts and keep them blameless till Christ's coming. That He will make all things work together for good, and finally bring them to heaven. There they are to be presented faultless before the throne of God, to be crowned with a royal diadem, to be introduced to the society of angels, to see the King in His beauty, to be like Him, and to sit with Him on His throne—in short, they are to inherit all things, being made heirs of God and joint-heirs with Christ. Now all these glorious things are free gifts on the part of God. But He condescends to engage Himself by oath to bestow them, and also to give us His dear Son as the Pledge or Earnest of them all.

But an important question occurs here. Who are those with whom this Covenant is made? There must be two parties to a Covenant. God is One. He gives the blessings, but who are those that receive them? God writes the Covenant, seals it with an oath, and signs it on His part with a "Thus saith the Lord." But who subscribes it on the other part? I answer that every man, woman, and child, who believes in Christ, signs the Covenant and thus gains a title to all its blessings. To as many as receive Him, to them God gives right or authority to become His children and heirs (John 1:12).

Have you subscribed with your hand to the Lord, or if not, will you now do it? I know you will not while you think yourselves rich and in need of nothing. But indeed you are poor and wretched, all the time you are destitute of a title to the heavenly inheritance. He that hath not the Son hath not life. Oh, strive to obtain a part in the Covenant! Despise not your birthright! Sell it not for the pleasures of the world. Hasten at once to secure "bags which wax not old, a treasure in the heavens which decayeth not." Or do you doubt whether you *may* sign it? Do you look at the gift and say, "Christ for a COVENANT! and with Him durable riches and righteousness, a crown, a throne, an unfading inheritance! How do I know it is offered to *me*?" Read the direction—"*I will give Him for a* COVENANT *to the people!*" Not the Jews only, but the Gentiles also, *all* people. *You* must be included in this description; for what is said of all is said of each; you have only therefore to take hold of the COVENANT and set your seal to it, and it is yours.

If one were to put into the hands of a needy man the title-deeds of some valuable estate and bid him look over them, he might give them back and say, "I am willing to make all this over to you. Here is a Covenant with my name and seal at the foot of it; put your name also, and it shall be your title to the estate, and a sign between us of this agreement." Do you think the needy man would hesitate? Would he not hasten to set his name to the Covenant and make it his own? Now, God in His word speaks just as pointedly to you and to me. "Incline *your* ear and come unto Me, and I will make an everlasting Covenant with *you*, even the sure mercies of David. I *give my Son to you* for a COVENANT or a Pledge of eternal life." Now you can truly say, "Lord, I *take* Thy Son for a COVENANT. I dare not doubt Thy sincerity. I embrace the offer, and set to my seal that Thou art true?" When, if your heart be sincere in this, all things are yours, whether the world, or life, or death, or things present or things to come, all are yours; and you have as much warrant as Dr. Doddridge or any other believer, to say,

> My God, the Covenant of Thy love abides forever sure;
> And in its matchless grace I feel my happiness secure.

Did I say just now that children may be parties to the COVENANT?—A little while ago, there lived a sweet little child who was a comfort to her parents and a favorite with all who knew her. She was taken ill and her life drew near to the grave. Her Sunday school teacher went to see her, and found her very weak but very happy. Wishing to know the ground of her happiness, he said—

"My dear child, you seem very ill; I am afraid you will not live long. Are you willing to die?"

"Oh yes, sir, I am quite ready to die!"

"But what makes you so happy in the prospect of death?"

"Because I hope to go to heaven to be where God is."

"But are you not a sinner, and is not heaven a holy place? How can you hope to go there?"

"Ah, sir, but I have read in the Scriptures, and you have often told me, that Jesus Christ is the Savior of *sinners*."

Wishing to try her a little further, he said, "But how do you know that He will save *you*?"

She hesitated a moment, and looked at her friends as if she wondered much at the question, but soon answered, "*Because it is written, 'Him that cometh unto Me, I will in no wise cast out.'* " Thus did this dear child take hold of the COVENANT and rest on Christ's promise. This was all her salvation and all her desire in the hour of death. O may the same faith and the same peace be ours when we are called to die!

But a few more words concerning the Covenant of grace. To this Covenant Jesus is the *Witness*; it is signed with His name and sealed with His blood. He is the *Surety*; undertaking to pay all debts and fulfill all obedience. He is the *Mediator*; He reconciles the two parties to the Covenant who were at variance— God and man. He is the *Messenger*; He came through a thousand dangers to bring it to us. Finally, He is the *Testator*. You know a deed is of unchangeable force, after men are dead; it cannot then be altered. Well, Christ *died*, and thus turned the Covenant into a last will and testament. May He not well be called the COVENANT, seeing that He is the Pledge of all its promises, the All in all in its execution, and Himself is the Grand Blessing conveyed in it?—Again, God has given Christ for a "CORNER STONE."

CORNER STONE (Eph. 2:20). The Corner Stone of a building is the first and principal stone that unites the parts of the building together. And Christ is called the CHIEF CORNER STONE of the Church, which is God's spiritual house. You know that usually when any remarkable building is to be set up, there is a great deal of ceremony at the laying of the Corner Stone. When men build a temple for the worship of God, the people of a whole neighborhood are summoned together and prayers are offered up to God that He would bless the work. And this is a beautiful observance, for "except the Lord build the house, they labor

in vain who build it." In ancient times, as well as in the present day, similar devotional solemnities used to be observed on like occasions. You may read in Ezra
3 an account of a service of this kind. "When the builders laid the foundation
of the temple they set the priests and the Levites to praise the Lord. And they
sang together by course in praising and giving thanks unto the Lord, because He
is good, for His mercy endureth forever toward Israel. And all the people shouted
with a great shout, when they praised the Lord, because the foundation of the
house of the Lord was laid—and the noise was heard afar off." The temple whose
foundation was celebrated with such rejoicing is now level with the ground;
there is not one stone upon another. And all temples on earth shall fall in like
manner. But here we read of a temple to be reared by the hands of the Almighty
which shall last forever, even a living temple made up of lively stones. And God
makes choice of a Precious Stone, a CHIEF CORNER STONE, for a Foundation on
which the building may rest and be firmly built up. And having made this choice,
He calls all the world to come and see it. "Behold I lay in Zion for a Foundation
a Precious CORNER STONE."

This Foundation is called a STONE, because a Stone is very strong and
durable. And this Divine CORNER STONE will stand any assault, and last forever.
It is called a *precious* Stone for the sparkling glory and brightness of its nature,
outshining the sun in its strength; also in that it is so rare. There is not such another Being in all the world as Christ. It is also *Elect*. God chose it for the purpose because He knew it would bear all the weight which was to be laid on it, for
He is God; and that it would be suitable to the other stones of the building , that
all might be compacted together, for He is Man. It is also a *Tried* Stone. It has
been tried by God Himself, and it answered His expectations. It has been tried
by Satan, and the gates of hell cannot prevail against it. It has been tried by men,
for thousands have laid their souls upon it, and have been unmoved amidst
storms and tempests. God may well call all the world to behold it. When the
Jews laid the foundation stone of the temple, God directed their minds to this
more Illustrious STONE (Zech. 3:9). As if He had said, "You see that stone, and
you glory in it; come, see another of which that is but the type. Behold the STONE
which I Jehovah have laid. Upon this STONE shall be seven eyes." It is of such
dazzling luster and beauty that it shall draw the attention of all. "And I will grave
the graving thereof, saith the Lord of Hosts."

Well, and did all those whose attention was called to this STONE hasten to
build their hopes upon it? Surely we might have supposed that those who saw
it laid by the hands of God would immediately build on it, that they might be
united with so precious a STONE. At least the builders, the scribes and rulers, if
not the common people, would perceive its worth. Alas! far from it. "This is the
STONE which the builders rejected": they were too blind to see its glory. And so,

instead of building on it they stumbled at it, and fell upon it, and were broken in pieces. It became a STONE of stumbling.

And how do you treat this STONE? Do you admire it? That is well, but you must come nearer. You must be joined to it. You must become one with it. There may be many stones lying around a temple that are never built into the walls. These will be all taken away. Ah! take care that you are not swept away among them. May God grant, in His great mercy and for His name's sake, that all of us may be laid upon this STONE, and, being polished after the similitude of a palace, be built into the everlasting temple so as to remain hereafter as pillars in the temple of God to go no more out forever! What can be so great an honor as to be a pillar in the temple of God? You may have admired some tall Corinthian column which you have seen in a palace or cathedral, beautifully polished and richly carved and adorned; standing firmly on its foundation, and crowned with an elegant capital which surmounts it like a diadem. Thus does the Christian rest all his weight steadily on Christ as the CORNER STONE, and then Christ also becomes to him an honor and an ornament—his "CROWN OF GLORY."

CROWN OF GLORY AND DIADEM OF BEAUTY (Isa. 28:5). There is a foundation spoken of, which a tempest of hail, the flood of God's wrath, shall sweep away, and the column that is built on it shall be overturned like the pillars which Samson pulled on himself and the assembled Philistine lords. For the hopes, which rest on any other foundation than Christ, shall be miserably disappointed. There is also a "Crown of pride and glorious beauty," which the prophet says shall be trodden under foot and fade away (Isa. 28:1). When the pillar falls, its capital is broken and all its beauty lies buried in the dust. Not so those who are joined to Christ, and built on the tried CORNER STONE. To be built on this STONE is simply to *believe* on Christ. Do this, and not only shall you never be confounded, but you shall be highly honored and esteemed. A Crown denotes honor and exaltation; and God will lift up your head. And whereas many wear Crowns who are loathsome and wicked, *your* CROWN denotes honor and exaltation; and God will lift your head. And whereas many wear Crowns who are loathsome and wicked, *your* CROWN shall be a DIADEM OF BEAUTY. For Christ will see to it that you shall be made meet for the Master's use, and worthy to stand before His throne and grace His temple. Let us then count all things but loss that we may be found in Him, resting all our weight on Him and deriving all our righteousness and beauty from Him. Then when He shall come to be admired in them that believe, He will not be ashamed to own us before His Father and before His holy angels. "In that day shall the Lord of Hosts be for a CROWN OF GLORY AND A DIADEM OF BEAUTY." Now let me point out what you ought to learn from the lesson of today.

1. *Learn to entertain right thoughts of God.* Do not think that the Father is full of anger and wrath, and that Christ alone is kind and gracious, and that He persuades God to be merciful to us. Our deliverance *began* with God. No one asked Him to show mercy; but of His own good pleasure He chose to redeem us. God contrived the plan of salvation, and sent His Son to work out His plan.

2. *Learn to have right thoughts of Jesus Christ.* He brings good news to *all* people. It is not for old people alone, but young people also. His business is with all who will attend to Him. And you are not left at liberty to attend or not, just as you please, but God "*commands*" you to "hear Him" and to believe on Him.

3. *Learn what true faith is.* It *takes* what God *gives*, and takes it thankfully. Unbelief is an insult to God. It is an intolerable thing that God should make us such great offers, and that we, though so poor, should be too proud or too idle to take them. Let us then comply with God's invitation and take what He gives. God says, "I *give* Christ for a COVENANT to the people." Do you say, "Lord, I am one of the people, and I *take* Him for a COVENANT?" God says, "Behold I lay Him for a CORNER STONE." Do you fall in with God's plan and say, "Lord, I build on Him as my only Foundation"? God says, "I give Him for a CROWN OF GLORY and a DIADEM OF BEAUTY." Do you say, "Lord, I will glory in Him alone, as my righteousness and beauty; and I will count all other crowns and ornaments as nothing in comparison with this"? They who thus treat God's offers truly honor Him, and shall be honored by Him; while they who despise or neglect them shall be themselves lightly esteemed.

> The COVENANT of the Father's love
> Shall stand forever good;
> For Jesus gave His soul to death,
> And sealed the gift with blood.
> To this dear COVENANT of Thy word
> I set my worthless name,
> I seal the engagement to my Lord,
> And make my humble claim.

13

Counselor. Comforter. Consolation of Israel.

WHEN a man undertakes an intricate journey, he will either ask his way or get a guide to go with him. And the seaman, if he means to get safe to port, will carefully observe his compass that he may steer his bark aright through the pathless ocean. Or if he be about to sail in strange seas he will hire a pilot, that under his guidance he may escape hidden dangers. The roads in many countries are very dangerous. They lead across mountains, over steep precipices, and through rugged ravines; and often they are blocked up with ice or covered with snow. Without a guide the traveler must lose the track, and either perish in the snow or be greatly hindered in his progress. But this delay may be his ruin; for if night overtake him, either he may be torn in pieces by ravenous wolves, or be frozen to death, or be attacked by robbers. Therefore the traveler who really means to get to his journey's end safe and sound, will secure the services of a guide.

My dear friends, you are all travelers. The moment you were born you began your journey, and when you die you arrive at your long last home. If you wish for a safe journey, and a joyful arrival, and a comfortable lodging at night, you must have a guide. And you must abide by his directions, for though there are many *wrong* ways, there is only one *right* way. That scornful infidel Voltaire thought he could shift for himself on this dangerous journey. He refused to have a guide and threw away his compass, the Bible, as a useless thing. And therefore, as you might suppose, he wandered far and wide from the right way and make a very unhappy end to his journey. When he was seized with sickness he sent in great alarm for the physician Dr. Tronchin, who, on attending the summons, found him in great agonies, exclaiming with the utmost horror, "I am abandoned by God and man! Doctor, I will give you the half of what I am worth if you will give me six months of life!" The doctor answered, "Sir, you cannot live six weeks." Voltaire replied with a dismal groan, "Then I shall go to hell!" and soon after died. His journey ended in the blackness of darkness. But the Christian's path shineth more and more unto the perfect day. "Mark the perfect man and behold the upright; for the end of that man is peace." And why? Because he commits his way to God.

Let me then recommend to you as your Guide Him whom God has given for a Leader, and whose name is "called Wonderful, COUNSELOR." Follow His counsel, so shall your journey through life be safe and your end peaceful; and your home through all eternity shall be in God's palace with angels and happy saints. I said your journey should be *safe*. It shall be *pleasant*, too. For Christ is the COMFORTER also of those who follow Him. They lean on His arm as well as walk in His steps. When the road is rough, "their shoes are iron and brass, and as their day is their strength." Not so the wicked. Their journey is very comfortless at times. Hear the complaint of one who rejected Christ as his Guide.

> Oppressed with grief, oppressed with care,
> A burden more than I can bear,
>   I sit me down and sigh;
> O life! thou art a galling load,
> Along a rough, a weary road,
>   To wretches such as I.
> Dim backwards as I cast my view,
>   What sickening scenes appear!
> What sorrows yet may pierce me through,
>   Too justly may I fear.

Behold! thus shall the man be who undertakes to be his own guide, and turns away from the counsels of God. But with Christ for a Guide as your journey shall be safe and happy, so shall your *end* be calm and peaceful. And when you stand on the threshold of your home you shall be like Simeon, who, holding in his arms the CONSOLATION OF ISRAEL, said, "Lord, now lettest Thou Thy servant depart in peace, for mine eyes have seen Thy salvation." These three titles of Christ, COUNSELOR, COMFORTER, and CONSOLATION OF ISRAEL, are to be the subject of this Reading. First,

COUNSELOR (Isa. 9:6). A Counselor is one who gives advice and direction. Those held in repute for holiness or wisdom are frequently applied to for their counsel. John the Baptist was held in great reverence among the Jews. Great multitudes were attracted by his preaching; and men of all ranks came to ask counsel of him. The people asked him, What shall we do? The publicans said, Master, what shall *we* do? And the soldiers demanded of him, And what shall *we* do? And you do not think it likely that young persons also came to him with the same question, What shall *we* do? We do not indeed read that such was the case; but we are certain that children went to John's Great Master, and that our Lord would not suffer them to be hindered. And the Savior is still willing to receive them and give them counsel. He is not the COUNSELOR of grown people alone but of the young also. The Bible was written for children (Deut. 11:19). The promises are for the children (Acts 2:39). Sabbaths and sermons are for children as well as for men and women. And Christ is a Guide for children. And why? Because children are *lost* and therefore need a Savior. They are exposed to many dangers and best with many difficulties, and therefore need a CounSelor as well as those who are older. Therefore, I pray you (ye younger ones), do not put these things away as if they did not concern you. With serious and attentive minds, I would have you all to ask at once of this wonderful CounSelor—What shall we do? I will imagine then that three sorts of persons put this question.

1. Some of you may say, "*We are uncoverted—What shall* we *do?*" Not converted? Then Christ's counsel to you is, that you neither eat, nor drink, nor sleep, till you are. For all the while you remain unconverted you are in the wrong road. Read Ezekiel 18:30–32. "Repent and turn yourselves from your transgressions, so iniquity shall not be your ruin. Make you a new heart and a right spirit, for why will ye die?" "Turn yourselves," that is, Change your minds. For instance: You have no mind to love God. This is very hateful, and therefore God requires that you should change your minds in this respect. God says, "My son, give Me thine heart." And is not this reasonable? Who made you? Who feeds and clothes you? Whose earth do you walk on? It is God who gives you all things richly to enjoy. And surely you should love Him. Therefore change your minds, and do it *now* before you eat, drink, or sleep; for except ye repent ye shall all likewise perish.

2. Some may say, "*We are awakened—what shall* we *do?* We feel sin to be a heavy load, and confess we are poor, miserable, and blind." To such the Counselor gives this advice—Come unto Me, all ye that labor and are heavy laden, and I will give you rest." And "I counsel thee to buy of Me gold tried in the fire that thou mayest be rich, and white raiment that thou mayest be clothed, and eye salve that thou mayest see." And make haste about it; believe now! Fly to Christ *now!* Would a man, pursued by a wild beast, stand still and gaze about him? Would he not run for his life? Wherefore "agree with thine adversary quickly whilst thou art in the way, lest he hale thee to the judge and the judge deliver thee to prison." There is no solid peace in life, and no security in death, for such as are *merely* awakened! The blessings of the gospel belong only to *such as have already come, and are daily coming to Christ*. And the way is open; Christ is ready to save you, and waiting to embrace you. However great your sins, however confused your feelings, whatever discouragements you have now pressing upon you, let them not keep you from Christ but rather drive you to Him. If you are ready to exclaim, "Oh, wretched being that I am! Who shall deliver me?" know that there is but one answer to all your inquiries—one remedy for all your complaints— You muSt Come to ChriSt. You need not carry your burdens away with you—you need not wait to hear more sermons, and read more books, and shed more tears—nor stay till you become more humble, more holy, more penitent, before you come to Christ; but you may come *now*, and come *just as you are*.

Come, and He'll cleanse your spotted souls,
    And wash away your stains,
In the dear fountain which He poured
    Forth from His dying veins.

Your heart, that flinty stubborn thing,
    That terrors cannot move,
That fears no threat'nings of His wrath,
    Shall be dissolved by love.

3. But, perhaps you are able to say, "*We hope we are converted—What shall* WE *do?*" The Bible is full of the directions of your heavenly COUNSELOR—Grow in grace and in the knowledge of your Savior.—Pray always; watch constantly.—Search the Scriptures.—Love one another.—Forgive and pray for your enemies if you have any.—Do good to all men.—Try to save wandering souls from death. Now these things are not grievous if you are converted, but delightful. It is "meat and drink" to follow Christ's counsels. I cannot stay to speak of them now. You must read them in your Bibles for yourselves. But I wish to impress it on your minds that you need not sit down on the seat of the slothful and idly ask, What shall we do? The youngest of you can store his memory with Christ's counsels and promises, and use them for the benefit of others; and like Naaman's little maid, who informed her master that she knew of a prophet who could heal him of his leprosy, you can tell your fell sinners that you know of a Physician who can heal their souls.—But we must pass on to the next Title. Those who obey Christ as their COUNSELOR, shall find that He will also be their "COMFORTER."

COMFORTER (Isa. 61:2; John 14:16). Our Lord in His sermon at Nazareth represented Himself as "anointed to COMFORT those that mourn." When about to leave the world, He promised His disciples that He would "pray the Father and He would send them *another Comforter,*" implying that *He* had been their COMFORTER hitherto. Great indeed was the comfort they had found in His society and conversation; and when He talked of leaving them it almost broke their hearts. Lord! said one of them, Why cannot we follow Thee? We will go with Thee to prison and to death. They spoke of a prison as if it would become a palace if He were there, too; and of death, as if life would not be life without Him, or as if they would surely die if they lost Him. When Christ once asked them, Will ye also go away? they were grieved at the question and said, "Lord, to whom shall we go? Thou only hast the words of eternal life; Thou art our only COMFORTER." They were ready to say to him, as Ruth said to Naomi, "How can we leave Thee or return from following Thee? Whither Thou goest we will go, and where Thou lodgest we will lodge, where Thou diest we will die, and there would we be buried."

Thus highly did they esteem Christ as a Comforter. And no wonder! There is no Comforter like Him. Job said of his friends, "Miserable Comforters are ye all"; and how often may we say the same of ours! Sometimes they cannot understand our grief, only our "heart knoweth its own bitterness." But Christ is the secret witness of our sorrow. And He puts our tears into His bottle; are they not in His book? Be not afraid that your complaints are too trifling for His ear. "They shall hang upon Him all vessels of small quantity, from the vessels of cups even to all the vessels of flagons" (Isa. 22:24). Sometimes our friends will not sympathize with us, even when we do unbosom ourselves. But Christ is touched with the feeling of our infirmities. None can feel for us like those who have been in the same trials themselves. He was a Man of Sorrows and acquainted with grief. Sometimes our friends are at a distance when we are overtaken with misfortunes. The comforter who should relieve us is far from us. But our Divine Comforter is always near at hand; we have only to knock at His door and it is straightway opened. "Thou shalt call and He will answer."

And when our eyes are opened to see the danger we are in of eternal death, because of the greatness of our sins, none but this Divine Comforter can relieve us. Friends may say, "Come with us—join in our merriment, and laugh away all melancholy feelings." Ah! but this will not do. Such joy is "like the crackling of thorns under a pot"; in the midst of this laughter the heart is sad. The very tears of one mourning for sin are sweeter by far than such empty mirth. And indeed even Christian friends may often in vain attempt to speak to our peculiar case. But Christ can speak "peace to him that is near, and to him that is afar off." For well He knows how to speak a word in season to them that are weary with the burden of sin; He was anointed to comfort those who thus mourn.

Again, sometimes we lose our friends by death. Perhaps we follow a pious mother or faithful sister or wife to the tomb; and there in the lonely graveyard, with many sighs and tears, we lay her precious remains. And we return to the dwelling, which was once gladdened by her presence; but all is changed. Her place is vacant. Her soothing voice is heard no longer. We miss the busy kindness, which sought to anticipate our wants and strove to make us happy. Alas! she is not. And our tears flow apace when we remember that we shall see her loved form no more on earth. Ah! who can comfort the mourner now? The voice of friendship cannot reach the wound. It is within. There in the hidden depths of the heart the pain is felt; and at every fresh attempt on the part of our friends to divert us, we say truly, Miserable Comforters are ye all. But oh, blessed be our heavenly Comforter! His divine consolations can reach us. He says, "I will not leave you comfortless (or orphans), I will come to you." And when He comes, it is to dry our tears and to remind us that He holds the keys of death, that with Him is the soul of this departed one, and that those who sleep in Jesus He will bring with Him, for that He is the Resurrection and the Life. Thus does He pour balm and oil into these painful wounds.

But we must die ourselves. And who shall comfort us in that solemn hour? Blessed Jesus! so precious are Thy consolations that like Thy disciples at Emmaus, we do entreat Thee not to leave us. With holy violence we would constrain Thee! Abide with us, for it is towards evening, and our short day is far spent, and our journey almost ended. And oh! what comfort will there be when we die if Thou be not with us! Where else can we lay our aching heads but in Thy bosom? Oh, be Thou near to speak comfortably to us when heart and flesh shall fail. When we must leave all our friends behind us, and go down into the dark valley and walk through it alone, then let Thy smile cheer us, let Thy rod and staff comfort us!

Yes, when we come to die all other comforts will fail us, but that which good old Simeon blessed God for, the

CONSOLATION OF ISRAEL (Luke 2:25). He saw at last with his eyes, and held in his arms, that which he had long waited for; and with joy unspeakable and full of glory he gave thanks to God. This was the CONSOLATION of the true Israel God, for which, during many ages, they had longed. In their darkest seasons this it was which consoled them. And the prophets, in the midst of their heaviest denunciations of wrath, often suddenly turn aside to solace themselves in Him. And still living and dying, there is no relief for any but in this Divine CONSOLATION OF ISRAEL.

I have heard it remarked by a Jew that the people of his nation always die very miserably. A gloom hangs over their dying pillow that nothing can dissipate. Ah! they reject the *only* CONSOLATION OF ISRAEL, and there remaineth no other. So common a thing is this dread of death among them, that if they witness anything different they are surprised. A Jew had a pious man in his employ as a gardener. This man died. And his master in a letter to another Jew says, "I am no longer disposed to laugh at religion, or to plead that Christianity offers no comforts in death. I witnessed the last moment of my worthy gardener, and I wish I may die his death; if there is happiness in another life this disciple of Jesus is assuredly happy. When the physician told him he was in extreme danger, 'How can that be,' said he, 'when God is my Father, Jesus my Redeemer, and heaven my country?' His last words were, 'I am about to die! but why should that trouble me? *My Jesus is the True God and Eternal Life!*'"

I knew "an old disciple," who enjoyed great peace in his last sickness, and before he fell asleep in Jesus spoke of Christ as his only but all-sufficient CONSOLATION. Among other things he repeated this verse—

My soul most surely prizes
The sin-atoning Lamb;
Thence all my hope arises,
Unworthy though I am.

His chamber, as I sat by his bedside, seemed like the porch of heaven; and the peacefulness of his end was exceedingly refreshing to all who witnessed it. I knew another devoted servant of Christ who wrote to me a little before his death, "I am a boundless sinner but Christ is a BOUNDLESS SAVIOR. There my soul finds her Rock, her Refuge; and thence I can look into Paradise." He also died soon afterwards, still sweetly reposing on Christ as the CONSOLATION OF ISRAEL.

Mr. Janeway, when he came to die, said, "I am through mercy quite above the fear of death, and am going to Him whom I love above life! Oh that I could let you know what I now feel! Oh that I could show you what I now see! Oh that I could express the thousandth part of the sweetness that I now find in Christ! *You little think what a Christ is worth upon a deathbed*! Oh the glory, the unspeakable glory which I now behold! My heart is full! Christ smiles—would you keep me from my crown? The arms of my blessed Savior are open to embrace me! the angels stand ready to carry my soul into His bosom. You would not have the heart to detain me if you could but see what I see!" Mr. Rutherford also died in holy triumph. These are some of his last words. "I shall shine! I shall see Him as He is and all the fair company with Him, and shall have my large share; I have gotten the victory! Christ is holding forth His arms to embrace me. Now I feel! I enjoy! I rejoice! I feed on manna. I have angels' food. My eyes will see my Redeemer!" He expired with the words, "Glory, glory dwelleth in Immanuel's land."

But many of God's people have been *tortured to death*. Was *their* end peace? and did the CONSOLATION OF ISRAEL lift them up above their sufferings? Yes, this is a sight which angels have often witnessed. A man suffering and yet joyful! A bush burning and yet not consumed! Christ's peace flowing in streams through the soul while the body has been writhing in anguish! In the year 1538, John Lambert was burnt to death in so cruel a manner that one cannot bear to speak of it. And yet God was with him and filled him with triumph. Just before he died he lifted up such hands as he had, all flaming with fire, and cried out with his dying voice, "None but Christ! None but Christ!" And twenty years afterwards, in the last year of the reign of that detestable queen Mary, a poor woman, Cicely Ormes, the wife of a weaver at Norwich, was burned alive for no other crime than that of love to the gospel. When led to the stake she kissed it, and amidst the kindling flames cried, "My soul doth magnify the Lord, and my spirit hath rejoiced in God my Savior." Then "she yielded up her life as if she had been in a slumber, or felt no pain."

But they were all grown-up persons; have *children* anything to do with these things in their dying hours? Oh, yes, the youngest child may have an interest in the CONSOLATION OF ISRAEL. There was one Sarah Howley who died at the early age of ten years. A little before her death she gave her Bible to one of her brothers, and said, "Oh, seek Christ for your soul while you are young! Put not off this great work till you come to a sick bed! Remember the words of your dying sister. *Oh if you knew how good Christ is!* If you had but one taste of His sweetness, you would rather go to Him a thousand times than stay in this wicked world! Oh! I would not for ten thousand worlds part with Christ! Will you not strive to get an interest in Christ?" The last words she was heard to speak were these, "Lord Jesus, help! dear Jesus! blessed Jesus!" And thus she died, like Simeon, embracing the CONSOLATION OF ISRAEL.

All this is as it should be, not only in death but in life also. When however we see Christian people pursuing their pilgrimage, burdened with a load of suspense and doubt as to their future, we are ready to say, "Can this be the will of God? Has He made no provision for stronger CONSOLATION than that?" Let us see. When Abraham received those great promises, which God gave him, his faith was hardly equal to the strain. He could scarcely "stand under" their exceeding weight. So God, to make an end of all controversy, added an oath; He sware by Himself, He backed His promises by His character. It was as if He had said, "Abraham, I Who am Jehovah say unto thee, Upon My Word and Honor, I will fulfill all these things."

And hath not God pledged those same "two immutable things" to every one who receives the gospel (Heb. 6:16–18)? Why did He think this necessary? Because He foresaw the endless controversies which would arise in our unbelieving hearts about such exceeding great promises. "Can they be true? Does God mean all that for such a one as I who am less than nothing and vanity, worse than nothing and sin?" "Well," saith God, "I will do all that can be done to make an end of this controversy, so hurtful to you, so derogatory to Me. I have given you My word, and surely the bare word of the Living God ought to suffice. But now hear! I pledge My character to you, I swear by Myself." Christian, why not take the "strong consolation" which it is the will of God you should have, and go on your way rejoicing?

One known as "Old Nanny" dwelt in a lonely cottage in the Highlands. She was poor and bed-ridden, but "rich in faith." A young minister was accustomed to visit the old saint, more for what he could learn from her than for anything he was able to communicate. One day wishing to try her faith he proposed this startling question; "Ah, Nanny, but suppose, after all your praying and all your trusting, God were to cast you off at last! What then?" The old woman raised herself on her elbow, and looked him steadfastly in the face and said, "Eh! mon.

Is that a' the length ye got to yet? Why, mon! God wad be the greatest loser. Poor Nanny wad lose her soul, to be sure; and that wad be a sair loss indeed, but God wad lose His character! He knows I've just hung up my soul and all my hopes upon His ain precious promises; and if they should be broken, the whole universe wad gang to ruin"; and then sinking her voice, "For God wad be a liar!"

And let this be engraved on the hearts of all who have not come to Christ, that if you have not Him for your COUNSELOR and Guide, your COMFORTER and Supporter through life, both your *way* and your *end* will be bad! Think not to live a life of sinful pleasure and indifference to religion, and then at the last to die a comfortable and a Christian death. This experiment has been tried and has failed. Thousands, under some sudden religious impression, have prayed, "Let me die the death of the righteous and let my last end be like his!" But they regarded iniquity in their hearts all the while they prayed, and the Lord did not hear them. No! the traveler in an unknown path, if he decline to follow the directions of his guide, must not be surprised if he stumble and fall. "The man that wandereth out of the way of understanding shall remain in the congregation of the dead." "Give glory to the Lord your God, before He cause darkness and before your feet stumble upon the dark mountains, and while ye look for light He turn it into the shadow of death and make it gross darkness" (Jer. 13:16). We must "give glory to God," by following Christ's COUNSELS. Then will He be our unfailing CONSOLATION in life and in death.

> For what can mortal friends avail,
> When heart and life and flesh shall fail?
> But, oh, be Thou my Savior nigh,
> And I can triumph while I die;
> My CONSOLATION is divine,
> And Jesus is forever mine.

14

Dear Son. Delight. Dew.

GOD promised Abraham a son in whom all the world was to be blessed, and in due time fulfilled His promise. And Abraham rejoiced greatly in this gift from the Lord. But one day God said to him, "Take now thy son, thine only son Isaac whom thou lovest, and offer him up for a burnt offering on yonder mountain!" Abraham, filled with surprise and grief, nevertheless prepared without delay to do as God commanded. It does not appear that he told Sarah his wife the dreadful secret, lest her maternal feelings should interfere with the performance of his duty to God. Rising up early in the morning, he saddled his ass, called his son, and went forth towards the place God had told him of. They traveled on for three days; and then lifting up their eyes, saw before them the mountain on which the altar was to be built. At once they began to climb the rugged steep; Abraham carrying the knife and the censer with fire, and Isaac carrying the wood. Abraham spoke not to his son; his heart was full. How *could* he explain this mysterious command of God? Together they walked on thoughtful and perplexed, till Isaac, unable to contain any longer, broke the silence and said, "My father, behold the fire and the wood; but where is the lamb for a burnt offering?" Then said Abraham, "My son, God will provide Himself a lamb for a burnt offering." So on they went. Presently they came to the top of the hill. And there the startling truth came out that Isaac was to be the sacrifice. What must have been the parent's feelings when he told him that! And what were Isaac's feelings when he found he was to leave the world in a way so dreadful, dying by a father's hand! And now the altar is reared, the wood laid in order, the victim bound and laid upon the wood! The dreadful moment is come! Abraham draws the glittering knife from its sheath, and with averted eye raises his arm to plunge it into the victim, when lo! in that critical instant the voice of the Angel arrests the stroke, and directs him to substitute another victim, even a ram just caught in a thicket close at hand. This the glad father takes and offers up. And Isaac, freed from his bonds, is received again as from the dead. And God could say to the obedient Patriarch, "Now I am satisfied that thou lovest Me. Now I know that thou fearest Me, seeing that thou hast not withheld thy son, thine only son, from Me."

This is an image, though a faint one, of the infinite love of God to sinners. He too had One Only Begotten Son whom He did not withhold from us—God's DEAR SON He is called in Colossians 1:13. "And in this was manifested the love of God towards us, because that God sent His Only Begotten Son into the world that we might live through Him" (1 John 4:9). Let us dwell awhile on this Title.

DEAR SON. God has many sons. The first man Adam was called "the son of God." The angels who shouted for joy when the world was created were "sons of God," and saints who are adopted into God's family are "sons of God." But Jesus Christ is greater than all, higher than the highest, the EQUAL OF GOD. And God loves this DEAR SON better than all the world beside, and will have all men to honor the SON even as the honor Himself, forasmuch as Both are Equal in power and glory. This is plainly taught in the Scriptures.

But about 400 years after Christ's ascension, there were found profane men in the Church who refused thus to honor God's DEAR SON. These men took wonderful pains to spread their hurtful opinions, and turned away many from the faith, amongst whom was the Emperor Theodosius. There was then living at Rome a bishop named Amphilochus, who was so grieved at the dishonor done to Jesus Christ, that he resolved to take some opportunity reprove the Emperor before the court. The Emperor had a favorite son Arcadius, whom he had proclaimed partner with himself on the throne. One day they both say in royal state to receive the homage of their subjects. Among those who attended on this occasion was our grave bishop. He bent before the Emperor, but took not notice of the son. "Know you not," cried the Emperor, "that I have made my son the partner of my throne?" Upon which the bishop placed his hands on the head of the young man and said, "The Lord bless thee, my son," and turned himself to go away. At this the Emperor was angry, and said, "Is this all the respect you pay him who is my equal in the throne?" "Sire," interposed the bishop, "you are angry with me for not paying your son equal honor with yourself—what must God think of you for encouraging those who insult His Equal SON in every part of your empire?"

This truth, which the zealous bishop took so singular a method to assert, is the very foundation of religion. We would sooner part with the sun from the firmament than give up the Deity of God's DEAR SON and His full Equality with the Father. But this DEAR SON God yielded up to the cruel death of the cross. Though He loved Him so greatly He sent Him into the world to be a Man of Sorrows. He allowed wicked men to spit on Him, to scourge Him, and to nail His sacred hands and feet to a tree, as if He had been the worst man that ever lived. And on that dreadful cross, scorned by His enemies and forsaken by His friends, He hung during six long hours of fearful anguish before He yielded up His spirit. How strange was this event! What is the meaning of it? The Bible says, "All we like sheep have gone astray, and the Lord hath laid on Him the iniquity of us all." Having agreed to bear our sins and take our place, God treated Him as if He had been a sinner. But, holy and undefiled, He was bruised for our iniquities, and endured all that bitter chastisement to procure our peace. This is the meaning of that strange and solemn sight, Christ Crucified; from which the sun hid its face, and angels turned away with amazement, while we who receive the benefit praise Him for His boundless love, and say, "Worthy is the Lamb that was slain to receive power, and riches, and wisdom, and strength, and glory, and blessing." We stand amazed at this most expensive proof of His love, in that He has not withheld His Son from us. We may well each one of us, cry out in astonishment, "Lord, I ask no other sign, I want no further proof of Thy love. Now I know that Thou hast loved mankind with an everlasting love, seeing that Thou hast not withheld Thy Son, Thine ONLY BEGOTTEN SON Jesus, from us! Hast Thou indeed given Him up for me? Stupendous thought! I will resist Thy love no longer. My heart relents. Lord, I believe, help Thou my unbelief"—A Title similar to that of DEAR SON occurs in Proverbs 8:30, where Jesus Christ, speaking of God's love to Him, under the name of Wisdom, says, "I was daily His

DELIGHT, rejoicing always before Him." This passage leads us back to a period "before ever the earth was, when as yet He had not made the dust of the world." It tells us God's DEAR SON was "as one brought up with Him," such was the sacred intimacy between "the Father of an Infinite Majesty, His Honorable, True, and Only Son, also the Holy Ghost the Comforter." Oh there is something very awful in the thought of that mysterious past, when the Glorious Three dwelt together so joyously, and there was neither man nor angel nor living creature beside! To think long about it is like gazing on the sun, which makes the eye to ache. Let us turn aside a moment and glance at something less oppressive to our sight. Imagine yourselves at Windsor Castle. The approach to it lies through parks of great extent. You go in at the gates and find on all sides great piles of buildings. On the right is the Round Tower from the top of which waves the royal standard. The gothic building on the left is St. George's Chapel, the sepulcher of many kings. You gain admittance at the palace, and are led through galleries of pictures, halls of music, chambers of state, drawing-rooms and saloons. You walk forth on broad terraces and look upon gardens and lawns and groves; and beyond you see houses for the officers and guards. Nothing is wanting to render this royal castle a proper habitation for a monarch. Well, suppose you have seen it all—the throne room of the kings, and the state rooms; you would then perhaps ask, "May we not just look into the inner apartments, and see the inhabitants of this princely place?" Not so. The royal family is concealed amidst towers and lofty walls. And their mode of living can only be known by those who are admitted to that part of the palace in which they dwell. Curiosity inquires in vain, for who dares intrude on the privacy of a monarch?

Now here is a little glimmering resemblance of the greater majesty of Jehovah; something that at least serves to illustrate it. The great Lord of all Power and Might has His spacious universe which is laid out, as it were, in public walks and gardens and everywhere supplied with convenient residences. These surround His palace; and in them His creatures may rove at liberty or live at ease. But the secret place of the Almighty none can find. He dwells amidst a blaze of light; and that "terrible brightness" hides Him from view as completely as though "clouds and darkness were round about Him." And yet our comparison will but confuse our thoughts, if it lead us to confine Him in solitary grandeur to one retired part of His dominions. "He filleth heaven and earth," and, which is a more wonderful expression, He "inhabiteth eternity." And Jesus Christ, who throughout that awful past dwelt in His bosom, has opened to us in this chapter of Proverbs "a door in heaven," through which we my look in to God's palace and see the Blessed Three infinitely happy in their mutual delight. And we even get a glimpse of their *employments* too. In that vast eternity when all things were planned, the great work of redemption was arranged. Christ's Delights were even then with the sons of men who should afterwards be born and be brought to believe on Him. And God delighted in them, too, and devised means with the Son and the Holy Spirit by which to secure their glory and happiness.

These two expressions, "I was daily HIS DELIGHT," and "I was as One brought up with Him," seem to refer to the pleasure a parent takes in His children, their conversation and employments, and all that concerns them. When Dr. Doddridge was a little boy, his mother taught him Scripture histories by the help of pictured Dutch tiles fixed in the sides of the fireplace. And often on a Sunday evening while the wintry wind whistled without, they two sat beside the blazing fire talking about righteous Noah, or meek Moses, or holy Daniel. And the happy mother felt great pleasure in her little soft-eyed intelligent boy, as he looked first at the pictures and then into his mother's face, asking her to tell him the meaning of them all. But she could not then foresee how useful he was afterwards to become, or she would have folded him to her bosom with ten times deeper emotions of joy.

A sorrowful mother once went forth to gather papyrus reeds from a riverside in Egypt. And then taking them home she twined them into a basket. And as she sat and wove them together her tears fell fast upon her fingers. Why did she weep? God had given her one of the loveliest of human babes. But not far away there were heartless men who would have killed him had they but heard his feeble cry. Determined to hide him somewhere, she thought of the reeds, which grew along the brink of the river, and made this boat or ark to hold him, as in a cradle, and keep him from the water. Now suppose as she sat weeping over her bulrushes an angel had called to her, "Fear not, poor mother, for that little babe shall live to be the greatest man upon earth; he shall talk with God face to face, and deliver His people from slavery." What effect would that have had on her? Surely her sobs would have been exchanged for smiles, while with all a mother's pride and fondness she would have redoubled her efforts to save her lovely babe.

Let me recount another history about "a wise son and a glad father." His mother died when he was young, therefore the father loved him the more and made him so many presents that his brothers envied him. One day they took him when his father was at a distance and sold him for a slave and then pretended that the poor boy had been eaten by wild beasts. But after many years tidings came that the son was still alive, and he had become Lord of Egypt. Who can describe the father's feelings here? It was hard to make him believe the report, but, convinced of its truth, he hasted to see his long lost son once more before he died. And what a meeting it was! They wept on each other's necks "a good while." Then the glad father went home with his son, and saw the all but royal state and grandeur in which he lived; and learned how his long lost Joseph became the distinguished Deliverer by whose wisdom and foresight Egypt and its surrounding districts had been saved from famine. Now is the joy of the old man full! His son had been his Delight years before when a little boy, dressed in his embroidered coat—how must more now! He loved him first because he was his own son; he loved him in childhood because he was so gentle and so good; and afterwards he loved him still more because he was so wise and so useful. Well now, this is the image by which God has chosen to set forth to us His infinite Delight in Jesus Christ. And from it we conclude,

First, that just as the parent delights in his child because he *is* his child, so God's own Son is HIS DELIGHT inasmuch as He is a Partaker of the Divine nature. Secondly, as a parent is pleased with his child's good character and disposition, so God delights unspeakably in the holiness and excellence of His Son. "Thou hast loved righteousness and hated iniquity, therefore thy God hath anointed Thee." Then, thirdly, as a parent takes pleasure in the son's works if they be wise and useful, so the God and Father of our Lord Jesus Christ had perfect satisfaction, from of old, in all His Glorious Son's works whether already performed or only foreseen. "By Him He made the worlds"; and as the work went on from day to day God "saw that it was good." So does He delight in Him as "upholding all things by the word of His power." But there is one of His works in which God takes special pleasure, as the most marvelous of them all—the work of Redemption. It was begun in eternity. It was then that God, foreseeing how Adam would plunge us all into ruin, contrived a plan to save the world, and the Son agreed to be God's Servant to do all that was required according to that most wise plan. It was arranged that man should be redeemed from prison and from judgment, only on condition that Jesus Christ should pay a great ransom. And what was that ransom? Would a thousand worlds do, or all the stars in the Milky Way? No, all these are of less value than one immortal soul. What then? The most precious blood of Christ! Nothing less. He must become Man, and suffer on the cross and pour out His life's blood for us, or we cannot be saved. And what did He say to these terms? Why, knowing all that it would cost—the wounds, the shame, the tears—He answered, "I will lay My life down for the sheep to deliver them from going down to the pit."

It was in the anticipation of this work that the Father delighted so greatly; and the Son delighted in it too; and thus Their delights were with the sons of men before the world was. And all that Jesus then undertook to do He has since done; and God loves Him for it. "I have kept my Father's commandment," says He, "and *abide in His love*," and "*therefore doth the Father love Me*, because I lay down My life for the sheep." But the great work which He finished, during His life upon earth, is inseparably connected with a divine process still going on in human hearts; in allusion to which He says, "I will be as the

DEW unto Israel, and he shall grow as the lily" (Hos. 14:5). The heavens have received Him out of our sight, but He sheds down sweet influence on His people below, causing them to grow holier and better. Thus also the Dew, having first risen from the earth, descends again to water it. Softly and silently do the precious drops distill through the air, but how wonderful is their effect! Did you never observe on a summer day, how withered the flowers look in the hot sunshine, how they hang their heads and seem all but dead? But go forth when the morning breaks, and how changed is the scene! Countless dewdrops sparkle like a shower of diamonds in the long grass. The thirsty flowers open their delicate leaves, and while they drink in the dew their colors brighten and the most delicious scents fill the air. In those parts of the earth where it rains but seldom, the plants depend almost entirely on the Dew, which falls during the night. After those refreshing showers, the lily opens its blossoms afresh, the olive smells sweeter, and even the towering cedar feels new vigor and pushes its giant roots still further into the earth. Thus is the Dew a lively emblem of the secret yet powerful influence by which our Savior carries on His work in our hearts by His Spirit. When a soul is converted, it is taken out of the wide wilderness and "planted in the house of the Lord." But it is a very tender plant. It cannot bear much of the sunshine of the world. Prosperity soon withers it up. But along with the night of sorrow there comes the heavenly Dew, which restores the Christian's spiritual health, and makes him fruitful among his brethren. And so the work goes on till he is ready to be transplanted to the region of "everlasting spring and never-withering flowers." And how must we gain this precious influence? We must turn the promise into a prayer. Does Christ say, "I will be as the Dew unto Israel"? Let us ask Him to fulfill that word unto us. David once complained that his strength was quite dried up by reason of sin. But he prayed, and God sent him again this sacred DEW, which restored his soul "like a well-watered garden." "And now," said he, "I am like a green olive tree in the house of my God."

But what principal lesson should we learn from the subject of this Reading? Why, just this—that if Jesus Christ be God's Delight, He must become *your* Delight also, and for the same reasons as render Him God's Delight.

1. *Consider His character and disposition.* How amiable He is! If you had seen Him on earth going about to do good, healing the sick, feeding the hungry, teaching the ignorant, and caressing little children—so gentle and tender and useful, like the Dew—how you would have admired Him! Well, the sweet story of all this is in your hands; and whenever you read it remember He is just the same still; as ready as ever to befriend the poor, and to bless children, and to be the Dew unto their souls, even in the early morning of their life.

2. *Consider His wonderful works,* and delight in Him on account of them. The huge planet which in its vast circuit takes eighty years to fly round the sun, the tiny mite to which one day seems a long life, the burning sun, the twinkling glowworm, are all His "handiworks," and, as they raise our wonder, should also provoke our love. But consider the great work by which He redeemed us! Think how He must have delighted in us to have done what He did! What bruises He endured, what toils He underwent, to save us from hell and bring us to heaven! Let your thoughts dwell on His works of love, all He has done and all He has promised to do, till your melting hearts move towards Him and you are prepared to say, "We love Him because He first loved us."

3. *Consider the glory of His Nature.* All the fullness of God is in Him. Ask now how can we take pleasure in an absent person whom we have never seen? Unseen He is, but then He is everywhere. In every place if you will but put forth the powers of your mind to feel after Him, you will surely find Him at your side. Nothing will hinder your delight in Him if your heart be inclined. And is it so, that your heart is *disinclined*? But what have you that can compare with Him? What will you name that can supply the place of God? Gain? Pleasure? Friends? All is short-lived like the grass and will soon fail. But delight yourself in Jesus Christ ever so much and ever so long, you will never find any deficiency in Him. If there is any reason why we should delight in Him today, there will be the same reason tomorrow; and to all eternity there will be infinite reason why we should delight in Him to the utmost. Abraham has been with Christ 3,000 years and more. He was glad on earth to see His day afar off; but how glad now to behold Him face to face and sit with Him in heavenly places! And does he grow tired of

his Lord's company? Weary of drinking of the Fountain of Living Waters all these years? Not at all, nor ever will, for he has got no nearer to the end of the "pleasures forevermore" than when he began.

Suppose a rich monarch, like Solomon, were to invite you to stay at his royal palace and do his utmost to entertain you, would you not promise yourself a world of pleasure? And at first all would be new. There would seem to be employment for a whole life. He would show you all his treasures. He would throw open his picture galleries and pleasure grounds. He would unlock to you his libraries and museums. And what a long time it would take to examine all these! But you would come to the end at last. There would be no new objects of wonder left to surprise with fresh delight. And you would begin to grow tired, and perhaps not feel sorry when the time came for you to change your place again.

But of the rich stores of Jesus Christ there is no end! You will never want anything else to delight in than that which He can furnish. Eternity will not suffice to explore all the pleasing wonders of all the beautiful worlds scattered through His great empire. And then the glories of His Divine character, and the heights of His amazing love, and the beautiful ideas of His glorious mind, are all boundless as immortality, and will abundantly entertain your happy spirit forever and ever. "Delight thyself in the Almighty, and He will give thee the desires of thy heart."

15

Desire of All Nations. Day Star. Day Spring. Daysman. Door. Defense. Dwelling Place.

IT is three or four thousand years since God told Abraham that in his Seed, the Messiah, "all nations should be blessed." And yet three-quarters of the world have not yet even heard His name. How is this? I will tell you. Just before He went to heaven, He told his disciples to go into all the world and preach the gospel to every creature. They began; and wherever they went men turned from idols to serve the Living God. But Satan stirred up great persecution, hoping thereby to frighten the followers of Christ from their work. But the more they were persecuted so much the more the word of God spread. Satan therefore tried another plan. He tempted them with riches and honor. And soon "the love of many waxed cold," they became worldly, and the work of preaching Christ almost ceased for ages. So that if God had not kept a "very small remnant" to be the salt of the earth, it would have been by this time like Sodom and Gomorrah. Of late, however, Christians have waked up again to a sense of their duty. They have scattered the Scriptures, they have sent out missionaries, they have gathered Sunday schools. In these and other ways they are trying to spread abroad the glorious name of the "DESIRE OF ALL NATIONS."

DESIRE OF ALL NATIONS. This grand Title is given to our Lord by the prophet Haggai, (Hag. 2:7). His words seem to imply that Christ should come at a time when all nations would be looking for the appearance of some extraordinary person. And so it was; for not only among the Jews but among other nations, there was a general expectation about this time, of the birth of some great one who should have dominion over all the world. The visit of the Eastern Magi to Jerusalem may be almost regarded as a proof of this expectation. Another proof is seen in the remarkable fact that Virgil the Latin poet who lived at Rome a few years before Christ, in one of his poems celebrates the birth of a "lovely boy with auspicious countenance," a "celestial seed" who should fulfill the DESIRE OF ALL NATIONS; under whose reign he says—

The serpent's brood shall die; the sacred ground
Shall weeds and pois'nous plants refuse to bear.

The jarring nations he in peace shall bind,
And with paternal virtues rule mankind.

Also the renowned Plato, that prince of philosophers, feeling in the dark after some guide, says, "We must wait patiently until someone, either a God or an inspired man, teach us our religious duties and remove the darkness from our eyes."

A few years ago, all France was moved at the birth of one who, from the delight expressed, might well be called THE DESIRE of the Nation. The Emperor earnestly desired a son to succeed him on his throne, and his subjects desired it too. One morning at six o'clock their fond wish was gratified. A son was born whose title was King of Rome. Royal births are usually announced by the firing of cannon. On this occasion it had been arranged that if the infant were a princess, 21 guns should be fired; but if a prince, 100. "At the first report the whole inhabitants of Paris wakened, and the discharges were eagerly counted, till when the twenty-first gun had gone off the anxiety of the people became almost unbearable. The gunners delayed an instant—and a hundred thousand persons held their breath; but when the twenty-second, double-charged, was let off, the whole inhabitants sprang on their feet" expressing unbounded joy. The news, carried by balloons, flew to distant towns and all the nations rejoiced as one man in the gratification of its DESIRE. But never were hopes more vain! There was nothing in that event to justify all this acclamation. Not long after the Emperor was a captive on a desolate rock and the child was carried to an early tomb.

But if a whole nation thus exulted in the birth of a puny infant on whom they thought proper to fasten their hopes because he was an emperor's son, how should the whole world have hailed the birth of the Holy Child, the SON OF THE HIGHEST! But no rejoicings awaited His entrance into life. In His own world He found no better place to lay His sacred head than a stable. And by whom was He thus treated? By His own people, the Jews. Less wonder then that the Gentile world was so indifferent to His claims. But why is He called their DESIRE when they do not even bid Him welcome?

1. Because He really is THE DESIRE of the wise and holy of all nations.

2. Because He richly deserves to be the DESIRE of all, since He only can furnish that which all feel the want of. For instance, among all nations, in ancient times, there were sacrifices offered up. This practice, whatever it arose from, proves that men everywhere felt themselves to be guilty—that they all believed there was no forgiveness without the shedding of blood—and that, notwithstanding their sacrifices, they felt their sin was not taken away and so they still continued to multiply them. The grand question they all seemed to ask was—

Where is the ONE TRUE SACRIFICE that will quite remove our guilt? And here is the answer!—BEHOLD THE LAMB OF GOD that taketh away the sin of the WORLD!

3. And then, although but few as yet are prepared to receive Him, yet at length all nations shall call Him blessed and own that He is the very Deliverer they have been waiting for. Go listen at the door of yonder lunatic ward. There lies one calling aloud for medicines and a physician. And yet at his side there actually stands the physician striving in vain to persuade him to take that which will relieve him. He is mad! And thus it is with the people. They cry, Who will show us any good? But, till they "come to themselves," they will not come to Him who alone can give them the desires of their hearts. So was it with the woman of Samaria. At first she plainly told the Fountain of Blessedness she wished to have no dealings with Him. But, when better instructed, He became "all her Salvation and all her DESIRE." What there is further in Christ which men find so suitable to their wants when once the veil is taken from their hearts, we will now consider.

A. They are in darkness and Jesus Christ brings Light. He is the DAY SPRING FROM ON HIGH and the DAY STAR.

B. They are at enmity with God and Jesus is the One Mediator—the DAYSMAN and the DOOR.

C. They are in danger and He is a DEFENSE and a DWELLING PLACE. Let us glance at these Symbols one by one. The first is the

DAY SPRING FROM ON HIGH who hath visited us, to give light to them that sit in darkness, to guide our feet into the way of peace (Luke 1:78). Darkness is both dangerous and dismal. It therefore well describes a state of ignorance and sin. On the other hand, light is safe and pleasant and is therefore a fit image of instruction and purity. As the world is a dreary place without the sun, so the soul is wretched and forlorn without Christ. Who is the source of knowledge and holiness. Welcome is the morning light to weary sailors rocking up and down on the tempestuous ocean in darkness and gloom. Refreshing is the dew to the lonely sufferer in the sick room who, throughout the long night, has been full of tossings to and fro. The rising sun cheers his spirits, and brings round him once more kind faces and soothing attentions. But far more welcome was the coming of Christ the DAY SPRING to the pious Jew. And sweeter still is the light of the DAY SPRING, when it visits the guilty conscience and dispels the dreary clouds of fear. The soul comes forth from its hiding place, and putting on the garment of praise, cries out, "O Lord, I thank Thee, for though Thou wast angry with me, Thine anger is turned away and Thou dost comfort me."

Did you ever think of the thick darkness, which for three days shrouded the land of Egypt in the time of Moses? It was a darkness that might be felt; and while it lasted, "they saw not one another, neither did any rise from his place." The clammy fog weighed down their spirits and put out their lamps. The laborer in the field and the traveler on the plain groped about in despair. The king in the palace and the trader in the market, each sat silent and horror-stricken till the gross darkness passed away. Three days they waited ere the sun appeared. But dismal as was that thick gloom, it was but a faint image of the darkness which covers the nations of the world on which the light of the gospel has not yet shone. A far deeper gloom broods over their souls—sin in the heart, ignorance in the mind, and sorrow and sadness in the spirit. "I am very ill," said a rich Abyssinian to a missionary, "and I will tell you the cause. I lived in sin till I became afraid of God's anger; I did not know how to get rid of my burden but tried many things. And first, I left my home and went among wild beasts, living all the while on roots, like them; but I found no peace in that way. Then I stood in a cold river for many hours every day. Then I bound a chain round my ankle till I was lame. After that, because my body was the cause of my sin, I wounded it with stripes till I was covered with sores. This has destroyed my health."

"But what did you do all this for?"

"I did it to please God."

"Ah! it is all of no use! you will find no relief so! God is not pleased with such things as these!"

"What!" cried the trembling man, "Is it indeed all in vain?"

The missionary explained the way of salvation, and showed him how the sufferings of Christ, and not our own, can take away the burden of sin. He listened and exclaimed, "How have I groaned to be delivered from the burden of sin! And now you tell me Jesus Christ says, Come to Me and I will give you rest—I will give up all other hopes from this time and go to your Savior."

It is to deliver men from such darkness as this that the DAY SPRING FROM ON HIGH hath visited us. The missionary who instructed the Abyssinian "was not that Light," which could relieve him, "but was sent to bear witness to that light." And as the poor wanderer listened and believed, the glorious Light shined into his benighted soul. Thus we read of a "Light shining in a dark place, to which we do well to take heed till the day dawn and the

DAY STAR arise in our hearts" (2 Pet. 1:19). By the DAY STAR rising within the heart, is meant the inward knowledge of the Savior. And His rising in the heart at the "dawn of day," refers to the gradual entrance of light into the mind—His "goings forth are prepared as the morning." We learn from these words of the apostle that we are to take heed to the Bible as to a sure guide; yet not to expect salvation from *it*, but from the glorious Savior to whom it directs us. So our Lord said to the Jews, "Ye search the Scriptures; it is well—they testify of Me; yet ye err if ye think ye have eternal life in *them*, but will not come unto *Me* that ye might have life." Let me illustrate this.

Just now I spoke of the gloom of Egypt during the three days of darkness. But all that time the sun shone as usual in Goshen where the children of Israel dwelt. "They had light in their dwellings." Imagine that you were passing through Egypt just at that dismal time. And suppose the darkness had continued—not three days only—but three weeks; and still it grew thicker and blacker, and no hope of dawn remained. As you sit on the ground in despair, suddenly a light flashes through the gloom. It is an Israelite from Goshen bearing in his hand a torch. He lifts you up and says, "Come with me, I will light your steps, and show you the way out of this dark land into one where there is sunshine." You gladly follow him. As you go along, the torch shows you the way and the dangerous places you must avoid. You travel on and there appears a little glimmer of daylight. Presently you see the dim form of a pyramid or a group of palm trees; and still your path shines more and more unto the perfect day; and at last you reach the lightsome land of Goshen where all is sunshine.

Now, take that benighted land for an emblem of your natural state of sin. The kind Israelite is a minister of God. The torch in his hand is the Bible, which shines like "a lamp in a dark place." The pleasant land of sunshine to which it will lead you is a state of favor with God—the "land of Beulah," on which the Sun of Righteousness shines all day long, and wherein all the people of God dwell. Now you would not value the torch only as it led you to the sun; so your knowledge of the Scriptures is useless except as it leads you to Christ. You are to take heed to it till that DAY STAR arise within. You are to follow on to know the Lord, till that Image of God shine in your hearts and you begin to "see the King in His beauty." The wise men of the East did not sit down to admire their bright star, but arose and followed it till it led them to the STAR OF JACOB. And when by its light they found Jesus, "they rejoiced with exceeding joy," as well they might. Now the Bible was meant to be to you just what that Star was to them—a guiding star to Christ, a lamp to lead you out of Egypt into His sunshine. Be careful, then, to find Christ by the light of the Bible. And when you have found your way into the pleasant path of righteousness and peace, pity those who have not the sure word of prophecy, and send them the light of truth. For all the dwellers upon earth in all countries and climes, whether learned or unlearned, are alike benighted without the Bible. The rich Brahmin trusts in the river Ganges that it will wash away his sins; while the poor Hindu hopes to gain heaven by a pilgrimage to Juggernaut. Heathenism is in truth the region of the shadow of death! How beautiful are the feet of those who carry the torch of truth into the gloom, and try to bring them to "sit in darkness" to where "the people have light in their dwellings." *This is the work of missionaries.* Who would not wish to help them?—Again, *Men are at enmity with God, and Jesus Christ is the only Mediator.* And when the Holy Spirit causes them to tremble at the thought of God's anger, they say, "Oh that there were a DAYSMAN to come between (God and us) and lay His hand upon both!"

DAYSMAN. You have this expression in Job 9:33. I do not say that Jesus Christ is here expressly called a DAYSMAN; but just consider what a DAYSMAN is and you will say, That is just like Christ. The business of a DAYSMAN is to *reconcile*. The word means Umpire, Mediator. Suppose a quarrel were to arise between two parties, who agree to refer the dispute to some friend in whose wisdom and fairness they can trust. That friend thus mutually chosen is a DAYSMAN. First he examines the case carefully; and then perhaps he says to one, "You must give up this point," and to the other, "You must give up that;" or he decides that the one most in fault shall pay over something to the other. To this they both agree, and thus their Umpire brings them together again. Well, Job was in great distress; he knew he had displeased God, but he also thought God had dealt hardly with him. He longed to lay his case before Him, but trembled because he had no friend to speak for him. "Oh," said he, "there is no DAYSMAN to come between us!" He might not have been thinking of Christ when he said this, but that very Friend he wished for so passionately, Jesus Christ is (1 Tim. 2:5, 6).

Suppose a steward robs his master of treasures, and is condemned by the judge to pay double its worth. But the treasure having been squandered, there is nothing wherewith to pay the fine. If that same judge were to say, "I will pay it," the faulter would be free. But is the deliverance complete? Not unless the man can be restored to his master's confidence. But suppose the judge persuades him to be reconciled to his unfaithful steward. Then indeed the judge would be fulfilling the part of a Daysman, an Umpire. Yea more, he would be at the same time a Surety and Advocate too.

And indeed Job needed just such a Friend with God as this, even more perhaps than he thought he did. And so do you and I and all the nations. For God has a controversy with all mankind. All have sinned and come short of the requirements of His law. But being willing to save us, He has appointed His dear Son to be DAYSMAN, referring the matter entirely to Him; "for the Father judgeth no man, but hath committed all judgment to the Son." Let us also refer our cause to this Just One, who, whether we choose Him for our DAYSMAN or not, is the ONLY Mediator between God and man. And think how fit a Person He is for this office!—at once God's Companion and Equal, and man's Brother.

And how does He decide the controversy? He first opens His mouth on God's behalf; and so far from allowing that the holy law is too strict, by His explanation of it He makes it appear more awful than before. Listen to His words—"I am not come to destroy the law but to magnify it; for whereas it is there written, He that *doeth* evil is a transgressor, *I* say, He that *thinketh* evil in his heart deserves to die." And what is His sentence on the transgressor? It is spoken in thunders from Sinai,

"Cursed is every one who continueth not to do all the things contained in the law." It is written in letter of fire over the gates of hell, "The soul that sinneth, it shall die." It is echoed in every one's conscience, "Thou art weighed in the balances, and art found wanting." Awful sentence! Must not the sinner's case be lost in the hands of so impartial a Judge? Fear not, trembling soul! For see! He leaves His judgment throne and lays aside His robes of majesty. He has spoken for God, He has upheld the law. And now He takes man's part—not by excusing his fault, but by paying his debt, and suffering his punishment. And then He intercedes with God on our behalf, presenting His own blood as the atonement for our sin; and at the same time to us He sends ambassadors to beseech us to be reconciled unto God. And (better still!) He sends also His Spirit to render those persuasions effectual. And throughout the wonderful proceedings, "all things are of God who hath reconciled us to Himself by Jesus Christ."

Now, if the nations did but know this DAYSMAN, would He not be their DE-SIRE? And do you not wish you could tell them of such a Friend? It is true, they feel quite satisfied with the intercessors and (which is quite as wise) some on wooden idols. Some look to angels, and some to the virgin Mary. But these cannot prevail. They have no righteousness to plead as Christ has, nor can they hear the prayers, which are put up to them from different parts of the world at the same hour. Folly indeed, to rely on such Mediators as these! There is only ONE NAME given under heaven among men by which we can be saved—only one "DOOR" whereby we can approach God with acceptance.

DOOR (John 10:9). The sheepfolds in Judea were shut in all around with stone walls to keep out wolves and bears, and could be entered only by the door. Perhaps Jesus Christ was walking beside one of these folds when He said, "Do you observe yonder sheep passing into the fold through the Door? Now I am like that DOOR. There is no way to life and salvation but THROUGH ME, and till you have come to ME, you are nothing better than stray sheep." But what is it to enter this DOOR?

First. You must steadfastly believe that Christ is the ONLY DOOR.

Second. You must be willing to part with everything that would hinder you from entering in. It is a *strait*, that is, a narrow gate. What will hinder you? Your own *unrighteousness. One indulged sin will bar you out.* Again, your own *righteousness* also, if trusted in, will hinder you. This therefore you must renounce. For although this DIVINE DOOR is wide enough for all the world to pass through abreast; it is yet too narrow to let in either a self-righteous person, or one who wishes to carry his sins along with him. An officer in the army, while in deep anxiety about his soul, had a dream. He thought he came to a place full of light and walled in all around. The people within seemed so happy he wanted very much to be with them. He looked for the door and tried to get in, but it was too narrow. He tried again, but his efforts were in vain. He thought it occurred to him that he had on a richly embroidered waistcoat. "Perhaps," said he in his dream, "if I were to strip myself of this I shall be able to get in." So he threw it off and tried again; and to his great joy he was able to squeeze himself through into the happy place, and directly felt as joyful as the rest. Upon this he awaked, and found it was a dream. But the lesson he learned from it was no dream. "Surely," said he, "this embroidered coat is a picture of my own righteousness, which I must throw away if I would be received by the Savior." Thus he passed through the DOOR into the fold of the Good Shepherd.

Thirdly. You must apply with earnest prayer. If you want admittance into a house you knock at the Door. If it be not opened you knock again more loudly. So do at this DOOR of Salvation. Strive to "enter in at the strait gate." "Knock and it shall be opened." Say with the burdened pilgrim—

> May I now enter here! Will He within
> Open to sorry me, though I have been
> An undeserving rebel? Then shall I
> Not fail to sing His lasting praise on high.

Again, *Men are in misery and danger; and Christ is a Refuge for them.* Nor can anything quiet the fears of the awakened soul but to be able to say with David, "The Lord is my DEFENSE."

DEFENSE (Ps. 94:22). A Door suggests the idea of security. For not only is it, when open, the way into a fold, but, shut, it makes the fold secure. The wolves may howl without but in vain. That which shuts the sheep *in*, shuts them *out*. Those who are "in Christ" are beyond the power of that "roaring lion who goeth about seeking whom he may devour." He may frighten them, but is not able to pluck them out of Christ's hand. Was Noah, as he sat in his floating house, afraid of the raging storm without? No, for God who shut him in was a sure DEFENSE from danger. Imagine the owner of a castle traveling homewards pursued by robbers. He rides fast with the hope of gaining his stronghold. His horse almost flies over the ground. Soon he reaches his castle, and, once within, bars the doors against his pursuers. The thieves soon follow. But the ironbound door is fast; and before they can reach him they must break it down. So the Christian's enemies must strike at him through Christ, who, like a strong castle gate, stands between him and them as their Shield and DEFENSE. And, believe me, you, like this traveler, are pursued by deadly foes. I pray you, do as he did. Fly to a place of DEFENSE! Make haste to Christ! Get within that DOOR; before Satan seizes you for his prey, and sinful habits, like fetters and chains, bind you fast, a helpless captive.

> Under the shadow of His throne,
>   His saints have dwelt secure;
> Sufficient in His arm alone,
>   And their DEFENSE is sure.

But we not only find shelter in Christ, but satisfaction and rest also. He is the HOME of our souls, our "DWELLING PLACE."

DWELLING PLACE (Ps. 90:1; 91:1). How refreshing is rest after toil! How delightful to stretch our weary limbs upon our own bed, in our own HOME! A most sweet and pleasant word is *Home!* It awakens delightful thoughts. Home may even be a lowly place; the windows, somewhat shaky, may not quite shut out the chill wintry blast; it may be devoid of many comforts—yet it is Home, and there is no place like it. The heart secretly longs for it, for there we always find something which we find nowhere else. Indeed we think we have said quite enough to convey a tolerable idea of earthly happiness, when we say of someone who has gained a comfortable situation, He has *found quite a Home.* Now, have you found a HOME for your *soul?* If you have really fled to Jesus Christ for refuge, you have; for they who have believed "do enter into rest."

> Here do I find a settled Rest,
>   While others go and come,
> No more a stranger or a guest,
>   But like a child at HOME.

When you see a poor beggar who has no home, you pity the destitute wanderer. But will you not weep for poor wandering homeless *souls?*—souls who have not yet found their way to Christ, and who have no hope for eternity. If you have indeed found rest in Him for yourself, I am sure you pity them that are without—and pray for them too.

That is one way in which you can serve the Missionary cause—you can *Pray* for it. And is there nothing else you can do? "Why," say you, "we should like to *tell* them of Christ; but they live so far away we cannot do that." But can you not give something to help to send preachers to them? Remember how highly our Lord speaks of the poor widow, and her little offering of "one farthing." He still sits over against the treasury and sees all you cast into it. And for all you devote to His cause out of love to Him you shall be "recompensed at the resurrection of the just." Do all you can, however little that all may be, to extend the glory and fame of Him who is well called THE DESIRE OF ALL NATIONS—for He is

A DAY SPRING to light their steps,

A DAY STAR to cheer their hearts,

A DAYSMAN to intercede for them,

A DOOR through which they may enter heaven, and

A DEFENSE and DWELLING PLACE—a safe and Happy Home for their souls in time and eternity.

16

David. Despised and Rejected. Deliverer.

"OLD FULLER" says, "Reasons are indeed the pillars of the fabric of a discourse, but Similitudes are the windows that give the best lights." And under the term "Similitudes" he includes that what he calls "Stories," which, whether they be true or fictitious, often convey instruction more forcibly than the clearest statements. Of this nature were most of the parables spoken by the Great Teacher. A parable is just a story with a double meaning; a little tale having a *natural* meaning, which can be understood at once; and a *spiritual* meaning which it sometimes requires much study to unravel. Some of our Lord's parables were stories of *real* events, others of *supposed* events, and both alike answered His purpose. They were as "nails fastened in a sure place" in the memories of His hearers, on which were hung some important lesson which else had been forgotten. And some parts of the Old Testament were meant to fulfill the same purpose—to be a sort of parable to lead the mind to higher truths. For instance, there were *Things* which were emblematical; such as the Altar, the Mercy-seat, the Manna. Then there are *Histories* which are typical; such as the offering of Isaac, the departure of the Jews from Egypt, and their settlement in Canaan. There were also typical *Places*; Canaan was a type of heaven, Jerusalem was a type of the church, and the Cities of Refuge, of Jesus Christ. Then again certain *Persons* are types of Christ, such as Melchizedek and Moses. No one *entirely* represents Him because of His perfection; and therefore there are many. Neither are they types in all things, but only in some particulars. A man may be a type of Christ, as a king, a lawgiver, a deliverer, or a priest; and yet not in his private capacity. Now, one of the most remarkable of these typical person is undoubtedly David, the valiant king of Israel.

DAVID. The meaning of the name is Beloved. And so closely are the type and the antitype connected together, that hundreds of years after the death of the Hebrew monarch, a King is foretold under the same name (Hos. 3:5); who can be no other than the Root and Offspring of David—his Son and his Lord. Israel's great prophet-king is the most complete of all the personal types of our Lord. It is worthy of observation, too, that his history occupies a larger space in the sacred records than that of any other of the great historic personages; no less than sixty chapters being devoted to it. Added to which, very many of the psalms are taken up with the detail of his inner history and experiences. It has been well said that "he not only *uttered* prophecies about Christ, but *lived* them. His place in history, his labors and sufferings, were typical and prophetical of the Savior. And while depicting his own experiences, he was all the while picturing, though less clearly, the experiences of Christ who was to be born of him." Other prophets portray the outward sufferings of Christ; but David displays a wonderful insight into those of His soul. And, in describing them, he did undergo in his own spirit much of the anguish, which he so passionately expresses. We must now, however, forget that David's mental agony was often on account of sin—his own sin; whereas Christ suffered only for the sins of others. Also, that the sufferings of the one must have fallen immeasurably below those of the other.

Except the history of Joseph, there is no biography in the Bible that takes such hold of the youthful mind as that of David. If I were to go into a Sunday school, and ask the children one by one to tell me something about him, I should be able amongst them to make up a complete history of that famous man. Who was he? "The man after God's own heart," says one little boy. "He was raised from a shepherd to a king," says another. A little girl remembers that he was the youngest son in the family, and kept his father's sheep in the wilderness. Another tells me he was a "cunning player" on the harp, and that he was a poet too, and composed many of the psalms; and she thinks it very likely that in this way he employed much of his time in the fields; for God was with him and taught him from his youth. From another I should receive a graphic account of his encounter with the lion, which carried off one of his flock. How, instead of running away and hiding himself among the rocks, he gave chase to the savage robber; and how the Lord delivered him out of the paw of the lion, so that he even slew him and rescued his poor little kid. Then there is the wonderful story of his battle with Goliath, which every child in the nursery knows. David is sent to visit his soldier brothers on the field of battle. There he sees the two hostile hosts covering the valley far as the eye can reach, their banners glittering in the sun, their plumes waving in the breeze, and their helmets and spears flashing on every side. In front of the Philistines stalks the giant Goliath, defying the armies of Israel, and shouting aloud his challenge to single combat. David's indignation is aroused, and he says, "I will fight that monster of a man, and the God by whose help I killed the lion will give me strength to bring down the proud boaster!" His words are reported to the king, his offer is accepted, and the hour is fixed for the combat.

What a scene must that field of battle have presented when David and the giant advanced to meet each other! The two armies drawn up on either side, and in the wide space between behold the two champions, and mark the difference!

Goliath is twice as tall as David: his head is protected with a huge helmet, his body covered all over with brazen armor and in his hand he brandishes an immense spear like a weaver's beam. And looking at David with scorn he cries, "Com on, proud boy, and I will give you to the birds for food." The modest young shepherd lad has neither shield nor sword, but he looks up to the God who has delivered him from the lion; and then, holding some small stones in his left hand and balancing a sling in his right, and fixing his bright eye on the foe, he advances to the conflict. "This day," he shouts aloud, "will the Lord deliver thee into my hands; for the battle is the Lord's, and all this assembly shall know that the Lord saveth not with sword and spear." The people look on almost breathless while David carefully fixes a pebble in his sling. He whirls it swiftly round, and, taking aim with practiced eye, lets fly the stone. The giant reels! His spear drops from his grasp, and down he falls headlong. The sling-stone has hit him right in the forehead. At the unexpected sight all the hosts of Israel clap their hands and shout aloud. The Philistines take to their heels, while David, with the giant's own sword, cuts off his head and carries it away as a trophy of victory.

Well, after many strange adventures on which we cannot dwell, God raised him to the throne. "He took him from the sheepfolds and brought him to feed His inheritance. So he fed them according to the integrity of his heart and guided them by the skillfulness of his hands." It is a wonderful history. No man was ever brought through greater trials; none was ever raised to greater honor than David; and both in his low estate and in his exaltation, he was a figure of Him that was to come. But the principal point of resemblance is his Royal Dignity as the Lord's Anointed, the King "set on His holy hill." In the days of Samuel, it will be remembered, the Israelites desired a king; and God appointed Saul to reign over them. But he did evil and came to a bad end. Then the Lord appointed David, and promised him that a member of his family should always occupy a throne. This promise could only be fulfilled in the person of Christ. For the throne of Judea has been long swept away; "but the Lord shall give unto HIM the throne of His father David,"—that is, the throne typified by David's, "and He shall reign over the house of Jacob forever; and of His kingdom there shall be no end" (Luke 1:32, 33). And David understood God's promise, and spoke of his Royal Son as the "Just One who should rule over men in the fear of God, and be as the Light of the morning" (2 Sam. 23:1). And if we take Dr. Pye Smith's translation, he spoke of Him as God too—"Even as the Light of the morning shall He arise—JEHOVAH THE SUN—a morning without clouds for brightness."

But, as in the case of David, before this honor must come the deepest humiliation. David was scorned by his own brothers; his life was frequently threatened; he was cursed and stoned and reviled; he was betrayed by his bosom friend, and finally he was driven from Jerusalem by his own son, and deserted by thousands of his subjects. In these and many other particulars David was a type of the Lord Jesus. For He also was "DESPISED AND REJECTED."

DESPISED AND REJECTED of men! (Isa. 53:3). His own brethren did not for a long while believe on Him. The Jews "went about to kill Him." One of His twelve chosen friends betrayed Him. And at last all classes of men among the Jews, when they came to learn the true nature of His kingdom, pursued Him with frantic hatred, loudly crying, "Away with Him! Crucify Him!" They renounced Him with the utmost contempt. They even mocked the Majesty of their Divine DAVID. They pressed on His royal brow a crown composed of prickly thorns, which caused the blood to stream from His sacred temples. They threw over the shoulders of their princely Shepherd a purple robe in profane mockery of the title He claimed for Himself. In His holy hands they placed a reed for a scepter; and, thus disfigured, they pointed the finger of scorn, and said, "Behold the Man!" Then they bowed their knees and laughed in His face, and spat on Him and smote Him!

DESPISED AND REJECTED of men! How awful these words sound when applied to such a One as He! The DELIGHT of the Father, the Lord of men and angels, the CREATOR and UPHOLDER of all—DESPISED by His own creatures! REJECTED by those whom He came to save! How deep the depravity, how fearful the doom of those "sinners against their own souls!" Yet think not that to the Jews alone this guilt belongs. Whosoever among you turns from the invitations of the Savior with indifference and sets at naught His advice, is chargeable with the same crime. There is no middle course between *despising* Him and adoring Him—between *rejecting* Him and serving Him. When Christ stood before Pilate, that base hypocrite washed his hands to signify, as he said, that he was "innocent of the blood of that Just Person." Vain and hollow pretense! for in the same hour he scourged Him and "delivered Him to be crucified." And equally vain, careless sinner, is your pretended complaint against the Jews for killing the Lord of Glory, while all the while in refusing to own Him as your Savior you *act* as if you thought they had done well in crucifying Him, and had only rid the world of an impostor! You start at such an accusation. But do you not see that *your* sullen indifference, *your* wicked neglect countenance them in *their* violent hatred? and that both are equally insulting to Him? Like Pilate, then, *you* must be considered to share in His murder—to be guilty of his blood—to consent to His death—all the while you only witness against it with your *voice*—but continue to countenance it with your *actions.*

So felt one of Whitefield's hearers at Plymouth while that great preacher was one day describing the atrocious crime of crucifying the Lord of Glory. He was an ungodly man, a shipwright, and had first mingled with the crowd that surrounded Whitefield with the intention to "knock him off the place where he stood." "I stood at his left hand," he writes, "he was not at this time looking towards me, but had just said, 'I suppose you are reflecting on the cruelty of those inhuman butchers who imbrued their hands in innocent blood! On a sudden he turned himself towards me, looked me full in the face, and cried out, '*Sinner! thou are the man that crucified the Son of God.*' I felt the word of God sharper than a two-edged sword. I was at once convicted. My heart bursting, mine eyes gushing forth floods of tears, I dreaded the instant wrath of God, and expected that it would immediately fall upon me." But he found forgiveness, and afterwards became a fervent preacher of the gospel he had opposed, a devoted humble servant of the Savior he had once "DESPISED AND REJECTED."

But Jesus Christ is also like David as the appointed "DELIVERER" of them that trust in Him.

DELIVERER (Rom. 11:26). David delivered his flock from lions and bears. Afterwards he delivered his country from Philistines and other foes. And in doing this he necessarily became their Destroyer. But David's Greater Son is known as the DESTROYER of Satan and of Sin, the two gigantic foes who hold us in such disgraceful bondage. Of these we shall find occasion to speak at some future time. Let us now confine our attention to the following—He is the DEATH of Death; the DESTRUCTION of the Grave, and our Deliverer from the Wrath to come.

First. He will be the DEATH of Death. Indeed, hath He not "abolished" Death already? You ask, how can that be when none escape its penalty, whether believers or unbelievers? Well, though we dare not say, the Christian's death doth in no sense partake of the nature of penalty; yet we do say, the penalty is commuted into a blessing. Its bitterness is taken away. Would it not be a thousand times worse than death to "live always"? For when the Christian pilgrim arrives at the postern of life, that which men call the gate of Death is to him the gate of Paradise. Gloomy as it looks on the near side, it opens on the radiant avenue which David terms "the path of life," the direct road to "fullness of joy and pleasures forevermore." When the "earthly house" is dissolved, the soul steps forth serenely from amidst the crumbling ruins, and climbs the mount of God. So that even Bunyan's description is too severe and forbidding. For there *is* no black cold river for the Christian to plunge into. It exists only in imagination. Sometimes, indeed, he may have to wait awhile on this side of the gloomy portal, in pain and full of tossings to and fro, eagerly listening for the turning of the key and the unfolding of the leaves; but knowing all the time Whose hand is on the lock. Is it not Him who says, "I am He that liveth and was dead; and behold I am alive forevermore, and have the keys of hell and of death"? Ought the Christian to be startled or panic-stricken?

> Is thy earthly house distressed,
> Willing to retain its guest?
> 'Tis not *thou* but *it* must die;

> Fly, celestial tenant, fly!
> Burst thy shackles, drop thy clay,
> Sweetly breathe thyself away.

But if still you urge, All this is true, but you see the Christian does die, after all, whether or no. And, if till the resurrection his body must lie under the ban of the grave, in the very clutch of Death, how can it be said to be abolished? Just as when one is condemned to be executed, he is from that moment *legally* dead, and in a few days will be actually dead; so is it with the last enemy. Death is *legally* abolished now, and in the purpose of God is *already dead*; will be dead *actually, finally,* when not one captive will be left under lock and key in the gloomy caverns of his grim jailer the Grave. The dread sentence, Thou shalt die, is fulfilled in the temporary death of the body. The soul never dies at all, not even for a moment, after it has been once "quickened together with Christ" from its death in trespasses and sins.

Second. But His work as a Deliverer involves the DESTRUCTION of the Grave too. "O Grave, I will be thy Destruction" (Hos. 13:14). In the sixth Reading we introduced BREAKER as a title appropriated to Christ. What a triumphant ring there is in the passage where it occurs, when read in *this* connection (Mic. 2:13). We behold Him first breaking His way out of the Grave wherein He himself is a prisoner. Before the entrance is placed a great stone which His enemies seal with cement and make fast. A centurion with sixty Roman soldiers surround it, keeping watch and ward over the Illustrious Captive. Hour after hour He lies silent and motionless, wrapped in the cerements of death, till the morning of the third day, when He breaks through the impotent barriers which enclose Him and flings them aside (as Samson did "the gates of Hebron, bar and all") and goes forth THE FIRST-FRUITS OF THEM THAT SLEPT. Weeping disciples seek Him where they had laid Him, but His place is empty. "He has passed through the gate" of Resurrection, "and gone out by it," the FORERUNNER of the "many sons whom He is bringing to glory."

Equally impotent will prove all the barriers built up by Death and the Grave around His people. Nothing will be able to withstand the Almighty power of the BREAKER, when He shall *descend* to force open the sealed receptacles wherein—sown in weakness and corruption—lay His redeemed dead. He will break the bars asunder, and recover His buried treasures from the tenacious grasp of the powers that hold them. Then the cave of Machpelah will restore the sleeping bodies of chosen patriarchs. The populous catacombs will surrender the multitudes of holy martyrs deposited in their endless labyrinths. And the innumerable graves, which cover every spot of earth, will give up their uncounted millions of sleeping saints. And all will reappear, "refashioned, recast, remolded, and possess of a new organization adapted to the new sphere into which they are to be introduced. And each will be endowed with immortal beauty and strength, and fitted to share the highest glory with which the manhood of the risen Savior Himself is crowned." "Thy dead men shall live; together with my dead body shall they arise. Awake and sing, ye that dwell in dust, for the earth shall cast out the dead." And the king shall pass before them and the Lord at the head of them. But every man in his own order; Christ the First-fruits, afterwards they that are Christ's at His coming.

But third, Jesus Christ is expressly spoken of as our "Deliverer from the Wrath to come" (1 Thess. 1:10). Oh how should such a Deliverer be hailed by us! The wrath to come! Consider what that is! It includes the loss of everything that is worth having, and that forever! The favor of God, the love of friends, the comfort of life, all blotted out. On earth there are dismal dungeons and captives loaded with fetters! Sad spectacles of woe! Do you see yonder stone cell lighted from a little grating? There lies a poor unhappy man who has lost his all. He once had riches but he has squandered them. He once had friends but he abused them, and one by one they left him. He once had liberty; he could go where he pleased; but he has forfeited that also. His bright hopes have all faded, and instead of health he is covered with disease. Forsaken and desolate, he sits in the dark dungeon with no company but his own remorseful thoughts. There is none to comfort him, none to heal his wounds, none to wipe away his tears. All is lost. If you were to visit such a one you could not witness his woe without tears. You would pronounce his condition dismal indeed! But what is that compared with the dungeon of hell? If we were doomed to be miserable for a year, we should think it a long time to suffer. But the year would come to an end, and the hope of that would sustain us. A thousand years would be an appalling prospect, but if there were certainty that at the end we should be happy, there would still be some comfort. But to go on suffering for a thousand years, and then another thousand—till they amounted to a million—and when all these were past, then for it to be still *the wrath to come!*— Oh what heart can dwell on the thought without horror and trembling?

> Most wretched souls! ah! whither can they flee?
> No friend, no hiding place is nigh,
> And onward rolls the storm!

And still it grows deeper, and heavier, and darker. No sounds but of weeping and wailing and gnashing of teeth! No prospect but a "certain fearful looking for of judgment and fiery indignation." Who so bold as to endure the thought without quailing? But, perhaps, you say to me, Why do you dwell on such a doleful subject? I will ask you another question—Are these sayings *true*? Does this representation agree with the statements of Christ? You dare not say to the contrary. Then let me entreat you to consider seriously,

1. *How fearful a thing it must be to fall into the hands of Jesus Christ otherwise than as a Savior.* I said just now He is known as a DESTROYER. This may seem a very unsuitable title for Him who is the Prince of Peace. Have you then never heard of "the wrath of the Lamb"? Is not that quite as strange—the meek and gentle Lamb to become angry? Yes, hear it with the deepest concern—All who DESPISE and REJECT the Savior now, shall hereafter be Despised and Rejected by Him. They who will not hail Him as their DELIVERER, nor serve Him as "DAVID their King" in this world, shall tremble before Him as their DESTROYER in the next, when He shall say, "Those mine enemies, who would not that I should reign over them, bring hither and slay them before Me." Then reflect, further.

2. *How necessary it is that you should, with all haste, flee from "the wrath to come."* God says to Job, "Hast thou seen the treasures of hail which I reserved against the time of trouble, against the day of battle and war?" Oh brave not the unknown "power of His anger," the sword of avenging justice. Whitefield once preached from Matthew 3:7. In the midst of the sermon he suddenly paused. And then bursting into a flood of tears, he lifted up his hands and his streaming eyes and exclaimed, "Oh my hearers, my hearers! The wrath *to come*! The wrath *to come*!" There was a young man present into whose heart those fearful words thus vehemently uttered, entered like a dagger. For weeks he could think of nothing else. The awful sentence rung in his ears wherever he went; till broken and humbled, he sought remission of sins from "the DELIVERER who came to turn away ungodliness from Jacob."

Have you never felt afraid of the bitter pains of eternal death? Is your heart never saddened with the dread of future woe? Oh do not stifle this feeling with laughter or cares. Ask Jesus Christ to convince you of the exceeding sinfulness of that which has brought so many thousands into that place of torment, and which brought Him to the dust of death. Seek from Him this one blessing above all other things, that you may be washed from your sins in His most precious blood, so that you may never come to that place of despair. Two young boys, Adam Clarke and James Brooks, were intimate friends. One day they went for a walk in the fields and entered into serious conversation. "Oh, Addy," said James, "what a solemn thing is *eternity*! and oh, how dreadful to be put into hell and to be there forever!" They both wept bitterly and begged God to forgive their sins; then they separated with full and pensive hearts. This little "Addy" was afterwards known as Dr. Adam Clarke, one of the most learned men of his day; and he says of this conversation, "The impression of it never wore away; I was then truly convinced that I was a sinner and liable to eternal punishment, and that nothing but the mercy of God could save me from it."

3. *How certain is the safety of all those who put their trust in Him?* David was a Shepherd, and most careful he was to guard his poor lambs from the lion; that

was the work his father, Jesse, had committed to him. And Jesus Christ delighted to speak of Himself as the Good Shepherd. And He is ever ready to deliver the young, the feeble, the tempted; for in Him is fulfilled the saying of the Prophet, "He shall carry the lambs in His bosom." Try Him, go, ask Him to be *your* DELIVERER, and you shall find how ready He is to hear your prayer. And when once "He takes you up," no roaring lion, no foul spirit, shall ever be able to "pluck you out of His hands."

> By His unerring Spirit led,
>   You shall not in the desert stray;
> You shall not full direction need,
>   Nor miss your providential way;
> As far from danger as from fear,
> While love, Almighty love, is near.

17

Ensign. Equal with God. Express Image. Everlasting Father. Elect. Eliakim. End of the Law. Example. Eternal Life. Exceeding Great Reward.

IN a former Section Jesus Christ was presented as the DESIRE OF ALL NATIONS. It is sad to look abroad and see how little He is loved as yet, but delightful to think that He who is so DESIRABLE will one day be the Desire of the whole world. But how is this to be brought about? By the blessing of the Holy Spirit upon the preaching of the gospel; in allusion to which Isaiah says, "There shall be a Root of Jesse which shall stand for an Ensign of the people, to which the Gentiles shall seek."

ENSIGN (Isa. 11:10). Of old an Ensign was the figure of an eagle, a lion, or a dragon, or some such symbol, fixed on the top of a pole; or it was a large plume of ostrich feathers; or if wanted in the night it was an iron basket with a blazing fire in it. But it matters not what the *form* of the Ensign was. Its use is the thing intended here. It was to have some particular meaning, and to be lifted up on high so that all might behold it. And the application of the figure to our Lord teaches us that the gospel is to be plainly preached, so that he "may run that readeth it." "Thou hast given a banner to them that fear Thee, that it may be DISPLAYED because of the truth." Forty Standard-bearers went to the South Seas in the ship "Duff" more than sixty years ago, and planted the ENSIGN among the islands there, and a goodly number of the natives have enlisted under it. And by-and-by men will everywhere "fly as a cloud" to the red Standard of the Cross of Christ. Princes shall come out of Egypt, and Ethiopia and China shall "find His rest to be glorious." The outcasts of Israel and the dispersed of Judah shall gather themselves from the four corners of the earth, and come to their Shiloh to Whom "the gathering of the people shall be."

But we have said an Ensign has some particular mark upon it. If it be the Royal Standard it bears the Imperial Arms. Or if it be the Ensign of the King's Representative, an Ambassador or Viceroy, there will be seen on it the sign of his official dignity. Now Jesus Christ is both the King and the King's Representative. On this Ensign therefore men read Equal with God—Express Image of God—Everlasting Father. They see also the seal of His official dignity; for He is the Elect, or Chosen Servant of the Father, His eliakim, or Chief Administrator, appointed to treat with mankind. And the preacher who would draw men to Christ must so display the Ensign that these Titles of our Lord may be plainly seen. Then when men are persuaded that Christ as God is *able to save*, and as God's Servant is *sent on purpose to save*, they will feel that they have every reason to come to Him. And when they do come, they find His rest to be glorious indeed, since He is the End of the Law for their justification; an Example for their imitation; and their Eternal Life and Exceeding Great Reward, to afford them strength and encouragement. All these glorious Titles may be plainly read on this Ensign. Let us take them one by one. First, Christ is "Equal with God."

EQUAL WITH GOD (Phil. 2:6). "*He* thought it no robbery to be Equal with God." And are there any who think otherwise? Not a creature in heaven or hell. Only on earth, and among those whose nature this Illustrious Being condescended to take upon Himself, are there to be found any who hold disparaging opinions of the Son of God. But God "thought it no robbery" when He said to His Equal Son, "Thy throne, O God, is forever and ever"; and spoke of Him as "the Man that is my Fellow." There is another Title given Him which teaches the same truth, namely, the

EXPRESS IMAGE OF GOD'S PERSON (Heb. 1:3). Do the Scriptures call God the King of all the earth (Ps. 47:7)? They also say of Christ, He is Lord of Lords and King of Kings (Rev. 17:14). Do we read that God hath made all things for Himself (Prov. 16:4)? We read also that all things were created by Christ and for Him (Col. 1:16). Do the Scriptures call God the Preserver of man and beast? They say also that by Christ "all things consist." Are we assured that only God knoweth the heart (1 Kgs. 8:39)? Jesus Christ says of Himself, "I am He that searcheth the heart" (Rev. 2:23). Thus we think it no robbery to give honor to Christ as in all respects God's Equal. Yea we call it a most wicked robbery to say the contrary, and make our boast in Jesus Who is "God over all, Blessed forever," and Who is expressly called by that magnificent Title,

EVERLASTING FATHER (Isa. 9:6). Or the Author of the Eternal Ages. Eternity?—Boundless ocean! All our thoughts are drowned in it! Duration without beginning or end! Who can think thereon without growing bewildered? "Father, what is eternity?" said a little boy to a learned doctor. But the father was silent; for the question was too deep for him to solve. "Child, what is eternity?" asked a visitor of a deaf and dumb boy, writing the question on his slate. The child thought a little, and then wrote under it "The lifetime of the Almighty."

The Milky Way, that stupendous pale arch which we see in a clear winter evening stretching right across the sky, when viewed through a telescope, is found to consist of countless millions of stars as thick as they can cluster. They are of all colors; deep amber, bright green, pale lilac, and white and yellow. God telleth the number of those worlds, but no one else can. A long time ago there were none. And perhaps God made them one by one. Perhaps He made the first, and then ceased a few thousand years; then another, and again ceased a long, long time; and so on till all were completed. Oh, thought cannot go back so far! And yet there are, it may be, archangels who lived ages before the first of them, and who have been present at all those creations. Yet even their long lives had a beginning. And if we fall back upon that far distant point, beyond the birthday of the most ancient of the sons of the morning, we come no nearer the commencement of eternity. It still stretches far away; so that the lengthened life of the eldest of archangels bears no more proportion to eternity than your life or mine, or the hour-long life of yonder gnats sporting in the sunbeams. Of that dark, awful, vast eternity, Jesus Christ is the Author, the Father. Oh, there is a greatness about this Everlasting Being, before which angels may well cover their faces with their wings. And yet it is He who is our Father.

Three men met together on the burning plains of India. "How do you call the Supreme Being?" said the Hindu to the Jew. "We call Him," said the Jew, "Jehovah, the Lord who is, and was, and is to come." "Your title," he replied, "is grand but it is awful too." The Christian then joined in the conversation, and said, "*We* call Him Father." They all raised their eyes to heaven as if struck with the sweetness of the name, and said, "Our Father." And then, taking each other by the hand, they said, "And we are brethren." Yes—Jesus is the Father of all men, but in a far sweeter sense is He the Father of "the children whom God has given Him" (Heb. 2:13). He has life in Himself and quickens them; He carries them in His bosom and watches over them with the most exquisite love; He feeds them with the sincere milk of the word and clothes them with the robe of righteousness. From the very commencement of their spiritual life He encourages them to look to Him for all they want. Are you a child of God? If you are, God hath sent His Spirit into your heart, and that Spirit leads you to call Him Father. As a little child, whatever it wants, whatever it fears, turns with imploring looks and cries, even before it can speak, towards its parent, so does the newborn soul to its Everlasting Father. Do you thus look to Him?

And He does not provide for present wants only; He lays up for His children against the time when they come of age. Earthly fathers have sometimes left stores of riches and houses and lands to their children. Yet the inheritance is but a fading one; they soon follow their parent to the grave, and all that remains to them of the "splendid property" is a little space in the family tomb.

But the EVERLASTING FATHER has treasures in the heavens which do not decay, mansions not made with hands, prepared before the world was formed, where "His seed will prolong their days" to all eternity. And do you not aspire to the honor of being one of this "royal family"? Are you content to stand "without" among "dogs and workers of iniquity," while, too, Jesus is saying to you, "Come away and be separate and touch not the unclean thing, and I will be a FATHER unto you, and ye shall be My sons and daughters"? Oh comply with His invitation. Go to Him at once. Take with you words; say, "Doubtless Thou art our Father, the Guide of our youth; receive us graciously and love us freely."

And now having read the first part of the inscription on our ENSIGN, which proclaims the Divine Nature of the Savior, let us turn to the next Title, which exhibits Him as God's

ELECT, His Chosen Servant (Isa. 42:1). We read of elect angels (1 Tim. 5:21); and elect men, (1 Pet. 1:2). Both are greatly beloved by God Who says excellent things of them. But Christ is the ELECT by preeminence, lifted up far above every name that is named. Many elect officers were in Pharaoh's court when Joseph stood before him. But who among them was THE Elect? It plainly appeared when the king rose up from his throne and put a gold chain on the neck of Joseph, called him the savior of the country, and arrayed him in a royal robe. We read of none honored as he was. He rode in the king's chariot, while heralds shouted before him, "Bow the knee!" And when God brought His Only Begotten into the world, He said, "let all the angels worship Him"; and eventually "to Him every knee shall bow and every tongue confess." Have you done Him homage? If not, "kiss the Son." Yield Him your confidence. And whatever you want, ask it in His name; for the Father loves Him so greatly, that there is nothing He will deny to the most unworthy when they go with this plea. For this is He Whom God hath made His Administrator—Sole Treasurer and Dispenser of His gifts. There is a type of Him in this capacity in Isaiah 22:20–25, (compared with Rev. 1:18; 3:7, 8) which must not be overlooked.

ELIAKIM. The terms in which Eliakim's investment is described greatly transcend the importance of his office. As we read we say, "Surely a greater than Eliakim is here." Accordingly, our Lord quotes almost the very words of Isaiah in affirming His own Headship of the Church. To "hold the keys" is a typical expression. It may indicate control as to stores and supplies—what shall be kept back and what distributed; as to admission and exclusion—who shall go in and who be shut out; as to concealment and explanation—what shall be kept secret, and what be made known. And since it is usual to lock up what we wish to preserve inviolate, it implies security also. But more particularly, (1) our Lord holds *The Key of Salvation*. Having opened the kingdom of heaven, He it is who admits each believer, one by one. (2) *The Key of Usefulness*. Every servant hath his appointed work according to his ability, concerning which the Master saith, "Behold I have set before thee an open door." (3) *The Key of Providence*. All providences are special, one event being as much under God's control as another. At the appointed hour He unlocks the two-leaved gates of brass, or cleaves asunder the opposing mountain, and reveals and accomplishes His hidden purposes. (4) *The Key of Death*. Each must die just at the moment He appoints, neither sooner nor later. But here is a delightful thought, Christians! It is He Whom, unseen, you have loved and trusted. Who will meet each one of you at the gate, which leads into the world of spirits. (5) He holds *The Key of Heaven*—not Peter, nor the priest, nor the pope. He who *here* saith, "Come unto Me," will *there* say to every one who accepteth this invitation, "Come in thou blessed of the Lord." (6) *The Key of Hell* is also grasped by Him; and when "He shutteth, none openeth" forevermore.—All this should be plainly set forth. For the Prophet says, Christ is to *stand* for an ENSIGN. The BANNER is to be lifted up—the truth (not preached with reserve, but) *displayed*. And when this is done faithfully, men will learn both His divine and His official dignity. They will see, not only that He is God, but also God's ELECT Servant, commissioned expressly to save sinners. He is the

END OF THE LAW for Righteousness (Rom. 10:4). What is the law? "Thou shalt love the Lord with all thy heart and thy neighbor as thyself." All men have broken this law, have lost their uprightness, and forfeited their happiness. Nor could any means of recovering either have been found if God had not devised the way.

> For all the souls that were, were forfeit once;
> And he that might the 'vantage best have took,
> Found out the remedy.

You may think that God might forgive them and take no notice of their trespass. So perhaps He might if sin were merely a personal affront offered to Himself; He could in that case perhaps pardon the offense on receiving a suitable apology. But sin is much more than that. "It is an enormous outrage perpetrated against the eternal law of righteousness, tending to the utter subversion of the order and well-being of the universe. For which the Great Judge and Administrator is under obligation to hold every transgressor personally responsible; and to demand full reparation from himself or a suitable substitute if such can be found." If one transgressor were unconditionally excused, then must all be. And what would become of Law and Righteousness and all Moral Government? Don't you perceive that, come what may, God *must* uphold the credit of the most holy law, and set an eternal mark of disgrace on its infringement? And here comes in that wonderful order of "means" which "He hath devised whereby His banished be not expelled from Him," which redeemeth men and angels are never tired of extolling. Jesus Christ is made Man in order to suffer the penal-

EXAMPLE   *145*

ties of man's transgression. Thus the law is maintained in all its glory, even while those who have broken it are freed from punishment.

The justice and mercy thus combined may be illustrated by a striking fact recorded in history. A just judge firmly pronounces a dreadful sentence on his own son who had incurred the penalty of the law—and yet, at the same time, contrives to spare that guilty son a part of the punishment by undergoing it himself. The penalty for the offense was nothing less than the loss of both eyes! And this inexorable judge and compassionate father, wonderful to tell, submitted to the loss of one of his own eyes, in order to compensate the law for sparing one of his son's eyes. Thus he saved the young man from the full extremity of the dreadful sentence, the utter deprivation of sight—and yet, at the same time, secured to the law its most rigorous demands! But God remits *the whole* of the sinner's punishment, even by bearing it Himself in the Person of His Son. And in this way He teaches all to revere that sacred law which He maintains at such infinite cost.

"I do not like this law; it is too strict," said the man. But the Lawgiver subjects Himself to that very law to show how much He loves it; and that He will have it magnified, even though He Himself must suffer. And mark! here is the END of the Law. The Law requires to be upheld, to be made honorable. Its END is fulfilled in Christ. Yet, in this way it is more honored than if Adam had never broken it. *The law makes no objection to your salvation and mine now.* Jesus Christ, the Just, died for the unjust that His precious blood might be our ransom; and obeyed the law perfectly that His righteousness might be our beautiful garment.

But that is not all. The LAW has another END which also we read clearly inscribed on our ENSIGN. The saved one must be taught to obey the LAW himself; Jesus Christ therefore hath set us a most perfect "EXAMPLE."

EXAMPLE (John 13:15). And people of every condition may see in Him a *lovely* Pattern of what they should be. First, He is an EXAMPLE to the *rich*. Though so exalted, He made Himself of no reputation and disdained not the condition of a servant, and even ministered to His disciples and washed their feet. Thus He condemns the proud and haughty.

2. He is an EXAMPLE to the *poor*. Being found in a state of poverty He was contented. He did not strive to raise Himself by hasty means. Some would have made Him a King, but He chose rather to remain a subject. He could have constrained the greatest men on earth to bow to Him, but He chose to be humble and unknown. His conduct then is a standing reproof to those who, being poor, are discontented with their lot.

3. He is an EXAMPLE to the *oppressed*. "He was led as a lamb to the slaughter, and as a sheep before her shearers is dumb, so He opened not His mouth." Behold Him standing at Pilate's bar, meekly suffering a thousand insults from those

whom in one moment He could have confounded, without so much as uttering a word or moving a finger. Thus His carriage condemns all passion and revenge, and all impatient attempts to vindicate ourselves.

4. He is an EXAMPLE to *parents and teachers*. How patiently He bore with the dullness of His disciples! How gently He corrected their mistakes and removed their ignorance! He gave them line upon line as they could bear it. His doctrine distilled as the dew and dropped as the rain.

5. He was an EXAMPLE to *children*. Of His early piety we have before spoken. Some young people, when a little instructed, grow proud and despise their parents, who in some matters may not have so much knowledge. So did not Jesus. He was so wise as to amaze the doctors in the temple with His wonderful questions, but still so docile as to be "subject to His parents." There are some amongst the young who, when they attend the worship of God soon get tired, and say, "What a weariness it is! When will the Sabbath be gone that we may return to our sports?" But the Lord Jesus loved His Father's courts, and left them not till He was fetched away. His example as a Youth rebukes the disobedient, the conceited, the idler, the Sabbath-breaker.

6. He is an EXAMPLE to the *afflicted*. "Father!" said He, "if it be possible let this cup pass from Me; nevertheless not My will but Thine be done." Thus He reproved the repining impatient sufferer who doth not "accept the punishment of his iniquity."

By example He taught us *how to live*. He was always occupied in His Father's business. By example He taught us *how to die*. He yielded to the dreadful death, which was appointed for Him without murmuring, and died praying for those who killed Him. In everything He is our Lovely Perfect EXAMPLE.

And where are they who walk as Christ walked? Are they to be found among the men of the world? Can those who are dead in trespasses and sins bring forth these excellent fruits? Impossible. We must be born again. We must have a new life within us. And wherein consists this LIFE? Christ dwelling in the heart, Who is "the True God and ETERNAL LIFE."

ETERNAL LIFE (1 John 5:20). "He that hath the Son hath Life." You know if you were to go to an apple tree and cut off a branch, it would never bring forth any more fruit, because it is separated from the root whence all its power to bear apples was derived. It is thenceforth good for nothing. Now man resembles this broken bough. When first created he received spiritual life in a direct stream from God, just as a branch receives virtue from the root. But being broken off from God by the fall he is become dead and withered. No more heavenly influence from God flows into the soul, and therefore no more holy fruit is brought forth. What is to be done to make him bear fruit? Must the broken bough be set upright in the ground, and be pruned and watered as though it were alive? Some try this plan but it does not answer. It will never bear until united again to God. The Holy Spirit must take the poor soul, the dry withered branch, and "graft it in again," uniting it to the Source of Life. This done, Christ becomes his LIFE, and by faith receiving nourishment from Him he brings forth fruit. All is vain without this. No one will follow Christ as his EXAMPLE who has not this LIFE within him. And sometimes God puts this LIFE into the tender hearts of the young. I will give you a wonderful instance. A little negro slave, only ten years old, who loved Jesus Christ, was cruelly beaten by the command of his wicked master for going to hear the gospel. While he was writing under the strokes of the whip the heartless man said, "What can Jesus Christ do for you now?"

"He helps me to bear it with patience," said the poor child.

"Give him five-and-twenty more." It was done. "And what can Jesus Christ do for you now?" "He helps me to look for a reward in heaven," said the little sufferer.

"Give him five-and-twenty more," cried the master in a rage. And as he listened to the dying groans of the child he asked fiercely, "What can Jesus Christ do for you now?" The noble little fellow with his last breath feebly said, "He helps me to pray for you, massa." And then his spirit fled to the bosom of Christ Who wiped away all his tears; but whether He answered the little boy's prayer for his murderer is not so certain. But this is plain; the dear child must have had Jesus Christ within him as his LIFE, or he would never have been so sweetly conformed to His Example Who, you know, prayed with His dying breath for His murderers.

And this SPIRITUAL LIFE is ETERNAL LIFE. The soul once reunited to God can never be broken off again. Satan tries hard to pluck the branch away—the winds of temptation blow them rudely about—afflictions like sharp knives threaten to cut them off; but nothing can separate the real believer from Christ, for it is written, "He that believeth HATH *everlasting* LIFE, and *shall not come* into condemnation."

Thus then, whenever Christ stands for an ENSIGN to the people, He is not only exalted as EQUAL WITH GOD—the EVERLASTING FATHER—and His ELECT Servant; He is also revealed as the END OF THE LAW for Righteousness to every one that believeth—the beautiful EXAMPLE to which we must be conformed—and ETERNAL LIFE within us. The prophet adds, "To it (this ENSIGN) shall the Gentiles seek," and not in vain, for "His rest shall be glorious." Glorious indeed! since to every one that believes He says, "I am thy Shield and thy EXCEEDING GREAT REWARD."

EXCEEDING GREAT REWARD (Genesis 15:1). He does not here say I will *give* you a great Reward; but "I *am* thy REWARD." Then we are rich indeed! If the EVERLASTING FATHER gives us Himself, surely all things are ours; this world and all worlds, the sun and the stars, earth and heaven, time and eternity. Yet are all these things nothing when compared with Himself.

That is the grandest inventory in the world which we have in 1 Corinthians 3:22, 23: "For all things are yours, whether Paul, or Apollos, or Cephas, or the world, or life, or death, or things present, or things to come; all are yours." But God is greater than His works and more glorious than His gifts. Infinitely so. And all heaven-taught souls are of his mind who said, "Yea, doubtless, and I count all things but loss . . . that I MAY WIN CHRIST."

> Thy only love do I require;
> I nothing else on earth desire,
>> Nothing in heaven above.
> Let heaven and earth and all things go,
> Give me Thine only love to know,
>> Give me Thine only love.

Let us conclude with four lessons.

1. *You should prize the preaching of the gospel.* It is the power of God unto salvation, and faith cometh by hearing.

2. *You should come boldly to the throne of grace.* What prevents the prayers of sinners from being heard? The offended law of God. But when you point to Jesus Christ as the END OF THE LAW for Righteousness, the law makes no more opposition. Come then with full confidence, and cease not in your prayers to

3. *Seek Spiritual Life from Jesus Christ by Whom you can bring forth fruit.* He came "that you might have life"; ask Him for it, and leave Him not to complain, "Ye will not come unto me that ye might have life."

4. *Keep in view the* EXAMPLE *of Christ.* If you hope to be saved by His righteousness you will love to follow HIS EXAMPLE. The gospel is not to make the law void but to establish it. "He that saith he abideth in Christ ought himself also so as to walk even as He walked." Jesus says to you, "Learn of Me, for I am meek and lowly in heart." Do you admire this lovely disposition? Have you tried to learn this lesson of Him? And are you striving to practice it every day? Again, the Father says to Him, "Thou hast loved righteousness and hated iniquity." Are you conformed to this beautiful pattern? Remember, "Without holiness no man can see the Lord."

18

Friend. First-Born. First-Begotten of the Dead. First-Fruits. Faithful Witness. Forerunner. Fairer Than the Children of Men. Former of All Things. First and Last. Fruit of the Earth. Faithful and True. Faithful Creator.

THERE lived some time ago two intimate friends. Sisters they were—beautiful, pious, and amiable. They loved each other most fondly, and could scarcely bear to be separated. The elder became dangerously ill. The younger watched her with the utmost anxiety; and suspecting that the sufferer was afraid to die, she said to her, "My dear sister, I fear you are about to die—I cannot comfortably part with you only to go to Christ, I hope therefore your interest in Him is clear." The elder turned to her and said, "What! sister, do they think I am in such danger? I must confess to you that if I thought death were near, my distress would be great, for I have not that full assurance for which I have often prayed." No sooner had she spoken thus than the other fell on her knees beside the bed and exclaimed, "O Lord, if one of us must die shortly, let it be me! For through Thy grace I have a sure hope of my interest in Christ. Wherefore I will willingly die, if it may but please Thee to spare my sister a little longer to make her calling and election sure." So saying, she kissed her sister and left the room. And so it came to pass—the elder began to amend and shortly recovered; while the younger, the ardent, the devoted, filled with the assurance of faith, was seized with illness and died! How sweet was the fellowship of these two! How beautiful the devotion of the younger! *Death* was not too great a price at which to secure the life of her beloved sister. Human love could go no further. But Divine love rises higher still. "Peradventure for a good man some would even dare to die; but God commendeth His love towards us, in that while we were yet sinners, Christ died for us." Then "there is a FRIEND who sticketh *closer than a brother.*"

149

FRIEND (Prov. 17:24). He is One who doth as far excel the most perfect pattern of friendship the world can show as the heavens excel the earth. Whatever is valuable in the best Friend exists in Christ to an infinite extent, with many qualities that no other Friend can possess. Tender parents pity their children and love to comfort them. But they are often at a distance when most wanted, and are sometimes doomed to see them perish before their eyes without the power to help them. Human Friends are liable to change, or the most devoted of them might not be able to help us—and so prove but broken reeds. Or we might number among our Friends the wise and learned, but if we are much inferior to them there could scarcely be a very cordial sympathy between us.

But *this* FRIEND is powerful to help us in every time of need, and never changes in His feelings. And He is fully prepared to accommodate Himself to us however lowly we are; for He loves to be known as the Friend of the poor and humble. *They were poor fishermen* to whom He said, "I have not called you servants, for the servant knoweth now what his Lord doeth; but I have called you FRIENDS—for I have told you all My heart." And *they were little children* whom He welcomed to His arms, saying, "Let them come to Me, for of such is the kingdom of heaven."

There dwelt at Bethany, in comparatively humble circumstances, two sisters and a brother; Jesus loved that little family and often rested Himself under their roof. What sweet hours those three spent in intimate conversation with the Man of Sorrows! What a privilege they felt it to sit in the same room with the Messiah and hear His wisdom! Oh! you think, if I had lived in Bethany then how I would have welcomed Him to *my* home! Would you indeed? Well, if you are sincere I can tell you of a greater thing than that! *He loves much more to be entertained in our hearts.* He asks for this. He invites Himself, "Behold I stand at the door and knock; if any one open, I will come in and sup with him, and he with Me." Will you be so rude and ill-mannered as to say, "I pray Thee have me excused"? What! decline the honor you thought just now you would be so proud of the privilege of entertaining the Lord of Glory? Think of the intimacy to which He invites you. Have you secret sorrows that you cannot reveal? Have you temptations that you do not feel at liberty to explain to any? You may unfold them all to Christ. Have you some fond wish which you shrink from imparting to any human being? Go speak of it to Jesus. It is to this intimate converse He calls you. This is what He wants—your entire confidence. This is what He means in Revelation 3:20, "I will sup with him and he with Me." Keep nothing from Him and He will withhold no good thing from you. Make your secrets known to Him and "the secret of the Lord shall be with you." I say again—There should be unrestrained intercourse; there is not a thing about which you ought not to converse with Jesus Christ. Cast all your burdens upon Him—

> Oh, let your weary heart
> Lean upon His! and it shall faint no more,
> Nor thirst, nor hunger; but be comforted
> And filled with His affection.

Ah! (say you) all this seems very sweet. We like the thought of *such* a FRIEND. But how can Jesus Christ be thus intimate with thousands at once? Because He is God! Behold He fills heaven and earth! Therefore He can deal with each one as particularly as if that one were alone in the world. Well, but stay! There is another difficulty still. We should like this friendship very much, and we can well imagine this kind of intimacy between equals; but will He Who, you say, is "Higher than the Highest" stoop to such worms as we? We can scarcely believe it. And then a bosom FRIEND ought to be able to enter into our feelings. To do this he must have been in similar troubles with ourselves. Exactly so! And Jesus Christ took part of your flesh and blood on purpose that He might be able to feel your infirmities and perfectly sympathize with you. Make no more objections then. But (first) observe that *There is in this Friend the closest Relationship.* He is "bone of your bone," and a Member of your family, the "FIRST-BORN."

FIRST-BORN AMONG MANY BRETHREN (Rom. 7:29). "He took on Him the seed of Abraham." God's "FELLOW" was not ashamed to be man's Brother! The rich are often ashamed of their poor relations, and find it hard to stoop to their level. But oh, the matchless grace of our glorious FRIEND! He was rich, yet so bent on owning us that He dwelt among us who were not only beneath such an honor, but sinful and altogether unfit for it. Admire this Holy One becoming the "FRIEND of publicans and sinners." He mingled with us but was not contaminated. He endured the stigma of our evil reputation and was numbered with transgressors, that He might gather around Him a great family and be the FIRST-BORN among many brethren.

These Titles, FIRST-BORN and FIRST-BEGOTTEN, (Heb. 1:6), point out His preeminence in all things. He is the Head of the family; the Eldest, the Heir; as well as the Leader to whom all the younger members of the family are to look up. But do we not read also that "it behooved Him in all things to be made *like* unto His brethren" (Heb. 2:7)? Observe, then (secondly), that *In this Friend there is not only Relationship but Likeness.* He is "the FIRST-BEGOTTEN OF THE DEAD."

FIRST-BEGOTTEN OF THE DEAD (Rev. 1:5). He was Partaker of our flesh and blood that He might hunger and thirst; that He might weep and suffer and be made like His brethren, and so be able to feel for them. Yea, and He died, and was buried like His brethren. He poured out His soul unto death, that through death He might deliver them from the power of death. But having died, He saw no corruption. Being buried, the grave could not hold Him. Three days He lay in prison, and then by His own power shook off the bands of death and became the "FIRST-FRUITS OF THEM THAT SLEPT."

FIRST-FRUITS OF THEM THAT SLEPT (1 Cor. 15:20). How astonishing is the doctrine of the resurrection! No wonder reason staggers at it.

"What! the dead arise?" cried an African king.

"Yes, all the dead will rise," said his informer, Dr. Moffat.

"Will my father arise, and all the slain in battle? And will those who have been killed and eaten by lions and crocodiles *rise again*?"

"Yes, and come to judgment."

"And those whose bones have been whitened on the plain and scattered by the winds—will *they* rise again?"

"Yes," said the doctor, "not one will be left behind."

"Father," said the Hottentot monarch, "your words are sweet; but the words of a resurrection are too great. I do not wish to hear them again. *The dead cannot arise.*" So said that untaught savage. And so said the learned Athenians when Paul preached "Jesus and the resurrection" on Mars Hill. And so say some in the present day. But Christ who is the AMEN and the

FAITHFUL WITNESS (Rev. 1:5) declares, "they *shall* arise." And if we want a proof that such a thing can be, He points to Himself and says, "I am He that was dead and am alive again." And being risen from the dead and become the FIRST-FRUITS of them that slept, He promises to raise up us also in like manner at the last day. And we believe His word, for "He is FAITHFUL who hath promised."

> The time draws on
> When not a single spot of burial earth
> Whether on land or in the spacious sea,
> But must give back its long committed dust.
>
> .   .   .   .   .   .
>
> His FAITHFULNESS stands bound to see it done.

All will share in this "rising again." But oh how different the state of the righteous and the wicked! These last shall rise to shame and contempt. But if you and I make Christ our FRIEND we shall rise to everlasting life, and be admitted within the veil "whither the FORERUNNER is for us entered, even Jesus."

FORERUNNER (Heb. 6:20). We have said that in all their *painful and humiliating things* He is made like His brethren. But it is in order that they should be made like Him in His *glorious* things. Did He rise from the grave? That is a pledge that they shall rise also. Has He gone into heaven? Oh delightful thought! It is as a FORERUNNER FOR US. A Forerunner is one appointed on behalf of others to hasten to some place to make ready for them who are coming after. This is the office assumed by our unfailing FRIEND. "In My Father's house are many mansions: I go to prepare a place for you." Is it so? Then surely if we mean to follow Him we should be getting ready for the journey. How are we to do this? We must "put off the old man and put on the new." We must part with the friendship of the world and cultivate that of Christ. We must cast away every besetting sin, and strive, and pray, and watch, that whenever He shall come for us, we may be found of Him in peace, without spot and blameless. We have said it behooved Jesus Christ to be made like unto His brethren, that they may be made like Him. Still the resemblance must be ever far short of the Original: for (thirdly), *There is in this* FRIEND *surpassing Beauty and Excellence.* He is "FAIRER THAN THE CHILDREN OF MEN."

FAIRER THAN THE CHILDREN OF MEN (Ps. 45:2). Moses and Joseph were fair; their beauty is said to have been extraordinary. Solomon must have looked fair in his royalties, surrounded with ivory and gold and precious stones. Fairer still are spotless angels. Kings in their greatest majesty cannot rival them. Their countenances are like the lightning, and their raiment white and glistening. But FAIRER than all is the Lord Jesus, "Beautiful and Glorious." Fair in the comeliness of His countenance, in the majesty of His person, in the grace of His lips, in the perfection of His character, in the sweetness of His disposition, and in all the magnificence of His kingly glory. Could we imagine all the beauty of men and angels collected together in one person, it would fall infinitely short of the beauty of Christ. Yea, being God as well as Man, He is the very Fountain of Beauty; for He is the Contriver and "FORMER OF ALL THINGS."

FORMER OF ALL THINGS (Jer. 51:19). He dresses the stately lily in its snow-white vest, and scents the rose with fragrance. He endows man with reason, and clothes archangels with strength and majesty. By Him the butterfly is arrayed in beauteous robes, and the bird of paradise adorned with elegant plumage. By Him the blue firmament was stretched out, which we behold sometimes "coated with woolly clouds, or laced with the curious rainbow; now all in a flame with flashes of lightning, and then made up again into serenity, and clear as a molten looking glass." And all His works are fair. Fair alike is the insect glittering in the sun, and the snowy mountain reaching to the clouds. Fair is the smooth lake, which reflects in its depths the fairer sun looking into it from above, or the moon walking in brightness. Fair is the "human face divine"; fair the unsullied courts of heaven. But infinitely FAIRER than all must He be who made them.

> These are His glorious works,
> His universal frame
> Thus wondrous fair—Himself how glorious then!

And as in His divine, so also in His human nature He if FAIRER THAN THE CHILDREN OF MEN. For He is "the

FRUIT OF THE EARTH (or Land), Excellent and Comely" (Isa. 4:2). Which simile must be referred (says Dr. J. P. Smith) to our Savior? "The term Branch of the Lord here stands connected with the Fruit of the Earth. The same person is the Son of Jehovah and a Child of the Land of Judea." The Fruit of the earth may signify that, as man is a kind of First-fruits of all creatures on the earth, and being formed of its clay and fed by its produce, might be fairly termed the principal production or Fruit on THE FRUIT—THE FIRST-FRUIT, the Principal Production of all—the Rod which, springing from the human stem, should fill the whole earth with its glory. Or understand it to mean the Fruit of the Land (Judea); then it points Jesus out as the Illustrious Child, who should be born of a virgin descended from the royal house of David, the Hope of the Jewish fathers, the Glory of Israel, the Joy of the Gentiles, and the Desire of all Nations. In either sense, as "the Fruit of the Land or of the Earth, He is Excellent and Comely." Then the expression, "Branch of the Lord, Beautiful and Glorious," evidently refers to His divine nature; which is also indicated by the Title,

FIRST-BORN OF EVERY CREATURE, or Chief of the Creation (Col. 1:15). It is a figurative expression for preeminence. In the early ages the first-born was heir to his father and lord over his brethren. In Isaiah 14:30, the "first-born of the poor" means the poorest; the "first-born of death," in Job 18:13, means the most terrible of deaths. And the Jewish rabbins were used to call the Holy and Blessed God the First-born of the World, to signify His supremacy over all created beings. He is also called the

FAITHFUL AND TRUE (Rev. 19:11). Let me here narrate a touching instance of a wonderful fidelity. A captain, on leaving his ship, gave his two young sons into the hands of his faithful Negro servant, saying, "Take care of my boys till I return." The captain had not been long absent when a dreadful storm arose which made an entire wreck of his ship. The people struggled into the lifeboat. In the midst of the confusion the poor Negro, faithful to his charge, took the two children and tied them securely in a wrapper, putting in a pot of sweetmeats for them; and swinging them across his shoulders, tried to get into the boat. But it was now quite full, and as the Negro was stepping in the mate cried out, "There is no room for you and the children too; either you or they must be drowned! for the weight of all three will sink the boat." The faithful man did not hesitate. "Very well," said he, putting the children into the boat, "give my duty to my master, and tell him I beg pardon for all my faults." Alone he stood for a brief interval upon the deck of the deserted vessel, but soon sank beneath the wave with the wreck and was seen no more. Who can but admire this instance of almost more than human faithfulness? As it is a wonderful instance of fidelity, so is it a beautiful picture of Him who was Faithful and True to His charge, even though it cost Him His life, which life He hesitated not to lay down for the sheep which

God had given Him to redeem. Oh, will you not commit your precious soul to such a "FAITHFUL CREATOR"?

FAITHFUL CREATOR (1 Pet. 4:19). Do so at once; entrust your all to Him. He will never leave you nor forsake you. But you must leave Him to judge what is really good for you. A little boy saw an old man sitting at the door of a cottage. He was lame and feeble, but he looked so happy that the boy wondered; for he thought that only the young, the healthy, and the rich, could be happy. "How happy you seem here!" said he to the old man; "I wonder you should be so, for I see you are aged and lame: shall I be as happy when I am old?" "My dear little boy, I will tell you what makes me happy. I have a FRIEND who is FAITHFUL and TRUE to me, though I am poor and old and lame. He loves me and I love Him. And this makes me happy." "Dear me!" said the boy, "Who is He? I wonder He does not help you out of this cottage." "He is very wise and good, my child," replied the old man, "and He knows what is best for me. And if a golden house and sound limbs were best, I should have them, for He can do all things." "*Do all things!*" said the child. "Why, nobody can do all things but God." "Well, my dear," returned the old man, "and my FRIEND is God. I have known Him ever since I was young. I have seen many troubles, but all things have worked together for good. And when I die I shall go to live with Him, and be very, very happy forever." At this the old man's face brightened, and laying his wrinkled hands on the little inquirer's head he said, "Good-bye, God bless thee, my child! May you love Him now, and not have when you grow old a life of sin to look back upon; may your hoary head be a crown of righteousness, and at last may you dwell with Him in Heaven." Then the little boy bade him good-bye, and went away thinking how good it must be to have Jesus for a FRIEND, since He can make people happy, even when they become old and poor and lame. He can do this, and everything else His people require; for (fifth) *To all his other qualities He adds that of Infinite Power.* Continue therefore in His love. Adhere more closely to Him, remembering whatever difficulties you may be placed in, He is able to bring you out of them; whatever troubles you may be called to bear, He is able to support you under them; whatever wants you are called to feel the pressure of, He is able to supply every one of them. Is there anything too hard for the CREATOR AND FORMER OF ALL THINGS?

Thus have I endeavored to tell you a little about this Exalted FRIEND. I have spoke of five of His excellent qualifications, viz., RELATIONSHIP—RESEMBLANCE—SURPASSING BEAUTY—UNCHANGING FIDELITY—and INFINITE POWER. And these five excellent qualities have been illustrated by thirteen most expressive Titles. Remember what I have told you of this

FRIEND: How of His great love wherewith He loved men, He determined to be made like them that He might be the

FIRST-BORN AMONG MANY BRETHREN. I have showed you that as they were subject to death, so He submitted to it too; but that death had no bands strong enough to hold Him captive, and so was compelled to yield Him up. "Now therefore is Christ risen" and become the

FIRST-BEGOTTEN from the dead; and the

FIRST-FRUITS of them that slept; all of whom shall be raised up at the last day according to His sure word; for He is the

FAITHFUL WITNESS whose word cannot fail. And then appeared the reason of His being made like unto us. It is that we may be made like unto Him, and be fitted to enter within the veil whither "the

FORERUNNER is for us entered," to make ready the heavenly places for our reception. Then we were reminded that our likeness to Him must be always indeed faint; for He is and ever will be infinitely

FAIRER THAN THE CHILDREN OF MEN; because He is God, and possessed of unapproachable excellence, being called the

FORMER OF ALL THINGS, THE FIRST AND THE LAST, the FIRST-BORN or Lord of all Creatures; at the same time we claim Him in His human nature as a Native of this world, or

FRUIT OF THE EARTH; but still Excellent and Comely above all others, for His holy soul knew no stain, His exalted mind no defect. Then we come to the conclusion that those who trust in Him will ever find boundless power combined with perfect uprightness. He is not only

FAITHFUL AND TRUE and a FRIEND; but, at the same time, as our FAITHFUL CREATOR, able to do for us above all we can ask or think. "This is our Beloved and this is our FRIEND."

19

Foundation. Fortress.

A ROCK is remarkable for strength and durability. Its weight and hardness render it immovable. The light sands of the desert may be drifted by the winds, the loose earth, which skirts the ocean, may be washed away by the waves. But the hard rock which lifts its stony front amidst the billows of the ocean, in form and size remains the same for ages, bidding proud defiance alike to the waves which roll at its base, the tempest which howl over its summit, and the more silent influence of time which gradually wears away all human monuments.

Opposite Plymouth, fourteen miles out at sea, there is a rock called the Eddystone. But though they toss themselves over it, and seem as if with angry roar they would swallow it up, yet when the storm has spent its fury, there it stands unchangeable, immovable, the same from one century to another.

A Rock, therefore, being more like that which is perpetual and everlasting than anything else, is often used in the Scriptures as an image of Him who is from Everlasting to Everlasting, the Ancient of Days, the Eternal Jehovah. In the Old Testament we read, "Who is a Rock save our God?" "He only is my Rock." And in the New Testament the same simile is applied to Jesus Christ (Isa. 8:13, compared with verse 14; Matt. 16:18; 1 Cor. 10:4). At the close of His Sermon on the Mount our Lord describes the building of two houses on two different Foundations. Both were assaulted with rains and winds and floods. One was washed away, while the other stood the shock because it was built on the Rock; which ROCK must be our Savior Himself, because it is written, "Other Foundation can no man lay" (1 Cor. 3:11).

FOUNDATION (Isa. 28:16). "Behold I lay in Zion for a FOUNDATION a Stone, a tried Stone, a precious Corner Stone, a Sure FOUNDATION, and he that believeth on Him shall not be confounded." O ye who read these pages, as you would not be ashamed in the great day of the Lord, see that you build on this FOUNDATION. Nothing will bear the weight of your soul and its eternal salvation but this solid Rock of Ages, the Lord Jesus Christ.

Marianne S., a beautiful girl of eighteen, was once under religious impressions, but put off to a convenient season that which required immediate attention. She was seized with typhus fever. The physician was summoned. He found her scarce able to speak, her tongue and lips covered with dark fur and her eyes almost closed. From her half-opened lips dismal moans were heard and bitter unearthly groans. The physician put his mouth to her ear and said, "Marianne, do tell me what mean these groans? What is the matter my dear child?" Upon which she opened her once beautiful eyes and lifted up her pale hand, and fixing upon him a look that made his soul ache, said, "Doctor! there is a difference between a life of amusement and a life of prayer. Oh, it is hard to *die without an interest in Christ!*" She closed her eyes, dropped her hand, and all was silent. She never spoke again.

It is a fearful thing to neglect this FOUNDATION till death put it out of your power to find it. But there are some who profess to believe that Christ alone is a Sure FOUNDATION, who yet do not come to this Living Stone, and are not therefore built on it and into it. *Their faith is a dead faith.* It would be well if there were no occasion for the caution. It would be more pleasant to think that there is no *wrong* way of building on the *right* FOUNDATION. Perhaps this mistake may be illustrated by a reference to the history of three lighthouses.

On the Eddystone Rock just now mentioned, about 150 years ago, an architect was employed to build a lighthouse. And, full of confidence, he speedily set up his tower without properly considering the great shocks to which it would be exposed. It stood eighty feet high. But so tremendous are the storms in that part of the sea, that sometimes the waves have been known to break more than a hundred feet over the top of the building. And at times the sea has covered more than half the side of the house, as though it were under water. One day, three years after it was finished, the builder went to see about the repairs. As he was leaving the shore with the workmen, some friends told him they feared his building would not long withstand the storms to which it was exposed. But he, pushing off, cried out "I am so sure of its strength, that I only wish to be in it during the most dreadful storm that ever blew under the heavens." This language was far too presumptuous. While he was there with his workmen there happened one of the most awful storms ever known. The next day, when it was over, the people went anxiously to look for the lighthouse, but there was not a fragment left. The bare rock was all they found. The lighthouse had been overset; and foundation and furniture and builders and all were swept away together.

However this lighthouse had been found very useful to the "night-o'er-taken mariner," and therefore was another set up taller and stronger than the last. This was built of wood. It stood for some time and was thought to be very secure indeed. But one night the lightkeeper went into the lantern to trim the candles and found it filled with smoke. Before he could give an alarm the whole building was in flames. The three men who had charge of it betook themselves to a hole in the rock for shelter, till the fire was seen from the shore and boats were sent to their relief. The poor men were almost stupefied with terror, and scarcely able to avail themselves of the proffered help.

Again another lighthouse was built. A more skillful architect was employed, who formed his tower of large stones fast locked and dove-tailed into each other, and into the rock on which it stands. It cost much labor and time. And often the sea broke in and interrupted their work and washed away their tools and materials. But they persevered, and at last it was completed. There it stands to this hour, "and lifts its massive masonry, a pillar of fire by night, of cloud by day," having endured the onset of the tempest for about 120 years without showing any sign of weakness.

> The startled wave leaps over it; the storm
>   Smites it with all the scourges of the rain,
> And steadily against its solid form
>   Press the great shoulders of the hurricane.
>
> And as each evening darkens, lo! how bright,
>   Through the deep purple of the twilight air,
> Beams forth the sudden radiance of its light,
>   With strange unearthly splendor in its glare!
> Steadfast, serene, immovable, the same
>
>   Year after year, through all the silent night
> Burns on forevermore that quenchless flame,
>   Shines on that inextinguishable light!
> And the great ships sail outward and return,
>
>   Bending and bowing o'er the billowy swells,
> And ever joyful as they see it burn,
>   They wave their silent welcomes and farewells.

We have said that a Rock is "more like" that which is everlasting than anything else, and therefore used to image the Ancient of Days. But, in common with all such emblems, it falls infinitely behind in the very quality for which it is remarkable. For though Smeaton's famous tower is as compact as ever and might last for ages to come, the rock on which it stands is found to be so worn by the action of the waves, that a new structure has become necessary. But so sound is the *principle* on which the old lighthouse is built that it will be adopted in the new one. And its *form* will be much the same; like the trunk of a great oak swelling outwards towards its base, and striking, right and left, its huge supports of dove-tailed stonework deep into the rock, as the tree does its roots.

But "OUR ROCK is not like that." The failure of the Eddystone Rock only adds increased emphasis to the lesson. Nor storms nor waves nor time nor change can affect the Rock of Ages, or render insecure the standing of any who believe in Him. "Therefore will not we fear, though the earth be removed, and though the mountains be carried into the mist of the sea."

You will not have read the history of these three lighthouses in vain if it serve to impress on your minds this lesson, that not only must you have a secure FOUNDATION to build on, but study the right way of building. Religion is no such easy, slight matter, as some think it. The apostle says, "I as a wise master-builder have laid the FOUNDATION." He means that he preached the gospel faithfully, and directed men to Christ alone for salvation. "But," he adds, "let a man take heed how he builds thereon!" Look again at the three lighthouses and receive instruction.

Remember the first, which not being properly made fast by joints and bands to the rock, was carried away—and beware of a false faith, which does not bind the soul to Christ. It is not enough to say, I believe; the devils believe and tremble. You must believe with the heart, and cleave to Him with your affections. There must be faith that worketh by love, and the influence of the Holy Spirit to unite you to Christ. O look for union to Christ by means of a real vital principle!

Remember again the wooden lighthouse which was burned up, and the attendants were scarcely saved, "saved as by fire." It was not the rock, the Foundation, which was in fault in this instance any more than in the last. The failure was caused by the flimsy nature of the materials erected upon it. Alas! how many there are whose religion has no more solidity than that wooden lighthouse! Their opinions are correct and their profession is plausible, their feelings are lively and they look well enough to the eye; but their piety melts away like wax when exposed to the fires of tribulation or persecution. Beware, as the apostle says, of building on the FOUNDATION "wood and hay and stubble!" such a religion or such a practice as will not endure the trial. "Look to yourselves that ye lose not those things which ye have wrought, but that ye receive a full reward."

Remember also the solid stone lighthouse carefully built into the rock, and which remains to this day firm as the rock itself—and let your religion be like that. Observe all the directions the Bible gives you. Who is he that is built on the Rock? "He that heareth My sayings and *doeth them.*" This is the man on the Rock, and here is the proof that he builds on the true Foundation. His piety flourishes. Like the lighthouse, which "hails the mariner with words of love," his life is useful to all around. He is the beacon "set on a hill," the taper "set on the candlestick." His light so shines that men are the better for it and God is glorified.

Dig deep for a FOUNDATION. Make a study of salvation. Oh beware of unsound work in this matter. There are thousands who "do many things," but who fall short of real faith. "They can find tears as Esau. They would like to die the death of the righteous like Balaam. They will fight for the Lord like Saul. They value the prayers of good people like Pharaoh. They can put away gross sins as Jehu. They hear the gospel gladly as Herod." They may seem to be on the right FOUNDATION; and yet there is some flaw at the very bottom, which ruins all, and they fail in the hour of trial. Alas, how many there are who, if we were to ask them what is their hope, would say "We trust in Christ alone, we build on the true FOUNDATION," when all the while they do no such thing.

Some workmen were once making a trench round a large plat of ground. "What is this for?" said a passerby. "We are digging," said they, "for the foundation of a church." Presently they thought they had got deep enough and threw aside their pickaxes in order to prepare for the next stage. By-and-by the architect came to see the progress of the work. He got into the trench and tried the bottom with a spade. And coming out he shook his head and said, "This will not do. You must go much deeper yet. You must take away all this loose earth and rubbish, nor desist until you reach the solid rock." Now this is just the mistake of several sorts of men who build for eternity. They do not go deep enough for their FOUNDATION. There is still much rubbish between them and Jesus Christ. And when they build on this loose earth and sand, no wonder their house totters and falls to the ground in the night of storms. One says in his heart, "Surely I (if any) may come to Christ with confidence, seeing that I am baptized and confirmed, and observe regularly all the prescribed forms of my church."—See you not that forms and ceremonies are this man's Foundation, and not Christ? Another says, "I am honest, I pray, I strive to keep Christ's commandments, *therefore* I will take to myself the promise of forgiveness in Christ." This man makes his own righteousness his Foundation and not Christ. Another says, "I have sweet devotional feelings glowing within me, and other evidences that I am a Christian; may I not come boldly to Christ *on this ground?*" To such a one I would say, "No indeed! Not on that ground. If you do, it is at your peril. Those feelings and evidences of yours (all the while you trust in them as you do) lie between you and the true FOUNDATION. You must go lower yet if you will build safely." In short, all those who do not come to Christ on *His bare word*, but are emboldened to apply to Him on the consideration of something good in themselves, fall short of building on the sinner's FOUNDATION. Oh, it is rare to build on Christ ONLY—to come to Him without money and without price—to receive salvation for nothing—to believe on the footing of His bare word of promise! But to this we must all be brought if we would be safe and steadfast.

And if you truly believe on Jesus Christ you perceive great glory and excellence in Him. In the eyes of the world this Rock is but a common Stone; yea, worse—it is a Stumbling-stone, which offends them. But to them that believe He is precious. In their eyes He is as a "FOUNDATION laid with sapphires and fair colors," a Stone that sparkles with ten thousand beauties, and they greatly admire Him. A missionary was once addressing a congregation of slaves from the words, "Lovest thou Me?" In the midst of the sermon he paused and said, "Is there no poor sinner here who can answer this question? Not one poor slave who will confess Christ?" Upon this a poor black boy, unable to restrain himself any longer, stood up and lifting up both his hands cried out with eagerness, "Yes, massa, me love Christ! me do love Him! me love Him with all my heart." But now it is time to speak of a second point of resemblance between Christ and a rock—*A Rock is a place of Defense.* Rocks have often been used for this purpose. In allusion to which it is said, "Thy place of Defense shall be the munitions of rocks." David when pursued by Saul fortified himself in rocks. Not that he trusted in these. No! he knew these rocks would be of no use without the Lord, therefore in Psalm 18:2, he said, "The Lord is my Rock and my

FORTRESS; my Deliverer, my Strength, and my High Tower." Whenever he forgot this and only looked at his earthly rock, he began to feel afraid. But whenever he retreated to his Divine Rock, the Lord his FORTRESS, he could say of his foes, "Let them compass me about like bees; in the name of the Lord I defy them." Oh, it makes one bold and courageous indeed to feel that God is his FORTRESS! Have you never admired the spirit of Nehemiah when his friends besought him to hide in the temple from wicked men who sought to slay him? This was his answer, "Should such a man as I flee?" But why not? Who was Nehemiah that such a man as he should not flee? Was he armed with a coat of mail from head to foot? Was he stronger than other men? No, but he was such a man as had God for his FORTRESS. *Therefore* was it he said, "should *I* flee? No. I scorn to run away and hide myself in the temple or anywhere else; the Lord is my Hiding Place." Betake yourself to the same Holy FORTRESS and dwell under the shadow of Christ. Plant your feet by faith on this Rock of Ages, and you shall not be moved. Though there be fears within and fightings without, though sickness and death threaten to do their worst, you will yet be able to say, "Should such a one as I yield to fear? If Christ be for me, who can be against me? What time I am afraid I will trust in Thee." But there are assaults of a more inward nature with which every Christian is exercised, and which can only be resisted in the strength of Christ. As His soldiers you are called to fight with unseen foes, led by an experienced general whose name is Apollyon. Till life closes expect no cessation of hostilities. When one means of ruining you fails, another is tried. Thus the foe hopes to tire you out and worry you into sin. Sometimes it is a corrupt desire of your own depraved heart, which you have to withstand; then a suggestion from some wicked spirit. At another time it is a sinful companion or a well-meaning friend through whom the mischief is attempted. But put it down as a settled point that there is always some plot in hand for your destruction.

In carrying on a war the first thing wanted is a strong castle to retreat to. When the Duke of Wellington entered on the famous Peninsular campaign in which he drove Bonaparte's armies back to France, he built a stupendous Fortification at Torres Vedras forty miles in circuit. Six hundred cannons were mounted on 150 towers, while every jutting rock bristled with weapons of defense. No such Fortress was ever seen before. Massena, the French general, thought he was sure of Wellington and his troops, and came down with eighty thousand men, like a whirlwind, expecting to drive them all into the sea. All at once they saw before them this appalling entrenchment stretching right across their path. Immediately they came to a halt, while their general rode to and fro for days, in hopes of finding some weak point at which he might enter. But all in vain. Torres Vedras was impregnable. He shook his head, and with shame gave orders for a retreat.

Now the Lord is your "Torres Vedras," your FORTIFICATION. No weapon formed against this FORTRESS can prosper. In it you may hold out against a siege for a whole lifetime. Iniquity shall never be your ruin if you do but cleave to Christ. Let me just name one of Satan's chief devices. When he sees you off your guard, he employs an evil thought to enter under some pretense and engage you in conversation. While you listen there comes another and another, each more and more evil, till at last they muster strong enough to drag you down from the walls of your FORTRESS and plunge you into sin. Oh how many to their great cost have experienced this stratagem! Yea, who is there that has not been thus many times cast down? Do not think I am picturing the danger in too strong colors; but engrave on your memories the command, *"Flee youthful lusts."* Not stand and fight! Not stop and hold a parley! that is the way to be beaten; but flee! In this warfare, flight is not cowardice, it is the truest courage. Immediately on the first appearance of temptation, *make good your Retreat to Christ.* Thus doing you will get His help directly. This is the best method of carrying on the war, an approved stratagem in dealing with the adversary. And then, though the blast of the terrible ones be as a storm against the wall, you shall hurl back the waves of sin as Wellington's strong Fortress did the attack of the Grand Army. But if you will be venturesome, and be unwatchful against small beginnings of sin, I warn you it is the way to be ruined. Cain went on from envious thoughts to murder; and Judas, it may be, began with thinking he would just take one small coin from the bag, and ended with the awful crime of selling his Divine Master for thirty pieces of silver, about £4 10s.

A man who was hung at Carlisle for housebreaking, declared that his first step to ruin was taking a halfpenny out of his mother's pocket whilst she was asleep. Another offender, convicted at Chester of housebreaking, before he underwent the dreadful sentence of the law, said to the people, "You are come to see a man die. Oh take warning by me. The *first beginning of my ruin was Sabbath-breaking:* it led me into bad company, and from bad company to robbing orchards and gardens, and then to housebreaking, and that has brought me to this place." Well do the Scriptures say, "Enter not into the path of the wicked, and go not in the way of evil men—avoid it, pass not by it, turn from it, and pass away."

During the long frosts of Russia, when for many months the rivers are frozen over, the people engage in a favorite amusement. Upon the frozen water they build high stages, with inclined planes slanting from the top and carried a long way out. Then they pour water down, which freezes so that the slanting surface becomes as smooth as a sheet of glass. When all is ready, they ascend to the top, seat themselves in sledges, slide down the slanting plane, and shoot along to a great distance as swift as lightning. But, you observe, when once they begin to slide they cannot stop: on they must go; and this is just a picture of the path of the wicked. It is a SLIPPERY path. All those who set out in it find it *exceedingly difficult* to stop; and most of them find it *quite impossible!* Therefore, "enter it not, turn from it, and pass away." A certain youth was awakened by the preaching of the gospel but was drawn aside by bad company. Then he repented but went astray again; once more he struggled back into the right path. But again he sinned, and came back no more. One day a friend met him, and sought to impress him with his danger and the necessity of resisting temptation. "Ah!" he said, "I know it—I wish I could—but I feel I cannot." The next week he was drinking with loose companions, became ill with a sore throat, and in three days he was a corpse. If that poor wanderer had but made Christ his FOUNDATION and rested all his weight on Him—if he had but made Christ his FORTRESS and resisted in His strength, he might have maintained his ground and inherited the promise—"He that overcometh shall be clothed in white raiment, and I will confess his name before My Father and the holy angels."

20

Fountain of Living Waters. Fountain Open for Sin.

IN the last Reading, I led you to "the Rock that is higher than we"—the Lord Jesus Christ. We saw Him to be a sure FOUNDATION and a safe FORTRESS. And so far the similitude of a Rock seemed very applicable. But rocks are dry places; and in this respect, at first sight, the figure does not seem so appropriate. But have you never heard of the wonderful "Rock in Horeb"? There is a dreary place not far from the Red Sea, called the Desert of Rephidim. It is enclosed with splintered rocks and stony peaks, hundreds of feet high; and all around it in solemn grandeur rise dark mountains, with barren slopes abruptly broken here and there into frightful precipices. It was on a vast plain in the midst of this desert, many centuries ago, that upwards of three million travelers pitched their tents, while on their way from Egypt with their little ones and their flocks and herds.

Three million people! that is thirty hundreds of thousands. You can scarcely realize the vastness of this multitude from the mere mention of their number. But just look at one page of this book, which you hold in your hand. It would be quite a task to count the letters that compose it. Now turn over all the leaves slowly, and consider what a multitude go to make up the entire book! Then consider again that you require above two such volumes as this before you can number three million letters! Three million people! And all wanted water to quench their thirst and fresh their panting animals, but found neither well nor water-brook.

Perhaps you have never thought of the enormous worth of water, and how impossible it is to live without it. In this country, God has given us a fair supply. But in many parts of the East it is very scarce; especially in the deserts, where, perhaps within a distance of 300 miles, the traveler will only find three or four springs of water. In those frightful wastes multitudes often perish, victims of the most horrible thirst. "It is then that the full value of a cup of cold water is really felt. In such a case there is no distinction. The servant will not part with a drop for his master. If he be a rich man, the owner of the caravans, and is dying for a cup of water, no one gives it to him. If he offer all he possesses no one hears him. The camels lie down and refuse to rise; no one has strength to walk. Only he who has a glass of water lives

165

to walk a mile further, and then perhaps he lays himself down and dies also." To be thirsty in a desert without water, and without shelter, exposed to the burning sun, is the most terrible situation a man can be placed in. But if in these circumstances, before things get quite desperate, a Fountain can be discovered, what expressions of joy are heard throughout the caravan! Men and camels, masters and servants, all rush forward in wild disorder, eager to quench their raging thirst.

And thus it was with the multitude we have mentioned. We left them encamped in Rephidim, tormented with thirst amidst barren rocks and burning sands. They first became impatient, and then enraged; and then they surrounded their leader with eager cries, "Water! Water! Give us Water!" and wildly threatened to stone him if he did not comply with the demand. But he, poor man, had not a draught of water for himself; much less could he supply three million mouths. However, he did what every wise man would do when placed in difficulty. While they loudly complained, he silently prayed to God. No sooner was the prayer uttered than from the midst of the cloud a voice was heard, "Call the elders and go forward to yonder Rock in Horeb and take thy rod with thee, and I will stand before thee there on the rock; and thou shalt smite the rock and water shall flow out." Immediately Moses summoned some of the leaders of the tribes, and bade them follow with him the way the cloud of glory was leading. Now Horeb is a day's journey from Rephidim. Imagine then, if you can, the state of the people while this journey is being accomplished. Some of them refuse to believe the promise, and, half delirious, lie rolling in anguish on the ground: while others strive to keep up their spirits, cheered with the hope of relief. The flocks bleat piteously as they lie down panting in the sun; and the thirsty oxen, with stretched-out necks and distended nostrils, snuff up the air.

But yonder goes the bright cloud followed by Moses and the elders. It leads over the rising ground towards the mountains at the head of the valley. Hours pass away; and still the weary elders are pursuing the cloudy pillar. But see! the sacred symbol pauses. It rests on the summit of yonder lofty Rock, which overlooks the plain. They halt, while Moses by himself climbs the rugged steep till he reaches the foot of the divinely selected Rock; and then, amidst the solemn stillness, he puts forth his rod and smites its stony front. Immediately a gurgling sound is heard high overhead. A jet of water leaps from the rock, and splashing from crag to crag, scatters the spray all around. The tide increases every moment, pouring down a copious stream into the hollow beneath till it soon becomes a river deep enough to swim in. And then the miraculous torrent suddenly makes for itself a channel among the rocks, and rushes forth headlong towards the camp. It is not long in accomplishing its errand. But who can describe the delight of the famished Israelites when on their listening ears the welcome "sound of many waters" is heard? It comes nearer. A shout of joy rends the air! Then there is a tumultuous rushing towards the crystal stream. Some catch up the water in their hands. Some kneel down to lap with their tongues. Some bring water skins that they may first relieve a child dying in the tent, or revive a drooping parent. On every side all is motion. All are making toward the watercourse till they discover a shorter way to the attainment of their desire; for see! the bountiful river, more precious than liquid silver, hastening to do the errand on which its beneficent Giver has sent it, spreads quickly on all sides and diving into numberless streams flows down to the utmost edge of their long rows of tents. No words can describe the comfort this supply yielded to the Israelites. It was so refreshing and so seasonable, that many years afterwards when Moses alludes to it he says, "Israel sucked *honey* out of the flinty Rock." We read, "this Rock followed them" for many years. Not that the Rock moved from its place; but that wherever they afterwards encamped among the many valleys which surround the hills of Sinai, there they found rivulets flowing from that wonderful Rock in Horeb ready to supply their wants. "He clave the Rocks in the wilderness, and gave them drink as out of the great depths; He brought streams also out of the Rock, and caused water to run down like rivers (Ps. 78:15, 16). Thus then you see that though rocks are mostly barren, the Rock in Horeb was a Fountain. So Jesus the ROCK OF AGES is also a FOUNTAIN—"THE FOUNTAIN OF LIVING WATERS."

FOUNTAIN OF LIVING WATERS (Jer. 2:13; 17:13). You must be aware that the Scriptures contain very frequent allusions to Rivers and Fountains, as emblematical of Christ and the blessings of salvation. And very likely the inhabitants of eastern countries understand better than we do the force of such comparisons. A recent traveler in Egypt describes the intense enjoyment with which they drink it there. "No idea can be formed in this climate (England) of the luxury of drinking in Egypt. Little appetite for food is felt. But when after crossing the burning sands you reach the woods on the borders of the Nile, and pluck the fresh limes and mix their juice with the soft river water, you feel that there is no refreshment so delicious, and that no boon can be compared to water."

And then it is not to Water in a cistern, which can be emptied out, that Christ is compared, but to a Fountain which cannot be exhausted. Nor to Water in a lake or reservoir ever so large, which might be muddy and stagnant, but to "LIVING WATER," pure spring Water, always fresh and flowing and sparkling with life, cool in the heat of the summer noon and clear in the storms of winter. There is a Fountain called the Ravensbourne, not far from London, which incessantly pours forth its rich treasure without ceasing at the rate of a ton every minute. Thus it flowed many centuries ago when the Romans first visited this country, and attracted by the flight of ravens towards the spring, encamped around its borders. Thus it has flowed ever since; and still it furnishes several thousands of people with their daily supply of this necessary of life. Beautiful Emblem of the

Fountain of the Water of Life, which remains undiminished, though millions of angels have been ever drinking from it full draughts of blessedness.

Angels? Yes, *they* may drink of it, but what of us sinners who have "forsaken the Fountain"? Is not God angry with us? Indeed he *was* angry with us, but His anger is turned away and now He comforts us, and gives us back our forfeited right to the Fountain! He gives us His Beloved Son! The grant is made in so many words, *to all the world*. It is for you and for me. "The Spirit and the Bride say, Come! and let him that is athirst come: and *whosoever will*, let him come and take of the Water of Life FREELY." Well may we say, "Thanks be unto God for His Unspeakable Gift!" Consider it! God's own Son, given to you and to me! and all we have to do to make Him truly our own, is to appropriate Him to ourselves—to receive Him with all His unsearchable riches.

When the manna fell around the tents of the Israelites, it was given to them all, but each had to gather his own portion. When the Water streamed out of the Rock in Horeb, and ran in a thousand rivulets down the mountainside, it was God's gift to all the Israelites who were willing to take it, without exception; but each must lift the precious liquid to his own lips. So free is God's Great Gift of His Own Dear Son to us! And just as the Israelite gathered up his manna or fetched his Water from the running stream, nothing doubting his right to it, or just as a man takes his part of the dainties of a feast to which he is invited and appropriates them to his own use—just so are we warranted to receive Jesus Christ; that is, as He says, "to eat His body and to drink His blood." Wherefore come boldly to the Fountain of Living Waters; put in each of you your humble claim, and God will not disallow it, but rejoice over you to do you good. "Ho! every one that thirsteth, come to the Waters."

Fountains in all countries are places of common resort. The inhabitants of eastern cities have not wells in their own gardens; but there is a public well or Fountain at no great distance from their abodes, from which they may procure the precious treasure. Around those Fountains, in the cool of the evening the people assemble with singing and mirth, and having enjoyed each other's conversation, they fill their vessels, lift them upon their heads, and return to their homes. In the sandy deserts also, here and there, are copious springs, which are places of resort. Travelers gather round them in troops to procure a supply of that object of universal desire—Water. Thither also bands of robbers direct their steps, not to supply their wants only, but to plunder the shepherd and the merchant. Of such conflicts at Fountains we often read in the Scriptures. In Deborah's song of praise, Judges 5:11, "those who have been delivered from the noise of archers at the places of drawing Water," are called on to "rehearse the righteous acts of the Lord towards the inhabitants of the villages"; and to do it "there"—that is, at the very Fountains, which, though once infested with archers, were now cleared of the marauders.

The prophet Isaiah has these sweet words in the midst of a beautiful song of praise: "With joy shall ye draw Water out of the Wells of salvation" (12:3). And I think we shall not do violence to the language if we apply it to the means of grace. The ordinances of worship are "Wells of salvation," all supplied from the LIVING FOUNTAIN. Come to "the place of drawing Water," come with bucket and cord, faith and prayer, and take each of you the supply you need. Be not absent when Christians assemble with joy to keep holiday round these "Wells." Come with great expectations. "Sing ye to it, Spring up, O Well!" Pray for a plentiful blessing; so shall you "drink of the river of God's pleasures," and be "satisfied with the fatness of His house."

And surely those gatherings of neighbors at even tide around the eastern city Fountains, are not inapt pictures of the assemblages of Christian worshipers in quest of spiritual supplies, on Lord's days in houses of prayer. Or perhaps those meetings at lonely wells in the desert are more to the point, where oftentimes pilgrims and wayfarers were unexpectedly confronted with a gang of thieves, and furious battles ensued. For do Christians come alone to the house of God? Or are they only friends who meet them there? Are there no enemies lurking in ambush ready to attack and plunder them? It is true, we are not forced, as our forefathers were, to worship in caves and woods, at the hazard of being seized and hurried off to noisome jails. It is true, mounted dragoons no longer scour the hills of Scotland to silence the hymn, and scatter the pious worshipers to a thousand hiding places. Let us thank God those times have gone by. We are "delivered from the noise of archers in the places of drawing Water." Our "Wells of salvation" are not infested with bands of cruel persecutors. But are there no foes present? When the sons of God come to present themselves before Him, Satan comes with them and evil angels are there. When you try to pray they resist you. When you would praise the Lord they distract your thoughts. When you hear the gospel they strive to take away that which is sown in your heart, "lest you should believe and be saved." Oh be watchful lest you fall a prey to their devices.

But there are also HEALING FOUNTAINS; Mineral Springs which avail for the cure of disease. They abound in the Pyrenees and other mountain districts, and are not unknown in our own land. But wheresoever they exist, they are restored to for the virtue which is supposed to reside in them. Thither from far distant places many a poor exhausted invalid undertakes a laborious pilgrimage, animated with the hope of relief. Some of these Fountains are curative of one malady, and some of another. The virtue of some of them is best secured by bathing, that of others by drinking. But however appropriated, have we not in the Healing Fountain a beautiful emblem of Jesus Christ, by Whom alone the diseases of our souls can be cured and our spiritual health repaired? Nor is this symbol unrecognized in the Scriptures.

In Zechariah 14:8, we read, "LIVING WATERS shall go forth from Jerusalem." And in Ezekiel 47, their HEALING use is specified. The waters gush forth from the threshold of the temple; and still, as they flow, widen into broader streams, till they become "Water to swim in, a river that cannot be passed over." And whithersoever they flow they convey healing to every living thing. All beautifully emblematical of the gospel, or rather of His infinite virtue Whom the gospel makes known and conveys. Just thus the Glorious Lord becomes a Place of Broad Rivers and brimming Streams, ever deepening, and still overflowing with incalculable blessings to all who know Him. Come, poor sin-disordered soul, come to this HEALING FOUNTAIN, and prove its infinite efficacy. And as Naaman, plunged seven times in the Jordan, was instantaneously cured of his leprosy; as the poor paralytic stepped into the pool of Bethesda, and on emerging from its bubbling waters, found he had left behind all his weakness, and could climb with agility the rock-hewn stairs down which he had just now been helplessly borne—so come thou to Christ, and thou shalt experience His mighty power to communicate health and cure, to cleanse thy leprosy of long standing, to heal thy broken heart, and to make thy dislocated spirit whole and sound.

A FOUNTAIN has yet another use, namely, *to fertilize or render fruitful.* The church of God is often compared to a garden; and Christ is, in relation to it, a FOUNTAIN OF GARDENS, a Well of Living Water, and Streams from Lebanon (Song 4:15). I need not say how needful water is to the very existence of a garden. Without it the plants would all die. Therefore when Solomon made gardens and orchards, he also opened Fountains to supply them with the life-preserving fluid (Eccl. 2:6). He brought streams from the hills, and prepared reservoirs in which to treasure up the water for use. Lebanon is a range of lofty mountains in Judea whose summits are always covered with snow. This snow, dissolving in summer, feeds the rivulets that run among the hills. The river Jordan is one of those streams from Lebanon. It takes its rise at the foot of the mountains, and then winds it course through hot and sandy plains and barren wilds. But whithersoever it goes it carries fertility along with it. Both its shores are "lined with continued grass plats of the brightest green; and fringed with groves of slender shrubs, and forests of willows and tall osiers and Persian poplars, with flowers of every color spreading on all sides."

Those Streams from Lebanon, becoming in their course a "FOUNTAIN OF GARDENS," are emblematical of the Water of Life (Ezek. 47:3–10). If you look into the Bible you will see that God calls His church a garden. And a sweet and fragrant garden it is. And His children—are they not all "trees of righteousness, the planting of the Lord," which flourish "beside Rivers of Water," and bring forth fruit in their season? Look into this garden and you will find many promising plants. Pious children like lovely violets, whose sweet fragrance enlivens the family circles in which they live; young Christians like shrubs and saplings planted in the courts of the Lord, giving promise of future excellence; and more mature Christians like the green olive bearing much fruit. You will see also strong oaks and towering cedars and flourishing palm trees, reviving those who dwell under their shadow. These are "the ministers of our God," who benefit the church by the ripeness of their knowledge and the strength of their faith, and stretch in the fullness of their stature towards the skies. Then there are aged trees, which though they bend under the weight of years, still bring forth fruit in old age and are fat and flourishing, "to show that the Lord is faithful," in that He does not cast His people off when they are old.

Some of these plants are weak and some are strong. Some bring forth plentifully already. And some are urged that they may bring forth more fruit. But the secret of all their greenness—the source of all their beauty—what is it? The LIVING WATER from the great FOUNTAIN that nourishes their roots. The influences of the Holy Spirit which, like streams from Lebanon, bring with them whithersoever they come life and verdure, strength and beauty.

> There grow Thy saints in faith and love,
> Blest with Thine influence from above;
> Not Lebanon with all its trees,
> Shows such a comely sight as these.

But wherever this influence is absent there is the sandy desert, there is the barren heath, there are the stony ground and the desolate wilderness.

There are in this garden of the Lord some very young and tender plants. Let me describe one. From his infancy he was a sweet little boy, and he grew in favor with all till he was seven years old. Then it was he heard a sermon, which made him feel, as he said, *that he was wrong* and that he was *lost* in common with all others. He was filled with distress and often wept; but he prayed for pardon and grace till he found peace in believing. And soon the fragrance of his youthful piety became very sweet indeed, so that his parents greatly rejoiced over him. This dear child had his heart set on being a minister; and there were many lovely blossoms, which gave promise of future usefulness. But

> There came One who loved the flower,
> And took it home to deck His bower;
> Bore it away beyond the skies,
> To bloom in His own Paradise.

For the Divine Husbandman daily walks in His garden to see the trees of righteousness, which He has planted with His right hand. And one day when young Samuel was about thirteen years old, the Lord of the garden transplanted him to the heavenly PARADISE, where he now flourishes in immortal vigor, far away from the boisterous winds of temptation and the blight of sin.

There is a Reaper whose name is Death, and, with his sickle keen,
He reaps the bearded grain at a breath, and the flowers that grow between.
He gazed at the flowers with tearful eyes, he kissed their drooping leaves;
It was for the lord of Paradise he bound them in his sheaves.
"My Lord has need of these flowers gay," the Reaper said, and smiled;
"Dear tokens of the earth are they, where He was once a Child."
O, not in cruelty, not in wrath, the Reaper came that day;
'Twas an angel visited the green earth, and took the flowers away.

And what shall I say more of this glorious FOUNTAIN? The subject is as inexhaustible as the FOUNTAIN itself. Eternity will not suffice to drain it. For a FOUNTAIN has yet another use besides this; viz., to cleanse that which is polluted. So the Lord Jesus is the FOUNTAIN FOR SIN. The

FOUNTAIN OPENED FOR SIN AND UNCLEANNESS (Zech. 13:1). It was to be opened "in that day"—the day of redemption, the day wherein this Sacred Rock was smitten and "forthwith came there out" a wondrous stream of mercy and grace for the washing away of human sin. And such is the virtue of this FOUNTAIN that it cleanses from ALL sin. In illustration of which another prophet compares Christ to "FULLER'S SOAP," which leaves no stain on the garment to which it is applied. See Malachi 3:2. And all of human mold, if they would wash their robes, make them white in the blood of the Lamb. "It was in this FOUNTAIN that Abel, so amiable and innocent, sought cleansing, and confessed to a more excellent sacrifice than that which smoked on his own altar. It was there that Enoch found the white robe in which he walked with God. It was hither that Manasseh carried his raiment, red like crimson, and found it suddenly white as snow. And it was there that the dying thief, blackened with many an atrocity, washed away his stains and was that same hour fit for Paradise."

What can be fouler than murder? There was a man who caused an upright servant of his own to be killed. And when he saw that his raiment was stained with "blood-guiltiness," he was filled with anguish. But, confessing his sin, he ran to this FOUNTAIN; and washed his robes and made them white as snow. There was one too who helped to murder Stephen, that innocent martyr. He approved of the deed and consented to his death. Afterwards his conscience smote him for that crimson crime; and betaking himself to the FOUNTAIN, he too obtained mercy as a pattern to them who should afterwards believe. Ah! and there were even men worse than they! There were those who stained their hands with the blood of the Lord of Glory—the most horrible act that ever was perpetrated. At which the earth quaked and the rock staggered, the sun hid himself and all nature groaned. They killed the Prince of Peace! And yet the moment their hearts began to ache for their monstrous offense, they were directed to this FOUNTAIN, and were assured that because Jesus had prayed for them, the black guilt of that most dreadful murder would never be mentioned against them. They went; they washed.

And now they sing the song of the saints in glory—"Unto Him that loved us and washed us from our sins in His own blood, be glory and dominion forever." Thus all-sufficient is this precious FOUNTAIN to take away every stain of sin. And, what is more wonderful still, though it has washed away the scarlet sins of 10,000 guilty sons of Adam, the WATER of this DIVINE FOUNTAIN has contracted no defilement, nor has it lost any of its wondrous efficacy. Still it flows for everyone who comes to it. Mountains of guilt are swallowed up in it the moment the sinner believes.

> It rises high and drowns the hills,
> It has neither shore nor bound;
> Now if we search to find our sins,
> Our sins can ne'er be found.

And still God is glorified in our pardon and forgiveness. Justice is not affronted though Mercy goes on bringing in millions more of transgressors. God is still a Just God and a Savior—Just and the Justifier of every one that believeth.

And now do not forget that Jesus Christ is compared to a FOUNTAIN, in the four uses to which water is applied.

First. He is the FOUNTAIN OF LIVING WATERS, which you have all forsaken, but to which you may immediately return; for Christ says, "If any man thirst, let him come unto Me and drink."

Second. He is a HEALING FOUNTAIN from which you may derive an infallible cure for all the maladies of your soul. You may be lame, halt, or blind; you may be a spiritual leper or a paralytic; your soul may be bruised, wounded, maimed, dislocated—here is a specific remedy of universal application. Make full and immediate proof of it.

Third. He is the FOUNTAIN OF GARDENS, by which the trees of God's planting are all watered and nourished. May you be early planted in the Garden of the Lord! May you be blest awhile with that influence which will make you flourish in His earthly courts and bring forth fruit; and, when the Husbandman shall see fit, be transplanted to the Heavenly Garden, and in that Paradise of God bloom forever in unfading verdure and beauty.

Fourth. He is a FOUNTAIN OPENED FOR SIN AND UNCLEANNESS, to which you must constantly resort, that your guilty soul may be cleansed, and your daily sins washed away. "My little children, these things write I unto you (not that you may become indifferent to the defilement of sin, but on the contrary) that ye sin not"; for all sin leaves a most malignant and foul stain. "But if any man sin," let him remember this FOUNTAIN and be encouraged to come by the inscription placed over it, "*The blood of Jesus Christ cleanseth from all sin.*" So shall he find that "If we confess our sins, He is FAITHFUL AND JUST to forgive us our sins and to cleanse us from all unrighteousness."

21

God. Guest. Governor among the Nations. Governor of Israel. Guide. Glory.

"TELL me," said the king of Greece to Simonides, "what is the nature of God?" "The question is difficult; give me," said the philosopher, "two days to consider it." The two days passed away. "Give me four days more." This period finished, he begged eight days more. The king impatiently demanded a reason. "Be not angry, O king! for indeed the more I think about God the more unable I am to understand Him." That was a wise answer, and it had more force even than the philosopher thought. We know more of God than he did, for we have the Scriptures, which he had not. Yet the very fullness of the revelation, while it brings with it a wonderful increase of light and blessedness, at the same time greatly multiplies the wonders of the theme. For these same Scriptures tell us not only that the Lord is One God, but also that there is a plurality of Persons in the One God. For the Father is GOD; the Son is GOD; the Holy Ghost is GOD. Are there then three Gods? Not so. These Three constitute One. Can we explain this? Not at all. But we are not so unreasonable as to demand to understand this mystery before we believe it. A pert young fellow boasted that he had made up his mind to believe nothing but what he could understand. "Then," said his friend, "your creed bids fair to be the smallest creed that ever was."

Look at that little fly. He can neither think nor speak. But suppose he could do both; and you were to overhear him and his playmate talking together as they buzz and bounce against the panes of glass. You listen and a tiny voice says, "Do you think, my six-legged friend, that those huge men in yonder college can really calculate how many miles it is to the sun?" "No, indeed," says the other, "it is nonsense; they cannot even rise so high as you and I." And away they fly out of the open window, and mounting aloft are soon out of sight. Such conceit, were it possible, would seem very absurd. But now if it would be presumptuous for an *insect* to limit the power of a *man*—between whom and himself there is *some* proportion, both being *finite*—what shall be thought of proud *man*—between whom and the Infinite *Creator* there is no *proportion* whatever—presuming to cavil at what God has been pleased to reveal concerning His own Incomprehensible Nature?

But of what use is it to talk to people about the Trinity? A great deal of use indeed! None can be saved but through Christ. But if there be not Three Persons in the Godhead, Jesus Christ is not God. And if He be not God, then He cannot save, for God says, "Beside Me there is no Savior." But let us see what the Scriptures say on this point.

And first, *Jesus Christ is in the Bible expressly called*

GOD. In Isaiah 9:6, He is named "The Mighty GOD." In Hebrews 1:8, we read, "Unto the Son He saith, Thy throne, O GOD, is forever and ever." In John 1:1, "The Word was GOD." In 1 John 5:20, "This is the TRUE GOD." In Jude 1:15, "The only Wise GOD." In Romans 9:5, "Christ who is over all, GOD blessed forever"; and in Revelation 21:7, "I will be his GOD."

Secondly, *He does those things that only GOD can do.* For instance, He can *see into the heart.* One day, when He was in the temple, the Pharisees brought to Him a sinful woman, and loudly accused her. They had forgotten their own sins, but found that Christ had not. They felt His eyes like a flame of fire darting into every corner of their hearts, till all within them was naked and open in His sight; and not being able to bear it, they stole away one by one, ashamed and confounded. He used also to read the troubled thoughts of His followers, and hastened to comfort them ere they could make known their wishes. He knew what was in man, and needed not that any should testify of him. Must He not then be GOD? Could anyone but GOD see what is passing within? "Lo! He that formeth the mountains and createth the wind, and *declareth unto man what is His thought,*"—who is He?—"The Lord, the Lord of Hosts is His name" (Amos 4:13). Then He can *hear prayer wherever it is offered up,* all over the world, though in a million places at the same hour. He is *with every one of His Ministers always,* even to the end of the world. And every Sabbath day He is *in the midst of thousands of congregations* met together in His name, at the same time. He can *create what He pleases,* (Col. 1:16); He can *raise the dead* when He pleases (John 5:21); and He has *power to forgive sins*—all of which are things only God can do.

Thirdly. *He says things that only GOD can say.* Who but GOD could say, "I am the First and the Last"; "I am He Who is, and was, and is to come, the Almighty"; "He that hath seen Me hath seen the Father"; and "I will send the Holy Ghost"? It is true at other times He speaks of Himself in very different terms. But the reason is plain. For either in those instances He speaks as a man—and you must never forget that He is truly a Human Being as you or I; thus He says, "My Father is greater than I," "My God, why hast Thou forsaken Me?"—or else He speaks in His character as Mediator or Servant of God; thus He says, "This command I have received of My Father."

You know blasphemy is one of the greatest of crimes. Of this the Jews accused Jesus because He said He was the Son of God. "Why," cried they, "this is making yourself equal to God." That was what they understood by the term "Son of God." And did our Lord explain to them that He meant no such thing? No. He confirmed their impression (John 5:17). Twice they threatened to stone Him for the same assertion. And did He say, "You have misunderstood My words; I did not mean that"? No, He left them in the full persuasion that He intended them to understand that He was Equal with God. It was of blasphemy they accused Him before the chief priests. It was for this they condemned Him to death, first taking care to hear it again from His own lips. Would He have suffered death for saying that He was Equal with God when He meant nothing of the kind? Impossible.

Fourthly. *He accepts from men and angels that worship which is due to* GOD *alone.* It is written, "Thou shalt worship the Lord they God and Him only." When the people at Lystra brought sacrifices to Paul and Barnabas, those holy men were distressed beyond measure, and forcibly prevented them from committing so great a crime. When John proposed to worship the angel who talked with him, the angel said, "See thou do it not; beware of such a sin, for I am only a created being—worship God." But Jesus Christ allowed Thomas to say, "My LORD AND MY GOD," without rebuking him. He heard Peter say, "Thou knowest all things," and did not contradict him. He permitted as many as were willing, to fall down and worship Him and did not hinder them. Can we understand this conduct on any other ground than that HE IS GOD? And in heaven, where there can be no mistake, angels and men fall down before Him, and pay Him such honors as are due to Him, only on the supposition that HE IS GOD. From all which it plain that Christ is God, and in all respects EQUAL IN POWER AND GLORY TO THE FATHER.

Thou, O Christ, art JEHOVAH! Thy goings forth have been from everlasting! Thou hast formed all those stars of light! Thou dost marshal their hosts and call them by their names and uphold them by Thy strength! Who would not fear Thee, O Thou Lord of all Power and Might! Who would not stand in awe of Thee, O Thou King of Saints! Thee we honor even as we honor the Father; and to Thee do we offer divine worship, for to Thee doth it appertain.

Since Jesus Christ is GOD, you see why His blood is so precious. Had He not been *Man,* He would have had no blood to shed, no life to part with, no capacity for suffering. But so closely joined together are the two natures in His One Person, that what the one suffered, the other perfectly sympathized with, and thus His sufferings and blood acquired an infinite worth and grandeur. The blood of every individual man is a sacred thing. None may presume to shed it. But what shall be thought of the blood of Him who is JEHOVAH? No wonder such consequences are traced to it! It is the price of our redemption, the means of our cleansing, the cause of our salvation. No wonder the Father sees much virtue in it! For the sake of it He is willing to forgive the most flagrant crimes, and treat with favor the greatest offenders. Oh, prize the blood of the God-man, and seek to feel its virtue!

And you see why men may trust Him so confidently. If He were a created being, He might not be able to perform all His promises. His strength might fail; His word might be forfeited. His purpose might change, He might forget, or He might be opposed by some stronger being. But none of these things can happen to the Blessed and Only Potentate, and therefore the Christian need not be afraid to trust Him constantly and entirely.

This glorious being became man's GUEST, a Visitor on His own earth. A wayfaring Man, He turned aside to tarry for a night. A Pilgrim and a Sojourner, He lodged with men during the term of His mortal life. He wore their very nature, and shared their sorrows. In the most mysterious manner, He emptied Himself of His glory and submitted Himself to the humble conditions of their mode of life. But more wonderful still, He proposes Himself to each of you as *your* GUEST in particular. Not to *visit* you in your house for an hour, but to *abide* in your heart always. We will put *this* down then, as one of His Titles, that Jesus Christ the GREAT GOD will be man's

GUEST. During His lifetime on earth, it was one day remarked with surprise that "He had gone to be GUEST with a man that was a *sinner!*" And this may be still said even of every Christian. All are sinners and unworthy of so great an honor; yet "this honor have all the saints,"—"We will come and make Our abode with him"; "I will come and sup with him"; "Whose house are we"; "I will dwell in them and walk in them." Yea, the apostle says we are *reprobates* (disapproved), if Christ be *not* in us. But how must I know whether Christ be in me? Some find it easy to answer this question. They remember loud knocks at the door of their hearts as from One who will take no denial, and much ado about binding the strong man and casting him out, as also the gladness which followed. In other instances, there was not so much stir at His entrance.

When He lived on earth, considerable diversity marked His visits. Some, as soon as He arrived, prayed Him to "depart out of their coasts." He took them at their word and went. Beware you treat Him not with insult and neglect, lest He leave you and say as He goes, "Woe unto you when My Spirit departs." But there were some who sent pressing messages to Him, "Sir, come down ere my child die." Others watched for Him with eager eyes till it was announced, "The Master is come!" These remind us of such as pray always and faint not. "They shall not be ashamed that wait for Him." If you want anything done for you which only Jesus can do, wait on Him, and remember He can accomplish in one moment that for which you have been praying for many months. Take your place before the throne of grace, and say,

> Here, Lord, in vehement hope I rest,
> Nor put Thee off nor urge Thee on;
> The secret lies in Thine own breast,
> Thy time and way to Thee are known.

With some He was a self-invited GUEST. Zaccheus, the man of little stature, climbed a tree to see Him pass. But to his surprise, the Lord made a full stop at the sycamore, and espying him among the branches, said, "Come down, for today I must abide at thy house." With joyful haste he descended from his observatory to give this willing GUEST a welcome; and received Him into his heart as well as his house. But He will not stay where He is not wanted. Clopas and his friend at Emmaus, charmed with the unknown Stranger, entreated Him to stay a little longer and be their GUEST; so He stayed to supper. Unawares they found they had entertained the Lord of Angels! and cried, "Did not our hearts burn within us while He talked?" And do you ever feel your hearts burn within you under a sermon? Neither your minister nor teacher has power to produce that effect; nor an angel hovering near. It is Jesus Christ who by His Spirit makes that powerful impression. Detain Him! Now is the auspicious moment. Do not let Him go; entreat Him to abide with you.

Is there difficulty here in any mind? Do you say, We can only pay one visit at a time to our friends; and we must leave one, in order to call upon another? Ah! but Christ can converse with angels in heaven and saints on earth at the same hour, as well as if they were all in one place. He can cheer the drooping heart of a poor sufferer in Madagascar and whisper words of encouragement to the spirit of a dying Christian in England, at the same moment. Yea, it is as easy for Him to enter into the secrets of a thousand hearts at one time, or to heal the smart of a thousand consciences, as of one. For He is everywhere to see all that is to be seen, to know all that can be known, to do all that requires to be done, to be the joyful GUEST of each individual heart that makes room for Him, as perfectly as though that heart were the only one in the wide world.

> Lover of souls! Eternal Light!
>   If Thou wilt stay with me,
> Of lowly thoughts and simple ways,
>   I'll build a nest for Thee.

> Who made this beating heart of mine,
>   But Thou, my Heavenly GUEST?
> Let none possess it, Lord, but Thou,
>   And let it be Thy rest.

But again, do you ask the question, How may I know whether "Christ is in me," *my* GUEST? Let me tell you it matters not so much *how* He enters, whether with whirlwind and storm, or whether more silently—whether He comes suddenly, as to Zaccheus, or whether you acquire His company after long and earnest prayer. But *here is the point.* If He be in you, these things do follow. You own His authority as your GOVERNOR. You follow Him as your GUIDE. You make your boast in Him as your GLORY.

Let us take these three particulars. First GOVERNOR.

GOVERNOR AMONG THE NATIONS (Ps. 22:28). What joy it is to realize the glorious fact, that while crafty politicians are pursuing their crooked paths towards some wild or impracticable result, He is surely fulfilling His own counsels and turning theirs into foolishness. Thus will it ever be with the potsherds of the earth and their see-saw policy. "He that sitteth in the heavens shall laugh," and hold their vain projects in derision. For the kingdom is the Lord's. Upon the earth there may be distress of nations, famines, wars, and rumors of wars. The political heavens may grow dark and the mountains be cast into the depths of the sea. Among professing Christians, exploded heresies may reappear, together with a grim resurrection of buried superstitions. The love of many may wax cold. The perverted ingenuity of others may toil to undermine the inspiration and authority of the Scriptures. Yet the Great GOVERNOR Whom God hath set on His holy hill, reigns all the same, and presides over the seething chaos, out of which He will bring forth truth and beauty, justice and holiness. For He shall reign till He hath put down all authority and power. To our troubled gaze the fountains of the great deep may seem to be broken up, and nothing but wreck and ruin appear on every side. But fears for the safety of His church and cause amidst these commotions should find no place. Is not Christ at the helm? And will He not steer His own bark safely through the billows? For this very end He is constituted GOVERNOR AMONG THE NATIONS. And God hath put all things under His feet for the Church's sake, but for whose interest the world would have come to an end long ago. But in Matthew 2:6, He is called the "GOVERNOR that shall rule My people Israel."

GOVERNOR OF ISRAEL (Matt. 2:6). And as His kingdom is *within*, let us bring this Title home to our own hearts in a parable. There was once a beautiful palace built for a great King. And servants there were whose whole work it was to take care of it and guard it from the spoiler. One day the Prince went on "a far journey, and called His servants and gave to every one his work, and commanded the porter to watch." All went on well for a time. But one day while they slept, there came a strong man armed, who seized the palace and the servants. And some he chained, some he blinded, some he corrupted; till soon no trace of their former happy state remained. After a long time the Prince came back and demanded admittance; but in vain. A constant noise of revelry and strife within drowned all His remonstrances. After a while, however, one whose name was *Conscience* heard His words and repeated them to the rest. At first they would not attend; but he waked up one *Fear*, and they both together begged and prayed so earnestly that the rebels relented and agreed to open the gate. But Beelzebub, seeing the turn things were taking, fought desperately to retain his hold. Yet notwithstanding all he could do the gate was forced, and the Rightful Prince stood once more within the walls of His own palace. And first He bound the strong man who had spoiled his goods and cast him out. Then He summoned all the servants to give an account of their wicked rebellion. But they were afraid and hid themselves. However the Prince caused the trumpet to be blown, and announced forgiveness for their unfaithfulness.

Then came they all forth to offer their homage. First came *Godly Sorrow* with downcast looks, and kissed the feet of the Prince and did bathe them with tears. Then came *Faith* and *Hope* who received a written covenant of pardon from His hands. Upon which they all raised a shout and said, "O Lord, we will praise Thee; for though Thou was angry, Thine anger is turned away and Thou dost comfort us." Then *Self-will*, the leader in the rebellion, yielded up his authority; but being made free indeed, his Lord gave him back the keys of the palace, enjoining fidelity. *Understanding* renounced the dominion of "that other lord" and desired to know the pleasure of his Rightful Sovereign. *Love* mourned that ever she had acted so unworthy a part, but fell at His feet and vowed loyalty. *Conscience* hoped he should never sleep again as his post but watch with greater zeal; while *Memory* undertook to write up the Prince's orders in great letters on the walls in full view of all the inmates.

But among the woods and waste places which surrounded the palace, some of those who had been inmates (*Corruptions* they were called) put themselves under the command of one *Carnal-mind*, who would not be subject to the new laws. These caused much trouble. They tried with craft and subtlety to seduce those who had returned to their allegiance; and sometimes they even resorted to violence. They therefore required constant watching. And so it came to pass that their hostile endeavors only served to prove more fully the loyalty. Again He rules in His own palace, and all the powers of the renewed heart own their GOVERNOR and promise obedience to His commands.

And now, if you have understood my parable, apply it to yourselves. If Jesus Christ has come into your heart as your GUEST, it is to set up His kingdom there. If He be in you it is to rule over you, for you have yielded your entire being to Him in the bonds of an unalterable, unreserved, everlasting covenant. All you have and are have been placed at His disposal. Every secret recess of your heart has been thrown open. Henceforth the first question is not, How shall I please myself? but, How shall I please my Lord? You crave permission and direction of Him in reference to all you do. Conscious of much evil within, and suspecting more, you are often saying,

> Tell me, my God, if aught there be
> of Self which wills not Thy control;
> Reveal whate'er impurity
> May still be lurking in my soul.
>
> Is there a thing beneath the sun,
> That strives with Thee my heart to share?
> Ah! tear it thence, and reign alone,
> The Lord of every motion there.

Thus then "the kingdom of God is within you." Jesus Christ dwells in your heart and you submit to Him as your Governor. You also consult Him as your "Guide."

GUIDE. See Psalm 48:14, where we read, "This God is our God forever. He will be our GUIDE even unto death." A Guide is one who undertakes to show a traveler the way. Every ship has someone on board appointed to be the Guide or Pilot; but many a gallant vessel is lost through ignorance or carelessness. Paul was once on board a ship in which the Pilot resolved on a wrong course. The apostle advised him to change his plan, but in vain. The ship was wrecked, and Paul said, "Sirs, ye should have hearkened unto me, and not have loosed from Crete to have gained this harm and loss."

Not far from the place of Paul's shipwreck in the Mediterranean, a noble frigate once set sail from port, and plowing her way through the waves, was soon out of sight. A gallant admiral, Sir Cloudesly Shovel, was her commander, and thought himself fully competent to guide her course. But there was an experienced seaman on board who knew better than he the dangers that surrounded them. However, on his venturing to say so, he was immediately hanged at the yard-arm for his impertinence. Not long did the cruel commodore survive him. In the darkness of the night the ship struck on the fatal rock concerning which the seaman had uttered his warning voice, and soon became a total wreck. A few escaped a watery grave, but the greater part, with the headstrong Sir Cloudesly himself, were drowned. You see, then, the importance of skill in him who undertakes to be a Guide, and the dismal consequences of the want of it. You see also what must become of them that refuse the counsels of experience. "He that being often reproved hardeneth his neck, shall suddenly be destroyed, and that without remedy."

Now learn a lesson here. You are all voyagers on the tempestuous sea of life, exposed to winds and waves of temptation and sorrow. And directly in your course are sunken rocks and dangerous reefs; and all around are the sad remains of former shipwrecks. If you have not Jesus at the helm you will surely be lost in some unlooked-for storm; for none can get safely to port without Him.

> I saw a wreck upon the ocean flood—
> How sad and desolate! No man was there;
> No living thing was on it. There it stood,
> Its sails all gone, its masts were standing bare;
> Tossed on the wide, the boundless, howling sea!
> The very sea-birds screamed, and passed it by.
> And as I looked, the ocean seemed to be
> A sign and figure of eternity.
> *The wreck an emblem seemed of those that sail*
> *Without the Pilot* JESUS, *on its tide.*
> Thus, thought I, when the final storms prevail,
> Shall rope and sail and mast be scattered wide,
> And they, with helm and anchor lost, be driven,
> In endless exile sad, far from the port of heaven!

But with Jesus at the helm none of you can founder. You shall outride the most terrible storms the Prince of the power of the air can raise against you. You shall plow your way triumphantly through the weltering seas, and sail straight into the "fair haven" of immortality, amidst a thousand welcomes from the Shining ones who line the happy shores.

At the point of death, Vara, a converted native of the island Aimeo, received a visit from his missionary. "Well, Vara, my brother, are you afraid to die?" "No, dear missionary, I am not afraid! The canoe is on the sea; the sails are spread; I am ready for the gale. *I have a good* PILOT *to guide me,* and a good haven to receive me; I am not afraid." Thus spake the converted islander, Vara, concerning his late-found GUIDE. How different from the false god "Eatooa," in whom his forefathers had gloried! That God, under whose wings he had now learned to put his trust, was the "Light which lightens the Gentiles and the GLORY OF HIS PEOPLE ISRAEL."

GLORY OF HIS PEOPLE ISRAEL (Luke 2:32). "Glory" means something weighty, precious, well worth having. That which constitutes the glory of an individual or a nation, is the possession of something excellent, which others have not. The bride might say to her attendants, "You have your ornaments, your embroidery, your jewels, but I have the bridegroom—this is *my glory!*" The son might say to the servants, "You have your liberal wages, your plentiful supplies of food—but it is *my* glory to have a claim to the inheritance, the mansion, and the paternal domain." The people of Ephesus gloried in their "great goddess Diana"; for no other city, they thought, could show an idol so magnificent or a temple so gorgeous. Great in their estimation was "Diana of the Ephesians whom all Asia and the world worshiped." While the glory of Athens were its beautiful marble structures, its unrivaled sculptors, its poets, orators, and philosophers.

But the people of Israel had something to glory in far better than any of these. Was it that they had Abraham for their father, who was the friend of God? Was it that they had a magnificent temple, which no city in the world could rival? Was it that their law came from heaven, their prophets were divinely inspired, and their priests divinely appointed? Was it that the fire on their altar was originally kindled from on high, or that the light of God's actual presence shined over their ark? To them indeed pertained all those glorious things; and no other people in the world were so highly favored. Yet none of these was the GLORY OF ISRAEL. But the Angel of the Covenant, who spake to them from the cloudy pillar, and was their Savior in every time of trouble, their Messiah King whose goings forth were from everlasting, and of whose dominion there shall be no end—He was the GLORY OF HIS PEOPLE ISRAEL. It is true they were constantly prone to glory in something far inferior, but were as constantly reminded by the bitter failure of every other hope, that "he that glorieth must glory only in the Lord."

And the GLORY OF ISRAEL is the Christian's GLORY. And if you are a Christian and Christ is in you, then here is the proof of it—you make Him your GLORY. But how, you ask, may one be said to make Christ his GLORY? I will show you by briefly adverting to the Titles brought forward in this Reading.

1. *You rejoice in Jesus Christ as the* TRUE GOD. You would not give up this for the world. If it could suddenly come to pass that you were convinced that Jesus Christ is not God, you would feel as though the sun were blotted out of the firmament. Darkness and gloom would settle on your heart forever. You could not trust Him with your eternal interests any longer. "Oh," you would say with the perplexed disciples at Emmaus, "we trusted that it had been He Who should have redeemed us; but this is 'another Jesus' (2 Cor. 11:4), not the One in Whom we had believed." The admiration you have cherished for Him would give place to suspicion and distrust. You could no longer regard Him as a Faithful Witness, for He certainly did, as the Jews said, "make Himself Equal with God." But away with the hateful insinuation! Jesus Christ *is* GOD.

> Should all the forms that men devise,
> Assault my faith with treacherous art;
> I'll call them vanity and lies,
> And bind the gospel to my heart.

"Oh," said good Mr. Venn on his deathbed, "in what a state should I be now if I had *only the Socinian's god to trust to!*" And Dr. Owens writes in the same strain—"Take heed of them who would rob you of the Deity of Christ. If there were no more grace for me than what can be treasured up in a mere man, I should rejoice if my portion might be under rocks and mountains."

There were two sisters who were brought up in the Socinian faith. One of them was seized with dangerous sickness. Her minister offered her such consolation as he thought would meet her case. Did he speak to her of the "blood which cleanseth from all sin"? or exhort her to trust in Jesus as the "Lord her Righteousness"? No, but he reminded her that she had lived a virtuous life, and that as to the little she could have to repent of, God was merciful, and on these grounds assured her that she had nothing to fear. But, as might have been expected, such considerations failed to dissipate the gloom that had settled on her mind. And as there was no one at hand acquainted with a better ground of hope, in this sad, comfortless state the poor young lady died. When the first shock was past, and the survivor was sufficiently composed to reflect, she was so struck with the melancholy cloud which had hung over her sister's dying pillow, and so convinced that Socianism was inadequate to secure any well-grounded hope for eternity, that she determined to search the Bible afresh. She soon saw reason for renouncing her former belief, and having received the atonement, united herself with those who glory in Jesus Christ as the "TRUE GOD and Eternal Life." Again, if you are a Christian,

2. *You glory in this* TRUE GOD *as your* GUEST. Some natives of South America, after having heard the statements of the missionaries concerning the attributes of the Christian's God, made the following answer—"We do not like the God you describe; you say He is everywhere present, and sees all that is done. Your God is too sharp-sighted for us! We do many things we do not wish to have known, and like to live in our woods unrestrained, without the inconvenience of having a perpetual observer over our heads." Those ignorant men did but speak the natural language of every guilty conscience. You meet with crowds in this country who are precisely of the same way of thinking. The thought that God's eye is always upon them is irksome. They therefore try to persuade themselves that He is too August and Magnificent a Being to take such special notice of poor insignificant man. But it is that very point which gives the Christian such satisfaction. If, therefore, you feel as you ought, you do indeed revere Him as the High and Lofty One that dwells in the High and Holy Place, but you also love to think of Him as willing to make a temple of your spirit—

> He to the lowly soul
> Doth still Himself impart,
> And for His dwelling and His throne,
> Chooseth the humble heart.

You are not shy of Him as though He were an unwelcome intruder. But as a man throws open every part of his house to some beloved and honored Guest, so you desire that He should have access to your inmost soul. You know that there is very much there to offend Him; but all *that* is burdensome to you also, and you wish Him to see and know it all, in order that He may help you to get rid of it. It is then your cherished hope that Christ has thus entered your heart, and you tremble whenever you suspect the contrary.

3. *You glory in this Heavenly* GUEST *as your* GOVERNOR. First, to rule over you *spiritually.* You love His service; you keep His statutes; to be a subject of His kingdom is the highest honor you aspire to. Some of His precepts are indeed very difficult, and much there is within your heart that struggles against His authority. But you know this DIVINE GOVERNOR can subdue your iniquity, and therefore you go to Him with the prayer, "Let these Thy foes be made Thy footstool." Then, again, you glory in Him as your GOVERNOR *providentially.* You would not have the control of the events which concern you, even if you might. And when things fall not out as you desire, you comfort yourself with the thought that nothing happens by chance, but that Jesus Christ is managing everything. In the reign of that cruel bigot Queen Mary, a minister named Gilpin was seized, in order to be conveyed to London and tried before the Popish authorities. While on the journey he broke his leg by a fall, which caused him much suffering and put a stop to his progress for some time. The guards who had the custody of him, took occasion from this circumstance to retort upon him an observation he was often accustomed to make, "That nothing happens to the people of God but what is intended for their good," asking him whether he thought his broken leg was so. He told them he "made no question but it was." And so it proved, for before he was able to travel, Queen Mary died, and he was released, and returned to his parish through crowds of people, congratulating him and blessing God for his deliverance.

> God nothing does, or suffers to be done,
> But thou wouldst do thyself, if thou couldst see
> The end of all events as well as He.

4. *You glory in Him once more as your* GUIDE—a GUIDE by His Word, by His Spirit, by His Providence. Oh, how much sometimes depends on a single step! One dark night, a poor woman, in trying to reach her home, missed her way. She became bewildered and wandered about, till all at once it was strongly impressed on her mind to sit down and wait the return of morning. She did so, and in extending her feet to relieve her weary limbs, they splashed in some water. Imagine her feelings when, after sitting there all night, the dawn of day showed her that if she had taken one more step she would have plunged into a deep river, the Ouse, on the very brink of which she had seated herself, she scarce knew why. Thus it often happens in the path of life. We are led, we hardly know how, to adopt some course to which it plainly appears afterwards, we are led by an overruling providence; for by it we have escaped some great danger, or been led to the enjoyment of some great blessing. Happy are you if you have chosen Jesus Christ for your Guide. Blessed shalt thou be and it shall be well with thee. In

every time of difficulty and doubt thou canst repair to Him with the prayer of faith; and "thou shalt hear a voice behind thee saying, 'This is the way—walk therein.'"

Such a God as the Lord Jesus, such a Guest, such a Governor, such a Guide may well be your Glory. As you follow Him, sing in the ways of the Lord, and let your song be—

> This God is the God we adore,
>> Our Faithful Unchangeable Friend,
> Whose love is as great as His power,
>> And neither knows measure nor end.
> 'Tis Jesus the First and the Last,
>> Whose Spirit shall guide us safe home.
> We'll praise Him for all that is past,
>> And trust Him for all that's to come.

22

Highest. Head of All Principality and Power. Holy. Husband. Heir of All Things.

WHENEVER in a thoughtful mood we contemplate that which is either vast or high, or mysteriously inaccessible, or of profound depth, we are conscious of a mental sensation stealing over us, compounded of fear and reverence. This emotion we term *awe*. The desert of the ocean across which the eye sweeps without finding any limit, the cataract descending with stupendous roar from amidst towering rocks overhead, and shaking the ground on which we stand, the terrible precipice over whose verge we peep with swimming heads and aching nerves—the mighty mountain with its unexplored gorges and dizzy untrodden peaks,

> On whose barren breast
> The fleecy clouds do often rest,

all these impress us with the feeling of awe. There is, for instance, Mont Blanc in Switzerland, of which no traveler ever gets a near view for the first time without being forced to yield to indefinable emotions of this sort. It lifts its hoary head and looks as though it leaned against the blue vault of heaven. There it rests in solemn grandeur, its huge sides covered with a white mantle of snow, its prodigious breadth glittering in the sun. And as men gaze on the great mountain, they feel their own littleness and are humbled. But what if that icy mountain were the abode of some mighty angel who had charge of winds and tempests, and used it as his storehouse wherein to treasure up hail and snow? Surely, if men stand in awe of the frosty pile itself, they would tremble much more at the lofty spirit of the mountain, enthroned among its frozen caves wielding whirlwinds and thunderbolts. The traveler, winding round the base of the mount, would quake for fear of its mysterious inhabitant; and they who dwell in regions near would be afraid to do anything which would bring down his vengeance upon them.

But "Is not God the height of heaven? And behold the heights of the stars, how high *they* are!" (Job 22:12). How much more reason have men to feel this solemn *awe* at the thought of One greater far than that imaginary Spirit of the storm! Dominion and fear are with Him; and before Him all the inhabitants of the earth are reputed as nothing. Before Him let us bow, Who is the "HIGHEST."

HIGHEST (Luke 1:76), "the Lofty One who inhabits eternity and dwells in the high and holy place." The venturous wing of the highest archangel never soared to the dizzy summit of that throne. Not even in thought could he climb the glorious eminence. And immeasurable distance forever separates between the Self-Existent Eternal and all creatures, however great they may be. In comparison with Him nothing is high. Angels and men, kings and paupers are alike mean. From that infinite height, He who is "HIGHER THAN THE HIGHEST" looks down on all worlds. And the wide creation thus lying beneath His footstool is subject to His absolute control; for He is "the HEAD."

HEAD OF ALL PRINCIPALITY AND POWER (Col. 2:10). He is Prince of the kings of the earth, and the powers that be are ordained by Him. His designs, however reluctantly, they *must* further. According to His sovereign pleasure He setteth them up and putteth them down. He raised up Pharaoh and buried him in the Red Sea. He removed Saul from the throne and called David from the sheepfolds to occupy his place. In the upper world all reverently wait on Him, and angels are ever on the wing to do His will. And as they fly to and fro they sing "Blessing and honor and glory and power be unto the Lamb forever." They celebrate Him as alone worthy to rule. But amongst those excellencies which qualify Him to be HEAD OF PRINCIPALITIES, there is one attribute which they admire most of all. Can you say which that is? It is His Infinite HOLINESS. He is that "HOLY ONE," spoken of in Isaiah 41:14.

HOLY ONE. Holy and Reverend is His Name. This most lovely part of His character calls forth their constant praise, since they know that it is this that insures the happiness and safety of all. Isaiah, too, was deeply impressed with the Holiness of the Lord. Twenty times he mentions this beautiful Title. At the beginning of his ministry he was honored with a vision of Christ's glory (John 12:41). A flood of light filled the temple where he was. In the midst he beheld a lofty throne, and One like the Son of Man, clothed with astonishing Majesty, sitting thereon. Above were spotless angels shading their eyes with their wings, as though abashed in His presence. But yet, as if they were scarce able to contain their admiration, they were heard calling to each other, "Holy, HOLY, HOLY, is the Lord of Hosts!" and the lofty pillars trembled at the voice, while a cloud of incense arose from the altar and partly veiled the glorious scene (Isa. 6).

Let us also "give thanks at the remembrance of His Holiness." Oh! the very thought of an unholy being possessed of infinite power and knowledge is dreadful. None could feel any confidence in him. All would seek to hide themselves from his sight. Angels would curse the day of their creation, and men would wish they had never been born! The good and bad would be dealt with alike. All creatures would become unholy, and heaven itself be just like hell. What motive would remain for the cultivation of holiness, if God were unholy and cared not whether His creatures were righteous or not? But let us rejoice! Holiness is an essential part of the divine nature. And we may place entire confidence in Christ Who "loveth righteousness and hateth iniquity." And when He united Himself to our nature, He was still the HOLY ONE. This Satan found out to be his shame, for he thought to corrupt Him as he had all other men. But no fault was found in that HOLY ONE and JUST. Alone among men He stood HOLY, harmless, undefiled, irreproachable. Else He could not have become our Sacrifice. But being "without spot," He offered Himself unto God for His Church, in order that He might make it also holy, and "present it to Himself a glorious Church not having spot or wrinkle or any such thing"—for this HOLY ONE is the HUSBAND of the Church, as we read in Isaiah 54:5, "Thy Maker is thine HUSBAND; the Lord of Hosts is His Name, and thy Redeemer the HOLY ONE of Israel."

HUSBAND. I have called on you to stand in awe of the loftiness of the Savior Who is "Higher than the highest" and Holier than the holiest. What shall I now say of His condescension in calling Himself by *this* endearing Title? If the greatest prince that ever lived were to marry the meanest person in his dominions, the wide world would ring with the news. But what would that nine days' wonder be to this wonder of wonders? Here you have that which will be wondered at in millions of worlds forever and ever. Would you not like to see the Lamb's wife "prepared as a bride adorned for her HUSBAND"? John, from the mountaintop, enjoyed a sight of her glory as she will appear at the great day of the espousals. And if you will ascend the Mount of Contemplation, and look through the telescope of the Word of God, you shall enjoy that sight, too. See Revelation 21:9. And may you all be there when the marriage of the King's Son shall be celebrated amidst angel songs and joyous melodies sounding from all the harps of heaven!

On earth there are grand celebrations. A king's coronation, a great victory, or a royal wedding is kept with great pomp and splendor, with shouts and music and sound of cannon. At Venice, once a year, there used to be a curious marriage ceremony performed. The Doge, or chief magistrate, sailed into the Adriatic Sea in a gilded ship covered with an awning of purple silk, banners flying and trumpets sounding, and attended by the nobility in gaily adorned gondolas. At a certain part the procession paused; and when all was hushed, the Doge leaned over the side of the vessel and dropped a ring into the rippling waves beneath, saying, "We marry thee, O Sea, in token of true and perpetual dominion." Then they all returned again to the city, and guns were fired, and the bells pealed from every steeple for joy.

But I can tell you of an event that will gloriously outshine all the festive scenes of earth. However grand, they will be all quite forgotten when the Divine BRIDE-GROOM, having arrayed His happy Church in "fine linen pure and white," will own her before His Father and the holy angels. Oh, the transporting sounds, like the noise of many waters and mighty thunderings, which will greet that morning of overflowing joy! Angels singing, harpers harping, and the arches of heaven ringing with the shout, "Alleluia! let us be glad and rejoice for the MARRIAGE OF THE LAMB is come, and His Bride hath made herself ready. Blessed are they who are called to the marriage supper of the Lamb!" But what if some of you should find the door of heaven shut! And when (as though you thought there must be some mistake) you knock more and more loudly, and cry, "Lord, Lord, open to *us*"; and a voice from within answers, "Depart!"—oh with what shame will you turn away! How you will wish the rocks to fall on you when you see coming from the east and the west crowds of people brought up in heathen lands, all pressing in, but you yourselves shut out! How dreadful to behold that bright place and yet not enter! to hear the rejoicings but to retire afar off, and see between you and the happy company a great gulf fixed forever! Ah! will you not make your calling sure before that day comes—while the Bridegroom says, "Knock and it shall be opened"? But if you have come to Christ already, love and cleave to Him more and more. Who but He deserves to be your sole treasure and glory? Some ladies of high rank once paid a visit to a queen, and all their talk was about their jewels and ornaments. One said, "Oh I have such a valuable necklace." And another, "I have such a beautiful set of bracelets." Each boasted of some piece of finery. And then they asked the queen what jewels *she* had—what she most prized as her greatest treasure. Her answer was, "My husband is my treasure." "But what else?" said they. "My husband, my illustrious husband, Leonidas," she answered, "*he* is my sole treasure." Nor could they get from her any other answer but that. So Jesus Christ, the HUSBAND of the Church, is the One Treasure and Joy of all true Christians, compared with which other things cannot be named. "Oh, I have *heard* of Christ often," said a pious young person, "but now I *know* Him to be just such a Savior as I want. People try to tell of the excellence there is in Christ, but their tongues are all to short to express His beauty and worth. Oh I wish my relatives could see how lovely Jesus Christ is!"

I have only to add, on this wondrous Title of our Lord, that by the great mystery of this alliance redeemed men are more exalted than angels, since He who is "HIGHER THAN THE HIGHEST" wears their very nature, and calls Himself their HUSBAND. This places them at the head of creation, seeing they are thus more nearly related to God than any. Thenceforth "the Bride, the Lamb's wife," is endowed with "*all things*," for she sitteth down on the throne of her HUSBAND, and becomes joint-heir with Him who is the appointed "HEIR OF ALL THINGS."

HEIR OF ALL THINGS (Heb. 1:2). All things are His, for He made them. But He receives this investment as the Redeemer of His Church and entirely for her sake. The meaning of the word "heir" in that part of the world where the Bible was written, differs a little from its meaning here. *There* an heir is not necessarily the successor of some deceased person. He does not always have to wait till he from whom his portion comes is dead. The son often receives his lot or inheritance in his father's lifetime. The term denotes any rightful *possessor by grant* from another. HEIR OF ALL THINGS then means, Proprietor of all things.

What a glorious inheritance is here! You know when an heir succeeds to valuable property someone is employed to make out the inventory. But there is *nothing* that does not belong to *this* HEIR. All things that are, or ever shall be, are His. Eternity, therefore, will not suffice to reckon them up in order. Heaven is His; with its jasper walls and golden pavements, its sapphire foundations and gates of pearl. His is the tree of life which grows in the midst; and that river of pleasure, which waters the lovely Paradise, flows from His throne. Life is His and He quickens whom He will. Death and hell are His, for He holds the keys of their gloomy caverns. The beautiful earth in which we live, with its mountains and mines, its fields and plantations, is His. And that curious world far away up yonder in the height of the firmament, which has seven moons and a vast shining ring encompassing it; and those other worlds which constantly revolve round our bright and burning sun—all belong to Him. But look upward at the sky, in an autumn evening towards midnight. How vast are yon fields of space that stretch over us and around us! Survey it all around from north to south. How thickly those sparkling worlds cluster! They all belong to Him. Observe them! They seem crowded together as though they must almost touch each other. But they are separated by spaces so amazing as quite to bewilder the mind.

If you could soar 2,000 miles a minute, it would occupy you more years to reach the nearest fixed star than have passed since Enoch went to heaven. And some such space as that which separates this world from those intervenes between one star and another. Sir John Herschel says, "There are stars twelve million of millions of millions of miles from our earth! So that light, which travels with a swiftness of twelve millions of miles in a minute, would require two million years to come from those distant orbs to our own! while the astronomer who should record the appearance or changes of such a star, would be relating, not its history at the present day, but that which took place two million years gone by." So we conclude that although the astronomer has counted six hundred million yonder suns, yet he can but see one little corner of the vast estate of Him who is HEIR OF ALL THINGS!

It is no unusual thing for kings to make grants of whole countries to their favorites. Napoleon, when he had conquered almost all Europe, said to his brother-in-law Murat, "You shall be king of Naples." To his brother Joseph Bonaparte, he said, "You go and be king of Spain." To his brother Louis, he appointed Holland; and to Jerome, Westphalia. Then his son-in-law, Eugene, was to be viceroy of Italy, and another relative to be prince of Lucca. And each went to take possession of his throne; but each found a very uneasy seat. One grew tired of his crown and resigned it. Another was driven away by hostile armies. A third was killed; and the rest soon gave place to more fortunate rivals. Thus they all came to nothing.

Now Jesus Christ has promised crowns and kingdoms to His followers. And you see it would be as easy for the glorious Heir of all things, such is the extent of His dominions, to say to one of His joint heirs, "Be thou over five planets"; and to another, "Be thou over ten worlds," and so on, as it was for Napoleon to appoint his relatives to be princes over the various countries he had conquered. While the crowns and principalities thus distributed among His brethren would last as long as His own, even forever and ever; if indeed such "principalities," and such rewards as these, were deemed by Him to be a fit expression of His love and bounty. But now I want you to learn two very important lessons from this day's Reading.

1. *What encouragement to prayer there is in these Titles of Christ*! He who is called the Highest and the Head of Principalities is surely *able* to help us. He who is the Holy One *will not break His promise*. He who is a Husband to His people and "hateth putting away," will acknowledge the tie that binds us to Him; while He who is Heir of all things must have stores equal to our largest wants. We read of the "*unsearchable riches* of Christ." Unsearchable riches! Think of that whenever you kneel down to pray. Imagine a poor beggar coming to a grand mansion. He knocks at the gate and asks for some small gift. The master of the house takes the poor man by the hand, and has him into a vast storehouse piled up to the roof with heaps of gold, and all sorts of treasure. And he says to the beggar, "You ask for alms. Behold, here are treasures. Come, make your choice. You shall have as much as you can carry away." The poor man's eyes sparkle, and he looks round on all the stores, and fastening on the best things within reach he says, "Good sir, may I have this bag of gold?" "Yes." "And that box of jewels?" "Yes." "And yonder bundle of raiment?" "Oh yes, take them all," says the bountiful man, "and when you want more you may come again." Now here is just a picture of Christ and His unsearchable riches. Your soul is the poor vagrant. It is in want of all things. It wants clothing and durable treasure and health and food and lodging. Well, you hear of Christ what a rich and noble Giver He is, and you come to Him in prayer. And He says, "Ask what you will; for everyone that asketh receiveth." And you look round and see great stores everywhere, gold tried in the fire, white raiment and pearls of great price, crowns of glory and

rich inheritances; cordials and sovereign remedies for every disorder, plenty of wine and milk and fat things full of marrow, and you say within yourself, "What shall I ask? My heart is a very bad one, I will ask for a new heart. My eyes are dim, I will ask for some eye salve. I have got two or three bad wounds that make me lame, I will ask for some Balm of Gilead. I am hungry and thirsty, I should like some manna and milk and honey; and I am very poor, let me beg for 'durable riches' and a bright mansion in heaven." Well, all these things, and many more, which your soul wants, I say again, *you may have for asking.* You have only to look round on the rich stores of blessings that are promised, and think what you most want; and then "Ask and ye shall receive, see and ye shall find." Oh what a rich and bountiful Person is this HEIR OF ALL THINGS! And though each of you may have as much as you can carry, they who come after will not be the poorer, for there is still as much left in the storehouse as there was before the treasures began to be distributed; they are *unsearchable riches.* Will you not pray to Him?—Then secondly,

2. *What inducements to a holy and religious life are here!* What is more honorable than to belong to a royal family? And what more glorious than to belong to the royal family of heaven? to call the HEAD OF ALL PRINCIPALITIES your HUSBAND, to be joint heirs with God's HOLY ONE, the POSSESSOR OF ALL THINGS? Yet this honor have all the saints.

But where, one may ask, are these joint heirs of Christ? I should like to see them whom the King thus delights to honor. Some of them live in garrets and some in workhouses; some are slaves and some are captives; most of them are poor and all of them are despised—the world knoweth them not and laughs to scorn their expectations. But what does that outward disguise matter? Wherever you see a follower of Christ, there you see one destined to wear a diadem compared with which all earthly honors are but empty baubles. A Christian lady greatly reduced, was obliged to pass her last days in the workhouse. One day a minister went to see her. And while he talked to her about the joys of religion, he saw an unusual luster beaming in her eyes; and he said, "Mrs. M. what thought was that which passed through your mind just now, and made your countenance so joyful?" "Oh sir," said she, "*I was just thinking what a change it will be from the* POORHOUSE TO HEAVEN!" Who would not strive to possess the character with which such sweet consolations and exalted privileges are connected?

23

High Priest.

THE writer of the Epistle to the Hebrews gives us this direction—"Consider the Apostle and HIGH PRIEST of our profession, Christ Jesus." Let us now follow His advice; and as this is the most important and conspicuous of all the Titles of the Mediator. we will devote a whole Section to it.

HIGH PRIEST (Heb. 3:1). What is a *Priest?* One appointed to offer sacrifices. At first every worshiper might offer sacrifices. Afterwards, in order the better to represent what was to be done by Jesus Christ, this sacred service was confined to a chosen family, the members of which alone were eligible as Priests; and the HIGH PRIEST was the Chief of the Priests. By him some particular works were to be performed which the other Priests might not attempt. It is *this* office that more completely prefigured the work, which the Lord Jesus accomplished for the salvation of man. But come, let us pay an imaginary visit to the camp of Israel in the wilderness. Let us suppose today to be the tenth of the seventh month, Tizri (September), the day of the great Annual Atonement. Yonder are the twelve tribes encamped not far from the foot of Sinai. How goodly are their tents, and how vast the number of them! How beautiful the encampment looks, stretching as far as the eye can reach, adorned with family standards and banners glistening in the morning sun! It covers twelve square miles, and is like a large city laid out in streets and lanes. There on the right is the banner of Judah, the most numerous of all the tribes, numbering seventy thousand men. On the left you see the camp of Reuben. They are forty thousand strong. Now we come to a wide space, and now again we plunge into a labyrinth of tents. This is the quarter where Zebulon dwells; behold the great ensign of the tribe. But stay! yonder is the smoke of the morning sacrifice curling slowly upwards from the very center of the encampment. And all the ways are thronged with women and children who have been out gathering the manna and are hastening home with it. They will not partake of it till the afternoon; for this is a strict and solemn fast—the only one in the whole year.

At last we have reached the central square of this vast city of booths. This is the place where the tribes assemble for worship. It measures more than a mile from side to side. In the midst is the tabernacle, and over it hovers perpetually a beautiful, bright cloud like a great pillar. And now we stand before the entrance of the tabernacle itself, which is about fifty feet long and eighteen feet broad, (the size of a small church). It is adorned with carved pillars covered with pure gold, resting on foundations of silver. Curtains and costly tapestry and red skins of leather joined together to keep out the weather, cover the top and hang down within a short distance of the ground. And at the entrance there is a still more beautiful curtain hanging between two golden pillars. But here we must stop; we may not enter. But surely we may just *look* in? No. He who (not being a Levite) dares to pry into the secrets of that palace of the great King must die for his presumption. That chamber is called the Holy Place, and into it the priests alone may enter. It is lighted by the seven lamps of the golden candlestick. On one side is the golden altar of incense, and on the other a table covered with gold on which are placed twelve loaves, called showbread, fresh every Sabbath day. And at the upper end of that solemn chamber, separated from it by a curtain, is the Most Holy Place into which not even priests may go; only the High Priest, and he but once in a year, namely, on this great day of atonement. The ark of the covenant is there, with carved figures of cherubim overshadowing the mercy seat; from above which there shines perpetually that mysterious glowing brightness called the Shekinah, which fills the room with dazzling light, and is the sign of Jehovah's immediate presence.

It is the third hour of the day (nine o'clock) and the time of service approaches. And lo! yonder are two priests with silver trumpets in their hands. They lift the trumpets to their lips and blow a long blast loud enough to be heard to the remotest corners of the camp, and to waken the echoes of surrounding mountains distant many miles. There is something unusually touching in the voice of those trumpets today. It is not a note of joy which they utter, but a note of admonition—almost of reproach—that thrills through the heart, for they summon a whole nation of guilty men and women to afflict their souls and confess their sins before the Lord. And yet there is a mingled note of encouragement too, for do not those trumpets, waxing louder and louder, seem to say, as with a voice from heaven, "Come and let us reason together, and though your sins be as scarlet they shall be white as snow"?—But hark! hear you not a confused noise like the hoarse sound of many waters? It seems to answer the trumpet's clang. It swells on the ear. It is as though the whole camp were in motion. It comes nearer and nearer. And now every avenue between the tents pours its stream of worshipers into the vast square, like countless rivers emptying their waters into some great lake. The outer court fills first. The Levites take their place there, and the leaders of the tribes cluster around the venerable Moses who is "King in Jeshu-run." And it is not long before the great square without is thronged with an immense assemblage, far too large for a religious meeting such as we are accustomed to see, for no human voice could make them all hear. But the instruction to be conveyed today is not by words addressed to the ear, but by symbols displayed to the eye, and the worship is for the most part performed in solemn silence. Far as the eye can reach, unnumbered thousands crowd together.

But who comes here? who is that old man with long, flowing beard and plain white dress, advancing with solemn steps towards the tabernacle door? It is Aaron, the High Priest. He approaches the altar leading a bullock and a ram, the offering appointed for his own sins and those of his house. Then the princes of the people advance with two goats and a ram for the congregation, and all these innocent victims stand trembling before the Lord. The priests ascend the platform before the altar and heap fresh wood upon the grate, while the High Priest, assisted by the Levites, proceeds to kill the bullock and cut it up, placing certain pieces upon the burning bars. The fire soon fastens on the quivering flesh, and melting the fat, bursts forth into a lurid flame, with clouds of black rolling smoke. Is not that a terrific picture of Justice consuming a guilty sinner?

While this is going on, Aaron pours some of the blood into one of the bowls of the altar. Then he takes a handful of sweet incense, and sprinkles it on a pan of burning coals, from which a cloud of fragrant smoke arises and spreads all around. And thus enveloped in smoke, he takes the bowl of blood in one hand, and in the other the censer with a quantity of fresh incense, and goes into the tabernacle. He is now lost to the sight of the people.

Picture him to yourself prostrate upon the sacred floor, with many tears confessing his own sins and the sins of his house. "Have mercy on me, O Lord, according to Thy lovingkindness; Oh blot out my transgressions. Wash me and I shall be whiter than snow." And then a still small voice whispers to his heart, "I, even I, am He that blotteth out thy sin and will no more remember it." The joy of pardon is more overpowering than the sorrow of repentance. It thrills through him; he sheds tears of delight, and amid the solemn silence meekly answers, "O Lord, I will praise Thee, for though Thou wast angry with me, Thine anger is turned away and Thou dost comfort me." Gladly would he prolong the delightful interview, but he must go forth to the waiting congregation; and his reappearance fills the whole assembly with gladness, and causes a movement among the people, like the waving to and fro of a field of standing corn as the gentle wind fans its surface.

Lots are next cast on the two goats, which shall be slain and which shall be the scapegoat. That on which the "Lord's lot falls," is offered up for a sin offering, and Aaron "does with the blood as he did with the blood of the bullock." He goes once more into the holiest of all, and while the incense smoke softens the too dazzling light, sprinkles it on the Mercy Seat, and makes penitent confession of Israel's transgressions, while all the people without fall on their faces weeping and praying. For now is the important question to be settled—Will God accept the mediation of our High Priest and send him forth with a blessing, or will He refuse the offering and punish our transgressions? "Oh, he has never seen sorrow," says an early Jewish writer, "who has not seen Israel during the absence of their High Priest!"—But whence that sudden burst of joy? It spreads through all the assembled host. It is the welcome with which they hail their High Priest as he issues from the tabernacle proclaiming God's acceptance of their offering. For "he has never seen joy," the same writer says, "who has never seen Israel when their High Priest reappears!"

Then the other goat is brought. With both hands placed upon its head, Aaron solemnly confesses their sin, and thus in a figure transfers or imputes it to the victim. After which it is led away, a doomed thing, carrying with it all their sins, and turned adrift into the wilderness where it will never be found any more at all. At this stage the High Priest retires to change the plain dress he has worn up to this time, and presently comes forth again arrayed in his grand official robes. How glorious he looks in that beautiful attire, as the afternoon sun shines full upon him! His vestment is of deep blue and gold with broad rich fringes. The ephod covers his breast and shoulders, beautifully embroidered with purple and gold, and scarlet and blue. On each shoulder is a large precious stone which glitters like the morning star. His golden crown is enriched with blue and white, and shows the words HOLINESS TO THE LORD upon its front, and his breastplate sparkles with twelve precious stones set in burnished gold.

But look again! "What!" you say, "is not this long service over yet?" Not quite. One thing yet remains. Aaron must offer a burnt sacrifice for himself and one for the people, after which the Levites must remove all that is left of the slaughtered animals and carrying them forth without the camp, make a great fire and burn them to ashes. When that is done, the High Priest spreads forth his hands and pronounces the blessing (Num. 6:24, 25).

"The Lord bless thee and keep thee," and all the people say "Amen!" How sublime that utterance from a million voices at once! It seems to rend the heavens.

"The Lord make His Face to shine upon thee, and be gracious unto thee." And again that wondrous "Amen" reverberates like thunder through all their ranks.

"The Lord lift up His Countenance upon thee, and give thee peace." A third time, more loudly still, the people answer, "Amen!" from every side, and then with glad thanksgiving in happy groups, repair to their distant tents.

Thus the ceremonies of that great day are finished. "The gospel has been *preached* to them" (Heb. 4:2), not plainly to their *ears* as it is to ours, but to their *eyes*, by means of expressive emblems and bleeding victims. The mediation of their Priest has been accepted; God has renewed His Covenant with them, and the faithful among them, though not able "*steadfastly* to look to the end of things to be abolished," have dived a little into their meaning, seen the promises afar off and embraced them, and gone home thankful and refreshed.

I have dwelt so long on this recital, because the whole was a living picture of the work of Christ in the salvation of men, *which work we should never have understood so well without the typical ceremonial.* The things we have looked at were *shadows* of good things to come; but the *body* or substance is Christ.

In the Epistle to the Hebrews, chapters 7, 8, and 9, Paul gives us the key to the whole. That beautiful tabernacle, he tells us, was a picture of a far more glorious Sanctuary on high; one which "the Lord hath pitched" somewhere beyond the glittering stars in the third heavens; those bleeding sacrifices were emblems of the spotless Lamb of God who was afterwards to be offered for the sin of many. The two Altars were types of Him, and the Mercy Seat, the Sacrifices, and even the Tabernacle itself. But the Chief Sacrificer in the Jewish church was especially intended to be the living image of the Lord Jesus Christ our Great HIGH PRIEST, who is "called of God as was Aaron, and consecrated forevermore."

That grand official dress which he wore pictured Christ's preeminent dignity—greater than Moses, greater than the angels, higher than the highest. And whereas you saw Aaron lay them all aside, and put on his plain white dress, *that* was to show the lowly form in which Christ should appear to put away sin by the sacrifice of Himself. Again, while Aaron was accomplishing those services, there was to be no other priest in the holy tabernacle. He must do it alone. So we read of Christ, that "His own arm brought salvation, and of the people there were none with Him."—But just look at Aaron's work again.

1. *He offered up sacrifices.* He killed an innocent lamb or a costly spotless heifer, and burned it on the altar. But why did the High Priest shed that innocent blood? Ah! the conscience of every beholder supplied the answer, "Either that substitute must die, or God must proceed against *me*! So foul is my sin in God's sight, that He cannot forgive it except as He thus declares His hatred of it, and teaches me by the entire burning up of that poor animal the fearful punishment due to it." What a picture was that smoking victim of Him who was afterwards to leave the blessedness and joy of heaven, and be led as a lamb to the slaughter, and die in anguish on the cross! And when the High Priest transferred the sin of the congregation to the Scapegoat, and sent it into the wilderness, was not that also an affecting picture of Him who was "made a *curse* for us"?

The Scapegoat on his head,
The people's trespass bore,
And to the desert led,
By them was seen no more.
Thus did our Surety seem to say,
"Behold, I bear your sins away."

But we must remember Jesus Christ was both the PRIEST and the SACRIFICE too. He took our sins upon Himself. He made His own pure soul and innocent body an Offering for them. Had He searched all through the universe He would have found no sacrifice good enough, no substitute able to bear the burden. There could be no value in the blood of bulls and goats however multiplied, only as their death and sufferings testified of His. But the blood of Christ is so precious, God sees such value in it, that for the sake of it He can even pardon the blackest crimes and receive to His favor the vilest sinners. That, therefore, was the SACRIFICE, which Jesus the HIGH PRIEST must offer. But

2. *Aaron made intercession for the people.* So Jesus Christ has entered into heaven with His own blood. He looks "like a Lamb that has been slain," and ever lives to make intercession for us. He taketh these poor prayers of ours, and putting them into His Golden Censer, offereth them up with His much incense (Rev. 7:3). But He does not stand before the throne of God like Aaron; nor prostrate Himself on the sapphire pavement while He maketh intercession. No. He is God's EQUAL, and sitteth at the right hand of the Infinite Majesty. And He saith to His Father, "Let not those that wait on Thee be shamed, for My sake."— "Father, I will that yonder poor suppliants be accepted and their prayers answered; I will that they be with me where I am, to see My Glory and to share in it, too." And all the angels and elders see Him interceding; and the noble army of martyrs, and the goodly fellowship of the prophets and apostles, and the happy souls of children, a countless throng from every clime rejoicing upon the everlasting hills; all these accompany this temple service of heaven with their harmonious anthems and enraptured songs, and make the place ring again with the joyous music of their harps. But there was another work that the Jewish Pontiff performed—

3. *Aaron came forth and blessed the people.* This the Master of Assemblies does *now*. While His people wait before Him He comes out of His ivory palaces to bless them. Not yet in His full glory. But He still comes. "Wheresoever I record My name, there I will come and bless you." But the hour cometh when He will issue from yonder Holy temple in a much more glorious manner. He will come arrayed in the visible robes of His Divine Majesty, and all the holy angels with Him. "To them that look for Him will He appear the second time without sin unto salvation."

Thus the transactions of the great day of atonement present a picture in miniature of the redeeming work of Christ. He first appeared on earth to put away sin by His One Offering. That done, He appeared next in "the true Sanctuary which the Lord pitched," and there He ever liveth in the exercise of "an Unchangeable Priesthood." Nor will He leave His place at the right hand of the Majesty on high till that Ministry is fully accomplished. For, just as Aaron's intercession, offered anywhere else than in the Holy of Holies, would have been out of order and unavailable; so, it would appear, Christ's intercession must be made there alone.

The fundamental laws of the office are laid down in the Epistle to the Hebrews. These seem to include the following—

First. That only by virtue of Priesthood is Christ able to save sinners (Heb. 7:25).

Second. That the office cannot be accomplished in this world (Heb. 7:4; 9:24).

Third. That His appearance yonder, in person, is absolutely needful for the Church as long as she continues in her state of imperfection (Heb. 1:3; 4:14–16; 7:24; 8:1; 9:11, 12, 24; 10:12, 21, 22; Rom. 8:34; 1 John 2:1).

Fourth. That therefore He will not lay aside His censer nor issue from the Holy place, till He can say of His Ministry of Intercession what He said of His Work of Propitiation, IT IS FINISHED.

But as these things must be obvious to all who study the Epistle to the Hebrews thoughtfully, in connection with other portions of the Scriptures, no more need be added here.

Now let me give you two rules to remember. First, Acknowledge no other for your PRIEST but Jesus Christ; and, secondly, Trust in Him with all your heart, and make constant use of His good offices.

But, you inquire, Are there any who dare to assume this sacred office? Lives there a man so presumptuous as to thrust himself into the Priesthood, and pretend to play the part of Mediator between God and my soul? My friends, there are many such deceivers, mortal men like ourselves, who with bare-faced effrontery tell us we cannot go to God but through them! Against whose crafty falsehoods it is our duty to protest. They claim to offer sacrifices and make atonement; they undertake to heal the smart of a guilty conscience, and pronounce forgiveness of sins! Vain pretensions! Oh, when will such cruel deceits perish from the earth? Jesus Christ is the ONLY PRIEST and INTERCESSOR. And the vilest man or the meanest child on the face of the earth has full liberty to come *directly* to Him, and through Him to God. He need not accuse himself before men, but humbly confess his sins to God Who knows his history and is willing to put away his guilt. He who would attempt to hinder this course on the part of sinners or teach any other doctrine of forgiveness, is a murderer of souls!

Well then, *You must acknowledge no one for your Priest but Jesus.* That is the first rule. The second is this: *Trust in Him with all your heart and make constant use of His good offices.* Do not neglect such a glorious Friend at court. Come to Him every day confessing your failings that His blood may cleanse you. Do not think any of your interests beneath His notice. In everything you are to make known your desires. Bring your prayers daily and put them all into His Golden Censer. He loves to gather "the prayers of all saints," and offer them up before the throne with His "much incense," which will render them acceptable. Do you want daily bread and other temporal supplies? Put all your wants into prayers, and bring them to the Golden Censer of your High Priest. And whenever you go to the house of prayer, expect to meet Him there who is the Minister of the Tabernacle. Put Him in remembrance of His promise to come and bless you, and He will be as good as His word—for blessed are all that wait for Him.

The parents of a certain well-instructed Irish lad were ignorant Papists, so blinded by superstition as to believe that their priests alone could secure salvation for such as were passing into the world of spirits. When their son became ill and was drawing near his end, they sent for the priest to insure him a passport to heaven. But the boy steadfastly refused his offices and said to him, "Sir, your visit is quite unnecessary, for indeed it is not your help which I want at all. I have got a PRIEST already, a GREAT HIGH PRIEST He is, who sits at the right hand of the Majesty in the heavens. He is able to save to the uttermost all that come unto God by Him. He lives forevermore to make intercession, and he is just such a PRIEST as my soul requires." This poor boy was well versed in the two rules just named, and practiced them, too; for he afterwards said, "I am not afraid to die. My Redeemer is Lord of the dead and the living. I love Him for His love to me, and soon I hope to be with Him to see His glory."

> We other priests disclaim,
> Their laws and offerings too;
> None but the bleeding Lamb
> The mighty work can do—
> Within the veil, He by His blood
> Alone secures our peace with God.

> He, and no other one,
> Deserves our confidence,
> Who pleads before the throne
> And sends forgiveness thence;
> The PRIEST who on His breastplate wears
> The names of all whose sins He bears.

24

Head of the Body. Hope of Israel. (Our) Hope. Hiding Place. Habitation. House of Defense. Help. Head Over All. Horn of Salvation. Head of the Corner.

UNION to Christ is not only a most important subject, but also a very profound one. And yet, though there is much in it which the greatest theologians cannot explain, the familiar illustrations by which the Scriptures set it before us render its main features level with the meanest capacity. If I were to take a child and set him on my knee, and say to him, "My dear child, if you wish to be really good and do things pleasing to God, you must be united to Christ," he would not understand me. "*United to Christ?*" he would say with a shake of the head, "I do not know what you mean, sir." I should wonder if he did. I must try another plan. I must use for illustration some similitude. I must say to him, "Come with me into the garden. See yonder beautiful grapevine. Its slender branches seem ready to break with the weight of those large clusters. Do you not wonder how such dry sticks as the boughs appear to be can produce such rich fruit? Well, look more closely, and you will see that the bough is united to the trunk; and the trunk is joined to something buried deep in the earth out of sight. That is the root. It sends up the sap to every part of the tree, through little hollow pipes like the veins in your body. And that sap, circulating through all the branches, causes them to bring forth leaves and fruit. Observe well what I say. For this is the pattern (one among many) which Christ has given of the wonderful union between Himself and His people. *He* is this root, and *they* are the branches. Their good works and holy dispositions are the fruit, and the grace of the Holy Spirit is the sap, the life, that produces it; and this life is 'hid with Christ,' just as the life of the tree is hid in its root." The child's notion might still be misty. But at any rate, he would learn more from the illustration, in five minutes, than from the most elaborate explanation. And even we children of a larger growth may often learn more from one symbol than from half a dozen essays. But to pass on to this day's subject—Of all the emblems of this union, none is more striking than that which you have in Colossians 1:18, and Ephesians 4:18, where Christ is called the

HEAD OF THE BODY. Can you think of anything more closely connected together than your head is with your body and its several members, the hands, the feet, the nerves? One life fills the whole. The same blood circulates through every part. If an injury befall any member—if only your little finger be pricked with the point of a needle, or a drop of hot water fall on your foot—quick as lightning, the nerves inform the head of the injury, and the brain directly feels for it and suffers with it. This is the image under which the Scriptures represent to us the intimate union of Christ and the church. Converted persons, whether "fathers in Christ" or "little ones that believe in Him," are all His "members in particular." And all of them are "by joints and bands knit together" with Him, and also with one another. Does your head feel for your members when they are injured? What may not the members of Christ expect from their HEAD? Will He not feel for them? Oh yes! "In all their afflictions He is afflicted." He has warned men not to touch them. Better far to be drowned in the sea than offend those whom He regards as parts of Himself.

See that persecutor hunting up Christ's disciples and dragging them to prison. He rides furiously along, breathing out slaughter and threatening what he will do with those whom he can seize. But lo! a dazzling light from heaven flashes in his face. He falls from his horse and hears a voice, "Saul, Saul, why persecutest thou *Me?*" Astonished he cries, "Who art *Thou*, Lord?" As though he would say, "Persecuting Thee? I did not mean that—my aim is those that have turned the world upside-down." But now he had to learn that those whom he had scorned so were parts of Christ, "members of His body, of His flesh, and of His bones." He could not assault the members without injuring the HEAD. "He that toucheth you," saith Christ, "touched the apple of Mine eye." And as the HEAD sympathizes with the members when they are wounded, so He is pleased when they are taken care of. When, out of love to Him, anyone takes pity on a poor believer in trouble, and ministers to his wants, Jesus Christ says, "*I* was the stranger whom ye then took in, and that which ye did to him ye did to *Me*." So completely is He *One* with His people.

But once more, the head is the seat of knowledge and judgment. My head guides all my members. It tells my hands and my feet what to do, and my mouth what to say, and my eyes where to look. It is watchful against that which would be injurious, and contrives for the support and safety of the whole. So all the members of Christ may expect their Glorious HEAD to contrive what is best for them in their difficulties, and to defend them from danger. There is another beautiful title in Jeremiah 14:8, which teaches this delightful truth very plainly. He is there called "the HOPE OF ISRAEL."

HOPE OF ISRAEL, the Savior thereof in the time of trouble. Under this Title the Jewish Church addressed their great Head, for He was indeed the Hope of their fathers (Jer. 1:7). Once, they wanted a path made through the Red Sea. They looked to Him, and He directly hollowed out a road for them and made the waters to stand on either side like a wall. But the night was dark and the road was slippery and rough, and they could not find their way without light. And they looked to their Hope again. So He sent them a bright pillar of fire, which went before them like a tall flaming beacon to show them the way. Then their food failed, and He rained bread on them from heaven. After that they wanted water—three millions of people in the midst of a desert where it never rained, and far away from all rivers, wanted water! But when they betook themselves to their Hope, He brought forth streams out of the Rock. Many a time they were in difficulties, but when they asked His help, He never failed them. The Head of their Church was their Hope and Savior, and while they clave to Him they never wanted for anything.

Did you ever in the height of some holiday, feel an inward dissatisfaction gradually creeping over your heart till at last it grew to downright vexation? Vexation that the day's amusement you had looked forward to with so much delight afforded you so little pleasure. And you broke off suddenly with the hope that something else you thought of would repay you better. Or have you ever had this disappointed "feel" in the midst of a party of friends, and wondered that you could not enjoy their laughter and enter into their jokes? And some such turn of thought has passed through your mind as this—"I do not know why, but this does not make me happy as I hoped it would. And it is almost over too! Well, never mind! I have a scheme for next week, and I hope that will answer better than this." And so you have gone on getting that comfort, or trying to get it, from hope of the future, which you could never get from the real thing while actually present.

Would you like to know the cause of this feeling? Go to the seaside, and perhaps you would espy just under the water, hanging to some great stone, a thing neither a fish nor a plant, but something between both. It has several long feelers floating about on the wave, with mouths at the end with which it gropes about in search of something that will suit its appetite. Those feelers are always twirling about, and sometimes they catch a little shrimp and sometimes a fly, but still they always seem hungry. Now this polypus (as the naturalist calls it) is a picture of your heart, and of every human heart. It has its feelers, it *hopes*, always searching about. God has given it an instinctive appetite for happiness. And so it gropes about constantly if haply it may find something that will suit it. It meets with what pleases it—perhaps a day's pleasure; it seizes on it, but it does not satisfy. It swallows the next thing it lays hold of, but is still as hungry as ever. It wins no real content. It has not yet found the one thing that will make it happy. As Dr. Hamilton expresses it (from whom I have borrowed this illustration, but with a different application), "there is a joy in existence which it has not yet struck out, a secret of more solid bliss which it hitherto has not hit upon." And without the information the Bible gives, it never will hit upon that secret. Try what you will, there is the worm of disappointment gnawing at the heart still. But that very boon which every human heart (like the polypus) is so eagerly feeling after in its darkness, is to be found in Him who is the HOPE of Israel—and there alone. You may refuse to listen, you may not believe it, or you may forget it as soon as you hear it; but I say it again, that busy industrious heart of yours will never be satisfied till it fastens *there*.

There is a text in Jeremiah 17:5, which asserts this, "Cursed is the man that trusteth in man (or created things) and maketh flesh his arm; but blessed is the man whose HOPE the Lord is." Let us glance at some aspects of this subject a little more definitely, as presented to us under another head. The apostle styles the Lord Jesus Christ, OUR

HOPE (1 Tim. 1:1). OUR HOPE. Not the highest angel nor all the angels in heaven could be OUR HOPE. No created being, let him be who or what he may, could possibly become the Trustee and Depositary of our interests for eternity. *He must be God* Who is to be OUR HOPE. And

1. *Jesus Christ is God.* And that is why we can make Him OUR HOPE. What can we want which He cannot supply? Where is the foe whom Omnipotence cannot vanquish? But He is OUR HOPE on another ground.

2. *He is the Appointed Savior of sinners.* His business is to rescue the lost. This is the one work that He lives to do. For this end was He born, and for this end He retains His office, that He may bring many sons to glory from among the vile and the undone. Again,

3. He is OUR HOPE not only because of what *He is*, but also on account of what *He hath done*. He took our nature, He bore our sins. He assumed our place and endured the penalty due to us. He has finished the work and brought in the righteousness by virtue of which we are justified and saved.

4. He is Our Hope because of what *He hath said*. Having done all that was required to insure our acceptance, He gives utterance to the most living and assuring words that can be conceived. His instructions, His invitations, His promises alike concur to drive away our distrust, disarm our suspicions, vanquish our unbelief, and awaken in our timid hearts the most implicit confidence, and excite and sustain the most glowing anticipations.

> Yes, all Thou *Art*, and all Thou *Doest*, and Thy sweet *Sayings*, too,
> Lay a foundation for OUR HOPE as firm as it is true.

Blest Savior! help our unbelief, confirm our feeble faith,
And we will cling to THEE OUR HOPE, constant in life and death.

"It is a bold word," writes Mr. Spurgeon, "but it is true, Our Lord exists for the benefit of His people. A Savior only exists to save. A physician lives to heal. The Sinner's Friend lives for sinners, and sinners may have Him and use Him to the uttermost. He is as free to us as the air we breathe. What are fountains for, but that the thirsty may drink? What is the harbor for, but that storm-tossed barks may there find refuge? What is Christ for, but that poor, guilty ones like ourselves may come to Him, and look and live, and afterwards may have all our needs supplied out of His fullness?"

Thus He Who is known as the HOPE OF ISRAEL is OUR HOPE. And the particulars I am about to mention will further illustrate it. This Hope is a "HIDING PLACE."

HIDING PLACE FROM THE WIND, and Covert from the Tempest (Isa. 32:2). Winter sometimes brings with it such a blasting, withering wind that we instinctively echo the exclamation, Who can stand before God's cold? At such a time the lee side of a wall is hailed as a shelter; how much more a Strong Habitation! And yet there are icy winds so biting that no precautions seem adequate to protect us. We may well shrink from the power of such an element, and provide against all avoidable exposure to it.

But how is it men do not thoughtfully revolve another question, Who can stand before God's anger? "Oh," say some, "that is easily answered. There is no such thing. It is a mere figure of speech. God loves His creatures too well to be seriously angry with them."

But what then is the meaning of the deluge? of the overthrow of Sodom? or of the solemn words which fell from the lips of the Friend of sinners touching the pains of hell? Yea, what is the meaning of His sufferings and death? Others urge that the uses of punishment are remedial, and that therefore the fires of hell will be short-lived, and be quickly followed by a universal restoration. But conjecture has no legitimate place here. What say the law and the testimony? Their invariable verdict is that the Great Judgment is destined to be the manifestation on a vast scale of the justice of God, and that the awards of the tribunal will be emphatic and final. Can any soberly imagine that, immediately it is past, the Judge will turn it all into a solemn mockery by proclaiming an amnesty to those who could not stand in the judgment, and fresh term of probation? Vain are all the Hiding Places that such conjectures afford. They will turn out to be a tottering wall and a bowing fence. There is but one HIDING PLACE from the tempest of tribulation and anguish, which is so solemnly denounced, against the impenitent. There is safety for those who avail themselves of the provision made through the sacrifice and righteousness of Christ—and nowhere else.

> From impending storms of wrath where can guilty sinners hide?
> No salvation can be found save in Jesus Crucified.
> Under heaven no other name is proclaimed to men beside,
> Other Refuge none is known, only Jesus Crucified.

COVERT FROM THE TEMPEST. This image calls up before the imagination a fearful picture. I see a tempestuous ocean lashed into fury by howling winds, and white with foam. "There is sorrow upon the sea," and stout hearts tremble with fear. It is night. But through the gloom I can discern a small vessel with ten or twelve frightened sailors clinging to the rigging. "They reel to and fro, and stagger like drunken men, and are at their wits' end." One moment the ship is lifted upon the crest of a huge billow, and now again it dives out of sight. Then it mounts another watery hill, and again as quickly rushes headlong into the gulf below, which yawns to receive it and threatens at each fresh plunge to swallow it quite up in its depths. More and more the storm rages! The voice of God's thunder is in the heavens, and "the forked lightning leaps from cloud to cloud." The poor seamen are in despair; "their soul is melted because of trouble"; for amidst the driving rain and pitchy darkness they cannot race their way. Oh, but do they not see yonder red light glimmering from afar? Ah! it is gone! Nay, there it is again, just peering through the gloom! That must surely be the lighthouse at the entrance of the harbor. Oh, if they could but reach it! The sight revives them. They venture to hoist up one small sail. The wind catches it instantly, and the little bark bounds from wave to wave. And now the harbor itself is dimly seen! The steersman, fearful of striking the pier, strains his eyeballs to discern the narrow entrance. A hoarse but welcome voice calls out from the shore, "Put your helm aport!" The command is obeyed, and the creaking ship shoots straight in, with the swiftness of an arrow, and rights herself in smooth water. "Then they are glad because they are quiet, so He bringeth them to their desired haven."

What is this but a picture of the convinced sinner full of horror and dread on account of his sins, or the afflicted and tempted saint "tossed with tempest and not comforted," who, when he flies for refuge to the appointed HIDING PLACE, is at once safe and peaceful? Oh blessed storm that drives a soul to such a Haven! Thrice-blessed sorrow that ends in such joy! We do not wish you to suffer anguish for its own sake. Far from it! But we wish you might, from this time, begin to feel in your heart such uneasiness on account of your danger as may drive you to Jesus, "the Hope set before you." For they only that trust in the Lord are truly "blessed," because they can say to Him, "Thou art my strong HABITATION, whereunto I may continually resort."

HABITATION (Ps. 71:3). Oh what a wonderful HABITATION the believer has! It is richer than a palace, stronger than a castle, and ancient as Eternity. All other habitations are liable to destruction. Sometimes whole cities have been swallowed up in a few moments by an earthquake. But it is the glory of this Divine HABITATION that no destruction can reach it. It has been the saints' HABITATION in all generations, and when the world shall be burned up and the skies rolled together like parchment, this imperishable HABITATION shall remain—the glorious happy *Home* of the children of God.

You know a man's habitation is the place where he dwells, eats, drinks, and sleeps, and where, most likely, he dies at last. Just so Jesus Christ is the believer's HABITATION. Into it he enters at his conversion—he is "a man *in* Christ." Therein he dwells all his life—he "abideth in Christ." He will live there till he dies, and then he will "sleep in Jesus"; and you know where it is written, "Blessed are the dead that die in the Lord." Oh, if you would not like the thought of having no place to lay your head in, no home in the world for your body, how much more should you dread the thought of having no HABITATION for your poor soul! If therefore there be any consolation in Christ, or any comfort of love, make haste! come! partake of it. Will you enter? or are you resolved to remain without? Well, you may not be fully sensible of your loss during life's brief day; but how dreadful it will be at the end of your journey to find no lodging at night! How dreadful to have to lie out, as it were, in the open field throughout the dark night of eternity, exposed to all the horrors of a tempest of fire, with nothing to shield you from its fury! But they that trust in the Lord can say, "Thou art my strong Rock, a 'HOUSE OF DEFENSE to save me.'"

HOUSE OF DEFENSE (Ps. 31:2). Where do men want to be when a tempest is raging, when the wind howls and the lightning darts to and fro, striking down tall trees, and hail and rain flood all the pathways? Do they not want to be in their Houses? Certainly. And at such a time, happy is he who has one to go to. But the kind Savior knew that there were worse storms than wintry blasts or sweeping hail, against which His followers would want a HOUSE OF DEFENSE. And so He forewarns them, "In the world ye shall have tribulation, but in *Me ye shall have peace.*" He points out beforehand the Retreat where they must hide themselves, "Come, My people, enter into thy chambers and shut thy doors about thee." Let us all comply with his affectionate invitation, and then—

> As Noah, humble, happy saint,
> Surrounded with the chosen few,
> Sat in his Ark, devoid of fear,
> And sung the grace that steered him through—
>
> So shall *we* sing, in Jesus safe,
> While storms of vengeance round us fall.

Again, it is said, "Ye that fear the Lord, trust in the Lord; He is their HELP AND SHIELD."

HELP AND SHIELD (Ps. 115:11). And surely the thought of this may well make the Christian a *Dreadnought*. Thus Luther, when one asked him where he would find shelter if the Elector of Saxony should desert him, replied, "Under the Shield of heaven." His confidence in his Divine HELP made him as bold as a lion. When his friends would have dissuaded him from going to Worms to contend for the truth, because many foes would be there who thirsted for his blood, his answer was, "Though there be as many devils at Worms as there are tiles on the houses "*I'll go*." And it was said over the grave of John Knox, the great Scottish Reformer, "Here lies one who never feared the face of man."

And you may all lean on the same Mighty HELPER whose support made those men such "*Greathearts*." "May I indeed?" says one, "but I am poor and everyone despises me. Will Jesus be *my* HELP?" Oh yes. He says, "Fear not, I will help thee." Who but He has helped you hitherto? When you were a little smiling babe hanging on your mother's breast, God took care of you; and when you were sick and no skill could heal you, the eye of God was still upon you; and many a time His hand has been stretched out to save you when you have not thought of Him. And if you pray to Him He will help you more and more. There may be sorrows and dark clouds before you and a weary journey through life, and the lonely grave as the end of it, and after death the judgment! But if you have Christ for your HELP, you need fear none of these. "Fear not, thou worm Jacob," says He, (and what can be weaker than a worm? but) "fear not—I will help thee."

HEAD OVER ALL THINGS TO THE CHURCH is another of the magnificent Titles of the Glorious Hope of Israel. In Ephesians 1:22, it is said, God "gave Him to be the HEAD OVER ALL THINGS to the church." This may mean He gave Him this Title and dignity or gave Him to the church to be all this for her benefit. And how gloriously this august Title becomes Him! It is no empty unmeaning name, like some that are conferred on mortals by their fellow worms, but one descriptive of His actions. For by Him God administers His providential government. Let us look at some of His wonderful doings on behalf of His people.

It was at His command savage lions restrained their thirst for blood and suffered Daniel to sit in their den unhurt; and raging bears came forth out of a wood to revenge the insult offered to His servant Elisha by those forty-two wicked youths who mocked the prophet, saying, "Let us see now if thou canst not go up into the clouds like old Elijah!—go up, thou baldhead, go up!" It was He that sent that great fish to be a floating ark for His disobedient prophet Jonah; and when Jonah prayed, "spake to the fish" and told it to carry him safe to land. It was by His directions the ravens daily winged their way to Elijah's hiding place in the desert, with a breakfast every morning and a supper every evening, till it was time for him to go forth in God's service again. At His bidding rocks became rivers, (Ex. 17:6); rivers became high roads, (Ex. 14:21, 22); and water was turned into blood, (Ex. 7:20), or into wine (John 2:6–9), whichever the occasion demanded; whether the church's enemies were to be confounded, or her friends comforted. He controlled the devouring element when three young Jews trod unhurt the red-hot pavement of the oven seven times heated. And when a company of fearful disciples were to be saved from shipwreck, the tempestuous winds owned the presence of the HEAD OVER ALL THINGS, and ceased their raging at the sound of His voice; while the deep waters of the lake bore Him up walking on its surface, and thus acknowledged His right to suspend the laws by which He had bound them.

All these, and many more such things are recorded for our encouragement. He does not now manifest His interests in His church by such astonishing miracles. But enough has been done to prove the greatness of His power, and to secure the confidence of His people; who are persuaded that if the church still required miracles for her deliverance, miracles would not be wanting which would prove His right to the exalted Title, HEAD OVER ALL THINGS TO THE CHURCH. Well may Zechariah sing in the name of the church, "Blessed be the Lord God of Israel, for He hath raised up for us a HORN OF SALVATION."

HORN OF SALVATION (Luke 1:69). This is another Title descriptive of His power to deliver. A Horn is a symbol of strength and conquest. The image refers to the horns of animals in which the power of so many of them lies. Herds of huge elks and buffaloes swarm in some parts of the earth, the force of whose horns renders them the terror of man and beast. Thus Moses said of Joseph in Deuteronomy 33:17, "His horns are the horns of unicorns, with them he shall push the people together to the ends of the earth." And David says of the great head of the Church, "Through THEE will we push down our enemies." Jesus Christ then is the Mighty HORN which wounded the dragon, and bruised the serpent's head, and which shall in due time, push down all your foes, ye "little children and young men in Christ." He will rid you of sin, Satan, and the world, just as a powerful unicorn would clear the field and drive away all assailants by the terror of his horn.

A Horn is also a symbol of glory and dignity. In eastern countries persons of rank may still be met with wearing a horn on their foreheads. This is not uncommon amongst the tribes of Lebanon. And it is also an emblem of royalty. For instance, "the great *Horn* that is between his eyes is the first *king*" (Dan. 8:21). "The ten *Horns* which thou sawest are ten *kings*" (Rev. 17:12). When Zechariah therefore spake of a HORN OF SALVATION, he used a well-known figure to express the glory of Jesus Christ, as the long-looked-for King of Zion, the HEAD OVER ALL

THINGS TO THE CHURCH, in whose days Israel should dwell safely, and the People of God "being delivered from their enemies should serve Him without fear all the days of their life."

This is the HORN that will destroy Antichrist, and toss to the winds all the vain pretenses of popes and priests, infidels and false prophets. The HORN OF SALVATION must prevail till He hath put all enemies out of the field, and the joyful song be heard in heaven and echoed on earth, "Now is come salvation and strength and the kingdom of our God and the power of His Christ." And then those words which are written in the Psalms will find their full accomplishment—"The Stone which the builders refused is become the HEAD OF THE CORNER."

HEAD OF THE CORNER (Ps. 118:22). This figure is applied by our Lord to Himself in Matthew 21:42. We are told by Jewish writers that while Solomon's temple was being built, a certain stone was selected as a Headstone. This stone, they say, the builders for some reason rejected as unfit for the purpose and were about to substitute another. But an express command from God obliged them to make use of it. And thus they explain the remainder of the passage—"This is the Lord's doing and it is marvelous in our eyes." Whether this story was invented by the Jews to explain the passage or whether something of this kind actually took place, the real application of the words, as pointed out by the Lord Jesus, is to Himself, who, though refused by the rulers and abhorred by the people, is nevertheless, "by the Lord's doing," elevated "far above all principality and power, and might and dominion, and every name that is named, not only in this world, but also in that which is to come."

1. *Let the subject lead you to Self-examination.* Ask yourself, What is my HOPE? (1) When a feeling of unhappiness comes over me, do I turn for consolation to the vain world, or do I run to Christ as the HABITATION and HOME of my soul? (2) When sad thoughts about sin fill me with fear, do I take refuge in my tears and duties and think God will pity me for the sake of these, or do I flee to Christ as my HIDING PLACE and build all my hopes of forgiveness on Him alone? (3) When I have been overcome with temptation, do I trust in my own resolutions, or do I cry to the strong Deliverer, "Be Thou my HELP and the HORN OF MY SALVATION"?

2. *Let it stir you to offer Praise.* Say, "What shall we render unto Thee, O Thou glorious HIDING PLACE and Savior? But for Thee storms of wrath would have beat upon us. But for Thee Satan would have seized us. But for Thee our sins like the wind would have carried us away. Thankful we are we ever heard Thy name. And since we have trusted in Thee and known Thy worth, we prefer Thee above our chief joy. Whom have we in heaven but Thee? Whom on earth do we desire beside Thee?"

25

Image of the Invisible God. Invisible. Immortal. Incorruptible. Immanuel. I Am That I Am. Interpreter. Intercessor.

IF you ever went to the National Gallery in London, you saw there a picture by *Vandyke* of a man named *Govartius* which almost startled you, for its eyes glisten as though the water really stood in them. It is an image of *a real form.* He whom it represents once looked just like that portrait. Or if we take a walk in some cathedral, we shall see in its solemn aisles images of *invisible* things. What is that on yonder monument? I see the figure of an aged man with a long beard and a scythe and an hourglass. That figure represents *time.* And a little farther on stands *Justice* with a pair of scales and a great sword. And just by are statues of *Fame* and *Victory.* But how can they be images of these things? No one ever SAW *Time* or *Justice* or *Fame*, any more than he could see the wind. True, but they are symbolical figures. For instance, the hourglass, which Time holds in his hand, signifies that our days are numbered; his wings show the swiftness with which he passes away; and the scythe reminds us that he soon cuts us down like the grass. Ingenious men thus express invisible qualities by visible forms. And were they to confine themselves to the lawful use of such things, there would be no evil in it. For even in Solomon's temple there were images of cherubim and forms of angels embroidered on the curtains of the holy place. They would not have been placed there by the direction of God if it had been wrong to form such things.

But here is the origin of the idol worship of the ancients. They presumed to make images of God Himself or of His attributes, and then they soon began to worship those images as so many separate gods. For instance, they knew God was powerful, so they made an image to represent strength. It was a tall, muscular figure with a huge club. Him they called *Hercules.* They knew that God was the Ruler of the world. So they formed a venerable image grasping thunderbolts, named him *Jupiter*, and built temples, and offered sacrifices to his honor.

But the second commandment strictly forbids the making of images to represent God. Why? Is it only because He is a Spirit? Is it wrong to make images of invisible beings? No. What then? Because the best representation that can be made of Him is only a *mis*-representation, a gross affront to the Most High, conveying most unworthy thoughts of Him. If someone were to draw a deformed picture and write your name under it, and say, "There is a representation of your character," would it not be offensive? But the ugliest caricature would be much more like you, than the most perfect image of beauty would be like the most Blessed God. Did you ever mark that awful question which God asks in the Bible, "To whom will ye liken ME?" And how do men answer it? Some say, "We liken Thee to ourselves, to four-footed beasts, and to creeping things." The Persian said, "I compare Thee to yonder bright sun." The Greek pointed to the figure of Jupiter or Saturn and said, "That is like God"; the Egyptian compared Him to the river Nile, the crocodile, or the beetle! But what is God's own answer to the question? He points to His Beloved Son and says, "This is the Man that is MY 'FELLOW'—I send Him into the world to be to all, the True, the Only Likeness of Myself, to be the sole IMAGE OF THE INVISIBLE GOD."

IMAGE OF THE INVISIBLE GOD (Col. 1:15). My words must be lowly and cautious lest I utter that which I know not, while offering a few observations on this Title of our Lord.

1. *He is just like God, and yet not a mere representation of Him.* You look into the glass, and you see the very image of yourself. It smiles when you smile, and imitates your every action. No art of man can so represent you. But it has no separate being. You go away, and it vanishes directly. I need not say the Lord Jesus is not such an Image of God as that, though there have been some who have been foolish enough to assert such a thing! The sculptor can hew out of a block of marble such a resemblance to reality, that the statue seems actually to claim a place among ourselves. Yet there is no soul, no life. The eyes see not, the lips move not. But Jesus Christ is God's Living Likeness, the Exact Counterpart of that Glorious Being. He is "in the form of God," but not a mere imitation of Him. Adam was created in the image of God. Saints are created anew in the same image. But Jesus Christ is the *Uncreated* Equal of God. "In Him dwelleth all the fullness of the Godhead bodily"; He has all the attributes of God in reality—the same Perfect Knowledge, the same Infinite Power, the same Glorious Goodness.

2. *He is a distinct Person from God, and yet not another God.* An image, you know, is a separate thing from that which it resembles. The sun looks down from the sky into the smooth lake below, and sees another sun reflected in its watery depths, but its image is distinct from itself. One twin child is sometimes so completely the image of its little brother that we scarce know them apart, but yet they are quite distinct from each other. And so the "EXPRESS IMAGE of God's Per-

son" is a distinct Person from God Himself. For God speaks of *Him*, and He speaks of *God*. But remember He is not *another* God, but One with the Father and the Holy Spirit in nature and essence.

3. *Jesus Christ is and must be God in order to afford a proper Representation of God to us.* God chose to make Himself known by an IMAGE or Representation adapted to our feeble powers; and whom shall He send for this purpose? You know a man cannot impersonate an angel, any more than a horse or a sheep can be made to act like a man; still less can the highest angel suitably represent God. But one man may represent another man, both being on the same level. So the only fit Representative of the Divine Being must be one of the Divine Persons. Else the representation would fall below the mark, and only mislead those whom it was meant to instruct. But now the honor of the Great Three-in-One can be safely trusted in the hands of One of the Three. God therefore sends His Only Begotten Son to be His Image. No less a Person can represent Him, and nothing less than His dying for us on the cross can fully exhibit the love of God. In Jesus Christ all God's Greatness, all His Glory, all His Goodness is gathered up, as it were, into a finite space that we may comprehend it. How kind it is of the Great Eternal to send us so Glorious a likeness of Himself. It is His picture set in a frame—all the fullness of the Godhead in a human body. Let us study every feature of God's beautiful character as it is displayed in the life and words and actions of Christ, and so become acquainted with God through Him.

Surely every thoughtful person must long to be acquainted with the Lord of all things. The Emperor Trajan one day said to Joshua the Jewish Rabbi, "You say your God is everywhere, but you boast that he resides peculiarly among your people—I should like to see Him."

"God's presence is indeed everywhere," said Joshua, "but He is invisible; no mortal eye can behold His glory." But still the emperor urged him, till he said, "Well, come with me. I will first show you one of His ambassadors."

He led him into the open air. It was the hour of noon, and the sun looked down from a cloudless sky.

"Now," said the Rabbi, "look steadfastly at the sun."

"How can I, man? The light dazzles my eyes and blinds me."

"Art thou unable to endure the light of one of God's creatures? And yet dost thou expect to behold the infinitely brighter glory of the Creator? Such a sight would not dazzle thee only—it would destroy thee; for thus it is written, 'Thou canst not see My face; there shall no man see Me and live.'" Ah, the Jewish Rabbi known as the Lord Jesus, He would have been able to furnish Trajan with a better answer. He would have proclaimed *Him* as the only proper Manifestation of God. Thus, when Philip, the disciple of our Lord, said, "Show us the Father, and we shall be satisfied," Jesus said unto him, "Have *I* been so long time with you, and yet hast thou not known *Me*, Philip? He that hath seen Me hath seen the Father." He had before said, "He that seeth Me seeth Him that sent Me," but Philip had forgotten this.

"Sir," said a poor woman to Mr. Cecil, "I have no notion of God. You talk to me about God, but I cannot get a single idea that is satisfactory."

"But" replied the clergyman, "you can conceive of Jesus Christ as a Man, can you not? Now just think, God comes down to you in Him, full of condescension and love."

"Yes, sir. That gives me something to lay hold on. There my mind can rest, I think I *can* apprehend God in His Son."

"Well then keep to that, and remember that God was in Christ reconciling the world to Himself, not imputing their trespasses unto them."

That seems a bold prayer that Moses offered up, "I beseech Thee, show me Thy glory." Yet it was a very acceptable one. And God is willing to show you this great sight too, even the glory of the God of Israel in the face of His Beautiful SIMILITUDE Jesus Christ. Urge the prayer, and see if God will not cause all His glory to pass before you. Ye who are fond of studying the beauty of the works of God, Oh say, will ye not like to behold the Beauty of the Lord Himself? Come then to the Son, for He it is who must reveal Him. Say, "Show *me* the Father," for such a sight will suffice to make you happy here, and will still surpass your expectations forever. And when you go to the house of God, offer David's prayer, "One thing have I desired of the Lord, that will I seek after, that I may behold the Beauty of the Lord while I inquire in His temple." If you have no such desires as these, it is because you are still like the "natural man who discerneth not the things of God." Your mind is dark and your understanding blinded. Away then to Christ, and beg for that "eye salve" of which He speaks—spiritual discernment. Say to Him, "Son of David! Light of the World! grant that I may receive sight."

Thus we have inquired how Jesus Christ is the IMAGE OF THE INVISIBLE GOD. God's Infinite Nature can never be explained to us. But Jesus Christ comes to exhibit in Himself all we can know of it; to temper the too dazzling rays of the Godhead, that we may not be afraid, but meekly acquaint ourselves with Him. In this sense He is "IMMANUEL."

But before we speak of this, let us pause an interval to recognize two or three august Titles pertaining to the Godhead of the Lord Jesus. First, He is

INVISIBLE. In 1 Timothy 6:15, 16, we find these sublime words applied to Him, "The Blessed and Only Potentate, the King of kings, and Lord of lords, Who only hath immortality, *dwelling in the light which no man can approach unto; Whom no man hath seen or can see*, to Whom be honor and power everlasting." And in 1 Timothy 1:17, we read, "Now unto the King Eternal, Immortal, INVISIBLE, the

Only Wise God, be honor and glory forever and ever." That all this unquestionably refers, in the first instance, to the Lord Jesus Christ, is proved by the connection in which it occurs. But it evidently embraces also the entire unity of the Godhead, and belongs alike to each distinct Person of the adorable Trinity. The Divine nature of Christ is equally INVISIBLE and Incomprehensible with that of the Almighty Father and the Holy Spirit.

But you ask, perhaps with some feeling of perplexity, is there not downright contradiction here? Christ the IMAGE OF THE INVISIBLE GOD, Seen of angels, Manifest in the flesh, and yet Himself INVISIBLE? How can these things be reconciled or explained? Reconciled they can be—explained never. Consider what is written as to the Divine Essence: none can by searching find it out. Who can *see* that which fills immensity and inhabits eternity? But from the moment when Christ assumed the office of Mediator, He is "God manifest in the flesh." In His visible Manhood He is the Representative and IMAGE OF THE INVISIBLE GODHEAD. For "In Him dwelleth all the fullness of the Godhead bodily." Yet, in its essence, His Deity must forever remain INVISIBLE and Inscrutable. No man hath seen Him or can see Him. But now let us glance at another of His Divine Attributes. He Who, as to the one nature was *born*, is as to the other Eternal and

IMMORTAL (1 Tim. 1:17). And again, "He only hath Immortality" (1 Tim. 6:16).

We speak both of God and man as IMMORTAL. But while the One is the Great Lord and Originator of Immortality, to the other it will be communicated by degrees as to a dependent creature. The One inhabits it as He inhabits infinite space. The other passes into it from stage to stage. But since, when we think of underived, absolute Immortality, we feel lost in a blaze of dazzling light, let us try rather to get some idea of what our own Immortality will be. Not everlasting duration merely. Think what growth there will be in our capacities, what a constant building up on the past, till the stature of the glorified spirit will reach to something stupendous. As Dr. Bushnell writes, "Take for example the memory. As we pass on there will be more and more to remember, till there shall be gathered into the storehouse of the soul more than is now contained in all the libraries of the world!" And all our faculties will have a similar power of expansion. How will the understanding grow while still occupied in ever enlarging visions of God! How love will increase by that on which it feeds! What inconceivable transformations from glory to glory will the soul experience, while still it gazes on the dazzling Original which itself is to reflect! If such the grandeur of each separate individual instance or stream of Immortality, what will the great aggregate be, when the participants will be numbered by countless millions? And what must the great Fountain be, which forever and forever will maintain the overflowing supply? But there is yet another Title which we must appropriate to Christ for the same reasons.

INCORRUPTIBLE (Rom. 1:23). He is incapable of deterioration. His power can know no decay, His wisdom can never be at fault. His righteousness cannot fail. Nothing outside Himself can affect Him. What can He gain by injustice or respect of persons? "An infinite Being with boundless resources, by what conceivable motives can He be swayed, under what temptation can He possibly come to do anything inconsistent with the most stainless rectitude?" He is the INCORRUPTIBLE God.

Let us stay here just to make a passing remark. Though in many qualities we are necessarily unlike God, in this, at least, redeemed man will hereafter resemble Him. He shall be Incorruptible. Already there is the germ of this. He is born again "of incorruptible seed." The Christian, alas, may and often does sin. The new nature never. "Whatsoever is born of God overcometh the world." "His seed remaineth in him." And that "good thing in his heart," is destined to a glorious development in the next world. There, untempted and untemptable, incorruptible and incapable of falling, he will shine in the beauty of the Lord forever. What a radiant future is thus outspread before the Christian! How elevating and sanctifying this glorious hope of His calling! But now we pass on to

IMMANUEL, God with us (Isa. 7:14; Matt. 1:23). Now, is it not a strange and fearful thing that men should despise as they do this wonderful contrivance of God to make His creatures acquainted with Himself? And yet at first sight it seems to be just the very thing they have been feeling after in all ages. For,

First. Did they not seem to desire a God who could sympathize with them? Yes, for they loved to represent Him as a Being of like passions with themselves. And yet when God met this wish and actually came down as low as possible, even in the very form and nature of man, they turned away from Him with contempt.

Secondly. Was it not because they grew weary of worshiping an *invisible* Being, that they made to themselves graven images? "Yea, they changed the glory of God into an image made like to corruptible things," on purpose that they might have some outward form before their eyes. But when Jesus Christ actually came to man, the EXPRESS IMAGE, the Living Form of God, they shut their eyes and refused to acknowledge the glory that shined in Him.

Thirdly. Did they not yearn after familiar converse with God? It was not enough to have images of their gods in their temples—they must have them in their houses; yea they would even carry them in their bosoms. But that very boon, the thought of which they professed to love so much, they rejected when God sent His Son on purpose to be IMMANUEL, GOD WITH US.

GOD WITH US! How full of meaning is this Title! Let us look into it a little. To be "*without* God in the world," is to be in the most wretched state imaginable. To have God *against* us, is so terrible as not to be thought of without consternation. But to have God *with* us, is to have everything that can insure our well-being in all conditions of life and death. For an army in the thick of the fight, and just ready to give way at the fierce onset of the foe, to hear the sudden shout, "The general is come! The king is with us!" how inspiriting! Such a cry in such a crisis has many a time entirely changed the fortune of the day. "Little boy, why are you so calm? Do you not see how fearfully the crested waves are falling? Hear you not the wind how it howls? And mark the seamen as they toil at the oar, do they not look pale with dread and disquietude?" Thus whispered one amidst the dangers of a storm at sea to a child sitting by his side. "Aha!" said the boy, "do you wonder why I feel so easy? See there! *My father is with us!* He it is who guides the helm." An industrious man strove in vain to make his way in his native land, and determined to "emigrate." When we heard it we said, "How sad and lonely to go so far from his friends!" "Oh! but all his family, wife, sons, daughters, and many more beside, cousins and acquaintances, are going along with him." "Oh!" said we, "that alters the matter."

So then, soldiers struggling at the cannon's mouth revive at the mention of their leader's name. The little boy, only half alive to his danger amid the raging sea, is calm because his father guides the vessel. The immigrant to strange shores hardly feels his exile, because around him are smiling faces and familiar forms and sympathizing friends, whose company solaces him. How much more must the Christian soldier, the Christian voyager, the Christian exile for his father's house, feel the sweetness of that word IMMANUEL! The sacred spell, GOD WITH US! Whatever his circumstances, he has always with him the Captain of Salvation, the Everlasting Father, the Omnipresent Companion. Is he in poverty or sickness? Is he lonely or deserted? Is he even just entering the valley of death? It is a cordial to his heart when one whispers in his ear that delightful word, "IMMANUEL."

There is a poor lad yonder who works hard for his living. He rises early and is often up till very late. And after all he scarce gets enough to keep him. His crust is oft moistened only with a little water, and his clothes are mended all over. But still he strives. Well, brave boy! we honor you for your contentment and your industry. Is there nothing in what we have said to suit you? What! would it be no comfort to reflect, when you bend beneath a heavy load, or pant over your work under the hot summer sun, or turn your weary steps homeward at dusk—would there be no consolation in the thought, "Jesus Christ is 'with me,' here in the field? He does not despise such a lowly one as I am. He many a time wearied Himself with hard work and long foot-journeys. He was often hungry and thirsty, and thankful for a piece of bread or a broiled fish from the basket of some loving follower, and was glad to sleep at night in a boat or a mountain crevice, or *any* place where He could lay His Head: and He, who once stooped to all the lowliness of such a life, is here now. I can speak to Him. He hears my whispers. His name is GOD WITH US. Yea, He is God with *me*."—Thus "acquaint yourself with Him, and you shall be at peace; yea, thereby good shall come unto thee." Thus walking with God, "the commonest thing shall appear clothed with beauty and grace; you will learn to take your morsel of bread as a blessing provided by Himself to lengthen life, and a pledge of that better bread with which your soul shall be fed to everlasting life. You will come to regard your neat little home as a shadow of His mansion in glory; your comfortable bed, and your lying down thereon, as a type of leaning your head forever on your Savior's breast; and your clean and refreshing change of garments, as indicating that 'fine linen, clean and white,' with which you shall be clothed forever."

Remember then this lovely Title of our Lord, "IMMANUEL, GOD WITH US." Read it as you will, it is most sweet. You may read it—GOD WITH *US* (laying the stress on the last word), and you will remember of the delightful fact that He is God INCARNATE, or made flesh, God in *our* nature, not in the nature of angels. Or read it—*GOD* WITH US; then you will be directed to the glorious truth that however great His condescension, He is still the True God whose Name is I AM THAT I AM. Or read it—GOD *WITH* US; then you will think of Him as God *at* our side to be an INTERPRETER or INSTRUCTOR; and *on* our side to be an INTERCESSOR who ever liveth to plead on our behalf—and if God be for us, who can be against us? Let us look more particularly at the three Titles just mentioned. I have said that to Christ belongs that most magnificent Name (EJAH) "I AM THAT I AM."

I AM THAT I AM. You will find it in Exodus 3:14. The angels, you know, are God's messengers. In the Old Testament you often read of their visits to good men. But there was one Glorious Angel who was known by the Name, "the Angel of Jehovah," or the Angel Jehovah. It was He who appeared to Moses in the bush, and said, "I am the God of your fathers." Observe, the Glorious Angel did not say, I am come from the God of your father, but I AM THE GOD. Moses was very much amazed, but when he recovered himself he asked the Glorious Angel to tell him His Name. And this was the answer, I AM THAT I AM. That Great Angel was the Lord Jesus. For He applied this Name to Himself when He told the Jews, "Before Abraham was I AM"; and again, "If ye believe not that I AM, ye shall die in your sins." And what does this great Name signify? Oh none can explain it. But it certainly includes the following particulars—

1. He is SELF-EXISTENT, that is, He lives by His own power. He maintains His Own Life, which only God can do.

2. He is ETERNAL. I AM—not I was or shall be. He lived infinite ages before anything was brought into being. There was a point in eternity when every cre-

ated thing began to be, and before that He could say in a peculiar sense, "I AM all the universe."

3. He is UNCHANGEABLE. He always will be what He always was. He does not grow wiser every year as we do. Millions of years ago He knew as much as He does now. And He knows everything that will happen in every future year of time and all through the ages of eternity, so that never having occasion to alter His plans, "He is in one mind, and who can turn Him?"

4. He is INCOMPREHENSIBLE. "I AM THAT I AM," What no man, no angel, shall ever be able by searching to find out. We can say much about what He *is not*, but what He *is* can neither be described nor imagined. Our strongest words fall infinitely short of the truth. But once more,

5. He is ALL-SUFFICIENT. When Moses was directed to go to his people he said to God, "They will ask Who sent me? what is His Name? and what shall I tell them?" "Tell them," said God, "I AM hath sent you." "He doth not say (writes Bishop Beveridge) 'I am their Light, their Guide,' but only 'I AM.' He sets His hand as it were to a blank, that His people may write under it what they please that is good for them. As if He should say—Are they weak? I AM strength. Are they poor? I AM riches. In trouble? I AM comfort. Sick? I AM health. Have they nothing? I AM all things. I AM power, wisdom, mercy. I AM glory, beauty, holiness. Whatever is desirable to them, that I AM. Whatever is great, good, or needful to make them happy—that I AM.

And if some anxious inquirer, who has been long groping in the dark after the way to true peace but cannot find it, and is wondering how he can be relieved of the load of guilt which presses so heavily upon his heart; if such a one is eagerly asking, "Who can dissipate this gloom and lead me forth to daylight and liberty?" let him know that there is only One who can do this thing. Only He Who claims to be the Revealer of this very mystery (as of all others), and Who says of Himself, "I AM the Light of the world: whoso followeth Me shall not walk in darkness but have the light of life."

In Job 33:22, we read of one brought down to the gates of the grave. His sickness is painful enough, but his great distress is about his soul. How shall man be just with God? is the awful question which troubles him most. This painful solicitude is not uncommon; oh that it were still more frequently met with!

Suppose some friend reads the Word of God to one in this state of mind, and explains God's way of saving sinners and the methods of His grace. He may have the tongue of the learned, and even know how to speak a word in season to him that is weary, yet, if the veil is still on the heart of the anxious one, can the instructor apply the word of promise or insure the entrance of the consolation which he seeks to convey? Ah no!

In vain Thy creatures testify of Thee
Till Thou proclaim Thyself. Theirs is indeed
A teaching voice; but 'tis the praise of Thine
That whom it teaches, it makes prompt to learn.

The poor, disconsolate soul requires something that the All-sufficient I AM alone can supply. If He be at hand, there is immediate relief. "If there be a MESSENGER with him, an INTERPRETER, ONE AMONG A THOUSAND, to show unto man His uprightness," then his soul is delivered from the pit. Now this Welcome Messenger is the Lord Jesus Christ. He is this INTERPRETER.

INTERPRETER (Job 33:23). Make room for Him. He and no other one knoweth the secret avenues, which lead to the inner man, the recesses of the heart. And His sole prerogative it is to *give* the peace of which other interpreters can only *speak*. His is the voice that saith, "Peace to him that is near and to him that is far off, and I will heal him." "The hour is come, and now is, when the dead hears the voice of the Son of God and lives and believes." Straightway, ere he is aware, the wondering soul finds the coveted peace diffusing itself within and filling him with new and unknown delight. Fresh feelings well up like those of childhood or youth, when everything looked bright as the light of the morning; and henceforth "he will pray unto God and He will be favorable unto him, and he shall see His face with joy." But what did the INTERPRETER do to him? He "showed unto him His uprightness," that is, a righteousness which would satisfy the law, and clothed in which he might appear upright and without dread before the judgment throne. And whose righteousness was this? Not the sinner's own. That was but filthy rags. Surely not *that*, but the Savior's.

One Sunday morning there lay a young man in his sick chamber alone, and with the Bible before him. Long time he had been distressed about his soul; he had sought the Lord sorrowing, but had found no rest. There had been all along a mist before the eyes of his mind, so that he could not understand the gospel or apply it to his own case. But that morning the mist all at once passed away. He was in a new world. He had just been praying to God to remove his perplexities and "show him His salvation." After which he opened his Bible and read John 14 till he came to the sixth verse, "I am the Way, the Truth, and the Life; no man cometh unto the Father but by Me." On reading this the darkness suddenly cleared off, and the way of salvation opened before him, appearing as plain as previously it had been obscure. He saw that Jesus Christ was waiting to save *him*, and wondered he had never seen it before. He felt that he had only to *go* to Christ and to fall into His hands, renouncing all his own righteousness, and God would freely, fully, and forever, justify and save him. Oh how glad he felt! How the tears coursed each other down his cheeks—tears of sacred joy—while he thanked the INTERPRETER again and again for his lovingkindness, exclaiming,

This is the way I long have sought,
And mourned because I found it not;
Till late I heard my Savior say,
"Come hither, soul, I am the Way."

Lo! glad I come, and Thou, Blest Lamb,
Shalt take me to Thee as I am;
My sinful self to Thee I give,
Nothing but love shall I receive.

But whence this great change? Was there any new revelation? Did the young man hear a voice from heaven? Had he read anything in the Bible that he had never seen there before? Nothing of the kind. This was the secret—the "INTER-PRETER" was "with him." He Who could make rough places plain, and crooked things straight, removed all his objections, opened his understanding that he might understand the Scriptures, and satisfied him that God's thoughts toward him were thoughts of peace and not of evil. Life and light accompanied the word, and a power, which made his heart vibrate. Unbelief and darkness fled away, and gratitude filled his breast. His soul was "flooded with a wondrously luminous joy; and its whole horizon was filled with light, the light of Christ revealed within."

And, my friends, I say not you must have precisely this experience, but you must have some degree of this inward light or you will never see the kingdom of God nor understand the Bible. A commentary is a very good thing. It is very necessary that ministers and teachers should expound the Word. But there must also be an *inward light* imparted by the Divine INTERPRETER. "Wherefore awake thou that sleepest, and rise from the dead, and Christ shall give thee light." Then you shall become a "disciple indeed," and shall not only have Him *at* your side as an INTERPRETER, but *on* your side as your "INTERCESSOR."

INTERCESSOR. It is written, "He wondered that there was no INTERCESSOR, therefore His own arm brought salvation" (Isa. 59:16). We read also that "He maketh intercession for the transgressors"; and says, "Deliver them from going down to the pit, I have found a ransom."

Before a bench of judges in ancient Rome there appeared one day a supplicant with only one arm. He asked the life of his brother lying under sentence of death, justly condemned by the laws of the country. "But," inquired they, "what reason hast thou to show, what sufficient argument to offer, on the ground of which thy brother should be spared?" The Intercessor made no answer, for his brother's crime could not be extenuated; but he silently threw off his cloak from his shoulders, and held up the stump of his lost arm. The judges felt the appeal, for this man had fought valiantly to deliver his country from foreign enemies, and in that conflict had become thus maimed. The plea was irresistible; his request was granted; the brother's life was spared. So Jesus Christ, our Brother, appears before the Majesty of Heaven *for us*, acknowledges the justice of our sentence, but shows the wounds in His hands and His feet. The Father beholds Him "like a Lamb that has been slain."

> Five bleeding wounds He bears,
> Received on Calvary;
> They pour effectual prayers,
> They strongly speak for me;
> "Forgive him, oh forgive," they cry.
> "Nor let that ransomed sinner die."

Those wounds have satisfied Justice, paid the demands of the Law, and made amends to the Glory of God. His plea prevails, and the offender is forgiven. Would you have Him for *your* INTERCESSOR? Read in John 17:9, 20 *how* He maketh intercession, and for *whom*. "I pray not for the world, but for them whom Thou hast given Me out of the world, and for them who shall believe on Me through their word." If then you "believe on Him,"—joyful thought!—you are one for whom He intercedes. Nor can He fail of success. "Who is he that condemneth? It is Christ that died, yea rather that is risen again, who also maketh intercession for us."—Now review the principal points in this Reading and see what you can learn from it.

1. *You see the wickedness of Image worship whether Popish or Pagan.* Christ only is the True IMAGE OF GOD, not in His *Human Person* so much as in His *Divine Character*, which we cannot see with the eyes of the body, but with those of the mind.

2. *You see the impiety of all those who refuse to honor Christ as they honor the Father*, since, being God's Exact Image He must be His EQUAL; besides which He distinctly claims the incommunicable Title of the Godhead, I AM; and is IMMORTAL, INVISIBLE, INCORRUPTIBLE.

3. *You see where you will find sympathy and relief in all your temptations.* IMMANUEL can *feel* for you, for He has been in similar circumstances, God in our nature; and He can *help* us because He is Jehovah, always WITH US in our humble homes and when we go abroad; WITH US in the dark, silent, sleepless night, and through the weary, laborious day; WITH US in all the busy scenes of life and in the lonely valley of death.

4. *You see that human teaching alone is insufficient to enlighten the mind, and remove the dark cloud of indifference and guilt.* Christ Himself must instruct each individual learner *personally* in the truth, and without this none will learn the way of salvation. O Thou Divine INTERPRETER! Let Thy Spirit be with each one

of us, to open our eyes, to remove our difficulties, to persuade and incline us to receive Thy atonement and submit to Thy righteousness.

5. *You see the certainty of the believer's salvation.* He has God on his side as INTERCESSOR, Whose honor is pledged for the security of all for whom He pleads. With such an advocate, who can lose his case?

> For when the grand twelve-million jury
> Of our sins, with direful fury
> 'Gainst our souls black verdicts give,
> Christ pleads His death, and so we live.
>   Sir. W. Raleigh

26

Jehovah. Jah. Jehovah-Jireh. Jehovah-Nissi. Jehovah-Shalom. Joseph. Joshua the High Priest.

PROPER names among men are of no use but to identify and distinguish one person from another. They do no describe the person. They do not tell us what is his trade or occupation. They convey no hint whatever of character or rank or standing. They may be and often are altogether out of harmony with either. On the contrary, every Name appropriated to the Divine Being contains unfathomable depths of meaning, and conveys inestimable instruction. There is one Name appropriated to the Almighty that may well be called His Proper Name. It is the Hebrew Title, JEHOVAH.

JEHOVAH. This august Name is incommunicable, and totally inapplicable to any save the Supreme Being of beings. And untranslatable, too. There is no equivalent term in other languages. So that when the apostle would render it into Greek, he writes, "Who was, and Who is, and Who is to come." There are three modifications of the glorious Name—JAH, EJAH, JEHOVAH. Serle says, "The first implies absolute Being. It means HE IS. It only occurs once (Ps. 68:4). The second, EJAH, being in the future tense, means HE SHALL BE. This also occurs but once (Ex. 3:14), where it is translated I AM THAT I AM (see last Reading). The third, JEHOVAH, includes the past, the present, and the future."

Who can search out the meaning of this Lofty Name? When we have said that it is the Symbol which stands in the Hebrew tongue for the Eternal, Independent, Self-subsistent One, the sole Source of Life and its Preserver, we feel how feeble words are to express ideas so sublime.

Let us here refer you to some Scripture proofs that this great Name belongs to Jesus of Nazareth. You need scarcely be told that wherever the word "Lord" is printed in small capitals (LORD) the word so translated is JEHOVAH in the original language. The Jews were afraid to pronounce that awful Title, JEHOVAH, lest they should be guilty of blasphemy. And to this day, whenever the Jews meet with it in their Scriptures, they say "That Glorious Name," or substitute ADONAI.

The translators of our English Bible have so far respected their example as usually to substitute Lord for it. Now then if you will consult the following passages and *think* over them a little, you will find that He Who is there called JEHOVAH or LORD is no other than Jesus of Nazareth: Zechariah 11:13; Isaiah 33:22; 43:11; Jeremiah 23:5, 6. Compare also Joel 2:27–32, with Acts 2:32, 33; Ps. 68:17, 18, with Ephesians 4:7–10; Isaiah 40:3, with Luke 1:76; Isaiah 6:1–5, with John 12:37–41; Obadiah 1:21, with Luke 1:32, 33; Zechariah 14:9, with Revelation 11:15. And these are but few among many.

In Psalm 68:4, it is said, "He rideth upon the heavens by His Name

JAH. "By which metaphorical description is expressed the great fact that He controlleth all the powers of the universe by virtue of the grand properties which the Name imports; disposing and molding them all to His will, just as the prowess of a skillful horseman bridles and curbs the movements of a fiery steed.

The elements of nature obey His behests; and tempests scour the main, and earthquakes shake the solid earth, and famine and pestilence stalk abroad, to chastise crime or discipline to repentance; all alike fulfilling His purpose whether of justice or mercy.

Political and national elements are subject to Him. When wars and revolutions sweep across a continent, when kingdoms are subverted and crowns are rolled in the dust, it is He Who guideth all to wise and merciful issues.

Moral and spiritual powers are subservient to His command. The wrath of man is made to praise Him. The *good* angel is sent forth to minister not only to Elijahs and Daniels, but to you and to me. And the *bad* angel is arrested in hot pursuit with the question, "Whence comest thou?"

In patriarchal times, devout worshipers, when they received some surprising token of Divine favor, were accustomed to call upon God by a new name; or they made some appropriate addition to the original name, as a memorial of the remarkable event. For instance, when Hagar fled into the wilderness, an Angel came to the fountain beside which she sat, and spake comfortably to her. But before the interview was finished, His words betrayed the presence of a greater than angels, even Jehovah Himself. And in that august presence, overwhelmed with a gratitude that almost swallowed up the feeling of awe, she said, "Thou God seest me. Have I wandered hither to find that my master's God is no respecter of persons, and that he doth not overlook, much less despise, even Sarai's outcast slave?" And she devoutly invoked Him by a new Name, The God of Vision; adding her memorial to the Name *El* (God) by which she knew the Almighty.

So Jacob, having overnight sent his family across the brook, stayed behind for prayer, not dreaming of the surprise which awaited him. During the starlit hours after midnight, there came One to him Whose presence and words were so grateful, that Jacob laid hold of Him to detain Him. The Stranger resisted, and a struggle ensued, in which Jacob kept his hold, till he became aware that the "Traveler Unknown" Whom he held in his tenacious grasp was more than a man, for He did but touch a muscle of his thigh and its strength was withered. "Let Me go," said the Wrestler, "for the day breaketh." But the patriarch, though partially disabled, clung to Him with both arms and "wept and made supplication to Him" (Hos. 12:3–5), and said, "I will not let Thee go." And so he prevailed, and carried away from the field of conflict a new name for himself, and a blessing weightier than all worlds. And as the sun rose and warned him to depart, he tore himself away from the scene of that hallowed interview, halting as he went. But he could not leave the place without stamping a monumental name upon it, Peniel (God's Face); "for there," said he, "I have seen God face to face." The lively impression of that memorable event accompanied him to Shechem. There he built an altar, and called it EL-ELOHE-ISRAEL—God, the God of the prince who had power to prevail with Him.

We see then that when a new name was appropriated to God, it was a usual and very natural practice to secure for it a permanent place in the memory by identifying it with some locality, or attaching it to an altar or a pillar. And thus it was that Abraham had, many years before this, called God JEHOVAH THE PROVIDER, and bestowed the Name on the place where God met him with so signal an interposition, as a memorial thereof.

But what authority is there for appropriating this and the two following compound Titles to Jesus Christ? To this question we answer, First, we have proved that the Title JEHOVAH itself belongs to Him. Therefore, of course, its adjuncts or accents must. Second, those three sacred appendages did but anticipate subsequent equivalent unfoldings of the Redeemer's grace especially in the New Testament; which indeed we need not stay to point out, so numerous are they. And Third, in two of the instances we have a Messenger described as The Angel of the Lord. But that He is at the same time One of the Sacred Three is evident; for when He speaks it is *as God*, and not as one who is only a Messenger from God. A Messenger from God He is; but He also actually *personates* God. He speaks in the first person. And surely none would have dared to do that but He who was God. And this is precisely the office that the Scriptures claim for the Mediator. He is JEHOVAH at the same time that He is the Messenger of JEHOVAH's Covenant.

There are also other appended Titles. The most remarkable are Rofi and Tsidkenu. But as these are not rendered into English in the authorized version, they do not come within the limit of our enumeration. But for the first the reader is referred to PHYSICIAN and for the second to The Lord our RIGHTEOUSNESS.

JEHOVAH-JIREH (Gen. 22:14). The three days occupied by Abraham in the journey from his peaceful homestead to the place appointed for the sacrifice, must have been full of anguish to the patriarch. "Few passages in literature," writes Dr. Dykes, "carry a deeper pathos than the words which tell how, in the fresh dawn, the aged lord of the camp crept away on foot out of the midst of his retainers' tents, while the cattle, marshaled with merry call and tinkling bell, were going forth in long strings to their several grazing grounds, and all the landscape grew busy with cheerful stir. How willingly would he have purchased, by the lives of all those lowing herds and bleating flocks, that one dear life which was going forth at his side to return no more! Not to a single soul that we know of did the old man dare to confide his purpose. The entreaties of a mother less resolute than himself might have overborne his firmness. The quieter anguish of a young and gentle heart, shrinking from too early death, might have proved more than he could endure. He must steal, as it were, from his home—the only wretched heart in all that pleasant camp; more wretched for this, that he must dissemble his wretchedness."

The Apostle indeed says, He counted that God was able to raise Isaac from the dead. But for that faith underlying all his troubled thoughts, the trial would have proved insupportable. But did it keep all within perfectly quiet? Far from it, we think. Faith had to wrestle hard with fear and doubt and all the affections and instincts of nature. Had it been otherwise his journey would have been a triumphant progress, and the temptation altogether unreal. But many tumultuous questions must have agitated his bosom all the while. What would Sarai say? How would Isaac meet it? And what will the surrounding heathen think?

To be sure, the sacrifice of children was not unknown among the idolatrous tribes of Canaan. But that made it all the more amazing that Abraham's God should "appear even for a moment to reduce His Own worship to a level with the inhuman rites of Baal." Abraham therefore was for the time left without a single ray of light upon the torturing question, What can be the meaning of this dreadful requisition on the part of Jehovah?

But all this was the dark background on which were to be emblazoned God's faithfulness, and the exhaustless depths of His resources in relation to all human extremities; as well as the greatness of Abraham's peerless act of obedience, and his entire consecration to God. And, may we not add also, the prohibitory lesson (as the same writer suggests), conspicuously taught—not by words, but in accordance with the usage of the age, in scenic fashion—that the True God has no pleasure in such unnatural offerings? "Lay not thy hand upon the child, neither do thou anything unto him."

But when all the bitterness of Abraham's patient endurance was past, and the moment appointed for the interposition arrived, must it not have been like a veritable resurrection even from the dead? "from when, also he received him in a figure."

In the overflowing joy of that memorable experience, did not his faith espy in the future a grander interposition still? So that standing upon "that place," which, if the ancient tradition is correct, was to witness the sufferings of the God-Man, the words were fulfilled, "Your father Abraham rejoiced to see My day; he saw it and was glad." At any rate, it must have been Abraham who first set that saying afloat which has passed into a proverb, "to this day," in the mount Jehovah shall be seen. Does it not read like a prophecy of Christ? especially when taken in connection with "My son, God will provide Himself a lamb for a burnt offering."

But even if we are to restrict all this to providential interpositions, it shows the high order of the patriarch's faith. He might have gasped out, "Thank God, He has helped me thus far"; and there have stopped. But he boldly grasps the conclusion, "The Lord *will* provide. So long as I live that shall be His Name to me; and I will maintain my confidence that in every extremity He will help me." This was worthy of the man who had "offered up his only begotten son, accounting that God was able to raise him up even from the dead."

And do we know of no places that *we* ought to have called by this name? no passages in our history where we ought to have said, "So signal is this answer to prayer, that we will never distrust God again?" Surely there must be many. But perhaps our faith never rose so high as Abraham's. We raised a grateful pillar, and wrote on it, *Thus far*. But our faith died not, like his, embrace the future; and so when the next trial came, we were as full of fear as ever. Let us revisit our sacred places, and call to remembrance this and that memorable incident in our history, when God has made us ashamed of our fears; and so get our faith invigorated for future exigencies. Let us boldly say with Abraham, The Lord *will* provide; and with Paul, "He who delivered us from so great a death, and doth deliver, in Him we trust that *He will yet deliver*."

Therefore, Christian pilgrim, (while carefully guarding against any abuse of thy privilege into which thy lower nature might betray thee), go in this thy might and walk up and down in the Name of the Lord—JEHOVAH-JIREH, The LORD will provide, The LORD will see to it, The LORD will show Himself. The Title includes these three senses and means a great deal more.

Poverty is not an unusual lot of God's children. They would be all rich, they would all live in splendid mansions and ride in gilded chariots, if it were good for them. But indeed it is not. Art thou even now in a strait, not knowing what to do? Art thou without employment? Is thy home smitten with sickness? Does want stare thee in the face? Tell thy trouble to thy PROVIDER. Say to Him, "Thou hast told me to call upon Thee in the day of trouble. Here is an utter extremity. O my Lord, appear for me and show Thy marvelous lovingkindness in this my pressing need." To such as do business in these great waters we say, Only pray in faith and pray without fainting, and you have your Lord's Word: I will deliver.

> Just in the last distressing hour
> The Lord displays delivering power;
> The mount of danger is the place
> Where you shall see surprising grace.

Or doth Satan accuse and harass thy hunted soul? Refer him to Christ and say, The Lord will see to it. Or are you tempted to ask in anticipation of coming storms, What shall I do in the swellings of Jordan? Or what, when this friend is gone and the other resource fails? What if the brook Cherith should cease to flow, or the gourd should wither, or the cruse of oil fail?—then resolutely answer, I do not know what *I* will do, but this I know, *The Lord* will appear.

> In some way or other the Lord will provide;
> It may not be *my* way, it may not be *thy* way,
> But yet in His own way, the Lord will provide.

George Neumarck, a German poet at Hamburg, obtained a livelihood by his violoncello. Becoming ill, he fell into straits. As a last resource he pawned his instrument on hard terms to a Jew. "May I just play one more tune?" asked the desponding musician. "You don't know how hard it is to part with that instrument." He seized it and played with such tenderness that even the Jew was touched. As he played he sang part of his own hymn, "Life is weary; Savior take me." Then he changed the key suddenly and sang again, "Yet who knows? The cross is precious." And then laying down the instrument rushed out of the shop.

In the dark he stumbled against a stranger who had been listening perfectly charmed. "Can you tell me where I can get a copy of that son?" said he. "I'll give a florin for it." "My good friend," said Neumarck, "I will give it to you for nothing." Then the poet told his trouble. The stranger went straight to his master who was an ambassador from some foreign court. He happened just then to want a private secretary, and engaged Neumarck at once. Here was an end to his troubles. He got his instrument out of pawn, and calling his neighbors round him sang to its music his own sweet hymn,

> Leave God to order all thy ways,
> And hope in Him whate'er betide;
> Thou'lt find Him, in the evil days,
> Thine all-sufficient Strength and Guide.
> Who trusts in God's unchanging love,
> Builds on the Rock that nought can move.

JEHOVAH-NISSI, The LORD my Banner (Ex. 17:15), was the new title appropriated to the God of Israel, and inscribed on His altar, on the occasion of a great victory gained by the combination of effort with prayer. Israel fought while Moses made his appeal to God. Only while his hands were lifted up did the enemy give way. A lesson for God's spiritual Israel. Do we find ourselves put to the worse before our foes? Is some lust of the flesh or spirit gaining upon us? covetousness, discontent, irritability? Then there has been some falling off in our prayers. They have declined in spirituality or fervor. We have forgotten to raise our Banner, or surely Amalek would not have prevailed. Let us look to it, lest we encounter disastrous defeat.

Sometimes, however, the danger lies on the other side. One cries day and night, Why art Thou so far from helping me? But is the man helping himself? or has despair paralyzed action? In vain would the hands of Moses have been uplifted if Israel had not fought out the battle. So prayer is useless without corresponding effort. The BANNER is not given to us to be used as a charm, but to encourage hope and incite to effort.

JEHOVAH-SHALOM, The LORD Our Peace (Judg. 6:24). Of this Title also it must be said that it belonged not to Gideon's rude altar, but to the God of the altar. Gideon had just received God's promise, that He would send peace. And this is his response, The Lord our Peace. How often has Gideon's previous complaint been echoed by us!—"O my Lord! if the Lord be with us, why then is all this befallen us?" When business is blighted; when all effort to retrieve our standing fails; when the bank breaks and poverty threatens; when some dear relative, the prop and stay of our hopes, is smitten with death; when temptations assail us, and gloom shrouds our path—unbelief rushes to the conclusion, Surely God hath forsaken us, His dealings falsify His promises, and prayer is useless. But it is no new thing for faith to have fainting fits. It was so with Gideon. He feared he should die immediately after God had assured him of peace. Child of sorrow, be of good courage. He will not only *speak* peace, but *send* peace. "Fear not! thou shalt not die." And soon He will break the rod of thine oppressor, "as in the day of Midian."

Thus all through the ages the Divine Being has been clothing Himself with new Names and Titles. Some claimed by His own authority, some appropriated by grateful, adoring recipients of His grace. And each furnishes a fresh claim to our confidence. Every Name is descriptive of some previously unknown beauty or dimly described characteristic, and all redolent of glory, majesty, and grace. For us it is one thing indeed to read these Titles, and another to know them. But when God Himself "graves the graving thereof," in deep lines upon the heart, while it is quivering in the midst of the fires of some distressing experience— O then, Thou God seest me, JEHOVAH-JIREH, or I am the Way, stands out in the souls' history in indelible inscriptions of living, burning light. Then the believer feels that behind the idea expressed in the words exists the glorious reality itself. He wants not the evidence of his sense nor of outward demonstration. The witness is within; for none could invent such a God, such a Christ! As the sun is its own witness, and the man who can see needs not to be told that it shine, so the

Name of God radiant with its own beauty and glory proves the existence of God—and not only that He is, but that He is what He is. And we rejoice with joy unspeakable and say, "This God is our God forever and ever."

Three historical types of Christ next claim our notice—JOSEPH, JOSHUA the Captain, and JOSHUA the High Priest.

JOSEPH. On the question, Is JOSEPH a type of Christ? The Rev. Andrew Fuller writes, "God prepared the way for the coming of His Son by a variety of *things*, in which the great principles of His undertaking were prefigured. And He pursued the same object by a variety of *persons*, in whom the life and character of Christ were in some degree previously manifested." In the opinion of that sound theologian, JOSEPH claims to be one of those typical persons. Let us trace the parallel in a few leading points.

When Jacob's beloved son was sent by his father to his brethren, "they conspired against him to slay him." So when from the bosom of His Father, Jesus Christ came to His own, they received Him not, but said, "This is the Heir, come let us kill Him."

JOSEPH was sold for twenty pieces of silver, at the suggestion of Judah; and Christ for thirty, by one known by the same name, Judas.

JOSEPH was falsely accused and imprisoned for sins he had never done; "whose feet they hurt with fetters; he was laid in iron. But the king sent and loosed him, and made him lord of his house and ruler of all his substance." Thus he was loaded with honors. Men cried before him, "Bow the knee"; and Pharaoh gave him a new name, Zaphnath-paaneah; which in one dialect is said to mean, Savior of the world, and in another, Revealer of secrets. Both singularly appropriate to one who is to be considered as a Type of Christ. So the Holy One, the Undefiled, was "rejected" and "abhorred"; judged and condemned: and finally led as a lamb to the slaughter. But "God hath highly exalted Him, and given Him a Name which is above every name: That at the Name of Jesus every knee should bow," in earth and in heaven.

Then his care for his brethren's settlement in Goshen recalls to our remembrance our Lord's request, "Father, I will that they whom Thou hast given Me be with Me where I am, that they may behold My glory." And his accumulated stores remind us of Christ, in Whom are all unsearchable riches, and of Whose fullness we receive, and grace upon grace. And Pharaoh's direction to the people when they clamored for food, Go to Joseph, serves as a finger post to us; that whatever strait we are in, whatever pressure lies upon us, we betake ourselves direct to Christ, in Whom are hid all the treasures of wisdom and knowledge, and inexhaustible resources of light and life, power and grace.

Finally, how forcibly do the words of Joseph to his brethren (Gen. 1:20), lead our thought to the dark deeds which earth and hell, Jew and Roman, conspired to perpetrate against the Lord's Anointed, and the hidden purpose of God which did underlie all that mystery of iniquity. "Ye thought evil against me," said Joseph, "but God meant it unto good, to bring to pass as it is this day, to save many people alive." So of Christ, Peter said to His murderers, "Him being delivered by the determinate counsel and foreknowledge of God, ye have taken and by wicked hands have crucified and slain" (Acts 2:23, 24). Wicked men acted with all possible freedom in just carrying out the atrocious devices of their own malicious hearts. But all the while "God meant it for good, to save many people alive." And now through this Crucified "Man is preached to every creature the forgiveness of sins; that by Him all who believe might be justified from all things." Turn we now to JOSHUA, the Captain of the hosts of Israel.

JOSHUA was a man of irreproachable character and eminent loyalty to God. But it is not that which places him amongst the Personal Types of our Lord, but the post he occupied and the great service he rendered as the Successor of Moses and the Subjugator of Canaan. His name was originally Oshea, but was changed to Jehoshua, which is synonymous with Jesus. No doubt this was done by the same authority that gave him his commission.

Nor were there wanting many authentications thereof, in the way of miraculous interposition. There was first that dryshod march across the bed of the Jordan of two or three million people, at a time when that deep and rapid river had overflowed all its banks; its breadth increasing from twenty yards, its ordinary channel, to a quarter of a mile, with corresponding increase of depth and augmented force of current. But that enormous volume of water was so disposed of as to leave the bed of the torrent dry while the tribes passed over.

Then followed the supernatural fall of the walls of Jericho, assailed as they were only by the trumpets of the priests and the shouts of the people. And there was, besides this, much miraculous help vouchsafed in the subjugation of the people. Witness the startling miracle implied in the command (Josh. 10:12, 13):

> Sun, stand thou still upon Gibeon,
> And thou, Moon, in the valley of Ajalon!

There are those who would have us suppose that this is no more than a quotation from a collection of natural songs, which they seem to regard as of about as much authority as the old English ballads which celebrate the doings of Robin Hood. But we dare not allow ourselves such serious liberties with the narrative.

Whatever allowances we are to make for the exaggerated diction of poetry, there remains proof enough that we are in the presence of some great miracle wrought in compliance with Joshua's prayer, when, in the hearing of the people, "he spake to the Lord." But the manner of its accomplishment is not indicated. It is possible the light was prolonged for many hours by means of refraction produced by natural causes, in strict accordance with the laws that govern the diffusion of light. But it seems more probable that the effect was due rather to some supernatural suspension of those laws. Either would be easy enough to the Almighty. If the latter, we are confronted with a miraculous intervention as marked in the drought in answer to Elijah's prayer, or the fire from heaven which consumed his sacrifice. But that the result was as here described, however produced, namely, the continuance of daylight for many hours beyond the usual time, it requests great effrontery to deny. To do so, we think, impugns the authority of Scripture.

We need not race the parallel between Joshua the Captain of the Israelites, and Jesus the Captain of Salvation, further than to say, The first was a type of the last, in that he was divinely named, divinely commissioned, divinely encouraged and sustained. He was constituted Leader of the Lord's host, and was appointed sole Judge and Umpire in determining the lot of each of the tribes and families of Israel, and settling them in the land of Canaan (Josh. 1:2–6).

But, however important the operations of Joshua, and admirable his fidelity, the mission and work of the Type have no glory by reason of the glory which so greatly excelleth. For the commission of the Great Captain of our salvation embraced not three million Jews and their descendants only. That "was a light thing" indeed contrasted with *this;* which involves the spiritual interests of the whole world, now and to all eternity. Nor will He leave the many sons whom He is bringing to glory, till He hath subdued all their foes, led them through death, and settled them in their heavenly inheritance.

> One army of the Living God,
>   To His command we bow;
> Part of the host have crossed the flood,
>   And part are crossing now.
>
> Our spirits too shall quickly join
>   Their ranks with glory crowned,
> And shout to see our Captain's sign,
>   To hear His trumpet sound.

Besides this Joshua, there is another spoken of by Zechariah.

JOSHUA THE HIGH PRIEST (Zech. 3:6). He was associated with Zerubbabel the prince in rebuilding the temple, and was the first to exercise the High Priest's office therein. When Cyrus gave permission to the captive Jews to return from Babylon to their own land, only a portion of them were willing to embrace the offer. Multitudes preferred to remain where they were. Yet they did not renounce their religion, nor forget the temple of God, but continued to send from time to time valuable gifts and offerings. When the first deputation of this sort arrived at Jerusalem, the prophet was directed to take the treasures from their hands, and cause the precious metal to be melted down and formed into two crowns. And then, before the eyes of these messengers, he was to place both crowns on the head of Joshua (or Jesus), the miter and the coronet; indicative, the one of priestly and the other of regal authority. Then he was to bid them behold in JOSHUA a Representative of Him whose Name is the BRANCH, the Messiah (Zech. 6:12, 13).

> Behold the Man Whose Name is the BRANCH;
> And He shall grow up out of His place.
> And He shall build the temple of the Lord;
> Even He shall build the temple of the Lord;
> And He shall bear the glory,
> And shall sit and rule upon His throne;
> And He shall be a Priest upon His throne;
> And the counsel of peace shall be between Them both.

After this ceremony the crowns were to be laid up in the temple, a perpetual memorial of this transaction, and a material sign of the coming of the Messiah. Not only would those messengers carry back to Babylon "the gospel" which had been in this way preached to them, but many would ask the meaning of this twofold coronation at Jerusalem, where it was enacted; and many more in future times would ask why those two crowns were preserved with such care; and by the interest thus excited there would be begotten and kept alive in thoughtful minds the expectation of Christ's appearing; and the truth would also be impressed upon them, that He would come *as a Priest to offer sacrifice,* as well as a King to rule. The whole was thus a grand scenic prophecy of the work of God's Anointed King and Mediator.

But do we not understand that prophecy much better than they? The tender BRANCH did sprout and grow up out of His appointed place, Bethlehem. And we know Him as the sole Foundation and Cornerstone of the temple (Zech. 3:9). As the great Master-builder, He is rearing the church from age to age. He had indeed first to endure the cross and the shame. But now He "wears the glory," an exceeding weight of glory. And He sits a Priest upon His throne, in the "true sanctuary which the Lord pitched and not man," where alone His priestly office can be exercised. He rules as a King at the same time that He intercedes as Priest. Nor will He abandon His priesthood up there till there will be no longer upon earth any who need His services "in things pertaining to God." His unchangeable priesthood can be no more abrogated than transferred, till the last soul shall have been saved that is ordained to eternal life.

Thus have we glanced at three typical persons, each illustrious in his own destined department, and each honored by being at the same time a Representative of Him who was to come. They were like the golden clouds which we have seen clustering in the east ere the sun has risen, and which vanished at his presence. Each personal type transmitted a reflected ray or two to keep expectation alive. But when the Sun of Righteousness appeared, they were alike lost in His all-absorbing effulgence.

> The TRUE MESSIAH now appears,
>> The types are all withdrawn;
> So fly the shadows and the stars
>> Before the rising dawn.

> JOSEPH the Savior so renowned
>> That title bears no more;
> THE WORLD'S REDEEMER we have found,
>> Let all the world adore!

> JOSHUA must both his crowns disown,
>> And doff his priestly vest,
> For CHRIST Himself ascends the throne,
>> The SOVEREIGN and the PRIEST.

> The elder JOSHUA too lays by
>> His helmet, sword, and shield;
> A loftier standard waves on high,
>> For JESUS takes the field.

27

Jesus. Just.

THE Bible tells us that no man hath seen God at any time. No one ever heard His voice or saw His shape. But do we not read that God *appeared* to Abraham, that Moses *saw* the God of Israel, that Jacob *wrestled* with Him, and said directly afterwards, "I have *seen* God face to face!" What then must we suppose? Why surely that the Divine Nature is indeed *invisible,* but that the Second Person in the Godhead, JESUS, who is called the IMAGE OF THE INVISIBLE GOD, did put on his bodily form from time to time; and thus gave His people an earnest of His future, more wonderful appearance upon the earth. And how delightful were those visits! An old-fashioned poet, George Herbert, says,

> Sweet were the days when Thou didst lodge with Lot,
> Struggle with Jacob, sit with Gideon,
> Advise with Abraham; when Thy power could not
> Encounter Moses' strong complaints and moan,
>   Thy words were then, Let Me alone.

> One might have sought and found Thee presently
> At some fair oak, or bush, or cave, or well;
> Is my God this way! No, they would reply,
> He is to Sinai gone as we heard tell;
>   List, ye may hear great Aaron's bell.

Ah! those days were sweet indeed! but sweeter far were "the days of the Son of Man," when He was seen in Judea, day after day, walking about the country and healing all manner of diseases. *Before,* He had but "turned aside as a wayfaring man just to tarry for a night." But *now* He becomes flesh, and *dwells* among men. Formerly He only called on one and another to converse awhile, as a prince might with one of his subjects; but now He stoops to be born one of the family, and joins His glorious nature to that of the little, smiling Babe of the manger at Bethlehem. For thus it was spoken to Joseph concerning Mary, "She shall bring forth a Son, and thou shalt call His name JESUS; for He shall save His people from their sins" (Matt. 1:21).

JESUS. This was the proper name of the Son of Mary amongst men. It was common enough with the Jews; as much so as James or Thomas is among ourselves. But the angel who directed Joseph to call Him JESUS, lifted the name high above the familiar level, by the surprising and most glorious meaning that he attached to it. The world has seen many wonderful births, but none that deserves to be named at all in comparison with this. Consider the first child that was ever born; oh! with what new, joyful feelings must Adam and his wife have gazed upon him! They fancied they already held in their arms the promised Seed! Moses was an extraordinary child, and regarded by his parents as one born for a great work. Then there were Samson and John the Baptist, both announced beforehand by an angel from heaven, and hailed as prodigies by their parents. But whatever peculiar circumstances attended the entrance of these into the world, they were mere human children. But here you see the Great Lord of Angels, the Glorious Ancient of Days, Jehovah Himself, stooping to be born in our nature.

> *This* Infant is the MIGHTY GOD,
>   Come to be suckled and adored;
>   The ETERNAL FATHER, PRINCE OF PEACE,
>   The SON OF DAVID and his LORD.

What a birth is here! Well might the angel say to the shepherds, "Fear not, for I bring GOOD TIDINGS!" and cherubic hosts shout, "Glory to God." Well might the shepherds say, "Let us go now even to Bethlehem to see this great sight,"—and wise men arrive from far countries with gifts and gold, asking, "Where is He?"—and we might old Simeon cry out, "Now let me die for I have held in my arms the greatest Wonder in the world, the Holy Child Jesus." And what an honor was conferred on Mary, that she should be singled out to be the mother of the promised Seed! She might well say, "My soul doth magnify the Lord!" And how highly was little Bethlehem exalted in being made the birthplace of the Savior, and so becoming the most renowned city in the world! But the honor is shared by us all. "He hath put down the mighty from their seats, and exalted them of low degree." There are many thousands of worlds, but *ours* is the favored stage on which the Proprietor of the vast creation ministers to His own creatures. There are, it may be, a thousand different orders of rational beings, inhabitants of those various world, and yet our disgraced and guilty race is the chosen bride of the Son of God. "Unto US the Child is born, unto US the Son is given." And what was the great work, which He came to do: "Thou shalt call His name Jesus; for He shall save His people from their sins."

First, He saves from the GUILT *of sin.* I do not mean that He changes the nature of sin, and makes that innocent which is vile. Sin must always be an abominable thing, an atrocious affront to God. And once committed it can never be undone. But I mean that the moment a sinner receives Christ, his sins are no longer charged to him. They are reckoned to Christ's account, for He suffered for them: while His righteousness is reckoned to the sinner. Thus "by the obedience of One many are made righteous." So there is salvation from the *guilt* of sin. But this is not enough.

Yonder is a garden railed in on all sides; beyond is a field, and in that field there is a deep and dangerous pit. The owner gives his children leave to play in the garden, but cautions them by no means to venture into the field beyond, on pain of his displeasure and severe punishment. Well, to play they all go. By-and-by, one boy, more forward than the rest, sees a butterfly and is determined to have it. So he gets over the rail, and running heedlessly across the field, falls over the sides of the pit. At first he is stunned by the fall, but on coming to himself he makes loud lamentation. His cries draw the attention of the other children, who make haste to report the accident and convey the boy's penitent apology to his affronted parent. Suppose now the father, on hearing the story, merely sends word to him that he *forgives the trespass.* Will that save him? Will a pardon lift him out of the pit and heal his bruises? Not at all. Someone must come with ropes and ladders to get him out. Else, notwithstanding his repentance and forgiveness, he must suffer the penalty of his transgression and be starved to death. And so it is with mankind. It is not enough that they be saved from *guilt,* therefore

Secondly, Jesus saves them from the PUNISHMENT *of sin.* By punishment I mean all those sufferings that flow from sin and are the penal wages of it. Suffering is inseparable from sin, and always follows it. But JESUS comes between the sinner and his punishment, and receives it in Himself. He has borne our griefs and the chastisement due to our sin, and so delivered us from it. He drank the dregs of the cup, which contained the *curse,* leaving none for His followers; for that cup of suffering which is sometimes put into *their* hands contains only wholesome medicine. There is no more *curse* in it. Thus He delivers from punishment. But even this is not all. It is not enough that we be delivered from the *guilt* and *punishment* of sin; something else still is necessary. Therefore

Thirdly, JESUS *saves us from the* POWER *of sin.* An unfaithful servant was imprisoned for robbing his employer; but he found a friend who was willing to pay what he had taken away; and on this footing he asked to be restored to his situation. "No," replied his master, "I do indeed free you from punishment, since the amount stolen away is restored to me; but perhaps you are still a thief at heart, and therefore I can never receive you into my service again." What was wanting in this case that would have made it safe to take back the offender? What? Why a change of disposition; which, you know, no man can produce, and none answer for in another. But JESUS not only pays our debts and delivers us from punishment; He also changes our hearts. He turns the thief into an honest man, the liar into a lover of truth, the swearer into one that feareth an oath. Having raised lost sinners out of the gulf of despair and freed them from condemnation, He cleanses them from the pollution of sin, and delivers them from the power of hurtful lusts and evil tempers and bad habits, and fully reconciles them to God.

Now you must have the whole of this salvation or none at all. All its parts are joined together. And if even it were not so, a *part* of it would be of no service. What good would pardon do you *by itself?* It would leave you in all the filth of your natural state. God could hold no communion with you nor admit you into heaven; or if you were to enter heaven, your unholy disposition would effectually render you miserable. Then what good would regeneration do *by itself?* The burden of sin would still be on your conscience and be recorded against you in God's book. Or of what service would both be, if the pains and sorrows of this life, to say nothing of hell, were entailed on you forever? If therefore you will have Jesus to be a Savior *to you*, it must be in His own way. You must allow Him to take away the love of sin as well as its guilt and its wages. And He cannot and will not save you in any other way; for we read that He is the "JUST ONE."

JUST, and having Salvation (Zech. 9:9). This is a very instructive Title of our Lord. It shows us that He is a HOLY SAVIOR and will have a holy people. He saves *sinners* indeed, but it is that He may purify them and make them "zealous of good works." And His salvation is not only *holy*, but *just* and *honest* too, for He does not save at the expense of God's law. *That* is upheld in all its glory, for He has answered all its demands. Thus His salvation is suited to the taste of the renewed man, who has now a "good and honest heart," and could not bear to be saved in a way dishonorable to God.

An upright man was thrown into prison for debt. There he lay a long time. But one morning the jailer said to him, "Yonder is the door—you are at liberty to depart." "Oh," said the other, "I am glad enough to get out of this doleful place, but tell me how this unexpected release came about." "What matters that?" said the jailer, "You have got your discharge, is it not enough?" "Not exactly; you know there are my creditors, how can I look them in the face or my neighbors either?" "Oh! set your mind quite at rest about your debts; a kind friend has discharged them all the very last farthing; you need not therefore fear to meet your creditors or anyone else; and look! here are all the receipts in full." Ah! that was just what the honest debtor wanted to learn. *His release was an honorable one;* otherwise as an honest man he must hang down his head all his life. But now no one can point to him and say, "There goes a man who has defrauded his creditors."

Now *we* were debtors in prison. And Jesus Christ proposed to redeem us; but He is "JUST AND HAVING SALVATION." Therefore He said to the Law, "What must I give thee, O Law! to let these go? what is the price of their ransom?" The Law made answer that not one of its requirements could be relaxed. It would have "an eye for an eye, and life for life"; perfect obedience or the full penalty. And to these terms the Deliverer agreed. He did not desire our admittance into heaven without making a full reparation for all our trespasses, and establishing our claim to eternal life by His own perfect obedience.

Rejoice then, Christian! "Rejoice greatly, O daughter of Jerusalem! Behold thy King cometh to thee; He is JUST AND HAVING SALVATION." You will not be looked on as an intruder in heaven, who, if strict justice were done, would not be allowed a place there. Oh no! Strict justice *has been* done. The Surety has paid the price and borne the penalty, so that through Him you will have a *righteous claim* to be in heaven, a claim which none can dispute. For to all who receive Him, this JUST ONE "gives *right* to become the sons of God"; and "*right* to eat of the tree of life." Oh do you not admire this just and righteous salvation that Jesus bestows? The just cannot help loving it and glorying in it. But as for you who care nothing about the honor and justice of God so that you may but get to heaven, know that heaven is designed for no such dishonest people.

But now you who love this just salvation, will you not love to praise the Just One who saves so gloriously? Oh! I call upon you all to love this Just Savior more and more; you can never love Him sufficiently. Extol Him to the skies, you can never lift Him high enough; and say to your friends, "Come magnify the Lord with me, and let us exalt Him together; for He hath done great things for us, and Holy is His Name."

In a dark cell there sits a felon, condemned to death, and waiting the hour of execution. The prison bell tolls his knell. Presently it ceases. There is a dead silence. Suddenly he hears steps in the corridor. A key rattles in the lock. The door opens, and a faint, cold shiver convulses the frame of the wretched victim. But instead of the jailer with the dreaded death warrant, a benign-looking stranger enters holding out a pardon, signed and sealed by the Sovereign's own hand. This precious document the visitor has procured by his own intercession. He explains the purport of the paper. What a change immediately occurs in the feelings of the prisoner! He is almost frantic. He falls at the feet of his benefactor, and covers them with kisses and tears. He pours out confused words and broken sentences meant to express a gratitude that cannot be uttered.

When the first overwhelming emotions have passed, the friend sits down to talk with him, and he says, "You must not think this pardon is procured without great expense on my part, of trouble, shame, yea liberty itself. I have even sold myself for a slave for a period of years to procure your release!" Amazement, grief, and gratitude contend together within the breast of the released malefactor. He knows not whether to rejoice at his own escape, or to mourn because of the sufferings he has brought on his deliverer.

But will he ever forget his savior? Will not his very name be precious to him as long as he shall live? Will he ever grow tired of sounding his praises? Yea, can he do less than say (as Ruth to Naomi), "Think not I will ever leave thee or return from following thee; for whither thou goest, I will go; and where thou lodgest, I will lodge. The Lord do so to me and more also, if aught but death part thee and me. I will even share thy toils, dear deliverer, and soothe thy sufferings, and be thy devoted servant forever!"

There was once a ship in mid-ocean, sailing before the wind and cutting her way through the waves at a rapid pace. All at once the cry was heard, "A man overboard!" Every heart sank at the voice; for before the boat could be lowered or the ship brought to, they would have left him far behind. And amidst those mountain waves how should they ever find him again? To add, too, to the difficulty, it was now nearly dark! There was a brave man on board, an excellent swimmer, who saw where he fell, saw him vainly contending with the waves, and felt there was not a moment to be lost. In an instant he threw off his clothes, and calling for the boat to follow him, plunged into the surge. He reached the sinking man just in time to save him from destruction, and succeeded in holding him up till the boat arrived and took them both to the ship. They lifted the half-drowned man on board. They warmed him and rubbed him and give him cordials, and at last succeeded in restoring him.

And do you think he could forget his deliverer? No indeed! His first inquiry was for the man that had saved him. One feeling seemed entirely to absorb his mind, that of gratitude to his deliverer. He clung to his feet. He clasped his knees, and seemed as if he would never loose his hold. It was quite affecting to see him. He poured forth the feelings of his overflowing heart in the most affectionate terms, and told his benefactor over and over again how deeply he felt the debt he owed him. And can you wonder at it? Are you surprised that during the rest of that voyage the saved one could never meet the man who had risked his life for him without the most passionate expressions of love and gratitude? No, you do not wonder at it. It was quite natural that such magnanimous conduct should produce just such a return. But surely you *do* wonder that the salvation of our souls, through the arduous efforts and dreadful sufferings of Christ, does not affect our hearts more than it does. Oh, it *ought* to do so! It is indeed shameful that we require Him so ill for the great love wherewith He has loved us! I pray God to shed abroad His love more and more in your heart and mine. I fear some of you have heard the story of Christ's sufferings and love so often, that it has become like a worn-out tale. Your spirit is not moved by it. Indeed you do not feel so much interested in the story, as in a newspaper report of robberies, or a piece of scandal circulating in your own neighborhood. But what a fearful state of insensibility is this! and how dreadful in such hardness of heart! How shall you be awakened from this state of torpor? Shall I arrest your attention if I remind you that every common blessing comes to you in the channel of Christ's mediation?

> There's not a gift His hand bestows,
> But cost His heart a groan.

Shall I offend you if I say you are more senseless than the brutes? Even the dog requites with gratitude the kindness of his master, and caresses the hand that feeds him. "The ox knoweth his owner and the ass his master's crib," while you, less impressionable than they, remain unmoved by all the kindness God has lavished upon you. Nay, but I will strive to arouse a spark of emulation in your breasts by telling you how the story of redeeming love affected the heart of a heathen when he heard it for the first time.

A missionary sat in the midst of a little circle of South Sea Islanders. He read the Bible to them and talked of JESUS. Presently he came to that verse, "God so loved the world that He gave His Only Begotten Son, that whosoever believeth on Him should not perish but have everlasting life!" On his reading it, one of them started from his seat and exclaimed, "What sounds were those I heard? What words did you read?" The missionary repeated the verse. The native again rose up from his seat, and earnestly asked his instructor, "*Is* that true? *Can it be* true that God *so* loved the world? God's Own Son came to die that man might not die? Is it true?" The missionary assured him "it was *all true; it was the very message* he had come so far on purpose to deliver, and happy were all they who would receive it." The man burst into tears, and, overpowered with his feelings, went into the bushes to think and pray over the glad tidings. Will not that poor heathen, think you, rise up in judgment against many who have heard the gospel every Sunday, and yet never once in their whole lives retired by themselves to meditate on the wonderful love of Jesus? How different will their thoughts of the importance of such subjects be, in that day when the Lord Jesus will sit upon His great white throne, as the "JUDGE OF QUICK AND DEAD!"

> King of Majesty tremendous!
> Who dost free salvation send us,
> Fount of Pity! then befriend us.
> Righteous Judge of retribution,
> Through Thine own great substitution,
> Grant, O grant us absolution.

28

Judge of Quick and Dead.

LAST Sunday we had under consideration that name of our Lord by which He was familiarly known as a Man among men—JESUS—together with its illustrious meaning, a SAVIOR FROM SIN. This He will continue to be to the end of time, to all who are willing to be saved. And then—A SAVIOR no longer—He will present Himself under the awful character of a "JUDGE."

JUDGE OF QUICK AND DEAD (Acts 10:42). "For God hath appointed a day in which He will judge the world in righteousness by that Man whom He hath ordained." An old and well-known book contains a graphic description of one "rising out of bed who, as he put on his raiment, shook and trembled so much as to provoke the inquiry, 'Why does this man thus tremble?' Then did the man answer for himself and said, 'This night, as I was asleep, I dreamed, and behold the heavens grew exceeding black; also it thundered and lightened in most fearful wise, that it put me into an agony. So I looked up in my dream and saw the clouds rack at an unusual rate; upon which I heard a great sound of a trumpet, and saw also a Man sit upon a cloud attended with the thousands of heaven; they were all in flaming fire, also the heavens were in a burning flame. I heard then a voice saying, "Arise, ye dead, and come to judgment!" and with that the rocks rent, the graves opened, and the dead that were therein came forth; some of them were exceeding glad and looked upwards, and some sought to hide themselves under the mountains; then I saw the Man that sat upon the cloud open the book, and bid the world draw near. Yet there was, by reason of a fierce flame which issued out and came before Him, a convenient distance between Him and them, as between the Judge and prisoners at the bar. I heard it also proclaimed to them that attended on the Man that sat on the cloud, "Gather together the tares, the chaff, and stubble, and cast them into the burning lake"; and with that the bottomless pit opened just whereabout I stood, out of the mouth of which there came in an abundant manner smoke and coals of fire, with hideous noises. It was also said to the same persons, "Gather my wheat into the garner." And with that I saw many catched up and carried away into the clouds, but I was left behind. I also sought to hide myself but I could not, for the Man that sat upon the cloud still kept his eye upon me; my sins also come into my mind and my conscience did accuse me on every side.'"

But I think I hear you say, "that was only a dream." Be it so. But the day is surely coming which shall "burn as an oven," wherein men shall not dream of judgment, nor talk about it, but astonished and affrighted, cry out, "The great day of his wrath is COME! and who shall be able to stand?" On that awful morning the trumpet voice of the Archangel will awake the slumbering world. The sun will grow dark, and the heavens be covered with a black pall; the skies will shrivel up like a scroll scorched with burning heat. The dead will start into life and the living undergo a wondrous change. The Ancient of Days will come in the clouds of heaven, and before Him shall be gathered all that have lived from Adam to the end of time.

They shall come from graveyards where they have slept in moldering heaps for ages. They shall assemble from battlefields where they were slain by thousands at a time. The dark caves of ocean, and old populous cities long ago deserted, will yield up in crowds the dead they have concealed. From all their hiding places they will be mustered. The wicked inhabitants of the old world drowned by the flood; and those who lie buried in the salt lake of Sodom; and all Pharaoh's host who perished in the Red Sea; and Sennacherib's great armies who were smitten by the Angel of death at Jerusalem—wheresoever the bones of human beings have been cast away, there will they be seen starting into life and putting on immortality. Not one child of man will be missing in that great assembly. Cain, the first murderer, will be there, and Judas, the betrayer of our Lord. And *you* will be there—and I—and everyone.

What an overwhelming sight will it be! John says, "I saw the dead, small and great, stand before God." That which he saw in vision, you and I, my friends, shall one day see actually in all its real and awful grandeur. We shall behold that wondrous multitude, and the great white throne towering high over all, and the glory of the JUDGE sitting thereon, and the hosts of angels ministering to Him, and the fiery stream which shall "issue before Him," and the forked lightnings leaping from cloud to cloud, and the whole world in a blaze! We shall hear the thousand times ten thousand chariots of God rolling in the heavens, and the reverberation of God's thunder, and the wailings of the lost as the angels bind them in bundles to be burned, and the yells of wicked spirits dragged to judgment in chains of darkness, and the shouts of the redeemed when they shall see the Savior who died for them coming in the clouds of heaven. And we shall not only witness it as men who watch some fearful sight from a distance, but mingle in the crowd and be personally concerned in the inquiry—not as accusers or witnesses or judges; nay, but to be ourselves judged, "for every one of us must give account of himself" before that JUDGE OF QUICK AND DEAD.

With such a prospect before us, well may we give utterance to the awful inquiry—"*Who shall be able to stand?*" Who will endure the solemn scrutiny of that day? In Psalm 1:5, we read that "the *ungodly* shall not stand in the judgment." But multitudes, who do not pass under this description among men, will share in the same condemnation. Among these will be found some who were

Members of Churches. For, remember, you may be baptized without being regenerated. You may be approved by your fellow Christians and be esteemed by judicious ministers, and yet be an abomination in the sight of God. You may have your name entered on the church books, while it is nowhere to be found in the Lamb's Book of Life. Again, there will be some who were

Preachers of the Gospel, who will not be able to stand; men who have held the truth in unrighteousness, or pursued the ministerial calling only for a livelihood. *Here,* admiring crowds hang upon their lips while they pour forth eloquent exhortations. *There,* their auditors will start to see them among the weeping and wailing on the left hand of the Judge! There will also be many so-called

Death-bed Penitents, who will not be able to stand. Many under apprehensions of death have made earnest vows of reformation, which, on their recovery, have evaporated like the morning cloud. Had they died while the pious resolutions were upon their lips, survivors would have spoken with confidence of their safety. But their recovery dissipated the fond conceit. May it not be feared that the great day will reveal many a one who lived without God till death came, and then, with hasty professions of repentance, "died like a lamb"? They deceived themselves, they deceived their neighbors, but they could not deceive their JUDGE, and they will not be "able to stand." But there is a numerous class of seemingly religious people who may be comprised under the term

Almost Christians. They hear the word gladly. They make long prayers. They weep over their sins. Perhaps they are tract-distributors or Sunday-school teachers. Surely *these* will be able to stand! Not if this be all. Many tears are wept over sins that are never forsaken, and millions go far in religion without going far enough.

But though many who now expect to be saved will then be condemned, none will suspect the JUDGE of unrighteous dealing. No such aspersion will rest on His character. Examination the most impartial will be made, and justice the most exact will be dealt to every individual. For do we not read that "*the Books will be opened?*" What Books can these be? The imagery is doubtless borrowed from the usages of men. God is represented as appealing to records and producing proofs. There is the stamp of righteousness, correctness, and truth. But "the Books," though emblematical, represent something real. What then are these Books?

1. *The Book of Memory* will be opened, wherein everyone will read his own personal history, and find his forgotten, secret sins set in the light of God's countenance. And everything will be as vivid as if only done yesterday. "On such a day," you will read, "I rebelled against God; in such a place I fell into sin; in such a company I went astray." Oh what a fearful record! Not a thing omitted; every idle word set down, and every page written by your own hand! "By your words you shall be judged," and "be condemned out of your own mouth."

2. *The Book of Conscience* will be displayed, and there you will find registered all its faithful reproofs, how it struggled and resisted, how it warned and entreated every time you put forth your hands to iniquity, but you would not hear. And what will you be able to say to its accusations?

3. *The Book of Providence* will be unrolled, where you will read the long catalog of God's abused mercies; how He sent you message upon message, and warning after warning; how He allured you with mercies, and alarmed you with judgments, and waited for you with long patience; but you went on still in your trespasses, and hardened your hearts, and would not let His goodness lead you to repentance.

4. *The Book of the Law* will be opened, and that will witness against you—how reasonable all its requirements were and how salutary, and yet you did not obey them! and how dreadful its threatenings, and yet you were so hardened you would not tremble at them! "But the words which I have spoken," says Christ, "they shall judge you at the last day."

5. *The Book of the Gospel* will be opened. And oh! this will be the most terrible book of all, to those of the wicked who were acquainted with it during their lifetime; for on its open page they will read of the blood of Christ, and feel that they have trampled on it; of the love of Christ, and feel that they have returned hatred for it. They will read its promises and invitations too, but with the bitter reflection that the opportunity of salvation is lost forever! "The harvest is past, the summer is ended, and they are not saved!"

And as men read what is written in these books, every mouth will be stopped, and all the world will be convicted.

6. But "another book will be opened." Ah! what book is that? *The Lamb's Book of Life*—that Book which contains a catalog of all His saints, and out of which "He calleth His own sheep by name." Nothing written in any of those other books will condemn you if your names are found written there. But oh! hear it, ye despisers of Christ! "Whoever shall not be found written in the Book of Life, *shall be cast into the Lake of Fire!*"

Thus all will be judged out of the books. None will be overlooked through haste or forgetfulness; no mistake will happen; each will be separately dealt with, and everyone's conscience will own that the judgment awarded to his particular case is just and righteous. For the wicked will not be punished all alike, but each in proportion to his crimes. Some are to be beaten with many stripes, and others with few. And among the righteous too there will be a difference made, and some will receive a greater reward than others. For there is still another Book to be opened, which you may read of in Malachi 3:16. It is called

7. *The Book of God's Remembrance*. And what will be found recorded there? All the good works which saints have performed out of love to Christ. "I was hungry and ye gave Me meat, I was naked and ye clothed Me," or "I know thy works and charity and service, thy tribulation and poverty." For "God is not unrighteous to forget their labors of love." It is written, "Do ye not know that the saints shall judge the world?" Whatever further explanation this may admit of, it is plain that their good works shall be brought forth and manifested to the condemnation of all who belong to the ungodly world; and that the righteousness of God's judgments against wicked men will thus be evinced. So DR. OWEN: "See," saith Christ, "these are they whom I own, whom you so despised and abhorred; and behold their works following them! This and that they have done while you wallowed in your abominations." And their future station in glory will exactly agree with what the Book of God's Remembrance records of their usefulness and faithfulness while upon earth. A cup of cold water given away out of love to Christ will not lose its reward, while "they that turn many to righteousness shall shine as the stars forever and ever."

And when all these books shall have been opened and examined, then shall follow the final sentence. And oh! who can describe the rapture of those on the right hand of the JUDGE, when He shall address to them the words, "Come, ye blessed of My Father, inherit the kingdom prepared for you!" On the other hand, with what despair and horror will the wicked hear their sentence, "Depart from Me, ye cursed, into everlasting fire prepared for the devil and his angels!" Is not the thought of such fearful language being addressed to ourselves, enough to make us tremble? "And these shall go away into everlasting punishment, but the righteous into life eternal."

What a proof is here that Jesus Christ is truly God! "The Father judgeth no man, but hath committed all judgment to the Son." A work like this could not possibly be performed by any created person. The JUDGE of all the Earth must be the Lord God Omnipotent and Omniscient. And Jesus Christ is JEHOVAH. He is Omnipotent, and therefore able to raise all the dead and compel them, however unwilling, to stand before His dread tribunal. His is Omniscient, and therefore well able to search the depths of all hearts, and unravel the mysteries of iniquity and tear away every disguise from the wicked. He is All-wise, and therefore qualified to weigh the motives and perceive the characters of all with perfect accuracy. He is Holy, Just, and True, and therefore incapable of wronging anyone in the smallest degrees. He is Goodness itself; He cannot be vindictive or cruel. His name is Love; therefore, though strict, He must needs be impartial and disposed to make every allowance consistent with righteousness.

In our last Sunday's Reading and that of today, we have dwelt on two grand offices of our Lord—SAVIOR and JUDGE. I have just a word or two more to add on both these.

1. Remember He is not a JUDGE *now*, but a Savior. He says Himself, "I judge no man"—that is not my business *now*—"I came *not to judge* the world but to save the world" (John 12:47). Think of this lest your consciences make you afraid. Luther once thought Him a severe JUDGE requiring what he could not perform, and this filled him with despair. Afterwards he learned that Jesus does not as an *exactor require* anything of us; but rather as a Friend and Helper will *perform* everything in us and for us. Do not be afraid of Him. He will not frown upon you, but will pity your infirmities, pardon your faults, and help you to do better. His language is, "Neither do I condemn you. Go and sin no more." Call Him not therefore JUDGE when you come to Him, but JESUS, a Savior. And oh! What a Savior!

He is a *Gratuitous* Savior—He will save you for nothing. Come, destitute, guilty, helpless; come with your hard heart, come just as you are. He is a *Loving* Savior—He meets you with expressions of love before you take the first step to Him. He loves to be beloved by such as you; for He says, "I love them that love Me." He is a *Mighty* Savior—He is JEHOVAH, able to supply you with everything required to make you blessed forever. He is a *Holy* Savior—Just and having salvation. He has fulfilled all righteousness for you, and—what an honor!—He is willing to make you like Himself and worthy associates for angels. He is a *Waiting* Savior—how He presses you to come to Him at once! Oh! do not loiter any longer as if unwilling to be saved, nor hesitate as though afraid to take Him at His word. He is the *Only* Savior—if you reject Him there remains no other. He is a Savior *for* YOU—this you must believe or you will never truly come to Him. He is not only a Savior for others—for David, and Paul, and Luther, but for *you*.

When Bishop Butler lay on his death-bed, he called for his chaplain and said, "Though I have endeavored to please God, yet, from the consciousness of my infirmities, I am still afraid to die."

"My lord, you have forgotten that Jesus Christ is a Savior."

"True," said the bishop, "but how shall I know that He is a Savior *for* ME?"

"Because it is written, 'Him that cometh to Me, I will in no wise cast out.'"

"So it is!" answered the prelate, "and I am surprised that though I have read that scripture a thousand times over, I never felt its virtue till this moment—and now I die happy!"

A young lady on the brink of the grave was very disconsolate. "There was no salvation for *her*," she said, "she was *such* a sinner!" One day, after a long conversation with her minister, during which he had set forth the love of Jesus, and tried, but in vain, to remove her difficulties, he ended by saying, "But you say you believe Christ is willing to save *all* that come to Him repenting of their sins, do you not?"

"Oh, yes."

"And you say that *you* repent?"

"Yes, I do, indeed."

"Now trust with all your heart in the promises which He has made, and believe that He is willing to save *you!*"

In a moment a new light entered her mind, a smile of joy illumined her countenance, and she exclaimed, "*Is that it?*" and, trusting in Christ, from that hour she found joy and peace; and some weeks afterwards welcomed death as a friend.

Yes, "*that was it*"; there was salvation in Christ, and it was here the moment she believed. And whosoever will come to Him in the same way will surely find joy and peace. The same path to salvation is alike open to the learned bishop and the dying child; nor is there any other.

But how many there are who refuse to believe that Christ is waiting to receive, and ready to forgive, *them*, though it be affirmed ever so often. They say they must be more penitent and contrite before this can be, and they set themselves to acquire the requisite state of mind. Or they say they cannot *believe*. "If they could but exercise faith, then they know God would forgive. They are praying for faith, trying to believe, and hope to succeed soon." They reason as if the case were, The Divine Being is reluctant, and we must persuade Him; instead of, He is ready to forgive, and we are to take the offered pardon.

Mr. Moody used to tell a thrilling story about a lost brother in illustration of this subject. He left his widowed mother and went forth a homeless wanderer. Years passed, and no tidings of him came to that broken-hearted mother. But she continued to cherish the hope that she should yet again embrace her lost son, long after every one else had given up all expectations of ever seeing him again.

One day a stranger, with long beard and bronzed face, stood in the garden path. His mother did not know him. He gazed at her a moment or two, and then great tears began to course each other down in his cheeks. She knew him by those tears. She sprang to her feet, rushed to the door, and threw her arms round his neck, exclaiming, "My boy! my boy! come home at last? Come in, my boy, come in." He gently disengaged himself from her embrace, and said, "Mother, I have vowed I will never cross your threshold until you have forgiven me." Did she keep him waiting? Did she pause to take the question into consideration? Oh no! She was "ready to forgive" on the instant. The son wronged his mother's yearning heart by that momentary expression of distrust.

So does the returning sinner wrong God and Christ when he looks askance at their loving invitations, as if he suspected their sincerity. Oh believe it instantly! What can the Holy Spirit say more of the love of the Father than that He is "READY TO FORGIVE"? And again, "He waiteth to be gracious—He is full of compassion—He delighteth in mercy." And what can the Loving Savior say more to banish your suspicions forever, than what He hath said already, and which you have heard so often, and appreciated so unworthily—"Him that cometh unto Me, I will IN NO WISE cast out"?

Thus Jesus Christ is a SAVIOR NOW and not a JUDGE. But I beseech you, observe that word *Now;* and flee to Him instantly, for the Last Day is coming; and remember, secondly,

2. He will be JUDGE *then*, and not a Savior! Rabbi Eliezer told his disciples that they should turn to God ONE day before death. "But how shall we know the day of death?" said they. "True," said he, "you know not when you will die; it may be *tomorrow,* therefore you must turn to God TODAY; so shall you be sure to do it before death comes." But if you delay your repentance till a future day, and death should come in the meantime and put it out of your power, think on what a terrible sight you will open your affrighted eyes when the voice of the archangel shall rouse you from your grave! Oh! with what horror will you behold "the Lord revealed from heaven with His mighty angels, in flaming fire, to take vengeance on them that have not obeyed the gospel." The day of the perdition of ungodly men has at last arrived! He who was once the Compassionate Lamb is now the Avenging Lion of Judah. The doors of mercy, which once were open day and night, are now closed forever and ever! And for those who are without, there remain only the "furnace of fire," and the "undying worm," and the "unquenchable flame," and "weeping and wailing and gnashing of teeth" to all eternity! The full meaning of these dreadful phrases none can tell! But ought they not to make your hearts tremble? The wrath of God! Oh, who will be able to stand before His indignation? Who will be able to abide the fierceness of His anger?

Oh, ye sons and daughters of pious parents! ye children of the Sabbath school! and all who have been taught the truths of religion, but who stifle conviction, and will not pray nor come to the Savior—consider the aggravation of your sin. Ye who know what God requires but will not repent, think how insulting and provoking your contemptuous conduct must be in His sight! If ignorant heathens and neglected outcasts will be beaten with *few* stripes, surely ye who do despite to the tenderest remonstrances of parents and ministers, yea, of Christ and the Holy Spirit, will be adjudged worthy of "much sorer punishment!" Surely, if one "undying worm" of regret shall gnaw the heart of an *igno-rant* transgressor, a thousand stings of remorse may be expected to torment *your* consciences if you live and die impenitent, and "MANY STRIPES" be your portion forever! But who can dwell with devouring flames? Oh that ye were wise, that ye understood these things, that ye would consider your latter end!

> Sinners, awake betimes; ye fools, be wise;
> Awake, before this dreadful morning rise;
> Change your vain thoughts, your crooked works amend,
> Fly to the SAVIOR, make the JUDGE your Friend;
> Lest like a lion His last vengeance tear
> Your trembling souls, and no deliverer near.

29

Keeper. King. King of Kings and Lord of Lords. King of Jews. King of Saints. King of Glory. Leader and Commander. Light of the World. Life. Love.

YOUNG people are often induced to become readers by the lure of entertaining fictions or fairy tales. But soon, it may be, voyages and travels to far-off lands, and stories of adventure, take the place of those early favorites. And when the readers grow a little older still, these, in their turn, are displaced by history, or biography, or poetry. And happy will it be if they escape the danger of acquiring an enervating taste, in early life, for novels and more sensational literature.

But there is one book with which some readers become enamored in early life to their own great advantage, which to a remarkable extent includes all the features named. For instance; it details the particulars of an eventful *journey* to a glorious land that is very far off. It unfolds a variety of *biographies*, in which readers of all sorts may see their pictures drawn to the life. And many *beautiful personages* make their appearance, much more charming than the best fairies that were ever invented, and with elements of substantial truth underlying the representations too. Again, *giants* and *giant killers* sometimes flit across the stage, and heroes of sterling mettle stand out here and there in the narrative. And the entire book is pervaded by *poetical feeling* of the highest order; although it is in plain vigorous prose that the author traces the surprising adventures of *Christian* and *Christiana*, in their Pilgrim's Progress from the City of Destruction to the Celestial Country.

So fascinating is this book of travels, that some young ones have been known who have read it through ten times before they were ten years old. And to some of these it has since become more interesting still. For why? Just because they have followed the pilgrim's example, assumed the pilgrim's garb, and become travelers in the same road; and like them, they have picked up many pleasant companions by the way; they have passed through many strange and startling adventures; and they hope by-and-by to reach the same happy home in the Paradise of God.

> A thousand ways in ruin end,
> *One only* leads to joys on high;
> By that my willing steps ascend,
> Pleased with a journey to the sky.

No doubt some of you have read that bright story of *Christian's* adventures and exploits; and you have a lively recollection of the interest you felt in it all, and in his joyful arrival at last where he wished to be. And when you have seen him safe through the river, how pleased you were to find that his wife *Christiana* had made up her mind to go after her husband, with her "four sweet babes" and *Mercy* her companion.

To this new dream you sat down with new pleasure, and eagerly followed them throughout all the ups and downs of their eventful course. You praised the courage with which they prepared to leave the condemned City, and the haste with which they fled across the wide field towards the Wicket-gate. You were sorry to see them struggling in the Slough, but rejoiced much when they got through. You admired the earnestness with which they knocked at the Gate, especially the violent assault which *Mercy* made upon the knocker; and you felt grateful to *Goodwill* for the kindness with which he granted their request and let them all in. When they slept at the *Interpreter's House*, you rested with them. When they were welcomed at the *Palace Beautiful*, you went in too, and heard all their talk; and you admired as much as they the wonderful things that were showed them. Then you lingered with them in the sunshiny *Valley of Humiliation*, and thought as they did, that it must be a sweet place to live in. But through the next Valley you made your way as quickly as possible, lest its gloomy horrors should seize on you.

In short, all the scenes of that wonderful book are painted with such power and life, that there is not an incident in the whole history that did not fasten itself on your memory. So that even when you ceased reading, you still seemed to be trudging the same road with them, or listening to the prattle of the children and the grave discourse of the guide, or—still more entertaining—to be standing by while the valiant champion demolished the giants who disputed their progress. And at night you dreamed that you too had become a pilgrim, and were on your way to the glorious golden city where those once weary pilgrims have been resting these many years, clothed with white robes, and crowned with pearly diadems.

Oh that it were so! I wish you were all travelers together in that good old way. For the Pilgrim's progress is no dream after all, as they can testify who are engaged in it. And the glorious rest at the end is no cunningly devised fable, but a solid reality, as they know who now inherit the promises. Come then, cast in your lot with us who are travelers to Zion. Hasten! for time wears; the night is far spent, the day is at hand. Lose no more precious hours. Escape for thy life! Up and begone!

> There is a path which leads to God—
> All others go astray;
> Narrow, but pleasant is the road,
> And Christians love the way.

> It leads straight through this world of sin,
> And dangers must be passed;
> But those who boldly walk therein,
> Will get to heaven at last.

> How shall a youthful pilgrim dare
> This dangerous path to tread?
> For on the way is many a snare,
> For thoughtless travelers spread.

Yes, let me not deceive you. The road is not all strewed with flowers. The enemies who withstand you are *real* giants, though spiritual ones, and more mischievous by far than lions or bears. *Worldly Wiseman* spoke the truth when he told *Christian*, "Thou art like to meet with wearisomeness, painfulness, hunger, perils, swords, lions, dragons, darkness, death, and what not." But he did not tell him *all* the truth. For notwithstanding all these and other evils that beset our path, we have a faithful KEEPER who is pledged to defend our every step; and One well able to protect us too, for He is the KING OF KINGS. He will also see us safely home, for He is given to be a LEADER to His people. He is the LIGHT that lighteth every one of us, the LIFE that quickens and supports us, and the LOVE that embraces us all in its affectionate arms. I invite you to take a nearer view of this Glorious Person as these Titles represent Him, that so the desire of your souls may be to Him, and to the remembrance of His Name. We read in the Psalms, "The Lord shall be thy

KEEPER, thy Shade upon thy right hand" (Ps. 121:5). "He that keepeth Israel shall neither slumber nor sleep." It was somewhat hazardous to travel about in Judea, when this Psalm was penned. There were poisonous reptiles hid in trees and crevices; there were lions and wolves thirsting for blood; and thieves and murders watching for plunder. In the daytime the sun was so hot as to be destructive to those exposed to it, and at night the moon had an equally injurious effect. When therefore the pious Israelite had to take his yearly journeys to be present at the great feasts, he would naturally comfort himself with the promises of this Psalm, and sing it as he went along. Dr. Watts has turned it into verse thus:

> My feet shall never slide,
>   Nor fall in fatal snares,
> Since God, my Guard and Guide,
>   Defends me from my fears.
> Those watchful eyes that never sleep,
> Shall Israel keep when dangers rise.
>
> No burning heats by day,
>   No blasts of evening air,
> Shall take my health away,
>   If God be with me there;
> Thou art My Sun, and Thou my Shade,
> To guard my head by night or noon.

Now that traveler, "making God's statutes his song in his pilgrimage," was a picture of you who are on your way to the Holy City, the New Jerusalem; and his enemies were emblems of yours. First, there is a swarm of evil spirits rising up out of the bottomless pit, invisible but active, who like scorpions "have power with their stings to hurt men." And they have a king over them whose name is Apollyon, who daily leads forth his armies to battle and slaughter; and fearful is the havoc they make with immortal souls! Then there are your own sinful passions and tempers. Every human heart has one master passion, which is the strength and stay of all its other sins. In some it is pride, in others envy, in others covetousness. There are also sinful companions ever calling to you and saying, "Come with us!" and worldly baits spread out to allure your affections, and crafty men who strive to poison your souls with false and destructive doctrines. All these are *spiritual* foes. They do not fight against you with swords and guns, but with still more deadly weapons they aim at your souls. And who can shield you but the Keeper of Israel? Let me entreat you then to commend your soul with earnest prayer into His hands every morning, and say, "Lead me not into temptation, but keep me from the evil one." Then "He will not suffer thy foot to be moved; He that keepeth thee will not slumber." And even if all the powers of hell and earth were to combine against you, they shall not prevail. His Name itself is a Tower of defense. He is God's Anointed Mediatorial King, Whom He hath set on His holy hill, and Whom He calls "My King."

KING (Ps. 2:6). The Lord Christ is The Blessed and Only Potentate and the veritable King of the Universe in His own right, and His Kingdom is everlasting. But this Title belongs to Him as Ruler of a Kingdom *within* the everlasting Kingdom. It is a Kingdom, which was not *from* everlasting, for it had a beginning.

Neither is it *to* everlasting, for it will come to an end. It is that Mediatorial King-dom, of which the apostle writes so grandly in 1 Corinthians 15. It was set up for two purposes: That the Son might give eternal life to all whom God had given Him, and that He might put down all authority and power; "For He must reign till He hath put all enemies under His feet." Then cometh the end of this interregnum, when He shall deliver up the temporary Kingdom and once more merge it in the everlasting Kingdom of the Godhead.

How glorious will that crisis be! Let us imagine the judgment day to be past. The MEDIATORIAL KING has finished the work that God gave Him to do. He hath brought the many sons unto Glory whom the Father had committed to His care. He hath overcome the arch-fiend and his allies, the beast and the false prophet; and "the last enemy that shall be destroyed, which is death," He hath swallowed up in victory. He hath rent asunder the bars of the grave, and rifled it of its ac-cumulated stores. He hath invested the saints with glorious bodies like unto His Own. And what remains but to present His beloved, redeemed Church to His Father, and to say, "here am I and those whom Thou hast given Me—*not one is missing*. I have put down all authority and power, and subdued all Thine ene-mies under My feet—*not one remains*. And now to Thee, O Father, I deliver up the Kingdom. I lay down my credentials at Thy feet, I restore to Thee the seals of office, and abdicate My temporary Kingship, surrendering it to the One Di-vine Sovereignty of the Godhead."

This special form of Messiah's Royalty therefore is destined to cease because there will be no further occasion for it. There will remain nothing for Him to do as MEDIATOR, for He hath presented, to the last man, all the saved to His Father. Nothing more as CONQUEROR, for He hath finally disposed of all God's enemies and theirs. But His relationship to His redeemed, as the King of Saints, will sur-vive this abdication, and abide in all its freshness and glory forever and ever. That tie eternity will not invalidate.

But before that grand consummation there is much to be accomplished upon the earth. "I saw heaven opened," said the Seer, "and behold a white horse; and He that sat upon him was called Faithful and True; and in righteousness He doth judge and make war. And He hath on His vesture and on His thigh a name written,

KING OF KINGS AND LORD OF LORDS (Rev. 19:16). How frequently in the history of the Church has the Lord Jesus proved His claim to this glorious Title! You have read of the hardened king of Egypt who said, "Who is the Lord that I should obey His voice to let Israel go? I know not the Lord, neither will I let Israel go." What became of him? Where did he leave his glory. Where were all his chariots and war horses, his captains and armed battalions, when Miriam cried out, "Sing ye to the Lord! for He hath triumphed gloriously?"

Sing! for the pride of the tyrant is broken,
His chariots and horsemen all splendid and brave;
How vain was their boasting! the Lord hath but spoken,
And chariot and horseman are sunk in the wave.

Who shall return to tell Egypt the story
Of those she sent forth in the hour of her pride?
The Lord hath looked out from his pillar of glory,
And all her brave thousands are dashed in the tide.

Egypt never recovered that tremendous overthrow. With all her efforts she could not regain the grandeur and supremacy she had previously possessed. And the time would fail to tell how the King of Kings has dealt with those rulers who have been enemies to His people; how He smote King Nebuchadnezzar with madness, and brought him to "extol the King of Heaven" as "able to abase them that walk in pride"; how He sent an angel to smite King Herod, who was immediately eaten of worms, and died miserably, because he gave not the glory to Him to whom alone it was due; or how Julian the Apostate, Emperor of Rome, who madly fought against Christ and His cause, expired with those words on his lips, "O thou Galilean! Thou hast conquered at last!" Truly, "in vain do the kings of the earth take counsel against the Lord and His Anointed," for "He that sitteth in the heavens shall laugh, He will have them in derision."—Among our Lord's Regal Titles, there is one eminently conspicuous, which demands insertion here.

KING OF THE JEWS, (Mark 15:26); or, as Nathaniel expresses it, King of Israel (John 2:49). Its first public recognition was in the form of a criminal charge, an accusation written upon His Cross—"The King of the Jews." That which is His glory and ours is imputed to Him as a capital crime. And this Royal Title was bandied about from mouth to mouth, by the brutal soldiery and the vulgar rabble, as if it had been the veriest term of reproach or the oddest joke they could think of. Nor was there wanting corresponding investiture of crown, scepter or royal robe, to make that uncouth celebration; for all was done that could be done to express derision and mockery. His crown was wreathed of prickly thorns. His scepter was a hallow reed. His "gorgeous robe" was most likely some discarded purple appendage of Herod's wardrobe. And, invested with such insignia as these, "Herod and his men of war set Him at nought," did spit upon Him, and insult Him with impious gibes and taunts, while He, "oppressed and afflicted, opened not His mouth."

Did e'er such love and sorrow meet,
Or thorns compose so rich a crown?

And when they crucified Him—because it was customary thus to specify the crimes of which men were convicted—over His sacred Head was posted up "His accusation," THE KING OF THE JEWS. This was all that could be substantiated out of the "many things, which they laid to His charge." All the rest fell to the ground. This, at least, was true. To this He declined to plead "Not guilty." Blessed be God, He *was* The King of the Jews, and the cynical Pilate insisted upon having the only charge of which He had been convicted thus prominently announced to the world. And so—when, against the Anointed One, Herod and Pilate, with the Gentiles and the people of Israel, "are gathered together to do whatsoever God's counsel determined before to be done,"—His judge pronounces Him, over and over again, an innocent man—the witnesses against Him are self-convicted of perjury—and He is condemned to die, on the sole ground that He claimed to be the Promised Messiah, the long-expected Offspring of David, the great KING OF ISRAEL, in Whom all the nations of the world are to be blessed!

What a trinity of mysteries meet together here! An infernal mystery of iniquity—an infinite mystery of Mercy—an unfathomable mystery of Divine Wisdom! Thus doth God make the wrath of man to praise Him; and in various ways compels the rulers of the world to witness to and acknowledge the authority of the King Whom He hath set upon His holy hill. But there is a race of kings, invested with a royalty far higher than theirs, who need no compulsion, but who love to bow their necks to His righteous scepter, and to join with those who sing, "Just and True are Thy ways, Thou KING OF SAINTS."

KING OF SAINTS (Rev. 15:3). Every saint is a King; therefore it is a great thing to be a saint. The saints think so, although the world scoffs at the term, and all that it involves. But the world scoffed at the KING OF SAINTS Himself, and even called Him Beelzebub; and should His followers expect to be honored where He was despised? If you have set your faces Zionward, marvel not that your religion is ridiculed as puritanical, your hopes deemed chimerical, and you yourselves stigmatized as hypocritical or mad. After the example of your KING Who "endured the cross, despising the shame," bear the world's contempt with meekness, for before honor is humility. In the next world the tables will be turned; the KING OF SAINTS is the

KING OF GLORY (Ps. 24:8), Who says, "Them that honor Me, I will honor"; and "where I am, there shall My servant be also." Those "everlasting doors" which lifted up their heads at the entrance of the KING OF GLORY, when He ascended up on high, are open night and day, offering glad welcome to all His followers when they leave this world to ascend the holy hill. Fear nothing, beloved pilgrims to the Holy Land. Only watch and pray and keep the KING's high road. He that is with you as your KEEPER and KING is mightier than all those who are against you—But you need to be *guided* as well as *defended*, and we read that God has given the Lord Jesus to be a "LEADER."

LEADER AND COMMANDER to the people (Isa. 60:4). In the way to heaven, as I have just intimated, there are all sorts of snares and soul-traps to catch benighted or careless travelers; there are pitfalls which plunge men into deep mire where there is no standing; and many a by-path which leads to entangled woods and dark mountains, where Giant Despair still builds his castle and prepares his dungeons. The only way in which you can avoid all these, is to keep close to your glorious LEADER, and consult Him in every step you take.

In Switzerland there is a frozen district, called the *Mer de Glace* (Sea of Ice); it is some such a rugged place as would result from the instantaneous freezing of the huge waves of ocean, while tossing and rolling themselves to and fro. Fast fixed in their billowy form, they are far more dangerous to pass over than the stormy sea itself. Immense clefts with edges slippery as glass, and too deep to be fathomed, arrest the traveler at every step. He who would pass safely over that sea, must have a Leader well acquainted with the way. Otherwise, it is likely he will lose himself or be dashed in pieces; and he must mind what the LEADER says too. "Would you traverse yonder *Mer de Glace*? Then watch also my movement. When I leap, do you leap; where I plant my foot, there do you tread, and in the spot where I fix my staff, do you place yours; you must imitate me carefully; otherwise I will not answer for your life.

Now this is just what our LEADER says to His disciples: "If any man will come after Me, let him deny himself and take up his cross and follow Me," and "Learn of Me, for I am meek and lowly." We must study "so to walk even as He walked," and to be "in the world even as He was in the world." There is no part of the journey in which His bright example does not show us how He wishes us to conduct ourselves. He is our FORERUNNER through the Valley of Humiliation, with its self-denial and poverty—through the Shadow of Death, with all its horrors. Throughout the journey our Glorious LEADER goes before to show us the way. And consider His fitness for such a work. He claims to be the

LIGHT OF THE WORLD (John 9:5). David also calls Him "THE LIGHT OF THE MORNING" (2 Sam. 23:4); and Simeon, "A LIGHT TO LIGHTEN THE GENTILES" (Luke 2:32). He is the Glorious Source of all Light, natural, mental, and spiritual. He made those great Lights, the sun and moon. He is the Author of instinct, that inward light, which in the absence of reason teaches the bird how to form its nest, and the bee how to construct its marvelous cells, which makes the dog so ingenious and serviceable, and the spider and the elephant so dexterous in their contrivances. The greater Light of reason is also from Him. Man can calculate to a moment the movements of yonder planets, notwithstanding they be hundreds of thousands of miles away. He can turn the winds and waves to his purpose, and manage the steam of boiling water so as by it to transport fleets and armies to and fro with marvelous speed. But it is Jesus Christ who gives him, together with the materials to work with, the wisdom to make use of them all. He "lighteth every man that cometh into the world."

Take away the sun from our system, and all would be darkness and death. Deprive the animal of its instinct or the man of his reason, and what would either be but a kind of walking shrub, useless and shiftless? So man without a Savior is a ruin, and his soul without a spiritual sun to enlighten it, a desolation. But Jesus says, "I am come a LIGHT into the world, that whoso followeth Me *should not walk in darkness but* HAVE THE LIGHT OF LIFE." There are some who "say they have fellowship with Christ," but "they walk in darkness, and lie, and do not the truth." All sin is darkness, and "he that walketh in darkness knoweth not whither he goeth." But let it be our care to "abide in the light," so "there shall be none occasion of stumbling in us," and "walking in the light as He is in the light," that is, striving always to know and do His will, we shall at last get safe to glory.

And if you ask, Where is our strength to come from for this dangerous journey and constant effort? I answer, We must seek it in Christ alone. Many set out in the way and seem to run well for a time who afterwards fall away, and are never more heard of in the paths of godliness. Vain are all a traveler's precautions, his helmet and his sword, and vain the light shining on his path, if his strength give way! Solomon's guard of "three-score valiant men, all holding swords and being experts in war, every one with his sword upon his thigh because of fear in the night," would be no defense against disease and death. David felt this when he called the Lord the "LIFTER UP OF HIS HEAD"; and Paul felt this when he spoke of Christ as his "LIFE." As the first Title is included in the last, let us consider Christ as our "LIFE."

LIFE (Col. 3:4). In the Interpreter's house, *Christian* saw a fire burning against a wall, and one standing by it casting *water* upon it, yet did the fire burn higher and hotter. At this he greatly wondered, till he saw One behind the wall secretly casting *oil* into the fire. That fire, he was told, was a picture of the work of grace in the heart. "He that casts water on it is the devil, but Christ with the oil of His grace maintains the work, notwithstanding all Satan can do to destroy it." This lesson *Christian* was to remember all through his race. For in the arduous journey to heaven, they only "who *wait on the Lord* renew their strength, and walk and do not faint, and run and do not grow weary," and live to reach at last their glorious home in the skies. But if they attempt the race *in their own strength,* "the youths faint, and the young men utterly fail."

Here is the secret of many sad failures and terrible apostasies. Reader! let me speak freely to you. Tell me, do I not utter truth when I say that you have often felt a heavy weight on your spirits which you could not explain, but which was somehow connected with a painful conviction that there was *something wrong within*? This melancholy feeling has sometimes made you almost wish that you had been anything but a human being, having a soul that must live forever and a conscience that would be still stinging and wounding you every day. And have you not sometimes, under such feelings, resolved that you would strive to repent and be a Christian? Well, perhaps you began, and you broke off some of your sins, and forsook your evil companions; you said your prayers regularly for a few days, and you read your Bible and tried to become better. But soon all this passed away as a morning cloud, and left you more unhappy than before.

And, it may be, this has been done over and over again, till your heart has become like a bar of iron hardened into steel. But you are not happy. The secret yearnings of young spirits cannot find complete satisfaction in youthful pleasures; neither can the hearts of grown-up persons find perfect happiness in their more important occupations. All is vanity and vexation of spirit. And you have a suspicion, though you do not heartily like religion, that religious people are the only people in the world who have found out the right way to be happy. And it is his suspicion that has led you to make the feeble effort I have spoken of towards a religious life. Now is it not so? If I could have a little talk with you in your more sedate moments, should I not draw from you some such confession as this?—"I would be glad to become religious, but I do not know how to go about it. I have failed so often I am quite discouraged. I have prayed, and I have sometimes wept over my sins, and I have made resolutions that I would lead a better life, but I could never make anything of it."

Well now, here is the secret. You set out in your own strength—you did it all *without Christ*. No wonder it all came to nothing. Try another plan. Why even the great Apostle Paul felt "he had no sufficiency *of himself*" to do anything. What did he do then? He "besought the Lord" for help. And then he was able to say, "Now I can do all things through Christ who strengthen me," and "I live, nevertheless not I, but Christ liveth in me." That was *his* plan; do you try the same. Christ was *his* LIFE, and He must be *your* LIFE, if you will be successful and happy.

Go to Him for help, pray in dependence on Him, and read His Word, looking to Him for instruction. Often fall down before Him, and tell Him you have heard of the tenderness of His heart, how gracious He is and kind, even to the greatest sinners. Tell Him you are come to beg the help of His Holy Spirit to breathe on your dead soul, and change your desperately wicked heart, and sweetly incline it to Himself. Confess to Him that you really have no relish for good things, and require to have your disposition entirely changed. Tell Him all your bad feelings, and ask Him to give you a new nature, that so you may lead a new life. *Throw the whole weight of your salvation on Him.* Go to Him for the remission of your sins, for the righteousness that shall justify you, and the strength that shall sustain you. Do *this* and you will begin to make some hopeful progress. "Believe," *thus* "on the Lord Jesus Christ, and THOU SHALT BE SAVED." Trust in Christ is the essence of all true religion.

May the Holy Spirit graciously incline you to seek the Lord from this hour with new determination. But if you would find Him, you must *seek Him with all your heart.* An old man once lost a bank note in his barn. He looked for it several times, but could not discover it. At last he said to himself, "That note certainly *is* in the barn somewhere, and *I will even search for it till I find it.*" Accordingly he went to work and carefully moved straw and hay, hour after hour, till at last he found the note. A few weeks afterwards the old man sat by his fire musing on his spiritual state, for he knew his soul was not right with God. Presently he turned to his wife, and asked, "What must one do to become a Christian?" "You must seek for it," she replied, "*as you sought for the bank note.*" She said no more. But her words made a deep impression on him. He followed the advice, and soon found the "Pearl of great price." Go then at once to the Savior. Seek thus diligently of Him who is the great LIFEGIVER, the grace which alone can quicken you, and make you constant and faithful. It is to be found only in Him, and you *shall* find it if once you are *resolved* to find it.

But observe how Christ became our LIFE. You may have seen a bird represented in the act of drawing blood from her own breast with her bill, and thus feeding her young. It is the pelican that is thus represented. It was formerly believed that she did actually thus nourish her young brood. But though this is fabulous of the pelican, it is true of Christ. He communicates life to us by His blood. He gave His flesh for the life of the world. He died that we might live through His death.

> Oh, the sweet wonders of that cross
> Where God the Savior loved and died!
> Her noblest LIFE my spirit draws
> From His dear wounds and bleeding side.

John says, "God is LOVE." And this is alike true of each manifestation of God—the Father, the Son, and the Holy Spirit. Therefore, Jesus Christ is "LOVE."

LOVE (1 John 4:16). Observe, it is not said He is kind, tender, loving—that might be said of an angel, or a man—but He is LOVE. If He had not been LOVE, the race of man would have been swept away from the earth long ago. He would not have borne with the vast wickedness of which the world is full. And so the bright sun shines on from age to age, and the rain still falls, and trees flourish, and fruits grow, because He is LOVE. The birds make sweet music from season to season, and the flowers send forth delicious scents, and the ground is clothed with verdure, because He is LOVE. There is nothing in Him but LOVE; there are no angry passions. It is true He is angry with the wicked every day. But His very anger is only a proof that He is LOVE. If the Lord of Glory frowns upon sin and punishes it severely, it is because He loves His creatures so much that He cannot see them defiled and destroyed by sin, without showing His infinite displeasure.

Then He is the Fountain of *all* Love wherever it exists. The love which dwells in the little bird towards its young, and which leads her to rear them with such gentle solicitude, is but a drop from the great ocean of Divine love. He "by Whom all things consist," puts those tender feelings into the lower animals. And there is no friendship or kindness you ever met with which did not first come from Him. But the most wonderful proof that GOD IS LOVE is the Father's parting with His Beloved Son from His bosom to die for us; and the Son's consent to suffer and bleed that we might have life and salvation. It was because the Father is LOVE, that He contrived a way by which wretched wanderers might come back to Him again. And because the Son is LOVE, He came down to construct that way, to prepare and cast it up; to become Himself "THE WAY, THE TRUTH, AND THE LIFE." And because the Spirit is LOVE, He enters our wicked, wayward hearts, and sweetly persuades and encourages till He prevails on us to set out in this Glorious Way to heaven.

Pilgrims to the Celestial City! Remember that Jesus Christ is not only your KEEPER, your KING, your LEADER, your LIGHT, and your LIFE—but His name is LOVE. With what entire confidence then may you trust Him! How certainly may you reckon on His help! How gently and affectionately will LOVE do everything for its favorites. "He will collect the newborn lambs with His arms, and carry them in His bosom, and will *gently lead*" those who require this delicate treatment. What more would you have to win your heart than this—Jesus Christ is LOVE? LOVE also is the home to which you are to look forward—you are to rest at last in the very bosom of Almighty and Unchangeable LOVE! What will not that do for you? What wish will remain unsatisfied! How sweetly will eternity roll on! How will it seem, as it passes, one bright day without a night, one continued feast without weariness!

But I have now said enough about this pilgrimage. It only remains for me to give you all a pressing invitation to set out immediately in the narrow way. When God's people were traveling to Canaan, Moses said to his friend, Hobab, "We are journeying unto the place of which the Lord said, I will give it you; come thou with us and we will do thee good; for the Lord hath spoken good concerning Israel." And what was the answer? "He said unto him, I will not go" (Num. 10:30). And is not this just the treatment our invitations receive among you? When we say, "Come with us; we are traveling to the place where God is, and He hath promised us glory and immortality"; do you not answer by your conduct, "We will not go"? But we remember the course Moses took with Hobab, and the success he met with, and we feel we must not be discouraged.

Moses would take no denial from his friend, but still urged him to go—Hobab must and shall go. And his kind importunity at length prevailed. Hobab made no more objections; for some few years afterwards, we find his family comfortably settled in Canaan along with the Israelites.

Well, we follow this example; and though you have many times said "No" to our importunities, we will still try and try again, all the while praying to the God of grace to give you the spirit of repentance; for we know that He can persuade effectually, though we cannot. Once more then I beseech you to cast in your lot with the people of God. Enter in at the strait gate, and accompany us in the paths of wisdom, which, though arduous at times, are nevertheless pleasantness and peace; while the end whither they lead is glorious beyond description. When you reach your home you shall wear a crown of glory brighter than the sun, and dwell in a mansion prepared for you by the Lord of the country, and built of pearls and jaspers. There you shall every day see the King in His beauty, and sit at His table. You shall walk and talk with angels of glorious form, in streets paved with burnished gold. You shall stand side by side with the noble army of martyrs, and help them to sing the song of Moses and the Lamb. You shall climb the everlasting hills and view the length and breadeth of Immanuel's Land, and feel that it is all yours. Yea, your bliss shall know no bounds, your joy shall run over, for "the Lord shall be your everlasting Light, and the days of your mourning shall be ended."

But if you will not choose the way that leads to such a home, what way will you choose? If you will not go to heaven, whither will you go? There is only one alternative. The same voice that will say to faithful pilgrims, "Enter into the joy of your Lord," will say to those who travel in the broad way, "I know you not. Depart from Me, ye workers of iniquity." And for those to whom this language is addressed, there remains nothing but "THE BLACKNESS OF DARKNESS FOREVER!"

30

Lion of Judah. Lamb That Was Slain. Lamb of God. Lamb in the Midst of the Throne. Lord Our Righteousness. Lawgiver. Lord of the Sabbath.

WHO has not heard much of the LION, "the strongest amongst beasts, that turneth not away for any"? (Prov. 30:30). Those who have visited his haunts tell us of his stately walk as he roams free and undaunted on his native plains, and of his majestic presence. In the dark night he makes the forest of Africa tremble with his deep-toned roaring, which swells on the ear and then dies away like the muttering of distant thunder. His two eyes glare like balls of fire and his long, shaggy mane sweeps the ground. He will attack the strongest quadrupeds, or boldly face a thousand men. And who has not often watched the LAMB, that pure, gentle, innocent thing frisking in the meadows, whose very look awakens our pity? Defenseless and harmless, it falls an easy prey to its devourers. What a contrast there is between the Lion and the Lamb! And yet Jesus Christ is compared to both. He is at once the LAMB THAT WAS SLAIN and the LION OF JUDAH. John heard the angel speak of a Lion which had "prevailed to open the book," but when he looked round to see the LION, behold a LAMB with the marks of bleeding wounds upon Him! How surprising that He Whom the angel described as a fearless LION, should look like a meek, suffering LAMB! But so it was. Such wonderful extremes are blended in Christ, and excellencies so different, that they could hardly be supposed to exist together in the same person. First, let us look at the "LION."

LION OF THE TRIBE OF JUDAH (Rev. 10:5). When Jacob was about to die he said to his son Judah, "Judah is a lion's whelp: from the prey, my son, thou art gone up: he stooped down, he couched as a lion, and as an old lion; who shall rouse him up?" This prophetic language might have referred to Judah's descendants, who many years afterwards marched foremost through the wilderness, and bore for their ensign the figure of a lion; yet there is no doubt it had reference also to the Messiah, Judah's great Descendant, the Root of David. But why is He called THE LION OF JUDAH? Everywhere and in all ages the Lion has been almost a synonym for strength, victory, courage, supremacy, and royalty. In one or more of these senses the title is used here as emblematical of Christ; and, "OF JUDAH" stamps His human descent, and identifies Him with the renowned ancestor of David, whose tribe was the leading one of the twelve.

Would it be dangerous to provoke the anger of a lion? Such things as these are written also of the LION OF JUDAH. "He is terrible out of His holy places." "At His presence the earth doth quake." "His eyes are like a flame of fire"; "His voice is like the sound of many waters; it shaketh the wilderness; the voice of the Lord is full of Majesty." "He shall roar like a lion, and when He shall roar the people shall tremble," for "dominion and fear are His." See Hosea 11:10; 13:7; Jeremiah 25:30; Amos 1:2. From these passages we may well infer that, as it must be a fearful thing to fall into His hands as our Enemy, so it must be grand thing to have Him to be our Protector.

Who would be afraid that had a lion to fight for him? Perhaps you remember an ancient story of a man who had a lion to be his champion. He was a slave, and ran away from his master into the woods. Tired with his journey, he lay down to sleep in a cave, but was soon awakened by the entrance of a huge lion. The man was greatly alarmed. However the lion showed no fierceness, but approached the terrified fugitive holding up his paw as though it were in pain. It appeared to be wounded; and viewing it more closely, the slave espied a large thorn that had run into it. He had sufficient courage to draw out this thorn, upon which the lion showed evident signs of gratitude. From that time he was his friend and defender, and would suffer no one to touch him. The slave was now in a condition to defy all his pursuers, for who would dare injure a hair of his head who had a lion to protect him? Thus happy and secure ought the child of God to feel, in the persuasion that he has the LION OF JUDAH to be his Almighty Shield and Defender. But the LION OF JUDAH is also the "LAMB," the

LAMB THAT WAS SLAIN (Rev. 5:6). This is a typical representation of the Priesthood of Christ, and of His atoning sufferings and death. When He was crucified, He appeared like a defenseless, unresisting LAMB in the mouth of Satan, the savage and roaring lion; yea, He was slain by his devouring jaws. And yet it was in that hour of His greatest weakness that he even conquered His very devourer; and in His turn triumphed gloriously over the adversary, and, "for the suffering of death was crowned with glory and honor."

"Crowned with glory for the suffering of death!" Yes, in heaven Jesus Christ is more admired for His *sufferings* than for His *victories*. Listen to the burden of their songs! Do they sing, "Worthy is the LION that slew His foes"? They might well sing that; but they sing rather; "WORTHY IS THE LAMB THAT WAS SLAIN!" For the Lord Omnipotent to be victorious is a thing of course; but for Him to *suf-*

fer and to *die* is a matter for infinite amazement and rapturous praise. The atoning work of Christ more delights saints and angels than any other manifestation
of His glory. We read that "Angels desire to look into these things"; let us also inquire into the meaning of this wonderful Title of our Lord, the LAMB THAT WAS
SLAIN, and the

LAMB OF GOD which taketh away the sins of the world (John 1:29). Three
questions occur here. 1. *Why is He called a* LAMB? A lamb is an emblem of patience, meekness, and gentleness. You cannot provoke a lamb, nor did you ever
hear of a lamb doing anyone an injury. Innocence and harmlessness are inseparable from all our ideas of a lamb; and thus it is a figure of Christ. In His
strength and majesty the LION is His emblem, but in His meekness and humility He resembles a LAMB. Thus we read, "He is brought as a LAMB to the slaughter, and as a sheep before her shearers is dumb, so He openeth not His mouth"
(Isa. 53:7). But He was called a LAMB principally in reference to His sacrificial
death; since it was a Lamb that was used for the Passover and the morning and
evening sacrifice. And that the figure might be more suitable, it was to be without blemish or imperfection. Why was the Lamb offered thus continually? Surely
to teach the worshiper, who stood by and saw it slain, that his sins deserved
death, but that God would accept of a substitute. And yet that the substitute
then offered before his eyes, could not really take away his guilt; and that therefore the sacrifice must be repeated again and again, and be cleansed by other
sacrifices, until God should provide some Victim that would really take away
the dreadful stain of sin.

> Not all the blood of beasts
> 　On Jewish altars slain,
> Could give the guilty conscience peace,
> 　Or wash away the stain.
> But Christ, the Heavenly LAMB,
> 　Takes all our sins away;
> A sacrifice of nobler name
> 　And richer blood than they.

2. *Why was He called* THE LAMB OF GOD? Because He is not a sacrifice of our
choosing but of God's appointment. God hath not left us to inquire "Wherewith
shall we come before the Lord?" But He Himself "provides a LAMB for a Burnt
Offering"; even His Only Begotten Son Whom He loved better than all worlds.
In Psalm 40:6, 7, and 8, we read that God had no pleasure in burnt offerings for
sin. Why? Because by them justice was not satisfied, sin was not removed. Therefore He hath provided another Sacrifice, even Christ, who accepts the appointment and comes to do His will. It is in allusion to this will of God that our Lord
says in Luke 24:26, "Ought not Christ to have suffered these things?"

3. *What is the* Lamb of God *appointed to accomplish?* He "taketh away our sins." Among the Jews, the priest was said to *bear* their iniquity, but he did not suffer for it. He *put* it upon the lamb, and the lamb *suffered* for it. But Jesus, our Great High Priest, bore our sins Himself. And the sins of the world were such a load even to Christ, that he bent under it and sweat great drops of blood, while He bore them in His own body and carried them away. O what an agonized death did He die! Who can contemplate without shuddering the poignant smart of those wounds in His hands and feet, as He hung for hours suspended on the cross? Yet not one word of complaint did He utter, till to all His other sorrows was added the sense of God's absence or *desertion.* And then there fell from His lips that bitter and mysterious cry, "My God! My God! why hast Thou forsaken Me?"

Behold a fearful picture of the anguish of mind that will surprise the lost sinner when he shall feel himself finally abandoned of God! See what will then befall him! When God forsakes His Son, all sorts of evils are let loose upon Him, and He dies in the midst of aggravated horrors. Priests and rulers, soldiers and servants, all conspire to insult Him. He is deserted by friends, taunted by enemies, assaulted by wicked spirits! A deadly sorrow, a mortal agony oppresses Him, which, after a few hours, brings Him to the stillness of death. He dies of a wounded spirit, a broken heart. It is not bodily pain, great as that must be, but insupportable grief, that causes His death. Behold the Lamb of God in that last hour of His mortal conflict! Doth He not seem to say in the words of the prophet, "Is it nothing to you, all ye that pass by? Behold and see if there be any sorrow like unto My sorrow, wherewith the Lord hath afflicted Me in the day of His fierce anger"?

And why all this? Because He stood *in our place* and suffered what was due to *our sins.* He was the Victim on whom the fire of God's wrath fastened that we might escape. But if any of you despise that wonderful intervention, and neglect to apply with earnest prayer for an interest in it, then we do most solemnly warn you, the fire of God's wrath will fasten on *you.* And can you endure to think of so fearful a fate? Oh, make haste! fall down before Him, and say, "Lord, let that blessed Sacrifice avail for me! Give me an interest in all the benefits that flow from it! Let that precious blood cleanse me from all my sin. Let its atoning virtue remove all my guilt, and let its sanctifying virtue, applied by the Holy Spirit, purify me from all defilement! Let me be numbered with those who have washed their robes and made them white in the blood of the Lamb!"

But now, having gazed with deepest reverence upon the Lamb Slain, turn with me for a few moments to the contemplation of the glorious vision of the Lamb Enthroned; the

LAMB IN THE MIDST OF THE THRONE, as depicted by the seer in Revelation 10. You will observe three circles of worshipers surrounding the throne, who with loud acclamations fill the vast empyrean. The innermost band is the

Church, represented in mysterious hieroglyph by the "four Living Ones"—and the four and twenty Elders

> With vials full of odors sweet
> And harps of sweeter sound.

These sing "a new song" (vv. 9, 10), while the Angels stand round with silent rapture, listening to a strain they cannot reach. Not long are they mute, however. At the first pause they join the song; yet, you observe, with a variation suited to the circumstances (v. 12). They go as far they are able, but *they cannot sing it all.* Still that second company of worshipers does its very utmost to exalt The Lamb that was Slain.

But just as when one casts a great stone into some still lake, the water first forms a circle where the stone goes down; then there is another, and again another circle; and still there appear others widening out one knows not whither. So, when that mighty anthem strikes upon "the sea of glass before the throne," behold, the circling praises widen and expand, till presently thundering voices come rolling in from all the outlying creation. The outermost circle (or as Watts says),

> The whole creation join in one,
>   To bless the sacred Name
> Of Him who sits upon the throne,
>   And to adore the Lamb.

In Psalm 148, the Psalmist invites all the universe to contribute its praises. And as we read his sublime ode, we seem to hear the sun and the moon, and all the stars in the milky way, and in the regions beyond, returning their joyous echoes; and the sea roaring forth its thundering response. And so all worlds with all their inhabitants, all nature with all its tributaries, swell the chorus, and sing and shout to the praise of Him "without Whom was not anything made that is made"; and Who took upon Himself a created frame, as one of themselves; and all to manifest the mighty love of God's heart, and to redeem and glorify His church.

Now, should we be right in regarding all this as if it were merely meant to describe just one act of worship on one particular occasion? Does not this most resplendent vision rather present to us the Lord Jesus, in His Person and Acts, as One everlastingly enthroned in the estimation and affection of all intelligent, virtuous beings? their Well-believed, their Chief Joy; the Manifested Glory, the Very Beauty and Crown of all Creation, outshining in His peerless preeminence all other displays of grace and glory in the universe. What He is, and what He does, is so surpassingly beautiful and glorious, that all in heaven and all on earth are perfectly enamored with it. He is therefore "exalted, and extolled, and very high."

Every fresh manifestation of His beauty, every new work, every inward thought of His, as it comes into action, fires afresh the passions and lights up the joy of all beholders and participators. It floods their hearts with unutterable exultation, and admiration perfectly boundless. It fills their mouths with loudest and most hilarious praise, which they cannot restrain if they would. Their joy overflows. Their adoration, their intense delight, must come out. And so heaven's high arches ring with it. The thunder of it travels, like the sound of many waters, far and wide, awakening responsive echoes everywhere as it goes. From the uttermost parts are heard "songs, even glory to the Righteous One"; while still the chorus swells and grows and reverberates all around God's universe.

And does it not appear as if the church is destined to *lead* the praise of heaven? For here have not the inner circle of worshipers the first word and the last? *They* pitch the tune. *They* start the keynote. And when the grand chorus flows in, *they* confirm it all with their loud "Amen!" Yes, it is the church that strikes the chord and leads the magnificent hymn—

> "Crown Him with many crowns!
> The Lamb upon the throne."
> Hark! how the heavenly anthem drowns
> All music but its own.

Who but the church can *sing*,

> All hail! Redeemer, hail!
> For Thou hast died FOR ME?

But the myriads of angels, though they cannot compete with *that* chorus, can respond with all their hearts,

> Crown Him the Lord of Love!
> Behold His hands and side;
> Rich wounds, still visible above,
> In beauty glorified.

And who *should* head the praise? Surely they who, raised up out of the lowest hell, now stand on the very heights of heaven and inherit the throne of glory. In full remembrance of "the hold of the pit whence they were digged and the rock whence they were hewn," now that they are invested with all the glory of heaven—if *they* did not sing the loudest of all—if *they* were not first and foremost in praise—if—nay! in the very nature of things it could not be otherwise. As they owe the mightiest debt, their praise must soar higher than any besides. And so they sing a song the loftiness of which no other choristers can emulate.

But now we must turn from the enchanting vision, and go on with our expository theme.

I have said that our sins were *imputed* to Christ, or "laid on" Him. That was in order that His righteousness might be *imputed* to us. And this explains why He is called "The LORD OUR RIGHTEOUSNESS."

LORD OUR RIGHTEOUSNESS (Jer. 23:6; 33:16). We read in the Bible of two Adams—the first, the father of us all, and the second, the "Lord from heaven," Jesus Christ. Each of these was a "covenant head." A covenant head! Perhaps the younger ones would like to have this expression explained. Well, suppose I were to say to the boys of a school, "Next week I will give you a holiday and treat you all to an excursion, on *condition* that one of your number commit to memory the whole of the Book of Ruth. I will select that boy from among you who has the best memory, and he shall undertake the task." Now the boy to whom this duty was committed would be a sort of "covenant head" to the rest. On him would entirely depend their enjoyment or their disappointment. If he should accomplish the task, the treat would be theirs; but if he should fail, it would be forfeited. You see how his learning or not learning the Book of Ruth by heart would be *imputed* to the rest, or reckoned to their account, for they would all share in the fruits of his triumph or his failure; also, how if he were to fulfill the task, *his* performance would constitute *their* title to the proposed reward, on the ground of my promise or covenant.

Now we gather from various parts of the sacred writings that when Adam was placed in Eden, the future happiness of all his children was in some such manner committed to him. Had he done well, his obedience would have entitled them (as well as himself) to the possession of that Paradise, and the continued favor of God forever and ever. But he did evil, and "by his disobedience many were made sinners," and had entailed on them the curse of the broken covenant. Ruined thus in our first covenant head, God gave us another. This "Last Adam" had certain duties to discharge, on condition of which all His seed would become entitled to a better Paradise and better blessings than those forfeited by the first Adam. And Jesus Christ fulfilled the conditions of this New Covenant, and His RIGHTEOUSNESS in so doing is imputed to all who believe. Thus then our RIGHTEOUSNESS is of Him. He suffered for our sins and we are rewarded for His RIGHTEOUSNESS, or as the Scripture has it, "He was made sin for us, who knew no sin; that we might be made the RIGHTEOUSNESS OF GOD in Him."

> Jesus! how glorious is Thy grace!
> When in Thy Name we trust,
> Our faith receives a RIGHTEOUSNESS
> Which makes the sinner just.

Observe, we must *believe* on Him in order to enjoy the benefit of His RIGHTEOUSNESS. Suppose the boy I spoke of just now had accomplished the task—he repeats the whole of the Book of Ruth. Immediately I announce that "every boy who wishes to share in the promised reward must set his name down on a certain sheet of paper." You see that by so doing he would not *merit* the reward—he would only secure it for himself; the boy who repeated the lesson *deserved* or *earned* it for him. And faith is just like the rest setting their names to that paper. Faith is *necessary* to salvation, but it does not merit it. All the *merit* is in THE LORD OUR RIGHTEOUSNESS, and it is faith that makes that RIGHTEOUSNESS ours. When the Lord Jesus healed a sick man and said to him, "Thy faith hath made thee whole," He did not mean *literally* that his faith had cured the dropsy or the palsy. It was the power of Christ that did that. And in the same manner, when we read that faith makes us righteous, it is not our faith which justifies us, but the RIGHTEOUSNESS of Christ in which our faith interests us. Thus He is THE LORD OUR RIGHTEOUSNESS. He fulfilled the law for us, and thereby procured a title to heaven and all spiritual blessings for everyone who believes. Then He is also our "LAWGIVER."

LAWGIVER (James 4:12; Isa. 33:22). He does not fulfill RIGHTEOUSNESS for us that we may go on living in sin. Not so! He redeems us from the curse of the broken law that He may teach us to love that law. The law of the ten commandments is still the law of Christ, and though we cannot be saved *for* keeping it, we are saved *in order that* we may keep it. And though none of us can keep it perfectly—only Christ could do that—yet we must ask continually for strength and grace, that we may walk before Him in holiness and righteousness all our days. Moses was the great Lawgiver of the ancient church. Before he died he foretold that God would raise them up a "Prophet like unto himself,"—a TEACHER and LAWGIVER. Christ is that LAWGIVER, and is to be "counted worthy of more glory than Moses, inasmuch as He who hath built the house hath more honor than the house." Some of Moses' laws He abolished, some he enlarged, and some He altered, for He is Lord over the Law. I might here show how sweet all His Laws are, and what great reward there is in keeping them. But I will only direct you to one—"Remember that thou keep holy the Sabbath day," for to that the next Title draws our attention; the Son of Man is "LORD OF THE SABBATH."

LORD OF THE SABBATH (Luke 6:5). Indeed He is LORD of *all* days, and therefore has a full right to require them to be put to any use He pleases. We are not at liberty to spend our days as *we* please. Our LAWGIVER says distinctly, "Six days shalt thou labor." Life requires labor; we cannot live without it, and six days are given to us for this use; but the seventh is the Sabbath of the Lord, which He requires us to keep holy. He first gave this command to Adam in innocence, and often repeated it afterwards. Nor has it ever been withdrawn; God still requires a *seventh* part of our time. But the precise day of the week on which the Sabbath is to be kept, has been altered from the *seventh* to the *first* day. And why was this alteration made? The *seventh* day of the week was, as you all know, appointed to be kept in commemoration of the glorious work of creation. But we read in Isaiah 65:17, that there shall be a new creation, so much more glorious than the first that it shall be commemorated instead of it, and that the former "shall not be remembered or come into mind" in comparison with it. What can be a greater work than creation if it be not the work of redemption? And ye know that work was finished on the *first* day of the week, for it was then our Lord rose from the dead; and it has been kept sacred ever since as the Lord's Day. It was on the first day of the week our Lord so frequently appeared to His disciples during the forty days He continued upon earth. And there can be no doubt that the apostles were instructed to keep that day sacred, since they all observed it as their day of meeting. And Paul must have had directions from Christ concerning it also, because, though he says "he gave them no other commandment than that which he received from the Lord," yet he gave orders that the collection for the saints should be made on the first day of the week. Why but because it was their practice to come together on that day for worship? John also, in Revelation 1:10, speaks of "the Lord's Day." And the Christians of the first age walked by the same rule. It was even a test of their religion. A martyr was asked by the Roman Governor, "Hast thou kept the Lord's day?" He replied, "I am a Christian"; as much as to say, "All Christians do this, therefore of course I have done so." Thus we conclude that the change was made by the express command of the Lord of the Sabbath, since it was enforced by His own example and that of the authorized teachers of His laws, as well as practiced by the Christians who lived immediately after them. "This, then, is the day which the Lord hath made; let us therefore rejoice and be glad in it."

But do not forget that although the day has been altered by the Lord of the Sabbath from the first to the seventh, the Bible breathes not a word of any alteration in the proportion of time to be thus set apart. It is still the *seventh* part—one day in every week on which we are to "rest from labor." And you must be careful not to mistake the intention of it. True, you are to *rest* on the Sabbath, but you may not spend it in idleness and sloth. It is a *holiday* too—you are to "rejoice and be glad in it"; but this language does not refer to carnal recreation and amusement. For the same authority that enjoins the observance of the day, informs you how you are to employ it. "You shall keep My Sabbaths, and *reverence My sanctuary*." "The people shall *worship before the Lord* on the Sabbath." "Remember that thou *keep holy* the Sabbath day." There are, indeed, some necessary works which we are allowed to do. We may relieve the distressed, and instruct the ignorant. We may partake of food ourselves, and supply what is necessary to "the ox or the ass." But we must be very careful how we appropriate its holy hours, ever remembering that we are not at liberty to spend the Lord's day otherwise than in accordance with the will of the Lord of the Sabbath.

And what a kind indulgent institution it is! "The Sabbath was made for man," for his benefit and relief. Besides which, God's special blessing is promised to all who observe it, while His displeasure is many times denounced against all who "despise His Sabbaths." No greater curse can befall any country than that threatened in Hosea 2:11—"I will cause her Sabbaths to *cease*"; and so bitterly complained of in Lamentations 2:6—"The Lord hath caused the Sabbaths to be *forgotten* in Zion." In France the Sabbath is shamefully abused *now*, but once it ceased to be observed altogether. The *week* was abolished in defiance of God, and divisions of ten days adopted instead. And the history of that period shows a frightful increase of violence and bloodshed and universal confusion. May God preserve England's Sabbaths! and convince Sabbath-breakers of the great guilt they incur in polluting that holy day; and frustrate the reckless efforts of some (who ought to know better) to break down its most salutary sanctions.

31

Lord of Lords. Lord God. Lord from Heaven. Lowly. Lord of Hosts. Lord of the Dead and Living. Lord of Glory. Lord of All. Lord of the Whole Earth. Lord of the Harvest. Last.

THE wise man saith, "I considered the oppressions that are done under the sun, and beheld the tears of such as are oppressed; on the side of the oppressors there was power, but they had no comforter." And who among ourselves has not often, with mingled emotions of anger and grief, done the same? In all times men have wept over wrongs which no power on earth could redress; and have passionately prayed for the interposition of heaven, as though they would themselves (if they could) grasp the sleeping thunderbolts of vengeance and smite the insolent oppressor to the earth. And God's ears are not heavy that they cannot hear the cry of the oppressed, nor is His arm shortened that it cannot save them. "If thou seest the oppression of the poor and violent perverting of judgment and justice in a province, marvel not at the matter; for He that is Higher than the highest regardeth." And the wisdom, which hath permitted the injustice for some worthy purpose, will put an end to it whenever the proper time shall arrive. "The Lamb will overcome those who make war with Him, for He is LORD OF LORDS and KING OF KINGS" (Rev. 17:14). Let us now consider this, and some high Titles similar thereto, expressive of His universal Lordship.

LORD OF LORDS AND KING OF KINGS. He is also called LORD OF KINGS, in Daniel 2:47. By Him kings reign, and princes decree justice. Their hearts are in His hand, and He can turn them whithersoever He pleaseth as the rivers of water. All their movements are under His control. He will frown on the kings and scatter the people that delight in war, and it shall be said, "Come, see what desolations He has made—He burneth the war chariot in the fire, and maketh wars to cease to the ends of the earth."

Never was there a more remarkable instance of the exercise of His power in frustrating the schemes of wicked princes, than when the king of Spain sent a vast fleet of 150 great ships to England in the reign of Elizabeth, to bring our forefathers under the yoke of popery. Vast were the preparations of the invaders, and dreadful their threats! They set out with the determination to take away the Bible from the people, to torture and burn, imprison and destroy all who would not submit to Rome. The pope, always the friend of oppression and cruelty, praised the undertaking and solemnly blessed the fleet, giving it the name of the Invincible Armada. "How vain was their boasting!" The LORD OF LORDS refused to ratify the impious act of His pretended vicegerent, or to favor the cruel scheme of Philip. Long ere the fleet reached the shores of England it was scattered and wrecked by fearful tempests; and the broken timbers of nearly ninety of those proud ships strewed the shores of the favored island they were appointed to invade.

It was many years after that happy deliverance that Bunyan, in his Pilgrim's Progress, described the pope as a feeble old giant, "grown so crazy and stiff in his joints that he can now do little more than sit in his cave's mouth grinning at pilgrims as they go by, and biting his nails because he cannot come at them." But the wholesale slaughters of the Church of Rome are not forgotten. It is said the Inquisition alone has destroyed more than five million men! In the Bartholomew massacre, 25,000 Protestants were cruelly butchered by the Papists. Nearly a million and a half of the Waldenses and Albigenses were put to death, amidst unmentionable barbarities, in thirty years! It is impossible to estimate the entire number of victims who have been immolated to this hideous Moloch, in the various countries where the Church of Rome has had her way. According to some authorities, she has destroyed fifty million men and women, *not for crimes, but for holding what she terms heretical sentiments!* Well may she be said to be "drunken with the blood of saints." And the time draws nigh when it shall be said, "Rejoice over her, thou Heaven, and ye holy Apostles and Prophets, for God hath avenged you on her" (Rev. 18:20). How avenged? Why, in the destruction of her whole system of priestcraft and its final disappearance from the earth, together with all the pernicious principles of which it has been the mainstay for ages. Over this and all kindred evils Jesus Christ will eventually triumph, and all the world will rejoice in the downfall of the gigantic impostures. "I heard as it were the voice of a great multitude, and as the voice of many waters, and as the voice of mighty thunderings, saying, Alleluia! for the LORD GOD OMNIPOTENT reigneth."

LORD GOD OMNIPOTENT (Rev. 19:6). And is anything too hard for the Omnipotent? A few years ago, there were wise and far-seeing men, who "considered the oppression" of the four million slaves in the Southern States of America, and the "power of their oppressors," and who shook their heads and said, "Not this generation, nor yet the next, will see the captive race emancipated!" But what hath God wrought? In less than seventy years after the utterance of that doleful prophecy, we behold slavery utterly abolished; and the power of those who bought and sold their fellow creatures like cattle, forever broken, throughout the vast territory of the United States. THE LORD GOD OMNIPOTENT hath many more controversies to settle with "oppressors." And though selfish tyrants may think He delayeth His coming, and that therefore they may do as they please, "He that shall come will come, and will not tarry" and hour beyond His time. And then let them see to it; for "strong is the LORD GOD Who judgeth them."

LORD GOD (Isa. 40:10; Rev. 18:8). This Title belongs only to the First of Beings, Whose throne is forever and ever. But you see it is here appropriated to Jesus Christ, for it is added, "He shall feed His flock like shepherd. His reward is with Him, and the recompense for His work before Him." This language may sound strange as applied to the LORD GOD; but of course it refers to the commands that the Son receives from the Father to save Adam's guilty race; in connection with which there is granted to Him a kingdom. And that His authority might not be questioned, the decree is publicly declared in Psalm 1:7. The Scriptures lay great stress on this Mediatorial appointment, and so must we, or half the Bible will remain unexplained to us. As the LORD GOD, He is in His own right the Possessor of all things, but as Mediator, He is *appointed* to this authority over all things for the sake of His church.

LORD FROM HEAVEN (1 Cor. 15:47), is another Title which points out His Divine nature and origin. He that cometh from heaven is above all. It also reminds us of His astonishing condescension. How great was the glory He left behind when He came to be the Despised and Rejected One! How vast were His riches, ere He became poor that His poverty might make us rich! And yet, though He was in the Delight of God and the Adored of Angels, He came to Jerusalem in great humility and poverty, even as it was foretold of Him— "LOWLY, and riding upon an ass, a colt the foal of an ass."

LOWLY (Zech. 9:9). From first to last His life was LOWLY. What babe ever came into the world in more humble circumstances—an outhouse His birthplace, a manger His cradle, a bundle of straw His pillow? And so poor was the mother, that when she presented Him in the temple she could only offer the sacrifice appointed for the LOWLY, a pair of turtle doves. His home was in a despised country town; and a carpenter had the care of His early days, who, as soon as He was able to handle the tools, taught Him to hew the timber, to saw it into planks, or to plane it for the common uses of His LOWLY trade. And for more than sixteen years He persevered in the dull monotony of a "working man's" life.

In the days of his brief public ministry He still took His place among the Lowly. His associates were for the most part poor. His mission was among publicans and sinners. His disciples were fishermen, and He was ever followed by the poor, the sick, and the miserable. He had no house of His own, nor place wherein to lay His head. In preaching the gospel of the kingdom, His long and weary journeys were accomplished on foot; or, when it was otherwise, He moved to and fro on the lake of Gennesaret in a boat that was borrowed. And when at last He was buried, it was in another man's grave.

Thus His outward estate on earth was LOWLY; but this was because He was "LOWLY IN HEART." And we are to learn of Him to be Meek and Lowly too; so shall we find rest to our souls.

LORD OF HOSTS is a Title given to Him in Isaiah 54:5, and in many other places; and LORD OF SABAOTH, which has the same meaning, in James 5:4, and elsewhere. This august description places before us the vast teeming multitudes in heaven and on earth and under the earth—all subject to His absolute dominion. The Hosts of heaven count it their highest happiness to obey Him. Even during the days of His humiliation, "angels, authorities, and power" were still subject to Him and loved to do His pleasure, "hearkening to the voice of His word." And the Hosts of hell trembled before Him, owned Him for their LORD and Judge, and cried, "We beseech Thee, torment us not. Send us not into the deep." He is the LORD of the Hosts marshaled upon earth's battlefields, and holds in His hands the balances of victory. The great and the small alike own His LORDSHIP over them. He is LORD of the Hosts of worlds that glitter in yonder sky, with all their "sweet influences." He looseth the bands of Orion and guideth Arcturus with his sons. Yea, He called them all by their names, and not one faileth to do His bidding. And He is LORD of the Hosts of insects, oft summoned from hidden repositories, to inflict His dreadful judgments. At His word, nauseous Hosts of lice or flies issue forth to devastate the land of Egypt; or, still more fearful, Hosts of locusts sometimes spread themselves over fruitful districts, devouring every green thing. He is LORD of the "Living" Hosts of men and women that swarm upon the earth, and LORD of the still more numerous "Dead," that lie buried beneath its surface, or drowned in the depths of the sea.

LORD BOTH OF THE DEAD AND LIVING is the description of him in Romans 14:9. He is LORD OF THE DEAD, for "with Him are the souls of the departed." He hath the keys of their respective habitations and knows them all by name. And though nothing but dust remains of their bodies, He has laid it all up securely against the morning of the resurrection, when He will bring them to life again. Twelve hundred million and more of the "LIVING" crowd the earth at this present hour! How vast the multitude! how vainly the mind strives to realize it! But what is that to the number of the "DEAD"? All earth's teeming populations who died before the flood; and all who have died from Noah to Moses, and from Moses to Christ, and from that day to ours. Thousands upon thousands of millions!—DEAD indeed as to their bodies but ALIVE as to their souls. More ALIVE, in truth, than ever they were upon earth; and all gathered in some mysterious world under the universal LORDSHIP of Christ. From those unknown regions none ever return to inform us of the manner of their life, their joy, or their grief. But we are not altogether ignorant. "I heard a voice from heaven saying unto me, Write, Blessed are the DEAD WHICH DIE IN THE LORD, from henceforth. Yea, saith the Spirit, that they may rest from their labors; and their words do follow them." And, as to those who did not die in the Lord, we know the LORD OF THE DEAD hath them all in His righteous charge, for He holds the keys of all the departments of Hades.

He is LORD OF THE LIVING also; for "He fixes the bounds of their habitation, and the number of their months is with Him." It is His to kill and to make alive. As no accident or disease can remove you till He please, so no skill can prolong your life when He shall say, "Return ye children of men." In that moment He will change the countenance of the LIVING, and send them away to the abodes of the DEAD. "I will not die! no, I will not die! exclaimed one when informed that death was near. Rising from his sick bed he rushed into the garden, still declaring "that he would not die." But his time was come! Affrighted friends bore him back fainting to his bed from which he never rose again. Death called for this man before he was ready, and would take no denial. On the other hand, there are some for whom death seems so long a-coming that they find it hard work to maintain their patience to the last. See that ancient woman. She is the mother of Dr. Dwight. She has reached the advanced age of 102 years. The bell tolls for a funeral; upon which she bursts into tears and exclaims, "Oh, when will the bell toll for *me*? I am afraid that I shall never die!" We must all abide His pleasure Who "hath the keys of Death and Hades, Who shutteth and no man can open, Who openeth and no man can shut"; and leave Him to determine the length of our life and the time of our death, Who is LORD BOTH OF THE DEAD AND LIVING. He is also the LORD OF GLORY.

LORD OF GLORY (1 Cor. 2:8). His glory fills heaven and earth. The skies declare it; the sun publishes it; the moon makes it manifest. Everywhere it is visible. But it is most conspicuous in the heaven of heavens. There in His "ivory palaces" is His starry throne, and round about it a rainbow like unto an emerald. No mortal eye could bear its dazzling brightness. But it is His will that all who love Him should see His glory; and for that vision He will prepare you if you ask Him. And the effect of that wondrous sight will be, even as you look upon it, to change you from glory to glory into the same likeness.

LORD OF ALL (Acts 10:36). LORD OF ALL power and might; ALL worlds, ALL persons, ALL things, ALL events: "He hath left nothing that is not put under His feet."

He is LORD of the Seasons; He causeth plenty to crown the labors of the husbandman, or He "calls for a famine" to chastise the crimes of an ungrateful nation. He is LORD of the Elements; the winds are His ministers, and earthquakes and volcanoes fulfill His word. At His righteous command the earth opens to swallow up populous Lisbon with its busy inhabitants; or a river of fire pours forth from burning Vesuvius, and overwhelms the cities of Pompeii and Herculaneum. "Oh LORD, our LORD, how excellent is Thy Name in all the earth!" The prophet Micah calls Him the "LORD OF THE WHOLE EARTH" (Mic. 4:13). He is seen to be

LORD OF THE WHOLE EARTH, in the particular Providence that He exercises over the circumstances of each individual life. Nothing is too trivial for His notice. Not a sparrow, not an insect falleth to the ground without Him. How much more doth He dare for man, choosing the place of his birth and fixing the bounds of his habitation. The same sovereign hand continues with him in his passage through life. "A man's heart deviseth his way; but the Lord directeth his steps." Success does not depend upon talent, nor education, nor wealth, nor friends; nor upon anything else that is human, but on the Lord alone. "Promotion cometh neither from the east nor the west; the LORD is Judge, He setteth up one, and putteth down another." It is His prerogative to determine who shall be poor, and who shall be rich; who shall occupy a throne, and who shall serve in the meanest offices. And it is a man's place cheerfully to acquiesce in the choice thus determined for him by infallible wisdom and infinite goodness. And then God will make all things work together for his good. "Along the streets of the town of Bedford," writes Dr. Upham, "the poor and illiterate preacher, John Bunyan, is conducted to prison. Years roll on. To human appearance all his earthly prospects are cut off; he has no books, with the exception of the Bible and the Book of Martyrs. Had he not been imprisoned, he would have lived and died as do many other men; known, perhaps, and useful within the limits of a single town and for a single generation. But, shut up in prison, and cut off from worldly plans, God was able to work in him, in His own wonderful way, and to guide his mind to other and higher issues. It was there he wrote that remarkable work, *The Pilgrim's Progress.* Had his enemies not been allowed to prevail against him it probably would not have been written. It was thus that the LORD turned that which was designed for evil into good. It was a wisdom higher than man's wisdom that shut up the pilgrim himself in prison. *The Pilgrim's Progress,* which was the result of the imprisonment of the pilgrim whose progress it describes, free as the winds of heaven, goes from house to house, knocks at every heart, teaches all classes, visits all nations."—But, again, He calls Himself by this Title,

LORD OF THE HARVEST (Matt. 9:38). The field is the world. The harvest is that of redeemed souls, and the laborers are ministers, parents, and religious teachers of all sorts. In short, all the Lord's people, whoever they are, are laborers in this harvest. See how it is in husbandry. One drives the plow, another dresses the ground; one sows the furrowed field, another "reaps the bearded grain," or binds the golden sheaves. There is work for everyone whom the master calls into the field. So it is in Christ's great harvest field, the world! There is something for each to do, while the Great LORD OF THE HARVEST, by His Spirit and His Providence, superintends the labors of all.

He calls some to special works of difficulty or danger. He appoints one minister to almost solitary toil and unknown hardship in barbarous lands, far away; and another to less arduous duties at home, where he is surrounded by many sympathizers. He distributes to each his peculiar gifts and qualifications, severally, as He wills—"to one ten talents, to another two"; and He it is who determines their term of service. He calls one away from successful labors into a sick room for a season, or consigns him to enforced inactivity for life. While another scarcely begins his work, when he is summoned away to higher occupations in heaven.

1. *Let us* PRAISE *the* LORD OF THE HARVEST, that ever since He ascended up on high, He hath not failed to "give gifts unto men," fitting them for high and honorable service. Prophets, apostles, martyrs, confessors, reformers, evangelists, in long succession, have been raised up for the world's requirements in all ages. And still they come. For what would become of the HARVEST if the laborers were to cease?

2. *Let us* PRAY *to the* LORD OF THE HARVEST, that it may please Him to "send forth more laborers." For the wants of the world are pressing, and much ground is totally unoccupied. "The HARVEST is plenteous, but the laborers are few." And let us each say, "Lord, what wilt Thou have *me* to do?" And when we have proved what is His acceptable will, let us devote ourselves to our work, "always abounding therein, forasmuch as we know our labor shall not be in vain in the Lord."

> How many serve, how many more
>   May to Thy service come!
> To tend the vines, the grapes to store,
>   Thou dost appoint for some;
> Thou hast Thy young men at the war,
>   Thy little ones at home.
>
> Employ me in Thy service, Lord,
>   And train me for Thy will;
> For even I in fields so broad
>   Some duties may fulfill;
> And I will ask for no reward
>   Except to serve Thee still.

The only Title which remains for me to mention today, is one that first occurs in Isaiah and is afterwards claimed by our Lord in His Revelation to John, "I am the LAST."

LAST (Isa. 44:6; Rev. 1:17). This Title, taken in connection with "THE FIRST," teaches us the eternity of His duration. Yea more; it intimates that he is the AUTHOR OF ETERNITY, the FATHER OF SUCCESSIVE AGES, and the ONLY LORD AND PROPRIETOR OF IMMORTALITY. Yet there are some other ideas that it naturally suggests.

1. *He is* LAST *in the estimation of men*; He is even "abhorred by the people." At the moment of His greatest humiliation, when He hung upon the cross, we are struck with the amazing extremes that met in Him. We see Him who is THE FIRST, being God over all, THE LAST, in the amazing depth of His outward degradation. No being in the universe seemed so abandoned as He. The two thieves who were crucified with Him were probably commiserated, and their last moments left undisturbed by reproaches. But upon Him was heaped all the scorn of almost all Jerusalem! The soldiers seem to have behaved with more brutality than usual, and the people too have gone out of their way to deride and insult Him. He was looked on as at once the most presumptuous and the most worthless of mankind. And in their zeal to mock His claims to be the FIRST, they were determined He should be the LAST and LOWEST OF ALL! And God permitted it, for it was "their hour and the power of darkness."

And is not Jesus Christ Last in the esteem of men still? Does not almost all the world either openly oppose Him, or inwardly despise Him? Is He not the Last to whom we turn for happiness? Yea, even when we become anxious about our souls, do we not usually try everything else before we go to Him for salvation? We go about to establish our own righteousness, or we trust in our own strength; we must be *driven* from every hold and every idol—it may be by painful discipline or agonizing conviction—and at length hardly come Him. He is the Last. It is many hundreds of years since our Lord said He would "draw all men unto him"; and, it seems, hundreds more must elapse before His words shall be fulfilled. "Beautiful and Glorious" as is the "Branch of the Lord," He will be the Last who will win the admiration of the world. Not until it shall have grown weary of every other object of desire, and disappointed in every other pursuit, will it "turn to the Lord." But it shall come to pass in the latter days. He who is Last in the esteem of the wide world will then be First. And every knee shall bow to Him, and every tongue confess, saying, "Asshur shall not save us, neither will we say any more to the work of our hands, Ye are our gods."

2. *He is the* LAST *who shall reign on the earth.* His kingdom shall "break in pieces and consume all other kingdoms, and fill the whole earth." When "all other thrones shall be cast down," there will be "given to Him dominion and glory, and all people and nations and languages shall serve Him." He will con-

quer all other conquerors, and upon the battlefield He will be the LAST. And then great voices of many people will be heard, saying, "Alleluia! salvation, and glory, and honor, and power, unto the Lord our God! His right hand and His holy arm hath gotten Him the victory."

3. *He is the* LAST *authority in judgment;* final Umpire and Judge of all men and things. Now—a sentence obtained in one court is often reversed in another. Disputes which were decided centuries ago are revived again; and arguments against God and the Scriptures, which have been answered a thousand times over, are urged afresh as if they were new. But when wise men shall have said all they can, He will have the last word. His voice—not bearing all down by force— but carrying with it full conviction, will determine every controversy and end all strife. "Who shall be the greatest?" is now the daily subject of dispute; but that question will be then settled once and forever. All things that have ever been done will come up for a final review; after which, men will no more stand in doubt, nor look for further trial; for He who will then acquit and condemn, re- ward and punish, is the LAST.

4. *He is the* LAST *who occupies the thoughts of the dying Christian.* An Irish girl who was once so depraved, that she would sit at her mother's door and throw stones at other children as they passed on their way to school, after a time thought she might as well go there herself. She did so, and soon a happy change came over her. By-and-by she became ill. She grew worse, till one day the clergy man came to see her, and found her dying. "Jane," said he, "you are just about to die; do you fear death?" "O no, sir. I know that my Redeemer liveth; He has passed through the valley of death before me, and though dark, it is only the *shadow* of death." Then, clasping her hands, she said, "Wonderful—Counselor— Mighty God—Everlasting Father." Her sister fell on her neck and kissed her, and, weeping, said, "O my darling sister! sure you will not leave me!" But Jane said, "The lips you kiss will soon be cold—'Kiss the Son!'" Her voice grew weak; her head sank on the pillow; she was just heard to whisper, "Jesus, the Way—Truth— Life," and then she ceased to breathe. Thus she passed away; Jesus was LAST in her thoughts and on her tongue, and the music of His Name refreshed her soul in her parting hour.

And we sometimes see, in the case of some aged pilgrim whose mind is gone, and who is in his second childhood, that the Savior is the LAST in His re- membrance, surviving every other idea. The poor man may not recognize his friends, and does not know his own children, but the name of his Savior still awakens in the lonely chambers of thought a sweet and thrilling echo. For some time before the death of the Rev. Joseph Slatterie, of Chatham, the faculties of his mind became entirely shrouded, so that he took no notice of any of his for- mer friends. One day Dr. Leifchild called to see him. He was announced by name, but that name, once so valued, awakened no emotion. "Brother Slatterie," said his visitor, "don't you remember me?" An incoherent sound was the only answer, and vain was every attempt to arouse him, till the question was put, "Do you know the Lord Jesus?" Then all at once the spell, which bound his faculties, seemed for a moment broken, and he exclaimed with glistening eyes—

> Jesus, my Lord! I know His Name,
> His Name is all my trust;
> Nor will He put my soul to shame,
> Nor let my hope be lost!

Jesus Christ was the LAST and never to be forgotten Friend, whose Name alone possessed this magic charm.

5. *He will be the* LAST *object of delight to saints and angels in heaven.* You know what the feeling of dissatisfaction is, for it is experienced more or less by all the world. Men try one thing and then another, and run an endless round, but are still dissatisfied, and so they will ever remain till they come to Christ. But even those who have learned His worth often lose their hold on Him, amongst the many things which occupy their thoughts and ensnare their affections; and just in proportion as they do this, their old feelings of dissatisfaction returns. But in heaven there will be no danger of their forgetting Him. He will fill their whole hearts and leave no room for a rival. Therefore the feeling of dissatisfaction will never be known there. They will never want to try some new source of joy. But still, as they follow the Lamb to fresh "fountains of living water," they will prove the truth of His promise, "*Whosoever shall drink of the water that I shall give him, shall never thirst.*"

32

Messiah. Man. Man of God's Right Hand. Man of Sorrows. Man That Is My Fellow. Mighty God. Maker. Most Mighty. Mighty One. Mighty to Save. Most Upright. Most Holy.

THE descendants of Abraham, from the first commencement of their history, were taught to expect the coming of a Great Personage into the world, who should be born among themselves and in Whom all nations should be blessed. He was to be at once King, Priest, and Prophet; to be victorious over all His foes; to set up a kingdom which should never be moved; and to take precedence of all other authorities in God's church. And the church in all ages looked out for His coming. Four thousand years they waited. Hymns were composed in honor of Him. Prayer also was made for Him continually, and daily was He praised. They used to pray Him to make haste and show Himself. "Be Thou like a roe or a young hart upon the mountains of separation." They used to sing, "Gird Thy sword upon Thy thigh, O Most Mighty, with Thy glory and Thy majesty, and in Thy majesty ride prosperously." And God sent heralds from time to time to reveal the date and manner of His approach. He was to come, they said, like the rain, and steal upon them like the dew; for to the outward eye, His appearance would be without form and attraction. Well, in process of time, after they had waited and prayed, He did come—this "Desire of nations," the MESSIAH.

MESSIAH THE PRINCE (Dan. 9:25). And He came, as had been foretold, softly and silently. No sound of a trumpet proclaimed Him near. No cry lifted up in the streets called the people from their labors to come and behold Him. But as David, when he went up against Goliath, refused to put on Saul's glittering armor, and chose the sling and the stone, so Christ would not clothe Himself in kingly power and outward glory, but came in all simplicity, with scarcely anyone to attend Him. With a still small voice He told them that He was the great Person they looked for. And some said, "We will not have such a man as this for our MESSIAH"; but some believed and said, "This is He." With what joy did the first disciples of our Lord greet their brethren with the exclamation, "Hail, companions! We have joyful news—we have found the Messiah!"

"What! Him, of Whom Moses and the Prophets did write?"

"The very same."

"Nay, we cannot believe it. It is too good to be true."

"Come and see then for yourselves. We will lead you to the very place where He lodges." And when they saw the Lord, they owned it was a true report, and cried out, "Rabbi! Thou art the Son of God! Thou art the King of Israel." We wonder not at their conclusion, but we wonder much that the Jews still reject Him. For if He be not the Messiah, all the prophecies have forever failed, and cannot now be fulfilled. For was it not foretold that He should come while the second temple was standing? But that temple has been in ruins for many a long century. Was He not to be put to death before the sacrifices should cease, and at the expiration of 490 years from a certain date? But the sacrifices have ceased, and, calculate it how they will, the number of years specified must have come to an end about the time when our Lord suffered death. Then He was to come before the Jews should totally lose their "scepter" (or *rule*—for scepter does not necessarily imply *royalty*), and their "lawgiver" (or judge). But the last trace of authority passed away from them within a few years of the coming of Christ.

Some Jews in India, who were in the habit of reading their Scriptures together, were much impressed by that prophecy of Jacob in Genesis 49:10. "How is this?" they said. "Jerusalem has been destroyed, and the Jews are scattered, without the slightest trace of government remaining to them. Surely, if the Shiloh did not come before that event, Moses was a false prophet. But as we cannot admit that, surely the Christians must be right. We will embrace the Savior of the New Testament." So they declared their new convictions, and were baptized.

But even if all that evidence could be evaded, there remain many minute prophecies of the Messiah, fulfilled in Jesus of Nazareth; which are too remarkable to be set aside. For instance, He was to be born of a Virgin, of the Tribe of Judah and family of David. His birth was to take place at Bethlehem. It was foretold that He should ride into Jerusalem on an ass—be betrayed by a friend—be sold for thirty pieces of silver, which money should be immediately paid for a potter's field. Also that He should be smitten with a rod upon the cheek—be spit upon—be pierced in His hands and feet; that His enemies should give Him vinegar and gall in His distress, and part His garments among them, casting lots on His vesture; and that he should be numbered both with the wicked and the rich in His death and burial. You can search all these out, and many more in the Bible for yourselves. And while you compare the prophecies with their minute fulfillment, you will not be astonished that many an obstinate unbeliever has been forced to submit to the overwhelming evidence thus furnished. Particularly was this the case with the Earl of Rochester, who has been described as "a great wit, a great sinner, and a great penitent." He was a most determined infidel till, one day, he heard the fifty-third chapter of Isaiah read, whereupon "he felt an inward force which do so constrain him" that he could resist the truth no longer. "The word," he said, "had an authority, which did shoot like rays of light into his mind." His infidel objections all vanished. He learned that wonderful chapter by heart, and often spoke of its contents with a heavenly pleasure; and "did ever after as firmly believe in the Savior as though he had seen Him."—Let me just add that the strangest contradictions were declared of "Him that should come." Though born to occupy a glorious throne, higher than the kings of the earth, He was yet to be despised and rejected of men. He was both rich and poor, both a Priest and a Sacrifice—a King and a Servant—the Lord of Life and yet subject to death—David's Lord and David's Son—the Mighty God and the Child Born—the Great I AM and at the same time a "MAN."

MAN (Acts 13:38). A real MAN He was to be: a Child that should be born, and grow, and acquire knowledge by degrees. "The Word was *made flesh.*" He had a body capable of pain and hunger, and which required sleep and food; and a soul susceptible of anguish and enjoyment. But why did He become MAN? That He might be capable of suffering, which, as God, He could not be. That He might have a life which He could lay down, and blood which He could offer for the washing away of human guilt. But He is such a MAN as never was before, and never will be again, He is the "MAN OF GOD'S RIGHT HAND."

MAN OF GOD'S RIGHT HAND. See Psalm 80:17, where the Jewish nation is compared to a vineyard, in which should grow up a BRANCH, called also the SON OF MAN (vv. 15, 17). The psalmist prays that God will remember the royal house of David, well-nigh wasted, for the sake of King MESSIAH Who was to spring from it; and bring this HOPE OF ISRAEL into the world. And blessed be God, He hath heard this prayer; and when He united the human nature to the Person of His own Son, He made Him strong for Himself and equal to the work He had given Him to do. This glorious MAN is spoken of as sitting *at* GOD'S RIGHT HAND; as exalted *by* GOD'S RIGHT HAND; yea, He *is* GOD'S RIGHT HAND— His Servant by whom He will gather Israel, save sinners, and accomplish His will. God hath given Him "dominion and glory and a kingdom, that all nations and languages should serve Him. His dominion is an everlasting dominion which shall not pass away; and His kingdom that which shall never be destroyed." But all this joy set before Him must be reached through seas of suffering. Therefore must He be a "MAN OF SORROWS and acquainted with grief."

MAN OF SORROWS (Isa. 53:3). Sorrow came upon this holy Sufferer from all sources at once. There were sorrows caused by the wicked, for they hated, rejected, and killed Him. There were sorrows from beneath, for the gates of hell assailed Him with all their strength. There were sorrows from the hand of His Father, for "it pleased the Lord to bruise Him." The greatest sufferer that ever lived was not so deeply acquainted with grief as this MAN OF SORROWS. "His visage was marred more than any man, and His form than the sons of men." We are apt to suppose that He must have ever had at hand a store of alleviations, because He was God. We forget that He suffered as a MAN, and that it was "so ordered that His Divine nature should not prevent the full tide of anguish from flowing over His soul."

There is an enclosed garden, just outside the city of Jerusalem, which is said to have been the scene of our Lord's agony. And we are told that eight ancient olive trees still remain, casting their broad shadows over the earth, which once received the precious drops of the Savior's blood. There He spent part of the last night, previous to His death. His three disciples, unable to comprehend His sore amazement, sought refuge from their perplexing thoughts in sleep. But how did He pass that dark hour? We see Him restless and agitated, pacing to and fro beneath those gloomy olives. Three times He waked up His slumbering attendants, as though He longed for their sympathy and wondered that they could rest. "He trod the winepress alone; He looked for some to take pity but there was none, and for comforters but He found none." How bitter must have been the mixture in that cup to have wrung from Him the thrice-repeated cry, "Father, if it be possible, let this cup pass from me!" But it could not pass. It was the cup of gall and wormwood, of justice and penalty, due to sinners whose Substitute He was. But in vain we pay visits to Gethsemane, whether real or imaginary, and in vain we weep at the recital of His agonized sufferings upon the cross, while we miss their deep meaning and solemn lessons. What lessons do they teach? These two among many.

First. *That sin and suffering are inseparable.* Either you must take your sins to the MAN OF SORROWS, and ask Him that His sorrows may avail for their remission—that "by His stripes you may be healed"; or you must say to sorrow, "Be thou my companion henceforth and forever." Ponder, I pray you, this alternative. And if, convinced of sin and danger, you seek refuge in "Jesus crucified for you," then there follows,

Secondly, *Conformity to His sufferings. You must be crucified with Him.* Let me explain this. Jesus Christ has two natures, with one of which He died for sin. And every Christian hath two natures. One of them is called "the flesh." This he must crucify, with all its corrupt affections and lusts. The process may be painful, agonizing, protracted; for still it begs and prays to be spared. But, just as Jesus Christ resolutely immolated His pure and sinless body, for your sake, in obedience to His Father's will; so, in subjection to the same will must you offer up in sacrifice, crucify, and kill, the old man, the body of sin, for Jesus' sake; that so you may "reckon yourselves dead indeed unto sin, and alive unto God through Jesus Christ." This is to "know the fellowship of His sufferings," and to be made conformable to His death. But we must proceed. Having looked at the Human side of Messiah's Person, let us now glance at the Divine. God, speaking of His illustrious Son, calls Him "THE MAN THAT IS MY FELLOW."

MAN THAT IS MY FELLOW (Zech. 13:7). This word means Companion, Next of Kin; and can imply nothing less than that He is God's Associate, His Equal in Nature and Rank. Not *another* God, for John says, "The Word that was *with* God in the beginning *was* God." And what does Jehovah say concerning this MAN whom He calls "MY FELLOW"? Well, in one place He says, "This is My Beloved Son," and in another, "Behold Mine Elect in Whom My soul delighteth." That is just what we should have looked for. But what He says here is the strangest and most appalling thing that can be imagined—"Awake, O sword! Smite the Shepherd." It is as if He had said, "Come from all quarters, ye troubles, and fight against Him. Come storms of persecution, and buffet Him. Come, legions of Satan, and harass Him. Come, cruel Jews and Romans, and crucify Him, for into your wicked hands do I deliver Him."

Oh! it is easy for us to say, "Forgive us our sins"; but do we consider at what infinite cost the power to forgive sins has been procured on the part of the Savior? If *we* escape the two-edged Sword of Justice, it is because its stroke fell upon *Him* as our Shield and Substitute. The Bible is full of the idea of substitution, sacrifice, propitiation. Its constant testimony is, "Die HE, or else the sinner must." There may be much, which we cannot explain in this doctrine, and we may not be able to meet every captious objection against it. But when men have said their worst, *there it remains*, and only he who receives God's gift as a little child can partake of the great salvation. Some of the ancient Jews deemed the things written about the MESSIAH so contradictory, that they invented the notion of two MESSIAHS—a suffering MESSIAH and a triumphant MESSIAH. But the two are one. The MAN OF SORROWS is the MAN, GOD'S FELLOW. He who hid not His face from shame and spitting, is the same Whom the hosts of heaven extol, as "worthy to receive honor, and glory, and praise, and blessing."—But there is another glorious Title under this head, "MIGHTY GOD."

MIGHTY GOD (Isa. 9:6). If, as was proved under the Title, God, (page 170), our Lord is *expressly called God, did things which only God can do, said things which only God can say, and receives from men and angels that worship which is due only to God*—why, what but prejudice, or dislike to the Savior, can induce anyone to dispute the fact? We maintain the glorious truth, that He is the MIGHTY GOD, the great I AM, clothed with majesty, and girded with strength. The divine work of creation is attributed to Him. For the Husband of the Church is called her "MAKER."

MAKER (Isa. 54:5). "Without Him was not anything made that is made." In Hebrews 1:10, these words are expressly addressed to Him, "Thou, Lord, in the beginning hast laid the foundation of the earth, and the heavens are the work of Thy hands." When the Great Father planned the work of salvation, He took care to lay help on One that is MIGHTY, who possesses all the power His Titles indicate, so that the work should not fail. Centuries before He came into the world, David called upon Him in the spirit of prophecy, "Gird Thy sword upon Thy thigh, O Thou MOST MIGHTY."

MOST MIGHTY (Ps. 45:3). Such language would sound like the keenest mockery, if addressed to any created being. It pertains to one "Fairer than the children of men," and Mightier than they. We read of exploits in history, which are considered "great," and of warriors who are called "Mighty." You can see in 1 Chronicles 11, an account of David's thirty captains, who were distinguished by this title; and of those among them who were called "the first three," the "three Mighties"; and also of the occasion of their obtaining that rank. You know the story of Samson, the lion killer, and the terror of all his foes, who bore away on his huge shoulders the gates of the city, bars, bolts, and all. And the story of Gideon, "the Mighty man of valor," who, with 300 men, vanquished an army many thousands strong. But all those were Mighty only *by comparison* with their fellow worms. Their strength was *derived* also. It came from the great Source of all strength. Our Redeemer is MIGHTY in His own right, the sole Sustainer of His own power, and that of everyone else. But why talk we of Mighty ones? "Who among the sons of the Mighty can be compared to the Lord, the MIGHTY ONE OF JACOB?"

MIGHTY ONE OF JACOB (Isa. 49:26). Around a grand mausoleum, amidst a proud display of funeral pomp and splendor, were once gathered all the nobility of France. They met to do honor to the remains of one who, for half a century, had been called, by universal consent, "The Great." Louis *the Great*! In one instant, at the touch of death, all his greatness vanished, his crown fell from his brow, his scepter was wrested from his grasp. On that solemn occasion the eloquent preacher, Massillon, stood forth to pronounce the funeral oration. Amidst breathless silence, he began with the slow utterance of these weighty words, "GOD ONLY IS GREAT." "How appropriate," writes Dr. Upham, "this utterance on such an occasion! How emphatically did it remove the arrogant title from the dishonored head of the poor mortal who had presumptuously worn it, and restore it to Him to Whom alone it belonged!" For "Thine, O Lord, is the greatness, and the power, and the glory, and the victory, and the majesty; for all that is in the heaven and in the earth is Thine" (1 Chr. 29:11).

Great indeed is this MIGHTY ONE. How great must he be Who is the Self-derived, the Self-subsistent!

> He was not born! There is no fount
> From which His Being flowed;
> There is no end which He can reach,
> For He is simply GOD.

Great; for He is the Fountain of Life to all who live, and all who have ever lived, and all who ever shall live. He telleth their number, He calleth them by their names, He appointeth their mission and shapeth their history. He hath formed all yon multitudinous host of worlds, which we discern in the calm depths of the midnight sky. Their measurements stagger us! Their distance from each other confounds us! Their number bewilders our imaginations at their utmost stretch! Yet if I know no more than science and observation teach me of the greatness of this MIGHTY ONE, I might indeed say, "O how I fear Thee, Living God!" But I could scarcely say, "O how I love Thee!" As one says, "There would be little consolation for us all in this glory, if the crowning glory of His grace were not to abide. Every other song in His praise would be altogether silenced if we might not sing, 'His mercy endureth forever.'" Those Mighty ones to whose exploits we have referred, were for the most part Mighty to destroy. But the MIGHTY ONE OF JACOB is expressly described as "MIGHTY TO SAVE."

MIGHTY TO SAVE (Isa. 53:1). This is the work He came to do, in which His soul delights, and on which He expends His greatest strength. True He is MIGHTY to create, and MIGHTY to keep creation a-going. But this is His greatest glory, and it is this which most endears Him to us, that He is MIGHTY TO SAVE. Then surely,

First, *None should despair of his own salvation.* What, though your sins seem to be the worst that ever were, it is the darkest sin of all to harbor the thought that they cannot be forgiven.

Second, *None would despair in reference to others.* No case is so desperate as to be beyond His reach. Lady Mary Fitzgerald was a devoted Christian mother; and when her son was justly condemned to suffer death for a deed of darkness, she was instant in prayer for the salvation of his soul. She continued her fervent supplications till the hour struck at which the sentence was appointed to be carried out—and then ceased. To the two ministers who attended him to the scaffold and continued their exhortations to the last, his case seemed one of hopeless impenitence. But the rope broke! And then ensued a marvelous scene. He begged the sheriff to grant him a little time, if it were but one half-hour, that the minister might return to him; declaring that during the few seconds of his suspension, he had had such a sight of the enormity of his sins, and their dreadful consequences, as had quite changed his mind towards the gospel he had despised. The sheriff gave him the short reprieve. The minister returned and again preached the rejected gospel; and the penitent man continued in prayer during the allowed interval, and then submissively acquiesced in the just sentence of the law. Again,

Third, *None should forbear efforts to save others because he feels himself to be such a feeble instrument.* Salvation depends not on the instrument, but on Him who is MIGHTY TO SAVE. Sometimes out of the mouth of children "God has ordained strength" to overcome the impenitence of obdurate hearts.

At the door of a Welsh cottage sits a little girl reading her Bible. A dusty traveler who is making the tour of the Principality on foot, tired and thirsty, stops and asks her to give him a little water. "Water! sir," she said, "if you will come in, my mother will give you some milk." The tourist enters, and the child resumes her reading. After he is rested he goes forth, saying, as he passes, "I see you are getting your task, little girl." "Oh no sir," she replies, "I am reading the Bible." "Aye, getting your task out of the Bible I suppose." "No, sir, it is no *task* to me to read the Bible, it is a *pleasure.*" These are simple words, and the speaker is only a child. But the infidel, for such he is—Hone, the author of the Every Day Book—receives a lesson, which, by the blessing of God, sets its stamp upon his future existence. The words impress him so strongly that he determines to read the Bible for himself. And not long afterwards he is found amongst the foremost in defending Scripture truth. But Christ Jesus is not only MIGHTY TO SAVE; He is also MOST UPRIGHT in His method of saving, and in all that pertains to the dispensation of forgiveness to the penitent and believing.

MOST UPRIGHT (Isa. 26:7). Our misery and helplessness establish no claim upon Him; nor do our sorrow and reformation. But if He deign to bind Himself by promise, THE MOST UPRIGHT can do no other than keep His word. And is not His promise to the returning sinner most absolute? What more could He have done or said to assure *us,* and bind *Himself?* Did He not expire in agonies and blood on purpose that He might have the power, the pleasure, the privilege, of forgiving the transgressor without dishonor to His Great Father, or disparagement to the eternal principles of justice? And is not His invitation a virtual promise? For what should He call us to His feet if not for forgiveness? Doth He not command us to believe? And what do we believe for, if not that we may be justified instantaneously? Has He not left orders to His Church that the world should be flooded with ambassadors, whose business it is to press forgiveness on every creature, and to beseech sinners to be reconciled? Has He done all this, and when we go to Him and ask Him to make good His word will He send us away unforgiven, unjustified? Oh, what do our suspicious, distrustful hearts take Him to be, that we should judge Him capable of dealing with us thus?

Again, He is MOST UPRIGHT in His judicial awards. This is most important. For the Father judgeth no man, but hath committed all judgment to the Son. And He, MOST UPRIGHT, doth accurately try the path of the just and of the unjust; He pondereth all his goings and weigheth them in unerring balances with strict impartiality. And so every man shall receive his own reward, and every transgressor a just recompense. Nor is He unrighteous to forget the labors and gifts of love. The two mites of the poor widow outweighed all the costly donations of the rich Pharisees. These in comparison were lighter than air. The hypocritical "charities" in which they wrapped up their covetous extortions only increased their condemnation. There is yet another Title which claims insertion here. You will find it in Daniel 9:24. The

MOST HOLY. It was no wonder if the Jews sometimes felt a little impatient for the arrival of their Messiah. But God assures them by His prophet, that He should be certainly *Anointed* or Consecrated to His great work at the appropriate time. That he should then, as Dr. Owen translates it, *"be made a* Messiah *of."* "Such a High Priest became us, Who is Holy, harmless, undefiled, and separate from sinners." If this be not the meaning of Most Holy—if instead of describing the Person and Character of the Savior, it refers to a *place* (as has been affirmed)—then it can only belong to the Most Holy Sanctuary not made with hands, into which the Most Holy Priest was to enter, to accomplish His Ministry of Intercession. But whichever is the correct interpretation, we can scarcely read this sublime Title without remembering Isaiah's awful vision of Christ in His glory, narrated in Isaiah 6:1–8. For that it *was* Jesus Christ, John informs us (John 12:37–41).

But what a reproof does the solemn, awe-stricken worship of those glorious seraphim, "first among the songs of glory," convey to us, whose reverence is so deficient, and whose acts of worship are sometimes disfigured by the downright absence of reverence! In the great congregation do we never yield to inattention and drowsiness? In the family service are the devotions never slurred over because of pressing occupations? And as to our place of seclusion for solitary prayer, what does He Who seeth in secret behold there? Let us judge ourselves, that we be not condemned with the irreverent world.

Let us often recall the theme of the seraphim's praises. It was not, Merciful, Gracious, and Long-suffering is the Lord of Love. Not, Mighty, Majestic, All-victorious is the Lord Omnipotent. Either would have been a grand hymn to raise. But "Holy! Holy! Holy! is the Lord of Hosts." Oh, how shall we who were shapen in iniquity, hope to tread the unstained pavement of heaven, and venture to stand with the seraphim before the Holy Lord God? What comfort have we but from the persuasion that our standing will be on *His* right, not *our own*? In Him alone is our hope, "Who offered Himself without spot unto God," and Who, by virtue of that one offering, is "able to present us faultless before the presence of his glory with exceeding joy."

> Holy! holy! holy! all the saints adore Thee,
> Casting down their golden crowns around the glassy sea;

Cherubim and Seraphim falling down before Thee,
Who wast, and art, and evermore shalt be.

And now, upon the great theme of this day's Reading, permit me just to build one exhortation; Rest not till you have found the MESSIAH for yourselves, and made Him by personal application your own Savior. You need not wander about asking, "Master, where dwellest Thou?" nor say to friends, "Sirs, we would see Jesus." Behold He stands at the door waiting, with your consent, to enter your heart and "make His abode with you."

"Does Jesus Christ live here?" This startling question came from a rough Indian boy, as he struggled through a hedge towards a lady who sat under a bamboo shelter, superintending a native school. "Does Jesus Christ live here?" he demanded almost impatiently, as he rushed up the steps of the veranda and threw himself at her feet.

"What do you want with Jesus Christ?"

"I want to see Him—I want to confess to Him."

"What have you been doing, then?"

"Does He live here?—I want to know that. I want to see Him, for I have heard that He can save us from hell! O tell me where I can find Jesus Christ! I want to stop doing wickedly, but I don't know how—what can I do?"

"But you cannot see Him now," said the lady. The boy uttered a cry of disappointment. "But," added she, "I am His servant, and He has sent me to teach all those who wish to escape from hell, how they may do so." At this his face brightened again.

"Tell *me*—Oh tell *me*. Only ask your Master to save me, and I will be your slave. Do not send me away. I want to be saved."

Of course he was not sent away but received further instruction; and of course (for what else could be the result of such earnestness?) he became a Christian. He lived several years after that; and when he had become a young man, he died and went to heaven's gate, not to say, "Does Jesus Christ live here?—tell me where I may find Him"; but to enter, unchallenged, and to sit down at the King's table, a welcome and honored guest. O let not the earnestness of this poor Indian boy bear witness against *you* at the last day! Follow his example. Let all things go that may seek acquaintance with THE MESSIAH. And at last you shall hear His welcome invitation—

To see My face thou long hast striven;
Come, see thy place prepared in heaven.
Sit down and take thy fill of joy,
At my right hand a bidden guest,
Drink of the cup that cannot cloy,
Eat of the bread that cannot waste.

33

Moses. Messenger of the Covenant. Minister of the Circumcision. Master. Master in Heaven. Morning Star. Man of War. Michael.

"How is it that I can remember your sermons better than other people's?" asked someone of the Rev. Andrew Fuller. "I cannot tell," replied he, "unless it be owing to arrangement. I pay particular attention to that." And then he illustrated his meaning by a comparison something like the following: "If I were to ask you to fetch my spade, some sealing wax, a garden rake, a little ink, a hammer, a pen, a hoe, a sheet of paper, and some nails, you might well say, 'Pray mention them again, for I have forgotten most of them already.' But if I were to say, 'I am going to write a letter, and shall want pen, ink, paper, and sealing wax; and afterwards I am going to work in the garden, and shall require a spade, a hoe, a rake, and a hammer, with some nails to fasten up the grapevine'; you would easily remember them all. Why? Because the several articles would naturally range in your memory under the two divisions, the letter-writing and the garden." The rule, thus familiarly illustrated by the great Baptist theologian, is a very good one. Pity it cannot be oftener observed. Let us follow it, as far as we can, in arranging the subjects that come next under observation. You know the Bible attributes to our Lord three principal offices—

> Christ is a Prophet, Priest, and King;
> A Prophet full of light,
> A Priest Who stands 'twixt God and me,
> A King Who rules with might.

Under these three heads, then, we will marshal the next ten or twelve subjects. And, first, let us consider His Prophetical office as illustrated by a Type and three Titles. The Type is Moses; the three Titles are Messenger, Minister, Master.

MOSES (Deut. 18:15, 18). "The Lord thy God will raise up unto thee a Prophet, from the midst of thy brethren, like unto me—unto Him shall ye hearken." In these remarkable words Moses refers to the Messiah, of whom he claims to be a Type. Not one of the prophets who succeeded him bears any specific resemblance to the Great Prophet-King in Jeshurun. In vain, therefore, we seek to trace any fulfillment of his prophecy till He came, of Whom Moses and all the prophets did write. A wonderful history, truly, was that of Moses, from first to last. His abrupt introduction to us, at three months old, is most interesting. You know the story well. His mother, afraid lest he should be slaughtered, and unable to hide him any longer, made for him a little ark or boat of the papyrus reed, coated with pitch; and, putting him into it, laid it down among the flags beside the river, charging Miriam, his sister, to keep her eye upon the precarious treasure. Presently Pharaoh's daughter draws nigh, perhaps to take her evening walk with her maidens, or, it may be, to perform her daily rite of absolution. And soon, one of them, espying the little ark, exclaims, "Yonder is something among the flags at the water's edge—it looks like a boat. I wonder what is inside!" "Shall we go and see?" says another. They receive the royal lady's permission, and, amazed at its contents, they lift up the ark with care and bear it to their mistress. She looks into the little skiff and there beholds the most beautiful child that ever was seen. His skin is soft and smooth, and his little lips round and ruddy. He fixes his large, dark, lustrous eyes full upon hers; and while she gazes and admires, behold the babe weeps. Oh those infant tears, how eloquent they are! Will she harden her heart against their appeal? No, she cannot withstand it. "This sweet babe shall not perish," she cries; "notwithstanding royal decrees, I'll keep the boy alive. I cannot suffer the little innocent to be devoured by crocodiles. It shall be mine!" Just then Miriam saunters by as if by accident, and hearing the words of the princess, offers to call a nurse, and receiving permission, forthwith fetches the child's mother. Well, under her fostering care, MOSES grows up a beautiful, fascinating boy. He is constituted heir to the king's daughter, and is brought up in all the grandeur this world can afford. But he cannot forget the counsels instilled into him by his mother. Finding, therefore, the court to be full of temptations, "when he was come to years," he refuses to be called the son of Pharaoh's daughter and abandons his royal home with all its attractions, "choosing rather to suffer affliction with the people of God, than to enjoy the pleasures of sin for a season."

Almost the next time we meet with him, he is become a venerable man of eighty. He is in the wilderness standing before a bush, all ablaze but unconsumed. Tread softly; for this is sacred ground. Moses is talking with the Great I AM; and from this time is in continual correspondence with God. No prophet in Israel was ever honored like Moses, who was forty days alone with God in the mount, and "whom the Lord knew face to face."

It was many years afterward, indeed just before his death, that he gave utterance to the remarkable prediction which stands at the head of this section. "A

Prophet like unto me." Wherein does the similarity consist? It would be interesting to trace it in the particulars of their lives. For instance; Moses was preserved in spite of Pharaoh's determination to have all the male children destroyed. So Jesus Christ was saved, when Herod ordered the innocents of Bethlehem to be massacred. Moses fled from his country, fearing the wrath of the king; but in his exile received a message—"Go, return; for all the men are dead which sought thy life." And Christ in His infancy was a fugitive too; and his parents were directed by a similar message to carry Him back again—"For they are dead which sought the young child's life." Moses fasted forty days in the mount, and Jesus Christ forty days in the wilderness. On the evening of deliverance Moses instituted the Passover. So Christ, the Lord's Supper, the night before the redemption of the world—Coincidences like these might be traced throughout the whole history. But I will not pursue the parallel any further in such points, but confine what I have to say to his official character. Moses delivered the Israelites from slavery; so Jesus Christ is our Deliverer from the bondage of sin. He was their Mediator with God, their Leader through the wilderness, and their Lawgiver and Ruler. So Jesus Christ is the Mediator, the Light and Leader of His people, and their Lord and King. Just a word or two on each of these particulars.

Are both DELIVERERS? Mark the parallel. Moses was commissioned to emancipate a nation of slaves from the bondage of Egypt. Christ comes to rescue a world of captives from the thralldom of Satan. Moses proved his divine legation by supernatural prodigies. Christ appealed to miracles as the credentials of His mission. Moses was withstood by Jannes and Jambres, magicians under the influence of evil spirits. Christ was opposed by the powers of hell, as well as by wicked men who were "of their father the devil."

Are both LEADERS? Again observe the analogy. The Hebrews did not reach their Canaan at once, but had to pass through a waste howling wilderness under the guidance of Moses. Believers in Christ do not immediately enter heaven, but are led through conflicts, perils, difficulties innumerable, ere they gain the promised land; and must pursue their pilgrimage ever looking to Jesus as their Captain.

Are both LAWGIVERS? Moses had authority from God to make laws, institute sacrifices, regulate worship for the Israelites, and forbid their departure from "the pattern," in the least particular. And with what jealousy God guarded the reputation and official dignity of his servant! "Were ye not afraid to speak against my servant Moses?" said He to Miriam and Aaron. And what swift retribution followed the arrogant attempt of Korah and his crew to overthrow his authority! So Jesus Christ claims absolute rule in the church that He hath constituted. And woe to them who add to His word, make void His laws, and pervert His Gospel! Neither popes, nor priests, nor prelates; neither councils, nor synods, nor convocations, have a right to enjoin aught in Church government or in matters of doctrine or worship, which have not sanction from the Great LAWGIVER. Nor will He fail to reckon with those who make themselves "lords over God's heritage" in any of these matters.

Are both MEDIATORS? Paul gives Moses this title in Galatians 3:19. Again and again he stood between God and the wayward people of his charge. So Christ is our MEDIATOR—In all these particulars, does He not stand out as the only One in whom the words of Moses are fulfilled—"A Prophet like unto me"?

But the chief thing for us to observe is that Moses was God's Minister in all that he did—God's Ambassador, sent to do it in His name, and by His authority. That is the principal point to be observed. He was the great Apostle and Prophet of the Jewish Church for the time then present, and their sole Authority in all religious ordinances. But when the time came for the great Jewish institution to vanish away, it was superseded by that which it prefigured—the Christian Church. And therein Jesus Christ occupies a similar prominent place, being the Head of the Church and the great Apostle of our profession.

Moses had the high honor of being the Messenger and Mediator of the national covenant between God and the Jews, and transacted all the business that pertained to it. But that covenant was "done away for the unprofitableness thereof," to make room for an everlasting covenant that should never be broken, because it was both a better covenant and established on better premise. All the business connected with this last covenant, Jesus Christ is engaged to arrange; Who is therefore called the ANGEL or "MESSENGER OF THE COVENANT" (Mal. 3:1).

MESSENGER OF THE COVENANT. He is God's MESSENGER to the whole world, Jew and Gentile, as Moses was to the Hebrew nation alone. He is therefore a MESSENGER to *you* and to *me*, as much as if we were addressed by name. But what is His message? It may be briefly summed up thus:

"The Father, Who sent Me, hath given Me a commandment what I should say. Thus saith the Lord, Incline your ear and come unto Me; hear, and your soul shall live; and I will make an everlasting COVENANT with you. I will sprinkle clean water upon you, and ye shall be clean. A new heart also will I give you; and I will put My Spirit within you, and cause you to walk in My statutes. For this is the will of Him that sent me, that everyone that believeth on the Son may have everlasting life, and I will raise him up at the last day. And here is my solemn attestation: Verily, verily, I say unto you, Him that cometh unto Me, I will in no wise cast out."

Observe, the message that Christ brings is in the form of a veritable COVENANT. It is an attested Conveyance, a Deed of Gift—sealed with the royal signet of the Great King who sends it—signed in characters of blood with the name of the MESSENGER who brings it; and countersigned by the Holy Spirit, who certifies all its promises to be yea and amen. What can be more sure than this Covenant, affirmed, as it is, by the "three that bear record in heaven"? But it wants one thing more to render it valid *for you*. It awaits your consent; it asks your acceptance; it requires your signature. You must put your name to it and "deliver it as your act and deed," if you would have it for your own.

If the Great MESSENGER Himself stood here now, confronting you with the roll in His hand, written within and without (not like Ezekiel's with lamentation, mourning, and woe, but) inscribed with all the precious promises and assurances which His lips have ever uttered, and were to ask, "Who among you will set his seal to this COVENANT? Here are made over unsearchable riches, an incorruptible inheritance, a crown, a mansion, a place on my throne. Who will sign his name and make it all his own?" Could any resist such an appeal? Would there not be voices responding on every side, I will—and I also—and I? "Oh, wilt Thou indeed accept my unworthy name?" each of you would be ready to cry. "Thou shalt surely have it, Lord. With all my heart and soul I will subscribe with my hand even now." You feel you could scarcely do otherwise. But why not do this as it is? Is the invitation less real, and the promise less sure, than if proposed by the MESSENGER personally? Nay, you dare not insinuate that. Why then hesitate any longer? Oh, while the Father calls you—while the MESSENGER beseeches you—while the Spirit and the bride say, "Come, hasten to receive the proffered grace, and with the sealing act of faith makes salvation your own."

But know, all ye careless ones, that just as the law hath its promise, Do this and live, on the one side; and on the other its penal sanction, Cursed is he that doeth it not; so hath the gospel two aspects towards you. He that believeth shall be saved, but he that believeth not—what shall become of him? There is a revealed way of escape for the man who hath infringed the law, but there is none for him who despiseth the gospel. And God is not slack concerning His promise, so He is not to be trifled with in relation to His threatening. We may learn from Jewish history, past and present, how ruinous a thing it is to refuse Him that speaketh to us from heaven. And this brings us to another Title, which belongs to His Prophetical office, namely,

MINISTER OF THE CIRCUMCISION, (Rom. 15:8); that is, MINISTER of the Jews, they being distinguished by the observance of that rite. He was God's MESSENGER first to them to whom, indeed, He almost entirely confined His *personal* ministry—"I am not sent but to the lost sheep of the house of Israel." Yet they rejected Him and His message also, and you know the dire consequences of that sin. But this Title hath a most benign aspect towards the future of that scattered people. They shall in the last days turn to the Lord, the veil shall be taken from their hearts, and they shall say, "Hosanna! Blessed is He that cometh in the name of the Lord!" They will then hail Him as their MINISTER, the Prophet like unto Moses—their great Rabbi, their Divine "MASTER,"—theirs and ours.

MASTER (Matt. 8:19). A Master (or Rabbi) is one who instructs, at the same time that he exercises authority, in familiar words, a schoolmaster, a tutor. Oh, there never was such a MASTER as Jesus Christ. He is not only a most learned Rabbi, but also "apt to teach." Job may well ask, "Who teacheth like Him?" For He can do that for His scholars which no other master can. If a boy is dull, can his teacher make him quick and clever? But this Divine MASTER of ours can make the most stupid of learners to be "of quick understanding in the fear of the Lord."

> No matter how dull the scholar whom He
> Takes into His school—He'll cause him to see;
> A wonderful fashion of teaching He hath,
> And wise to salvation He makes him by faith.

This present world is God's training college, where every heir, as long as he is a child, is "placed under tutors and governors," until the time appointed of the Father. And they are received into their Father's house only when they have completed their education. In Christ's great university there are many masters and monitors. And there are not wanting hard lessons and tears and chastisements, and these things make term time a time of great trial. Yet there are holidays occasionally, and times of refreshing and rest, and great prizes also for the diligent and persevering.

But who are the teachers and tutors? The *Holy Spirit* must be named first, for He is the Moderator, and the entire education of each scholar is superintended by Him, for without Him no one can think a good thought. Another teacher is *Creation*. He declares the glory of God and shows the learner His handiwork. And *Providence* is another. He teaches difficult problems by the algebra of mysterious signs and perplexing events. There is *Revelation* also. She is a wise and holy matron whose "every word is pure." Oh what wondrous things doth she unveil to those who are prepared to receive with meekness her engrafted words! What beautiful histories doth she relate to her pupils! What enchanting pictures doth she display!

Then the *Law* is also our schoolmaster. With him it is but a word and a blow. No transgression is overlooked; excuses, tears, cries, all are in vain. Indeed this hard taskmaster would drive all to despair if the Holy Spirit did not, at the proper moment, change the discipline. Then there is a place, forbidding-looking usher, named *Adversity*, who bears a great rod in his hand. With many stripes he makes both beauty and strength to consume away like a moth. But strange to tell, his students are very thankful for his treatment, and often say, "Before I was afflicted I went astray, but now have I kept Thy word." Next I will mention

Disappointment. What shall I say of him? He draws bitter tears, exacts many forfeits, and often takes away jewels and treasures, however highly prized, and dashes them to the ground before our very eyes. Nor must we forget *Prosperity,* with his smiling face. He is a great favorite with every one. But, it must be confessed, his mild methods do not suit all; at any rate, not long together. So, when the learners grow sleepy and idle under his hand, they have to be subjected to more severe discipline. I will only mention one more; *Poverty* is his name. A very stern teacher is he, and those who attend his classes often have a hard life of it. However, there are no unnecessary lessons taught in this college; for there is an "iron sinew" in our proud wills which it often requires much suffering to subdue. But let us not fear. Our MASTER has a very tender feeling for us. He will not lay upon us more than we are able to bear. And when patience shall have had her perfect work, we shall attain rich rewards, which shall make amends for all, even glory, honor, immortality, eternal life.

Oh, if you could read over the records of Christ's school, you would see how heartily the pupils of the GREAT RABBI endorse the painful methods He adopts with them; and how wonderfully they thrive under His tuition; by means of which they are trained for usefulness on earth, and fitted for sublime and holy service in the higher world. Thus far the Prophetical Office. Let us now turn our attention to Christ's Kingship. What have we to do to illustrate His Kingly Office?

We will begin with this same Title considered under another aspect. For Christ is not only a TEACHING MASTER, but a RULING MASTER. The apostle, in enforcing the mutual duties of masters and servants, sustains his appeal to the former thus, "For ye also have a

MASTER IN HEAVEN" (Col. 4:1). Jesus Christ is accomplishing a wonderful work upon earth in quickening the dead children of men, and building up the temple of His church with these recovered "living stones." At this He works incessantly, and the Father also, with the Holy Spirit. And He condescends to summon man "to the help of the Lord" in this work; a great honor indeed to be conferred upon earthen vessels, as fragile as they are, insignificant and unworthy.

First. It is the Great MASTER'S prerogative to *choose* His own servants; for His service is so noble and estimable, that no man can take this honor to himself, but he that is called of God as was Aaron. It is true the servant freely chooses Christ for his MASTER. But it is always because the MASTER first chooses him. And, what is very wonderful, He sometimes selects the most unlikely people in the world. He accosts a raging persecutor in the heat of pursuit, and says, "Go, work for Me"; and he obeys. He arrests a blaspheming infidel while busy plotting mischief among his companions, and says, "Come away! I have something better for you to do than that"; and he comes. He goes among Satan's roistering recruits, and beckons a thief, a drunkard, or a gambler, and allures him to His own sweet service. The man straight-away abandons old haunts and old pursuits with shame, and engages himself to his new MASTER. And not only does the MASTER engage the most unlikely people, but calls them often in the most extraordinary and remarkable ways.

A certain Christian traveling on the continent, and bent on doing good and making known the gospel, was walking alone through a mountainous district. Striking into a path, which bordered a deep ravine, he suddenly heard voices; and, looking through the bushes, he espied a number of banditti at their evening repast; for the sun was setting. His first thought was to hasten forward as quickly as possible. But his second thought was, Here is a fine opportunity to make Christ known, if indeed the attempt is not too hazardous. He hesitated a few moments. Then he thought he would take just another peep at the formidable gang below; when suddenly the loose earth crumbled beneath his feet, and he was precipitated right into the midst of them.

"A booty! a booty!" shouted the marauders.

He sprang to his feet and cried aloud, "Yes, a booty such as you have never had before."

There was a scowl on their faces, but he went on without heeding it, "I bring you good news of a Powerful Friend, who is able and willing to save both body and soul."

A tall, dark-featured man took up his words, "Save my soul? No one has ever cared for my soul. I have been a castaway from my birth."

The traveler opened his pocket Bible, and as the light was fast waning, repeated from memory several gospel invitations and promises. Finding their attention riveted, he went on a little, concluding with the verse, "This is a faithful saying, and worthy of all acceptation, that Jesus Christ came into the world to save sinners."

"Let us shake hands upon that," said one.

The traveler, thankful at hearing this speech, proposed prayer; and they all knelt down under the blue vault of heaven; he in the midst, and the robbers all around him. Upon rising, the dark-featured man begged a favor of him. "Will you give me your Bible, sir?"

"Will you promise to read it with prayer?" asked the other.

"I will," he answered.

"You shall have it," said the visitor.

Then they parted. Three years afterwards these two met again in Piccadilly. The traveler heard a voice addressing him—

"Excuse the liberty, sir, but did you visit such a place in such a year? And do you know *this book?*" And then the well-remembered, dark-featured man produced the Bible from his pocket, *well worn.* They grasped hands, and the former bandit said, "This gift of yours has been blest to my soul. And often have I prayed that I might meet you on earth to thank you for the inestimable boon."

We know not the subsequent history of that wandering sheep, thus strangely sought and found, and in such a sovereign manner rescued from his vicious and dangerous course. But can there be any doubt that his afterlife was devoted to the business of the MASTER Who had in this singular way enlisted him in His service? But,

Second. The MASTER *trains* His servants for their work. For all, even the most orderly and well-conducted among them, are totally unfit for His service in their native condition. They are worth nothing till He has made them willing; and educated them, and furnished them with the gifts and graces of His Spirit. For all were originally "servants of sin"; "afar off"; "dead in trespasses." And all had to be "turned from the power of darkness, in order to be translated into His kingdom." Strange materials out of which to mold servants for so sacred a work! Again,

Third. He *appoints* each to his place and directs him what to do. If a householder, who had announced his purpose to hire servants for his establishment, were to be surrounded with applicants who demanded, one to be appointed steward, and another to be installed as butler, and a third to be made coachman, would not such proceedings be very unseemly? And would not these self-elected functionaries all have to learn that the decision belonged not to them but to the Master? So must Christ's servant put himself entirely at the disposal of the MASTER IN HEAVEN. He must not say, I wish to do this kind of work, or I feel competent to that. Rather, " 'As the eyes of a servant are to the hands of his Master, so mine eyes wait on Thee,' until Thou shalt show me what Thou wilt have me to do."

In a great house there are vessels appointed to honor, and others for inferior uses. Of Eliakim, upon whose shoulder the key of the house of David was laid (Isa. 22:22–24), it was said, "They shall hang upon him all the glory of his father's house; all vessels of small quantity, from the vessels of cups to all vessels of flagons." That Lord Treasurer at Jerusalem, of whom such great things are written, was a type of the MASTER IN HEAVEN; Whom to serve in any capacity, whether as a hewer of wood or as a doorkeeper in His house, is a greater honor than to rule over an empire.

And whatever is the work which the MASTER gives us to do, be it ever so lowly, we are to do it with a will so as to please Him, whether we please man or not. Our common, ordinary work comes under this rule, as well as that which (if we use the term restrictively) we miscall our religious work. George Herbert has a quaint little poem, which he entitles "The Elixir," in which he says,

> Teach me, my God and King,
> In all things Thee to see;
> And what I do in anything,
> To do it as for Thee.
>
> All may of Thee partake;
> Nothing can be so mean
> Which, with this tincture—For thy sake,
> Will not grow bright and clean.
>
> A servant with this clause
> Makes drudgery divine;
> Who sweeps a room, as for Thy laws,
> Makes that and th' action fine.

Fourth. The MASTER *superintends* His workmen, carefully inspecting all they do. He says to each, "I know thy works."

Fifth. He *supplies* all necessary qualifications, furniture, and materials for their work: is with them always, to defend and sustain; and will never fail to afford them all the help, counsel, and encouragement they require.

Sixth. He *pays* them most munificent wages above all they can ask or think. The best services of the best of His servants are mean and unprofitable. But they will all be recompensed with an exceedingly rich reward, infinitely beyond all proportion to their value. A cup of cold water lovingly administered to a disciple, for Christ's sake, shall not pass unrecognized. For He regardeth the *spirit* of the service; not the amount of work got through merely, nor the place it occupies in the esteem of men. And so it will be no wonder if it shall come to pass that "many that are first shall be last, and the last first." But of all who serve Him He says, "Where I am, there shall My servant be."

All this belongs to the LORDSHIP of Christ—His KINGLY office. Let us now take the next under this head.

MORNING STAR (Rev. 22:16). We have before spoken of this symbol, and may hereafter have something more to add. We have now only to do with it in reference to His Royalty. A Star, in the Scriptures, is the well-known emblem of a Governor. In Balaam's prophecy—"There shall come a Star out of Jacob, and a Scepter shall arise out of Israel,"—the *Scepter* evidently fixes the meaning of the *Star*, and both refer to some future king. Who that is, it is not hard to say; for in the closing words of Revelation, our Lord, by adopting the simile, connects the ancient prediction with its glorious fulfillment in His own Person in the last days.

The MORNING STAR it is which brings up the train, and is the brightest and best of all; for, when it appears, daylight is at hand. So, after all rulers shall have had their little season, like flaming comets or blazing meteors, scattering terror and distress all around, He will come last and take the place of all the rest. He will come, shedding a mild, bright, clear light, that shall gladden every heart, and usher in the glorious millennial day. After the long night of darkness and misrule, the full establishment of His beneficent kingdom shall gladden the weary world, and be "like the light of the morning when the sun riseth, even a morning without clouds." But so great is the opposition, that He must be a Conqueror before He can enjoy His kingdom in peace. And so we pass on to another Title belonging to His Kingly office—Jehovah is a

MAN OF WAR (Ex. 15:3). When our first parents were overcome by Satan, God promised to raise up One Who should espouse their cause and revenge their defeat. In due time this Great Champion, this Seed of the Woman, entered the lists, single-handed and alone, to encounter all the strength of hell. At the first, indeed, the battle seemed to go against Him. Satan bruised the heel of his Opponent, who fell beneath the stroke. He was carried off the field covered with wounds, and lay three days concealed in the grave. For a time the issue seemed doubtful. Satan wondered whether he had gained the victory or no; while Christ's followers complained of their disappointment and were ready to give up their cause for lost (Luke 26:21). But on the third day all uncertainty was at an end. Christ rose from the dead, burst the bars of the tomb, came forth to the light, and openly declared Himself the CONQUEROR. "O sing unto the Lord a new song, for He hath done marvelous things; His right hand and His holy arm hath gotten Him the victory."

On the part of Conquerors there are usually great rejoicings and triumphal processions. Nor can we suppose that the victory won by our Lord, was destitute of a triumphant commemoration. The Psalmist says, "Thou hast ascended up on high. Thou hast led captivity captive." We read of a chariot of fire being sent to grace the ascension of Elijah. And "the chariots of God are twenty thousand, even thousands of angels." And shall they be wanting to grace the triumphal ascent of the Mighty Conqueror over sin and hell? Shall the morning stars sing and shout when the work of creation is completed, and shall they be silent when the greater work of redemption is finished? Shall they who hastened to sing His birthday song when the MAN OF WAR entered the field of battle, be absent when He returns from His mighty work, laden both with the scars and the spoils of victory? Without doubt, the angels escorted Him to the heaven of heavens with joy and praise, as in like manner they will when He comes to judge the world (Acts 1:11).

Forty days after His glorious victory He led His followers out to Bethany. There He blessed them and gave them His last commands, when suddenly a cloud veiled Him from their sight. He stepped into His fiery chariot, and went up into the skies. The mighty MAN OF WAR "having spoiled principalities and powers, made a show of them openly, triumphing over them." Then was the Lord received again among His angels, as in Sinai, in the holy place. There was the great multitude which no man can number, of the spirits of just men made perfect—all having the harps of God, and arrayed in white robes, with palms in their hands. There were the ten thousand times ten thousand chariots of God rolling in the heavens—the innumerable company of angels and archangels—the thrones and dominions, the principalities and powers in the heavenly places—all coming forth to greet Him.

> Legions of angels strong and fair,
>   In countless armies shine,
> And swell His praise with golden harps,
>   Attuned to songs divine.

> They brought His chariot from above,
>   To bear Him to His throne,
> Spread their triumphant wings and cried,
>   "His glorious work is done!"

And who can describe their heavenly music? The harpers harping with their harps, the sound of the trumpet, and the voice of the angels round about Him—the number of whom was ten thousand times ten thousand, and thousands of thousands—coming on the ear like the sound of many waters and the voice of mighty thunderings. And what is the burden of their songs? Listen! as they answer one to another: "Let us be glad and rejoice and give honor to Him, for the marriage of the Lamb is come! We give Thee thanks, O Lord Almighty, which wast and art, and art to come, because Thou hast taken to Thee Thy great power and hast overcome. Worthy is the Lamb that was slain to receive power, and riches, and wisdom, and strength, and honor, and glory, and blessing! Alleluia! for the Lord God Omnipotent reigneth." And as the glorious company soars upward, Oh what mighty joy fills all their hearts! While the attendant seraphs that lead the way to heaven's gates answer one to another in hymns of triumph: "Lift up your heads, O ye gates, and be ye lift up, ye everlasting doors, and the King of Glory shall come in. Who is the King of Glory? the Lord Strong and Mighty, the Lord MIGHTY IN BATTLE." And again the grand chorus bursts forth from all the choir—"Lift up your heads, O ye gates, even lift them up, ye everlasting doors, and the King of Glory shall come in."

Thus He passed into the heavens. But the sword of this Mighty MAN OF WAR is not yet sheathed. In Revelation 12:7, we have a glimpse of the Royal Warrior, under the name of "MICHAEL."

MICHAEL, with His Angels, is still fighting against the devil and his angels. I will not detain you on this Title, but refer you to the sealed book of the Apocalypse, and say, "Come and see!" For therein are depicted, in mystic symbols, the battles of this MAN OF WAR. Come and see Him *going forth to His conquests* (Rev. 6:2). "Behold a white horse, and He that sat on him had a bow; and a crown was given unto Him, and He went forth conquering and to conquer." And turning over a few leaves, you will come upon another vision of the mighty Conqueror *completing His triumphs.* Again the havens open and disclose the white horse, and Him that sat on him, clothed with a vesture dipped in blood. See Revelation 19:11–16. Most Mighty Warrior! glorious in Thine apparel, traveling in the greatness of Thy strength; gird Thy sword upon Thy thigh, with Thy Glory and Thy Majesty! Ride prosperously, and let Thy right hand perform terrible things!

> With force of arms we nothing can,
> Full soon were we down-ridden;
> But for us fights the proper Man
> Whom God Himself hath hidden.
> Ask ye who is this Same?
> Christ Jesus is His Name,
> The Lord Zebaoth's Son,
> He and no other one,
> Still Conqueror in the battle.
>
> LUTHER.

34

Melchizedek. Mediator. Mercy Seat. Minister of the Sanctuary. Merciful and Faithful High Priest.

THE desert of Arabia is, for the most part, a scene of savage wildness. Rugged rocks and shapeless blocks of granite are piled up around the barren mountains in the wildest disorder. The little spire of grass cannot grow there; the sweet flowers never blossom there. But frightful chasms abound, the haunts of slimy serpents, and steep precipices whereon the eagle and the vulture build their nests. It is in the midst of the most terrific part of that dreary scene that Mount Sinai, the place where God gave His law to the Jews, lifts its rugged summit.

At the foot of that mountain were once gathered the ten thousands of Israel, that they might meet with God, and hear His own awful voice enunciate all the words of the Covenant. Three days were given them to prepare for the solemn interview. And now the third day had arrived; and before Jehovah's awful throne they trembled with utmost alarm and terror; for in the early morning of that well-remembered day they had been aroused by the rolling of thunder and the voice of a trumpet exceeding loud; so that all the people in the camp trembled greatly. And well they might; for "Mount Sinai was altogether on a smoke because the Lord descended upon it in fire. And the Lord talked with them face to face in the mount out of the midst of the fire."

Now there was a fence set up around the foot of the mount, lest bold men, breaking through to gaze, should perish; and at the top of the mountain was the "fire and thick darkness where God was." And clouds went up like the smoke of a great furnace, covering the sky over their heads with a black curtain. From the midst of the darkness dreadful lightnings flashed and crashing thunders pealed. And all the mountains quaked and trembled greatly. But above all the din of the tempest the sound of the trumpet is distinguished.

> For still on Israel's awe-struck ear
> The voice exceeding loud,
> The trump that angels quake to hear
> Thrills from the deep, dark cloud.

309

It grows louder and louder, and then suddenly ceases. There is silence throughout the camp. And now the awful voice of God, louder than all, falls upon the ear, and fills every heart with terror and dismay. So dreadful were the sights—so fearful the sounds of that day, that even Moses exclaimed, "I exceedingly fear and quake!" Well might the people say to him, "Let not God speak to us; we cannot endure it. We shall die if we hear that awful voice again. Do thou speak to us, for thy voice we can bear." That was at Mount Sinai.

But we are come this afternoon to another Mountain. Its name is Mount Zion. And God also manifests Himself here. But, oh how differently! Is this the same God Who once came down with such terrible majesty? The same. There is but one God, and His Name is LOVE. He is a serene, happy, and merciful Being. But when He deals with sinners, it is needful to let them know how greatly He hates their sins. A milder morning has dawned upon us, wherein we also are summoned from our beds of sloth—"Awake, thou that sleepest, and Christ shall give thee light." As on Sinai, so on this Mountain there is brightness; but it is the mild light of the Day Star, not the fierce blaze of the lightning. There is the sound of a trumpet, but it is the silver trumpet of the gospel; not harsh and terrible to hear, but inviting and cheering as well as awakening. There is a "pillar of smoke" also going up towards heaven, but it is the smoke of the incense of Christ's intercession. There is the voice of words, but it comes to us in tones of peace and love: the still small voice of pity and compassion—"Come unto Me, and I will give you rest." The voice does not say, "Keep this law which I have engraven on stones, and live"; but it speaks of a *New* Covenant, and says, "I will write My laws in your hearts." It does not say, "Away, get you down!" but "Rise up, My love, My fair one, and come away!"

Jesus the Mediator has taken away all that was terrible; and sprinkled the Mountain with His "blood, which speaketh better things than the blood of Abel." The fierce glare of the lightning and the commotion of the tempest have yielded to the quiet sunshine of God's love, soothing our minds and inviting us to gratitude and thanksgiving. At Mount Sinai Moses said to the people, "Stand afar off; come not nigh, lest ye perish!" But at Mount Zion we hear an invitation from the New Testament—"Draw nigh with boldness. Come with assurance." Let us seek to comply with this invitation, and gaze on the glory of Christ, the Mediator, through Whom alone we can approach the holy God, who was justly angry with us on account of our sins. There is a mysterious Personal Type of the ME-DIATOR referred to in three remarkable passages of the Scriptures. His name is

MELCHIZEDEK (Gen. 14:18; Ps. 110:4; Heb. 7). The traveler, as he wends his way through strange countries, sees here, it may be, a tall tower perched on a commanding rock, and there a ruined, weather-beaten castle on a distant hill. No sooner does he descry the dim outline than he eagerly asks, "What is the name of yonder ruin? Who built it? What is its history?" Perhaps no one knows. But the very mystery that veils the venerable structure increases the traveler's interest, and stirs up endless inquiries and conjectures. So is it with many a mysterious personage, who suddenly makes his appearance upon the page of history, and as quickly vanishes out of sight. All we can gather about him is, perhaps, his name, and the legend of some remarkable virtues for which he is famed, or some great exploits that he is reported to have performed. It is one of these historic figures, whose venerable outline thus faintly emerges for a moment from amidst the haze of ancient centuries, who claims our attention today.

In Genesis 14:18, we read that when Abraham returned from his rescue of Lot, this priest and king brought forth bread and wine, and blessed him. His name occurs no more till many centuries after, when David, in Psalm 110:4, hails One whom he terms "My Lord," as a "Priest forever, after the order of MELCHIZEDEK." These two notices are all that the Old Testament contains concerning him. And yet the writer of the epistle to the Hebrews represents him as one of the most illustrious among all the types of our Lord. "Consider," he says, "how great this man was." And thus challenged, theologians of all ages have given a license to their ingenuity, in hazarding some very extraordinary conjectures concerning him. He was an angel in human disguise. He was the patriarch Shem. He was the Son of God Himself. Or, more startling still, He was the Holy Ghost. But Josephus says he was the Prince of a tribe of immigrants that had settled in the country. This may be a conjecture, too, but one likely to be much nearer the truth than the others.

But turn to the passage in Hebrews 7:3, and say if it does not read very like a riddle—"Without father, without mother, without descent, having neither beginning of days nor end of life." But the language can easily be explained. It seems to mean no more than that there was "no account of his ancestry; that his title to his office did not rest on *descent;* and that neither the beginning nor the end of his history is recorded. Unlike the sons of Aaron, he was not one of a race of priests, but stood alone; having no forerunner nor successor in his office. And let us not be surprised that we can discover nothing more of him than what is here recorded. For certainly, if he were not a very mysterious personage, the apostle's argument would be spoiled. God intended him for a Type of Christ; "he was made like unto the Son of God"; and He ordered the Type in such a manner, that it might show the truth which was to be fulfilled.

But, says one, we read "He abideth a priest continually,"—is he a priest now? Certainly not, except as all God's people are "made priests unto God." The meaning of this seems to be, that his priesthood continued as long as his life lasted; whereas the Levitical priests began their work at the age of thirty, served only by turns certain days in the year, and ceased to serve at all at fifty. In the psalm quoted, an intimation is made of a future change in the priesthood. Just as Moses foretold a future Prophet, to supersede his authority in the church, so David predicted a new priesthood. And the apostle, in maintaining that Jesus Christ is that very Priest, makes use of such points as the history furnished, to prove his argument.

Again, the priesthood of Aaron was restricted to the Hebrew Church; whereas that to which MELCHIZEDEK belonged had a worldwide aspect. It was instituted from the beginning, for all mankind. To this illustrious order belonged the first martyr Abel, and Noah the preacher of righteousness, and Job, who offered sacrifices and made intercession for his three friends, and all the heads of families who worshiped the One Lord of heaven and earth.

The sum of all, it has been well said, seems to be, that "Melchizedek's dignity, his glorious titles, the place where he reigned, his belonging to the universal priesthood, his solitariness, the very mystery that surrounds him, were a likeness of the grandeur and preeminence and eternity of the Son of God," after Whom is no priest. He is "the First and the Last"; for by one offering He hath perfected forever them that are sanctified. His mediation has always been in force. He is the Lamb slain from the foundation of the world.

And those high titles with which Melchizedek is honored, King of Righteousness and King of Peace, can only properly belong to Him who is the Lord our Righteousness and the Prince of Peace, "anointed with the oil of joy above all" His similitudes.

For MELCHIZEDEK is only a dim likeness after all. Like all other symbols, he falls infinitely short of the Original. And that "because of the infinite distance there must ever be between Christ and the poor creature," however great. He is above them all as much as the heavens are above the earth. For He it is of whom the apostle says, "There is ONE MEDIATOR between God and man, the Man Christ Jesus."

MEDIATOR (1 Tim. 2:5). The meaning of this word is, *one who reconciles parties at variance or between whom there exists a controversy.* But as this definition does not quite meet the case—since the "variance" is all on the side of man, and the reconciliation originates with God—shall we try an illustration? Imagine the inhabitants of a province in a state of rebellion. The king shrinks from destroying them; but yet feels that to offer them pardon unconditionally, would confound all law and order and bring his government into contempt. What is to be done?

We will suppose that, in this dilemma, he seeks the services of a neighboring potentate as Umpire. This friendly prince goes among the disaffected and remonstrates with them. He apprises them of their king's unwillingness to punish, and urges them to desist from their hopeless and insane course and seek reconciliation. He gains their ear; they listen to his counsels. He tells them further, that besides their instant submission and ample apology, some amends will have to be made for their atrocious doings—some sufficient atonement to law and justice. Not only the king's honor must be saved, but the authority of law and justice must be upheld at all hazards. To secure these ends he proposes a heavy fine, which they, poor wretches, are quite unable to pay. On learning their inability, so bent is he upon seeing the quarrel thoroughly made up, that he generously offers to pay the whole redemption price himself. That noble potentate acts the part of a Mediator. He transacts this difficult matter for the king with his rebellious subjects, and thus makes them one again.

You can easily see how far this imperfect picture represents the case between God and man, and where it falls infinitely short. However, if it helps ever so little our idea of a MEDIATOR'S work, it serves the purpose. Here we have the clemency of an injured sovereign, the good offices of a friend, his disinterested efforts and great generosity, and the due maintenance of the claims of law and justice in effecting the reconciliation.

And precisely these are the great principles brought out in the plan of salvation. On the part of God we see a display of infinite love. On the part of the Son the most wonderful condescension and self-sacrifice. There is the emphatic condemnation of sin, as such an atrocious evil that it cannot, must not go unpunished. While, as to the law, the perfect righteousness of God is so magnified in its sacred supremacy, that He appears as Most Just while justifying the ungodly. But it is no easy payment of a munificent fine, out of unsearchable riches, that would have the honor of law and justice in our restoration to God's favor. No! The redemption must be effected by entire self-sacrifice—stripes, sufferings, and obedience to death, on the part of our great MEDIATOR; for death is the penalty of treason. The soul that sinneth shall die.

Consider then what *you* have to do in this great matter. Is your hard heart softened? Would you gladly be reconciled to so living a Father, so gracious a Sovereign, through such affecting means? Would you enjoy the holy fruits of this Mediatorial work? You must cordially give in your consent to it. If you *neglect* the salvation, it is all one as if you *rejected* it. But, we beseech you, be ye reconciled. Accept the boon deliberately, close with the proposals, and set down your name to the covenant, of which He is expressly called the MEDIATOR. God will stand to His promise. Never fear *His* fidelity. And if thou shalt "believe in thy heart," and confess with thy mouth thy glad and thankful consent to be saved in God's own way, thou *shalt be saved* with an everlasting salvation.

The next illustration of Christ's Priestly office is "MERCY SEAT."

MERCY SEAT (Ex. 25:17; Heb. 9:5). We have just been seeking to gain a little insight into the Mediatorial work of Christ, by the aid of an illustration borrowed from an occasional method of settling controversies. We have now before us an illustration of the same truth, far more sacred, because one of God's devising. The MERCY SEAT was a massive slab of pure gold, resting upon the top of the ark, which stood in the Holy of Holies. This ark was a chest about a yard and a half wide, made of very durable wood and covered with plates of gold; and in it were deposited the two tables of the law. There was a "crown of gold," or rim all around the top, into which the MERCY SEAT fitted closely, thus serving the purpose of a lid or cover, and at either end there was the figure of a cherub with outstretched wings overshadowing it. These were molded out of solid gold, their faces turned towards each other, their eyes looking downward upon the MERCY SEAT. And, over all, perpetually hovered that mysterious awful light, which was the appointed symbol of the presence of Jehovah.

So here we see at the foundation of all, the holy law; for "justice and judgment are the habitation of his throne": and over all, the Shekinah, the emblem of Him Who is of purer eyes than to behold iniquity—and between the two, the MERCY SEAT or Propitiatory sprinkled with blood. And thus the great truth is brought out, that Jesus Christ, with His atoning sacrifice, must come between God and the condemning sentence of the law, or there can be no reconciliation. The Jewish Church had thus a standing testimony, that while God is the Holy One, He is also the Merciful One; and that, in perfect consistency with His spotless holiness, He can, through sacrifice, pass by sin and receive the penitent transgressor.

Have you not often observed, that those holy men who wrote the Psalms often use the phrase, "the shadow of Thy wings?" The allusion is to this MERCY SEAT, with the outspread wings over it, and the light of God's presence beaming upon it. And the suppliant thus recognizes the mercy of God, as pledged to His people in that divinely appointed symbol. There was something very grand, notwithstanding its obscurity, in that figurative method of preaching the gospel to those ancient believers. But how grateful we ought to be, who have Christ, "evidently (that is, plainly without a figure) set forth crucified before us," and who enjoy the full revelation of those truths, which were so dimly seen by the fathers. Their Holy of Holies was a figure, for the time then present, of the heavenly temple, whereinto Jesus Christ hath entered, as the "MINISTER OF THE SANCTUARY."

MINISTER OF THE SANCTUARY, and of the true Tabernacle, which the Lord pitched and not man (Heb. 8:2). We talk of heaven as the Golden City, lighted with the glory of God; also as a temple wherein solemn, rapturous worship is offered. In that holy place the Great MINISTER OF THE SANCTUARY appears for us, "as a Lamb that has been slain." He is there as our Advocate; and in all His Mediatorial acts He is attended with the songs and joyful acclamations of holy ones. A vast multitude is gathered there, whose worship cannot be merely mental and silent, because it consists much of praise, simultaneously presented by a harmonious assembly. And these surround Him as He gloriously "ministers" before the throne. Oh could we but catch the distant echo of their songs! But these things we are not able clearly to conceive, and therefore cannot rightly express. "For Christ is not entered into the holy place made with hands, which are the figures of the true, but into heaven itself, now to appear in the presence of God for us," our "MERCIFUL AND FAITHFUL HIGH PRIEST."

MERCIFUL AND FAITHFUL HIGH PRIEST (Heb. 2:17). When we are in distress, and forced to apply somewhere for help, what is the first thing we look for? Ability, to be sure. We ask, Is he to whom we apply *able* to help us? And if satisfied of that, we then think within ourselves, Is he kindly disposed? Will he help us if we go to him? If we are satisfied on these two points, and feel very much pressed, we shall resolve to make the application.

Now, I think you must own that we have much more than this to encourage us in our application to Jesus Christ. As to His ability, I suppose we never had a doubt. We know He is "able to do for us exceeding abundantly above all we can ask or think." He is Mighty to save—can save to the very uttermost. Of that we entertain no doubt. The difficulty generally lies here—Are we not so vile, so wicked, that He really does not care to save such unworthy creatures? Is there not some specially atrocious feature in our case, which will quite alienate His heart from us?

Now, from this Title, we learn that He is as MERCIFUL as He is Mighty. He is *disposed* to help—*inclined*, because of the great pity He feels for all who are in sin and trouble. He has "compassion on the ignorant and them that are out of the way." His bowels yearn over the wanderer. Fear not. He is "MERCIFUL."

But read on—"and FAITHFUL" also. That is, He has promised and undertaken to save, and feels obliged, by His own word and a jealous regard to His own great reputation, to save them that trust in Him. What! Can the "FAITHFUL WITNESS" break His word, even to the vilest? Would we make Him who is the Truth a "liar"? Let us be ashamed of our distrust.

> Engraved as in eternal brass,
>   The mighty promise shines;
> Nor can the powers of darkness rase
>   Those everlasting lines.

Here then is a threefold cord, MIGHTY, MERCIFUL, FAITHFUL. Trust all your weight on it. Nothing can break it.

But there is still something behind, which we often lose sight of. It is this. *He delights to save.* He takes a special, yea an infinite, pleasure in saving. He layeth the wandering sheep on His shoulders rejoicing. Yea, beloved, believe it, He rejoices more in saving you and me than we do in being saved. Doth He not Himself say, "It is more blessed to give than to receive?" You cannot afford Him greater pleasure, you cannot do Him greater honor, than to place yourself in His hands, to be pardoned, saved, sanctified. Do not think He stays to rejoice till He can see you perfectly holy. He rejoices *now*, at once, whensoever He first finds the bleeding, bruised, perishing soul, and takes it up into His arms. "He taketh pleasure in them that hope in His mercy!"

From the subjects of today's Reading let us learn

First. *To beware of limiting the mercy of God by our own poor contracted notions.* What saith the Scripture? "As high as the heavens are above the earth, so high are My thoughts above your thoughts, and My ways above your ways." Let us give God the glory that He here claims. A popular teacher, writing lately of David's sin and penitence, insinuates that those fervent petitions in the fifty-first psalm "might have been answered after his death, but scarcely before." That is, twenty years after they were offered! Alas! when those who undertake to preach the gospel so misrepresent God's heart of love, and His methods of grace, how can we be surprised that men should mistake the path of life, and pine away in their iniquities?

Dear old Fleming's account of a repentant malefactor at Ayr seems much more in accordance with the word of God, above quoted. He says, the man "was wonderfully wrought on while in prison and was brought to a most kindly repentance, with great assurance of mercy; insomuch that when he came to the place of execution, he could not cease crying to the people, under a sense of God's favor, '*Oh! He Is a Great Forgiver, He is a Great Forgiver!*' adding the following words, 'Now hath perfect love cast out fear. I know God hath nothing to lay against me, for Jesus Christ has paid all; and *those are free whom the Son makes free.*'" And who, remembering our Lord's words to the dying thief, could dare to contradict him, malefactor though he was?

Secondly. *We should take care not to misrepresent the mercy of the Savior, by the terms we use in inviting sinners to come to Him.* After all I have said today, should I do well to call upon you to "*venture*" on Christ?—to *venture* to believe? As well might I speak of a poor, little, penitent child *venturing* to hide his tearful face in the bosom of his affectionate mother—who, indeed, is only too glad to soothe and comfort him. And yet it is in this hesitating and timid way many are induced to come to the tender-hearted, loving Savior of the lost.

"It is just a year today," writes an eminent Christian lady, "since I entertained hope in Christ. Reflecting on the words of the lepers at Samaria, 'If we enter the city we die, and if we sit still here we die also,' I felt that if I returned to the world I should surely perish—if I stayed where I was I should perish—and I could but perish if I threw myself on the mercy of Christ. Then came light and comfort such as I never knew before." And in the same spirit an old minister, speaking of his conversion, says, "I was reading a sentence from Luther, 'I would run into the arms of Christ if He stood with a drawn sword in His hand,' when this thought came bolting into my mind, So will I too—my burden dropped off, my soul was filled with joy and peace. This *'venturesome believing'* was the means of setting me at liberty."

Thus they found their way to Christ. And since they did actually come, it matters little how. But was there not some wrong notion, some erroneous teaching at the bottom of this *"venturing"*? Do not the words of the venerable Dr. Simpson exalt Christ much more, and show unto us a more excellent way? "When," said he, "I consider the infinite dignity and all-sufficiency of Christ, I am ashamed to talk of *venturing* on Him. Oh, had I ten thousand souls, I would at this moment cast them all into His hands with the utmost confidence."

> For you and for me He died on the tree;
> His work is accepted, the sinner is free;
> That sinner am I who on Jesus rely,
> And come for the pardon God cannot deny.
>
> My pardon I claim, for a sinner I am,
> A sinner believing in Jesus' Name;
> He purchased the grace, which now I embrace:
> O Father, Thou knowest He hath died in my place.

35

Myrrh and Camphire. Manna. Nazarene. Offspring of David. Only Begotten. Only Wise God Our Savior. Omnipotent. Offering for Sin. Propitiation. Peace Offering. Passover.

WONDERFUL are the virtues with which the Creator has endowed the plants of the earth. Some restore and preserve life as food and medicine. Some are fragrant in their scent, and others beautiful to the eye. Among many lovely things in nature used to set forth the exceeding grace of our Lord, the Rose of Sharon and the Lily of the Valley, mentioned in the Song of Songs, have been favorite emblems with old writers. Rutherford constantly makes this use of them. In one of his letters he describes Christ as "The Flower of Jesse, the Plant of Renown, the Choicest, Fairest, Sweetest ROSE ever God planted." Again, "Christ is His Father's Noble ROSE casting a sweet smell through heaven and earth. He is a ROSE that beautifieth all the Upper Garden of God. A leaf of that ROSE of God for fragrance is worth a world." And Dr. Watts says,

> Is He a ROSE? Not Sharon yields
> Such fragrancy in all her fields;
> Or if the LILY He assume,
> The valleys bless the rich perfume.

They both seem, however, by fair interpretation, to belong rather to the Bride than to the Bridegroom. But as MYRRH and CAMPHIRE refer undoubtedly to the latter, we will include them in our list of symbols.

MYRRH AND CAMPHIRE (Song 1:13, 14), are both shrubs bearing flowers and berries, and producing a gum exceedingly odoriferous. Myrrh is supposed to preserve from putrefaction and infection. It is also used as a medicine, and for healing wounds, and by Persian ladies, as a perfume. Camphire is a beautiful plant, with large clusters of pale yellow flowers of a most delicate scent. These flowers are high prized by the people of the East, and have various uses. Amongst others, they serve for friendly gifts, and are carried in the bosom as remembrances. Those who persist in believing, in spite of the conclusions of modern criticism, that the Song of Solomon is intended to celebrate the mutual love of Christ and His church, recognize in this passage a declaration of her devoted love to her Lord, "My Beloved is unto me as a CLUSTER OF CAMPHIRE in the vineyards of Engedi." She declares she will bear on her heart the constant remembrance of His love, just as an eastern female might wear in her bosom a cluster of the fragrant Camphire flowers, or the odoriferous Myrrh—whether for the sake of its scent, or in remembrance of some friendly hand which had presented it. Thus the desire of the believer's soul is towards Christ, and "the remembrance of His name."

> As MYRRH new bleeding from the tree,
> Such is a dying Christ to me;
> And while He makes my soul His guest,
> My heart shall be His constant rest.

Strong perfumes are sometimes used to arouse people when overcome with drowsiness or faintness. So when the Christian, dwelling in the deadening atmosphere of the world, feels spiritual sloth creeping upon him, nothing is so effectual to arouse him as a timely remembrance of Christ.

> The vital savor of His name
> Restores his fainting breath.

But it is amidst Sabbath worshipers, and in God's house, that this fragrant odor is more eminently shed abroad; and the believer goes back, again to tread the dusty paths of life, revived, and invigorated with fresh power to resist temptation. Perhaps he took his seat just now, and sighed to think how cold his heart was toward spiritual things, and how far from God his Chief Joy. Then the preacher, with earnest prayer for God's blessing, opened the Bible and preached Christ. On this Plant of Renown great and precious blessings grow in rich profusion, like clusters of CAMPHIRE and bundles of MYRRH. And while he divides to each his portion in due season, the Holy Spirit takes of the things of a Christ and shows them to the listening congregation. To some it is a savor of death, for they scorn it. To others it is a savor of life. The drooping pilgrim hears again of the faithfulness of his Savior, of the blood of Christ which cleanseth from all sin, and of the eternal weight of glory to which he is called; and straightway arises, strong in the Lord and the power of His might. His heart is nerved and his spirits are refreshed, and he rejoices as a strong man to run a race. The Lord Jesus is to him as MYRRH and CAMPHIRE. He presses Him to his heart as one would a cluster of reviving spices, and goes on in the strength of that refreshment many days. He "had fainted unless he had believed, to see the goodness of the Lord in the land of the living."

I stay a moment to ask you whether the name of Christ is thus refreshing and pleasant to you, and whether you delight to hear and think of Him. Happy are they who thus know the joyful sound! They walk all day in the light of God's countenance. But alas! it is not everyone that can perceive the fragrance of Christ. Most people are so taken up with other gratifications, and are so besotted, that they even wonder what strange sweetness the Christian can find in communion with the Savior. Oh do no rest satisfied till you do understand it, and can enjoy the Lord Jesus as the Christian does; till you can say, "My Beloved is unto *me* as a CLUSTER OF MYRRH AND CAMPHIRE in the vineyards of Engedi."— And let us pray, in order that this day's lesson may be profitable to us—

> Breathe Thy Spirit—so shall fall
> Unction sweet upon us all,
> Till by odors scattered round,
> Christ Himself be traced and found.

The next subject—namely, MANNA, will form a very convenient band, helpful to the memory, by which to unite the particulars, which follow in order. The MANNA was *despised* by the people—*promised* before it was sent—*came down* from heaven—and *was given* for the life of men. So Jesus Christ was *Despised* as the NAZARENE—*Promised*, as the OFFSPRING OF DAVID—*Came down* from heaven, for He was God's ONLY BEGOTTEN SON—and *Given* for the life of men, for He was the OFFERING FOR SIN, our PEACE OFFERING, PROPITIATION, and PASSOVER. We will begin with that instructive Type of our Lord, the

MANNA (Ex. 16:15). You all know the ancient story. Three million mouths, and not a loaf to be had! and nothing but barren mountains and uninhabited deserts all round! And you know how they despaired and complained, and how God said He would, on the morrow, open the windows of heaven, and rain down bread upon them. Well, the morning comes, and while yet the dew is abundant, and every spire of grass is hung with liquid diamonds sparkling in the sunbeam, they turn out in crowds to look after the strange provision. They search in all directions, and one calls to his neighbor, "Have you found anything yet?" "No," replies the other, "I can see nothing but the heavy dew that covers the ground." By-and-by the sun grows hot and the dew begins to evaporate, but there is still nothing like bread to be seen—neither wheat, nor flour, nor grain of any kind. Presently one calls out, "What is this?" "It looks like hoar frost," says his companion. "It cannot be that," cries a third. "Here is some more," exclaims a fourth, "and look! It is scattered everywhere, and is just like little pearls." They taste it. It is sweet as honey, and soft as oil. Lo! here is the promised bread. And they name it MANNA, which means "What is this?" or "It is our portion." And soon the pearly beads bestrew "thymy slope and stony vale," and cluster at the foot of every jutting rock, till the face of the wilderness all around grows white; and exulting myriads eagerly gather in the welcome harvest. The dear children are in high glee, and as they run and scramble, cry, "Who will get the most?" But there is no room for covetousness, for it covers the ground for many a mile. When they carry it to their tents, they find they have got as much as will supply all the dwellers in the camp with, at least, two quarts apiece. The next morning, there it was again; and the next day it was just the same; and this miraculous supply came every day, for forty years, except on the Sabbaths; and to provide for them, a double portion fell on the previous day, which did not become corrupt as it did on other days, if kept till the morrow.

Now St. Paul calls this MANNA "spiritual meat," by which he means it had a spiritual meaning or reference. And if you want to know what that is, Jesus Christ Himself will tell you. "Your fathers did eat MANNA, and are dead; I am the LIVING BREAD which came down from heaven. If any man eat of *this* BREAD, he shall live forever. And the Bread that I will give is My Flesh which I will give for the life of the world" (John 6:51). Our Lord seems to say to the Jews, "You think that MANNA an excellent thing, so it was; yet they who ate of it died. What will you think of BREAD, of which if you eat, you shall never die?" "Oh," cried they, "evermore give us this Bread." Let us all offer the same prayer, but with more simplicity and a better understanding than they.

When the Jews extolled the Manna as Bread from heaven, Jesus Christ did not discountenance their words; but, reminding them that it was provided merely for temporary use, and had a special typical reference, He claimed to be Himself that True Bread from heaven, the Living Bread given for the life of the world. The typical Bread could not save even from natural death them who ate of it. But the Living Bread possesses such transcendent virtue, that it saves the souls of all who partake of it from *spiritual* death, imparts an incorruptible life, and insures to their bodies a glorious resurrection. All who eat of it shall, in their entire nature, and in the most glorious sense, live forever. And He explained the eating to mean (not partaking of the Lord's supper with which they could have nothing to do at that time, but) *coming* to Him and *believing* on Him.

How does a hungry man make Bread available? By gazing at it? handling it? extolling it? Nay, but by using it in the only appropriate way—eating it, masticating it, that thus it may be incorporated with his frame. That is the emblem of the cat by which we are to make Christ available for salvation and life. We must appropriate Him, believe in Him, receive Him into our hearts with full consent, and make constant use of Him for the purposes indicated in the instructions and promises of the gospel. "As the Living Father hath sent Me, and I live by the Father, so he that eateth Me, even he shall live by Me."

Now there are some great fundamental truths taught here. God is the Chief Good, and therefore He alone can satisfy the soul's hunger, fill its insatiable void, and nourish its intellectual and emotional powers. But because man has fallen away from God, and is in a state of separation, he requires special methods of treatment. Christ therefore comes to reunite him to God by drawing him first to Himself. As the Mediatorial, Redeeming God, He adapts Himself to the special wants of men as sinners, and, on certain conditions, becomes the Chief Good of all who receive Him. In Him they find propitiation for their sins, healing for their maladies, light and life and strength for all their exigencies, a Treasury of all fullness. In Him man's reason finds all it requires to meet its eager inquiries, and gratify its expanded capacity and thirst for knowledge. At the same time, his affections find in Christ that which infinitely transcends his utmost powers of admiration and complacency. For there is everything in His beautiful life, His glorious nature, and perfect character to provoke and gratify the most intense adoration of which intelligent beings are capable. "He that cometh to Me shall never hunger, and he that believeth on Me shall never thirst." And thus, in coming to Christ as a penitent sinner, through Christ he re-enters a state of union and fellowship with the Godhead; Whose favor is life, and Who is the soul's true Bread, the only satisfying Food in the universe adequate to its wants.

But let us see what further correspondence there is between the figure and the thing signified. The typical MANNA was *plentiful*. So in Christ are unsearchable riches, grace enough and to spare for all the word. Again, it was *seasonable*, for they were starving. So without Christ we must perish. It was a *free gift*. And so is Christ; "Let him that is athirst come." But though they did nothing to deserve it they were obliged to gather it, and it cost them some trouble too, for they could only do it early in the morning. So we must "seek the Lord while He may be found," that is, early, immediately. Then, again, the Manna was very *palatable*. It was suited to everyone. It was a milk to babes, as medicine to the sick, a cordial to the faint, strong meat to the robust; and the Scriptures that illustrate this, as it applies to the Savior, are so numerous, that we cannot stay to examine them. Yet, notwithstanding all these excellent qualities, this Bread from heaven was *loathed;* and garlic and onions, and I know not what, were preferred before this "angels' food." And just so, Jesus Christ, the true BREAD from Heaven, was (how shall we utter it?) "*abhorred by the nation*." And among other ways of showing their contempt, they called Him, in scorn, the "NAZARENE."

NAZARENE (Matt. 2:23). "But that only means a native of Nazareth," some might say, "and it does not sound to us a *very* harsh expression." Pray consider a moment. If the inhabitants of the town where you live bore a very bad character, would it be no injustice if that were to be cast in your teeth as a personal stigma, notwithstanding you hated their wickedness? Now *that* was the case with our Lord. I suppose God told Joseph and Mary to go and live at Nazareth, and bring up their Holy Son there, as a part of His humiliation. For its inhabitants were held in very low esteem on account of their vice and ignorance. "What!" said Nathaniel, with a sneer on his honest features, "Can any good thing come out of Nazareth?"

In fact, Galilee, where Nazareth was situated, was the most disreputable part of Judea, and Nazareth was even a byword in Galilee! What more could be wanting to render it infamous? The mere fact, therefore, that He was an inhabitant of Nazareth, was regarded as an indelible stigma on His character.

But someone says, "It is stated that He dwelt there in order to fulfill what had been spoken by the prophets; but no prophet has these very words that we can discover." No, but several of the prophets write of the contempt in which He would be held. And you see how the *spirit* and *meaning* of what they said were fulfilled in the letter of His history. For enemies and friends alike knew Him, not as Jesus of Bethlehem, which would have been an honorable title; but as Jesus of Nazareth, which was an opprobrious title. "He was despised, and we esteemed Him not." This seems to be the most obvious solution. However, some explain the enigma by reference to the original meaning of the name, Nazareth. It is derived, they say, from *netser*, which means a branch; and so, "by His residence at Nazareth, or the City of Branches, He, whose Name is the Branch, fulfilled the meaning of the ancient prophecy."

But, again, the MANNA was *promised* before it was given. "Tomorrow," said God, "ye shall have this provision." Just so, Jesus Christ was a Promised Gift, promised expressly for ages before He came, as the OFFSPRING OF DAVID.

OFFSPRING OF DAVID (Rev. 22:16). He claims this title Himself, evidently, with express allusion to the prophecies, which had preceded His coming, so many of which declared that the Messiah should spring from the House of David. There are two genealogies of David's lineage preserved in the New Testament. That in Matthew traces the descent of Joseph, the supposed or legal father of our Lord, from the tribe of Judah and the house of David. The other traces that of Mary. For Heli, called Joseph's father, there can be no doubt, is really Mary's father, and so Joseph's father-in-law. Thus "Jesus Christ our Lord was made of the seed of David according to the flesh"; but also "declared to be the Son of God with power."—The MANNA is called "Bread from heaven." So Christ says, "I am the Living Bread which came down from heaven"; and He calls Himself the

ONLY BEGOTTEN SON, Who was in the bosom of the Father (1 John 4:9). All we know of the Person of the Savior is most wonderful, and much of it quite inexplicable. On this lofty and mysterious title, many words have been expended, but in vain. For who shall declare His generation? Who describe the nature or unfold the mystery of His mysterious kinship to the Father? But though we cannot fully comprehend it, what we can know in reference to it is very plain. Though God is said to have many sons, He is THE SON in a sense quite unique— the only One of them who is Omnipotent, Omniscient, Omnipresent, a Partaker of His Infinite Nature, and a Sharer in His Uncreated Glory. Therefore Jesus Christ is God's Only One, Infinitely Beloved, His Elect, His Delight. He was with God, "in His bosom," from eternity, and shared, with the Great Spirit, all His counsels. For He is styled by Jude the

ONLY WISE GOD OUR SAVIOR (Jude 1:25). He bears a Name, which belongs exclusively to the Great Three in One—the highest Name in heaven. To be supremely WISE is peculiar to the Godhead. No creature, however exalted, can wear such a Title as this. Therefore the appropriation of it to Jesus of Nazareth asserts in the most unqualified way possible His Essential Deity. And this is not the only instance in which that which is the common property of the Godhead is distinctly appropriated to Him as One of the Three Co-equal Persons. He is "the Blessed and Only Potentate, Who only hath Immortality." He also claims to be the Wisdom of God (Luke 11:49). And in Proverbs 8:27–31, He says:

> When He prepared the heavens, I was there;
> When He set a compass upon the face of the depth;
> When He established the clouds above;
> When He strengthened the fountains of the deep;
> When He gave to the sea His decree,
> That the waters should not pass His commandment;
> When He appointed the foundations of the earth;
> Then I was by Him as One brought up with Him;
> And I was daily His Delight, rejoicing always before Him;
> Rejoicing in the habitable parts of His earth,
> And my delights were with the sons of men.
> But again, the Lord Jesus is described as

OMNIPOTENT in Revelation 19:6, while in Psalm 148:5 the understanding of Him Who telleth the number of the stars is said to be INFINITE. A theorizing infidel, lately deceased, Mr. Mill, rejecting the revelation God hath given of Himself, preferred to believe in a god of his own invention—a sort of would-be infinite being who, with stupendous effort, is trying to carry out great purposes; and finds himself helplessly thwarted by opposing powers of evil, so that still evil prevails against good; and what the result will be no one can guess.

If this be the most sagacious theory a thoughtful infidel can propound, the Christian is under no temptation to envy him. In what midnight darkness must the belief of that horrible dogma envelop the mind! It is a relief to turn from the dreadful nightmare to the glorious God of the Scriptures, Who, from His lofty height, surveys the universe, and can say, "Is there a God beside Me? I know not any." Rebels against Him there are many. Rivals there are none.

A being less infinite, were he ever so benevolent, would be no god at all. We could not trust him. On all sides his power must encounter limitations and obstructions insuperable. The teeming multitudes of creatures would overwhelm him. His attention would be too distracted to embrace them all. And who amongst us would not be tormented with dread lest he himself should be found among the unfortunates who must be overlooked, and his interests be drowned in oblivion? But now under the outspread wings of the God of the Bible, there is room for all to nestle in the joyous "carelessness of faith," and ample space wherein the meanest and the youngest finds his own sphere clearly marked out from that of all others, and guarded from interference. Here also there is absolute security against chance. For nothing can elude the eye of the INFINITE, and no unforeseen disaster disarrange the plans of the OMNIPOTENT.

> O Majesty unspeakable and dread!
> Wert Thou less Mighty than Thou art,
> Thou wert, O Lord, too great for our belief;
> Too little for our heart.

> But Greatness which is Infinite makes room
> For all things in its lap to lie.
> We should be crushed by a magnificence
> Short of Infinity.

> Great God! our lowliness takes heart to play
> Beneath the shadow of Thy state;
> The only comfort of our littleness
> Is that Thou art so great.

And yet God so loved the world that He gave this Only Begotten Son for its redemption. None inferior to the ONLY WISE GOD, the OMNIPOTENT, the INFINITE, could be our Savior.

Observe then, once more, that as the MANNA was *given* to sustain life, so Christ was Given "for the Life of the World." His Holy Soul was made an

OFFERING FOR SIN (Isa. 53:10). All He did while on earth he did *for us*. All He suffered He suffered *for us*—as our Substitute. A familiar illustration will explain to the youngest what a Substitute is.

Two brothers, Paul and James, were together at a certain school. James had been so obstinate as to incur punishment; which the master was about to inflict, when Paul stood forth begging that he might suffer instead of his brother. "Why, Paul!" cried the good man, "you are one of my best boys, I could not give *you* pain."

Paul replied, "It hurts me to see my brother suffer; he is younger than I; do allow me to take the punishment instead of my naughty brother." James looked at his noble brother, but said nothing, while Paul still entreated with tears. "But," said the master, "did you ever hear of anyone who bore stripes to shield others?" "Oh, yes sir; the Lord Jesus gave His back to the smiters, and by His stripes we are saved. Oh, sir, let me endure the pain, and pardon James for my sake. I know he has broken the rules, and I know you must keep your word, but pray, sir, punish me, because I am stronger than he." And then the affectionate Paul threw his arms round James's neck, and wetted his hardened face with his tears. This was rather more than James could stand; so he, too, began to cry. His heart was at last melted; he embraced his brother, and begged forgiveness. The good schoolmaster, overcome with emotion, clasped both in his arms, and prayed for them to Him who was "wounded for our transgressions and bruised for our iniquities."

In Leviticus, chapter one, we have a full account of the institution of the BURNT OFFERING. Every Israelite who desired to have his sins pardoned, was required to choose a bullock or other animal mentioned, without spot or blemish, and bring it before the Lord to the door of the tabernacle. There he was to lay his hand on the head of the victim, and (as the Jewish Rabbis say) to confess that he had done evil in the sight of the Lord, and left undone that which he should have done. Thus was signified the transferring or putting off all his sins on the animal that it might suffer in his stead. Then the priest killed it, and burned it entirely on the altar.

Thus were the Jews taught that they were sinners; that sin brings suffering and death; and that God was willing to forgive on this only ground—*that someone else should suffer* in their stead. It must have been plain to them that the blood of bulls and goats could not take away sin; or would they not have ceased to be offered? "For the worshipers once purged, would have no more conscience of sin." The mind of the thoughtful worshiper, therefore, while he stood by and saw the bullock or lamb cut up and laid on God's altar, was directed to anticipate some better sacrifice, of which this was only a shadow. For was not God's continual acceptance of those confessedly insufficient sacrifices a pledge and promise that He would, at some future day, "provide a Lamb for a BURNT OFFERING," who should by one sacrifice forever put away sin? All the sacrifices imply these lessons. They teach the truth, most impressively, that as the unoffending animal had never committed the sins for which its blood was spilt, so Christ, the great Substitute and Surety, the Lamb without spot, should in like manner pay debts He had never contracted, and die for crimes He had never been guilty of.

To what extent the more spiritual and heaven-taught worshipers of that age were able to discern the end foreshadowed by their types, cannot be determined. But if they did see the truths and doctrines indicated, it must have been "through a glass darkly." We live, thank God, in a clearer day, and can see more plainly the meaning of those ceremonies that are abolished. Christ has come. And now there is nothing further required than His One True and All-sufficient Offering. Oh let not the Israelite, who say the way of salvation is through so obscure a medium, rise up in judgment against us who see "Christ evidently set forth crucified amongst us." Let us go to Him and say,

> My faith would lay her hand
> On that dear head of Thine,
> While like a penitent I stand
> And there confess my sin.

But, again, our Lord is said to be the

PROPITIATION, or Atonement (1 John 2:2). This word signifies that which makes reconciliation, and has reference to the Mercy Seat as sprinkled with the blood of sacrifice. In this PROPITIATION, the Apostle says, "God declares His righteousness for the remission of sins." This PROPITIATION, then, completely meets the necessities of an awakened conscience, and furnishes an answer to the question: Wherewith shall I come before the Lord? a question anxiously asked throughout the world, but only satisfactorily answered where the light of the Gospel is known. A poor heathen, performing a long journey with spikes in his sandals, to make atonement for his sins, sat down, weary and sore, under a tree. It was a preaching station; and soon a missionary arrived and preached from the text, "The blood of Christ cleanses from all sin." Long before the sermon was over, the poor man had thrown off his prickly sandals, calling out, "This is just what I want, just what I want." It was as the water-brook to the thirsty hart, for he saw that pardon and peace and blessedness are only obtained through the divinely appointed PROPITIATION. The same truth was taught by the Hebrew Sacrifice known as the

PEACE OFFERING (Lev. 3:1). Behold yonder Israelite just restored from dangerous sickness. How shall he show his thankfulness? Well instructed in the law, he selects from his flock a spotless heifer, and calls his friends; and, together, they lead it to the temple. Then the pious offerer puts his hands upon it, and it is killed at the door of the enclosure; for Christ is the only Way to the Father. Next the blood is sprinkled upon the altar as a token of the satisfaction of the claims of justice. Then some of the inward parts are burned upon the altar. Perhaps this taught him that God must have the heart, and that praise must glow from deep inward feeling, for thus Christ made His inmost Soul an OFFERING. Then God's portion of this PEACE OFFERING is burned upon the altar, the priest has his share, and the remainder is borne away by the offerer and his friends that they may hold a feast of joy in their own home.

Now, there must be some meaning in all this. It cannot be a mere empty ceremony. Doth it now shadow forth the delight God hath in the work of Christ, because of the peace and happiness that follow from it to His people? It is called an "OFFERING of a sweet savor," and "food," and "bread." Thus God rejoices over His people to do them good. And doth not Jesus, the Priest, get His portion too? Certainly, He "sees of the travail of His soul, and is satisfied." And the believer gets *his* share, for the sacrifice satisfies his conscience, and he feasts upon Him who giveth His flesh for the life of the world. It is indeed a PEACE OFFERING, for God and His people feast together in token of reconciliation. But perhaps the most remarkable of all the Jewish Offerings, and which, more plainly than any, shadowed beforehand Christ Crucified, was the

PASSOVER (Ex. 12:11). The story of the plagues of Egypt, and of the institution of this feast, which is still observed by Jewish families, is very interesting. But we must not dwell at length on it now. You can read it in your Bibles. After many punishments against which Pharaoh hardened his heart, God threatened to *pass through* the land and smite all the firstborn. But He promised that He would *pass over* the dwellings of His people, leaving *their* firstborn unharmed. But only on this condition. They were to kill a lamb in every house, between three o'clock and six, and sprinkle its blood upon the posts of the door; afterwards, they were to roast it and eat it, and by no means to venture out of doors.

And God said, "When I see the blood I will pass over you." And they did as they were commanded; and at midnight, as they stood silent and awestruck, there rose upon their ears a loud and bitter wailing. The destroying angel had fulfilled his dread commission, and death was in every Egyptian house. But God was true to His promise. The Destroyer *passed over* every house where was the blood-red signal. Not a Hebrew died that night who had observed God's directions. And these were minute and significant. The lamb was to be without blemish. You know what that means. It was to be killed and roasted with fire. So we read in 1 Corinthians 5:7, "Christ our Passover is sacrificed for us." Then, not a bone was to be broken. This was also prophetical of the Lamb of God, and, by a special providence, His sacred Body was preserved from fracture "that the Scripture might be fulfilled" (John 19:36). The blood was to be sprinkled upon the doorpost, which teaches us that nothing stands between us and God's judgments but the blood of Christ. It was not enough to have the slain lamb in the house; the blood must be upon the door. So no compliance can save us, unless the blood of Christ be appropriated to ourselves by a real faith. And as no Israelite died where the red sign was, so, whoso believeth shall not perish. Again, they ate their sacrifice, and were strengthened for their journey. And Christ is given to be fed upon. "Our PASSOVER is slain for us, therefore let us keep the Feast." They were to eat it with unleavened bread. The apostle explains this, "of sincerity and truth," instead of the "old leaven of malice and wickedness." Once more, it was to be eaten with bitter herbs. I know not whether this refers to repentance, or whether it has some deeper meaning. We all know that, often, bitter medicines are administered to provoke appetite. And, just so, without conviction and repentance there will be no relish for the Gospel, no appetite for Christ, nor disposition to receive Him at all.

A German immigrant in America went out to hunt one Sunday, and had a bad fall from a high tree. The branch on which he rested broke, and down he went. In that moment, while falling, he prayed for the first time in his life. "Lord, have mercy!" he gasped, and straightway caught hold of another branch below, and was thus saved from a dreadful death. But his conscience was alarmed. "What if de limb dat I caught mit my hands had broke!" said he to a minister. "Oh, I had such ugly thoughts—such a load here in my breast. I got de Bible and said, No I will see what I must do to have de load taken away. I open de Bible. O it make me feel so bad. It said, de wicked are turned into hell, and I was wicked. I thought I would die. I eats little, I sleeps little. I get so thin as a skeleton. I keep in dis way a good while; one day I get de Bible, and read, and read, and *dare I see Jesus* standing between me and my sins! My load den was gone. O, I was so happy—just so happy as miserable before. I could jump mit joy so high as de fence. I go and tell my bruders dat I found Jesus, dat He had taken away my sins, but dey take me to be crazy! *Dey had never seen dare sins* nor Jesus in de Bible."

Here is the secret of delight in Jesus Christ. The bitter herb of conviction of sin prepares the heart to receive the gospel with joy. May the Holy Spirit awaken your conscience and convince you of sin. Then will Christ be to your soul what MANNA was to the hungry wanderers in the desert, and what the PASSOVER was to those who were delivered by it from bondage and death.

> While still absorbed in things of earth,
> The soul in Christ perceives no worth,
>   Nor heeds the heavenly call;
> But when the Spirit shines within,
> The soul forsakes its life of sin,
>   And Christ is All in all.

36

Polished Shaft. Power of God. Prince and Savior. Peace. Prince of Peace. Prince of Princes. Place of Broad Rivers and Streams.

WE shall make use of the Symbols on our list today, principally, to illustrate the sinner's translation out of darkness into the kingdom of God's Dear Son. You know an unconverted person is in the Bible spoken of as "dead,"—not *literally*, but *spiritually*. He seeks his happiness in self and sin, and, being alienated from God, is quite cut off from the true source of life. This melancholy condition is the opposite of that intended in the expressive phrase of the Apostle, "*alive* unto God." This poor soul is *dead* unto God. Alas! the inward eye sees not the worth of Christ, and therefore there is no movement of the affections towards Him. The inward ear hears not His loving words, and so there is no response in the heart to His wakening call. It is as though there were no speech nor language addressed to it.

There is a thrilling story brought from the Arctic Seas, which, though oft repeated, never loses its impressiveness, because of the weird-like interest that gathers around it. Fifty years ago and more, some mariners sailing amongst the icebergs discovered a ship fast locked amidst the encircling ice. They hailed the strange-looking craft, but there was no response. With great effort they succeeded in boarding her, and on entering the cabin were petrified at the strange scene that presented itself. At a table in the center sat one who seemed to be the captain, the pen still grasped between his fingers; while, open before him, lay the log book, as though he had just been making notes of some passing event. The startled visitors looked at him, half suspecting he would speak, so lifelike was his aspect. They saluted him, but there was no response. And round the cabin, sitting or reclining on the lockers, or lying on the floor, were the crew, attired in their usual dress and presenting a similar appearance of life. Half affrighted at the spectacle, some of them shouted; but none heard, none moved hand or foot. While the glassy stare of their eyes, and their inflexible posture, soon convinced the most incredulous among them that they were gazing upon inanimate corpses. They had been in this state for years, and were thus strangely preserved by the frost, which had arrested and congealed the vital stream in their veins. For aught we know, that ship, with its ghastly freight, is drifting about to this day, amidst inaccessible hummocks of ice far beyond human ken; the hapless crew dead, notwithstanding the attitude and appearance of life; just as we find whole communities of souls dead towards God, notwithstanding dorms of godliness and attitudes of devotion.

How is this state of things to be altered? Ask some and they would say, "Startle them into life by signs from heaven. Send an angel to arouse them, or one raised from the grave." Thus *the Jews require a sign*. Alas! that would be like galvanizing a dead body. The muscles might move, the dead man might sit upright, but he would be a dead man still. Ask another, and he might say, "Convince him by argument, allure him by persuasion, set before him his own interest, and the claims of religion." Thus *the Greeks seek after wisdom*. But what saith the Scriptures? Go, tell him the story of Christ Crucified. This, (not the mere story, but the Christ in the story), is the

POLISHED SHAFT in God's Quiver (Isa. 49:2) which, faithfully presented, is the proper instrument of conviction and awakening. It is God's own ordinance for this end. And it will be effectual whenever the demonstration of the Spirit accompanies it. "Of what use," might Ezekiel have said, "is it for me to prophesy to dead men's bones? How can that wake them up?" It could not wake them up. It was the power of God accompanying His own means that was to do that. "What good will seven plunges into the waters of the Jordan be to a leper?" asked Naaman. None at all, ordinarily. But it was God's plan in this instance, and song, when tried, it was effectual.

On the inhospitable shores of Greenland, devoted missionaries long labored without success to teach the savages in the first elements of religion. One day, when the missionary sat in his hut, translating a portion of John's Gospel, who should come in but the chief, Kajarnak, accompanied by a party of men as wild as himself. Seeing a pen in the missionary's hand, he said, "What are you doing?" "Writing," said the missionary. "Writing?—what *is* writing?" said the other. The good man explained what writing was; and then said, if he would sit down he would read to him what he had been writing. Kajarnak listened while the account of Christ's sufferings was read to him—the agony, the scourging, the mocking, and the crucifixion; and as the reader went on, the listener became deeply interested. At last he asked, "And why did they treat Him so? What had the Man done?" "Oh," said the missionary, "*this* Man did nothing amiss, but Kajarnak did. Kajarnak murdered his wife; Kajarnak filled the land with his wickedness, and deserved to go to hell. And this Man suffered in order to bear

Kajarnak's punishment, that Kajarnak might not go to hell." And then he explained the gospel plan, and told him all about God's love and Christ's work for sinners, till big tears were seen to roll down Kajarnak's cheeks, and, unable to restrain his feelings any longer, he rose to his feet, threw himself into the missionary's arms, and cried, "Oh, tell it me again—tell it me all over again, for I too would like to be saved!" The missionary told it him all over again. God blessed the words; he became a changed man, and was afterwards a useful preacher to his countrymen. Notwithstanding, then, that "Christ Crucified" is "to the Greeks foolishness, and to the Jews a stumblingblock," the Apostle glories in Him as the "Power of God,"—the

POWER OF GOD unto Salvation (1 Cor. 1:24). A mighty Power there is in the story of Christ Crucified. The 3,000 who were received into the church on the day of Pentecost, and the 2,000 who followed them within a day or two, were trophies of this power. Peter did but preach to them the Christ Whom they had killed, and this Christ was the Polished Shaft by which conviction was aroused, and their enmity slain; the Weapon, "mighty through God to the pulling down of the strongholds" of unbelief. And not only that. The convinced sinner sees that there is, in this Christ, exact adaptation to all he wants. "The Power of God!" he cries. "Why, power is just what I want. I feel that there is a dreadful power in sin to hold me fast, a terrible power in evil habits to enslave me still, a formidable power in Satan to withstand all my struggles in the right direction. And I require a Power on *my* side, a supernatural Power, a Power greater than all the power that is against me."

Well, this very Power is Christ Himself. No less an influence must be at work within you. "Can the Ethiopian change his skin, or the leopard his spots?" Then may ye who are accustomed to do evil, learn to do well. It is not mere *doing* good, but *being* good, that is required. Selfish and debased, there must be a holy nature imparted. Dead in trespasses, what is wanted is "newness of life." At enmity with God, you require a "right spirit." You cannot otherwise do what is right before God. But then the new life, the right spirit, the holy nature, cannot continue to act or even exist a day without Christ. The Living Christ is the Power that must actuate you from first to last. It cannot be too plainly asserted, nor too deeply pondered, that real religion is and must be a supernatural thing. It is Christ in the soul, Christ dwelling in the heart by faith. Nothing less than this is the Power of God unto salvation. Then there is another Title under this head, a most grand and imposing Title: "He is exalted at God's right hand a Prince and Savior, to give repentance and remission of sins."

PRINCE AND SAVIOR (Acts 5:31). Is the sinner distressed with the remembrance of his sins? This Savior Prince "hath power on earth to forgive sins." But observe, He never forgives without repentance. What is repentance? "Sorrow for sin," says one. True, but Judas was sorry—so sorry that life was too great a burden to be borne, and yet there was no true repentance. That holy disposition called *godly* sorrow is what we want—sorrow towards God, grief that we have offended our Father, and crucified our Savior. It means a change of mind, a turning from sin to God. Jesus is sent "to bless us by *turning us away* from our iniquities," teaching us to hate sin *as* sin. To grieve for it only because it has done us harm is but a selfish sorrow. We must abandon it because it is "the abominable thing which God hates." With *this* repentance there is connected forgiveness of sins. But let us not confound these things together. It is not meant that we are forgiven on account of our repentance. Not at all. Without it there is indeed no forgiveness, for God doth not throw away pardons on those who are bent on going on still in their sins. But the forgiveness is the free gift of Christ. The sinner is made to feel that he has not to do anything in order to be reconciled, but as soon as "he comes to himself," he finds that peace is already made for him by One who is called "OUR PEACE."

PEACE (Eph. 2:14). And God is waiting to be reconciled to him. All that is wanted is, that he should be willing to be reconciled to God. Oh, glorious gospel! Most gracious provision! Well may Micah sing, "*This Man shall be the* PEACE," and Paul responds, "*He is our* PEACE." He procured it for us by the sacrifice of Himself. "The chastisement of our peace was upon Him." To bring back peace to countries distracted by wars, great sacrifices are often necessary. The peace has to be conquered. Those opposed to it have to be overcome, and before there can be a settled peace, there must be an obstinate war. Half a century ago, Europe was distracted from one end to the other, through the restless ambition of the first Napoleon. In order to secure peace, the princes of various countries combined together to conquer it for themselves. This being done, many years of peace followed. But it was purchased by an enormous expenditure of human life, and millions of money, and years of precious time. So PEACE was not procured for sinners but at an enormous cost, by our great PRINCE OF PEACE.

PRINCE OF PEACE (Isa. 9:6), and LORD OF PEACE (2 Thess. 3:16). Single-handed He labored and suffered, fought and bled, in order to procure for us the precious boon. The word PRINCE here means Author, Originator. He *made* peace for us by the Blood of the Cross. Well, having made peace, what more does the Title suggest? That *he* dispenses peace to us. It is His prerogative to speak peace to our hearts; "Peace to him that is far off and to him that is near, and I will heal him, saith the Lord." How different the peace that He speaks to the troubled heart from that which men speak to each other! The world cries, Peace! when there is no peace. It tries to mimic the great PRINCE and AUTHOR OF PEACE, but succeeds no better than did the Egyptian magicians in imitating the miracles of

Moses. He gives not as the world gives, but in an effectual way. What He *says*, He *can* do and *will*, while the world mocks everyone who trusts its lavish promises.

A certain rich lady suffered from deep depression, though surrounded by all that wealth could procure. Riches, kind friends, gay pleasures, evermore cried peace to the gnawing vulture within her disconsolate heart; but her distress was only evermore aggravated. In the providence of God, there crossed her path one day someone who threw a tract into her carriage, entitled, "The Way of Peace." At first she was displeased at what she deemed an insult. Yet she was not able to resist the inclination to read the tract. It led her to the cross, and there she found the longed-for peace. Soon great afflictions came upon her. She lost her health, her husband, her children, her property; but she never lost the precious treasure, peace. "My peace," as our great Prince calls it, ruled in her heart, and throughout the remainder of her trying life, it soothed her sorrows, quieted her fears, and lit up her pale face with heavenly smiles. It is not always that conversion is so soon followed (and tested) by such varied tribulations as this afflicted lady endured. But be certain, so soon as the sinner is turned to God, the world, the flesh, and the devil, will array themselves against him in some form or other. But here is another Title, which brings with it assurance of help—

PRINCE OF PRINCES, and Prince of the Kings of the Earth. See Daniel 8:25 and Revelation 1:5. This Mighty Prince controls the proudest potentates, and sets limits to all persecutors, beyond which they cannot pass. We have spoken of this under other titles, and therefore will not dwell upon it here. What I want you to observe now is the restraint that He keeps upon the malice of the prince of this world, and the principalities and powers in alliance with him. You remember that it is our Lord Himself who names Satan the prince of this world; but surely it is in *irony*. He does but call the proud, fallen spirit by the title, which he claimed for himself, when he boasted, All the power, and glory, and kingdoms of the world are mine, and to whomsoever I will give them. And as long as there is so large a proportion of the world "lying in the wicked one," it is no wonder he still glories in his usurped titles. And incessantly doth this archenemy of our Great Prince and of His followers, "walk about, seeking whom he may devour." All the inward temptations and outward persecutions which assail us, are, more or less, traceable to him. For "we wrestle against principalities and powers, and against the rulers of the darkness of this world." But, take courage, all ye who are willing, heart and soul, to become the loyal subjects of our Prince of Princes, King Jesus. Fear not the prince of this world, nor his subordinate principalities, for

> The word that saves you doth engage
> A sure defense from all their rage.

Now, let us go on to observe that the sinner who is led to Him for Peace, soon finds himself "brought into a large place," where "the Glorious Lord is unto him a

PLACE OF BROAD RIVERS AND STREAMS" (Isa. 33:21). This beautiful figure occurs amidst promises of deliverance to the Jews. Not that there were any "broad rivers" near to Jerusalem. But God means to say that He would be to them *instead of* all such natural advantages. The figure is expressive of the Divine favor, and is typical of the blessings that pertain to the kingdom and subjects of Jesus Christ. And it seems to suggest,

1. *Safety*, as the primary and most obvious meaning of the figure. The broad seas that surround our highly favored island have done much, on several occasions, for our preservation. But neither seas nor rivers can absolutely insure safety. If you have read the History of England, you may remember that the Dutch once sailed up the River Medway as far as Upnor Castle, burning and destroying all along their course. In that case the river helped the foe. But God promised the Jews that in the River He spoke of "there should go no galley with oars, nor gallant ship pass that way," that is no ship of war. And this figurative promise meant that no hostile attack should avail while He was their Safeguard. So, of you who have fled for refuge to this Glorious Lord, it is said, "No weapon formed against you shall prosper," and "none shall pluck you out of My hand." The Broad Rivers and Streams interpose an effectual barrier against every assault, and garrison you all round. But the figure suggests,

2. *Abundance*. Not one river, but Rivers. Not narrow brooks, but Broad Streams. Everything here is superlative. There is overflowing profusion. The love of Christ "passeth knowledge"; the righteousness that justifies is an "everlasting righteousness"; His promises are "exceeding great and precious"; when He saves, it is "to the uttermost"; when He answers prayer, it is "exceeding abundantly above all we can ask or think." When He pardons, it is "abundantly," and the sin is removed "as far as the east is from the west." Yes, Christ's riches are "unsearchable riches." The arithmetic of angels cannot reckon them; nor can they be weighed in scales, for everything is light as air in comparison. Eternity will not only never exhaust them; it will not even diminish them one whit. Then the figure suggests the idea of

3. *Enlargement and Liberty*. Some travelers, exploring in Australia, years ago, traced the course of a winding river for a long distance with the hope that it would lead them to some fruitful district. They met with many hardships and sore disappointments. Their food failed, their powder was expended, and the wild men of the country threatened them. Hopeless of success, they were ready to abandon their attempt, when, all at once, their narrow stream, often choked with weeds, opened into a deeper channel. "A place of broad rivers and streams"

was spread out before them, widening for miles towards the sea, with fertile lands on either side. There they pitched their tent, and prepared "a city for habitation, and sowed fields, and planted vineyards which yielded fruits of increase."—Thus it is with the human soul in its pilgrimage through this world. Man pursues his way, exploring as he goes, and ever inquiring, Who will show us any good? Disappointment and darkness often attend him. If now he cries unto the Lord, in his trouble, the Holy Spirit will "lead him forth by the right way, and bring him to a city of habitation."

A poor mother of a family of little ones was smitten with consumption. She felt her end was near, and became very disconsolate. How can I meet death? How shall I part with my husband? And what will become of my poor babes? Such thoughts as these filled her mind with perplexity. A young lady who had often sought to console her, but hitherto always in vain, one day, finding her still dejected, said to her, "Will you like to hear me sing, Mrs. S?" The proposal being assented to, the lady, with a sweet and touching voice, sang Miss Elliott's well-known hymn, "Just as I am." And, as the gentle singer, with thrilling tones, passed on from stanza to stanza, the sufferer's eyes began to glisten and her face to glow. A secret but irresistible power went with the words. The dark cloud rolled away. The sun of God's favor shined brightly into her heart. Difficulties vanished, and from that hour she could entrust her soul to the care of her Savior. She could smile at death. She could cheerfully part with her husband, much as she loved him; and her dear children, too, who lay so heavily on her heart, she could leave in the hands of Him to whom she had committed her soul. She had entered a new world wherein was light, liberty, enlargement. The GLORIOUS LORD became to her a PLACE OF BROAD RIVERS AND STREAMS. It was no mirage, no deception, but an expanding enjoyment and prospect of soul-satisfying good, which led her to exclaim with the psalmist, "Thou hast set my foot in a large room."

> She looked with wonder at the sudden view,
> As when a traveler
> Through dark and desert ways, with peril gone
> All night—at last, by break of cheerful dawn,
> Obtains the brow of some high climbing hill,
> Which, to his eye discovers, unaware,
> The goodly prospect of well-watered lands,
> Which now the rising sun gilds with his beams.

But while we speak of "enlargement" let us carry our thoughts a little further. The state of reconciliation with God may well be called a "wealthy place" when contrasted with the hopelessness of the former state. But what will heaven be as contrasted with the best we can know here? "What will it be to be there?" For the Christian is not "out of the woods" yet! It is likely enough he will find the most trying passage of all at the close of his journey. There are to come the rendings of nature, painful farewells, and the unknown pangs of dissolution. And, it may be, with many a groan he will pass through death's narrow portals. But out of that dark passage he will emerge into what? Fear not to close thine eyes, dying Christian, for the next instant thou shalt open them upon all the dazzling brightness and blessedness of heaven! In one short moment the bitterness of death will be past, and then the arms of angels will encircle thee, the congratulations of sister spirits thrill through thy soul, the pearly gates of Paradise fly open at thy approach and the golden city spread itself out before thy wondering gaze. And, above all, the smiling countenance of thy Savior shall beam upon thee, filling thee with joy unutterable and full of glory; and there the GLORIOUS LORD will be unto thee a PLACE OF BROAD RIVERS AND STREAMS.

> Oh change—oh wondrous change!
> Burst are the prison bars;
> This moment there, so low,
> So agonized, and now
> Beyond the stars.
> Oh change—stupendous change!
> There lies the breathless clod;
> The sun eternal breaks,
> The deathless soul awakes,
> Awakes with God.

Let a closing word or two be added in confirmation of the subject of this Reading—The sinner's translation from darkness to light. You know our Lord insists on a great and vital change as indispensable to salvation. "Verily, I say unto thee, Except a man be born again—born of water and the Spirit—he cannot enter into the kingdom of heaven." Is that such a change as can be effected by the sprinkling of a few drops of water? The idea is too preposterous to be entertained for a moment. Does it then mean a merely outward reformation, a growing better by bodily exercise and self-improving efforts? Nay. This also, though better than the former, falls far below our Lord's meaning. Nor is it a literal recreation of the man, the new heart being another organ introduced in place of the old one. What then? Surely, it is the importation of a new taste, a new condition of the affections of the soul—a new love! The supreme love of self, and of the world, must give place to the supreme love of God; so that, thenceforth, the first question is not, How shall I please myself, and make the best of this world? but How shall I please God, and do His will?

You see this is a change so great, so radical, that it cannot be effected by any *natural* power within or around us. The power must be *supernatural*. It must come from God. Nor is the change so wrought as that, once effected, there needs no further exertion of the power that produced it. The newborn soul is united to God. Christ, the Power of God, lives in it as a consecrated temple, and by His Spirit illumines the understanding, quickens the conscience, brings the will into accordance with His own, disengages the affections from their idolatries, and fastens them on Himself. And so it comes to pass, that the life such a one lives in the flesh is no more according to the flesh, the corrupt principles of nature; but according to higher principles, "by the faith of the Son of God." *This is regeneration*, and anything short of this is mere religiousness, not true religion. Now, does anyone say, "This is a grand and glorious thing, but it seems far above, altogether out of my reach?" Of course it is. You cannot get at it. *It must come down to you.* Therefore,

First. *Ask for this supernatural influence.*

Second. *Make room for it.* Break off every evil habit, part with every evil companion and association. Turn out of that pre-engaged heart of yours every lust of the flesh, every idol of the spirit. "If you will have Christ, you must sell all to secure Him—part with all to create a void for Him to fill. For, as certainly as the light will pour into an open window, just so certainly will God reveal Himself in a mind that is open to His approach."

Third. *Appropriate the promise, which makes Christ yours on believing.* As the serpent of brass was set up that whoso looked thereon might live, so is Christ presented to you, on purpose that you may make Him your own, on the express warrant of His word: "If any man thirst, let Him come unto Me and drink—Him that cometh unto Me, I will in no wise cast out."

But if you will not have this salvation, and deliberately prefer the world and sin, then "hide it from yourselves, if you can, that you were made for God; but call it no severity that Christ has not opened heaven to such as you. 'Marvel not that I said unto you, Ye must be born again.'"

> For how can sinful flesh and blood
> Appear before the throne of God,
>   In that pure world above?
> The sensual heart must be renewed,
> And be with heavenly life endued,
>   The life of holy love.

37

Preserver. Plant of Renown. Pearl of Great Price. Portion. Precious.

WHEN Jacob blessed his grandsons just before his death, he used these words: "The God Who fed me all my life long unto this day, the Angel Who redeemed me from all evil, bless the lads." The God Who fed him was the Angel Who redeemed him. Without attributing a knowledge of New Testament theology to the patriarch, we may observe that to us there is a peculiar sense in which it is Jesus Christ "Who redeems us from all evil," Who also is the God who provides us with temporal supplies. He it is Who is the

PRESERVER OF MEN (Job 7:20). For the entire administration of the world is entrusted to His hands, with power over all flesh. In token of this He feasted great multitudes plentifully, once and again, upon half a dozen small loaves and fishes. These were great miracles quite out of the common way. But is not that providence of His much more wonderful, which causes the fruits of the earth to grow from year to year, and the beasts and fishes to multiply at such a prodigious rate, in order to supply the wants of the teeming inhabitants of the world? Think what enormous quantities twelve hundred million mouths must consume day by day continually! And what an enormous exertion of power and wisdom that must be which keeps up the amazing supply year by year!

Indeed, are we not often within five or six weeks of universal famine? If the harvests of the world did not come in their season, if they failed only for once, we must all die and the world must come to an end. But the Great Preserver of man and beast will not let it come to that, till He has completed all the grand purposes of His Mediatorial Kingdom. Seed-time and harvest will not fail till all the prophecies are fulfilled, and Christ is prepared to deliver up the kingdom unto the Father, together with the seals of office, having put all enemies under His feet (1 Cor. 15:25).

But not only doth the PRESERVER OF MEN provide food for us, but manifold gifts besides, which are essential to life. For man doth not live by bread alone.

There are countless gifts and providential arrangements and interpositions essential to our life and well-being, which we cannot reckon up in order, so great is the sum of them.

There are blessings that are insured to us by the ministry of angels; others that reach us through the ministry of friends; and others still that come to us through the ministry of multitudes whom we have never seen; some of whom have lived before us and others are contemporary. Some gifts are direct and others indirect. Some have relation to the preservation of health, and some to restoration from sickness. Some insure our physical well-being, and others our spiritual prosperity. Who can show forth all His mighty acts as the Preserver of Men? Indeed, who can enumerate the profusion of benefits of all kinds, which "load" us even during one day of our lives?

But we must pass on from this tempting topic to what next claims our thoughts. If for the four subjects which fill up the remainder of this Reading we were required to furnish an inscription, it would be, Christ an All-Comprehensive Good; or if to select a text, it might well be, "The unsearchable riches of Christ." Let us see how far our four subjects illustrate this grand theme. And first, in Ezekiel 34:29, it is written, "I will raise up for them a Plant of Renown."

PLANT OF RENOWN; "and they shall not more be consumed with hunger." The word "Plant" may be looked upon as a general term, including all the vegetable productions of the earth, in all their wonderful variety. "Plant" represents all sorts of food—wheat, rice, fruits, and all other things available for our subsistence. It stands for shelter, medicine, clothing—all. Since the timber, which forms our houses, and the flax and cotton, which clothe us, are all derived from the Plant. And all sorts of medicines too—aloes, gentian, rhubarb, bark. And some of these are Plants of Renown, for they are known throughout the world for their valuable qualities. There grew trees in Gilead renowned for their healing balm. And there were cedars in Lebanon unrivaled for their excellent timber. The islands of the Pacific boast their nutritious breadfruit tree. China is universally famed for its favorite tea plant, and Arabia for its odoriferous spices. The banian tree is remarkable for the vast extent of surface over which it spreads itself. While the palm—the beautiful, stately palm—furnishes food, clothing, cordage, shelter, timber, writing tablets, and I know not what besides, to the inhabitants of India and other countries.

But what if there could be found, somewhere, a species of tree, whose fruit and leaves and stem produced all that men are accustomed to derive from a multitude? Ah! that would be a Plant of renown indeed! All the world would ring with its praises. Well, though we find not this in the natural world, in the spiritual world Christ is that very Plant of Renown. The wants of the soul are far more pressing than those of the body. It needs shelter, nourishment, and relief, suitable to its nature, or it must perish. This world in which it dwells is like a vast desert. Nothing grows on its parched plains that will satisfy the poor hunger-bitten soul, save only in one verdant spot. The church of God is that oasis of the desert, that garden in the wilderness. "The Lord hath placed salvation in Zion for Israel His glory"; and there this Tree of Life flourishes all the year round.

Let us bear this ever in mind—it is not a great variety of things our souls require. We need not roam over the wide world in search of happiness. One thing is needful. While all things else disappoint expectation, here we shall find all we want, and more than we can ask for. Should God deprive us of every other source of gratification, were all our friends to die, all our property to be destroyed, all means of subsistence to fail, we may betake ourselves to the covert of this glorious PLANT OF RENOWN and sing, "Although the fig tree shall not blossom, and there be no fruit in the vine, the labor of the olive shall fail, and the fields yield no meat—yet will we rejoice in the Lord, we will joy in the God of our salvation."

Surely this PLANT richly deserves to be renowned, to be exalted and extolled, and to be very high in our esteem. And so indeed it is. In heaven, angels and saints constantly celebrate its worth; and on earth, its fame is spreading far and wide, and men of all nations pitch their tent under its branches. Come the glad day, when every tongue shall confess His preeminent beauty and preciousness!

But ah! we seem still far from that! What various treatment this PLANT OF RENOWN receives from different sorts of people! One traveler hears of its fame and turns aside to gaze. But not discovering at once that wherein its comeliness consists, he passes on. To him it is a Root out of a dry ground, and he leaves it for the shadow of some worthless gourd that will wither in an hour. A second draws near, and admires its goodly height and majestic proportions. But not feeding his necessities, he remains too far off to be the better for its cool shadow and refreshing fruits. But here comes one who is weary, and faint and ready to die. The fragrance of this PLANT of Life revives him as soon as he gets within its reach, and allures him to its shade. He tests its virtue; new life courses through his veins, and his resolve is taken—"Because Thou hast been my help, therefore in Thy shadow will I rejoice." It is a shelter from the heat, and a covert from storm and from rain. It will not, like the short-lived gourd, fail us when we most want its protection. No worm can undermine it; no sun can smite it. It knows no decay; it is the same yesterday, today, and forever.

Those three travelers are representatives of many among ourselves. Some despise God's glorious plan of salvation, and some talk about the Savior and even commend Him highly, but are ignorant after all of His virtues. There must be personal application out of a deep sense of need, or we shall not experience His worth in time of trial. One stormy winter day, the minister of Jedburg called upon a member of his block, an old man, living in great poverty in a lonely cottage. He found Him with the Bible on his knees, but in great outward discomfort. The snow was drifting under the door and through the rafters, and there was but little fire in the grate. "What are you doing today, John?" was the pastor's inquiry, "O sir," said the happy saint. "I am just sitting under His shadow with great delight."

I have read somewhere of a conflict between two animals—I think a snake and a toad. The former had a formidable weapon in the powerful venom with which it was endowed. But the other was more than a match, for he had an antidote at hand, which speedily relieved him of the effects of the poison. It was a plant growing close by, to which the toad had immediate recourse whenever he felt himself wounded. And the leaves of that plant seemed to possess the rare virtue of removing the ill result at once. The naturalist who witnessed this maneuver on the part of the wounded combatant, being curious to try the effect, plucked up the plant; whereupon the poor animal, having lost his antidote— his Plant of Renown—soon fell a prey to his opponent, and sank exhausted to the ground. You know the lesson to be drawn from this story. Christians have to fight with spiritual enemies; and when they get wounded by the fiery darts of the wicked one, they too would die if they did not apply to their PLANT OF RENOWN. May we all know its healing virtues!

And not only in our conflicts, but also in our troubles, we find the same blessing in constant application to Jesus Christ. You remember the story in the Bible, of fainting travelers in a desert arriving at a fountain. They eagerly rush forward to drink. But so bitter is the water that they reject it with disgust. In their perplexity they cry to the Lord. He tells them to cast a certain tree into the water; and when they do this it becomes sweet. And how often do we, in life's pilgrimage, come to fountains that we find embittered with vexation and sin. We trust in a friend and he deceives us; we lean on the promises of a patron and they utterly fail us; we repose on our possessions, and lo! while we count our gains, they take wing and fly away; we boast of our health and it is gone. Perhaps you occupy a subordinate situation, and have to do some things that seem degrading; or you have to suffer from the hasty tempers and froward behavior of fellow servants or others about you; or you may be misunderstood or misrepresented. Vexations may surround you on every side. Remember now the PLANT OF RENOWN. Bear and do everything as under the eye of Christ. Take Him with you wherever you go. Ask Him to put His blessing into all your "bitter fountains," and that will make them sweet, or if not sweet, at least salutary and medicinal. The PLANT OF RENOWN can remedy every evil. Christ *within* will turn the curse *without* into a blessing.

We mentioned, just now, the Balm of Gilead as a Plant of Renown; and in that aspect an emblem of the Savior. There is an allusion to it in Jeremiah 8:22, which suggests some instructive and searching thoughts on which it may not be amiss to dwell a few moments. The prophet, passionately deploring the miseries and sins of his people, asks, "Is there no Balm in Gilead? Is there no PHYSICIAN there? Why then is not the health of the daughter of my people recovered?" It may be well just to note that the Balm here spoken of was a gum flowing from a small tree peculiar to Judea. At Mount Gilead there were many groves of this tree, and from them the *best* Balm was procured. It was a favorite medicine, a sort of panacea, in the time of Jeremiah. And hence the touching allusion. Now, whether or not the famous Balm whose virtues seem to have been quite proverbial, was really possessed of all the efficacy attributed to it, it is certain that, for all *soul diseases*, Jesus Christ is the one specific, effectual, certain, never-failing Remedy. He is both the Remedy and the Healer who applies it—"The Balm in Gilead and the PHYSICIAN there!" And the remedy is so efficacious, so open to all, that when we look around upon our friends and neighbors, and see them still under the power of their various spiritual maladies, we may well exclaim, "Is there no Balm in Gilead? Is there no PHYSICIAN there? Why then is not the health of my people recovered?"

Friends and neighbors! Perhaps I need only name *some* symptoms, and your own conscience will instantly detect them in *yourselves*, and whisper, "Thou art the man—thou art the woman!" *Hardness of heart* is one form of spiritual disorder, wherein the mind and affections are averse from God and insensible to everything good. "Stony hearts"—alas, how common they are! and some "harder than the nether millstone." There is *Pride* too, a leprosy that renders you unfit to live amongst your fellow creatures. Satan was turned out of heaven for his pride, but not till he had infected many others with the same disease; and then he came to earth and communicated the fatal leprosy to our first parents, and they again to us. Then there is unbelief, blindness of mind, hatred, variance, envy, wrath, strife. All these different kinds of sins are so many destructive diseases, one of which is enough to ruin the soul forever; for they who indulge such passions shall not inherit the kingdom of God.

Now, if the Balm of Gilead or any other medicine were capable of curing all the maladies to which our bodies are liable, how men would esteem it! Neither danger nor expense would deter them from seeking to obtain it. Oh, that men would think as highly of God's remedy for *spiritual* disorders! Christ is the BALM that can cure them all. But how are we to get at it? Does it grow only in one favored country? Must we dig in the earth to look for it there? Or is it so expensive that we cannot find wherewithal to purchase it? No such thing. It is to be bought without money and without price. Have you thus sought it, and have you applied it? Is the cure begun in you? Or if not, *why* is not your health recovered? If sin still reigns in your mortal body, you have no excuse. Christ says to each of you, "Wilt thou be made whole?" Alas! how frequently have you turned away from Him, refused to be healed, and chosen death rather than life! And how often has He made this complaint of you—"Ye will not come unto Me that ye might have life."

But now I call to you once more. You may never be called again. And you must die of your sickness if you come not. The way is open. The cure is freely offered you. If you perish, you will not be able to plead that there was no BALM provided, no PHYSICIAN to apply to, and that therefore you were not healed. If you perish, it will be because you would not be saved; if you pine away in your iniquities, it will be because you rejected the Remedy, despised the PLANT OF RENOWN, and chose death rather than life. But let us now turn to the next emblem—the "ONE PEARL OF GREAT PRICE."

PEARL OF GREAT PRICE (Matt. 13:46). It may perhaps be more correct to apply this figure to the "kingdom of heaven," that is, the gospel, or Christianity. However, as Christ Himself is the Center and Substance of the gospel, the Jewel and Sun of Christianity, we think, without affirming that this was its direct reference, we may add it to our list. And what may this illustration suggest?

First. A PEARL is a *hidden* treasure. Who that did not know the secret, would think of finding such a thing of beauty inside a pair of rugged oyster shells? And was not Christ hidden from men even when He lived among them? They did not recognize their own Messiah under such a humble exterior, though "in Him dwelt all the fullness of the Godhead bodily." Had they known Him, they would not have crucified the Lord of Glory. And is He not hidden, now, from all men in their natural state? Alas! hidden from the wise and prudent, the most accomplished among them, till His beauty and worth are unveiled by the Holy Spirit. Then each cries with St. Augustine, "Oh Beauty of ancient days! ancient but ever new! Why did I not know Thee before? Too late I sought Thee; to late I found Thee! I have been poor in the midst of riches, and starving with hunger beside a table spread with the richest dainties!"

> Ah! why did I so late Thee know,
>   Thee, lovelier than the sons of men!
> Ah! why did I no sooner go
>   To Thee the only ease in pain?
> Ashamed, I sigh, and inly mourn,
> That I so late to Thee did turn.

Second. A PEARL is a *portable* treasure. The greatest pearl that ever was found, can be carried about either as an ornament or in one's pocket. And thus one who has a precious pearl might be "worth" thousands of pounds, no one suspecting such a thing. So a Christian is rich in the possession of Christ *within*—rich in faith and heir to a kingdom, and yet the world knoweth him not. When a man has Christ dwelling in his heart, he may be shut up in a prison, or banished to the snows of Siberia; he may be shipwrecked, or beaten, or burned at the stake; but his joy, his glory, his wealth, no man can take from him. When John Bunyan was shut up in Bedfordbridge jail, the prison was turned into a palace, and though he expected something worse even than imprisonment, he could sing,

> This prison very sweet to me
> Hath been since I came here;
> *And so would also hanging be,*
> If God would there appear.

Third. A PEARL is a *valuable* treasure. It is one, which the seeker ventures a great deal to obtain; for the oysters that contain pearls are at the bottom of the sea. Men must dive deep down after them, and grope about where they are beset with perils. They venture their all, their very lives, in the effort. And many lose their venture, and are drowned or killed by sharks. And are not all men busy adventurers or merchantmen seeking pearls? One thinks *wealth* a goodly pearl, ventures all for it, and drowns himself in perdition. Another thinks *pleasure* a fascinating prize, and in the pursuit of it loses both body and soul. And yet, after all, these are but *counterfeit* pearls. Oh! if men would but take the same pains to find the *real* PEARL, the PEARL OF GREAT PRICE, Jesus Christ, they would not lose their labor!

Would you find this precious treasure? You must take pains to find it, counting other things "loss" in comparison with it. It must have the first place in your heart—nay, the whole of your heart. And this explains the expression "he *buyeth* the pearl." So we read, "*Buy* wine and milk without money." It is true, the "goodly PEARL" is *freely offered* and yet it is true you must *buy* it. That is, you must part with sin and the world, not as a price but to *make room for it*. You cannot have these things and the PEARL too. But buy it! *Buy it*—be sure you BUY it, whatever it may cost. Sell all to gain it. It is worth your having at any sacrifice.

Of all jewels, the Oriental Pearl, with its glistening silvery radiance, was the most admired by the ancients. Sometimes one has been found as large as a walnut. Pliny speaks of one, which belonged to Cleopatra, worth £100,000. "What an amazing sum!" you say, "but I would rather have the money than the pearl." No doubt you would. But do you know, your words suggest a very painful thought. What is it? Just this—there are those who say the very same in reference to Jesus Christ, that PEARL of inestimable worth! One merchantman says, "Jesus Christ is a GOODLY PEARL, no doubt, but I think He is marked at too high a price. There is too much effort required, there are too many sacrifices demanded, in order to become religious." And another says, "I would rather keep my little share of the world's pleasures than give it up even to get Christ." But you say, "Surely no one would talk in this extravagant way." No! they do not say it in *words*, but in *deeds*—alas! to their eternal undoing. Happy he who can say, "Lo! I have left all and followed Thee. The Lord is my PORTION, saith my soul."

PORTION (Lam 3:24). This is the resolution all come to when once they gain a discovery of the exceeding preciousness of Christ. And what a PORTION! All-sufficient and everlasting, Christ alone, *with nothing else*, quite fills up the Christians' cup—fills it to overflowing. Sweet were the last sayings of that saintly man, Payson. "Christians would be saved much trouble," said he, "if they would but believe that *God is able to make them happy without anything else.* He has been depriving me of one blessing after another; but as each was removed, He came in and filled up the place. And now, when I am a cripple, and not able to move, I am happier than ever I was in my life before." And then he added, "Oh, if I had believed this twenty years ago, what anxiety I might have been spared!" And beautiful were the dying thoughts of Ebenezer Erskine. With a countenance expressive of the utmost joy, he told his daughter that this one sentence filled his soul to overflowing, and feasted him day and night—"I AM THE LORD THY GOD."

> The shinings of Thy blissful face,
> Thou All-sufficient God of grace,
> Salute mine eyes with beams so bright,
> I nothing need except Thy love,
> In earth below or heaven above,
> To fill my soul with pure delight.

A PORTION, you know, is an allotted share of an inheritance, and means much the same, in common conversation, as a *Fortune*. A mansion and a park, and a large income therewith, is the Portion or Fortune of some few. But how rich must he be, who has the Lord Jesus for His Fortune! He has, indeed, an estate of which it is lawful to boast; better than the whole earth—better than the heaven of heavens—better than the wide universe—even the great Lord of all Himself. Rich indeed! And he can never lose his Possession. It is inalienable. For, again, the word Portion means the share each child has in his father's property. It is his Inheritance. This is, perhaps, the leading idea connected with the word. So the prodigal said, "Father, give me the *portion* that falleth to me." Thus it comes to signify one's own special and peculiar Possession, which no one else has a right to interfere with, or can lawfully take away. So Christ, the believer's PORTION, is the gift of God and can never be alienated. It is the Father's good pleasure that nothing shall separate him from Christ. As Toplady beautifully sings,

> Things future, nor things that are now,
> Not all things below nor above,
> Can make Him His purpose forego,
> Nor sever my soul from His love.
> My name from the palms of His hands

Eternity will not erase;
Engrave it forever remains
In marks of indelible grace.

But now we must sum up what we have to say today. This Pearl of great Price, this PORTION is, as it well may be to them that believe,

PRECIOUS (1 Pet. 2:7). The believer loves Him because (1) He is PRECIOUS in Himself. Pray what qualities do you most admire among men? I think I hear one of you say, "I most admire genius, as we see it in Milton, Newton, and the great painters and sculptors." Another says, "But I admire skill and wisdom. What a great man Wren was, who built St. Paul's; and Watt, who invented the steam engine!" A third says, "Ah, but I love to think of such a man as Howard; what a great heart he must have had! and missionaries, too, think what hardships they undergo, even to the hazard of life, for the good of others!" But listen; there is yet another, a little one, who says, "I love Dr. Watts, because he wrote those dear little hymns for children—and John Bunyan, for his *Pilgrim's Progress*." Beloved ones, you may well venerate and admire all these, and others like them. But all their qualities, and every other you can think of that is excellent, exist in the human nature of Christ in their highest perfection. Whatever you can think of that is tender, beautiful, and loving—condescending and king, and strong and mighty, and skillful—that Jesus Christ is;

Add all the grace
You can in saints and martyrs trace;
And all in history you can find
Recorded, of vast powers of mind
And genius high—this Glorious One
Will all eclipse, e'en as the sun
Extinguishes each starry ray
That glimmers in the Milky Way.

And then, consider, He made all men what they are, gave to all the endowments which render them so attractive. He is the Fountain whence came their genius, their skill, their goodness. He is the great Originator of all. Thus, all right-minded people love Jesus Christ with a pure love apart from all self-interest, because He is all over glorious, "altogether lovely" in Himself. And then, (2) He is Precious in regard to what He is to us—Our Savior, Shepherd, Physician, Brother, Friend—our Helper in Life, our Solace in death. But if we go into this, we shall have to begin all over again. This entire volume is the comment on this head.

My God, my Portion and my Love!
My everlasting All,
I've none but Thee in heaven above,
Or on this earthly ball.

38

Prophet. Priest. Physician. Prince of Life.
Quickening Spirit. Resurrection.

LUTHER used to say of some grand and suggestive texts, that "each was a little Bible in itself." There is a text in 1 Corinthians 1:30, which may well deserve this appellation, so comprehensive is it, so full and exhaustless. "Christ Jesus, Who of God made unto us wisdom, and righteousness, sanctification, and redemption." It is customary to dissect and divide texts for their better elucidation. This text divides itself. Here are four points. We will illustrate the first, *Wisdom*, by the Title PROPHET; the second, *Righteousness*, by that of PRIEST; the third, *Sanctification*, by PHYSICIAN; and the fourth, *Redemption*, by PRINCE OF LIFE, QUICKENING SPIRIT, and RESURRECTION. First, He is made *Wisdom* to us as our PROPHET.

PROPHET (Luke 13:33). We have already spoken of our Lord as the INTERPRETER; and again as the MASTER or RABBI of His disciples; and we purpose to recur to the same subject one more, under the head of TEACHER. To these the reader is referred. We will therefore dwell but briefly on this Title, important and prominent though it be.

The most common notion of a Prophet is that he foretells things to come. The true idea is, that he makes known divine truth and conveys divine messages to men. And Jesus Christ is preeminently God's Revealer and Expounder, and Man's Instructor. He is "the Light that lighteth every man." Whatever skill men have to dive into the secrets of nature, to build cities, to construct ships and steer them across the pathless ocean, to weigh the stars, and calculate their movements, comes from Him, and none the less if not by direct revelation. For He it is who giveth man reason and understanding; that by inquiry, comparison, and experiment, under the guidance of Providence, he may make happy discoveries and hit upon useful inventions. And by industry and diligence he arrives at the wonderful results, which we behold with such admiration—crystal palaces, grand cathedrals, railways, electric telegraphs, and other works of art. And if all *natural* light, much more all *spiritual* light is from Him.

But our Great PROPHET does not merely *impart* "wisdom" to us as the ancient expounders of God's will did—He *"is made* Wisdom" to us. Does not this mean that He becomes our Wisdom, places His Wisdom at our disposal, and uses it on our behalf, both in the ways of Providence and Grace? It is as if a rich man were to say to a poor man, "I have plenty of money; look now—I will be your banker; come to me for every shilling you require, and you shall never want." Or as if a guide, who well knows the entangled ways across a pathless mountain, should say to a traveler who had never been there before, "Trust me—I will be instead of knowledge to you. Do as I tell you, and I will lead you past all the bogs and snowdrifts, and place you in safety on the other side." Or, as if one who had the full use of his eyesight were to say to a blind man, "Give me your hand, and I will be instead of eyes to you."

Thus Jesus Christ brings the blind by a way that they know not, and leads them in paths they have not known. He makes all His infinite wisdom as available for our right guidance as if it were our own. The reason why the people of God make mistakes and fall into snares is, therefore, because they persist in trusting in their own wisdom instead of His. Oh, if we would but withdraw our confidence from ourselves, and place it all in our Great Prophet, we should always take the right course, and avoid a thousand sad falls and bitter disappointments. Too blind to pick our hesitating way through the intricate paths of life, we should each of us find his hand grasped by Another, and hear Him say, "Poor blind one, give Me thy hand; and implicitly trust thyself to Me, and I will guide thee with *Mine eye*." But if, with the waywardness of a mule, we choose our own occupations for ourselves, our own situations, our own companions for life, and all without reference to His will and His wisdom, why then we shall incur the penalty denounced upon the blind who is led by the blind; for whoso undertaketh to guide himself in such things, hath a fool for his leader, and shall certainly fall into mischief. But, secondly, Jesus Christ is "made *Righteousness* to us," as our PRIEST.

PRIEST (Ps. 110:4). Of the special features of this Office of our Lord I have before treated, and therefore do not refer to them here. I will only ask you to consider Him under one aspect of His Priesthood implied in the words, "He appears in the presence of God for us"; that is, He is our *Representative* there. A barrister or advocate is said to *represent* the prisoner who employs him to plead his cause. But he does not bring in his hand a ransom to insure the prisoner's release; nor does he engage to stand surety for his client for the future. A member of parliament *represents* the citizens who vote for him on the understanding that he will watch over their political rights. But he does not so identify himself with every one of them, as to make the interests of each his own, nor seek advantages for them as personal favors to himself. The Jewish High Priest used to *represent* the whole nation in the holy place on the day of atonement, but not *meritoriously.* He did not plead for their forgiveness on the ground that his own obedience was sufficient to justify them all.

But our Divine *Representative* goes far, far beyond these, and all others known by this designation.

(1) He appears in the high court of heaven with a great Ransom in His hand. By that He hath redeemed us, and for the sake of that God will grant Him all He asks,

(2) He undertakes to be the Surety of every one who entrusts his person and his case to Him.

(3) There is a wonderful identity established between Himself and them. He takes their nature, and they are partakers of the Divine nature. Thus He speaks, "The glory Thou hast given me, I have given them, that they may be one, as We are One." He is the Firstborn among many brethren. And the Father loves them even as He hath loved Him.

(4) And all this, because what He did in fulfillment of His Father's will, He did, not for Himself, but for them; and His obedience, because of its perfection and glory, maketh many righteous. So we sing of Him, not only as Jesus Christ the Righteous, but as the Lord our Righteousness, and desire to be found in our great PRIEST, not having on our own Righteousness, which is of the law, but that which is of God by faith.

Remember then that God sees us only in our Righteous PRIEST and *Representative*, or we should be consumed. Think also, that in Him, one believer is as completely accepted as another—the youngest child, the poorest man, the greatest sinner, if penitent, who believes in Christ as completely as Job, the perfect man, or Daniel, the man greatly beloved. Again, Christians are as fully accepted now, while on earth and still imperfect, as they will be hereafter in heaven when presented to God without spot. This seems hard to believe; but so it is, because we are accepted through Christ our *Representative*, even as He Himself is accepted in the sight of God. He ever sees us in Him, not having our own Righteousness but His.

We have often spoken of the High Priest's loving ministry on behalf of His people; how He presents the prayers they offer, the services they perform, the obedience they render. Let me now add, in the appropriate words of another, this blessed encouraging consideration. "The Christian's poorest, meanest service is thus made as acceptable to God as if it were most perfect. The motive may be defective, the aim may be unsteady, the performance may be mean and unworthy (yea, is it not always so?) but his poor stammering prayers, his faltering attempts to comfort the depressed, or to teach the Sunday school children, or distribute the humble tract right and left; all this is as acceptable to God as the highest act of adoration offered by some lofty angel or burning seraph before the throne. Why so? Because it is accepted for the sake of Him Who presents it, and not for his sake who offers it.

"Don't let us ever allow ourselves to think, 'O this poor stammering prayer, this poor stumbling effort! Surely I might as well have done nothing at all, for I am quite ashamed of it.' Nay, if you did it in the name of Christ, if you took that poor service to Him to offer it, go thy way, eat thy bread with a merry heart, be of good cheer, God accepteth both thy person and thy offerings, and 'spareth thee as a man spareth his own son that serveth him,' " Let us then, with cheerful adoptive boldness, continually lift up our face to His God and our God, crying, Abba Father. But again, thirdly, we have said Christ is "made *Sanctification* to us" as our PHYSICIAN.

PHYSICIAN (Matt. 9:12; Luke 4:23). What a precious boon is health! Without it life cannot be enjoyed, and life's duties are accomplished with difficulty. The poor body, when out of health, drags on heavily, like a loaded wagon creaking and groaning its way through deep ruts and miry roads. But of far greater importance is spiritual health, the health of the soul. Holiness, you know, is health, and sin is disease. Christ alone can take away the latter, and impart to us the former. He presents Himself to us with the faithful saying, "I am the Lord that healeth thee." Oh we love to think of this work of our Lord, and of the gracious promise implied in that sentence; and also in the words, "The whole have no need of a PHYSICIAN, but they that are sick; I came not to call the righteous but sinners to repentance." Let us ask a few questions about this PHYSICIAN.

I. What are the qualities that recommend Him? To which I answer: *He is a most skillful* PHYSICIAN. Eminent skill is the first thing we look for when we choose our Physician. And Jesus Christ can "heal the broken in heart and bind up all their wounds." He can even "heal *backslidings*." And they are the worst cases of all; for relapses, everyone knows, are always dangerous to the patient and difficult to the Physician. Indeed there can never be a case brought to Him that shall baffle His skill. However delicate, complicated, or protracted, never fear that it will confound His judgment. Is anything too hard for the Almighty? Nay. He is able to save the uttermost all that apply to Him.

He is a most tender PHYSICIAN. No one can feel for us in our afflictions like those who have passed through similar troubles. And it is just thus that Jesus Christ has been qualified to sympathize with us. Therefore, "He can be *touched* with the feeling of our infirmities." He sees His poor wounded, weeping patient on his way to His door; and He calls him by his name and says, "Ha! what sound is that? Surely I did hear Ephraim bemoaning himself. Is Ephraim my dear son? Is he a pleasant child? Yes, yes, I do earnestly remember him, my heart is troubled for him, I will surely have mercy upon him. I have seen his ways and will heal him." And, as one whom his mother comforteth, He listens to the sorrowing one and soothes his complaints. I once knew a child whose life was despaired of by reason of the severity of his sickness, and his brothers and sisters were called to his bedside to take their leave of him. But, as a last resource, a second Physician was called in who, by God's blessing, was the means of bringing back the little patient from the very gates of death. That is sixty years ago and more, and he is alive still. But O if you had seen how the kindhearted old gentleman exulted over him, and what pride he seemed to take in his little restored patient! He had him to his house, and showed him to his friends, and seemed as if he could never make enough of him. Just so Jesus Christ rejoiceth over all His patients. To do them good in His delight, His glory. He undertakes their cure because He pities them from His heart. He continues His care, in spite of their dangerous and frequent relapses, because He loves them. And by-and-by, when the cure shall be perfected, how will He rejoice over them with singing, and rest in His love! With all His healed ones—a countless host—He will present them to His Father with exceeding joy, faultless, completely cured, with no spot of sin remaining in their souls. Again,

He is also a gratuitous PHYSICIAN. Some professors of the healing art cannot be had at all but at an enormous expense. I knew one (he practiced in Chile) who demanded a fee of £400 before he would undertake a certain case. And another (in England) who, though his patient had died under his hand, presented a bill for the modest amount of £500. It is a good thing that very few are like that. Still "the doctor's bill" is often a formidable matter to a poor man. But, in opposition to this, Jesus Christ saves freely, He insures healing "without money and without price." The only condition is, that we apply to Him, willing to be healed in His own way. All the advertisements of this most munificent PHYSICIAN run in this style: "Look unto Me, and be ye saved." "Come unto Me, and I will give you rest." "Whosoever will, let him come."

He is easy of access. Through a thinly-inhabited mountain district a tourist once took his journey on the outside of a coach. Heavy rain came on. He was ill when he set out; he was worse when, late in the evening, he reached the inn. He sent for the landlord immediately, and told him he required medical advice. "Very sorry," he replied, "but there is no doctor in the village." "How far off does he live?" asked the tourist. "Fourteen miles!" said the landlord. He might as well have been in America! But our Divine PHYSICIAN is never afar off. Wherever we are, He is always at hand. Nor is He so much engaged, at any time, as to be unable to attend to our case. Night and day He is ever ready to hear and help. If you are tempted to think otherwise, receive instruction from a child.

"What do you do without a mother to tell all your troubles to?" asked one child of another who had no mother.

"Mother told me who to go to before she died," answered the little orphan, "I go to the Lord Jesus, He was mother's friend, and He is mine."

"Jesus Christ is up in the sky," said the other. "He is a long way off, and has a great many things to attend to. It is not likely He can stop to mind you."

"I do not know anything about that," answered the child. "All I know is, He *says He will, and that is enough for me.*"

He is no respecter of persons. A prime minister of France, the Cardinal Dubois, once sent for an imminent surgeon to perform a serious operation. On his arrival the great man said to him, "You must not expect that I am going to be treated in the same rough manner as you treat the poor miserable wretches at yonder hospital." "My lord," replied the surgeon, "everyone of those miserable wretches, as your imminence is pleased to call them, is a prime minister (as good as one) in my eyes." The spirit evinced in this noble answer well illustrates the disposition of our Divine Healer. To Him the poorest man is as dear as the richest; and the black man's prayer as welcome as the white man's; and the little child is tended with as much care as the philosopher or the monarch. "Him that cometh unto Me"—any him, as Bunyan says—"I will in no wise cast out."—Thus far the qualifications of the Physician. But we have another question to ask.

II. What are the sicknesses that He cures? I answer, All the diseases wherewith we are afflicted. Their name is Legion. Their symptoms are endlessly varied. And yet the malady is one. Its name is Sin.

It is a universal malady. The whole race is smitten with it. True, the symptoms are very different in different persons. In some they are mild. In others they are virulent and dangerous, and carry destruction and death far and near. You may read a list of some of its worst manifestations in Galatians 5:19–21; and there is another terrible statement in 2 Timothy 3:2–5.

It pervades the entire nature. Not only everyone, but the whole of everyone is tainted. The prophet's vivid description of the state of the Jewish nation is applicable here: "The whole head is sick, the whole heart is faint; from the sole of the foot even to the head, there is no soundness, but wounds, and bruises, and sores." The heart is rendered deceitful by it, the conscience is stupefied, the mind darkened, and the affections defiled; while it turns the will into an iron sinew.

It is a fatal malady. If not cured it will be sure to kill. It will never die of itself, but gather strength every hour, and become more and more difficult to deal with. Take immediate steps to get it cured, all ye who have not yet come under the care of the Great Physician. Rest not until, by real conversion to God, the fatal malady shall receive its death blow.

III. What are the remedies He makes use of?

The remedies are various. Were you to walk through the wards of a hospital with the surgeon, you would perhaps see that he has a different medicine for every patient; for that which would cure one might kill another. So is it with Christ. He has many remedies in store. There are fierce temptations, afflictions of all sorts and sizes, losses, disappointments, bereavements. There is pain in various degrees, poverty, reproach. From these He carefully selects what is suitable to each case, for He has a perfect understanding of all the symptoms. You may have seen some Christians rich and healthy, and happy as to their outward lot. And they do not seem the worse for it in a spiritual sense, though occasionally they may need an alternative. But you see others poor and afflicted, and unsuccessful in everything they put their hands to. Perhaps these last could not bear what was given to the first, without downright ruin to their spiritual interests. And perhaps the first would be utterly discouraged by the treatment to which their more afflicted brethren are subjected. Our Physician knows what He is about. Only let us trust Him, and He will bring the cures that He undertakes to a wonderful issue.

The remedies are often severe. That is, they seem so to us who are ignorant and short-sighted, and who wince at every touch. A gentleman who had passed through great affliction, saw a gardener pruning a pomegranate tree. He was a careful workman, but he cut the poor tree almost through in one part, so unmercifully as it seemed, that the visitor paused to inquire why he had treated it thus. The man told him, the tree was a good one but was unfruitful, and if he indulged it, it would continue so. "So I must make it bleed," he said, "in order to render it fruitful." "Ah," said the afflicted one, as he turned away brushing a tear from his eye, "I see—it is thus the Divine PHYSICIAN deals with me; His sharp strokes make me bleed, but it is that I may be holier and more heavenly-minded." "Every branch that beareth fruit, He purgeth it (pruneth it), that it may bring forth more fruit."

The remedies are saving and effectual. The PHYSICIAN does not willingly afflict. He takes no pleasure in grieving us. Quite the contrary. Why, would you not despise a surgeon who was fond of trying experiments and inflicting unnecessary pain on his patients? Of course you would, and take special care not to put yourself into his hands. Shall it be thought that Jesus Christ ever inflicts one pang too many, or protracts the suffering one minute longer than is needful? Oh, no! we wrong our tender-hearted PHYSICIAN when we harbor the suspicion. He hath a special aim in every infliction and variation of pain and sorrow, and when that aim is gained the affliction is withdrawn or moderated. Trust Him, He will not lose His labor. He has undertaken to "bring us health and cure," and heal us He will, let the cost be what it may to Himself or to us. The remedies shall certainly effect all He intends, and "the light affliction which is but for a moment, will work out for us a far more exceeding and eternal weight of glory."— One more question remains.

IV. As to the cures He performs. In each instance the cure is *gradual*—it is *certain*—it is *glorious*. But on these topics we cannot enlarge. His success is perfectly astonishing. The cases of cure can never be detailed. All the books in the library of the British Museum could not contain the history. There is not one of all the human race now in heaven, who was not, while here, under His care. And know, all ye who will come and enter your names on the list of His patients, you shall be effectually cured of every spiritual ailment; you shall be made whole and sound every whit. And when you are fit to be discharged from the hospital of this world and ready for a loftier life, you shall ascend to heaven, and become dwellers in Immanuel's land "where the inhabitant shall no more say I am sick,"—and

> Sin, your worst enemy before,
> Shall vex your eyes and ears no more.

But it is time to go on. Fourthly, Jesus Christ is made unto us *Redemption*, which in this passage refers (we think, without restricting the meaning of the word) principally to the Resurrection—"the adoption, to wit, the Redemption of our body" (Rom. 8:23). It is important to observe that the Lord Jesus does not confer the promised salvation all at once, but in several grand installments. First, there is the new birth, which is gradual and progressive. Next, there is the state in which the spirit is made perfect in Paradise. That is a wonderful attainment in the onward progress. But still the salvation is not complete, for where is the body? Was it not Redeemed as well as the soul? It was; but it remains in the prison of the grave, under lock and key. Death holds it and will not give it up, till, as the last enemy, he shall be destroyed. And when he can retain the bodies of the saints no longer, then comes the last grand result, the *Redemption* of the body. This is what falls under our notice now, as effected by the "PRINCE or AUTHOR OF LIFE."

PRINCE OF LIFE (Acts 3:15). The earth teems with life. Organized living beings are everywhere. Ocean is full of them. The forests resound with their music. Yea, every drop of water swarms with forms of life. Of insects alone there are at least four hundred thousand varieties; and what millions there are of each kind! Of all that varied life Jesus Christ is the PRINCE or Author. He calls them into joyous existence in all their myriad forms; and He dismisses them to make way for their successors. And when they pass away, they live no more. The beautiful, happy, wonderful life, so far as we know, is extinguished forever. But "if a *man* die, shall *he* live again?" Will the dry bones ever be raised from the grave and be clothed again? Reason, Philosophy, Science, have no answer to this inquiry. But Revelation has. Jesus Christ has spoken—"The hour is coming in which all that are in the graves shall hear My voice, and shall come forth."

And now that the Lord of Nature has spoken to our *ears*, Nature herself steps forth, and offers a few feeble illustrations of the doctrine to our *eyes*. The wonderful change that comes over the earth, when dreary winter gives place to spring, is a Resurrection. A month ago the boughs looked like dead sticks, and, moved by the wind, rattled like dry bones. But now the almond trees starts into sudden beauty, and every tree is bursting with leaves and blossoms. The glorious dawn that succeeds the dark-long night, the beautiful butterfly that springs from the shapeless grub, the living flowers that shoot up from dry roots and seeds, far gone to all appearance in a state of decay, seem to us like whispered confirmations of the doctrine of the Resurrection, made known with certainty only in the Bible.

"If a man die, shall he live again? 'It is impossible,' said a certain man of science. 'But is *this* possible? tell me,' said his friend. 'A servant received a silver cup from his master, and let it fall into a vessel of aquafortis [nitric acid]. It was speedily dissolved. The servant, seeing it disappear, concluded that its recovery was impossible. But the master came, and knowing more of the secrets of nature than the servant, infused salt water into the solution. This separated the metal, which was then taken out of the water; and, remelted and recast, was soon molded by a silver-smith into a far more beautiful cup than before.' The objector was obliged to own that this was possible, and that things still more wonderful could be effected by science and skill. Why then should it be thought a thing incredible that God should raise the dead? As he thought and thought, his stumbling-block was removed, and he became a believer in the Resurrection of the body."

Yes, He that raised up Jesus Christ from the dead shall also quicken our mortal bodies. The Jews in North Africa have an affecting ceremony whenever they bury their dead. Plucking the grass from the sides of the open tomb and scattering it around, they sing in chorus, "O my brother, thy bones shall flourish, O my brother, my brother!"

But think now of the grandeur of the Resurrection! At least a hundred and fifty thousand millions of human beings have lived since the creation. Suppose we add only as many more. There will be hundreds of thousands of millions of dead and decomposed bodies for the PRINCE OF LIFE to quicken and re-edify! But we talk of *millions* without any notion of what a million is. Consider then, there are about a million of moments in ten days; again, there have been just about two millions of days since the creation. Dwell a moment on these two facts, and you will acquire a juster notion of *a million*; and be better prepared to realize what a commanding position the first Adam occupies as the father of this huge family! "Consider how great this man was!" And when you have done that, rise another step, and think how glorious is the Last Adam, Who to all this vast host will be a "QUICKENING SPIRIT."

QUICKENING SPIRIT (1 Cor. 15:45). "Quickening," that is, giving life; "in a moment, in the twinkling of an eye, at the last trump; for the trumpet shall sound, and the dead shall be raised, and we shall be changed." Yes, the long, loud peals of the trumpet blast shall roll round the globe, and echo from one pole to the other, and penetrate every grave, and reach the sleepers at the bottom of the sea, and waken all to new life. The rejoicing saints shall come in bright squadrons, to put on their new and beautiful bodies, which they left long since in the grave, weak, dishonored, corrupt, dead. They find them now, radiant like the sun in brightness, white like the snow in purity, strong and active, glorious and beautiful, endowed with deathless immortality, and swift to do the will of God.

With what exquisite joy and delight will those old companions, the long-sundered body and soul, hail one another! How will they rush each into the other's arms! The spirit delighted beyond measure to assume once more the control of the body, now become a spiritual body, holy and pure, and no longer as of old an inlet to temptation. And the beautiful, chaste, radiant body, rejoiced once more to receive into its embrace its lost inmate, again to serve her purposes and do her bidding! For, be it remembered, it is the same body and not another. It is a *Resurrection*, not a creation. For the QUICKENING SPIRIT is known by yet another Title; He saith, "I am the Resurrection and the Life."

RESURRECTION AND THE LIFE (John 11:25). O how consolatory to the mourner, hiding his weeping face under his sable cloak, as he slowly follows the coffin which holds all that remains on earth of some beloved relative, is that solemn, sweet, beautiful sentence of our Lord. "I AM THE RESURRECTION AND THE LIFE; He that believeth on Me, though he were dead, yet shall he live." It falls from the lips of the minister, as he joins the mourning procession at the iron gate of the cemetery, and seems to break the silence like a voice from heaven.

And so indeed it is. The RESURRECTION! Then that poor piece of inanimate clay, which I am about to see deposited in the grave (if indeed these flowing tears will let me see), will rise again! That same body, transformed indeed, but in its very identity, I shall again behold. I shall see it arrayed in ineffable glory, invested with immortal youth, endued with power, swift of flight, a spiritual body, like the glorious body of the PRINCE OF LIFE Himself, and "shining as the sun, in raiment white and glistening."

39

Rod and Root of Jesse. Root of David. Ruler in Israel. Rich unto All That Call upon Him.

WE observed, last Sunday, that *Nature* offers some contribution to the great doctrine of the Resurrection, and affords some help to feeble thought in its efforts to realize it. And so does *History*. But—only to name the one great fact round which all other facts cluster, as molehills round a mountain—Why should it be thought a thing incredible that God should raise the dead, when, from such a degraded race as ours there has sprung such a wonderful Being as Jesus Christ; and out of such an impoverished stock as the fallen family of David, which had been in the dust for ages, there hath arisen so illustrious a Descendent to be Ruler in Israel?

During a thousand years, and through a thousand perils arising from exterminating wars, treacherous massacres, and cruel captivities, this one family was preserved for the fulfillment of God's purposes. At a date so early in its history as a hundred and fifty years after the death of David, it was only saved from utter extinction by a marked interposition of Providence. The strands of the cord on which hung the hopes of the world, were sundered, all but one little thread, which the relentless sword failed to reach. Queen Athaliah, a human panther like her mother Jezebel, "arose and destroyed all the seed royal" (2 Kgs. 11:1). That is, she issued her mandate to that effect.

But the atrocious scheme failed. The purposes of God are not so easily set aside. Tidings of the murderous intentions reach the ears of Jehosheba, wife of the High Priest, who instantly contrives a plan by which to snatch from the terrible fate, one, at least, of the victims. A little babe, hardly a year old, is "stolen" from among the doomed ones, and hidden in the temple. Six years pass away before Jehoiada, the High Priest, reveals the secret; and immediately arrangements are made by stealth for a public recognition of the secreted prince. Levites, princes, officers, have their parts assigned, and the people are called together to the temple. The little boy is set up on high beside the central pillar, and they crown him with the royal crown, and anoint him with the sacred oil. Then "they clap their hands and cry, God save the king!" The blast of trumpets and the loud crash of martial music mingle with the shouts of the people, till the noise rises and swells like the sound of many waters, and reaches the ears of the queen. Forthwith she comes into the temple with all haste to see what can be the matter. And beholding the stranger boy, with the crown upon his head, standing in the place of royal authority, she cries, "Treason! treason!" But none side with the wretched murderess. She is immediately hurried "beyond the ranges," and put to death; while the young king is uplifted into the golden throne within "the king's gateway."

Thus wonderfully was David's family secured from utter extinction on that occasion. And that one small Rod out of the Stem of Jesse, the sole survivor of all his co-descendants, was preserved to carry on the royal lineage. For 400 years longer the family maintained its position, and then, without losing its identity, gradually sank into poverty and obscurity. It seems to be with some allusion to this depression of the royal race, that the prophet connects Jesus Christ with Jesse the private person, rather than with David the King, when he calls Him a

ROD OUT OF THE STEM OF JESSE and a **ROOT OF JESSE** (Isa. 11:1, 10). They both mean the same thing. Jesse was the father of David. He was a man of no rank in Israel, though, very likely, the chief man of the village of Bethlehem, where he lived. He might have been a sort of "Sheik," occupying the lands of Boaz, his grandfather, who, it will be remembered, was the husband of Ruth the Moabitess. But this humble "Stem" shot up to a great height of worldly grandeur in the person of David. It grew like a thriving forest tree, grew into a "great cedar"; for thus Ezekiel describes the royal family of Judea, 400 years after the death of its founder. But the glory of the family passed away at last. The stately Stem of Jesse was smitten by desolating storms. Rude winds rent it goodliest branches into fragments, and scattered its leafy crown upon the earth. It was hewn down, and its dishonored trunk leveled with the dust. Not rooted up, however, for still the stump remained; and there was life in it too.

Job says, "There is hope of a tree, if it be cut down, that it will sprout again, and that the tender branch thereof will not cease, though the root thereof wax old in the earth." This was the condition of the family Root of Jesse, when the long-looked-for Illustrious Rod out of the Stem was born. A thousand years had passed away, and the wonder was, not that the family had fallen from its high position, but that after the lapse of so long a period, and amidst so many narrow escapes from utter destruction, there was any trace of it left at all. But it was preserved for a special end, even the fulfillment of God's purpose to raise up a Horn of Salvation for us in the house of His servant David. And having answered this end, the family quickly disappeared from history, with all its records and genealogies. Jesus Christ is called also by a similar name, expressive of the same idea, but identifying Him with the royal Patriarch himself—

ROOT OF DAVID (Rev. 5:5). Rudely trodden down, and scarcely distinguishable from other decayed stems of the forest, this Root at the time appointed sent out a "Tender Plant," a "Branch," destined to become a "goodly Cedar, under the shadow of whose branches there should dwell all fowl of every wing" (Ezek. 17:23). "It shall stand as an Ensign to the people; to it the Gentiles shall seek, and His rest shall be glorious." But to the outward eye there was no indication of this. "A Root out of a dry ground" was all that was to be seen; a trunk so withered, that from it nothing could be hoped for of beauty or strength. All parties seemed to be agreed that such meanness and poverty were no signs of the true Messiah. But never were human calculations more at fault.

A little African boy, who had been taught to read at a missionary school, going some distance into the country, took with him his book to read in the fields. There, as Dr. Moffat relates, he met a shepherd boy, to whom he read out of his book the story of the angel's annunciation of the birth of Christ to the shepherds of Bethlehem. The young shepherd was much delighted with what he heard, and eagerly asked where this interesting Babe was to be seen. "Was He at the missionary station?" The boy with the book told him that "He was certainly there, for they prayed to Him, and sang hymns to Him." Whereupon the other resolved he would go as soon as he could in quest of the wonderful Child. Well, he set out on a journey of some days to the station. Poor boy! there was no star to guide him on his way. No bright light to go before, and show him where he might hear things which would make him wise unto salvation. But God guided him, and on the third day he arrived at the station.

It was Saturday evening. A converted native lodged him for the night; and in the morning, when the bell was rung for service, he went with the rest to the chapel. Strange to say, the missionary read from the pulpit the very birthday story that he had heard from the Sunday school boy. And he looked round eagerly for the Babe. And seeing a white child in the arms of the missionary's wife, so unlike the swarthy infants he was used to, he concluded at once, That surely is He! And he gazed at the unconscious babe till he was ready to fall down and worship it. After the service he was taken to the missionary, who explained the sacred story to him; how that, though once the Lord Jesus had been a Babe, carried about in His mother's arms, yet having become a Man, He died for our sins and rose again. This was his first lesson in the Gospel. But he soon learned more, and became a disciple of Christ.

Now, though this African lad was too late, by many centuries, to see with his mortal eyes the Blessed Babe whose birth had so interested him, there was a time when it might have been said, "Yonder, in that little village, you may actually see that great sight, the Holy Child Jesus!" Let us imagine ourselves ascending the little, hilly street at Bethlehem, and asking everyone, Where is the Holy Child? Very likely we should gain no information. No one knows, or no one cares. But pursuing our search, at last we stand in the entrance of a rock-hewn stable; and we peer into the dim recess till, behind that pair of camels with their ungainly humps, we discover the wonder of wonders we came so far to see. Yonder, sure enough, is the lovely Infant folded in His mother's arms, and asleep on her bosom.

May we enter? But will it not be thought an intrusion? We hope not. The highly favored virgin whom all generations will call "Blessed" as long as the world stands, though she would exclaim with the utmost horror if we were to offer our worship to her, will approve the reverential homage which we pay to her Great Savior Son. Let us kneel before Him and raise our psalm of praise, for this is He of whom it is written, "Unto us a Child is born, unto us a Son is given, and the government shall be upon His shoulder. And His Name shall be called Wonderful, Counselor, the Mighty God, the Everlasting Father, the Prince of Peace." Lo, the Root of David, which had waxed old in the earth, has "sprouted again"; and the Tender Plant is He of whom it is written in ancient prophecy, "Out of thee (Bethlehem) shall He come forth unto Me that is to be Ruler in Israel; Whose goings forth have been from of old, from everlasting."

RULER IN ISRAEL (Mic. 5:2). Happy, honored Bethlehem! to have been the chosen birthplace of the Great Savior of our race. But alas! the highest honor is closely allied with the greatest peril. Poor sorrowing Bethlehem! we say, when we remember thy mothers weeping for their children; this very prophecy being the occasion of a murderous outrage upon thy innocent babes! You all know the story. It is shocking enough, without being made worse by the exaggerations of monkish writers, who have reckoned those honored little martyrs at a thousand or two. But the whole population of Bethlehem scarcely reached a thousand altogether; and "all the coasts thereof" might furnish 500 more. The male infants "under two years" of age could not therefore exceed fifteen or twenty. But whether many or few, He Whom they sought to destroy was far away. For God had provided a faithful, kind-hearted guardian for the Divine Infant, in the person of Joseph, the husband of Mary, who, warned by a dream, had conveyed Him in safety to Egypt.

Ruler in Israel! Our Lord was not the first Ruler who came out of little Bethlehem. A thousand years before it had been the birthplace of David, whom "God took from the sheepfolds and brought him to rule Jacob His people." But his goings forth were not from everlasting. David was a Typical Ruler, and his people were a typical people. Both he and they were figures of something far more grand and glorious. The first was a type of Christ, and the second of the Church of Christ. For Christ is often called by the name David; and the Church is spoken of as Israel, Jerusalem, and Zion. And authority over the Church is described by sitting "on David's throne," or having "the key of the House of David." For ancient Israel was a Theocracy—that is, a government presided over by Jehovah Himself. Just consider what a beautiful form of government that was! Their laws were to be made by Him, and all their difficulties were to be referred to Him. Whatever enemies assailed, they were to rely on Him for help; whatever supplies they required, they were to seek them from the same Source. Whoever was their king for the time being, was to rule over them as God's Viceroy, and according to His commands. What a hopeful plan! Talk about forms of government, what could equal that?

Supposing the people and their princes had been obedient, what then? Why that ancient Theocracy, the kingdom of Israel, would have been an exemplary picture and figure of the inward and spiritual Kingdom of Christ in the latter day. It would have stood out as a lighthouse amidst surrounding darkness for the guidance of the nations; a morning star, "blazing on the forehead of the dawn" as a harbinger of the bright day that was at hand. But how different was the fact! Neither princes nor people were faithful to the covenant. They rebelled and vexed His Holy Spirit, and left God to complain, "O that thou hadst hearkened to My commandments! I would soon have subdued thine enemies, but thy time should have endured forever."

There was once in the British Museum a vase of wondrous worth and rare beauty. One day a miscreant shivered it into fragments with his cane. Everybody mourned it as quite lost. But a clever artist was employed to put it together again. He succeeded to admiration. And there it stands, a thing of beauty still, though in ruins; a monument of wicked recklessness on the part of its destroyer, and a triumph of skill on the part of its restorer.

Just thus the beautiful, delicate fabric of Israel's holy Theocracy, by which was to have been represented the Kingdom of God, was shattered even before it was nigh finished. And we can only get at the original idea by picking up one piece here and another there, and putting them together as best we may. One primitive fragment we discover in Moses' time, another in David's reign; another piece turns up under Hezekiah, and another into the days of that Eliakim who had the keys of the house of David laid upon his shoulder.

But who shall imitate the skilled workman by whom the Portland vase was reconstructed? and, out of the shivered atoms of the still unmolded materials, describe what that Divine Theocracy was fitted to become? Alas! it must ever remain in its effaced beauty and glory, a monument alike of God's marvelous patience, and man's appalling wickedness.

But though the fair *effigy* of the Church of Christ was demolished, the *reality* shall stand forever; for the gates of hell shall not prevail against it. Go forth! ye children of Zion, and behold, not King Solomon but our great Ruler, "with the crown wherewith He was crowned in the day of His espousals, and in the day of the gladness of His heart." Like Solomon, was He not *twice crowned*, with solemn acclamation and sublime sign of investiture? Once, when He left the dead, and was declared to be the Son of God with power, "God raising Him up to sit on David's throne"; (Acts 2:30–36)—that is, to be Ruler in Israel—and, once again, when He ascended up on High and led captivity captive, and God said to Him, "Sit Thou at My right hand till I make Thine enemies Thy footstool." Nor shall we see Him again on earth till the restoration of all things, when at the trumpet's sound the dead shall be raised, and Death itself shall die, having no further occupation in God's universe.

Thus when the old Israel has passed away, throne and all, never again to occupy its ancient place, or serve its original purpose, as a type of something greater. But, which is far better, it is destined to become part and parcel of the grand reality which it prefigured, and to be absorbed into the Church of the Firstborn. But the spiritual kingdom which it foreshadowed, according to Daniel's prophetic symbol of the "stone cut out of the mountain," has increased and is increasing, has demolished and is demolishing every obstacle, until, there being no room left for competition, it shall fill the whole earth. Even so, come Lord Jesus!

We must not dismiss the last portion of our Reading without marking the two lessons, which it seems so forcible to point.

First, *See the importance of knowing and seizing opportunity.* In the beginning of their history, the Lord told the Hebrews to go and take possession of Canaan, promising an easy victory. That was within a few months of their leaving Egypt. But, influenced by fear and unbelief, they refused to obey the command—so *that* golden opportunity was lost, and it was thirty-eight years and more before God gave them another. What then? Why, when they did enter Canaan, they strangely disregarded His directions in reference to the inhabitants of the land for the second time, and lost the opportunity of effecting a complete subjugation; which loss they could never retrieve till 200 years afterward.

During the rule of the judges, they repeatedly trifled with opportunity and paid dearly for their folly. In the days of Solomon, their prosperity having reached its culmination, there was a time of glorious opportunity. Had they been faithful to God, what a commanding position they might have held among the nations! But a most disgraceful departure from God, on the part of king and people, drew after it fatal judgments; and the kingdom was divided, never to be reunited. We pursue the history of the divided kingdoms with melancholy interest. We see them, with occasional faint efforts at reformation, going on from bad to worse; till first came the overthrow of the kingdom of Israel, with the dispersion of the ten tribes; and, a 135 years afterwards, Judah's captivity at Babylon. The first disaster was never retrieved at all. The last, after continuing for seventy years, was followed by a partial restoration. And God gave them one last opportunity, during "the days of the Son of Man." Alas! they despised and rejected their Messiah, and left Him no alternative but to weep over their folly, and to say, "O Jerusalem! how often would I have gathered thy children together as a hen doth gather her brood under her wings, and ye would not. Behold your houses is left unto you desolate!"

Thus, for 1,500 years, they trifled with God, and threw away all the opportunities He gave them of taking their proper position as His "holy nation." For 11500 years He bore with them. But destruction came at last, and their present state of dispersion and humiliation reads to all the world most solemn lessons, on the danger of neglecting opportunity, and wasting the day of grace.

But some may say, What about God's purposes? Were they not fulfilled in the history of His chosen people? We know nothing of God's purposes, but what He Himself reveals. And *these* were His revealed purposes: "If thou shalt hearken diligently unto the voice of the Lord thy God, to observe and do all His commandments, then the Lord will set thee on high above all nations of the earth"; but, on the other hand, "If thou wilt not observe to do all these things, and to fear this Glorious and Fearful Name, THE LORD THY GOD, then the Lord will scatter thee among all people, and make thee a byword." See Deuteronomy 28. And to us, doth He not use the same language, translated into gospel terms? "Now is the accepted time; now is the day of salvation. He that believeth shall be saved; he that believeth not shall be condemned." These are the decrees of God. Then,

Second. *Admire the long-suffering of God, but presume not upon it.* We have seen that God bore with Israel, during the long period of 1,500 years, before He poured upon them the evils threatened in case of disobedience. And is not that ancient history a picture of God's patient dealings with individuals? Has He not offered to *you*, for instance, many opportunities of returning to Him? Has He not sent you line upon line, and message after message? Perhaps it is not long since you felt some conviction of sin. God spoke to your heart. Conscience heard the voice and was aroused. You began to pray; and for a time you seemed not far from the kingdom of God. But those tender emotions subsided, and you have left off to be wise and are restraining prayer before God.

Perhaps you have experienced more than once such time of visitation. But the movement of your soul towards God has only been partial, and has ended in nothing—nay, worse than nothing. "You flattered Him with your mouth, but your heart was not right with Him. You were not steadfast in His covenant, but were turned aside like a deceitful bow." Ah! is it so? "Do this now, my son; give not sleep to thine eyes, nor slumber to thine eyelids," till thou hast, on thy knees, thanked God for His long-suffering and penitence, and told Him that thou art resolved to put them to the test no longer. What wilt thou do, what canst thou do, with that unstable heart of thine, with its fickle emotions, its vain thoughts, its faltering purposes? What, but take it to Jesus Christ, and put it into His hands, and employ Him to mold and manage it for thee, so that thou shalt no longer go astray from Him?

We have heard of one who, six times during his life, was aroused by deep conviction to feelings of penitence and professions of amendment; and who six times fell away again to indifference and sin; each time hardening his wretched heart more and more, till death came and fixed his state forever.

But pause awhile, ye careless, thoughtless ones! Does not God sometimes afford but one marked opportunity, one time of visitation, and only one? And what if that be cast away? "You see that great house up yonder?" said a happy young man to a minister, who spoke to him of immediate preparation for eternity—"that white house over there—Do you see it? Well, my uncle has just left it to me in his will, and I am going to get all the business of the estate settled, and then I mean to become a Christian." So saying, he shouldered an axe, and went into the neighboring wood with a companion to cut down a tree. As the tree vibrated to their strokes, a heavy, dead branch that hung loosely to the trunk, came crashing down through the boughs, and striking the young heir on the head, killed him on the spot!—"I will enjoy the world while I am young," said a young lady of fifteen, "and when I am a little older, I shall think of religion." Three weeks afterward the friend to whom she spoke thus, was summoned to attend her funeral. Accommodating the familiar lines of our great bard to the subject in hand, may we not well say—

> There is a tide in the affairs of men
> Which taken at the flood, leads on to—glory.
> Omitted, all the voyage of their life
> Is bound in shallows and in miseries;

and ends, alas! where? In tribulation, and anguish, and everlasting night! Let me say again, *Know and seize your opportunity. Admire the long-suffering of God, but presume not on it.*

But now, having said so much of the Jews, and their breach of covenant and forfeited privileges, we must stay a few moments just to glance at the next page of their history. The question of their territorial restoration cannot be entered upon. But we may just say that the theory of their supremacy over all the nations, and their precedence of all the rest of the church in respect to spiritual privilege, we deem to be a visionary speculation, which, however tenaciously clung to by some, has no fair Scriptural warrant. Far higher (infinitely indeed) is their return by repentance, faith, and prayer, to their much-abused Messiah, and their reception into the Christian Church. "For there is no difference between the Jew and the Greek. For the same Lord over all is

RICH UNTO ALL THAT CALL UPON HIM. For whosoever shall call upon the name of the Lord shall be saved" (Rom. 10:12, 13). Let us read this and the following chapter, and set them by the side of Zechariah 12:10—13:1; and learn to look and long and pray for the glorious period (the precise date of which none can conjecture) when "all Israel shall be saved." Not only "the remnant according to the election of grace" previously called, and still to be recognized "at this present time also," but "the whole bulk and body of the nation," as one says. And what shall be the receiving of them into the one undivided church, but life from the dead to the Gentiles, even the whole outlying world of unbelievers?

And first, the Spirit will descend upon them nationally; and, convinced by Him of crimes with which no other people is chargeable, they will mourn for Him "Whom they have pierced," and "be in bitterness as for a firstborn." Dr. David Brown, writing on this subject, says:

"Once He came to His own, and His own received Him not. But 'at the *second* time Joseph shall be made known to his brethren; and the house of Pharaoh shall hear the weeping.' Oh what an unexampled mourning will that be! . . . But the most glorious feature of it will be its *evangelical character.* . . . And oh, when they see that blood which as a nation they murderously shed, turned into a Fountain open to themselves for sin and uncleanness—when they find their robes washed and made white in that very blood of the Lamb—how will they water a free pardon with their tears! how generously will they detest forgiven sin! how will they exclaim to their Gentile brethren everywhere, 'Come, hear, all ye that fear God, and I will declare what he hath done for my soul!' "

When we take a survey of the world, whether Jewish or heathen, or so-called Christian, we gaze "o'er gloomy hills of darkness"; and our hearts fail us as we own to one another, "Truly the enemy hath come in like a flood." But when the great Head of the Church shall have reached the end of all the resources of which we have any conception, He will then unveil boundless reserves of unknown treasures of wisdom and power, which will suffice to sweep down all obstacles. And according to those "riches in glory," the work will be accomplished, and not according to our limited notions and experiences of the methods of His grace. "The Spirit of the Lord will lift up a Standard" against the flood, and roll back its desolating waters. For that Spirit of "Evangelical mourning," of which Dr. Brown speaks, will be also a "Spirit of supplication," and not upon them only, but upon the whole church. And shall not God avenge His own elect, which cry day and night unto Him? Yea, He will avenge them speedily, though He bear long with them. For He is Rich unto all who call upon Him.

Elijah was a man of like passions with ourselves. And he prayed once and again. And the Lord answered him. And that instance of successful prayer, connected though it was with miraculous interposition, is expressly proposed as an encouragement to all. Did God hear Elijah's prayer? and did He respond to the appeal of his successor, Where is the Lord God of Elijah? "The same Lord" will hear our appeal, and show Himself RICH UNTO US. Let us take Him at His word, and do with this record of Elijah's prayer as Elisha did with his mantle—smite with it every interposing barrier, every threatening foe, every insolent temptation, every discouraging fear; boldly invoking Elijah's God. By prayer Peter's prison doors were unlocked. By prayer Sennacherib's host was overthrown. By prayer a path was opened through the Red Sea. But those were all miracles. True. But it was "the same Lord." And He hath the same resources still, the same loving heart, the same open ear, and the same mighty arm. And He is still the "Rewarder of them that diligently seek Him," and "Rich unto all that call upon Him."

40

Redeemer. Ransom. Righteousness. Refiner and Purifier. Redemption.

THE limited space allotted to the subject of last Sunday, left no opportunity to say all that was desirable about the Great Ruler who was born at Bethlehem. Today, let it be further observed, that this Ruler, if He will have any subjects at all, must fight for them, ransom them, die for them. But will He do all this? Will He? He has done it all, and has become their Redeemer, Ransom, Redemption, and Righteousness. But more than that—He must fit them for their place in the kingdom. He intends them all to be princes, noble and royal like Himself, worthy to be the children of the Great King. As He must gather them from highways and hedges, and lift them out of the very depths of degradation and slavery, He has much to do to fit them for the stations designed for them. Which, indeed, could never be accomplished, but that He has a power by which He is able to subdue all things to Himself. So He is their Refiner and Purifier. Let us first take "Redeemer."

REDEEMER (Isa. 59:20). The word means Kinsman; and it was the Kinsman's duty, in eastern usage, to vindicate and befriend his relatives, and to be the avenger of the blood of such of them as were slain. For this office our Lord qualified Himself by taking our nature. Thus He became our Kinsman, our near Relative. No sooner had Satan brought about man's ruin than His gracious intention was manifested; and our poor dejected parents were comforted by a promise that, in due time, there should be born One who should avenge the whole race on their adversary, and punish that "murderer from the beginning," who "brought death into the world and all our woe." In two respects man wants a Redeemer. First, he is under the curse of a broken law and exposed to the penalty which that law enforces. Second, he is in captivity to his lusts and passions, and in these chains is led by Satan at his will.

Yonder stands a dark frowning prison surrounded with walls and battlements. And in a cell under one of the turrets, there can be seen, by a ray of light which struggles through the grating, a despairing convict sitting on the cold ground and chained to a stone pillar. He is condemned to death for breaking the laws. But what if some "Kinsman," having interest with the authorities, could get the sentence reversed? There is one who will make the effort. He hies to the tribunal, seeks an interview with the judges, and learns the conditions on which alone the pardon can be granted. There is a fine to be paid; he must also be surety for the offender, and render certain other services to the state in order to atone for the injury. The ransom demanded is very great; but so was the crime of the malefactor, and so is the love of the ransomer. And, costly and difficult as the conditions are, he is ready, on the day appointed, to meet all the conditions required, and to say, Deliver him from the prison, I have found a ransom. "And so the condemned one receives his discharge, and comes forth again to life, light, and liberty." Now the benefactor who accomplished all this for him deserves, in a very high sense, to be called his Redeemer.

But look at another picture. Two travelers are wending their way on horseback along a lonely road—a mountain pass it is, rugged and gloomy, with lofty rocks on either side towering upwards to the clouds. They ride on, mingling gay laughter with merry talk, and suspecting no danger. Suddenly the horses start, with ears erect and necks eagerly stretched out.

"Did you hear that?" whispers one to the other.

"Yes, I heard a low voice and a sound like the jingle of arms." In silence they draw forth their weapons, and go on warily looking from side to side. In vain their caution. From behind a huge pile of boulders there rush forth six or eight mounted robbers whose practiced adroitness renders resistance hopeless. They are made captives and are thenceforth doomed to a hard life. Robbed of all and burdened with a chain, they are obliged to do service to their hated masters who keep sharp watch over them. What hope is there now of release from the bandits' stronghold in the mountain recess?

But they have one friend who cannot rest. He makes ceaseless inquiry and careful search; nor tires till he has discovered the dreadful secret, and traced them to their whereabout. He ascertains the strength and number of the lawless band. He spares no expense. He hires soldiers, he plans a surprise, he comes upon them suddenly, and, overpowering them with superior numbers, scatters to the right and left all who cannot be seized, and rides off triumphantly with his rescued friends. That happy deliverance is a redemption, and that courageous noble friend is their Redeemer. The first instance represents a redemption by price, the second a redemption by *power*. And such is our condition, that we need both combined. Let us look at the second first.

1. *Jesus Christ is a* REDEEMER *by power*. We are captives. Satan, the tyrant, is our cruel jailer and hard taskmaster. But he does not *make* our fetters. Strange, but

true, the heavy chains wherewith he loads us are formed by ourselves. Each separate sin is a link. And as we go on sinning still, day by day, these countless links twine themselves into chains of imperious habits which we can in no wise break asunder. I say again, this dreadful chain we forge for ourselves, and Satan stands ever at our side, blowing the bellows for us, and helping us in the fearful work.

Behold the intemperate man. His ruinous habit grows by degrees. He never meant to become a drunkard. He thought the merry glass, which he took now and then, because his companions did so, was only a gossamer thread, a cobweb, which he could any day blow away with a puff. Not so. I have seen the thread become an interwoven cord, and the cord thicken into a rope, and the rope still twisted and twined, till it grew into a cable as thick as a mast! And, like a boa constrictor, it has coiled itself round the victim, paralyzing his strength and defying all his efforts to get free. The dreadful habit crushed everything in its progress. Away went money, business, health, till the mind itself failed, and the soul sank forever. But can nothing save him before it comes to that? Can he not throw off the dreadful thing? Not he. Only Christ the Redeemer can rescue him. And He will, too, if only the victim be honest, and take hold of the Savior's proffered help in the way the Savior prescribes.

"Well but," you say, "we are in no danger from intemperance. We should never think of such a thing. Some of us are teetotalers too, and all of us are perfectly sober." Ah! but that is not the only sin wherewith Satan fetters human souls. Alas, no. Their name is legion. Covetousness grows in the same way; uncleanness, pride, selfishness, envy. All these are alike fatal. And all are little rills at first, but swell into rushing rivers in time; or, to return to the first figure, each indulgence is a separate link, which, multiplied, forms by degrees chains of darkness, in which the miserable soul is held fast till the judgment of the great day.

O look to it! Is one of my readers fond of novel-reading? It is an ensnaring taste, and has beguiled many into the way of destruction. Are others devoted to cards, dancing, theaters? We enter into no abstract questions about what is or what is not sin; but we say, these things have an aspect in the wrong direction. There is a snake in the grass. Beware! Flee from the beginnings of sin and sinful entanglements. Search and see if any wrong habit is gaining on you, and abstain from the very appearance of evil.

But wherever you are now, at the present moment—by whatever evils ensnared—do not despond. Be the sin that fetters your soul a thick cord or a thick chain, here is One who can deliver you from this dangerous state of things. Take the worst cast that can be. Is it so that you are frequently prostrated by the terrible power that some imperious criminal habit has gained over you, and are compelled to own your utter inability to struggle against it? You have so long indulged your peculiar passion, that at length it has come to tyrannize over you as with a rod of iron. Your frequent acts have become habits; your habits have gained strength till they constitute a second nature, impel you with a force you cannot resist, and set all your resolutions at defiance. You have grown desperate, and are tempted to say, "There is no hope; I have loved strangers, and after them I will go!" But must you thus hopelessly resign yourself to destruction? *Will* you do this? Is there no one who can "take the prey from the mighty and deliver the lawful captive?" O yes! Christ is a REDEEMER Mighty to save.

Go show your galling chain or fascinating snare to Him. Confess your folly. Give Him your confidence. Put the case entirely into His hands. Expect Him to break asunder the links that bind you. He has done it for thousands. It is His business to preach deliverance to the captives, and His delight to throw open prison doors to them that are bound. He sees your despairing struggles, waits for your application, and is willing to afford you aid. What though your failures and falls amount to seventy times seven? Be not dispirited. Rise from the dust; however inveterate and incurable your case may seem, you will find Him well able to cope with moral maladies of long standing, "to subdue all your iniquities, and cast them into the depths of the sea." But again I say, be honest. The REDEEMER will help, only on condition of immediate and total renunciation, in His strength, of all sin, especially the sin which easily besets you. Follow this course and you shall yet set your feet upon your lust and say, "Rejoice not against me, O mine enemy! Though I fall, I shall arise, and though I sit in darkness, the Lord shall be a Light unto me."

> O my old, my bosom foe, rejoice not over me!
> Oftimes thou hast laid me low, and wounded mortally;
> Yet the prey thou couldst not keep; Jesus, when I lowest fell,
> Heard me cry out of the deep, and brought me up from hell.

The first thing, however, is to get it forgiven. And, blessed be God, there is no difficulty whatever about that. There were infinite difficulties, and obstacles insurmountable except by Divine wisdom and power. But Christ has taken them all out of the way, "having obtained eternal redemption for us." How "obtained" it? Not by power only, as we have said; for

Secondly, *Jesus Christ is a* REDEEMER *by purchase.* You have this in many texts. "He gave Himself for us" (Titus 2:14). "Ye are bought with a price" (1 Cor. 6:20). The church is "purchased with His own blood" (Acts 20:28). "He gave His life a Ransom for all" (1 Tim. 2:6). And here again, "The Son of Man came not to be ministered unto, but to minister, and to give His life a

RANSOM for many" (Matt. 20:28). The doctrine taught in these expressions is assailed, in the present day, on all sides, both by ridicule and by sophistry. And many, from whom better things might have been expected, have turned aside to "vain janglings" which invalidate or explain it away. But we refuse to surrender this citadel of the Christian religion. We will cling to it while we live, and glory in it when we die, and praise God for it eternally in heaven. For this assailed doctrine is part of the new song. Nor will the celestial arches ever hear the last of it. Through eternity they will echo to the chorus, "Worthy is the Lamb, for Thou wast slain and hast redeemed us to God by Thy blood, out of every kindred, and tongue, and people and nation, and hast made us unto our God kings and priests."

The Holy Spirit has, we have no doubt, chosen the best possible phrases for the instruction of the ignorant and unlearned. For such the Bible was principally written and not for the learned. The former have always been the great majority and are likely to remain so. And we believe the wayfaring man, as long as the world stands, will persist in understanding that the blood of Jesus Christ is the Ransom, the Redemption price, of man's salvation. Not a price paid to Satan their jailer, as some scoffingly affirm that we mean; nor yet to God as a mere expedient to show His hatred of sin, and to secure His honor in the release of the condemned ones, as others somewhat more reverently urge. How then?

The death of Christ is a real atonement for sin; a true and proper infliction of the penalty of a broken but inflexible law; a true and proper satisfaction to the unbending justice of a righteous Lawgiver and Judge.

What is law without the sanction of penalty? Can you imagine such a thing? If no punishment is attached to its infringement, the precept loses its character. It is no longer a law. It is just a piece of good advice, which, if we chose to follow, it is well. If not, we may expect the offense will be overlooked. What would become of the authority of God as the Sovereign of the world, if the law merely said, "Do this"; and did not add, "The soul that sinneth, it shall die?"

All have broken the precept, and incurred the penalty. And Christ died for all, that by His death He might discharge the claims of justice, render a sacrifice to Righteousness, and make the salvation of the redeemed a just (and a justifiable) salvation. We see not how it could be justified on any other ground. The inspired apostle lays down the law of the case thus: Without shedding of blood there is no remission of sin. Without a proper Ransom, it would not then have been right for God to grant a release. And who shall be the judge of what constitutes a true and proper Ransom, if not God? Whether therefore men will receive or reject Him, God hath set forth Jesus Christ to be the only Ransom and Propitiation, through faith in His blood.

I have somewhere read a story of a man, brought up in a heathen community, becoming distressed in conscience about his sins. He hears some vague reports of certain statements made by a missionary who had traveled that way, of a God who pays the debts incurred by transgressors against the Divine law. He inquires further, but can get no satisfactory information. He undertakes a long journey, asking still for the God who pays the sinner's debts. But the strange inquiry meets no solution. Some laugh at him, and others refer him to a country still farther off, where the Christian religion is professed. Thither he goes, still urging the same restless inquiry; till one day he enters a place of worship, and hears the glad gospel announced of Jesus Christ the sinner's Ransom. The wanderer is overjoyed. He has found the great secret. The God that pays the sinner's debt is "made unto him Righteousness."

RIGHTEOUSNESS (1 Cor. 1:30). The law cannot abate aught of its claim. "These offenders are my prisoners," saith Justice, "and I must have a perfect Righteousness, or they must lie here under condemnation forever; they can never have a release." Our Redeemer provides that which the law requires. His Righteousness is perfect. It knows no flaw. And, by His perfect, spotless obedience unto death, He maketh many righteous, even all that trust in Him. They are accounted righteous, treated as righteous, for His sake. As righteous as if they had done the very thing the law requires. Yea, as righteous as though possessed of the Righteousness of Christ, who fulfilled the law for them.

A certain man who had been unacquainted with this way of salvation drew near his end. And he said to himself, "How shall I fare when I stand before God? I am a sinner, it is true, but I will trust in God's mercy." By-and-by it occurred to him, "But God is *just* as well as merciful—suppose He should deal with me *on the footing of justice, where am I then?*" He sent for a minister, to whom he stated his perplexity; the minister said, "That is the very difficulty which the gospel meets; it shows us God as a *Just* God and a Savior, through Christ who is the END OF THE LAW." When this doctrine was more fully explained to him, the dying man caught at it as his only hope, and confessed, "I here see a solid footing to rest on, which before I could never find."

Come then to Jesus as your RIGHTEOUSNESS. Only believe on Him! and that majestic Law which now condemns you, will be no more contrary to you, for "there is now no condemnation to them who are in Christ Jesus." For Justification is more than pardon. God does not merely say to the penitent one, "My child, I forgive you. I will not remember your sin against you." But this rather, "I look on you as identified with my Son, interested in all that He did as your Surety, Substitute, Representative, invested and covered all over with Him. Therefore I accept you in Him and rejoice over you for His sake."

But again, the redeemed one, being invested with a title to the purchased inheritance, has to be trained, and ennobled, and sanctified; so that he may rightly enjoy it, and suitably grace it. For so it is written, "He gave Himself for His church, that He might sanctify and cleanse it with the washing of water by the word" (Eph. 5:26). And, again, "He shall be like a Refiner's Fire"; and again, "He shall sit as a REFINER AND PURIFIER OF SILVER."

REFINER AND PURIFIER (Mal. 3:3). This Title suggests the crucible, with the molten silver quivering therein; and the glowing furnace, urged to a white heat by the panting bellows of the silversmith; who all the while bends forward, intently watching the changes which the liquid ore undergoes while agitated by the fervent heat. And now the scum and impurity that discolored the surface have disappeared; and lo! the beautiful, clear metal reflects the image of his face as vividly as a looking glass. This is what he has been so patiently watching for— the sign that his end is accomplished, that the silver is purified from all its dross. A very instructive parable doubtless. But who can dwell upon it, with self-application, without shrinking? For that Scorching Fire is the emblem whereby the Lord hath chosen to represent the trials and afflictions by which He disciplines His children. "I will melt them and try them; for how shall I do for the daughter of My people?" "I will turn My hand upon thee, and purely purge away thy dross and take away thy tin."

"To the flesh fire is most agonizing. The torture it inflicts is exquisite. A single spark is enough to extort from the wincing sufferer the cry of terror. So indeed are the pains that accompany some forms of disease. They feel like fire. And they are meant to do so. They would not serve the purpose intended if it were otherwise. Other kinds of trial there are which torture the spirit in an equal degree. The temptations of the wicked one are fiery darts, which set the soul in a blaze. The words of slander are like coals of juniper which have a most vehement flame; and scorch, and tear, and exasperate the soul almost beyond endurance." The figure, however, is not that of fire applied to the quivering flesh, inflicting merely suffering; but that of a Refiner's Fire as applied to metallic substances for the purpose of purification. Note these five particulars.

1. *The Refiner's Fire has a* SEARCHING *power*. It penetrates into the very texture and tissue of the substance submitted to it. Nothing can evade its continued action. Urged by the blast of the bellows, it forces its way into every minute cranny, and finds out everything on which it can expend its force. Just so, Affliction pierces the inmost heart, and divides asunder the joints from the marrow. Now the drowsy soul starts from its sleep; for its most secret recess is reached, its hidden sore is laid open; it is touched in the tenderest part; the Fire is found to be quick and powerful.

2. *The Refiner's Fire has a* REVEALING *power*. It detects the nature of substances, proves what they are made of. Under its action the false tinsel betrays its base nature, while what is real and valuable is equally manifested. So is it with the Christian when he is put into the crucible of trial; many things which passed muster in the days of prosperity, come to be seen in a very different light. That worldly compliance—those over-keen business transactions—outbursts of unsanctified tempers—formality, selfishness, and sloth—force themselves on the

sight, and look very ugly. Perhaps, as the testing process goes on, and the fire grows fiercer, nothing else appears but that unsightly scum floating on the top; the genuine metal, if there be any, being, for a time, all out of sight at the bottom of the vessel. The new nature is obscured, the voice of the "old man" alone is heard. Thus Abraham, involved in perplexities, invents an unworthy evasion to screen himself. Thus Peter, when his trial is at the hottest, betrays the corruption which is hidden within, and denies his Master with oaths and curses.

3. *The Refiner's Fire has a* SEPARATING *power.* As the workman sits over the vessel, and still urges the fire to a white heat, not only is the metal proved, but that which is pure gradually separates itself from the dross that debases it. So is it when the Great Refiner subjects His people to the process of purification. The "sons of God are all comparable to the most fine gold." Each one is an ingot of genuine metal. But even the best of them is so alloyed, that go he must into the fining-pot of affliction. And nothing but the true gold will stand the fire. That which is spurious runs off as scum, and is thrown aside. Hear the mournful complaint of the prophet, "The bellows are burned, the lead (put in to assist the process) is consumed of the fire, the Founder melteth in vain. Reprobate silver shall men call them because the Lord hath rejected them" (Jer. 6:29, 30).

Not so was it with Job. He was "a perfect man," a real saint to begin with; and so bright and exemplary, that he, of all men, scarcely seemed to need the crucible. Yet his furnace seemed seven times heated. Nevertheless he stood the test wonderfully, nor ever lost the consciousness of his own integrity. At the worse he could say, "When Thou hast tried me, I shall come forth as gold." As yet the hidden depths of his heart were not probed, when it was said of him, "In all this Job sinned not." But more and yet more severe grew the trial. "The calamities of life, like a burning storm, seemed to tear up and melt his heart, as a fierce fire breaks up the silver and melts it into a quivering stream." The fire still waxed hotter and fiercer, and then the secret place was reached, the corruption of his heart flowed forth dark and unsightly—"Job opened his mouth and cursed his day." It was well the fire had revealed this "perilous stuff"; for it was revealed in order to be separated under the careful oversight of Him who sat as a Refiner, with His watchful, loving eye ever fixed on the sufferer.

4. *The Refiner's Fire has a* DESTROYING *power.* It consumes all that is noxious, the scum and refuse; or turns it into slags and cinders. And trials and afflictions have a like issue. Perhaps the man's sin was the love of money; and God said, "For the iniquity of his covetousness I was wroth and smote him." The property he had idolized was taken away. The bank failed, the ship went down, or the warehouse took fire; and thus the inordinate desire of possession received its death stroke. Or, it may be, the selfish desire of human applause was the sin. And this had to be slain by the intense mortification caused by treachery or in-

gratitude. Or it was the plague of a wicked ambition. And that could only be removed by a providential blow, which disappointed some lofty, fond expectations. "And thus every sinful passion was smitten or destroyed, till the hunted soul learned to find its center in God."

There is a story of a Christian whose personal piety was greatly injured by worldly prosperity. Very likely for consistency's sake he prayed for sanctification; and God answered him by "terrible things in righteousness." The REFINER could not sit by and see His child ruined, and He therefore put him into the crucible. His wife died. Still his worldliness was not cured. Then he lost his only son, but still without the effect aimed at. Then his crops failed, his cattle died, his person was smitten with a lingering disease. Still the cure was not effectual. Finally, his house took fire; and, as he was carried forth from the burning building, he was heard to say, "Blessed be God! I trust I am cured at last."

5. *The Refiner's Fire has a* PURIFYING *power.* It purges out from the gold and silver the mixtures which alloy them. And when this result is gained, the workman's task is ended and his fire is extinguished. And so is it with afflictions. We do not mean that sufferings of themselves can effect this purification. There is another Fire at work simultaneously; "He shall baptize you with the Holy Ghost and with Fire." And it is the two Fires together that work out the beautiful result. To refer again to the grand old patriarch Job—the wise man says, "Take away the dross from the silver, and there shall come forth a vessel for the finer." So was it with him. By his afflictions the REFINER purged away his dross, and molded him into a vessel of honor meet for the Master's use; and fitted him to shine, conspicuous in the sight of all men, in the gallery of Scripture heroes, where he still maintains his place as high as the highest of human worthies, bright and lustrous, reflecting the glory of heaven to all successive generations.

Well—have faith and courage, thou poor mourning, suffering, deeply tried Christian! You know who hath said, "When thou walkest through the fire, thou shalt not be burned, neither shall the flame kindle upon thee." And you can trust Him—can you not?—that He will not make the fire one degree hotter than necessary, nor keep you in contact with it one moment after His end is accomplished. He doth not willingly afflict you. It is not His pleasure He is pursuing, but your profit. He would bear it Himself if the benefit to you could thereby be secured. He has borne infinitely more "in His own body," for your redemption, than He sees it needful to inflict upon yours, for your sanctification. Patience then! In due time you shall come forth from the furnace, as the three Hebrew youths did from theirs at Babylon, with no trace of the fire, nor burning scar upon you. Your dross shall be burned, your sins shall be destroyed; but your souls shall be made glorious in holiness. And the sharp pain, and the bitter tear, and the poignant throb, shall be found to praise, and honor, and glory, when the

REFINER shall have completed His work, and shall "come to be admired in all them that believe." But the believer's salvation is not perfected; and therefore we must still add that Christ is "made unto him . . .REDEMPTION" in a further sense still (Rom. 8:23).

REDEMPTION. For it is not enough that he be pardoned, justified, emancipated from the bondage of sin, made a child of God, cleansed, refined, ennobled. Nay, the salvation is not complete even when the disembodied spirit, obtaining joyful release from the body, exults in its glorious liberty among the spirits of the just. As long as the dishonored body, though redeemed, and claimed, and watched over, remains in the tomb, the salvation is not complete. Death still triumphs over one part of him at least. But Christ is made Redemption, which includes the whole of salvation, and carries on the glorious work to the end. The trumpet shall should, and the dead shall be raised; and then shall be brought to pass in the fullest sense the saying, "Now is come salvation, and strength, and the kingdom of God, and the power of His Christ!" And Death shall be swallowed up in Victory. ALLELUIA!

> The slumbering bodies of the just
> Shall issue from their opening tombs,
> And every particle of dust
> Leap into life when Jesus comes.

41

Rain and Showers. Rock of Ages. Refuge from the Storm. Rivers of Water. Rock of Offense. Root out of a Dry Ground.

IT is scarcely possible to run the eye over the subjects of his afternoon's Reading, without being reminded of the very opposite feelings with which our Lord is regarded by different people. Upon some "He comes down as the RAIN, and as the SHOWERS that water the earth." They who receive Him thus are softened and renewed, and thenceforth bring forth the fruits of holiness in their lives. To these also He is "as RIVERS OF WATER in a dry place." They drink and are refreshed. They flee to Him as their ROCK, and hide in Him as their REFUGE. But very many (alas! must we not say the greater part?) regard Him as ROOT OUT OF A DRY GROUND, and stumble at Him as a ROCK OF OFFENSE. To these six Symbols let us now devote our attention—Christ's "coming down" is likened to

RAIN AND SHOWERS "that water the earth" (Ps. 72:6). Most countries suffer at times from the want of rain. Even when it is only withheld for a few weeks the consequence are often serious. The ground becomes chapped, the cattle are distressed, and vegetation languishes. But what a fearful state of things must that have been which ensued upon Elijah's appalling prediction in the reign of Ahab! For three years and six months there was neither rain nor dew! and "the famine was sore in the land." "Their nobles sent their little ones to the waters; they returned with their vessels empty; and they were ashamed and confounded and covered their heads." How welcome at last was "the sound of abundance of Rain!" It is astonishing how speedily the poor blighted earth recovers greenness after such a period. Rain hath a wonderful power to fertilize and refresh the parched ground. As the gentle shower distills, the dry earth drinks it in, and the dust, besprinkled with huge drops, sends up a pleasant scent as though it were grateful for the cooling gift. It is like life from the dead, for the face of the earth is renewed and transformed.

Now this wonderful, reviving virtue of RAIN is used by the prophet as an emblem of Christ's beneficent reign upon the earth. After long ages of blight and barrenness, he says, there should come into the world One who would "make the wilderness and the solitary place glad, and cause the desert to bloom like the Garden of Eden." This prophecy is fulfilled whenever religion revives after long depression, as was the case at the Reformation; and, again, under the preaching of the Puritans, and of such men as Whitefield and Wesley. It is fulfilled also in every instance of individual conversion from sin, or restoration after declension.

But how are we to know whether this precious Rain hath descended into our hearts? Just as we know when there has been Rain upon the tender herb—by the effects. Instead of the stony heart, there is a heart of flesh; and the fruits of the Spirit, instead of sinful words and selfish actions. What a beautiful change this is! Beautiful to our fellow creatures who cannot but admire it. It is like the smell of a field that the Lord hath blessed; like the fragrance which arises from beds of flowers in a well-watered garden. And grateful even to God Himself. Kind acts, loving words, gifts to the poor, when offered under the influence of love to Christ, are very acceptable to God. He is well pleased with such sacrifices. Just what an odor of a sweet smell is to our sense, such these Christian acts are to the heart of our Great Father.

And He will reward them too. What that reward will be we may not be able to say. But would it be nothing to be congratulated and thanked, in the golden streets, by some sister spirit who would say, "Thrice welcome to this Holy City, you who led me to Christ, or you who were such a help to me when on earth! I read your book—I heard you preach—or I was one to whom you gave the tract, or uttered the warning which led me to Christ, and brought me here." Oh, yes, verily there is a reward for the righteous. They shall shine as the brightness of the firmament; and they that turn many to righteousness as the stars forever and ever.

But let us not confound things. Good works are enjoined—they are pleasing to God—they are even rewarded. But, if we had all the merit of all that were ever performed, they would furnish no foundation for our hope of salvation. *That* must be built on the Only Sure Foundation, the "ROCK OF AGES."

ROCK OF AGES (Isa. 26:4). The words translated "everlasting strength" in this passage mean, according to the marginal reading, the EVERLASTING ROCK, or ROCK OF AGES. God is also called "the ROCK OF MY REFUGE," in Psalm 94:22. What is there in nature more durable than a Rock? The Matterhorn in Switzerland, for instance, a stony pyramid, rising three miles into the sky. Around its frozen summit and against its precipitous sides the storms of thousands of years have raged in vain. No frost, nor hurricane, nor lightning, can make any perceptible impression on the hoary giant. It defies the united force of all the elements. Every reader of the Bible knows how often our Divine Redeemer is compared to a Rock, for His eternal duration and impregnable strength. These two qualities are what we require in a foundation. And a house built on the broad ROCK, whose roots reach far down into the earth, may be said to have a *sure* foundation, so far as earthly things can be secure.

One dark night in 1830, a family, in the mountains of Vermont in America, had retired to bed. The night was cheerless, the wind howled, and the rain poured down in torrents, while the rush of a neighboring cataract, swollen with the rain, added its din to the deafening uproar. At the dead hour of night there was a terrific crash. The house moved! The next moment it was afloat, the water gushing in at every opening crack. The dreadful reality was too plain. Their house was being carried away with the flood! It tore its way madly through trees and over rocks till it approached the cataract. The father and his son plunged into the flood and reached the bank, while the dreadful shrieks of the wife and children rose loudly on the blast. It was but for a moment or two. The house, with its devoted inmates, shot down the cataract, and scarce a wreck remained to tell the direful story. They had made some fatal mistake in building their wooden house *where* they did, or *as* they did. The foundation was not sure; and in the night of storms it was swept away.

But so it shall not be with those who build aright on Jesus Christ the Rock of Ages. But for more about this Foundation, and the right and the wrong way of building thereupon, I refer you to page ???, and proceed to remark that this eternal Rock is also our safe RETREAT. We read in Isaiah 2:21, of those who "go into the Clefts of the Rock, and into the tops of the ragged Rocks for fear." During times of persecution the Clefts of Rocks have frequently offered a safe retreat from pursuers. In the wilds of Scotland there are many Clefts pointed out as the hiding places of the persecuted Covenanters, when the dragoons and moss-troopers of that infamous man Claverhouse, used to hunt them like hares upon the mountains. There is a cave in the hill of Garrickfells, which was used for this purpose; and it must have furnished an excellent retreat. Within, it was commodious, while the entrance was small, and covered with bushes and brakes, which effectually concealed it from sight. In those days the pious worshipers could not meet together in towns, as we do, "none daring to make us afraid," but were forced to get together on the hillside, or in the forest, or in some lone farmhouse or shepherd's cottage.

One day, there was a little party assembled in a shepherd's house at Closeburn in Nithsdale to hear Mr. Peden expound the Word of God. While thus engaged, the bleating of a sheep was heard. The noise disturbed the little congregation, and the shepherd was obliged to go out and drive the sheep away. As he turned it out to the heath, he lifted up his eyes and saw, at a distance, horse soldiers coming towards his cottage. He hastened back to give the alarm. All instantly dispersed and hid themselves. Mr. Peden betook himself to the Cleft of the Rock, the Cave of Garrickfells. And soon the clatter of horses' hoofs and the ring of armor told him that his foes were at hand. But safe in the Cleft he sat unmoved, and through an opening saw them gallop past, without any suspicion that he whose life they sought was so near. "His place of defense was the munitions of rocks." And there God hid His servant from his murderous pursuers.

Now just thus the believer, whenever he is alarmed, runs to Christ for shelter. He is the ROCK OF AGES; and He was cleft for us, that we might find in Him a sure HIDING-PLACE from the avenging sword of justice. For out of Christ there is no safety from the just wrath of God; nor yet from the power and malice of wicked spirits, who range up and down throughout the world, seeking whom they may destroy. From the Clefts of the Rock also there came forth those refreshing waters that followed the Israelites through the wilderness. So from the wounded side of Christ there flows a stream, which gives life and health, pardon and purity, to all who partake of it.

> Rock of Ages cleft for me,
> Let me hide myself in Thee;
> Let the water and the blood,
> From Thy riven side which flow'd,
> Be of sin the double cure,
> Cleanse me from its guilt and power.

Blessed Lord Jesus! Thou art indeed the Hope of Israel! Thou art the Savior thereof in the time of trouble! We bless Thee with joyful lips for all Thy sufferings on our behalf. Thou wast bruised for our iniquities, and didst pour out Thy life's blood for us, that in Thee we might find a Hiding Place. Thy sacred side was torn and pierced, that there we might be screened from danger. Teach us ever to regard Thine anguish as the source of our peace—Thy death as the spring of our life. With Thy stripes may we be healed, and every moment may we take refuge in Thy wounds!

REFUGE FROM THE STORM (Isa. 25:4). There are many kinds of storms in the natural world; snowstorms, and windstorms, and thunderstorms. All are terrific. But perhaps the most dreadful is the burning sandstorm of the desert, known as the Simoom or Sirocco. One morning some travelers, on leaving their tents, found all the dromedaries with their heads buried deep in the sand. "Ha!" cried the Arabs, "make haste, the Sirocco is coming!" Thus admonished, they retreated in all haste, stopped up the crevices of their tents, and then, covering their heads with their mantles, threw themselves on the ground. And not a moment too soon! A furious blast of hot wind suddenly rushed upon them, with whirling clouds of burning sand. Sixteen long hours did that dreadful tempest keep them imprisoned, half suffocating them. It ceased at last; and on venturing outside, they saw what would have been their own fate, had they been exposed to its fury. Seven or eight poor travelers lay dead on the burning sands, blackened and scorched as by the heat of an oven. Poor things! Either they were too late with their precautions, or their shelter was too slight to stand the stress. The others escaped because they believed the warning, and made the most of their few brief moments. Have you believed the warning voice, which tells of storms far more perilous, and have you made good your retreat to Jesus Christ, the only REFUGE? Then indeed, when the tempest of sorrow shall come, or the wild deluge of cares; when sickness and death invade, you will smile at the "blast of the terrible ones," securely nestled in the bosom of your Savior. Not otherwise. For oh, what thrilling histories we could unfold, had we space, of hopeless horror seizing upon some who have too late discovered that their hope was a vain hope! and that having missed or neglected the only safe REFUGE, they have lost forever their opportunity of salvation. Oh do not be beguiled. Throw away those frivolous books. Give up those ungodly companions! those baneful habits! those Sunday excursions! And "flee to the mountain, lest you be consumed!"

Nor safety alone will you find in this Rock of Ages, but also, all you want for happiness and pleasure. Jesus Christ is "as RIVERS OF WATER IN A DRY PLACE."

RIVERS OF WATER IN A DRY PLACE (Isa. 32:2). Long ago, one who had all but boundless resources, with every possible advantage for the experiment, made full proof of the utmost the world could do for its votaries. No king ever reigned in greater splendor than Solomon. His wealth was as astonishing as his wisdom. The richest monarch in Europe possessed not a twentieth of his vast income. The tribute, which poured into his treasure from all surrounding districts, was a most prodigious amount, reckoning the gold and silver talents how we will. The money he expended on the temple and its furniture, of his own and his father's accumulated wealth, amounted to hundreds of millions of pounds, enough indeed to pay England's national debt. Surrounding monarchs were bewildered with the glare—"The kings shut their mouths at him." The Queen of Sheba came from far distant lands to hear his wisdom, and feast her eyes on his grandeur, with expectations raised to the highest pitch by the voice of fame. But she found the half had not been told her, and overcome with admiration, she seemed to envy the very servants who stood in his presence, and performed his behests. But he who was thus raised to the very pinnacle of affluence and splendor, above all other mortals that ever were, pronounced upon it this sweeping sentence, "Vanity of vanities—all is vanity—emptiness, and vexation of spirit." And to Solomon's verdict all the votaries of the world, even without the spiritual discernment he seems to have possessed, do sooner or later subscribe.

"Their Rock is not as our Rock, our enemies themselves being judges." Yet say, is not theirs a brave Rock? And from its bosom does not many a flashing river flow forth into the desert, full of promise to the thirst and the dissatisfied? There is the glittering River of Wealth, rolling its golden sands to the very feet of its eager explorers. There is the sunny River of Pleasure, ringing from shore to shore with sound of mirth and jollity. There is the gay River of Fashion, radiant with rainbow reflections of azure and gold, amber and emerald. There is the River of Power for those who are courageous and strong of will. And the River of Fame for the sons of genius. All these, and many more, the world pours forth lavishly; but those who drink the deepest are the loudest in their expressions of disappointment.

Let us hear the very words of some of them. They are but the echo of Solomon's melancholy sentence. First take Lord Chesterfield's testimony, "I have enjoyed all the pleasures of the world, and I do not regret their loss. I appraise them at their real value, which is very low, while those who have not tried them always overrate them. They only see the gay outside, but I have been behind the scenes, and have seen the dirty ropes and smelt the tallow candles which move and illuminate the gaudy machine." And yet this man had everything the world could give, and denied himself nothing that his heart could crave.

"You must be a happy man," said one to Rothschild.

"I happy," answered the rich man, "What! when I have to sleep with a brace of pistols by my pillow? Why, the other day, just as I was going to dine, a letter came—'If you do not send me £500, I will blow your brains out.'—Happy indeed!" But this was one who reckoned his wealth by millions.

"A few weeks and I shall escape to the country, and find a short resting place between vexation and the grave."—These are the words of that most prosperous of men, Lord Eldon. Or take the testimony of Robert Burns, a poet of rarest powers. When life was nearly ended, he wrote, "I close my eyes in misery, and open them without hope." Or that of Sir Walter Scott, than whom no author ever enjoyed greater popularity, or climbed to a more dizzy height of distinction. But overtaken with reverses, he writes of himself as "lonely, aged, impoverished, and embarrassed. Sicknesses," he says, "come thicker, friends are fewer. The recollection of youth, health, and powers of activity neither improved nor enjoyed, is a poor strain of comfort. The best is, the long halt will soon arrive and close all." Campbell, another of the favored sons of genius, near the close of life, wrote, "My last hopes are blighted. As for fame, it is a bubble that must soon burst." And Talleyrand, who contrived to be ever at the top of the wheel of fortune, whosoever might fall to the ground, on his eighty-first birthday inscribed in his journal these melancholy words, "Life is a long fatigue."

None can say that these confessions of the world's most fortunate devotees are very complimentary to their idol. Very different is the testimony of the people of God to *their* Rock. But first, what are those Rivers that flow from it? David speaks of this world as "a dry and thirsty land where no water is"; that is, no water that satisfies the soul. But here are "RIVERS OF WATER in the dry place." Rivers that satisfy and never tire, of which we drink and thirst no more. Rivers of salvation, to refresh and heal and cleanse. There is the River of Justification, into which, the moment we plunge, all our sins are taken away; we are "abundantly pardoned." There is the River of Sanctification, in which we are to bathe and bathe, and, ever as we do so, we find ourselves "washed with the renewing of the Holy Ghost." And Rivers that make barren souls fruitful, so that instead of the thorn there may spring up the myrtle tree. Even in this world, the Christian often enjoys "Peace like a river, and righteousness like the waves of the sea"; and the volume still widens and increases as he nears eternity. The River of the Water of Life is a River to swim in—so deep is it; a River that spreads into oceans—so overflowing is it; a River that will flow on through eternity—so exhaustless is it. And what is their testimony who drink of these waters?

"Oh," said Lady Huntingdon on her death bed, "all is well for ever! I am cradled in the arms of love and mercy." And Doddridge said, in similar circumstances, "Such transporting views of the heavenly world as my Father now indulges me with no words can express." Hear also the dying testimony of Thomas Scott. "This is heaven begun. I have done with darkness forever. Nothing remains but light and joy." Such testimonies might be greatly multiplied. But turn we now to a similitude applied to Christ that seems, after all we have said, quite startling. To multitudes Jesus Christ is a "ROCK OF OFFENSE."

ROCK OF OFFENSE (Isa. 8:14). Two travelers, arrested by what they thought an enchanting scene, stood gazing upon it with intense enjoyment. A copious river, clear as crystal, ran babbling by at their feet, making its way, with many a playful cascade, over the rocks and boulders which seemed to challenge its progress. The arch of an old bridge spanned the river, from which there hung luxuriant festoons of dark green ivy. Friendly trees waved their branches over it, and, on either side, innumerable tall foxgloves swung their crimson bells to and fro in the breeze. But the crowning charm of the scenery was the stately mass of rocks which rose all round, piled up mountains high, in endless varieties of picturesque form, and sprinkled over with mosses and lichens of all colors; while on their ledges were proudly perched, at inaccessible heights, forests of pines and fir trees. As they stood thus, quite fascinated with what they saw, there passed a cottager who lived close by, with whom they fell into conversation. Presently he said, with an irreverent nod at the rocks, "I suppose you admire all that!"

"Yes, very much indeed—don't you?"

"No, not at all."

"Why? what is the matter with it?"

"Well—I don't know—what is there but rocks and stones? No, no! A level country is the place for me."

This man seemed quite insensible to any beauty there might be in the scene before him; and the rocks, which awakened their admiration, you see, were quite an OFFENSE to him. But now, what I want you to notice here is, that the state of the mind gives its own tint to all it sees. That Welsh cottager and the two visitors looked at the same scene, but, as it were, through glasses of different colors. They thought *theirs* were of a cheerful, bright tint, while his seemed to them discolored with discontent. Now here is the secret of the opposite feelings with which the ROCK Jesus Christ is regarded by different people. Some see in Him a thousand attractions, and make Him their ROCK, their REFUGE, their RIVER, and their All. These all "have their eyes anointed," so that they see. To others He is a ROCK OF OFFENSE; for Satan hath "blinded their minds so that the light of His glory doth not shine into them."

He is a Rock of Offense to some because He is so high. They will admit He is *eminent*—"to be sure they cannot see to the top of the Rock, but its height is only veiled. It does not really reach to heaven. As to His being anything more than a creature, that is a pure invention." They reject His claim of equality with God, though, in doing this, they leave upon His sacred character the stigma of imposture. To others He is a Rock of Offense because He is so low. "Is not this the carpenter who lives in the next street, Mary's Son, Simon's brother?" asked they of Nazareth; and they were offended at Him. The rulers were of the same mind. His birth, His station, His associates, all were so mean, that they would not own Him as their Messiah. And those men have their representatives among ourselves, who think the religion of Christ too unfashionable, and His people too vulgar, for them to identify themselves with either. He is an Offense to others because He demands too many sacrifices; and to others still, because His method of saving is too humbling for their self-righteous pride. Another emblem suggests the same sad fact. "He shall grow up as a

ROOT OUT OF A DRY GROUND" (Isa. 53:2). This "dry ground" represents the depressed condition of David's royal and stately house. The figure is that of a barren spot, where formerly there had flourished the goodly cedar and thriving trees of lofty stature. But the feller has been there with his axe, and nothing is now visible save a few starved and stunted growths. The principal descendant, perhaps heir, of the princely David, seems to have been Joseph the village carpenter. And, sharing in the lowliness and poverty of His family, our Lord grew up as a Root despised and not esteemed by the Jews. Nor were they peculiar in their neglect and contempt. They have many followers and sympathizers now. May God give to such repentance, and deliver us from their spirit of unbelief.

Two hundred years ago, a minister (Flavel, I think) preached from the text, "If any man love not the Lord Jesus let him be Anathema Maranatha." He had finished, and the people waited only for the usual benediction. But the preacher was mute. They lifted their eyes, and there he stood, solemnly looking down upon them. At length he broke the oppressive silence and said, "Why do you all gaze at me? Do you expect me to pronounce this blessing? What! a blessing on you that love not the Lord Jesus? not so! 'If any man love not the Lord Jesus, let him be Accursed;' but 'grace be with all you who love the Lord Jesus in sincerity and truth.' " At this the people broke forth into weeping; tears flowed on every side. Deep was the impression. And in many a heart there arose, in that solemn hour, an unquenchable resolve to know and love the Savior.

> Oh Beautiful, and yet Unknown!
>   The sinner cannot see Thee now;
> The veil across his sight is thrown,
>   Which shuts him from Thy shining brow.
>
> Friend of the lost, the sinner's Friend!
>   Who only canst the light impart;
> O Savior! haste that veil to rend,
>   And pour Thy brightness on his heart.

42

Star of Jacob. Sun of Righteousness.

ONE fine day in Autumn, soon after dawn, two friends set out afoot on a short journey. The Morning Star was glistening in the sky, and they said one to another, "Behold an emblem of the Savior." Presently up rose the glorious Sun over the hilltop, flinging abroad his powerful beams and shedding luster on all creation. And him they hailed as a still more illustrious emblem of the Great Redeemer of the world. By-and-by, on the hillside, behold a Shepherd led forth his flock to a chosen pasture; while on the furrowed plain below, a Sower with measured step scattered abroad in handfuls the precious grain. And our two travelers, glad to be reminded of Him whom they loved, went on still conversing of His care over His "little flock," and of His interest in "the children of the kingdom." After a while they felt tired, and were fain to rest in a cool recess which some quarrymen had excavated in a tall rock by the wayside. And there they sat a little, still "finding sermons in stones and Christ in everything." "Ah!" they said, "here is an illustration of that figure, THE SHADOW OF A GREAT ROCK in a weary land; and yonder threatening fragment overhead, of that other awful figure of the Stone falling upon the despiser, and grinding him to powder. And here are stones fit for corner stones and foundation stones, and even some lying about, as though they might be STONES OF STUMBLING, to trip up the unwary. All these, looked at in the light of the Scriptures, read us many a useful lesson." Presently, having secured the object of their journey, they resume their walk homewards. And you will not wonder that ruined castle by the roadside, over which formerly floated the royal standard, not only suggested Stronghold, but other symbols of Christ connected with His kingship; and among the rest, SCEPTER, SHIELD, AND SWORD. And then their home, at which they shortly arrived, reminds them of the SANCTUARY which all find in Christ who flee for Refuge to Him.

And now the walk is finished. But we have not done with the instructions that it suggested. Here are ten or twelve similitudes of Christ. Two furnished by the firmament; two found in the field; three or four suggested by the quarry, as many by the royal castle, and one by their now comfortable home. Let us follow this order. And first let "the heavens declare to us the glory of Christ." Yon lonely Star glistening from out of the clear, gray morning sky, seems to look down upon us from that lofty height as if it had something to communicate. Can we fail to interpret the lesson? Nay, we immediately think of Balaam's famous prophecy of Christ as the rising of a

STAR out of Jacob (Num. 24:17). Nor do we omit to couple with it those words of our Lord in which He applies the prophecy to Himself, "I am the BRIGHT AND MORNING STAR." Most of yonder Stars are really suns, mightier far than our own, yet, because of their vast distance, they appear but as points of light. So Jesus Christ appeared to the first fathers of our world. They strained their eyes to see His day, and then could only descry Him dimly, and at a great distance; like a twinkling Star rather than as the Sun, under which emblem He may be more appropriately apprehended by us. Again, the Stars are far up in the heavens, very high. So Jesus Christ is not of the earth, but is the Lord from heaven, Higher than the Highest. And again, the Stars are bright and beautiful. So Jesus Christ is "the Brightness of the Father's Glory, the Altogether Lovely";

> The pleasing luster of His eyes
> Outshines the wonder of the skies.

But what practical lessons are we to gather from this similitude? First. Admire Him, yea adore Him, and extol Him to others. Second. Be ever looking to Him. The mariner afar off upon the sea, throughout the long night calculates his course by the Stars. And happy indeed he deems himself if no envious cloud hides them from his sight. Steer your course by His bright example and His guiding sayings, and you shall never go wrong. "I am the Light of the World," saith He; "he that followeth Me shall not walk in darkness, but shall have the light of life."

> Is He a Star? He breaks the night,
> Piercing the shades with dawning light;
> I know His glories from afar,
> I know the BRIGHT AND MORNING STAR.

Third. Expect to be like Him. Is the Star of Jacob highly exalted? Every follower of Christ shall sit down with Him on His throne. Is He glorious and beautiful? "The beauty of the Lord our God shall be upon us." Christ says, "I will give unto him that overcometh the Morning Star." Is there not some reference here to the honors by which earthly princes distinguish their favorites? In this country one receives the grand cross of the Order of the Bath; and another the coveted riband of the noble Order of the Garter; and thenceforth they take rank among the proudest subjects of the realm. Jesus Christ also hath rewards and distinctions for them that serve Him. In different degrees they will shine, for "one Star differeth from another in glory." But everyone shall bear a badge, which shall infinitely excel the brightest star that ever glittered on the breast of the proudest peer. It shall distinguish him forever as a member of the Royal Family of the Almighty, the family which stands nearest the throne amongst all the principalities of heaven, and of which Christ is the Firstborn, the Eldest Brother, the Husband. Thus is Christ the Bright and Morning Star Who giveth to all his followers to be Morning Stars too. But the firmament hath another emblem. The Prophet says, "Unto you that fear My Name shall the Sun of Righteousness arise with healing in His wings."

SUN OF RIGHTEOUSNESS (Mal. 4:2). When the Sun disappears at the close of the day and consigns us to darkness, we console ourselves for his absence as best we can, and adopt such expedients for the supply of light as ingenuity can devise. If our occupations are within doors, we light the candle or the lamp; and, though at a considerable disadvantage, we still pursue our work, whether of the needle, the loom, or the pen. Or we gather round the table or the fireside, and with our companions pore over the instructive page of some favorite author. If we have occasion to go abroad, and no friendly moon should reflect the light of the lost sun upon our path, some poor artificial substitute—the gas lamp or the old-fashioned lantern—sheds a fitful ray to guide our wary steps.

But, perhaps, when the sun went down just now, the thick darkness which succeeded found some poor traveler far away from home, bewildered among the unlighted hills or all but boundless moors. While the sun was present, he could find his way well enough across the pathless waste. But when the pitchy darkness settled down and drew a black pall over every object, first he faltered, and then he came to a full stop. He had lost his track! The well-known clump of firs and the broken boulder of rock to which he trusted as way marks, he can discern no longer. And he abandons his task in despair, and watches and wishes away the weary hours, till the sun shall reappear with "healing" in his beams, and bring the longed-for release.

But the horror of the darkness, and the danger of the traveler, are greatly enhanced in countries where, "when it is night all the beasts of the forests do creep forth, and the lions roar after their prey." A recent traveler has a thrilling story of a "night-o'er-taken" hunter, who spent the hours of darkness so near to a wounded tiger, that he could every now and then see his two dreadful eyes glaring like burning coals, and even fell his warm breath upon his cheek! Crouched upon his knees, he durst not venture on the slightest movement, lest he should betray his presence to the infuriated beast on the other side of the bush; and all through that fearful night the dread silence was broken only by the hoarse growls of the tiger, and the sound of the gong striking the hours in the village close by. Imagine his relief when, on the first approach of daylight, the night-loving beast arose from his lair and slunk away across the plain. When the sun arose, what "healing" he brought with him! what balm to the distressed hunter!

Thus night is always a time of gloom, and sometimes of fear, notwithstanding we know the sun will soon reappear. But should the bright orb of light and heat forsake us for a few days or a few hours only—What then? How long would it take for the world to become a dark dismal chaos full of horror and desolation? There would be no more cheerful colors nor beautiful forms. The faces of our friends would cease to beam upon us. All the warmth of the atmosphere would speedily steal away and give place to universal frost. It would immediately "grow wondrous cold"; and, in attempting to feel our way about, we should find

> The ice is here, the ice is there,
> The ice is all around.

But in such a state of things no living creature could survive. The trees would be blasted and withered; the crops would die in the open field; beasts and birds must quickly yield their breath, and all mankind be involved in speedy destruction.

Or suppose it were possible (which, speaking scientifically, it is not, but let it pass as an illustration) for some few forlorn mortals to maintain a little warmth by nestling together; and to keep the lamp of life from complete extinction by recourse to some fast diminishing stores; oh with what earnest, ceaseless cries would they importune the Great Creator to restore to them once more their lost treasure, their precious, inestimable SUN! And what if, after many days of almost hopeless watching, the prayer were answered! Suddenly a broad streak of gray, misty light is discerned upon the horizon; and all immediately cry out, "Is it the Sun?" Yes, it must be, for the light increases. It becomes stronger, brighter. It begins to redden. And now a roseate blush streams across the sky. One by one the clustering vapors catch the crimson hue. And soon the whole sky is lit up with gorgeous colors, as though the clouds in serried ranks and decked in holiday attire, were marshaled to welcome the approach of majesty. All doubt is at an end. And presently, from behind the hills, the dear, old, friendly face of the sun once more shows itself. It is he! We cannot paint the joy of those who had breathlessly watched all the precursors of his approach, when at last they behold the dazzling monarch coming forth from his resplendent tabernacle, "with healing in his wings," rejoicing once more as a strong man to run a race. Who would wonder, if, like the fire worshipers of old, they were to greet the brilliant source of light and warmth with almost idolatrous words of welcome?

Who indeed can ever, without feelings little short of rapture, watch the Rising Sun? How beautiful to see him lift up his radiant head above the horizon, scattering hither and thither the heavy mists which overhang vale and river; flinging abroad, with affluent liberality, his dazzling beams over every object in the landscape, near and afar off! Surely, no comparison in the Scripture seems more apt than that of the Rising Sun, to set forth the healing, cheering, life-giving influences of the glorious Christ of God, the Sole Light of the spiritual world. All creation doth not afford any object so commanding, so imperial, as the Great Light that rules the day. It is the one source of illumination; for all kinds of artificial light have gathered their virtues from its central flame, our very coal mines being but, as one says, "magazines of sunbeams." It is the fountain of heat, the quickener of life, the spring of fertility, and the dispenser of all the colors that delight our eyes. It is the center of gravitation to all the planets, and the main spring of the order and well-being of the whole world.

Well, just what the sun is to the outward world, Jesus Christ is to the spiritual. All things are dark, cold, dead, without Him; and, when the soul has once tasted that He is gracious, and has known what it is to live and act in the sunlight of His love, if He withdraw Himself, if "earth-born clouds arise" and conceal Him from view, the soul is inconsolable, as well it may be and ought to be, and saith, "Where is God my Maker, my Light, my Joy? Where is He Whom my soul loveth? I pine away in this cold gloom. I cannot rest till I see Him once again."

For the true Christian, at least the healthy Christian, is like that flower which Hervey describes as manifesting such a "passionate fondness for the sun." It is of a bright golden color, rising on a strong and stately stalk. During the night it folds its leaves, and seems to mourn the absence of its beloved. But "no sooner are the eyelids of the morning opened, than it welcomes the returning light, and turns towards it all the day, nor ever loses sight of its charmer so long as he continues above the horizon. In the morning you may perceive it, presenting its golden bosom to the east. At noon it points upward to the middle sky; in the evening it follows the same attractive influence to the west."

> How she observes him in her daily walk,
> Still turning toward him her compliant stalk;
> And when he downward sinks, she droops and mourns
> And is bedew'd with tears till he returns.

Here is a lesson for us! Nor was ever sermon in lofty Gothic choir more eloquent than that preached to us by this bright flower of the garden. Oh, if we were half so constant to our divine SUN as that faithful heliotrope to the bright king of day, what lives we should lead! How full of praise and love we should be! Let us learn from it ever to be turning our faces towards Jesus Christ, as those who would court His presence, and cherish the light of His countenance, and rejoice in His favor. So shall we truly glorify Him, and at the same time drink in unknown draughts of bliss from His life-giving smiles; while He will beam brightly upon us from the third heavens, and seem ever to say to us, "Arise, shine, for thy Light is come, and the Glory of the Lord is risen upon thee."

Are any of you troubled about your sins, seeking the Savior and looking to Him for healing and light? Then "Follow on to know the Lord, for His goings forth are prepared as the morning." Or, did you once see the Sun of Righteousness, but are now walking in darkness? Does the Sun seem to be behind a cloud, or quite eclipsed? Let your resolution be, My soul doth wait for the Lord more than they that watch for the morning. Stay your hearts on the precious promise, "Unto you that fear My Name shall the Sun of Righteousness arise with healing in His wings." Pray for this, Pray on, and quickly "thy light shall rise in obscurity, and thy darkness shall be as the noonday."

> In darkness shades if He appear,
> 　My dawning is begun;
> He is my soul's Bright Morning Star,
> 　And He my Rising Sun.

Many analogies might be traced between the natural sun and the Sun of Righteousness; as, also, many dissimilarities. For instance:

1. *The Sun shines freely on all without distinction, great and small.* It illumines alike the trembling dewdrop and the stupendous snow clad mountain. The golden ray in which the tiny gnat disports itself, and the struggling light by which the unwieldy elephant traces out a path among the crowded turns of a primeval forest, flow alike from one center. So the child and the philosopher, the pauper and the emperor, have an equal hold on the sympathies of Christ, and the beams of His mercy gladden alike the cottage and the palace.

2. *The Sun, when its rays are admitted, discovers dust and motes where none could be seen before.* Step into an unfrequented room where the shutters are partially open, and you see nothing to remark. But, throw open the windows, admit the sunbeams, and the whole atmosphere is immediately seen to be teeming with motes and floating atoms; and every piece of furniture covered with dust. So is it with the human heart. It is full of defilement and pollution; for many hidden lusts are there. But all the while the light that "makes manifest" is not admitted, they are, for the most part, undetected. Then, when light enters, we begin to know ourselves, and not before. So did the Apostle: "When the commandment came, sin revived, and I died." Light discovers deformity.

3. *The Sun invests with beauty that which hath no glory in itself.* Looking westward towards the close of the day, you will sometimes see huge banks of leaden-colored clouds, lowering and unattractive. But, as the sun sinks to a point whence they can catch his rays, they are suddenly lighted up with unearthly splendor, and arrayed with indescribable beauty. A profusion of colors—crimson and orange and amber, emerald, and gold, violet and purple, feast the eye of the observer. That which a minute ago looked inky and monotonous, now glistens as though composed of rubies, opals, and amethysts. So when Jesus

Christ shines into a human heart, there is "beauty for ashes," light instead of darkness, and the glory of heaven and the glow of love, instead of the deformity and selfishness of sin.

But the natural Sun sets—Our glorious SUN knows no change. *That* shall wax old, as doth a garment; but to the SUN OF RIGHTEOUSNESS it is said, "Thy throne, O God, is forever and ever!" Again, there are spots in the natural Sun, unsightly patches of discoloration; but there are no such imperfections in the Sun of Righteousness. He is Light; Light itself, in which is no darkness at all. The Sun also has some baneful as well as beneficial influences, which accounts for its being sometimes used as an emblem of destruction. We read of a Sun that scorched men with great heat; and we have a promise to this effect, "The Sun shall not smite thee by day." Those who live in eastern lands would feel the force of such expressions much more than we can. However indispensable the influence of the Sun, its parching, blasting, midday glare is all but intolerable. The air is like the scorching breath of a fiery furnace to the over-wrought slave, hard at work under the open canopy of heaven, or to the fainting traveler exposed in the desert, far from the sheltering rock. Now there are no baneful influences in Christ. He is Light. He is Love. And yet, for this very reason, He is as a Refiner's Fire, separating the evil from the good and burning it up. "Our God is a Consuming Fire." And the obstinate and the impenitent, who refuse the shelter of His love and despise the "healing of His wings," in this great day of His grace, will seek in vain to hide themselves from His face under rocks and mountains, in "the great day of His wrath."

Alas! there are some who reject the light of this glorious SUN. They even deny that it shines at all, and are content to commit themselves to the flickering torch of reason, or to the dark lantern of science. Underneath almost the whole of Constantinople there runs a vast cavern, which the Turks call the "Swallowed-up Palace." It is a sort of deep underground lake of black waters, from the bottom of which spring up innumerable columns supporting an arched roof. At one spot only, where the ground is broken, does a ray of light enter the cave. Its extent no one knows. One day an Englishman determined to take a boat and a torch, and row himself through the watery waste, and penetrate its gloomy recesses. In vain the Turks entreated him to give up his foolish expedition. With singing and laughter the gay voyager pushed off; and soon the flash of his torch disappeared into the distance, and then the splash of his oars died away on the ear. Hour after hour they waited his return, but he came not. A night and a day passed ere they gave up hope, but he returned not. Nor was anything ever heard or seen of the rash traveler more. It is likely he lost himself amidst the endless avenues of pillars. Perhaps his torch burned out, and the darkness bewildered him, and after many ineffectual attempts to trace his way back, he yielded to despair and death. Behold here a picture of the condition of man without Christ. "Strong delusions" and all "deceivableness of unrighteousness" encompass him who forsakes Christ, turning his back on the SUN OF RIGHTEOUSNESS and preferring the sparks he himself has kindled, he gropes his way farther and farther into the blackness of darkness, and at last, bewildered with his efforts, he lies down in sorrow.

It is said of one of the Roman Emperors (Hadrian, who, to do him justice, though devoted to pagan institutions, was not a persecutor of the Christians), that on the near approach of death he composed some verses, bewailing his darkness as to the future world. The sentiment of his lines has been thus represented:

> Oh my fluttering trembling spirit,
> Just about to leave thy home,
> What strange world must thou inherit!
> What is thy impending doom
> All thy cherished pleasures here
> Vanished are, and gone forever;
> See! grim Death is drawing near,
> Soul and body to dissever.
> Striving hard to pierce the night,
> Nought my aching eyes descry,
> Save confusion infinite,
> Vast outspread vacuity.
> Could I only grasp some hand!
> Might I hear some cheering voice!
> Ah! how lonely thus to stand
> On this fatal precipice!

Thus this Pagan emperor to his bewildered soul. How different the happy lot of the believer in Christ who can say, "The Lord is my Light and my Salvation, whom shall I fear?" Truly the light is sweet, and a pleasant thing it is for the eye of faith to behold the SUN OF RIGHTEOUSNESS. But how will the light increase yonder! "The light of the SUN shall be sevenfold, as the light of seven days." Yea, there is no comparison between the vision the believer gets of Christ here by faith, and that which he shall enjoy when, without a veil, he shall see the King in His beauty.

Again, there are some who, though they do not reject this great SUN formally, nor are to be classed with infidels, yet are not careful to walk in His light; nor afraid to venture into dark places where they know the SUN OF RIGHTEOUSNESS shines not at all. An excellent friend of mine had a Sunday school, and often chose very singular texts for his addresses. One afternoon he made his appearance at the desk with a card, on which lay a large fly and a small spider. *That was his text.* He had just come from his garden, and proceeded to describe what he had seen.

A little spider had stretched his web across a round opening in a garden gate. The sun shone brightly on one side of the gate, throwing a deep shadow over the web. The place seemed deliberately chosen by the cunning weaver for the purpose of entrapping heedless flies. It was not long before a large bluebottle fly darted through the hole from the sunny side of the gate, and, not seeing the web so artfully hung in the dark, was caught in its meshes. The little spoiler bolted out in a moment and mounted the back of the fly, taking great care, however, to keep out of the way of the huge wings, which were flapping to and fro with angry violence. Presently they both fell clean out of the web, the spider still keeping his hold. No sooner had they reached the ground than he went diligently to work. First he tied up one leg, winding his threads round and round, and gluing it tight to the body of the fly; then he bound up another leg, and so on till he had quite disabled his poor captive. But just as he was about to begin his repast, my friend, who had been watching the whole proceeding, took them both up, and placing them on a card, bore them off, as I have said, to his school room.

He drew from it this moral. "There! my boys—learn from this little incident to keep in the light! Avoid all sinful society, all haunts of vanity and immorality—the low fair, the theater, and the race course. They are dark places where Christ shines not, and where you cannot expect, because you dare not ask, His presence and blessing. Be sure *that* is where the fowler lurks—that is where Satan spreads his snares; and he that plays on the hole of the asp, or ventures near the cockatrice den, is in danger of being entangled and caught, and led down a hapless prisoner into the chambers of death."

Well now, remember the lesson we have sought to derive from the stories of the lost traveler and the captive fly, and "Walk in the Light." Consider how the light has increased, and, with it, our responsibilities. Jesus Christ appeared but as a Star at first in the early morning of the world to the fathers of our race. Yet "when they saw the Star, they rejoiced with exceeding joy," and walked in the light of it, and waited and longed for His salvation. But He hath come nearer to us. We enjoy "the Light of the Morning, even a morning without clouds." On us He hath "risen—the SUN OF RIGHTEOUSNESS, with healing in His wings." Let us rejoice in our greater privileges, and be doubled careful to "walk in the light," lest we incur the greater condemnation, and be beaten with many stripes.

43

Shepherd and Bishop of Souls. Sower.

LAST Sunday the heavens declared to us the glory of Christ. The Star of the morning and the radiant Sun, Regent of the Day, were our instructors. But if the firmament over our heads hath voices, which talk to us about this grand theme, so hath the earth on which we tread. "Come, my beloved, let us go forth into the fields, let us lodge in the villages, let us get up early to the vineyards." And first, see in yonder Shepherd conducting his flock into green pastures, a favorite emblem of our Lord.

SHEPHERD AND BISHOP OF SOULS (1 Pet. 2:25). God calls Him "*My* SHEPHERD (Zech. 13:7). He calls Himself SHEPHERD (John 10:14). And His people love to recognize Him by this title (Ps. 23; Isa. 40:11; 1 Pet. 2:25; 5:4). He is "the CHIEF SHEPHERD," the "GREAT SHEPHERD OF THE SHEEP," the "GOOD SHEPHERD." And what similitude can be more expressive of His tender and constant oversight of His people? As to the term Bishop, it originally meant Overseer or Caretaker; and at length it came to be used exclusively for one whose business it is to watch over souls. God complains of some in Ezekiel's time whose duty it was to do this, but they were "hirelings" and neglected the flock, and then He gives utterance to those touching words of mingled reproof and promise: "I will seek that which was lost, and bring again that which was driven away; and I will bind up that which was broken, and I will strengthen that which was sick" (Ezek. 34:16).

The occupation of a Shepherd used to be reckoned very honorable. Jacob for many years kept the flocks of his father-in-law. And Moses and David were Shepherds; also other ancient worthies whose histories we have in the Bible. As to the work of a Shepherd, our Lord has described it in a few tender words, which are preserved in John 10. He knows his sheep individually, speaks to them, and calls them by name. The sheep hear and recognize his voice. When he leads them out to pasture, he goes before them, and they follow him. He also watches over them and protects them from the wolf. These particulars find their counterpart more completely in the usages of other countries than of our own. We have, indeed, seen a large flock *following* their Shepherd on a public road in England; but usually they are *driven*. Not so in the East; there they are invariably led; and there is also a better understanding between the Shepherd and his flock than exists here, and more tenderness displayed in their treatment.

And in Switzerland one might sometimes see, on a grassy slope on the hillside, a Shepherd with his little flock grazing around him. Sometimes he will speak to them, and two or three will run to him to eat from his hand the tufts of grass that he has plucked. Presently, it may be, someone comes along with a basket of flowers. These are wonderfully attractive to the sheep, and the whole flock is soon on the track. But the moment the Shepherd calls to them, they all come back immediately. In the evening he descends the hill and leads the way to the fold, the sheep following close at his heels. Among the Waldenses and in Greece, the Shepherds give names to their sheep, to which they respond as readily and with as much evident pleasure as a dog. A certain traveler, greatly interested in this sight, tried one day to imitate the Shepherd's voice, and called them by the same names. But "they knew not the voice of the stranger," and would take no notice of him or his calls. We will stay to offer just a word or two on these particulars before we proceed. Observe,

1. *The* SHEPHERD *has a special, personal regard for each one of his flock.* "He calleth His own sheep by name." The sun, when it flings abroad its dazzling rays, flashes upon every separate dewdrop, touches with lines of light each individual blade of grass in the field, and defines every rounded pebble on the shore. It cannot do otherwise. So, by the necessary perfection of His divine nature, the Great Shepherd is specially cognizant of each one of His followers; as much indeed as though each were the only one. He does not lose sight of you, doubting one, amidst the great multitude, which no man can number. Take care, then, not to lose yourself in the crowd. Do not fear to appropriate His eye, His heart, and His love, to yourself particularly. To each one, to you and to me, He saith, "I know thee by name." And thou art saved, and one beautifully says, "not as a man, or someone of mankind led forth in the general flock, but as the Shepherd's dear James or John, Appheus or Martha, whose name is so recorded in the Lamb's book of life."

2. *The* SHEPHERD *chooses for each one his appropriate pasture.* "He calleth them by name and leadeth them out." He doth not turn His sheep loose into the wide world to find their own way, but selects for each that which is best. He may see good often to change their way. "He leadeth them about," sometimes in green pastures beside still waters, sometimes through a waste howling wilderness. Moses must surrender his beloved retirement, and end his forty years of quiet communion with God in the secluded valleys of Midian, for God has other work for him to do. Israel must strike their tents in Horeb, for there comes a message, "Ye have dwelt long enough in this mount—turn ye northward"; and straight-

way the cloudy pillar moves forward in that direction. So is it still. Endeared ties must be sundered; favorite haunts of usefulness surrendered; health be exchanged for sickness, or prosperity for loss. Like Naomi, widowed and desolate, the bewildered one may sometimes be tempted to say, "Call me Mara, for the Lord hath dealt bitterly with me; I went out full, and came back empty." But courage, poor drooping heart! Thy Shepherd is leading thee by a right way; but perhaps He sees that bitter herbs and rough paths are, for a time, better for thee than crystal streams and quiet pastures. Take up thy cross, and follow thine unerring Guide, and all shall be well. As the heavenly-minded Tersteegen says,

> Ill that God blesses is our good,
> And unblest good is ill;
> And all is right that seems most wrong,
> If it be His sweet will.

But what if a Shepherd should lose one of his flock, and when he counted them at night there should only be 99 instead of 100? Doth he say, "No matter—it must take its chance; perhaps I shall find it again some day"? No. However late it may be, he lights his lantern, and calling his faithful dog, hies away among the hills to search for the lost one. And when he finds it he is glad, and layeth the silly wanderer on his shoulders, and whistling his dog, he trudges home with a glad heart to his supper and his bed.

Well now, the first thing Jesus the Good Shepherd has to do, is to seek after the sheep; for they are all lost to begin with. "All we like sheep have gone astray, every one to his own way." Some of us are lost in the woods and entangled in the thorns. Some have well nigh drowned themselves in perdition, and have to be "taken and drawn out of many waters." Some have stumbled on the dark mountains; and bruised, and broken, and blinded, they know not the way back to the fold. But wherever they are, His pitying eye discerns them; and in the cloudy and dark day of their dispersion He goes after them whithersoever they are scattered, and brings them back, rejoicing over them to do them good. He layeth them on His shoulders, or carrieth them in His arms, or gently leads them, or forcibly drives them, according to the treatment their condition and character may require.

And not only by various methods does He reclaim His lost sheep, but He gathers them from all countries and from all ranks. Some He takes from ragged schools and Sunday schools. Some He finds in hospitals and workhouses. Now and then He brings one from a palace, and oftener still, one from a cellar or an attic. Take the following case of a lost sheep recovered. One week-evening an old woman, very poor and very lame, heard the church bell ring for service. She had never been to church before, but took it into her head to go this once. Rather, let us say, God put it into her heart to do so. The minister preached on the parable of the lost sheep; and his words conveyed real news, and joyful news too, to the old woman. And she sat drinking it in as a traveler drinks at a well in the desert, to save his very life.

"What!" said she to herself, "be I then a sinner? Yes, surely I be. What! be I then just like a lost sheep? Aye, for sure I am just like that. And be there a SHEP-HERD searching about for *me*? Will He find me? Be I worth His while? A Savior for a poor thing like me! 'Tis wonderful loving."

These were her self-communings as she hobbled back, leaning on her crutches, to her dark cellar. A short time afterwards the clergyman received a message that the poor old woman was dying, and earnestly desirous of seeing him. The moment he made his appearance she exclaimed, "That's the man that told me about the lost sheep—I want to know more about it." So he sat down, saying, "I will gladly tell you more about it. I will tell you also about the sheep that was found."

"Yes," she exclaimed, "Found! found! found!" She did not live long after this interview, and she passed away, with the same thrice-repeated words on her dying lips, "Found! found! found!"

Oh, what stories are told in heaven of lost sheep found! How many singing—

> He followed me o'er hill and vale,
>   O'er deserts waste and wild;
> He found me nigh to death,
>   Famished and faint and lone;
> He bound me with the bands of love,
>   He saved the wandering one. Hallelujah!

Alas! while they still remain in this world, the sheep of Christ have a sad propensity to the old habit of wandering. But does their Shepherd give them up? Does He say, "I delivered them from death and brought them into a good pasture; and if they wander again I will abandon them quite"? Ah, not so! What! shall He lose one of the sheep of whom He says, "My Father gave them Me"? He would rather lose a thousand stars out of the Milky Way, than part with one soul whom He has taught to trust in Him. If indeed it were possible, what would become of us who have so often had to cry, with the good man who wrote the hundred and nineteenth psalm, "I have gone astray like a lost sheep; seek Thy servant, for I have not forgotten Thy commandments"? When He hears this plaintive bleat, He flies to the rescue, and rests not till the wanderer can say, "He restoreth my soul; He leadeth me in the paths of righteousness for His name's sake."

And why will He not lose them? Because He shed His precious blood for their redemption. The GOOD SHEPHERD laid down His life for the sheep. I have never heard of any Shepherd who did this but Jesus Christ. It would not be proper for a man intentionally to sacrifice his life for any such purpose. But many a Shepherd has hazarded his life, and even lost it, in pursuit of his calling. This very fate once befell a poor shepherd lad in Ireland under the following circumstances.

It was a bleak, wintry night, when his father, on counting his sheep, found one missing, and sent his son to look for it. The son, without knowing it, acted over again the parable in Luke 15:3–6. He cheerfully undertook the task assigned to him; pursued his weary journey amongst mountain steeps, through the whole of that dark night, in quest of the lost sheep; found it after a long search, and laid it on his shoulders and carried it home. It was morning when he arrived; and of course over that lost sheep found, his father and mother, with their neighbors, rejoiced. But the poor lad—ah! he took a cold that bitter night which soon brought him to his grave.

The sequel is intensely interesting, for his sickness unto death became the means of the salvation of his soul. A minister who visited him, when he saw his danger and found he was as ignorant as a heathen of the way of salvation, felt his heart sink within him. On hearing his story, however, he was struck with its resemblance to the gospel parable; and immediately seized on it as the vehicle of instruction. He turned to the four verses in Luke which express the SHEP-HERD'S care, and read them to the boy; and finding his interest awakened, pro-ceeded to explain to him the way of salvation from that text. God opened his heart. He drank it all in, received it with implicit faith, and believed on the GOOD SHEPHERD who laid down His life for the sheep. There was little time to expound any other portions of the Scriptures, for he only lived a few days after the first interview. But there was every reason to hope that, in that short time, he learned enough to make him "wise unto salvation"; for he died peacefully, if not joy-fully, with the words upon his lips, "Jesus my Savior and SHEPHERD."

But though this Shepherd lost his life in saving the sheep, he had not in-tended that. But I have heard of a father whose love for his child was so great that he intentionally sacrificed his own life to save him. He was a poor miner, and had an only son, tender and well-beloved, whom he used often to take with him when he went to his work down in the deep mine. One evening he put his little boy into the basket to be drawn up with himself, as was usual. When they got some distance up the narrow shaft, they heard something crack. The rope was breaking! The father saw in an instant that it would not bear the weight of *both*, and that the only chance of saving his *boy* was to sacrifice *himself*. He said, "Lie still, my child, and you will soon be safe at the top," and then dropped out of the basket—and was dashed in pieces. The poor child reached the top in safety, and the state of the rope, and his few artless words, told the tale of the father's self-devotion and sad fate. Do you think that this man loved his child as much as Jesus Christ loves each one of His people? Nay. The love that filled the father's heart to overflowing, was only one of millions of little streamlets, flowing from the infinite ocean of love, which fills the great heart of the GOOD SHEPHERD.

But it is written, "He shall gather the *lambs* with His arms, and carry them in His bosom." Who are the lambs? Young converts newly born into the fold, and children whose hearts are tender and who fear the Lord. The GOOD SHEPHERD, Who was once a child Himself, is very fond of children and loves to be beloved by them. See what countless multitudes of them He is taking to heaven every day, and hiding them there from the rough storms of life! It is roundly computed that 50,000 young children die daily throughout the world. What beautiful flocks, what endless processions of redeemed children are continually crowding "the path of life," ascending the ladder that Jacob saw, with songs and everlasting joy on their heads! See them pressing through the pearly gates, passing along the golden streets, welcomed by sister spirits and smiling angels, and presented before the throne of the Great Father by their loving Shepherd. "I heard a voice from heaven saying unto me, Write, Blessed are the dead which die in the Lord." Thrice blessed indeed, those spirits of departed infants! "From henceforth" they will be innocent and pure like the Holy Child Jesus, every taint of sin contracted through their short contact with this impure world, being washed away by the blood of Christ.

In this rough world the lambs of the flock are easily hurt. What hurts the souls of the young? Wrong teaching, bad examples, temptations, sin. And just as the little, playful lambs sporting on the upland pastures might be easily lost, so is it with children. They are unwise, and inexperienced, and prone to go astray.

A poor man in Scotland, going to work in a potato field, took along with him his little girl, three years old. It was October, and there were a few gay flowers scattered here and there on the wide moor just by; and these attracted the eye of the child. Presently the father missed her, and called, but there was no answer. By-and-by it grew dark, but no child could be found. The little thing had wandered he knew not whither. The distracted father went home in haste with the sad story. That was on Wednesday. For three days, and far into each night, they sought her everywhere. There were by turns frosts and rain and wind, and they gave her up for lost. But on Saturday, her grandfather found her among the heather, and with a beating heart picked her up. Was she dead? He put his hand upon her little heart. It was beating still. She was only asleep. Think how great was his joy! And when she opened her bright blue eyes, and gazed into his face and said, "Where's farder? Where's mudder?" no wonder the old man was fairly overcome, and was forced to sit down, with the child in his arms, to "have a good cry," before he could begin his homeward journey.

It makes us very sad to think that this little, stray child should be a picture of the moral condition of such multitudes. They go astray as soon as they are born.

Satan fills their hearts. Evil companions lead them away. Sin breaks forth in their lives. Alas! how quickly they learn to disobey their parents, to utter falsehoods, to quarrel, and fight, and steal! What tears can adequately deplore these flowers that have lost their fragrance, these lambs that have lost their innocence, and, wandering in forbidden paths, have defiled themselves in the mire? And will they ever come back? Not if left to themselves. Not unless the GOOD SHEPHERD "seek that which is lost, and bring again that which is gone away." Here is our hope. May He stretch forth His powerful arms and gather you to His bosom! But what is it to be, carried in His bosom"? Ah, you shall know if you will but come to Him.

> I heard the voice of Jesus say,
> Come unto Me and rest,
> Lay down, thou weary one, lay down
> Thy head upon My breast.

> I came to Jesus as I was,
> Weary and worn and said;
> I found in Him a resting place,
> And He has made me glad.

"Carried in His bosom."—Where doth the SHEPHERD carry them all to? Whither did the old man who found the little, blue-eyed wanderer, out upon the breezy moor, carry her? He carried her home to her father's house, of course. So doth Jesus those whom He gathers with His arms. A little, pious African boy named George drew near to death. Upon one asking him how he did, he said, "I thank the Lord, *He hold me fast.*" And, thus held fast in the SHEPHERD'S arms, he was carried safely through the river of death into the "Father's house." Oh, who would not choose Christ for his SHEPHERD? For just here the parallel ends. The sheep cannot choose its own shepherd; but you may choose yours. You may, yea, you must if you will be saved, leave the beguiling pastures of sin where you have been sporting, and put yourselves under the care of Jesus Christ the SHEPHERD and BISHOP of our souls.

> Bear me to the sacred scene,
> The silent streams and pastures green
> Where the crystal waters shine,
> Springing up with life divine.
> Where the flock of Israel feed,
> Guided by their Shepherd's tread,
> And ever sheep delights to hide
> Under the tree where Jesus died.

But yonder, with measured step, moves the Sower over the furrowed field. And, in the "field of the world," the Lord Jesus describes Himself as a "SOWER."

SOWER (Matt. 13:37). "He that soweth good seed is the Son of Man." This SOWER must not be confounded with the Sower in the other parables, in verses 18–23. The Sower *there* may be a minister, or a Sunday school teacher, or a Bible woman; and the seed sown is gospel truth. The SOWER *here* is the Master Himself; and the seed that He sows are "the children of the kingdom." He who spake the parable hath interpreted it for us. By a single line He here divides all people into two sorts, the children of the wicked one, and the children of the kingdom. The tares, in eastern lands, are said to be very much like the wheat; indeed scarcely to be distinguished therefrom when the plants are young. No wonder then that the householder charged his servants not to meddle with them till the harvest, when the produce would show which was which. Just so, in the field of the world, the good and the bad are to grow together till the day shall declare them.

It is not my business to expound the parable. Only let me say—It doth not teach us that we shall not be able to tell which side we belong to till the last day. It doth not teach us that we may freely associate with all sorts of people indiscriminately. Nor yet doth it warrant Christians to hold church communion with those whose spirit and conduct prove them to be the enemies of Christ. This would be to contradict rules, which the Master has Himself given us in other places. Again, perhaps the servants who asked the question, "Didst thou not sow good seed?" are the same as the reapers. If so, we learn that the angels are not able, any more than ourselves, to explain why the wicked are suffered to carry out their designs in the world. We think of course, (perhaps the angels have had this thought too), that it would be best to have them rooted up. But it is evident the Master does not think so; for He has certain designs to fulfill by their presence which could not otherwise be brought about. So we must bear with patience the evils which we cannot remedy, however we may deplore them; comforted by the thought, The harvest will come in due time, when all the good seed will be carefully gathered, and the bad be forever separated from it.

We observed that the Sower whom we saw in our morning walk flung abroad whole handfuls of seed at a time; seeming to care not a whit where each grain fell, provided that it was but among the furrows. But our Divine SOWER (unlike him in this) does not scatter the good seed at a venture; but He places it carefully in the spot that He has selected for it. And that is the best possible spot that can be for each particular grain of seed. Then He surrounds it with everything that is fitted to nourish and develop it. He visits it every morning. Lest any hurt it, He watches it every moment. And He waters it continually with morning dews and evening showers. And yet, the children of the kingdom, the good seed, about which the SOWER takes such infinite pains, are very apt to complain of His treatment; and, more particularly, as to the place where He hath fixed them. They could be so much more useful, they think, if He had but put them into another situation, or given them more money, or a more prosperous trade, or something else that they think desirable.

If now, the seeds cast into the ground by ordinary Sowers were to find a voice, we might not so much wonder if one of them were to exclaim, "Why did the Sower fling me out here under this wet dropping hedge? All my delicate fibers will be quickly rotted." Or another, "Why am I cast upon this hard rock? I shall surely be parched to death when the sun is up." But from the "Seed" for which the Divine Sower has selected the place with such careful, loving consideration, surely there should be no such remonstrance ever heard. But yet, some of the children of the kingdom have been heard to say, "We wish the SOWER had placed us on yonder higher part of the field where the sun shines. We feel sure we should get on much better than here in this deep shadow." Quite a mistake! The station you occupy, with all the surroundings, is the very best in the whole field for you. It is the place chosen by Divine wisdom. Where you are, you can best learn the lessons the SOWER means you to learn, and bring forth the fruits He watches and waits for; and also be best prepared for the place and the employment He designs for you in the higher world.

It may be that solitude and enforced seclusion are your portion. "You are left alone," writes Dr. Bonar, "in a quiet room—it may be a garret—and seldom are the steps of any sympathizing friends heard approaching. From day to day you are left thus lonely, and are often sick and weary. But do you not remember it once was thus with John the Baptist? He was hurried away from the scenes of a mighty movement, and lodged in the cell of a gloomy prison beyond Jordan. Very few were they who came or were admitted to see him. Months passed, and every day John hoped to hear the voice of his Master coming to the prison to speak a few words in person to His servant. But it was not so. No doubt for our sakes the Baptist was asked to be satisfied with knowing that this way of dealing with His saints seemed wise and good to the Lord, Who will explain all in the day of His appearing. 'Blessed is he who shall not be offended in Me,' was the word sent to calm the ruffled soul of the greatest among all the prophets. He was thus prepared to bear his lot of solitude, obscurity, and trouble in that prison, and then by the stroke of a soldier's sword to pass away, leaving his body to be buried anywhere. And yet the Master loved him with all His heart, and at His coming will crown that head of his with a glory that few in all the kingdom shall wear."

Yonder is one who has set his heart upon being a minister at home, or a missionary abroad, or a busy worker in some other line of usefulness. Highly commendable! But, dear young friend, perhaps that is not the sort of fruit that is required of you at all. You may have to learn lessons of patience and meekness in some obscure, out-of-the-way corner. You are to find out, it may be, how to be downtrodden and unsuccessful without being soured, and even with an actual increase of sweetness and gentleness. You are ordained, it may be, to bring forth the fruits of patience and longsuffering under sharp trials of pain or poverty. And with such lowly fruits as these, however despised by men, the Great Husbandman will be better pleased, than with the most costly sacrifices of the rich, or the most fervent labors of the active and the strong.

From these two symbols of our Lord let us draw one and the same lesson. You would think him a negligent SHEPHERD who did not look out for suitable pasture for his flock. And you would deem him a poor HUSBANDMAN who would sow his seed in a soil not adapted to its growth. And will you impute ignorance or negligence to Jesus Christ? No, surely not. Believe that He knew what He was about, when He chose for you, afflicted child of the kingdom, the station in which you find yourself. It was nothing less than Infinite wisdom, which placed you amidst those very circumstances that surround you. And, be they ever so trying, ever so forbidding, His grace can show you how to solve over again Samson's riddle, to get "honey out of the carcass, and bread out of the eater." If you find this very hard to do—that indeed you cannot untie the knot and bring your mind to your circumstances—then take your restless, froward spirit to Him and ask Him to subdue it; to attemper and adjust its feelings, so that you shall rightly meet those particular trials which He sees fit you should be exercised with. Indeed He will do it. For this is quite the sort of work He loves to undertake. Say to Him—

> I would not have the restless will
> That hurries to and fro,
> That seeks for some great thing to do,
> Or secret thing to know;
> I would be treated as a child,
> And guided where I go.
> I ask Thee for the daily strength
> To none that ask denied,
> A mind to blend with outward life
> While keeping at Thy side;
> Content to fill a little space
> If Thou be glorified.

44

Stone of Stumbling. Stronghold. Shadow of a Great Rock. Shadow from the Heat. Shield. Sword. Scepter. Solomon. Sanctuary.

WE are still going over the lessons we learned from the morning's walk. The firmament and the field have taught us something of Christ. Now let us listen to the echoes, which sound from the quarry by the roadside. I need not tell you that "Stone," in some form or other, occurs very often in the sacred volume as an emblem of our Lord. He is a PRECIOUS STONE, a TRIED STONE or STONE OF TRIAL. He is the FOUNDATION STONE on which God's holy catholic church is built; and the CORNER STONE, which, placed where two walls meet, is a uniting Stone, cementing Jew and Gentile, and making them one. Then He is the Stone rejected by the foolish builders, but exalted notwithstanding to be the HEAD STONE. Of these we have spoken. Once more we read of Him as a STONE OF STUMBLING.

STONE OF STUMBLING (Isa. 8:13, 14). In ancient times it was customary to consecrate great Stones as Altars of Sacrifice. And sometimes they used to connect with the Stone Altars the privilege of "Sanctuary," so that, if a man were pursued by an avenger, he might take his stand beside some sacred Stone and claim it as his Refuge. And in most cases the pursuer would recognize the claim and forbear to injure him. But you see how, if one were running in the dark, or too heedlessly even in the light, he might stumble over the very Stone which was meant to be his safeguard. And he might be hurt by the fall, or be overtaken while prostrate, and thus be "broken, and snared, and taken."

Now look at this. If the sinner pursued by Divine justice and the curse of the law, flees to Christ for refuge, he is safe. It is the law of the kingdom of grace that not a hair of his head shall perish. On the other hand, if he despise or neglect this Divine Stone, it will be the occasion of his destruction. In the days of Christ's humiliation the Jews rejected Him with scorn. They stumbled on Him and were broken. But we who live in these days are more inexcusable than they, if we turn away from Him. For He is now highly exalted, and His claims to our confidence are established. He is manifestly "made the Head of the Corner." This is the Lord's doing, and is meant to be marvelous in our eyes. If it is otherwise, we are under that denunciation, "On whomsoever this STONE shall fall, it will grind him to powder."

You see Christ is a TOUCH-STONE to try us all, to test what we are. Thus He becomes either "a savor of life or a savor of death" to each one. If, when we hear of Him, we embrace Him by faith as God's chosen Savior and ours, all will be well. Our foundation is on the immovable STONE, which God has laid in Zion. If, on the contrary, we disbelieve Him or neglect Him, nothing can shield us from the coming woe. "Behold, ye despisers, and wonder and perish." But is anyone whose eye rests on this page obnoxious to this dire storm? Ah! you need not be. Why will ye die? Think how numerous the symbols, which set forth the perfect security and blessedness of all who hide themselves in Him. And see! here are yet others to be added to all that have gone before. He is compared to a "STRONGHOLD."

STRONGHOLD (Nah. 1:7). Beautiful are the prophet's words! "The Lord is good, a Stronghold in the day of trouble, and He knoweth them that trust in Him"; and most encouraging also is the invitation in Zechariah 9:12, "Turn ye to the Stronghold, ye prisoners of hope." There are some who may be described as prisoners of despair. Such are they who have died without reconciliation to God. They are where hope never comes. But all who are yet upon earth are "prisoners of hope." The most hardened sinner in existence is not beyond hope, because he is not beyond the boundary within which mercy rules. If even He would turn to the Stronghold, he would yet be saved. But especially are those concerned in this invitation who are under religious impressions; poor troubled souls, who have light enough to see their dungeon walls, and sense enough to feel the weight of their chain, and who sigh for liberty.

When Lot fled out of Sodom, the angel urged him to get to the mountain, and not to stay in all the plain. But the mountain path was toilsome, and Lot was footsore and weary; and he preferred a request that he might stay at Zoar. But soon Zoar seemed unsafe to his affrighted spirit; and he fled farther away from the dreadful storm of fire that glowed so near at hand, and hid himself in a cave. And you also are under constant fear of danger, ever afraid of stopping short of a secure refuge. You feel as if you were hunted from refuge to refuge. You find that repentance is no STRONGHOLD, nor reformation, nor tears, nor pious feelings, nor sacraments. You must urge your way to that STRONG TOWER, the "name given under heaven whereby you may be saved," the STRONGHOLD Jesus Christ. Tarry not in all the plain; wait not to be holier or better prepared, before you apply for admittance; but come as you are, and without further waste of time.

Just as you are, without one trace
Of love or joy or inward grace
Or meetness for the heavenly place,
          O guilty sinner, come.

SHADOW OF A GREAT ROCK in a weary land, is another expressive similitude (Isa. 32:2). Delicious thoughts of refreshment after toil arise in the mind
when we meet with such words as these. Especially if the weather is sultry, and
they occur to us when we see a flock of panting sheep lying down to rest in the
dusty road and under a cool shadow. It is hard to tell which enjoys the respite
most, the sheep, the dog, or the driver. Or when we ourselves, heated with our
long walk and half choked with dust and thirst, have turned aside to recline on
the grass, in the shadow of high rocks from which the limpid stream trickles
down, then such words sound as if they had a deep meaning, and we call to
mind the verse,

Where is the Shadow of that Rock
Which from the sun defends Thy flock!
Fain would we rest among Thy sheep,
Among them feed, among them sleep.

But to whatever extent our own observations or sensations may help us to
understand this metaphor, we can never have half such vivid impressions of its
force and beauty, as those who traverse the "weary lands" of eastern climes. To
look round with aching eye and see nothing but miles and miles of hot sands;
to feel, with throbbing temples, the scorching sun beating down like the blast of
a burning furnace; this is the condition we must be in, before we can fully enter
into the meaning of "the SHADOW OF A GREAT ROCK in a weary land."

But can we not get at the thing signified without going all that distance to
understand the figure? I hope so. Let us try. This world then is the "weary land."
"What," you say, "this world? If that is all, we are so in love with it, that we care
for nothing but what it is capable of supplying us with." Well, you may think thus
withal the fresh, cool, gay morning of life lasts. But what of the noontide hour
with its blighting afflictions, its weary cares, its burning pains? Has the world any
shelter from these to offer to those who trust in it? Has it any cordial for fainting hearts? Will a novel or a sensational tale serve the turn? Can the theater offer
any solace for a time of acute suffering? Will cards or dice furnish any comfort
amidst the decays and infirmities of old age, any support for a dying hour? Ah!
full well you know the world will utterly fail its votaries under such circumstances as these. It has no "SHADOW FROM THE HEAT when the blast of the terrible ones is as a storm against the wall."

SHADOW FROM THE HEAT (Isa. 25:4). See yonder aged man. He has seen eighty summers. He is perhaps the greatest genius that ever lived. He has achieved such triumphs of art that his name will never die. He has climbed the pinnacles of fame, and covered himself with this world's glory. All that the world could do by the help of popes and princes for its greatest favorites, it has done for him. He is Michelangelo, the painter, the sculptor, and the architect of St. Peter's at Rome. And these are his words—

> My thoughts, once prompt round hurtful things to climb,
> What are they now when two dread deaths are near?
> The one impends—the other shakes his spear.
> Painting and Sculpture's aid in vain I crave,
> My one sole refuge is that love divine
> Which from the cross stretch'd forth its arms to save.

Romanist as he was, he had made his way through all the empty forms of his religion to the SHADOW OF THE GREAT ROCK, and there alone he found the Shelter he felt the want of. But methinks I hear a faint whisper from one in the bloom of youth—"Ah yes, we may be glad too to shelter ourselves under your Rock when we grow old and weary." Who told you that you would ever live to grow old? On yonder bed lies a young woman breathing out her life; but alas! she has no "SHADE upon her right hand" to shield her from "the blast of the terrible ones." "I inquired," says the minister who visited her, "if I should pray with her." She said, "No!—prayer is too late! I am lost forever." Anguish, deep and hopeless, was riveted on her countenance. Distressed at the sight, he knelt down and prayed for her; but it was, as she had mournfully said, too late! Her heart was hardened in despair. She had been at a former period seriously impressed, "but," said she, "my mother sent me to the dancing school, and I danced all my convictions away." And thus, having wandered out into the "weary" desert, far away from the SHADOW OF THE GREAT ROCK, she died in despair. She had wasted her short life and neglected the Savior, till she had neither time nor strength to reach the ROCK that is higher than we.

But let us pass on to the next similitude.

SHIELD (Gen. 15:1; Ps. 33:20). And what does this metaphor suggest? It calls to mind the battle of the warrior, the hurtling of arrows and clashing of swords, "the noise of the rattling of the wheels, and of the prancing horses, and of the jumping chariots." A Shield (or BUCKLER, Ps. 18:2, 30) was a piece of armor used by the ancient warriors to ward off the weapons then in use, which were chiefly arrows, darts, and spears. It was made of wood, covered with leather or brass. Arrows were shot from bows with great force by archers; and darts were hurled by the muscular arm of the soldier with unerring aim. These were either poisoned, or supplied with combustible matter and set on fire; so that wherever they entered they produced rankling wounds, which ended in death. But the shield of the ancient soldier would be a poor defense in modern warfare. Even King Solomon's 300 Shields of massive gold, which he made for those who guarded the house of the forest of Lebanon, would be quickly battered into atoms at the first onset. But the illustration stands good for all that. Let us learn from it a lesson or two. There are three kinds of arrows or darts, from which the spiritual warrior would suffer greatly if it were not for Christ his Divine SHIELD AND BUCKLER.

1. "*The arrows of the Almighty.*" Job complains (6:4) that "the poison of these drank up his spirits." David also says (Ps. 38:2), "Thine arrows stick fast within me." Both were saints, and yet they suffered greatly from these arrows on account of their sins. Oh then, if the righteous scarcely are saved from them, what shall become of the ungodly? Hear the Psalmist—"If they turn not, God will whet (or sharpen) His sword. He hath bent His bow and make it ready, and ordained His arrows against them." And in another place we read that His "arrows are sharp in the heart of the King's enemies." Now there is no defense against the dreadful arrows of the Almighty, whether for saints or sinners, except one, and that is the tried BUCKLER, the Lord Christ. He came between us and God's wrath, and making bare His bosom, received into His very heart the arrows of God's quiver. He expired beneath them, but now He lives again. And we are by faith to hold up this BUCKLER, and say, "Behold, O God, our SHIELD."

2. "*The fiery darts of the Wicked One.*" Satan is a warrior. He is fighting against the Most High. He has enlisted all men under his banner. And while they side with him and are at war with their Maker, he is satisfied with them, and promises them promotion and honor, ceasing not to persuade them that all is well. But the Spirit of God inclines some in this Apostate's army to come over to the camp of the saints. And from the moment they do so, Satan strives by all means to distress and annoy them. Among other weapons he uses *fiery darts*. He pours into the mind evil thoughts and blasphemies. These are called *darts*, because they enter suddenly and penetrate deeply, and wound sharply. And *fiery* darts, because they inflame and scorch the mind and consume the strength. And whereas the enemy is called the *Wicked One*, this is to denote the union there is among all the legions of devils by whom we are assaulted. They all aim at one thing—to devour whom they may.

Now then, Christian, there is no discharge in this war. From this conflict nothing can save you. The way to the crown lies straight through the very midst of the battlefield. But look to God for strength and courage, and take the Divine SHIELD AND BUCKLER for thy protection. Then, under cover of that, thou mayest easily with the Sword of the Spirit hew thy way through the ranks of thy foes. Be vigilant, be valiant; quit yourselves like men. And though thou art the very mark at which Satan daily shoots his poisoned arrows and hurls his fiery darts, yet go on. This Shield shall cover thy head in the day of battle; and God will "bruise Satan under thy feet shortly." Thou shalt inherit the blessing pronounced upon Joseph, concerning whom we read, "The archers have sorely grieved him, and shot at him and hated him; but his bow abode in strength, and the arms of his hands were made strong by the hands of the mighty God of Jacob (Gen. 49:23, 24).

3. *"The sharp arrows of the mighty"*; in other words, the reproaches of wicked men (Ps. 120:4). These are frequently compared in the Psalms to "spears and arrows" and "drawn swords." David suffered bitterly from them. And all who will live godly in Christ are liable to this kind of persecution. But Christ will guard their good name and shield them from reproach, hiding them under His shadow as in "a pavilion from the strife of tongues"; for "He is BUCKLER to all who trust in Him." If you are among those who have made their escape from Satan, and are engaged in "wrestling" against him; then, I may well congratulate you that you have such a SHIELD as "no weapon formed against you" can penetrate. Use well this SHIELD, and no artful thrust, no well-aimed dart, shot at you with most malignant skill, can wound you in any vital part. "Thy God (thy SHIELD) shall cover thee all the day long."

But do we not read in the New Testament that the Christian's Shield is faith? How does that agree with the statement that the Lord is his SHIELD? There is no contradiction here. It is called "the Shield of faith" because faith is the arm that bears it. Faith lifts it up against the foe, or thrusts it in his face. But faith, without Christ, would be a naked arm devoid of covering and incapable of defense. Christ then is the Christian warrior's Shield. "Happy art thou, O Israel! who is like thee, O people saved by the Lord! who is the SHIELD of thy help and the SWORD of thy excellency."

SWORD OF THY EXCELLENCY (Deut. 33:29). That is, the SWORD that shall defend thy exalted position, and conduct thee to certain victory. It is as if the lawgiver had said, "he is thy complete panoply—thy SHIELD to defend thee from the enemy's thrusts, and thy SWORD deal such heavy blows upon them as shall effectually beat them off and utterly slay them at the last." Whom dost thou fear then, O child of the Living God? Do thy sins affright thee? Well they may without Christ. But He Who died on the cross for them will be their destruction; thou shalt see them dead at thy feet one day. Is it Satan? No wonder, for he is a formidable foe indeed! But, against the "SWORD OF THY EXCELLENCY," he is powerless as a worm. Is it death? Ah! when he doth but shake his dart, he makes the stoutest heart to quail, and the boldest face to turn pallid with dread. But there is One who saith, "O Death, I will be thy Plague! O Grave, I will be thy Destruction!" In this battle you shall not need to fight. "Set yourselves, stand ye still, and see the salvation of the Lord." Courage, poor trembler! Christ will fight out the battle for thee; and thou, hidden safe behind thy mighty SHIELD, shalt find it easier to die than ever it was to live.

All this because He is the Prince of Princes, Prince over the prince of darkness, and King over the king of terrors. His Royalty is shadowed forth under the emblem of a "SCEPTER."

SCEPTER (Num. 24:17). "A SCEPTER shall rise out of Israel"—or a SCEPTER BEARER. This is the SCEPTER that is to break in pieces all other scepters. Thy throne, O God, is forever. It is not *He* who is the stone spoken of by Daniel in his magnificent prophecy—it is His *Kingdom*, which, cut out of the mountain without hands, and prevailing against all opposition, shall at the appointed time become a great mountain and fill the whole earth. "Yea, all kings shall bow down before Him, all nations shall serve Him."

But say, whose subjects are you? Some master you are serving. Someone's will you are doing. Look round, now, upon the leaders who claim your obedience, and choose which of them you will have for your king. Shall it be Satan? Ah! his is too dreadful a service for anyone to engage in deliberately, though vast multitudes are doing it thoughtlessly. Will you then attach yourself to some earthly patron, to be subject to all his caprices? That would turn out a most galling servitude, and leave you at last to wish, with Cardinal Wolsey, that you had chosen a better master. Will you then devote yourself to your own interests, your own lusts, your own pleasures, seeking your own way and your own will selfishly in all things? If this be your choice, you will serve a master who will never be satisfied, and whose demands will increase with every effort you make to meet them. There is not a more exacting tyrant than Self in all the world. Ah! be persuaded, in the strength of God, to pronounce a final, everlasting *No* to all these, and choose the Royal SCEPTER of Israel to be the sole Lord and Sovereign of your heart. Fairer than the children of men, no words can set forth His beauty or the grace of His service. His yoke is easy; His laws are meat and drink to those who observe them; and His love to all His subjects passeth knowledge.

But some thoughtful reader may ask, Ought there not to be a personal type introduced here, whose name was not noted by the two pedestrians in their morning walk (page 387), when the sight of the ruined castle, over which the royal standard had once waved, suggested to them SCEPTER, SWORD, AND SHIELD? You are right. To be sure

SOLOMON must be recognized as a Type of our Lord. But, like the rest of the historical types, only in connection with a prominent feature or two. The seventy-second Psalm seems to be a beautiful prophetical prayer, offered up by David, for him who was both the king and the king's son. And in it he foretells a peaceful and prosperous reign. But as we read, we find the bright and glowing colors introduced betray the fact that, to the writer's inspired gaze, a Greater than Solomon occupied the field of view.

Solomon's administration was, upon the whole, righteous; and so it serves as a dim picture of Christ's. It also lasted a long time, for his descendants occupied the Judean throne for hundreds of years; and so it pictures to us the endless reign of David's Greater Son, Who "shall reign over the house of David forever, and of Whose kingdom there shall be NO END" (Luke 1:33).

Solomon's kingdom was to extend "from sea to sea and from the river unto the ends of the earth." There are some who, having a theory to uphold, affirm (on insufficient grounds we presume to think) that as this promise was never fulfilled, it therefore remains to be. But it must not be forgotten that the promises God made to the kings and people of Israel, of prosperity and enlargement, were conditional on their obedience and loyalty to God. Did they keep their covenant engagements? Alas! for the most part, they flung them to the winds, kings and people too. But are there not two parties to a covenant? And oh not the failure of one to fulfill his part of the contract acquit the other also from its obligation? But observe, those very words are, 400 years afterwards, applied by the prophet Zechariah (9:9, 10) to the kingdom of Him Who should "come to Zion, Just and having salvation, Lowly and riding upon an ass." This cannot be held to refer to anything less than the worldwide dominion of the Messiah.

Again, David said, "All kings shall fall down before him, all nations shall serve him." And in a measure this was fulfilled in Solomon during his best days—his days of allegiance to God. See 2 Chronicles 9:23. "All the kings of the earth sought the presence of Solomon. . . . And they brought . . . a rate year by year." But all such expressions will find their perfect fulfillment only in the Omnipotent One, Who is King of kings and Lord of lords, and to Whom every knee shall bow.

Well, and now our morning's walk, having furnished us with lessons for three Sundays, is ended, and we arrive at our home; whence we derive one more symbol.

SANCTUARY (Isa. 8:14). A Sanctuary means a holy place. Heaven is a Sanctuary; so is a temple upon earth. The world is also used for a place of safety, a pavilion in which one may hide, an inviolable sacred spot where one may be sheltered from danger. Thus a man's own house is his Sanctuary, his Castle. It is in this sense that it is applied to the Redeemer. He is the "Strong Habitation" whereunto multitudes are every day resorting—the Home wherein they dwell.

But some little child may say, "Will so great a Savior regard a little one like me?" Yes, my child, He will. True, He is a Great SANCTUARY, large enough to take in all the world. But He is a LITTLE SANCTUARY also, small enough, and homely enough, and familiar enough, for your littleness and mine. In Ezekiel 11:16, we have these remarkable words, "I will be to them as a Little Sanctuary," which teaches us that Jesus Christ adapts Himself to our size, our age, our wants, whatever they may be. And well He knows how to do this. He understands the heart of a little child, for He was once a little child Himself. He knows the peculiar nature of a boy, a youth, and a man. For He has "passed through all the successive stages of weakness, growth, and education, that belong to a life like ours."

Behold yonder hen gathering her fluttering little chickens under her wings. How they come scampering from right and left, at her well-known maternal call, and, nestling close within the warm shelter of her feather, find protection and rest. It may be she sees some threatening danger, which we perceive not. What is that dark speck hovering in the sky overhead? Is it a hawk, or other bird of prey? In haste she summons her brood of helpless fledglings to hide themselves in their Little Sanctuary, the shadow of her parental wings. Dost thou observe how beautifully adapted those broad outspread pinions of the mother-bird are to be a retreat to her little brood? But none so perfectly as Jesus Christ to be a Little Sanctuary to thee, O thou helpless one! And hark! doth not the Savior expressly call you? "Suffer the little children to come unto Me."

Again, in your own little home, is there not a special place kept on purpose for you?—to which you are not only welcome, but where you are fully expected to appear. There is the little seat at the table, and the little corner at the fireside, and the little bed where you sleep at night—all for you. So in the heart of the Divine Sanctuary, there is not only ample room for all, but a place reserved for each. "I will be as a Little Sanctuary to you."

One more thing. This Sanctuary is easy of access. You must not think of it as like some lordly mansion on earth, which you would be afraid to enter without great ceremony. It is indeed more glorious than any earthly metaphor can set forth. But then, it is, at the same time, as free and familiar as your own home. And just as a child at his father's door, would not stand knocking, but lift the latch and pass straightway in, so you are to make use of your Sanctuary, "boldly," and whenever you will. And, in proportion to the constant use you make of it, you will find that it doth even seem to fit itself to your infirmities, and yield support to all your weaker powers.

There, little one! I have answered your question. But it is not on my authority but on the authority of God that you must take it for truth, that the Sanctuary is for thee; made expressly for thee; adapted to every infirmity, and adjusted to thy every want. Thou are the very one who mayest say to Jesus Christ, "Thou art my Refuge and Fortress," while He responds to thy humble trust, "I will cover thee with My feathers, and under My wings shalt thou trust!"

Thou art as much His care, as if, beside,
No man nor angel lived in all the earth—
The sunbeams pour alike their golden tide
To light a world, or wake an insect birth;
They shine and shine with unexhausted store.
Thou art thy Savior's darling—seek no more.

Thou! But what Thou? Can this language apply to all? Ah, no. But to all who have come to Christ. And whose fault is it, if any of you are still wanderers in the waste howling wilderness of an unregenerate condition, exposed to the fiery heat and storms of the wrath of Almighty God?

The STONE of Israel is set up on purpose to be a SANCTUARY, a STRONGHOLD for "the prisoners of hope."

As a mighty ROCK, He stands over in sight, able and willing to be to you a SHADOW FROM THE HEAT in this "weary land."

He is at once SHIELD, SWORD, AND SCEPTER, to those that trust in him, insuring defense and victory, and all He can do for them, as the most benign and powerful of Rulers—yea, even to the half of His kingdom, and a share in His throne.

And lastly, He says, "I will be a LITTLE SANCTUARY to you." Strong, indeed, but convenient and available, wherein you may hide yourselves from evil, and find all the advantages of a blessed, familiar Home for your immortal spirits: and where, when the world is all in arms, you may lay yourselves down and rest in quiet.

Whose fault is it, I ask, if you avail not yourselves of these infinite advantages? Have you no answer? Hear then the words of the Faithful Witness: "O Jerusalem! How often would I have gathered your children as a hen doth gather chickens under her wings—*and ye would not.*"

45

Son of God. Son of the Blessed. Son of the Highest. Son of Man. Son of David. Servant.

NEXT follow in order, three august Titles which set forth the Divine nature and glory of our Lord, namely, SON OF GOD, SON OF THE BLESSED, and SON OF THE HIGHEST. These show us what He is originally. Then follow three other Titles which display His Human nature and life, namely, SON OF MAN, SON OF DAVID, SERVANT. These show us what He became. And then three more which show for what purpose He thus condescended, namely, SECOND MAN, SEED OF THE WOMAN, SHILOH. These last, we shall have to reserve for next Sunday.

SON OF GOD (Matt. 4:3). This Title signifies no less than that he has the same nature and attributes as God—Self-existence, Omnipotence, Unlimited Greatness. Further than this we can say but little; for "no one knoweth who the Son is but the Father." We are afraid to meddle with the cumbersome definitions wherewith some have beclouded this mysterious and sublime subject. But we rejoice in the plain revealed truth that He is "One with the Father"; the Great I AM, the Eternal Son who dwelt in the bosom of the Eternal Father. The Everlasting Light and Glory of the universe is the Godhead; and Christ is the Brightness of that Glory, the Effulgence and Manifestation of its Infinite Beauty. The Godhead, the Tri-unity is the All-wise Contriver and Originator of plans embracing Infinity. And Christ is the Divine Word by Whom they are revealed, and the Almighty Arm by Whom they are executed.

In Hebrews 1:2, we read, "By Him God made the worlds." We are accustomed to speak of "the world," as if there were but one. Look around, and you will be able to reckon many worlds, and all of them the product of His power and wisdom. First, there is this great, round globe that we inhabit, with its mountain chains—

> Rock-ribbed, and ancient as the sun—its vales
> Stretching in pensive quietness between;
> Its venerable woods—rivers that move

In majesty, and the complaining brooks
That make the meadows green; and poured round all
Old ocean's gray and melancholy waste.

This beautiful world which is given to the sons of men, with its cattle upon a thousand hills; its groves vocal with the song of birds; its myriads of insects burrowing under the clods, or dancing in the sunshine, and flashing with colors that outvie the very rainbow itself; and last, yet greatest, its many millions of human beings, all "fearfully and wonderfully made," kept alive by His power, and subsisting daily on His bounty. Nor these living ones alone—

All that tread
The globe are but a handful to the tribes
That slumber in its bosom. Take the wings
Of morning, and the eastern desert pierce,
Or lose thyself in the continuous woods
Where rolls the Oregon, and hears no sound
Save his own dashings—yet the dead are there.

Everywhere, under our feet, there lie sleeping in the dust thousands of millions of the human race, who only wait the Archangel's summons to start into life again.

No spot of earth but has supplied a grave.

And there are worlds within this world—worlds in ruins, lower down still, dimly revealing their histories in fossil skeletons of huge lizards and salamanders, and monsters of gigantic size, all turned to stone, and deeply imbedded in ancient rocks. Those grim, silent witnesses testify that successive races of animals inhabited this globe ages before Adam was created.

There is also the world of waters, the great ocean with its deep abysses many miles down, abounding throughout with living creatures, both great and small. There roam those huge leviathans and giants of the deep, which God has "made to play therein."

There are worlds, too, which the microscope has brought to light, teeming with an endless profusion of life. We look through the magic tube, and in a drop of stagnant water we descry whole tribes of active little creatures, sporting in exuberance of gaiety. In a little particle of sour paste we see crowds of wriggling eels; and bits of decayed cheese are found to be alive with tiny mites; while every plant in the garden swarms with minute flies, arrayed in colors superb enough to grace a seraph's wing.

And there are worlds, great and marvelous and multitudinous, which the telescope has revealed. There was a time when, to the unassisted eyes of our forefathers, the stars looked like lamps depending from the sky as a mighty ceiling, which in its mystic motion daily revolved round the earth. But the telescope was set up; when lo! the lamps are transformed into suns, each mightier far than our own; and are found to shine from a distance so remote, that the very beam which darts into the eye that now looks upon them, has taken thousands of years to travel hither.

Then there is the vast, unknown world of separate spirits, and angels good and bad. And the SON OF GOD made that, and all the other worlds we have named. And even now He is preparing yet another that shall outdo all the rest in splendor and glory. "I go to prepare a place for you," said He, almost with His last breath. And to that world He will at last welcome His own with the words, "Come ye blessed." And without the SON OF GOD was not anything made that is made. It is Him Whom we extol when we sing, "Thou art worthy, O Lord, to receive glory, and honor, and power; for Thou hast created all things, and for Thy pleasure they are and were created."

SON OF GOD. In Ephesians 3:14, God is invoked as "the Father of our Lord Jesus Christ, of Whom the whole family in heaven and earth is named." Does this expression mean named *after* Him, or named *by* Him? Either way it is equally true.

Take the first sense. Are not the saints expressly called sons of God? Don't they bear Christ's very name? And are they not sons of God in such a sense as none of any other order or race can be? They are sons not in their own right, but in His in Whom they are accepted, and with Whom they are identified. And they can never lose a sonship with which they become invested thus, and on such a ground. For the privilege is not theirs apart from Christ. It is not a patent of divine nobility or royal sonship, merely conferred on them by the Father in honor of Christ's mediation, and in compliance with His intercession. They have it only in Christ *as they are one with Him*. Christ's Sonship is theirs because Christ Himself is theirs.

Or take the other sense, named *by* Him. It is He Who gives the power to become the sons of God. They have no right to the title, and no authority to appropriate it, except that which He Himself confers (John 1:12). It is because they belong to His Brotherhood that He gives them to share in His Filial and Family Relationship to His Great Father. The many sons, of whom He is the First-born, are all united together in a sacred, indissoluble family bond; so that they become joint-heirs with Him, heirs of His Father along with Himself. For, saith He, "The glory which Thou gavest Me I have given them."

This honor cannot belong to the angels, or any other beings that exist already, or shall be hereafter created. Why? Because the SON OF GOD doth not take their nature. But He does take ours, and will wear it forever in the sight of all "in beauty glorified."

Thus the saints become allied to Himself and so to His Father, somewhat in the sense in which we use the earth-born expression, blood-relationship. They are akin both to the Father and to the Son. For they are not merely adopted, they are begotten of God, born of the Spirit. And so intimate is their oneness with the SON OF GOD, that they are described as "members of His body, of His flesh, and of His bones"—"joined to the Lord and one spirit with Him." They are "bound up in the bundle of life" with Him as intimately as the branches of a tree are one with the tree. Yea they are made as completely one with Him as the members of a body are one with the body.

Are these things so? Then well may we wonderingly ask, what is man? Eternity alone will answer the question. God will show what man is, and what he is capable of, in the exceeding and eternal weight of glory wherewith He will surround him.

Young men and maidens! you were made for God. Can you think too much of such a birthright? Will you continue to slight the injured love of such a Friend? Will you still permit the trifles of time, and the fashions and pleasures of this world, to build up a screen between you and the brightness of such a destiny? Rather look at it thoughtfully, and consider what it involves. If you fall in with the purpose of God, you become sons and daughters of the Almighty; and—not honored members of Christ's special retinue only—but His everlasting associates, the very brothers and sisters of the Son of God, and co-heirs with Him of all the wealth of eternity.

> O strive to win that glory,
>   O toil to gain that light;
> Send hope before to grasp it
>   Till hope be lost in sight.

SON OF THE BLESSED (Mark 14:61). God is the Blessed God, the Happy Self-sufficing One. "In no sense whatever can His happiness depend on creatures. It can neither be increased nor diminished by what He Himself has called into being, with a perfect foreknowledge of its coming history." Whatever is meant in the Scriptures when words expressive of repentance, fury, scorn, or passion are used in relation to the Supreme Being, we do most certainly misunderstand them if we are led to impute human emotions to Him, otherwise than as they can consist with an infinitely Happy, All-blessed, Serene, and Self-sufficing Nature. So Blessed is He that to Him a thousand years are but as yesterday; for what is laps of time to One who is perfectly Happy? No disturbance can invade His Serenity; no disaster can take His Omniscience by surprise; no perplexity can disconcert His All-wise Counsels; no discomfort can interfere with His ever-joyful and placid Repose.

"Our Father in heaven," writes one, "is infinitely Wise, Holy, and Good. He is Love. No human mind can conceive the deep calm joy of such a Being. Perfect in power, in Him there is no weakness at all. Perfect in holiness, in Him there is no stain. Therefore in Him the two great fountains of sorrow are wanting. He is infinitely Happy because He is infinitely Holy. His peace is without disturbance, because His purity is without stain. His bliss can never cease, because His love can never fail."

Thus when the Great Father inhabited eternity, in equal fellowship with the Son and the Holy Spirit, They were infinitely BLESSED in Themselves and Each Other, without the existence or service of any created beings. Blessed also They were in becoming the Fountain of being and bliss to the whole creation. And the SON OF THE BLESSED is the Steward and Dispenser of all the rivers of God's pleasures. And every draught of bliss affords more pleasure to Him Who gives, than to him who receives. For so our Lord says, "It is more blessed to give than to receive." What man or angel can conceive the infinite happiness of Him who is the Hand, the Word, the Channel, by whom Jehovah communicates life and joy to all the creatures He has made? While, from out of His unsearchable riches, He is still pouring forth rivers of bliss which will widen, and deepen, and swell forever and ever.

The vast amount of enjoyment diffused among irrational creatures, throws wonderful light on the character of the Great Creator, the SON OF THE BLESSED. The innocent lambs gambol together in the meadows, frisking playfully around the graver matrons of the flock. The playful kitten finds exuberant fun in chasing a ball of cotton, or spinning round after its own tail. In ruder and more boisterous merriment, long-legged frolicsome puppies chase and roll over one another by the half-hour together. Gnats, in a network of endless mazes, dart to and fro in the sunbeam, while birds render the woods vocal with their thrilling songs. Why all this? but because their Creator is a "Happy God," and loves to diffuse happiness and joy among all living things. "He condescends to take an interest in all things He has made—to hear the songs of His own birds, to play with the shepherd's flocks as they sport on the sides of the mountains, and to rejoice with the young lions as He feeds them in the forest."

Again, what *endless variety* appears in the objects that meet our eyes! Go to the seaside, and from the miles of pebbles that line the strand, bring away a cartload if you will, and, if you can, discover among the heap two that shall be alike in every respect. Or go to the forest and collect as many leaves from one sort of tree, and try the same experiment, and you will meet with the same diversity. And if we find this among the most common things of earth, must we not conclude that it prevails everywhere? If there are no two stones, no two faces alike upon earth, we may conclude there are no two angels alike in heaven; no two worlds alike in yonder crowded sky. But not to soar quite so high, behold the clouds, those graceful folds of drapery which often veil the blue abysms from our sight. And did anybody ever see two clouds alike? Nay, verily, though endless processions of them have been ever passing across the face of the heavens from the creation till now. Beauteous forms they are, "wrought for us daily, yet varied eternally, and never repeated; found always, yet each found but once."

And why this endless variety? "Every single purpose of the sky," writes Mr. Ruskin, "might so far as we know, be answered, if now and then a great, ugly, black rain cloud were brought up over the blue, and everything were watered, and so all left blue again till the next time. Instead of this, there is not a moment of any day of our lives, when God is not producing scene after scene, picture after picture, glory after glory, and all wrought on such perfect principles of exquisite beauty, that it is quite certain it is all done for us, and intended for our perpetual pleasure."

The truth is, sameness would be wearisome to us. God hath made us capable of receiving both profit and pleasure from variety. Our very nature craves it, though alas, the nature being vitiated, the craving becomes so too. But this want of our nature is ministered to most benevolently, wherever we turn our eyes. Everything seems fitted to keep attention always awake, to reproduce pleasure, to arouse admiration, to provoke thought, and to allure and guide our inquiries after the Beneficent Contriver and Blessed Creator of all. And when men will not hear the still small voice in which He discourses so eloquently, no wonder if God complains as one disappointed. "None saith, Where is God my Maker? None regardeth the operations of My hands." And no wonder if He then speaks to them in the thunderstorm and the tornado, or by pestilence or famine. But another title is "SON OF THE HIGHEST."

SON OF THE HIGHEST (Luke 1:32). Height is a relative quality. The spire of a cathedral seems very high when compared with a house. But it would diminish to a point if looked at from the top of Mont Blanc. And where would that be if searched for from the height of yonder star? It vanishes into utter insignificance; yea, the great globe itself passes clean out of sight. A country squire is a very lofty personage in the eyes of the orphan boy at the village workhouse. An archbishop seems at a wonderful remove above the lowly station of a charity school child. And the queen is higher than all. But from that height, where the Son of the Highest sits enthroned, they are all seen as on a perfect level. There is no respect of persons with God. Be sure the meanest child is as great in His sight as the proudest sovereign. Aye, perhaps, he may be even the greater of the two. O SON OF THE HIGHEST! Dost Thou ask to what will ye compare Me? We fall upon our cases at Thy feet. We sink into nothing before Thee. Comparison? There is none! Only contrast, inconceivable! For Thou fillest heaven and earth, and we are "less than nothing and vanity." Thou alone art High, the High and Lofty One that inhabiteth eternity. And yet we know Thee also as the SON OF MAN.

SON OF MAN (Matt. 8:20). Behold this Great One, this Creator of men, becoming a SON OF MAN—this Lord of principalities and powers in the heavens, stooping to be a member of the fallen human race, in this mean far-off province of His vast universe! Behold Him whom the heaven of heavens cannot contain, limiting Himself to a human body, and submitting to human conditions of life—toil, hunger, thirst, suffering, death! Behold the SON OF THE HIGHEST emptying Himself, and becoming a SERVANT "of no reputation,"—the SON OF THE BLESSED, making Himself a Man of Sorrows, and submitting to be rejected and despised by creatures who lived on His bounty. O wonder of wonders! O unfailing subject for astonishment and admiration in all worlds! O matchless burden of everlasting songs of praise! What can we say? What words can we make use of which shall not degrade this most majestic of themes?

> Lord! what can earth and ashes do?
> We would adore our Savior too.
> But holy reverence checks our songs,
> And praise sits silent on our tongues.

The SON OF MAN began His human life where we all began ours, in the utter helplessness of infancy, with many "blank months" of unremembered, because unconscious, life. His expanding mind opened step by step, as did yours and mine. He had to learn to talk and to learn to walk, just as we do. Memory, thought, observation, were gradually quickened into active exercise; and education went on by little and little. "He grew in wisdom and in stature." Many years must have passed away, of that marvelous life, ere He was capable of understanding the work He was sent to accomplish. All this while, no external miracle marked the development of the powers and faculties of the Holy Child Jesus, except the one miracle which distinguished Him from all other human beings, His spotless purity. He partook not of the taint of our fallen nature, but passed through all the successive stages of infancy, childhood, youth, manhood, without ever committing a single fault, or ever being convicted of a single unsuitable word or failure of any kind. Rest and sleep He required just as we do. He "came eating and drinking." He wept, He rejoiced, He suffered. In all things He was as completely human as He was perfectly divine.

SON OF MAN. Every man can claim this title in its ordinary application. But, "Who is *this* SON OF MAN?" He is *the* SON preeminently. All else are alike involved in helplessness and ruin. None can redeem his brother or give to God ransom for him. But here is the "Brother born for adversity." Born into the family expressly to repair its disasters, to roll away its disgrace, to be "a glorious high throne to His Father's house," its Restorer and Redeemer, its Crown of Glory and Diadem of Beauty.

SON OF MAN points to His worldwide relation. As the Seed of Abraham He is identified with the Hebrews; and as the Son of David, with the regal family of that nation. But as the SON OF MAN He wears a universal aspect to the entire race. All the families of the earth have a common interest in Him, for in Him all are to be blessed.

Although the Title belongs to Christ's assumed nature, and therefore implies His infinite condescension, it is not expressive of humiliation. It is rather a Title of Glory and Royalty indicative of His Headship over all mankind. Thus He says, "God hath given Him authority to execute judgment, *because He is* THE SON OF MAN." Just as the final judicial function is vested in an earthly monarch because he is the head of the nation.

This was the usual, if not favorite, Title He made use of in speaking of Himself. And how unspeakably endeared to us! It places Him by our side, and makes Him one of ourselves, notwithstanding His infinite elevation above us. Entrust Him with all thy secrets, Christian. Cast on Him all thy cares. Confess to Him all thy infirmities; and be assured He will make all just allowances, as One who hath been tempted in all points as we are, though without sin.

The incarnation of the Eternal Son of God is the grandest and most marvelous fact that ever was or ever will be. After so stupendous a descent from such an infinite height, we are almost incapable of surprise at anything that follows. Yet it was not only man's nature that He took upon Him, but man's lowliest station. He was literally a poor, laboring man, although the SON OF DAVID.

SON OF DAVID (Matt. 20:30). His descent was indeed reckoned from a long line of royal ancestors, "kings and princes, sitting on thrones, and riding in chariots and on horses," whose genealogy had been carefully preserved in the national archives. But observe, He was born into the family when it had fallen into utter decay. Its glory had long passed away and was become matter of history only, when that Child of the royal house, in whom all the promises of God and all the hopes of men were centered, made His unnoticed appearance. The chief representative of the renowned family of David seems to have been Joseph, a village carpenter; but whose royal descent won no respect from his townsmen. Nor did the fact conciliate men's feelings towards our Lord during His ministry. He was indeed hailed twice or thrice as the SON OF DAVID, by the blind and poor. But with this exception (and that one burst of popular favor which attended Him into Jerusalem, with loud "Hosannas to the Son of David" from children's voices, just before His crucifixion), His claims to be considered on this ground were evidently not recognized. Neither His holy character, His useful life, His miraculous works, nor His royal descent, could save Him from the hatred of both rulers and people—to whom indeed He ministered as a "SERVANT."

SERVANT (Isa. 52:13). God calls Him "MY SERVANT." But we speak of Him now as the SERVANT of men, a "SERVANT of rulers" (Isa. 49:7). "I am amongst you as He that serveth" (or as the Serving One), He says of Himself (Luke 22:27). He "came not to be ministered unto but to minister,"—to serve, to wait upon, to deny Himself, and "to give His life a ransom" for others.

From His earliest life He was in subjection as a dutiful Son to His mother and Joseph. He "fulfilled all righteousness," and did His duty with exemplary humility to each member of the lowly household. At the proper age He learned, and afterwards practiced, a trade; one which is useful, yea indispensable, among men. We should speak with caution where the Bible leaves us without information. But we are not depending merely on tradition when we affirm that He wrought as a carpenter; for the contemptuous question of His fellow townsmen, "Is not this the carpenter?" conveys this information. Nor need we be at a loss to know what, in that capacity, His employment would be. Everybody knows what the work of a carpenter is. If one would build a house, it is he who is employed to make the frames for door and window, and to prepare the rafters for floor and roof. If one would cultivate a farm, or undertake a long journey, it is he who fashions the plows and yokes for the oxen, or prepares the gear for the camels and the poles for the tents. And this Illustrious Workman, like other artisans, (with reverence be it uttered), must often have executed such work as this, subject to the will of an employer—"a SERVANT of rulers."

Had you been living them, you might have walked past a humble workshop adjoining the little village street. And, looking in, you might have seen this wonderful Artificer carefully planing a board for domestic use, or diligently fashioning some implement of husbandry. The people of Nazareth saw all this going on continually, and thought it nothing extraordinary. And yet, all the while, there were illustrious visitors going and coming who felt and thought very differently. Angels, in their swift errands from the skies, would often rest their wings there, and pause awhile to gaze with adoration and awe. Nor, if we feel aright, will it abate our reverence for Him a whit, but rather increase it a hundredfold, to dwell, with fond and adoring interest, on this feature of our great Master's private life. "Time was," says Dr. Guthrie, "when He set His compass on the deep; time was when He stood and measured the earth. And now with line and compass and plane and hatchet, the sweat dropping from His lofty brow, He who made heaven and earth, and the sea, and all that is in them, is, in the guise of a common tradesman, bends at a carpenter's bench! What an amazing scene! Henceforth let honest labor feel itself ennobled, and let no man, whatever rank he has attained, blush at the meanness of his origin; or be ashamed of his father's trade."

When He began His public ministry He was still the SERVANT of all. You will remember that He fixed His home for a considerable time at Capernaum. This was then a large town; it is reported to have contained 16,000 people. One Sabbath morning He did but heal a sick person or two, and immediately the news spread through the whole place. People talked of it in every street and lane of the city, and when the Sabbath services were over, and the sun was setting (for the Jewish Sabbath ends at sunset), "the whole city was gathered together" at His door. They gave Him no rest, but brought all the sick people they could find, and with skillful hand and yearning heart, He healed them all. Surely, while He dwelt there Capernaum must have been the healthiest town in the country. For who would endure the pain of sickness for a single day when could get instant cure by application to this most beneficent SERVANT of all?

Nor must we forget that beautiful and instructive scene—so grand, when we consider Who was the central figure, and yet so quiet and lowly—the scene in the large upper chamber. After supper, "He took a towel and girded Himself," as a SERVANT waiting on his master would do, and went round among His disciples, and, to their great surprise—and ours—washed and wiped the feet of each. What a lesson for them! What a lesson for us! Oh when shall we learn that it is indeed "more blessed to give than to receive?" And more honorable to serve the poorest, in the spirit of love and in the will of God, than to command grand armies of men in the spirit of self-will and pride? The humble Bible woman going her daily rounds in dirty courts and narrow alleys, diving into damp cellars or climbing into squalid attics, is an object of far greater interest in the estimation of heaven, than a king and his courtiers, glittering in gold and scarlet, and surrounded with all the world's gayest pageantry.

We see then that not only was Jesus Christ made in the form of a SERVANT, but that He did the work of a SERVANT, ministering to the sinful, the ignorant, the sick, and the poor. But the great service He came to render was only indicated by such deeds as these. We propose therefore, in the next Reading, to consider the end and object the SON OF THE BLESSED purposed in assuming those lowly forms.

In the meantime let us take away with us this thought. Not only doth Jesus Christ thoroughly know, as God, the nature of all kinds of grief and distress, and our most secret sufferings, whatever they are; but, having as the Son of Man "His own self" borne our infirmities in His own body and soul experimentally. He feels for us in them all as a fellow sufferer and as only a fellow sufferer can. "He took our nature," writes Elihu Burritt, "and wore it in poverty-stricken babyhood first, that forever and forever, when He went back to His high heaven, He might know, and feel for, the little weaknesses, wants, pains, and joys of small human children. He wore it through the ardent years of eager, hopeful, ambitious boyhood, that He might know and remember forever what boys feel and think, and the temptations and trials that beset them. He wore it into the thickest cares, anxieties, and affliction of middle manhood, that He might forever know how they take hold of our nature; what manner of trial comes upon it in a moment to test its weaknesses; what sensibilities writhe under the touch of pain; what tears fall here and there on the road of life; and how these fret the immortal spirit within us, and weigh it down in dumb despondency." When, therefore, you are called to bear pain, or reproach, or poverty, or temptation, you may look confidently to Him for sympathy. The SON OF MAN is the "Brother born for adversity," Who can be touched with the feeling of our infirmities. He was made MAN, and suffered by personal experience, on purpose that He might know how to succor them that are tempted.

> The Man of Sorrows stoop'd to feel
> The woes He undertook to heal;
> He came to link His life with ours,
> And trace the path where tempest lours,
> Acquaintance personal to gain
> With every form of grief and pain;
> In His own world to find no home,
> Endure throughout a martyrdom,
> And finish in the lonely tomb;
> That in our every pressure we
> Might find completest sympathy.

46

Second Man. Seed of the Woman. Shiloh.

LAST Sunday's Title selection showed us *how low* the glorious SON OF GOD stooped, even to the form and station of a SERVANT; and from what a *height*, even the topmost place in the universe. We were obliged to reserve till today, our examination of the three Titles by which we proposed to illustrate the *purpose* for which He thus condescended. It was, as the SECOND MAN, to get back the inheritance the First Man had forfeited—as the SEED of the woman, to vanquish the old serpent, the author of our ruin—and, as the SHILOH, to gather together all the redeemed into a state of eternal rest and blessedness.

SECOND MAN, or Last Adam (1 Cor. 15:45–47). Adam was the earliest of the Savior's *Types;* just as the SEED of the woman was the earliest *Title* by which He was made known to men. He was "the figure of Him that was to come," in several particulars before adverted to (see pages 6 and 272). Both were "made upright." Only these two men of all the race came into the world holy, that is, without taint of sin or bias towards it. The one was a perfect man, the other a Holy Child. Then again, both were tested by temptation as *Representative men,* each standing for others as well as himself, and "sharing what he has with his own." Upon the conduct of each depended the weal or woe of multitudes.

Adam's fall involved the whole race in ruin. But had he stood, they would have shared in the advantages that would have followed his obedience. Among these we must reckon, dominion over the world, its creatures, and perhaps, its elements—purity of nature—friendship with God—exemption from disease and death—and growth in knowledge and bliss. This great estate and inheritance of honor was "vilely cast away." The serpent beguiled him into sin, the paradise was forfeited, and the race was ruined. "Man, being in honor, abode not, but became like the beasts which perish." "By one man's disobedience many were made sinners"—"death came by sin"—and so "in Adam all die."

But, you say, was not the offense a very slight one to be followed by such a punishment? Slight? Ah! think again; it was the violation of the only express command God seems to have given him. It was not some toilsome duty that was required, which would have taxed his strength to the utmost; but just this light and easy thing, "Of all the trees in the garden you may eat, only touch not yonder central tree of knowledge." That was a *severe test* of obedience to which Abraham was subjected when required to offer up his only son. And *that* was a severe test by which the Second Man was tried, when after forty days' fasting He hungered. No common hunger was it; yet He refused to exert His miraculous power for the supply of His wants, apart from the will of God. But Adam's test was the easiest that could have been invented, of loving loyal obedience, and therefore the failure was the more shameful and criminal. "Well," says one, "I must own that what you say is true enough: but there are other difficulties I should like to have cleared up." No doubt. But suppose I could clear them all up, what would that contribute to your deliverance? Nothing. Would a man seized with cholera be taking any step toward a cure by setting himself to find out how he caught the distemper? Nay, rather let him lose no time in applying the remedies, for death is at the door. And so it may be with the skeptic. While he is occupied with idle speculations and fruitless inquiries, the day of grace slips away, and his last hour is upon him.

Suppose you were heir to a fortune, which, on your coming age, is found to have been dissipated by dishonest guardians. And suppose some rich man were to propose to endow you with ten times as much as you have been defrauded of. Would you say, "Very kind indeed, sir, but first I must know how the estate has been wasted, and what has been done with the money, and why such unworthy people were trusted with it at all. In short, sir, I must find out the whole mystery of the injustice before I can accept your offer." You would not adopt a course so foolish. You would receive the offered boon at once, and afterwards, if it were worthwhile and you could find nothing better to do, you might search into the fraud.

Put away therefore your cavils and "perverse disputings." Trust the "Judge of all the earth," that He will do right, and hasten to secure the purchased possession, the redeemed inheritance, the lost favor of God. All the ruin introduced by the first man, augmented as it has been a thousandfold by our own personal transgressions, this Second Man undertakes to repair. Did the first man sell our inheritance for the small gain of a momentary gratification? and have we set our seal to the fatal deed and added our signature, by our still greater offenses? Behold the SECOND MAN, the Lord from heaven! Who having taken our nature, ransomed both us and our heritage at the price of His own illustrious life and precious blood!

> Extol the Son of God,
>   The Great atoning Lamb;
> Redemption, through His blood,
>   Throughout the world proclaim.

You who have sold for nought
    Your heritage above,
Shall have it back, unbought,
    The gift of Jesus' blood.

The year of Jubilee is come;
Return, ye ransomed sinners, home.

And then think for a moment how far the inheritance secured to us by the Second Man must needs transcend that which would have been bequeathed by the First Man, had he stood his ground. Grant that the human race, under such favorable auspices, might have been developed into something very grand and imposing, and, like a spreading tree, have filled the whole earth with its fragrance and its fruit; yet all would have fallen far short of the exceeding and eternal weight of glory which is the reward of the obedience and sufferings of the Son of God.

In the present state there is an immense difference observable between man and man. Once or so in an age, "a specimen occurs," as George Steward observes, "of unusual grandeur, a colossal being gazed upon wonderingly, as well by posterity as by contemporary millions." John Milton, for instance, among poets, Michelangelo in the department of art, and Sir Isaac Newton in that of philosophy. "Here is still *man*, but in such unwonted proportions that he seems to have assimilated for his production the human elements of an age, and to have given to the race a new conception of the stupendous powers of their own nature. But let the same nature be engrafted into the SECOND MAN, a stock of immeasurably greater excellence than its native one, and developed by all the chosen agencies of Omnipotent love, and what might not be predicated of its future?"

Man is made for God. His nature is eminently receptive, and especially adapted to receive Divine communications. And these native indications of his high destiny are found to agree with mysterious hints, scattered up and down through the Scriptures, like lights gleaming in the midst of darkness from the streets and battlements of some great city, indistinctly revealing its lofty situation and wide extent.

This very nature in the Person of Christ occupies a status above all principalities and powers, and every name that is named. It is uplifted to the topmost throne of the universe. And in some unknown way the church is to be associated with Christ, "sitting down with Him on His throne." For the church is Christ's Bride, His Companion and Consort, His complement and Fullness. Is it not in allusion to this He says, "The glory Thou hast given Me I have given them"? "To him that overcometh will I grant to sit with Me in My throne, even as I also overcame, and am set down with My Father in His throne." Let us now turn to the Title,

SEED OF THE WOMAN (Gen. 3:15). "I will put enmity between thee and the woman, and between her Seed and thy see. It shall bruise thy head, and thou shalt bruise His heel." Thus spoke the Divine Voice to the tempter immediately after the sin of our first parents. The Adversary of man was here told, that though he had induced Eve to accept his friendship and place herself under his guidance, the mischievous compact between himself and the seduced one should be immediately broken. "I will put enmity into her heart against thee— she shall become thy foe forthwith." Did not this involve an express promise of her personal conversion to God? Enmity also "between her seed and thy seed." Was not this a virtual promise that she should have descendants like-minded with her converted self? And that there should always be a seed to serve God upon the earth? Although Satan would have his seed—his party too—"the children of the wicked one," yet he was not to have it all his own way; I will raise up a godly seed who shall oppose thee and thy interests. Then there comes a sudden change—"It shall bruise thy head." Who is this Mighty IT here spoken of— this Illustrious One among Eve's descendants? Who but "the Lord Zebaoth's Son, He and no other one"? A great Protagonist to fight against and destroy man's antagonist is here promised.

And this was spoken in the hearing of the two transgressors. Poor trembling penitents! What a balm must the hope thus implied have been to their crushed hearts, when watering their steps with bitter tears, they went forth to encounter the toil and sorrow, the thorns and thistles of the outer world. No more were they to hear the "Voice of the Lord walking in the garden in the cool of the day," nor hold happy converse with angel visitants. No more, at the noontide hour, would they pluck their daily repast from clustering festoons of delicious fruit, nor lie down at night in Eden's amaranthine bowers, fearless alike of noxious reptile or evil beast. Henceforth they must eat their bread in the sweat of their brow; and everywhere meet that dreaded thing, the curse; and, some day, encounter that unknown phantom, death. But, courage! poor mourners! There is a Deliverer promised, a Champion who shall do more than avenge your cruel wrongs—much more. However long the race may have to wait for His coming, come He will and lift His restored ones to a height of glory far above the earthly paradise you have lost. Stay yourselves on this great promise, dim and mysterious indeed in its terms, but sure and certain in its fulfillment.

But so eager is the mother of mankind to embrace the Messiah, the Promised SEED who shall retrieve the mischief she had done, that, in the birth of her firstborn, she seems to have thought she had the fulfilled prediction. "I have gotten the Man from the Lord," she exclaimed. Alas! how misplaced was her exultation over that beautiful, artless, smiling babe! How bitter her disappointment when her darling, her firstborn, as he grew up, gave unmistakable indications of the passion, and pride, and envy, which should afterwards culminate in the murder of his brother!

Age after age rolled away, and still the vision tarried. But the faith of the patriarchs, those gray fathers of the world, was firm and strong, as they looked forward "over the gloomy hills of darkness." And, however it might have wavered, never did faith completely fail from among men till it was announced, The Shiloh is come! But we who live in this state of history of redemption, know much more than they, of this promised Seed, this glorious Champion, and of the nature of His struggle.

We know, for instance, that His was a lifelong conflict. It lasted thirty years and more. For "in all points He was tempted as we are," in childhood, in youth, in riper years. But through all He was more than a Conqueror. But just as in our own history there are times when temptation rages, and we are tried to the utmost verge of endurance, so was it with this Seed of the Woman. Three grand onsets did Apollyon make, in each of which he was signally foiled. The first was

In the desert of Judea. With insolent effrontery the Devil said, "Prove that you are the Messiah by turning stones into bread. Or do something still more wonderful; work a brilliant miracle by leaping from the top of the temple. Or win all the kingdoms of the world at one stroke by a single act of homage to the prince of this world." But the Second Adam did not swerve one hair's breadth from His allegiance. He would wait His Father's pleasure, and reach His crown through the appointed paths of sorrow and death. And herein, let me pause to observe, He is our Great Example. For this is the drift of all Satan's temptations, to whomsoever addressed, "Seek your own selfish interest, your own will, your own way. Do just what pleases yourself, without regard to the will of God." Watch, therefore, continually, against this subtle self-will, which can only be overcome by prayer and the sword of the Spirit. The second great assault recorded was

In the Garden of Gethsemane. "There," writes one, "beneath the cold moonlit olives, with eighteen long hours of shame and mortal agony before Him, there fell on Him a 'sore amazement.' He wrestled with it, but it threw Him on the earth. He prayed; He prayed more earnestly; He wept; He cried aloud in His agony; like blood drops His sweat fell upon the earth; till, after three several spasms of conflict, an angel came at length to strengthen Him." But who can comprehend the sore amazement and exceeding sorrow that came upon Him in that hour of the power of darkness? It is a quite imaginable mystery of suffering. We can but stand and gaze, and think how terrible the conflict which He is waging for our salvation. We hear His exceeding bitter cry, and "wonder and sorrow sit silent on our tongues." For the nature, both of the conflict and the victory, are only obscurely hinted to us by the thrice repeated prayer, "Father, if it be possible, let this cup pass from me—nevertheless not My will but Thine be done."—But the third great crisis of the battle was

On the Cross; where, by death, He destroyed him that had the power of death, that is, the devil. Then was brought to pass the saying, Thou shalt bruise his heel. So far the devil seemed to triumph—but *only seemed.* For *that* death was the appointed means of our redemption, the one effectual oblation and atonement for our sins, and the price of our ransom. Bitterly did the Adversary rue his supposed triumph. In that very moment he is made to lick the dust. His *"head is bruised."* His crafty device recoils on himself. The death he had brought about by means of the "wicked hands" of Jew and Roman, will be death and destruction to himself and his cause.

And his head is still being "bruised." When his Conqueror ascended up on high, He led captivity captive. When He poured out His Spirit on the day of Pentecost, the kingdom of darkness was shaken to its center. And He is taking the prey from the mighty day by day continually. "Whenever," says Dr. Vaughan, "one of us, grieved with the burden of his sins, comes to Christ for salvation; whenever one of us, feeling the yoke of some evil habit or wicked temper, kneels down before God and asks Him for Christ's sake to forgive and cleanse him; and when in answer to this prayer he is set free, gradually—tardily it may be— but really, and at last completely; then does Christ conquer Satan and 'bruise his head'; and then is the saying again verified, 'I beheld Satan as lightning fall from heaven.' and again, 'There was war in heaven; Michael and His angels fought against the dragon; and the dragon fought and his angels, and prevailed not.' " And the time draws nigh when the dragon's Great Conqueror shall lay hold on him, and bind him with a chain, and cast him into the bottomless pit. And then the joyful note shall echo round the globe, "Now is come salvation and strength, and the kingdom of God and the power of His Christ; for the accuser of the brethren is cast out."

The prophecy, traced in such dim outline before our first parents, became more plain in the age of the Hebrew patriarchs. Jacob, on his deathbed, uttered these remarkable words, "The scepter shall not depart from Judah, nor a lawgiver from between his feet, until there shall come the

SHILOH; and unto Him shall the gathering of the people be" (Gen. 49:10). Understand that the word in this passage translated "Scepter," does not necessarily imply royalty. It may mean a shepherd's staff, or a rod of authority and judgment. And the institution of the chief council of seventy judges, which, by Jethro's advice, Moses first appointed in the wilderness, seemed to have survived through many changes, among the descendants of Judah, till the end of their history. For we find it, with Caiaphas at its head, condemning their Shiloh to death. And since, as we have said before, all authority among the Jews ceased with their dispersion, either Jesus Christ was the Shiloh, or there never will be one.

But we are concerned now, not with proving that Christ is He, but with the meaning of this Title, and the nature of the work that it implies. The term is understood to mean the *Giver of Peace* or Rest. Most applicable indeed to Him Whose well-known words are ever ringing in the ears of all who know the gospel—"Come unto Me and I will give you rest." And what is the rest which He gives? Is it an earthly rest? Ah no. He is constantly driving us from that, as the greatest impediment that can be to the rest He loves to impart. As well might one try to build a house on the heaving waves of ocean, as expect to find rest from earthly sources.

"One night, ages ago," writes a popular author, "a fire broke out in an American wilderness. A spark dropped on dry leaves. The lighted leaves flew before the wind. The flames raced along the ground and glanced from tree to tree, till all the forest was ablaze, and night was turned into a terrible day. Certain Indians, driven out of their hunting grounds by the red storm, fled for their lives. Hour after Hour they ran until, half dead with fatigue, they reached a noble river. They forded it, and after scaling the opposite bank, their chief struck his tent pole into the ground, threw himself on the cool turf, and cried, *Alabama!*— here we may rest. But the land was claimed by hostile tribes. And so it came to pass that, having escaped the fury of the fire, they perished from the cruelty of man; and where they looked for the still delight of a home, found but the quiet of a grave. Let this tradition," he adds, "serve as a parable. Earth has no Alabama for the soul. Chased from refuge to refuge, the fugitives from trouble often say, as they reach the shelter of some cherished hope, Here may we rest! But God says, No! and sends the stern angel of calamity to wake them up with the cry, 'Arise ye and depart, for this is not your rest.'"

And yet there *is* rest for us while in the world, though it is not at all *from* the world: "*In Me* ye shall have peace." "*We who have believed* do enter into rest." It is thus, and not otherwise. And men may toil, and travel, and delve, and dig, till doomsday, but they will never change this order of things. There is no rest anywhere, nor ever will be, but under the Friendly Wings of our Great SHILOH.

> Heart broken and weary, whoe'er thou may'st be,
> There are no words like these words for comforting thee—
> When sorrows come round thee like waves of the sea,
> The Savior says, lovingly, Come unto Me.
>
> I will walk thro' the world with these words on my heart,
> Through sorrow or sin they shall never depart,

> And, when dying, I hope He will whisper to me,
> "I have loved thee and saved thee—Come, sinner, to Me."

And they who come to Christ shall find, even in this world, His rest to be glorious. Yes, the man has rest who can say, "Now I have found the true secret of happiness and no longer chase shadows; I have found the real way to righteousness and no longer vainly seek it by the deeds of the law; I have found the only way to holiness and no longer labor for it in my own strength; I have found the right road to heaven and inquire no longer, "What shall I do to be saved?" Has not he rest who can say all this? "Surely," says Bishop Hopkins, "his soul must be brimful of brave thoughts that is able to refresh himself with this meditation: God is my Father; Christ, my Elder Brother, is to be my Judge; the Holy Ghost is my Comforter; the Angels are my attendants; all the creatures mine for use; the world is mine own; heaven my home. God is always with me, before me, within me, overseeing me; I talk with Him in prayer; He speaks to me in His Word—sure, if these be our accustomed thoughts, we cannot but have rest."

It may not be, it is not, a rest without any conflict while the Christian remains here—but still a real rest it is. The soldier rests between arduous marches and fierce engagements and after painful victories, though still in an enemy's country. The artificer rests and rejoices as he sees his work daily growing under his hands, though it is still far from completion. The traveler often rests and is refreshed as he is still making his way to his loved but far distant home. Something like this is the rest of the Christian. Faith assures him that the promise on which he relies is true—Hope looks forward to the full enjoyment of the things promised—while Love rejoices in such foretastes as it already receives of future bliss. But the rest is in proportion to faith. "Thou wilt keep him in perfect peace whose mind is stayed on Thee, because he trusteth in Thee."

"To Him the gathering of the people shall be." "I, if I be lifted up, will draw all men unto Me." It was for this the Son of the Blessed became the Seed of the Woman, even that He might "gather together in One, the people of God that are scattered abroad." He has gathered great hosts already; He is still gathering every hour, and will pursue His great work, till all the world shall come beneath His shadow, and prove His rest to be glorious.

But *gathering* suggests *separation*. The fisherman draws his net to the shore, examines what he has gathered, and, retaining only the good, throws the bad away. The husbandman gathers his harvest, but carefully separates the wheat from the tares and the chaff. The merchantman seeking goodly pearls, from his gathered stock of gems carefully eliminates the counterfeits of glass and paste. So is it in the SHILOH'S gathering. "Many are called but few chosen." There are "the sons of God comparable to find gold," and there is "the reprobate silver which the Lord hath rejected." There are some of whom He says, "They shall be

Mine in the day when I make up My jewels." And there are others, "abominable and unbelieving," whom He will cast into outer darkness with the refuse of creation. The day will declare it. But your own position in relation to the SHILOH, you can ascertain *now*. Let each one ask himself, Am I among the gathered ones? Have I responded to His call, and found rest under the shelter of His outspread wings? How are you to know? Ask another question, How do I feel towards Him? Is He a hard Master whom I serve grudgingly, and whose claims I would rather evade? Or, penetrated with feelings of gratitude and love, do I gladly wear His yoke, and make it my meat and drink to please Him?

Let me recall to your recollection a well-known passage in the life of Doddridge. He had made an earnest effort to effect the deliverance of a convict, who, he believed, was innocent of the crime laid to his charge, but who had been condemned to an ignominious death. When the doctor went to see him after having procured the reprieve, the grateful man, overwhelmed with his emotions, fell at his feet and poured out heartfelt expressions of gratitude; declaring that "every drop of blood in his body thanked his deliverer, and that all his future life should be entirely at the service of him who had so generously exerted himself to save him from death."

Or let me remind you of another incident which, it is likely, may not be unfamiliar. A colored woman was exposed for sale in a South American slave market—an atrocious thing happily now impossible, for slavery, that "sum of all villainies," is abolished throughout the States. Bathed in tears and trembling with fear, she was seen by a benevolent stranger, whose sympathies were immediately awakened. He paid the price demanded, and at once prepared papers of manumission and gave them to her, telling her that she was free. Scarcely able to realize such an unexpected deliverance she still followed him. Again she was told she was at liberty to go whither she would, for her purchaser had relinquished all claim upon her services. But she refused to leave him. "Nay, but I will follow him wherever he goes. I shall only be too happy to be permitted to serve him. He has redeemed me!" she cried, "and saved me from a condition worse than death." And serve her deliverer she would; and she continued to do so, faithfully and devotedly, "to hoar hairs."

Now do we feel like this towards the SHILOH? What is a deliverance from slavery, or a reprieve from temporal death, compared with redemption and pardon through the blood of Christ, and life eternal? Oh may we all believe the love He hath towards us, and grasping the offered grace say, "Every drop of my blood thanks Thee, O Thou loving Redeemer! henceforth I am Thine."

> Now, my Savior, Thine I am;
> Now I give Thee back Thine own;
> Freedom, friends, and health, and fame,

Consecrate to Thee alone.
Thine I live, thrice happy I—
Happier still when Thine I die.

For still, what is the peace that the most favored ones enjoy, as the gift of Jesus Christ in this world, compared with their future blessedness? The true and final rest is up yonder, where a vast gathered throng of blessed ones cluster around their Great Shiloh, and sing His praise, Who hath "redeemed them out of every kindred, and nation, and people, and tongue"; and so filled them with joy, and perfected them in holiness, that not one desire remains ungratified.

47

Savior. Scapegoat. Sacrifice. Surety.

WHEN the Bible was translated into Eskimo, the missionary was somewhat puzzled by the word *Savior*. He could find no term in the language to represent it. How was he to get over the difficulty? One day it occurred to him to ask the people, whether they were not sometimes overtaken with storms while out fishing. "O dear yes," they answered.

"And you have been sometimes in great danger?"

"Yes, very often."

"But has it ever happened to some of you to fall into the water and to owe your safety to some brother or friend who has stretched out his hand to help you?"

"Yes," they said, "again and again."

"Then, what do you call that friend?" Immediately they named a term by which such a helper would be distinguished. And as promptly, the translator seized on the word, and wrote it against the title Savior wherever it occurs in holy writ. And was he not right? Such a deliverer was a Savior, in a high sense, and the word by which he was designated was as fitting a term as they were likely to find, by which to point out Him who is the

SAVIOR of all men (1 Tim. 4:10); "even Jesus, Who delivered us from the wrath to come." Flavel relates a story from Plutarch of the emancipation, by Titus Flaminius, of multitudes of Grecian slaves from long bondage under cruel oppressors. He sent a herald to explain the condition of their freedom. Upon him they so crowded, in their eagerness to hear the proclamation, that he was almost crushed to death. At first they could hardly believe their ears; and when they were assured, they were almost frantic with joy. They rent the air with their shouts, so that the very birds flew about scared with the uproar, which resounded on all sides. "A Savior!" they vociferated from one side of the camp. "A Savior! A Savior!" was re-echoed from the other. And throughout the rest of the day, and far into the night, those emancipated captives, with instruments of music, danced round his tent, and with songs of praise extolled their generous liberator to the skies. And all must confess that Flaminius did really deserve the title awarded to him by acclamation, in thus presenting liberty to the captives.

A notable Savior too was Joseph, whom Pharaoh made ruler over all the land of Egypt. But for his wise precautions during the seven years of plenty, famine would have desolated the whole country, as well as surrounding districts. And, whether the name by which Pharaoh called him, Zaphnath-paaneah, means, as some say, Revealer of Secrets, or Savior of the land, as others say, it comes to the same thing. For by means of the secret that he received from God, he saved the people from destruction. So he was their Savior.

But neither of these Saviors sacrificed himself in saving others, as did our Great SAVIOR. And the work they accomplished was confined to this world. The life and liberty conveyed did not at all affect the soul; did not extend beyond the term of this moral life. But He Whom we call SAVIOR breaks for us the yoke of Satan and sin, gives liberty to the spirit, and imparts eternal life.

Doubtless it is a noble thing to draw a drowning man out of the wave, and lift him into a place of safety. And it is a rare act of munificence, indeed, to give liberty to a multitude of despairing captives and send them back to their homes. And still a greater thing, so to order the affairs of a great nation as to save it from famine and death. But what a SAVIOR is He who rescues myriads from the depths of hell, and raises them to the heights of heaven! If *they* deserve to be hailed as Saviors who are great benefactors—if they deserve the most extravagant praise which their grateful admirers can lavish upon them—what adequate praises can we offer to our Great SAVIOR Jesus Christ? Ah! words fail; thoughts fail. We feel we never shall, and never can, do justice to *this* SAVIOR and His glorious work. We sometimes try now to sing His praise; we hope to do better when we get to heaven. But heaven's highest praises will be far too mean to set forth the greatness of the glory of His mighty acts. And this we shall realize still more deeply when, "with yonder sacred throng," we shall sing, "Worthy is the Lamb that was slain to receive power, and riches, and wisdom, and strength, and honor, and glory, and blessing."

But must we remain silent because our words fall infinitely short of the lofty theme? No so. For it is written, "One generation shall praise Thy works to another; they shall abundantly utter the memory of Thy great goodness, and talk of Thy power." So, however imperfect our words must needs be, let us proceed to say,

First. Jesus Christ is an *Efficient* SAVIOR. There is a beautiful amplification of this Title in Hebrews 5:9, "Author of Eternal Salvation unto all them that obey Him." We have referred to this before (see page ???). But as it opens up a mine of wealth, the depths of which we can never fathom, let us return to it again for a moment. The word Author, in this place, means a Causer, an Effector. As applied to Christ, it implies not only that He is *able* to save, that He *offers* to save, *begins* to save, but that he actually *does* save—carries out His purpose to a definite issue, brings the performance to a triumphant conclusion. "Ah," says one, "that is just the Savior I want; but I see it applies only to them that obey Him." But what then do you take that to mean? Salvation by works? That would be salvation in name only; a mockery; not a reality. We are saved not for obedience, but unto obedience. And *till we are saved* we can render no acceptable service at all. Therefore we add,

Second. Jesus Christ is a *Gratuitous* SAVIOR. We readily own there is something for you to do at the very threshold, if doing it may be called. Would you enter into life? Then understand, "This is the work of God, that you believe on Him Whom He hath sent." "This is His commandment." And it is obedience to this law of faith that gives access into a state of salvation. Call it a *condition* if you will, for without it you cannot be saved. But beware of attaching the slightest idea of merit or efficiency to it. For faith is but the empty hand of the beggar stretched forth to take a free gift. But then forget not,

Third. Jesus Christ is a *Holy* SAVIOR. "Obey" has still a further reference. All those to whom He is the Author of Salvation, He trains to loyal obedience. This is an essential part of the Salvation itself. "HE gave Himself for us, that He might redeem us from all iniquity, and *purify us to Himself.*" All who are justified are predestined to be conformed to His image. This is the Salvation. It consists in being turned from rebellion to allegiance, from enmity to loving service, from death in trespasses to life in obedience.

Fourth. Jesus Christ is a *Most Munificent* SAVIOR. Indeed, from first to last this Salvation is characterized by profuseness, affluence. There is a lavish expenditure of grace and love in it. See it as it emanates from the Father. When Absalom killed his brother Amnon, he fled from his father's anger, and remained in exile three years. At the instance of the wise woman of Tekoa (prompted by Joab), David relented thus far, "Let him return to his house, but let him not see my face." So for two years he dwelt at Jerusalem, and saw not the king's face. But beyond that there was no infliction of penalty. Surely this was mercy; for had he not deserved the murderer's death?

Suppose now God had dealt with us in a way somewhat after this pattern, and, remitting the extreme punishment, had only enjoined, Let not man see My face nor dwell where I dwell. Who can say there would not have been much mercy in this? If the angels had been consulted as to what had best be done in the direction of mercy, would their suggestions have risen higher? But how infinitely below what God has actually done! "Who is a God like unto Thee?" Who could have conceived such "plenteousness of mercy"? He sent His Only Begotten Son to die for us. It is an Infinite Gift! But in the exuberance of His grace He has added to it this Gift also, His co-equal Spirit to dwell in our unworthy hearts. The first is the promised Consolation of Israel. And the second is "another Comforter" equal in power and glory to the first.

But look at the munificence of the grace as it shines in the SAVIOR'S own share in the work. True, the Son was "Mighty to save." But what He did was not an achievement of mere Omnipotence, which commands and it is done; not a result which its Author could accomplish while still occupying in undisturbed tranquility His throne of glory. There were legal obstacles to be disposed of which would only be met by self-sacrifice. So, though He was rich, yet for our sakes, He became poor. Though He was "with God," One of the Sacred Three, yet He stooped to be numbered with transgressors. Though He was adored and served by holy angels, yet He encountered, in its most repulsive and violent forms, the despite of the wicked. And though He was the Prince of Life, yet He underwent the suffering of death, and became an inmate of the grave.

Fifth. Jesus Christ is an *Everlasting* SAVIOR. Eternal salvation is what you are to reckon upon, and that on His express authority. The work once really begun He never abandons. It is "the hireling," He says, "whose own the sheep are not," Not the Shepherd, who leaves his sheep to be scattered and lost. "I give unto My sheep eternal life, and they shall never perish." An incompetent pilot might run the vessel on the rocks. A faithless guide might betray the wanderer, who had confided himself to his care, into mischief. But we should be better taught than to distrust the Author of Eternal Salvation for a moment, or to think it possible for Him not to keep inviolate those interests which we have committed to Him on His express warrant.

What Jesus Christ confers upon us as our SAVIOR may be thus summed up. Forgiveness, Righteousness, Holiness. Victory over all evil, and perfect Blessedness in heaven at last. These five particulars we propose to illustrate by several Titles and Symbols. The first by SCAPEGOAT and SACRIFICE; the second by SURETY; the third by SANCTIFICATION; the fourth by STRENGTH; the fifth by SALVATION. The first that claims our attention is "SCAPEGOAT."

SCAPEGOAT (Lev. 16:26). Upon the grand Day of Atonement, amidst many impressive solemnities, two goats were led to the door of the tabernacle. One of these was appointed by lot to be slain in sacrifice, and the other to be sent forth alive, and abandoned among the mountains of the desert. Upon the head of this *Scapegoat*, as it was called, Aaron laid both his hands, confessing the guilt of the congregation; thus imputing it, as it were, to this innocent victim. Immediately after which expressive ceremony, it was led by the hands of a fit man into the wilderness, and left to its fate. What can be the meaning of that mysterious observance? Some would have the Scapegoat to be a type of the resurrection, but the application seems very doubtful. And some maintain that the devoted animal was killed by lightning, as a type of the sword of justice plunged into the heart of the sinner's Substitute. But the Scriptures nowhere say what became of the goat.

Was it not rather intended to teach that, after all their sufferings, satisfaction for sin was not yet secured, nor the true expiation as yet discovered? So the sin-bearing victim was committed to God to deal with. No one ever knew what became of it. Their sin was confessed to God, and pardoned, on the ground of some provision that was still in obscurity. For the observance seemed to say, Though the sacrifice is slain, the sin is not finally disposed of. Though carried away, indeed, so as to relieve the conscience and no longer obstruct the favor of God, it is still deposited *somewhere*, to be dealt with hereafter as God shall see fit. And did it not accumulate from age to age, placed to His account on Whom God did in the fullness of time lay the iniquity of us all (see Heb. 9:15), and Who, by one offering forever, did "make an end of sin" and perfect them that are sanctified? Let us, then, having just glanced at this mysterious type, turn to the great Antitype, who has at once fulfilled and explained the dim and shadowy Symbol.

SACRIFICE (Eph. 5:2). His whole life was SACRIFICE, while for three and thirty years He continued to forego His Divine Majesty, and to make Himself of no reputation. Born into the world a helpless Babe, and placed side by side with the defiled and the guilty, He both shared their sufferings and the shame that belonged to their fallen condition. In this SACRIFICE, He laid all upon the altar. "He pleased not Himself." He surrendered His will to His Father, accepting all that was prescribed, even to the extent of an ignominious and cruel death.

The agony in the garden was scarcely over, the midnight silence had but just now been broken by the sighs and prayers of the Holy Sufferer, and the celestial whispers of an angelic comforter—when, suddenly, the tread of a vulgar rabble was heard in the sacred enclosure. They came with "lanterns, torches, and weapons," headed by the traitor, Judas. To them He quietly yielded Himself to be led through the streets as a malefactor, knowing all that awaited Him. "He was brought as a lamb to the slaughter, and as a sheep before her shearers is dumb, so He opened not His mouth."

At the hour of early dawn the members of the Jewish Council, summoned on special business, were seen hurrying through the silent city towards the house of the High Priest. The "special business" was not as judges to *try*, but as enemies to *murder* the accused One under the forms of law. For, in their dark murderous hearts, sentence against Him had been pronounced long ago. "In His humiliation His judgment was taken away."

Then came the atrocious accusation, and the false swearing, and the hasty consultation, and the shameful indignities heaped upon Him by the servants of the house—all endured with unruffled forbearance. He turned not aside, "but gave His back to the smiters and His cheeks to them that plucked off the hair; He hid not His face from shame and spitting."

> Sinners did bind the Almighty's hands,
> And spit in their Creator's face!

And onward, from that hour till the moment of His death in the afternoon, He endured every sort of mockery and cruelty that the imagination of brutal men could devise.

"Behold Him," says a well-known graphic writer, "handed over to men of blood and stripped of His raiment! His wasted form—for it is He who speaks in the prophet's words, 'I may tell all my bones, they look and stare upon Me'—moves no pity. No more His meek and patient looks. They tie Him to a post. They plow long furrows on His back. And then cruel work is followed by more cruel sport. Laughing at the lucky thought, His guards summon all the band, and hurry off their faint and bleeding prisoner to some spacious hall. The expression may seem coarse, but it is true—they make game of the Lord of glory! And when the shocking play is at its height, what a sight there to any disciple who should venture to look in! Mute and meek, Jesus sits in the hall a spectacle of woe; an old purple robe on His bleeding back; in His hand a reed; and on His head a wreath, not of laurel but of thorns; while the blood, trickling down from many wounds over His face, falls on a breast that is heaving with a sea of storms. Angels look on, fixed with astonishment; devils stand back, amazed to see themselves outdone. While all around His sacred Person the brutal crowd swells and surges. They jibe; they jeer; they laugh; some, in bitter mockery, bend the knee, as to imperial Caesar; while others, to give variety to their hellish sport, pluck the reed from His unresisting hand, and beat the thorns deep into His brows. And ever and anon they join in wild chorus, making the hall ring to the cry, 'Hail! King of the Jews!'"

And then, in that one short sentence, "they crucified Him," what untold agony is implied! It was the most dreadful of all the torturing deaths that the Satanic cruelty of man has devised, and it was reserved for the most degraded criminals. But from no extremity of agony and dishonor and mental distress would our loving Savior shrink, that was necessary to perfect the SACRIFICE, and render adequate the expiation to justice which was demanded by our sins. "It pleased the Lord to bruise Him."

If, when encountered in some quiet home, and amidst the soothing attentions of friends, death sometimes brings with it strange bewilderment, and mysterious depressions, and pangs unknown; what must be the dire disorder of the nerves, the racking distress of the brain, the fever and excitement, which attend such a death as this? Oh, we know not! Whatever it was, the illustrious Sufferer encountered it all; not accepting even the poor relief that the narcotic drug offered in deadening sensibility to suffering.

And while He hangs there, nothing is wanting to fill to overflowing the cup of shame and grief. Reproachful taunts and bitter revilings continue to be hurled at Him by the crowd which surged around the cross—till their cowardly consciences are alarmed, and their blasphemies are silenced, by the deepening gloom of a supernatural darkness which settles down upon the solemn scene. But there are sufferings deeper than the eye can see. With wonder and awe, we hear from the lips of the dying Savior those mysterious words, "My God, My God, why hast Thou forsaken Me?"

In this wonderful death of Jesus Christ what have we? An Example to show us how to die? Yes, the greatest and most perfect that ever was. But much more than an example. What have we then? A Martyrdom? Yes, the most wonderful, and self-denying, and noble that ever was, or ever will be. But much more than martyrdom. As in life He stood alone the only Sinless One, so in death He suffered alone as never man suffered, the only SACRIFICE and Propitiation for sin. Or whence the contrast between the dreadful darkness that shrouded His holy soul, and the joy that has filled to overflowing the spirit of may a martyr, in the very extremity of torture? *They, conscious of sin,* yet exulting in the Father's favor. *He, never having failed* in a single instance, yet uttering the mournful, bitter cry, "My God! why hast Thou forsaken Me?" Ah! Do you not know? Is not the answer plain? Take it in Scripture phrase; "It pleased the Lord to bruise Him.—He hath put Him to grief.—He made His soul an offering for sin.—The chastisement of our peace was upon Him.—He gave Himself for us."

And thus is consummated the great Sacrifice by which the High Priest makes an end of sin. Now the veil of the temple is rent in twain. The way into the holiest is laid open. The mysteries of the Hebrew worship are explained and fulfilled. The priests may be disbanded; the altar may be overturned, and the victims cease to bleed. There remaineth no more sacrifice for sin—

> For Christ, the Heavenly Lamb,
> Takes all our guilt away;
> A Sacrifice of nobler name
> And richer blood than they.

But there is more than this in it. Let us look further into the great mystery of godliness, in our contemplation of Jesus Christ as our

SURETY (Heb. 7:22). What is a Surety? One who undertakes to pay another's debt; or who pledges his own character, possessions, or life, to secure another man's liberty or life. *Surety* is another name for *Substitute*.

There is a famous story, very ancient, and well-known to every schoolboy, which will, (perhaps all the better for being old and familiar), serve a little to illustrate this subject. There were two friends at Syracuse, one of whom, being condemned to death, obtained permission to bid farewell to his kindred and settle his affairs, on condition that he should provide a Surety who would undertake to suffer death in his stead, if he should fail to return at the time appointed. I need scarcely say that no such boon would have been granted, but that the thing was deemed impossible. But the accused one, Damon, had a dear friend, Pythias, who gladly undertook the service, and released him from prison. The day of execution arrived, but Damon had not returned. The hour appointed was about to strike but still he came not. The faithful Surety rejoiced at the prospect of becoming his friend's Substitute, whose life, he affirmed, was far more important than his own; and who, he was quite sure, was only prevented from honorably fulfilling his engagement by some insurmountable obstacle.

But things did not proceed to that extremity. Just at the last moment, a great stir was observed in the outermost verge of the huge crowd of persons assembled to see the execution. A shout was heard. Proceedings were arrested. And soon Damon rushed through the crowd and threw himself into the arms of his friend. Their embraces were so cordial and affectionate—the one rejoicing at having arrived in time to save his Substitute, the other lamenting that he had not been permitted to die for his friend—that the tyrant who had condemned Damon to death, and who had come to witness the execution, was overcome with surprise and admiration. So that he not only reversed the sentence but loaded the devoted pair with honors.

A Surety, you see, is much the same as a Substitute. And it is just in this capacity that Jesus Christ undertakes our cause, and consents to bear our sins, and endure the chastisement of our peace. And by that SACRIFICE of Himself, pardon is secured to all who accept the offered grace.

But we have said justification is something more than pardon. When a father forgives a disobedient son, what does that forgiveness do? It places him just where he was before, certainly no higher. But (as we understand it) the justification that Christ confers, lifts the sinner into a far higher state than he occupied before. God does not deal with him merely on the footing of forgiveness, that is, as if he had never sinned; but, as if he had performed some highly meritorious work—which indeed in *the person of his* SURETY he has—and because he is clothed in that SURETY'S righteousness, he is invested with a title to a glorious inheritance. He is an heir of God, a joint heir with Christ. For Jesus Christ imparts to the redeemed all that belongs to His own Sonship and His own Lordship, which they are capable of receiving. "The glory which Thou gavest Me I have given them."

And see by what high and sacred principles of Righteousness all this is characterized. Suppose now (to refer to the illustration we used just now) Damon had never returned, then his friend Pythias must have been put to death because he had assumed his place. And as the latter undertook the Suretiship voluntarily, the execution of Pythias, supposing the sentence to have been a just one, would have been a public homage to justice. Again, suppose Damon had returned, but too late to save his friend's life, and the king had executed him too, would not every one have exclaimed at the gross injustice?

And, if we may illustrate such a grand and holy transaction by such feeble and unworthy types, so it will be seen that the sinner's salvation rests on the firm footing of justice. God, having appointed and accepted the SURETISHIP of our Lord, will not, cannot punish those who comply with His will in availing themselves of the gracious provision. Yea, rather, He will not only forgive and justify, but delight to load with honor and rewards, those who trust in Christ, for the dear sake of His own Son Who died for them. So that, if, by-and-by, you who believe in Him should meet some lofty angel on the plains of heaven, who shall ask you by what right you tread those holy precincts, you may answer, "Heavenly Sir, know that I am here by a right that none in the universe can challenge. My title to be an inhabitant of heaven, and a member of God's royal family, is the Righteousness of your Lord and mine."

Have you received the atonement? Without this faith there can be no reconciliation with God; and without reconciliation, no holiness and without holiness, no heaven. This is the law of the kingdom.

48

Sanctification. Strength. Salvation.

LAST Sunday we were inquiring a little into what Christ does for us, answerable to the title SAVIOR; and we found that He procures pardon, as our SACRIFICE, bearing our sins in His slain body, like the *Victim*-goat on the great day of expiation; and bearing them away, like the *Scapegoat*, into the land of forgetfulness. Further, that He became our SURETY and Substitute, paying our debts, that we might shine in His righteousness forever. Let us pass on now to observe, that to whom He is "made righteousness," He is also made

SANCTIFICATION (1 Cor. 1:30). And much we need it. We must be renewed and made holy, as well as be forgiven, or heaven will be no heaven to us. It is a very melancholy picture that which the Holy Scripture draws of fallen human nature—your nature and mine. Shall I recall to your recollection a few of its faithful but humbling words? "The Lord looked down from heaven,"—and what does He see? this—"that there is none righteous, no not one!" "All have sinned and come short of the glory of God," are "dead in trespasses and sins," and "enemies in their minds by wicked works"—"all the imaginations of man's heart being only evil continually." Again, it is written, "The heart is deceitful above all things and desperately wicked." Therefore, it is plain, we "must be born again."

Have you ever considered these and similar statements of the Bible? And has your conscience ever whispered, All this is true? I also want a new heart. I must be renewed in the spirit of my mind, or where God is I never can go. And has that conviction driven you to your knees with the cry, "Create in me a clean heart, O God, and renew a right spirit within me"?

Know, then, that you are not to be justified in one way, and sanctified in another—justified by faith, and made holy by your own efforts. No; it is all of faith from beginning to end. You must believe in Christ for holiness as well as for pardon. Our Lord taught Nicodemus these important truths, in simple and forcible language, when, having described the inward change, which he as well as we must experience, He went on to show him the way in which we are to realize this holy transformation. And what is the way? "As Moses lifted up the ser-

446

pent in the wilderness, so must the Son of Man be lifted up, that whosoever believeth in Him might not perish but have everlasting life." The Hebrews were dying of the serpent bite, and they were to be healed simply by faith in God's own provision. We also must take this course. We die—we *are* dead. Yet, not so dead, but that we are called upon to look to God's Dear Son, as crucified for us, that we may have life and holiness and health.

This do, then, and thou shalt live. This continue to do, and thou shalt have life more abundantly. Watch, pray, study the Scriptures, avoid bad company, keep close to the worship of God, do justly, love mercy, give alms. Oh yes, all that—but not that alone. Faith is the great Sanctifier because faith it is which takes hold of Christ, as "made of God, SANCTIFICATION." Closely connected with this is the next head, for it is He Who communicates to us power for all needful purposes, Who gives grace to live and grace to die. He is the

STRENGTH OF ISRAEL (1 Sam. 15:29). What can be done without strength? Go to yonder poor invalid, and ask him at what price he estimates strength. Perhaps he rises from his bed with difficulty, and when he is up he can scarcely crawl from one room to another. And all day he is ready to faint at every fresh exertion. Oh, strength to him is beyond all price! It is with a mixture of wonder and envy that he sees those who have strength wasting it on trifling objects. Now, all God's people are in a spiritual sense "invalids." Their strength is small and they are apt to faint in the day of adversity. And nothing affords them greater encouragement than the assurance that "He giveth power to the faint, and to them that have no might He increaseth strength."

The marginal reference in Isaiah 40:31 is very suggestive. Read "*change* their strength" for "*renew* their strength." Suppose it were possible for some poor invalid to make such an exchange physically, and to receive into his impoverished frame all the imparted strength peculiar to some vigorous man in the full glory of perfect health. How gladly would the feeble one throw aside his own debilitated power in order to clothe himself with this tenfold might! And with this new-found energy what feats could he not accomplish? Before, it seemed huge labor to drag himself a mile. Now he boldly undertakes thirty miles a day. It was toil enough before to walk along the levels. But now he can scale mountains with the agility of a young roe. His feet are like hinds' feet, and nothing daunts him.

Spiritualize this; and is it not the very thing intended in the passage above referred to? To "rejoice in Christ Jesus and to have no confidence in the flesh" is the badge of a Christian. What does that mean but that he has thrown aside his native strength, and now trusts in the strength of another, even the everlasting Strength of Jehovah? That he takes hold of that Strength so as to make it his own; that he says to "the Strong Lord," Be Thou my Arm every morning, my Salvation also in the time of trouble.

And is not this the very thing Christ proposes when He says, "Abide in Me and I in you?" The very thing affirmed by the Scottish maiden, when, fastened to her stake a good way below high watermark (and having already witnessed the death of a fellow martyr), she calmly awaited the stifling wave that should end her own life; and to the taunts of her persecutors answered, "Think you that we are the sufferers? No. It is Christ in us—He Who sendeth us not a warfare at our own charges." And is it not the very thing Paul claims, when he says, "I live, yet not I, but Christ liveth in me"? And again, "I labored more abundantly than they all; and yet it was not I that did it, it was the grace of Christ." This is Paul's own account of his secret.

And the most instructive biographies must surely be those which are penned by the subjects of them—autobiographies we call them—for "who knoweth the things of a man save the spirit of a man which is in him?" When another writes the history, he may depict ever so correctly the outward actions, but he must often conjecture the motives that prompted, and the feelings that accompanied, those actions. But when a man writes the history of his own life, if he be a true man at all, those hidden springs are thrown open to our view. For instance, we read the biographical notices of Paul in the Acts of the Apostles, and we are charmed with the invincible perseverance and unquenchable ardor displayed. But if we would gain an insight into the principles that guided him, the motives that fired him, and the power that sustained him, we must refer to his own statements in the Epistles. We are thankful that he felt himself constrained by circumstances, as well as guided by the Holy Spirit, to lay open so much of his inner experience; and especially to speak so often of that which was the life of his life and the soul of his religion, namely, the divine element, the supernatural impulse which wrought within him, and sustained him throughout the whole of his wonderful history; and which we need as much as he, in the duties and difficulties which fall to our lot.

There is a passage in Philippians 4 which has been unspeakable dear to the saints in all ages, and which, in many an overwhelming trouble, has led them directly to the only SOURCE OF STRENGTH. When the Protector, Oliver Cromwell, lost his favorite daughter by death, the paternal heart of the grand old soldier was quite overwhelmed. He bade his attendant read that memorable chapter, Philippians the fourth. At the eleventh verse, "I have learned in whatsoever state I am, therewith to be content," he interrupted the reader with the remark, "It is true, Paul, *you* have learned this—but what shall I do? It is a hard lesson for me to take out—truly I find it so." But the thirteenth verse was read, "I can do all things through Christ Who strengtheneth me." These words re-animated his drooping faith. Christ's Omnipotence was felt within his soul. His heart found consolation, and he exclaimed, "Yes, I see it, I feel it; HE THAT WAS PAUL'S CHRIST IS MY CHRIST TOO."

And only they who can enter into the spirit of these words are able to perform duties or endure afflictions in a right spirit; or, in truth, to offer any acceptable service to God. See that aged pilgrim bending under the weight of years, and having to carry the heavy cross of poverty besides. He would have fainted long ago, had he not known where to go for Strength to sustain him in life's long and weary journey. Next door to him there dwells another, not so old, indeed, or quite so poor, but his cross is not less galling, for he is wasted with long sickness and worn with pain. He must have greater Strength than his own wherewith to meet this constant pressure, or he would quickly give way to impatience, and cry out, "O Lord, take away my life for me, for it is better to die than to live," yet he is tranquil and happy in the midst of his greatest sufferings, for underneath are the everlasting arms. Look again, and consider yonder harassed soldier of Christ wrestling with some master passion, some hard besetting sin. He would soon give place to the devil, and fall to rise no more, if power to maintain the arduous conflict did not continue to flow into his exhausted spirit, from Jesus Christ the great SOURCE OF STRENGTH.

And, if you are a follower of Jesus, you too are a soldier, hewing your way through opposing forces. The most dangerous of them all is that sinful self of yours, with its corrupt inclinations and appetites. If you could but rid your souls of these, there would not be much fear of such as are marshaled under the other two great leaders, the world and the devil. For it is the existence of these traitors within that gives to the external foes all their advantage. But the conflict will be a lifelong one; for thus the Scriptures describe it, "The flesh lusteth against the spirit, and the spirit against the flesh, and these are contrary one to the other."

Now, there are many wrong ways of fighting, but there is only one right way. In striving for the mastery, you must strive lawfully, or you will not prevail. Would you be strong? It must be "in the Lord and in the power of His might"; for His Strength is made perfect in weakness. To attempt the battle in one's own strength is a too common mistake, and leads only to discouragement.

> Too strong I was to conquer sin
>   When 'gainst it first I turn'd my face,
> Nor knew my want of power within,
>   Nor knew th' omnipotence of grace.
> In nature's strength I fought in vain
>   For what my God refused to give;
> I could not thus the mastery gain,
>   Or lord of all my passions live.

Again, some have thought to root up this sinful nature altogether and so get rid of the uncomfortable strife at a blow. And, for a time, they have deemed themselves successful; and have gone on their way bravely, supposing they had left all their enemies dead on the battlefield. Alas! it was a vain imagination, as they soon found out. All at once, perhaps in some unguarded moment, those slain foes came to life gain, and stood on their feet and confronted them, as bold and mischievous as ever; and the battle had to be fought over again, and every inch of ground reconquered. But that was not the Scriptural method. You cannot thus eradicate the evil from your nature, and become as holy as an angel at once; be your efforts ever so determined, or your faith ever so strong. There is a more excellent way; a way wherein you shall "strive lawfully," and therefore successfully, against your dreaded foe.

Hast thou a new nature implanted within? Do you hate all sin, and long to be delivered from it; yet still find that when you would do good, evil is present with you, always present? Now, instead of measuring swords with the old nature, and thus striving to beat it down, your endeavor must be to get the new nature fortified and fed, by ever fresh supplies from Christ the STRENGTH OF ISRAEL. It is through the Spirit, Whom He sends in answer to prayer, that you must mortify the deeds of the body; and only as the new nature thus grows strong will you be able to counteract and tread down the motion of sin within.

Let me quote here the words of another in illustration of this. "Sanctification does not mean mending the old nature which we inherit from Adam; it is cultivating and developing the new nature which we receive from Christ. The old nature cannot be improved; it is under a ban and a curse; it is to be crucified with its affections and lusts, and mortified in its members. We are to put it off as we put off a worn-out and defiled garment. Pride will never be humble, lust will never be pure, and selfishness will never think of a neighbor's interest, envy will never exult in a neighbor's joy. The only thing to be done is to turn out these tenants by bringing in others stronger than they, who will, little by little, get the mastery over them. The way to conquer pride is to cultivate humility; and if we would be gentle, we must practice self-control, and thus the old affections must be expelled by new."

Wherefore, then, poor, weary, wrestling soul, dost thou waste thyself in sighs and groans? "Oh," thou sayest, "those evil imaginations, those busy thoughts that rush to and fro, those wrong inclinations which struggle for the victory, do all threaten to destroy me. I bid them begone, but they will not go. I cry out against them, but they mock my prayers; they are too strong for me, I cannot manage them. For, though I renounce them, and pray against them ever so earnestly, there they are still; and there also is the discouraging consciousness that they are rooted in my very nature, and the disheartening fear that I shall never surmount them."

Courage, poor struggler! Thou canst not manage them nor conquer them? No! As well stop the revolution of a planet. But have faith in the STRENGTH OF ISRAEL. He can do it for thee, and He will. Go tell all to Him Who is manifested to destroy the works of the devil. He Who has made ten thousand thousand fainting, but still fighting, souls more than conquerors will help thee. Fear not, thou worm Jacob. Get thy new nature constantly reinforced by waiting on Christ. Wait, I say, on the Lord and He shall strengthen Thy heart, and enable thee to "tread upon the lion and adder, and trample underfoot the young lion and the dragon."

An instructive writer says, "One of the most fatal things in the conflict of faith is discouragement, and one of the most helpful is cheerfulness. We should *expect* to conquer. This is why the Lord says so often to Joshua, 'Be strong and of a good courage. Be not afraid, neither be thou dismayed. Only be strong and very courageous.' The power of temptation lies in the fainting of our hearts. Satan knows this well, and he always begins his assaults by discouraging us, if he can any way accomplish it."

The first thing, Christian wrestler, is to make up your mind, once for all, that you are not able to keep yourself from falling. The next is, to throw yourself resolutely and unconditionally on Him, of Whom it is expressly said, "He is able to keep us from falling." Devolve the responsibility entirely on Him as your STRENGTH, and see if He will not "hold up your goings in His paths, that your footsteps slip not."

Thus then there is Strength to be had, Strength wherewith to meet the greatest pressure in life; so that none need faint or abandon the conflict in despair. But someone says, "Death is before us also. Is there Strength to be had for that solemn hour?" Yes—

> Death cannot make our souls afraid,
>   If God be with us there;
> We may walk through her darkest shade,
>   And never yield to fear.

> Thanks be to God, there is no death
>   For them that trust His word!
> Thanks be to God for victory,
>   Through Jesus Christ our Lord!

> Instead of death's appalling frown,
>   The saints shall see the face
> Of Christ arrayed in smiles of love,
>   And rest in His embrace.

A Christian sat by the deathbed of his friend, and seeing him so long getting through the narrow portal, he was distressed for him, and said, "Brother, how hard it is to die!" Upon which the other, almost in the moment of dissolution, replied, "Oh no, no! easy dying—blessed dying—glorious dying!" And glancing at the timepiece he added, "I have enjoyed more happiness in dying two hours this day, than in my whole life! It is worth a whole life to have such an end as this. I have long desired that I might glorify God in my death, but oh! I never thought that such a poor worm as I could come to such a glorious death."

I was reading the other day of a young man who uttered such words as these in the presence of death, "I find now that the gospel is no delusion. My hopes are well founded. Eye hath not seen, ear hath not heard, the heart cannot conceive the glory I shall shortly partake of. Read your Bible; I shall need mine no more. Oh, can this be dying? My body seems no longer to belong to my soul. It appears only as a curtain that covers it, and which will soon drop off and set me at liberty. I rejoice to feel my bodily powers give way, for it tells me I shall shortly be with my Savior in glory."

And why did these meet death so calmly, so gladly? Because the Strength of Israel had despoiled Death of his sting, and thus in fact, "abolished death." "Then," you ask, "need none be afraid of death, since his sting is gone, and his power to wound is abolished?—is this what you mean?" Not exactly. The sting of death is sin; that is, one's own sin, not another's. Understand that your own sin it is which puts the sting into death's hands. You never thought of it, but you have been lengthening that sting, and strengthening it, and sharpening it all your life long. What then are you to do? Why, believe in the Lord Jesus Christ, and He will manage the matter for you. He will take away the sting, which Death hath in reserve for you, and enable you to say, "Thanks be to God who giveth us the victory through our Lord Jesus Christ." And you will be able to meet death with composure, or even with joy, as others have before you, and to say, "The Lord is my Strength and my Song, and is become my Salvation."

SALVATION (Ps. 118:14). Salvation is a wonderful word, full of the richest and most comprehensive meaning. It includes all that we have been speaking of, and much more. It is a great thing for the rebel to be pardoned—for the ungodly to be pronounced righteous—for the unclean to be renewed and sanctified—for the weak to be strengthened for all the exigencies of life and death. All this is grand and glorious. But there is much more beyond, of which those who die in the Lord gain a glimpse, and the sight makes them glad to die. The great Savior carries His salvation work to a glorious completeness. Ascending the typical ladder, which Jacob saw, we go from strength to strength, from one glory to another. We can trace the lower steps, but the top is lost in dazzling brightness. To have the last remaining spot and stain of sin finally removed from the spirit, so

as to be without fault, even before God—to enjoy the society of the blessed forever, beyond the reach of all storms and temptations—to live in the immediate
presence of our glorious Lord with exceeding joy, so as to feel that beauty and
blessedness of such a state is our proper home!—it is so grand a destiny that we
only seem as those who dream, when we try to grasp, and much more when we
try to utter, the idea of an experience so exalted.

> Oh bliss too great to be conceived
> By such as dwell in this low scene!
> But yet with joy to be believed,
> Despite its high transcendent sheen.

> How beautiful, with open face,
> Thy countenance, O God, to see:
> Thy wondrous attributes to trace,
> And be absorbed alone in Thee!

> To see Thy face without a cloud!
> Untired to gaze, nor shrink o'erawed,
> Nor want a veil between, t' enshroud
> The dazzling brightness of the Lord!

But, revealed in Scripture, there is an advance even beyond that; a great increase of glory at the resurrection of the body, without which the salvation is still
incomplete. But, as it makes the eye to ache that tires to gaze on the sun, so it
seems to strain the mind to search too curiously into that radiant future. "It doth
not yet appear what we shall be, for when we shall see Him, we shall be like Him,
for we shall see Him as He is." We will not, then, pursue our too adventurous
flight, but descend to seize some practical lessons, before we close this address.

1. *Consider the infinite danger of neglecting so great a Salvation.* If on a certain
day we had stood upon the banks of the Niagara, we might have seen a sight that
would have thrilled us with horror, and forever have lived in our remembrance.
Just above the place where the vast volume of water leaps over the rocks in two
stupendous cataracts, a canoe was seen gliding down the river. Swifter and swifter
was its motion. Was it empty? Nay, an Indian is soon made out, stretched at full
length in the bottom of the shallow boat. The bystanders, appalled by the danger, and quite incapable of affording him any help, shout their loudest with the
hope of waking him, that he may at least make one vigorous effort to turn the
boat out of the fatal current. In vain! Onward the little bark drifts with increasing acceleration, bearing its living freight, all unconscious to his doom. And soon
it nears the brink. Suddenly, the Indian is aroused by the terrific roar of the
cataract, now close at hand, and springing to his feet, seizes his paddle and stands

erect. One startled glance reveals all in a moment; and the next, paralyzed with terror, he shoots over the glassy edge into the seething abyss below.

Is it not just thus, that multitudes suffer themselves to be carried down life's rapid stream towards the eternal state, resisting, if not resenting, all attempts to arouse them till actually arrested by the hand of death? And then, o then! if he poor affrighted soul could but secure one week, or only one day, before the fatal plunge, "to wash away her sins and fit her for her passage!" But it cannot be. The hand of fate is on the curtain *now*. The dying lips are parted, and the doleful words are gasped out, "It is too late! too late!" There is one last sigh and all is over. The soul is wrecked.

Are you neglecting the great salvation that we have been endeavoring to unfold? The conduct of some of you makes it only too plain. But you do not mean to die without repentance, do you? "Oh no; that is far enough from our intention." Beware! or these delays will bring at last a fate infinitely worse than that of the sleeping Indian on the rapids of Niagara.

2. *Consider, Salvation, from first to last, rests on the atoning work of the Lamb of God.* In every land, and in every age, men have felt the want of some expiation on the ground of which they might secure reconciliation with the supreme Being, from Whom they have felt themselves alienated. Many strange and expensive devices have been invented to supply this craving of the conscience. But in none of them has the human heart found rest. This deep and universal want is only satisfied in Jesus Christ, and cordial faith in the atonement lies at the root of all true religion, all peace and holiness here, and blessedness hereafter.

"I have been in great trouble this morning," said an old warrior who was sick and blind, to John Williams the missionary, "in great trouble, but I am happy now. I saw a mighty mountain with steep sides, up which I tried to climb. But when I had reached a great height, I lost my hold and fell to the bottom. Weary and overcome with grief, I went to a distance, and sat down to weep. And while I was weeping I saw a drop of blood fall upon the mountain, and, in a moment, it was dissolved."

"That was a strange sight," said Williams; "what meaning do you attach to it?"

"That great mountain," answered the old man, "was my sins. And that which fell upon it was one drop of the precious blood of Jesus Christ, by which the mountain of my guilt is melted away." He added, "My desire is to depart and be with Christ, which is far better than to remain longer in this sinful world."

The missionary was with him when he breathed his last. During the interview he quoted many precious passages of Scripture. And, having exclaimed with energy, "O death! where is thy sting?" his voice faltered, his eyes became fixed, his hands dropped, and his spirit departed to be with the Savior, one drop of Whose blood had melted away the mountain of his guilt.

Our subject today, and last Sunday, has been the work and worth of Christ as a Savior. "Unto you is born this day in the city of David a Savior Who is Christ the Lord." That was the announcement that the angel made to the shepherds. And his words straightway awoke the music of heaven. For immediately there was heard in the air the exultant song of a multitude of the heavenly host—"Glory to God in the highest; on earth peace and good-will to men." And well might they sing thus. For this Savior came to secure pardon for rebels by becoming a Sacrifice for them—to justify the ungodly by becoming their Surety and Substitute—and to be the Sanctification, Strength, and Salvation of all who receive Him. "Look unto Me and be ye saved, all the ends of the earth."

49

Teacher. Truth. True God and Eternal Life. Treasure. Testator.

I THINK it was Lady Glenorchy who once remarked that she was under great ob-
ligations to the letter *M*. For if it had been the law that *not Any*, instead of *not
Many*, noble are called, she would have been passed by. But the letter *M* changed
the whole case in her favor, and so she found herself included among the "not
many," of noble birth, who were followers of the lowly Jesus.

So it has been in every age. Only a few, one here and another there, scorned
by their peers and half ashamed to "come out and be separate," have confessed
Christ before the world. In the days of our Lord's ministry, only one "noble,"
one "rich," and one "wise" man are found among his followers; and the last two
of these "secretly for fear of the Jews."

The one wise man after the flesh, was Nicodemus, the Rabbi. We may suppose, that many a struggle might have occurred within his breast, before he
could at all make up his mind to seek an interview with the Carpenter of
Nazareth. At last, it may be, he said to himself, "Why should I hesitate any longer?
I am resolved to shake off this fear of man, and go, let the consequences be what
they may." Let us watch him, as he proceeds to carry out his resolution. No
sooner does he reach the outside of his gate, than the great Doctor Famaliel
salutes him, and courteously offers to walk a little way with him. Very perplexing! But, such is his profound respect for his learned brother, he cannot decline
his company. So they walk on together till their brief talk comes to an end, and
the renowned Rabbi bids his friend farewell. Nicodemus keeps his eye on him
till he fairly turns the corner, and then resumes his way to the little street where
he had been told Jesus Christ lodged. But, just as he is about to cross the road,
whom should he espy, coming along, but Caiaphas the High Priest. "Oh," says
he to himself, "what shall I do now? He will surely suspect me." All the ruler's
good resolutions fail, and back he hies to his house, whispering as he goes, "Yes,
I see how it is; I am certainly observed—I had better not go till it gets dark." So
he bides his time. Presently the sun goes down. And when the city becomes so

wrapped in obscurity that a Rabbi can scarcely be distinguished from a beggar, he sets out afresh.

> The streets are silent. The dark houses seem
> Like sepulchers in which the sleepers lie
> Wrapped in their shrouds, and for the moment dead.
> The lamps are all extinguished; only one
> Burns steadily, and from the door its light
> Lies like a shining gate across the street.

It was as if the watchful Master were awaiting the timid inquirer. Before that door he pauses, and softly inquires, "Does the Prophet of Nazareth lodge here?" He is invited to enter, and then follows the memorable interview recorded in the third chapter of John; and that wonderful conversation, which will be read, and pondered, and discussed, and wondered over, as long as the world stands.

Just now we have only to do with the opening sentence of the conversation, "Rabbi! we know that thou art a Teacher sent from God," or rather the title by which he here salutes our Lord. But before we part Nicodemus, it is but just that we should remember to his credit, that, three years after this, in that hour of darkness and consternation when all the disciples usually in attendance on their Master were scattered, this one "wise" man, along with the one "rich" man, Joseph, the honorable counselor of Arimathea, both of whom had been His secret followers till that time, were not ashamed of their crucified Master, but with tender reverence took down His body from the cross and laid it in the garden sepulcher. And for that sacred service, devoutly and affectionately rendered to their Lord and ours, we feel that we each owe them, personally, an everlasting debt of gratitude. Let us now contemplate Christ as a

TEACHER (John 3:2). "A Teacher come from God." He is indeed the most wonderful of Teachers, whether we look at the things which He taught, or the method of His instruction, or the authority with which He spake, or the wonderful works whereby He authenticated His instructions. Well may He say of Himself, "The Lord God hath given Me the tongue of the learned, that I should know how to speak"; and well may they who heard Him, say, "Never man spake like this Man." What authority there is in His utterances! "I came from the bosom of the Father. As the Father gave Me commandment, so I speak. And the words are not Mine but His that sent Me."

And the condescension and simplicity of His teaching were equally remarkable. To render it suitable to the poor, and the ignorant, and to children even, His discourse is full of the most common and familiar illustrations. His similitudes were always near at hand, and were always such as could be easily understood. The housewife making bread, and mixing the leaven with it, was the type of his doctrine. The woman sweeping the room to find the lost piece of money, was a symbol of His own care to seek the sinner. The plate, well washed outside but dirty within, is made to convey a useful lesson on hypocrisy. A new patch in a worn out coat, a leaky bottle, a candlestick, children at play, wheat and tares, sheep and goats—these, and other common things, furnished all He wanted to convey the most important lessons into the minds, and fix them in the memories of His hearers.

No wonder that the fine ladies and gentlemen of that day, who prided themselves on their "culture," turned with disdain from such preaching, and "derided Him." No wonder at all if they even denounced it as vulgar and coarse! But "Wisdom is justified of her children." His own words show how He rejoiced in thus stopping to suit His lessons to the lowly: "Father, I thank Thee that Thou hast hid these things from the wise and prudent, and revealed them to babes." Indeed, a chief feature of His teaching was its adaptation to such. "The poor have the gospel preached to them," was His own statement. And it is noted by one who was a frequent if not constant hearer, "The common people heard Him gladly."

No doubt He uttered some things hard to be understood. But those truths that lie at the foundation, and are necessary to the right knowledge of the way of salvation, He would take care to state in terms not easily misunderstood by the ignorant and the unlearned. For instance, when He told His disciples that "He came to give His life a *Ransom* for many." He used that word, well knowing the meaning His simple hearers must needs attach to it. In His lips, it did not mean some very profound idea in reference to His atoning work, which could not be made out till the nineteenth century, when some wise men should arise to explain it to the wondering people. We prefer to think that this, and similar New Testament expressions, such as "bought with a price," "purchased," "redeemed," are intended to convey a meaning, much nearer to the idea which the common people connect with them, than that far-fetched signification which some in the present day have fastened upon them.

It may be conceded that there is infinitely more in such terms and the truths they symbolize, than ever *has been* made out, or ever *will be*. The mischief is, that the new explorer does not propose to *add* his marvelous discoveries to the accumulated stores of ages, but vaunts of them as worthy to supersede all that has gone before. Whereas, the fact is, each separate doctrine of revelation is like a vast mountain, which has its summit veiled in impenetrable clouds, and its roots buried deep down in the earth. And like the mountain, each truth is many sided, and we cannot see all its relations to other truths. We cannot get all around the great mountain, so as to survey it on every side. From where we stand, we can discern one small portion only, and that but dimly and imperfectly. Our neighbor's standpoint is not quite the same as ours, and thence, it may be, he sees the same truth in a different aspect. Yet, though his way of stating his impressions may not exactly tally with ours, it does not follow that he is wrong, and we are right. The divergence may arise from the imperfect and partial degree of acquaintance which both are able to attain, with the subject in dispute. Nor do we forget that we have the promise, that what we see of truth we shall see rightly, if we yield our minds unbiased to the Great TEACHER sent from God. Of course it must be on that condition. But alas! where is there an unbiased mind? Are not all warped, on one side or the other, by subtle, undetected prejudices of education or feeling? Hence our conceited notions and endless disputes. We must be "converted and become as little children," ere we can enter into the right understanding of the mysteries of the kingdom. Such "babes" will be more in sympathy with Christ's meaning than the "wise and prudent." But to get back to our subject—

The Great TEACHER taught by *deeds* as well as *words*. His every act was a lesson, a sermon. "When He healed the sick," observes a continental author, "when He unstopped the deaf ear, and opened the blind eye, what was it but an intimation, too plain to be misunderstood, that men must come to Him for the cure of their spiritual maladies; must look to Him to uncover the inward ear, and enlighten the dark understanding? And when He cast out unclean spirits, what an emphatic testimony it was that He had come to destroy the works of the devil, in a higher sense, and in every form in which he ensnares and destroys mankind."

Great Rabbi! we know Thou art a TEACHER come from God; for not only no man can *do* the things that Thou doest, but no man can *reveal* the things that Thou revealest, except God be with him! Questions, about which philosophy had been at sea for thousands of years, were solved by Him in a few words. "He uttered things kept secret from the foundation of the world." He has unveiled the unseen world to our wondering gaze, and brought life and immortality to light. He has taught us all that it concerns us to know—indeed, all we ever shall know, on earth—of His Father and ours, and how we are to please Him—of the holy angels—of the future judgment—of death, and heaven, and hell. And on all His words we can place the firmest reliance, as truth, infallible, unadulterated truth. He is the Amen, the Faithful and True Witness; or, as He calls Himself, the

TRUTH (John 14:6). I am the TRUTH. It is as if He were to say, I do not so much tell you the Truth, as present Myself to you as the very TRUTH itself. I AM THE TRUTH.

Truth may be contrasted with Types. What is a Type? It is the shadow of a coming Truth projected before it. It is a fact designed to prepare the way for something greater than itself, and to be a voucher for it as brought to pass by Divine wisdom and power. It may be a person, a thing, an event, a place, or an institution. But whatever it is, *it is designed to convey instruction relative to Christ and His Church.* Now Jesus Christ says:

I am the TRUTH of *all the Types*—the principal Antitype of all the mysterious things prescribed in the old law. They were only Shadows and Symbols. I am their ultimate Design, their Scope, the very Soul of them all. I am all that which they lead to and signify. They all find their center in ME, Who am the true Sacrifice, the only Altar, the proper priest, the real Mercy-seat, Tabernacle, and Holy Place.

I am the TRUTH of *all the Prophecies*—the Central Truth—their ordained Fulfillment. They all point to ME. I am Jacob's Shiloh—Isaiah's Tender Plant—Jeremiah's Branch of the Lord—Ezekiel's Plant of Renown—Haggai's Desire of Nations—and Malachi's Messenger of the Covenant. "The testimony of Jesus is the spirit of prophecy."

I am the TRUTH of *all Religion*—its Life and Substance. In harmony with this, He made Himself the whole subject of His preaching. "Beginning at Moses and all the prophets, He expounded in all the Scriptures the things concerning Himself." He proposed Himself as the only Door to heaven, the only Way to the Father; Himself, the Life by which they were to live; Himself, the Bread the were to eat. "Search the Scriptures," said He to the Jews. "You are right in thinking that therein is the secret of eternal life; but that is because they testify of Me. If you find not Me there, all else will be nothing. He only hath life who hath the Son."

But Who is this that claims to be not merely infallibly True, but THE TRUTH itself in the abstract? If He were other than God, might we not well say, Whom makest thou thyself? How can any but God know all Truth and be all Truth? Therefore, we wonder not that it is said of Him, This is the

TRUE GOD AND ETERNAL LIFE (1 John 5:20). He Himself complained that the Samaritans worshiped an unknown god. The True God they had not apprehended. No doubt this sounded very harsh and uncharitable. For did they not worship the God of Jacob? Indeed they professed to do that. But so transformed was He by their misrepresentations that Jesus Christ would not own him for the TRUE GOD at all, but pronounced this withering rebuke, Ye worship ye know not what. We wonder how many classes of religionists, tried by this rule, would be found to deserve similar condemnation, and upon the same ground, that what they worship is no God at all.

For instance: He whom the Moslems call Allah, they claim to be the patron of their violence, sloth, and impurity. Is that the TRUE GOD? Or do they "worship they know not what?" Again, He to whom the Papists build gorgeous temples, and offer the blasphemous sacrifice of the mass, expressly authorizes (so they allege) the sale of pardons, and indulgences in sin, for money; and He also sanctions their lying wonders and gross absurdities. Is that the TRUE GOD? Or are they also "worshiping they know not what"?

And what about the infidel's god? For most of them own a god of some sort. Can that be the TRUE GOD who, they assert, set creation a-going ages ago, as one would wind up a clock, and ever since that, has left the atoms to work themselves into fishes and birds and gorillas, till at last man luckily turned up? We are bound to add that this is very convenient god, for he takes no notice of men's actions. He is either too dignified or too easy-going for that. They may be as bad as they like, and indulge their appetites to any extent, he will never call them to account. Very like this is the god of multitudes of nominal Christians, the Pharisee, the lover of pleasure, the sentimentalist. He is not *quite* so indifferent as the last, but yet is "a god all mercy," and so indulgent that he would rather break his word than punish men for their sins. At any rate he will be quite content if people "pay everyone his own, and do the best they can."

Two friends were discussing the nature of God. One of them, for want of a better description, we will designate an orthodox believer; the other was what is called a Socinian. The latter argued against the Deity of Christ, and said, "Certainly, if it were true, it would have been expressed in the Bible in more unequivocal terms."

"Well," said the other, "suppose you believed in the doctrine, and were authorized to teach it in your own language, how would you express it so as to make it quite indisputable?"

"I would say expressly," replied the Socinian, "that Jesus is the True God."

"You are very happy," rejoined the other, "in the terms you have chosen. For you have hit upon just the very words used in the Bible, of the Son of God (John 5:20). This is the TRUE GOD AND ETERNAL LIFE.

Nor does this doctrine rest only on a few isolated passages such as this. It underlies the whole of Scripture from beginning to end. It is the cornerstone of revelation. Either the Socinian view is a mistaken one, or the Bible must be a gross imposture from beginning to end. The doctrine of Christ's Deity is the central sun of Christianity; without which the whole system of truth relating to the redemption of the world would fall into utter chaos. Adopt the Socinian system of interpretation, and every man will have to be his own savior, for Christ and the Holy Spirit have no place on the eternal throne.

We take leave to say that either the Unitarian must "worship he knows not what," or we are chargeable with that. For the contrast between his Christ and ours is quite irreconcilable; the difference between the two is immense, infinite. For let them invest the grandest created being imaginable with all the attributes possible to such a one; let them heap one imposing delineation on another, to any extent, and magnify all a million-fold, still there remains an infinite distance between that ideal being, grand as he is, and the Being of Beings.

Their Jesus, therefore, is altogether "another Jesus," (as Paul says), one quite incompetent to the discharge of the great work devolving upon him. For how can he fulfill his promise, "I give unto them eternal life?" He has it not to give. He is not eternal himself!—only in a dependent, subordinate sense, as we ourselves are.

We maintain, then, that the One Living God, the only Real and Actual God, is revealed nowhere but in the Scriptures. And that these most unequivocally teach that in the Eternal Godhead, not only the Father is God, but that Jesus Christ and the Holy Spirit are as truly and essentially God as the Father.

This Jesus then, of Whom we make our boast, is the TRUE GOD AND ETERNAL LIFE. TRUE—so that we may rely on all He says with absolute confidence. GOD—therefore abundantly able to do all He engages to do. He can give unto us ETERNAL LIFE, for He IS ETERNAL LIFE. Mark the words.

He *is* ETERNAL LIFE. He does not merely give to us ETERNAL LIFE just as He gives us food and raiment, health and prosperity, homes and friends. These are often bestowed upon such as neither have, nor desire to have Himself at all. Only they have ETERNAL LIFE who have the Son Himself, the Fountain of that LIFE. Who are they? Those who believe in Him, and none beside. Such only are possessors of this life. And it is theirs because Christ Himself is theirs; and on no other ground (1 John 5:12).

Again we say, Search the Scriptures. In them ye rightly think ye have ETERNAL LIFE. They not only make it known, but actually *convey* the blessing. For if you use the Bible aright you will discover in it the TRUTH to be received; you will come into personal acquaintance with the TRUE GOD, the Lord and Giver of ETERNAL LIFE; and you will find out also that you have in it a will, a testament, made in your favor; a veritable title-deed which assures you of the possession of an Infinite TREASURE.

TREASURE (Matt. 13:44). In this chapter our Lord discourses concerning the "kingdom of heaven." And, amongst several illustrations, represents to us two men, hard at work. One is seeking goodly pearls, and attains at last the reward of his perseverance in the discovery of "one PEARL of Great Price." The other is digging in the field without expecting any such thing, and suddenly lights on a "hidden TREASURE."

Having, for the reasons assigned, inserted PEARL in our list of sacred Symbols, we are bound to include TREASURE, on the same grounds. Two classes of converts are here represented to us; both reaching the same result through very different experiences; and both showing equal eagerness in securing the prize when once discovered. There are some who find Christ and salvation, after many weary efforts and long and painful inquiries. They hear and read and pray, industriously seeking salvation, and resemble a man diving in search of pearls, who leaves no stone unturned in pursuit of the much-coveted prize. Or, rather, (if we adhere to the terms of the parable) such a one is like a trader, traveling from his distant home to some seaside district where divers play their adventurous occupation, and knocking at many a door inquiring everywhere who has pearls for sale. Others there are who seem to find Christ suddenly, almost without seeking; and even while in pursuit of some other object. These are suitably represented by the husbandman striking against big lumps of gold with his spade, while only intending to turn up clods of earth. Perhaps the former kind of conversion is the most usual in our day. But here is an instance of the latter.

A few years ago a superintendent of a mission school invited a young man to come to it. After some hesitation, in a careless and unconcerned mood, he went to see what sort of a thing this school might be; or, perhaps, more likely, just to pass away the time. Seating himself on a back form he looked on listlessly. By-and-by the children sang a hymn, beginning, "I fain would be an angel."

There was nothing very poetical in the verses; nothing very musical in the voices. But soon he became conscious of new and mysterious emotions heaving within his breast. And then the tears began to course each other down his cheeks. The Holy Spirit was striving within him. Deeply affected, he went home, locked himself in his room, and falling down on his knees prayed for mercy. And there, as he afterwards said, "I dedicated myself to God, and gave my heart and my all away to Him, forever. And, God be praised that ever I was invited to that Sunday school."

Thus, at a time when he thought of nothing so little, he found the TREASURE which was to enrich him to all eternity; and, like the fortunate finder in the parable, who, for joy thereof, sold all that he had and bought the field, this young man from that time counted all things but loss for the excellency of the knowledge of Christ. To this class of conversions belongs that of Saul of Tarsus, who found the Savior even in the act of breathing out threatenings against His followers. And, nearer our own day, that of Col. Gardiner, who was surprised into deep conviction of sin, and visited with a saving manifestation of Christ, when deliberately planning some opposite course of evil. Add to this the remarkable case of the man who went to hear Whitefield in Moorfields, his pockets filled with stones wherewith to pelt the preacher; but who, being arrested by his solemn appeals, emptied out the stones from his pockets and received the TREASURE into his heart. Let me name but one more instance of this kind; that of the youth who went to hear a sermon by Rowland Hill, thinking of nothing but the "fun" he might get out of it; and who, borne from the chapel in a fainting state, and under deep convictions, found a HIDDEN TREASURE in the message he had made so light of, and afterwards became, himself, an eminent minister of the gospel.

I have said the former manner of entrance on a religious life is the most usual, among such as know the joyful sound, and are acquainted with the gospel. They hear so much of the happiness connected with true religion that they resolve to seek it for themselves. They listen while the beauty and worth of the Savior are portrayed, till their desires are awakened, and they say, "Whither is thy Beloved gone, that we may seek Him with thee?" From that hour difficulties spring up which were not before dreamed of. Every possible device is attempted by their spiritual foes to divert them from the pursuit. Sometimes they are assaulted by impetuous temptations, sometimes stupefied by suggested doubts, sometimes pursued by terrors, sometimes plunged into dejection. Often tempted to give up their pursuit, and as often urged afresh by an inward impulse they cannot resist, months—years pass away, it may be, and still they have not found the PEARL. But let them take courage. Like Gad, "a troop may overcome them, but they shall overcome at the last." In some favored hour, Christ will reveal Himself, and the PEARL OF PRICE will be their own.

With still less instruction as to what they really wanted, some have long groped in the dark after relief; but persevering, have at length come upon the ONE PEARL, the HIDDEN TREASURE, which has in a spiritual sense "made their fortune" forever. Dr. Bushnell relates how Clement the Roman was harassed from his childhood by questions which paganism could not answer. Incessantly haunted by thoughts relating to his being—whence he came, and whither he was going—he resorted to the schools of the philosophers, but became more bewildered than ever. Then he resolved to visit Egypt, the land of mysteries, and seek some magician who could summon spirits from the other world, with the hope that thus he might be furnished with some certain truth. But, in this agitated, inquiring state, he heard of the Christian's gospel, and in that found the TREASURE he had so long sought sorrowing, and, with it, rest for his aching heart, and peace for his agonized conscience.

This TREASURE—what is it, but "Christ in us the hope of glory," though variously described in Scripture, because, along with Christ, the believer is endowed with all His unsearchable riches? For some particulars of the nature and preciousness of this TREASURE, the reader is referred to PEARL and PORTION; while we proceed to add here a few words on its inalienable security. Admire the pains God hath taken to satisfy the heirs of promise of the security of their possessions. And as you read, pause a moment to admire His infinite condescension too. Let me transpose into this page a sentence or two on this subject from an eminent writer. "In accommodating Himself to the weakness of human trust, what men are fain to exact from their treacherous fellowmen, *that* the Faithful and True

God deigns to offer them. For this Promiser to ratify His word by a sign, to exchange guarantees with men, or to bind Himself with an oath, means that He acts just as suspected human promisers are required to act. To concession so touching does the All-truthful descend, that it may become a little more easy for our suspicious hearts to place reliance on the words of His grace." Various are the terms by which the heirs of salvation are certified of the soundness of their title. Every method in use among men, to make possession certain, is quoted as a comparison. Men come into possession (1) *By Inheritance;* the title to which is indisputable, because founded on right of relationship or adoption. (2) *By Promise;* in which one pledges his honor to another. (3) *By Oath;* which is considered to make an end of all controversy. (4) *By Covenant;* which is an engagement, not spoken merely, but written, legally endorsed and sealed, and registered in the proper courts. And, once more, as if to exhaust all the illustrations the usages of men furnish, there is added to all this the figure of (5) *A Will or Testament.* And Christ is compared to a Testator.

TESTATOR; that is, one who, having bequeathed his property to his heirs by his Last Will, doth by his death cause that Will to have all the force of an unchangeable law (Heb. 9:16, 17). A Will is the heir's title-deed, which not only *describes* the nature of the property bequeathed, but actually *conveys* it to the recipient, and constitutes him the legal possessor of it. And provided the Will is duly signed and sealed, and proved to be genuine before the proper authorities, no one can ever after challenge his rights. In like manner, "the writings of Scripture contain the last dying Will and Testament of Jesus Christ, full of munificent legacies to sinners"; and thus are both the Conveyance and the Title-Deed by which he is put in legal possession of the unsearchable riches of Christ.

An Irish lad was one day going to school with a Bible under his arm. A priest met him, and asked him what he had there.

"A Will, sir," said the boy.

"What Will?" asked the priest.

"The last Will and Testament which Jesus Christ left to me, and all who believe."

"What did Christ leave you in that Will?"

"A kingdom, sir."

"A kingdom! Pray where is it?"

"It is the kingdom of heaven, sir."

"Heaven?—but will not everybody get there as well as you?"

"No, sir, none but those who claim their title to the kingdom, on the ground of the Will."

Just here the conversation abruptly ended, and the priest went on his way. But the boy's account of the matter may admit of further elucidation from another story. A tract distributor said to a poor man whom he found breaking stones on the roadside,

"There is a letter at your house from a very rich person, who has made a Will in your favor."

"What, sir!—a letter at my house!—a Will in my favor? Where did it come from?"

"It came from the Lord. It is a message from Him. The Will is the Will of the Lord Jesus."

"Well, who would have thought that the Bible was a Will? And you say, sir, that my name is in it?"

"Yes."

"Well, I'll go home and search till I find it."

"Do so, and you will soon see your name there; for your name is *Sinner;* and 'Christ Jesus came into the world to save sinners.' Search it well and you will find that salvation is yours, Christ is yours, all things are yours, if you do but believe."

Yes, let a man with humble faith take hold of this Testament or Covenant of Grace, and "it guarantees to him the friendship and assistance of heaven under all circumstances. It gives the soul a lien, a clear lawful hold on Omnipotence, if only he will dare in the abandonment of a childlike faith to reckon upon the fidelity of God."

TESTATOR! But does this comparison hold good in every respect? No. None of the resemblances of Christ do this. Along with one or more points of *likeness,* there are always many of *unlikeness.* For instance, when a Testator dies he loses all interest in his houses or goods. Nothing remains to him of all his former possessions but, it may be, a little square recess in the family vault. But the Divine TESTATOR *"was dead* and is alive again, and behold, He liveth forevermore." And therefore He is still Possessor of all things. But His riches are so exhaustless, that when all the many thousands of millions of His joint heirs are endowed, each with his portion, the great TESTATOR has as much left as before He distributed His riches. And all the heirs have an equal portion; for each has all! Profound riddles these, which it will take eternity to unravel. But again, an ordinary Testator, being himself (poor man!) dead and buried, must have executors, as they are terms, to carry his will into effect. But our glorious TESTATOR is His own Executor. Having made His Will binding by His death, He rises from the dead that He may carry out its provisions, and see that all the legatees have their large portion; even glory, honor, immortality, eternal life. So far doth the Symbol fall beneath what it is intended to illustrate. Wherein then is the resemblance?

1. Christ is like a TESTATOR because the things He gives are His own to dispose of, just as He pleases, for He is "Heir of all things." They are also His own by another title, for He purchased them.

2. Christ is like a TESTATOR, because His death makes His Testament effectual and irrevocable. This is the great point intended. It is confirmed by His death—"otherwise," it is added, "it would have no force at all."

3. Christ is like a TESTATOR, because He alone, and no other—neither pope, bishop, nor priest, prescribes the way whereby we become possessed of the Legacy—namely, by faith in Himself. Note this last observation well; for upon it everything turns. It has sometimes come to pass that a rich man has bequeathed all his property to some individual on one particular condition. In all other respects the grant was absolute, the title perfect, and the conveyance thoroughly secured. That one condition might be that the legatee should take the name of the Testator. But, whatever it was, upon this all is made to depend. Compliance in this one point makes his claim unquestionable, and puts him in possession; while non-compliance forfeits it forever.

So is it in this case. Christ and His salvation are mine, are yours, on one ground alone. He that believeth shall be saved, while he that believeth not shall be condemned. Come to Jesus Christ then. For, "to as many as receive Him, to them gives He power to become the sons of God, even to as many as believe on His Name." And let us adore Him for His wondrous love. For not only has He made over to us glorious gifts in His last Will and Testament, but He scrupled not to die, in order to make that Testament available. For "otherwise it would have been of no force at all."

> Sweet is the memory of His Name,
> Who blessed us in His Will;
> And to His Testament of grace
> Made his own life the seal.
>
> I call that Legacy my own
> Which Jesus did bequeath;
> 'Twas purchased with a dying groan,
> And ratified in death.

50

Tabernacle. Temple. Tender Plant. Tree of Life. Vine.

SUPPOSE a convert of the Apostolic age, in ignorance of human history since he left the world, were to resume the body, and come to England to inquire into the progress of the Christian religion. Let him come in all the freshness of impressions made upon him in connection with the ministry of such men as Paul and Timothy. How could he reconcile what he would witness in some so-called Christian churches with what he remembered of old? Looking round upon altars decorated with gay colors, and candles burning at midday, and priests arrayed in vestments of green, and gold, and violet, bowing before a cross, with clouds of incense curling over their heads—what could he make of it all? In profound perplexity he inquires of his conductor, "Where are we? What do you call this place?"

"A Christian church, ancient sir."

"This is a Christian church?"

"Yes, indeed, a most correct specimen, modeled after the antique pattern."

"And do you call this Christian worship?"

"Certainly, sir, the most approved and refined style of worship."

"What! this strange mixture of Jewish and Pagan ceremony?—But listen! I hear the name of Jesus pronounced! And surely, a well-remembered passage from the writings of holy Paul is being recited. But as for all this idolatrous ceremony—it is not Christianity at all. It is contrary alike to all Apostolic precept and the practice of the early church."

"Excuse me, sir, our priests affirm it to be the true primitive method of worship, long lost sight of in the church."

"Say rather the substitution of a counterfeit, imposed upon the people under the name of Christianity. It is a libel on our holy religion and an insult to the King of saints." Some such words would, we think, express the disgust of this ancient adherent of Christianity, on beholding so pitiable an exhibition. And what justification do they allege? Among other weak excuses for all their vain ceremony and gorgeous embroidery, it is urged that with such things the Hebrew fathers were wont to embellish the worship of God in their day. But suppose they did, what is that to the purpose? Surely there is a wide difference between what was appointed by God, and what is invented by man; between that which had a real meaning, and that which has no meaning at all except such as unauthorized fancies are pleased to imagine.

The law, with its shadows and ceremonies, came by Moses, and was of Divine authority; and yet God has expressly abolished the whole system, and the apostle had denounced it as made up of weak and beggarly elements; and why, but for this reason, that "grace and truth have now come by Jesus Christ," who is the reality and substance of all that the law prescribed. Surely then, if it would be impiety to revive rites which God has abolished, it is scarcely less to parody them by pitiful caricatures.

The most prominent object connected with Jewish worship as instituted by Moses, was, as you are aware, "the TABERNACLE."

TABERNACLE (Heb. 8:2; 9:11). And what was the TABERNACLE? I have lying before me at this moment a picture of it. It does not pretend to be taken from sketches drawn by some artist of that day; nor yet is it altogether a fancy picture, but one designed from the description contained in Exodus 26. It must be confessed, its outward aspect, with the exception of the rich hangings at the entrance, is not at all attractive. It is a long, gloomy-looking structure, not very high, covered all over with dark-colored skins. But it is all glorious within, for it is overlaid with sheets of pure gold. The unattractive exterior conceals a vast amount of costly workmanship. The value of the gold and silver alone, used in the building and its contents, estimated according to its weight, would be £200,000 and more of money in present use. Beneath the outward cover are three others. The innermost consists of hangings of fine-twined linen, fastened with clasps of gold. Over that is another set of hangings, curiously wrought of goats' hair; a sort of rich, thick damask it seems to have been, embroidered in needlework of blue, and purple, and scarlet. And then, to protect all these rich curtains from the weather, there is a covering of "rams' skins died red"; and lastly comes the outside coating of badgers' skins. And all is in strict accordance with a divine pattern, which God showed to Moses in the Mount. Well, such was the tabernacle. It was, what its name implies, a moveable house, a capacious tent. It was divided by a rich veil or curtain into two chambers; and the whole was so put together, that it could be easily taken to pieces, and removed and put up again elsewhere.

For, as the children of Israel were "to walk through the wilderness" for forty years, sojourning in tents, God condescended to set up His Tabernacle among them, that He might "walk with them" (Lev. 26:12; 2 Sam. 7:6). So, wherever they pitched their tents, that royal pavilion was reared in the center of the camp, a constant sign that the Lord of Hosts was with them. Not as though He could be enclosed in "temples made with hands," for the heaven of heavens cannot contain Him; but He condescended to afford them this familiar pledge of His constant presence. While over the Tabernacle there rose, hovering aloft in the air, a pillar of cloud, which in the dark night glowed like flames of fire. And within, there was the Shekinah, that mysterious "glory" which beamed from over the Mercy Seat, and illumined the Holy of Holies.

It may not be amiss just to remark, in passing, that though this structure is often spoken of as if it had been but a temporary building, made use of only for a short period, it existed for nearly 500 years, as the central place of sacrifices and sacred services. Removed more than once after the settlement in Canaan, and renewed or repaired from time to time, it had a longer duration than the first temple, which was subsequently reared at such an enormous cost by Solomon. For the latter had scarcely stood 400 years, when it was rifled, and finally burnt by Nebuchadnezzar. But to return—

Consider all that curiously wrought and costly structure, what was it but a representation of the incarnation of Christ? If not fully to the people of that day, yet is it truly so to us. For Paul calls Christ's human body "the true Tabernacle which the Lord pitched and not man." Nor is this metaphor used to express the sacred body of Christ alone. Peter speaks of his own body as his "tabernacle." And Paul calls our mortal frames, all of them, "tabernacles." They are tents, which will be taken down at death, and set up again at the resurrection. This being our state, Jesus Christ also would have a Tabernacle. "The children being partakers of flesh and blood, He likewise took part of the same." So He saith prophetically in the Psalms, "A body hast Thou prepared Me,"—"a body which could be taken down, and folded up for a season, and be erected again without the breaking or loss of any part of it." This sacred TABERNACLE was set up when Christ was born. Then it was "the Word was made flesh and dwelt among us," (or tabernacled, as the word is)—and in that human nature of His "all the fullness of the Godhead dwelt bodily."

And the contents of the Tabernacle were alike typical of heavenly things, and had reference to our Lord. The golden altar and censer were typical of His Intercession; the Mercy Seat, and what was in it, of His Priesthood; while the "veil" is expressly called "His flesh."

Much that we have said about the TABERNACLE belongs to the TEMPLE also, which was no less a type of the human nature of Christ. Both are also emblems of the Church of God; but with that we have not now to do. "Destroy this TEMPLE," said our Lord, "and I will rebuild it in three days." "But," it is added, "He spake of the TEMPLE of His body," and in Revelation 21 there occurs this wonderful passage—the seer is describing the new Jerusalem, and he says—"I saw no Temple therein, for the Lord Almighty and the Lamb are the TEMPLE thereof." We will therefore add a few words on this Symbol of Christ, the

TEMPLE (Rev. 21:22). Solomon's renowned Temple it is to which the allusion is made. It occupied several years in building; but it does not seem to have been so remarkable for its size, as for the amazing value and richness of its materials. Indeed, it would appear to have been the most costly building, by far, that was ever reared; many hundreds of millions of pounds (estimated by our standard) having been expended on it! There were tons upon tons of gold, and a still more enormous quantity of silver, and precious stones besides. The walls and doors were (not *gilded* but) lined with plates of solid gold; the very floors were covered with pure gold. There were costly marbles, white, black, and colored, brought from great distances; and countless cedars from Lebanon; and brass in such prodigious quantities, that no account was taken of the weight. This metal is supposed to have been (more correctly) bronze—a compound of tin and copper. And it is believed by some that the tin was imported in the ships of Solomon and Hiram, from the British Isles, and that Cornwall thus contributed its share to the wealth and splendor of that wonderful and unrivaled edifice. And such huge stones there were for the foundation, as quite confound all calculation as to the mode of transporting them; for some of these remain even to this day, and astonish every beholder. Perhaps the vast multitude of hands engaged in the works may help a little to solve the difficulty; for 150,000 laborers were employed to assist and wait upon 3,000 skilled artificers!

And as it was meant to be (equally with the Tabernacle) a Type of Christ, it was not left to man's wisdom to devise. The whole was fashioned, just as the more temporary building had been, according to a pattern prescribed by God Himself. This David delivered to Solomon, with these emphatic words, "God made me understand in writing, by His hand upon me, even all the works of this pattern" (1 Chr. 28:12–19).

Indeed the whole system of worship was appointed by the authoritative directions of God. The various sacrifices and offerings, and the ceremonial observances connected with them; the solemn feasts and the one annual fast; the materials and embellishment of the priestly robes; the form and composition of the sacred vessels, down to the very snuffers and tongs used for the lamps and altar fires, were all minutely prescribed—while the hymns used in the sanctuary services were composed by men inspired by the Spirit of God. After the lapse of many centuries, this most elaborate system waxed old, and soon after the coming of Christ, vanished altogether; being superseded by the more spiritual worship of Christianity, and the simpler ordinances prescribed in the new Testament. These consist of prayer, preaching, thanksgiving said and sung, baptism also and the Lord's supper, together with some general rules touching the ministry, officers, and discipline of the church. But minute and special directions, like those that ruled the worship of the Jewish Church, there are none.

In the days of the Apostles, therefore, the outside world, both Jews and Pagans, were startled at the strange sight of a religion that claimed to subsist without temples, or altars, or sacrifices; without images, vestments, or defined ritual of any kind—or priests even—except as the members of this new sect, both men and women, claimed to be alike "priests unto their God." As for masses, crucifixes, holy water, incense—these, with all the rest of Rome's unmeaning paraphernalia, have been invented since. So has much that pertains to the worship of purer communions. But God is not to be pleased with ceremonies and forms. He rather "seeketh such to worship Him" as will do so "in spirit and in truth."

But what our subject more immediately teaches us is that even those few ordinances that are peculiar to Christianity, are to cease "when that which is perfect is come." For John saith of the redeemed, perfected church in heaven, represented under the similitude of a resplendent city of gold and gems, "I saw no Temple therein, for the Lord Almighty and the Lamb are the TEMPLE thereof." Whatever that may men, it evidently points to a far more sublime and spiritual worship than anything the best can attain unto here; but what it is we shall not find out till we are fitted to enjoy it. Only until the first coming of Christ were the Hebrew institutions of worship intended to last. And the gospel ordinances will, in their turn, be abolished when Christ shall come "the second time, without sin, unto salvation." For "the saints in heaven shall want nothing, and therefore shall not need a house of prayer—they shall know perfectly, and therefore will not need any pulpit instructions—they shall always see Christ, and so will not need sacraments whereby to remember Him; 'I saw no Temple therein.' "—But we must not dismiss the subject without a glance at some other lessons which may be derived from it.

First. God's Sanctuary, whether Tabernacle or Temple, whichever was standing, was the appointed place to which all the sacrifices were to be brought; and that which was offered elsewhere was rejected. So all our praises, prayers, and offerings must be presented to God by Christ alone. And their labor is worse than lost who come to God through the virgin Mary, or angels, or saints, or who offer prayer to any but Himself.

Second. The Sanctuary was the place to which all that were in distress even when ever so far away, were to look, and towards which they were to pray. So must all the weary and sorrowful look to Christ alone for relief, even "from the ends of the earth."

Third. The Sanctuary was furnished with everything requisite for worship, and purification, and light. So all holy things are laid up in Christ, even everything that belongs to the life, instruction, and happiness of the soul; all we want for pardon, holiness, joy, and peace, are treasured up there. "Surely shall (every) one say, In the Lord have I righteousness and strength; even to Him shall men come; and in Him shall all the seed of Israel be justified, and shall glory" (Isa. 45:24, 25).

And now, let the vegetable world furnish us with our three next similitudes. The first, TENDER PLANT, comes from the forest. The second, TREE OF LIFE, has its origin in the garden of Eden. And the third is contributed by the vineyard. We will take them in order. He who is called "the Arm of the Lord," that is, the manifestation of His power, is said to grow up before Him as a "TENDER PLANT."

TENDER PLANT (Isa. 53:2). Fit symbol of the history of our Lord in its feeble beginnings and grand results. A similar metaphor occurs in Ezekiel 17, where the royal house of David is compared to a cedar of Lebanon, its highest branch representing King Jehoiachim. The came to the forest a great eagle, "long-winged" and of gorgeous plumage, who "cropped off the topmost twig and took it away." That is Nebuchadnezzar carrying the king captive to Babylon. Then mention is made of another topmost bough or sprout of the cedar, a TENDER ONE, which Jehovah will plant upon a high mountain, where it shall grow to "a GOODLY CEDAR, under the shadow of whose branches there shall dwell all fowl of every wing." None less than the Messiah can be intended in the latter part of this parable. Ezekiel's TENDER ONE is Isaiah's TENDER PLANT.

Now, of all trees, we think a Cedar might most suitably be used to set forth Christ's grandeur and unchangeableness. It is one of the greatest and most durable among the trees of the wood. There are Cedars now upon the Mountains of Lebanon, the stems of which measure forty feet and more in circumference. They are of wondrous antiquity too; some being calculated to be 4,000 years old. Look back and see our Lord's original condition as a little Child, reared amidst poverty and hardship, unknown or despised; and then think for a moment what He is now, enthroned far above every name that is named—and you will confess the beauty and force of this illustration—a topmost bough, "a TENDER ONE," planted on a bleak mountainside, and growing into a majestic CEDAR, affording shelter to birds of every wing. But referring the reader to what was said under the heads, BRANCH, ROOT OF DAVID, BABE, etc., for further illustration of this, we pass on to the next—"TREE OF LIFE."

TREE OF LIFE (Rev. 22:2). The Bible contains the history, in outline, of the human family from the creation day till doomsday. It begins with a Paradise, and ends with a Paradise. The first Paradise must have been a most enchanting spot. We think of it as a garden of vast extent, planted and arranged by God Himself; and richly furnished with everything desirable to render it an attractive abode for pure and intelligent beings. Behold the goodly land! There are murmuring rills making melodious music amidst sweet-scented flowers of every hue—limpid waters falling gracefully from terraces of many-colored rocks—rivers widening out into beautiful lakes, surrounded with gentle slopes or lofty hills—and stately woods and tangled foliage, varied with opening glades of verdant grass. And there are birds of rich plumage and melodious note, warbling in the branches of the trees, while the spotted leopard toys with the meek-eyed kid, or the majestic lion with the playful lamb, beneath their shadow. Every object teems with beauty, and every living thing seems to talk to us of innocence and peace.

But Satan comes upon the scene and all is lost! Yet not irretrievably. Behold Another, Stronger than he, advances to the rescue! The contest is long, and while it continues, ages roll their weary courses. But when the clouds clear away, the Seed of the Woman stands forth as the Conqueror, and we see His foe and ours cast into the bottomless pit. Then the lost Paradise reappears. Nay, not the same, but one infinitely better. So rich, so grand, so glorious, that no specific description is attempted. We get only a dim and momentary glimpse of its beauty by the aid of imagery borrowed from the first.

The TREE OF LIFE was a central object in the garden of Eden, where it was a *real* and material tree. And it reappears as one of the principal attractions of the heavenly Paradise, where it must be regarded as a *symbolical* tree, representative of truths most instructive and glorious. To us indeed the Tree in Eden is plainly typical. But whether it was so to our first parents, or, if so, to what extent, and in what direction, we are unable to say. Some think it was so, and that it did, in some way, set forth Jesus Christ to them. Of this we shall say nothing, because we know nothing. But about the TREE OF LIFE as a very beautiful type of the Lord Jesus to us, we will now endeavor to say a word or two.

Suppose this identical Tree were to be discovered, still flourishing in some secluded and hitherto inaccessible part of Asia. Or, if that is too much to imagine, one of the same species actually descended from the original stock—what should we expect to find in the Tree? Should we not be greatly disappointed if it were not remarkable for its *Beauty*? Or if in *Fragrance* it were outdone by the almond tree or the citron? It would cast around also, we think, a very reviving *Shadow;* and its *Fruit*, and *Leaves* too, we have made up our minds, must possess qualities eminently valuable. What it really was in all these respects we cannot tell. But we may certainly transfer these supposed qualities, divinely spiritualized and ennobled, to the real TREE OF LIFE, the Lord Jesus.

Speak we of *Beauty!* Oh how rare, how stately, how peerless is His loveliness! "He is the Chief among ten thousand, yea, He is Altogether Lovely,"—the Brightness of the Father's Glory.

> Sweet majesty and awful love,
> Sit smiling on His brow.

Or shall we make mention of *Fragrance!* His very name indicates it. He is Christ, the *Anointed One.* His name is therefore "as ointment poured forth." All the letters of His name, "all His garments smell of myrrh, aloes, and cassia"; the scent thereof is "as the wine of Lebanon." From Him is the oil of joy, which makes the Christian's face to shine; and the oil of frankincense and myrrh to render Him fragrant—acceptable to God and attractive to men. For they who have been with this Anointed One will betray it by the "good savor" of their lives, and the sweet odor of their piety.

And then how refreshing is the *Shadow* of this TREE OF TREES! They that dwell under it shall "revive as the corn and grow as the vine." Oh it is a rare TREE! Beautiful and Glorious, Excellent and Comely. Call its name Jehovah—jireh. Expect all things from it. Abandon all the other Trees of the wood. Some are like the fabled Upas trees, scattering death to all who come within their reach; and the others are but withering gourds; they can shelter there but for an hour. Come, dwell under the shadow of this "Goodly Cedar." He shall cover thee with His friendly branches while life lasts, and when thine end is come, thou shalt find that the reviving odor of this Anointed One will refresh thy soul in death.

But what does the Bible say about the *Fruit* of this TREE OF LIFE? "It bears twelve manner of Fruits, and yields its Fruit every month." This does not mean twelve varieties of fruits and no more. "Twelve" evidently bears reference to the length of the year. It means that the TREE bears, all the year round, fruit adapted for every want, suited to every case and condition, fruit for the early months of childhood and youth, and fruit for the wintry season of old age. "Art thou oppressed with a sense of sin?" says an eminent preacher. "There is pardon on the TREE; take it and be at peace. Art thou thirsting after righteousness? Behold here are clusters which will make thee glad. Eat, and thou shalt find Jesus made unto thee wisdom, righteousness, sanctification, and strength. Is adversity thy condition? Oh, this TREE yields fruit in the cloudy as well as in the sunny day. Yea, it is when the heavens are overcast that its boughs are most thickly laden. And throughout the whole year of our lifetime, its twelve months of spring, summer, autumn, and winter, never is there a day when we can go to the TREE and not find upon it fruit—fruit just suited to the season. And still, when we get to heaven, the fruits will change with the season. They will be the same beneath the cloudless shinings of eternity as amid the bleak winds of time," but be still adapted to our growing capacities and ripened powers.

And the *Leaves*, what of them? They are "for the healing of the nations," says John. Not that the nations will want any healing in heaven, for "the inhabitant shall no more say, I am sick." You observe that the vision with which St. John was favored was not so much of heaven, as of the inhabitants of heaven in their perfected state. And, as He sees this Grand Tree towering, as it were, over the heads of the saved ones, he attributes to it all the salvation and life they have derived from it from first to last; as they do themselves, when they sing, "Worthy is the Lamb that was slain to receive power, and riches, and wisdom, and strength, and honor, and glory, and blessing."

In another aspect He is also a TREE OF LIFE to us; for He says, "I am the TRUE VINE, ye are the branches."

VINE (John 15:1). This parable is memorable, as for other reasons, so because it occurs among our Lord's last words to His disciples. This part of His discourse follows the words, "Arise let us go hence." It would seem, then, to have been spoken out of doors, and during their walk from the upper chamber, where they had partaken of the last supper, to Gethsemane. Perhaps, in their way thither, they had to pass through a vineyard. Sometimes the passengers would have to make their way amidst withered leaves and severed branches, gathered in bundles to be burned. Thus the spot might have suggested the simile, and the solemn lessons of this parable be rendered all the more impressive by the presence of the illustrations made use of. Is it not as if the Master had said, "Look at the Vine, with its substantial stem and unfailing store of living sap, and behold a symbol of Me. Look at each verdant branch, loaded more or less with clusters of fruit, and see an illustration of such as believe in Me. You observe it is not merely *tied* to the stem. It *grows out of it,* and is fed by it. And only by virtue of that living connection can there be any fruit. So there can be no spiritual life without living union with Me, and the continual taking in of grace from Me as the branch takes in the sap. And look at those withered boughs, which strew the path, and see a melancholy picture of such as do not really believe in Me. If anyone seeks to be religious in other ways he will turn out no better than the dead bough, which the vinedresser takes away as only fit to be burned. Severed from Me, he must remain devoid of a single pulse of life. Therefore see to this one thing, Abide in me. Only so can ye live and bear fruit at all." Is not this a fair statement of the Master's own account of this central doctrine?

Let us see what follows from this union. Imagine a dry stick picked up in a garden. Suppose the gardener knew the secret of grafting such dead things as that into a vine, so as to make it part of the very tree. We are aware he could not do this, but suppose he could and did. From that moment there would set in a flow of sap, which would impart life and make the dry stick green and flourishing. It has been taken into partnership with the vine, and the vine pours into it as much as it can receive of the vital juice. And now it puts on the very nature of the tree, and soon there come forth congenial buds and leaves and tender blossom, and by-and-by rich clusters of grapes.

Just that which the gardener is supposed to do with the dry stick, the almighty Husbandman does with you who are worse than a dry stick—wild and degenerate. The moment you truly receive Christ you are *in* Him, so that virtue flows into your heart continually. For now you are in full communion with Him. All that there is in Him, which you can make use of and are ready to receive, is at your service. His righteousness is yours; you are a partaker of the Divine nature and of His filial relationship to the Father, by virtue of His Sonship. You are capable of bearing fruit, which you never were before—"more fruit"—"much fruit," such as the Divine Husbandman looks for.

Why doth a branch bring forth fruit exactly according to the character of the tree? Because its union involves a most intimate oneness with the parent stock, and perfect assimilation thereto. How is it, for instance, that some Christian people are not patient, but fretful or irascible? We presume not to think they are pretenders. But there must be something wrong somewhere. What should we say of some particular branch of a vine—old enough quite, and large enough to bear good store of fruit—if it were to remain barren, or only produce wild grapes? Should we not conclude that some defect or disease prevents the proper inflow of the sap.

So must it be here. If we are Christians, and yet our spirit and temper are not like Christ's, then let us look to it. By some means we must be cutting ourselves off from the source of spiritual life and health. Let us bring the matter before the Great Husbandman; for who, otherwise, can understand his errors? Let us try to institute an examination, asking Him to bring the defect to light. The cause of unfruitfulness may turn out to be a self-dependent spirit, or an undevout life, or a haphazard sort of walk, which, as one says, "though it be the walk of a Christian, is not at all a Christian walk." Disciple of Christ! you must get closer to Him, and grow up into Him. "Whosoever abideth in Him sinneth not." This is not spoken of absolute perfection at all, but of that conquest over sins, which Christ always gives to those who are constantly looking to "Him Who is able to keep them from falling," with a full conviction that they cannot keep themselves.

"For without Me ye can do nothing." *This furnishes no excuse for sloth.* Some might say, "Oh yes, our Lord's words are quite true; I am powerless, yea dead, therefore I will sit still and not attempt anything." But suppose a father were to call his son, and say to him, "My dear boy, I have selected a task which I wish to have done, but I tell you beforehand you will not be able to do it without me." Suppose now the boy were to say, "Then I will not attempt to do it at all." Would that be an acceptable excuse for not taking the task in hand? No, it would only prove him to be a perverse, disobedient child. He could not master the lesson by himself, but no less was it his duty to set about it in dependence upon his father's help.

"For without Me ye can do nothing." *The words afford great encouragement.* A loving caution it is from Him who knoweth our frame. If one man were to bid another to beware not to step on a dangerous plank, not to sail in a leaky vessel, not to trust his weight to a rotten rope, that would indicate a kind interest on the part of the adviser. So when Jesus Christ tells us that without Him we can do nothing, it is that we may not depend on a reed, and so ensure to ourselves a fall. When a fond mother cautions her child in his first attempts to walk, or tells him as she lifts him from his falls, "You are not yet able to go alone, my child, you cannot do without me"—that is not to discourage him, but to induce him to keep by her side, and take hold of her hand, and give heed to her directions so that his attempts may be more successful. Oh, how often we trip like the child, and fall and wound ourselves, for want of habitual dependence on Christ! Oh, believe it, no fond mother watches her offspring more carefully than Jesus His people. His eye is ever on them, not to mark their falls with severity, but to lift them up, and guide them aright, and endear to them the promise of His grace. True, Christian, you can do nothing without Christ. You have no strength at all. What then? You learn to glory in your infirmities, for they bring you acquainted with the strength of Christ. And to be thus poor in spirit is to be rich in faith.

"For without me ye can do nothing." *This language conveys most important instruction.* It shows us the one thing we are to do at all times. We must cling to Christ, nor ever venture to do anything without Him. For that work will be wretchedly done, and end in confusion, which is begun in the spirit of the proud boast, "I can do it without help." Professor Upham cites the example of an experienced Christian, who, whenever he was asked to offer supplication at the prayer meeting, used invariably to begin with the words, "Lord give us a prayer." That was to pray in the right spirit. "As the branch cannot bear fruit of itself, so without Me ye can do nothing."

51

Unspeakable Gift. Water of Life. Witness. Word of God. Wisdom of God. Way. Wall of Fire.

GOD is a most open-handed Giver. What multifarious gifts He is ever distributing among the children of men! Those which are most coveted, such as health, rank, genius, are reserved for the few; and the fortunate possessors are often regarded with envy by those who are not thus distinguished. But the gifts that God distributes more generally, such as reason, health, eyesight, are greater and far more important. What are the former compared with these? And yet the latter are for the most part overlooked or undervalued, and the bountiful Donor receives but scanty thanks. But the most unreasonable treatment is reserved for the greatest of all God's gifts—that Gift which infinitely outweighs all the rest put together. Riches, rank, health, and even life itself, sink into very narrow dimensions when compared with it. Yea, a very competent judge goes so far as to reckon all things but as "dung," so that he might but win this one great GIFT. He uses a very contemptuous comparison indeed, that he may the more enhance its exceeding worth. And this Gift is not like riches and rank, accessible only to the few, but is brought within the reach of all, so that "whosoever will" may claim it. And our Apostle, having secured it for himself and recommended it to others, exclaims, "Thanks be unto God for His 'UNSPEAKABLE GIFT.'"

UNSPEAKABLE GIFT (2 Cor. 9:15). They who have a home and "food convenient," a kind father, a faithful husband, health, safety, should not forget to thank God for all; for words are insufficient to set forth their worth. But the GIFT we now speak of as much transcends them as the mightiest mountain towers above the anthill at his base; or the loftiest cedar above the violets and primroses that grow under its shadow.

The UNSPEAKABLE GIFT! When we look at it, it dazzles our eyes. When we think of it, it swallows up our thoughts; it quite confounds our imagination. There are no comparisons by which we can illustrate it. If we would talk to one another about it, words falter on our lips. If we would offer thanks to God for it, we know not what to say, and "praise sits silent on our tongues." For this UN-SPEAKABLE GIFT, what is it?—Nothing less than God's own Dear Son Who dwelt in His bosom from eternity. "For God so loved the world, that He gave His Only Begotten Son, that whosoever believeth in Him might not perish, but have everlasting life."

The *Motive* that prompted the GIFT is UNSPEAKABLE. Who can describe the love of God? He *so* loved the world. "So" is a little word; but oh the stupendous weight it carries in that sentence! The *Munificence* that marks the GIFT is UNSPEAKABLE; for all the universe cannot supply such another. The *Mercy* which characterizes the GIFT is UNSPEAKABLE; for who can describe the utter baseness of the recipients? And its *cost* is UNSPEAKABLE too; for the WORD must be made flesh, and the Equal Son of God must stoop to suffering and death. Who can utter the greatness of this sacrifice on the part of God? We cannot even imagine the feelings that would rend the heart of a parent called to surrender a beloved child to the hands of cruel murderers. And if *human* emotions, under such circumstances, are indescribable, who shall speak of the *Divine*, when the Father "spared not His own Son but delivered Him up for us all"? But though we cannot gauge the *motive*, nor measure the *munificence*, nor estimate the *mercy*, nor count the *cost* of this UNSPEAKABLE GIFT, we are thankful to say we do perfectly understand how we are to make it our own.

"Indeed!" someone objects, "but surely that sounds very like presumption." But is it so? If you were to stop half a dozen hungry men in the street, and say, "Here, all of you good people, hold out your hands, and I will give you each a piece of money to buy food with"; would you not wonder to hear one of them say, presumptuous for *me* to take the money? Or if one were to make a great feast, and send the crier into the lanes and courts where the poor live, to invite them all to come and partake of it without payment, would any stay away on the plea that they were too poor and unworthy? Nay, I think there would be no such difficulty in such cases. Nor should there be in the other. For God has given us distinctly to understand that we may all receive the UNSPEAKABLE GIFT, and make Jesus Christ our own, and with Him all things we want, pardon and holiness, repentance and a new heart.

Now do not rest in merely believing that these blessings are *for you*, or that they are *already yours* because God hath given them. There was something for the poor people to *do*, though nothing for them to *pay*, in order to secure their part in the feast. They must leave their poverty-stricken homes, and seat themselves at the plentiful board, and thus take each to himself his personal share of the bounty. And this is just what the sinner has to do, and *all* he has to do. He must come to Christ and make personal application. He must embrace the offer, believing in Christ for himself in particular, upon the gospel warrant—"Whosoever will, let him come." And thus he will make that which is, at first, only a GIFT *by grant*, to become to him a GIFT *in possession*. Receive then the UNSPEAKABLE GIFT *now* without loss of time. "The Spirit and the Bride say Come, and let him that is athirst come, and whosoever will, let him take of the WATER OF LIFE freely."

WATER OF LIFE (Rev. 22:17). Some things have been already written, in former pages, of WATER as a Symbol of Christ and of the blessing that He communicates. (See FOUNTAIN, RIVERS, PLACE OF BROAD RIVERS, etc.). A few words must therefore suffice here. Afar off upon the sea is an open boat, tossing up and down on the heaving billows. It contains a little company of sailors, only survivors of a shipwrecked crew. They have been a week or more beating about thus, straining their eyes all the day long, and eagerly scanning the horizon with the vain hope of discerning a friendly ship to which they might signal for assistance. When they first took to the boat, one of them secured a little cask of fresh water. Oh what a treasure was this! And how careful they were over it. But it wasted away, and at last they had to restrict each one to an allowance of a few drops at a time. And soon they reach the bottom of their cask, the end of their precious store. With dejected looks, they share out the last little pittance. The precious store exhausted, they grow wild with raging thirst, and some of them, though warned of the danger, drink from the briny ocean. The salt water renders their thirst ten times more excruciating than before; and, what is worse, the wretched victims become delirious, and with difficulty are restrained from casting themselves into the sea. The rest, more patient and discreet, hold out a little longer, and at last are taken up by a vessel which heaves in sight just in time to save them from death.

That thirsty voyager upon the ocean madly drinking the salt sea—of whom is he a picture? Of *you*, if you have forsaken the Fountain of the WATER OF LIFE, and are drinking waters that poison and inflame; or, to drop the metaphor, if you are living in neglect of the great salvation, and seeking happiness in the things of earth instead of Christ. Once more we warn you of danger, and tell you that you are destroying yourselves. We even hold the cup to your lips and press upon you full drafts of the WATER OF LIFE. Will you still turn from it? What can the world, what can the pleasures of sin do for you? Drink no more the deadly draft. Receive the UNSPEAKABLE GIFT. "Take the WATER OF LIFE freely."—The next Title in the List reads us a similar lesson. God saith of his Son, I have given Him for a

WITNESS TO THE PEOPLE (Isa. 60:4). Our Lord told Pilate, before whom He witnessed a good confession, that He was born to bear witness to the truth. In Revelation 1:5, He is called "the Faithful Witness." Look round and you will see that everywhere the Christ is opposed by some antichrist. The very elect are warned against deception because there are so many antichrists. Wherever the waters of Salvation flow which Christ gives, there are, not far off, waters of death which sin and the world supply. So there is a *False* Witness as well as a FAITHFUL WITNESS. Of both we read in Proverbs 14:25, "A TRUE WITNESS delivereth souls, but a deceitful Witness speaketh lies."

Here and there along the coasts of our island home, there rises a lighthouse, from the lantern of which a bright, unearthly radiance glares forth nightly upon the surrounding darkness. It is where danger threatens that the lofty tower lifts its head, and a Faithful Witness warns the mariner of hidden rocks or treacherous sandbanks hard by; or, with friendly welcome, it lights up the entrance to the secure harbor. And, year after year, when silent night approaches, the punctual monitor kindles afresh its flaming beacon, and seems intent on its sacred work of "delivering souls." One night, a little while ago, a bark, well-mannered and officered, was sailing not far from a harbor where one of these friendly lights is posted. Suddenly a man from the main yards called out, "A light on the port bow!" The captain saw the light, and the ship was steered accordingly. Too late he discovered the fatal error. A light had been mysteriously exhibited for some wicked purpose, in the wrong place; and that false light he had mistaken for the true. In vain they strove to reverse their course. Almost immediately they struck on a dangerous reef, and the gallant ship was wrecked. The "deceitful Witness spoke lies," and lured them to destruction.

Oh how many thus go astray, led by false doctrine, or delusive authorities, or deceitful friends, and do not awake to say, "Is there not a lie in our right hand?" till it is too late to stay the mischief. "Oh," said one on his deathbed, who had been thus beguiled by a false Witness, "I wish I had never read that infidel book; it sowed the seeds of my ruin and has led me to this untimely end." "Ah," said another, directing a fierce glance towards the person to whom he spoke, "It was you that led me astray! Yes, to you I owe my eternal ruin. Begone out of my sight!" "It is awfully dark," breathed another with a shudder, when just about to die— he had treated with neglect the counsels of the Faithful WITNESS—"awfully dark, and my feet seem on the edge of a great gulf. Oh for some—" and he stretched out his hand as if for a guide. "Christ is the only Hope; grasp Him!" whispered one who sat by. "Not for me, not for me." cried the other. "O, I shall fall! I am falling!" and the next moment, with a convulsed frame, he breathed his last.

The True WITNESS who delivereth souls, had they heeded His faithful words, would have saved them from thus making shipwreck of eternal interests. They who follow Him "shall not walk in darkness, but shall have the light of life." We may well trust the WITNESS, for He can make no mistake. His Name is called "THE WORD OF GOD."

WORD OF GOD (Rev. 19:13). This Name "no man knoweth but He Himself" (v. 12). But we may be allowed to say that one reason why He bears this Name evidently is because it is through Him God holds communication with men.

And thus it agrees with modes of expression in the Scripture somewhat similar. For instance, in Genesis 3:8, we read, "They heard the *Voice* of the Lord walking in the garden, in the cool of the day." It is not easy to discover in what sense a voice may be said to "walk"; but if we understand it of the Divine Person called the WORD OF GOD. "Who was in the beginning," the passage is plain. God is a Spirit. He hath no organs answering to our ears, or eyes, or mouth. Yet doth He represent Himself as hearing, seeing, speaking. This seems to be in condescension to our weakness; just as we talk to little children in their own way, using their own childish expressions, in order the better to make ourselves understood. So this Title would appear to be used by the Divine Being. When we want to communicate our thoughts and wishes to one another, we do it by *Word*. Christ, therefore, being the Medium through Whom alone God makes known His will to us and explains His thoughts, is called THE WORD OF GOD. Doubtless this is one reason for the use of this Name. In all ages, it is He Who has been the Great Revealer and Interpreter of God's will; and Who has visited and held communications with men. It was thus "the Word of the Lord came to Abraham in a vision," and talked with him (Gen. 15:1). And might it not have been thus that "the Word of the Lord came to" Jonah, and Nathan, and to others of the prophets? We forget now, however, that it was in "diverse manners" God spake to the fathers. Further into the mystery of this Name, we confess ourselves unable to penetrate. Similar to this is the next Title, "WISDOM OF GOD."

WISDOM OF GOD. This Title is given to Christ in 1 Corinthians 1:24 and in Luke 11:49, 51. He seems to appropriate it to Himself. Again, in Proverbs 8, there are certain things said of Someone, under the name of WISDOM, which have their complete fulfillment only in Christ; and there are words attributed to the same Person that are appropriate only in His lips. He therefore is justly thought to be the Person metaphorically presented under the name of WISDOM. Listen to what WISDOM says—"The Lord possessed Me in the beginning of His ways before His works of old. I was set up from everlasting, from the beginning. Then was I by Him as One brought up with Him; and I was daily His Delight, rejoicing always before Him, rejoicing in the habitable part of the earth; and My delights were with the sons of men." See Proverbs 8:22–31. Read also Colossians 1:15–19. These words lead back our thoughts to a very remote period, before "ever the earth was"; before the firstborn sons of creation were called from their nothingness into happy existence, when the Great Three-in-One did enjoy a universe in Themselves and each other. "We may well confess that over this relation of Father and Son and Holy Spirit, there hangs a sacred veil which none can pierce; for comparisons are wanting, and language is unequal to the weight of such thoughts," and imagination, however daring, unequal to the weight of such conceptions. Yet we seem to have here a momentary gleam of light, illuminating the depths, and "revealing a living, loving God, Who did not need to seek in a created world the object of His love, but found it in the Being like Himself, who is His perfect Image, and in the Co-equal Divine Spirit.

It was not to augment His blessedness that the Great Creator gave existence to other beings; but Infinite Love loved to diffuse itself, and scatter happiness in profusion over a wise creation. And so, by Him Who is the WORD and the WISDOM OF GOD, He made the worlds and all their teeming inhabitants. "And without Him was not anything made that is made." By Him all things consist. By Him are all things reconciled. And by Him alone Jehovah speaks to the children of men. He is the WORD and WISDOM by Whom God communicates with us. Not only is He God's Way to us, but also He is our Way to God; as He saith, "I AM THE WAY."

WAY (John 14:6). "Good Master," said one, "what shall I do that I may enter into life?" Do? Thou knowest the commandments—do them! Yes, this *was* the WAY, the most ancient and direct WAY; and *is* the WAY still for the unfallen. He that doeth them shall certainly live by them. But who doeth them? Where is the man that doeth all things that are written in the law? Ah! since Adam's failure, none has been able to discover that path. Thousands have made the attempt; but they have only found a flaming sword, turning every way, prohibiting their advance. The holiness and justice of God present an eternal bar to the salvation of any of the sinful children of men by the deeds of the law.

And yet there is a WAY. A new WAY, and a safe and certain WAY it is. Many obstacles there were to the preparation of this WAY; but they are all removed. *Sin* stood there, like an impassable mountain; but before the Great "Restorer of Paths" it became a plain. He made an end of Sin and took it out of the way. *The Law* was there, with its curses and threatenings, brandishing a fiery sword. And *Justice* demanded a penalty so dire that it cost the most precious life in the world to satisfy the claim. Not without the blood of the Victim could we be redeemed from the curse of the Law. So Christ became the WAY; and had He not done all this, there would have never been a WAY at all. But, traveling in the greatness of His strength, He finished the work given Him to do, and has set before us an open door, and unlocked the kingdom of heaven to all believers. But is the WAY so open and so free that no payment, condition, or qualifications at all are required? None. Your payment, your qualifications, would ruin you utterly if you trust in them. You must take the offered grace upon Christ's own terms, without money and without price, or you cannot have it at all.

"I am the WAY," saith He. "Go to the Father in My Name, and ask all you want for My sake; and you shall have all you require and more than you ask. The Father loves me so well that there is no spiritual gift He will deny to this plea. Go therefore! I, even I, am He that saith, 'Whatsoever ye ask the Father in My

Name, I will do it.' Why do you draw back? Do you doubt My word? I am the TRUTH! The AMEN, the TRUE WITNESS cannot lie. Go therefore, plead My promise and speak of My blood. Do you still hesitate? Do you say, Ah, I have no life, no power? Well, I am the LIFE. 'He that believeth in Me, though he were dead, yet shall he live.' My Spirit shall help your infirmities. My grace shall quicken your dead heart, and impart to you life, and power, and salvation."

"I am the WAY." This must be your clue in all later difficulties. Keep fast hold of it, and it will lead you aright through the most intricate paths. Beneath the streets of Rome, and extending to a surprising distance beyond, there is an endless labyrinth of dark passages and caves, where the early Christians used to hide themselves from their persecutors, and where great multitudes of them lie buried. A young artist was once engaged in these catacombs, alone, copying some of the tablets on the sepulchers. After wandering about some time, his lamp went out! Horror well-nigh overcame him, for the darkness was total. "Trying to find his way out, he stumbled to and fro among dead men's bones, and was half choked with the dust of bygone generations. But all his efforts were in vain. The longer he wandered, the more bewildered he grew. Hopeless, he at last flung himself upon the ground. As he fell, providentially, his hand touched something. What was it? Nothing less than a cord, which had been placed as a clue for explorers. He seized it, and carefully holding it in his hand, followed its guidance till it led him to daylight and safety." Imitate that confounded wanderer whenever you become entangled in temptations, or perplexed by difficulties in your religious course. Seize afresh this sacred clue, CHRIST THE WAY; and it will secure your escape from darkness and bewilderment.

And what more shall I say of this wonderful WAY? It is an *Ancient* WAY. A new WAY, indeed, because not the most ancient way of all; but as old at least as the time of Abel. Moses and David walked in this WAY. It is a *Beaten* WAY. Thousands upon thousands have traversed it, young and old, wise and ignorant, sinners of every degree, and it has led them all to heaven. It is an *Easy* WAY. In itself it is so. All difficulties arise from defect of faith. If you have faith, you may say to every mountainous obstacle, Be removed! "All things are possible to him that believeth."—It is a *Good* WAY, "the WAY of holiness." It makes those good who walk in it. "The unclean shall not pass over it." People become righteous the moment they take the first step in it. The WAY is honorable to God and delightful to the wayfarer. It is one of pleasantness and peace. It is a *Living* WAY. It sustains the life and keeps up the spirits of those who walk in it. And once more it is a *Safe* WAY. "No lion shall be there, nor any ravenous beast go up thereon; it shall not be found there." For He who prepared the WAY will be a "WALL OF FIRE," round about the pilgrims who walk therein for their protection and defense.

WALL OF FIRE (Zech. 2:5). The allusion here is to the practice of shepherds in eastern countries and early times, who used every night to enclose their sheep within high walls. And when they were too far from home to do that, they kindled great fires at intervals all around the flock, to deter the wild beasts and frighten them away. And travelers in Africa, and other countries where wild beasts are common, do the same thing now, whenever they sleep at night in their wagons; for lions and tigers, and all wild creatures, have a great dread of fire.

One night a little boy, scarcely more than an infant, was lying on his back in a Caffre's hut before a small fire of dry sticks. Presently a hungry lion came that way; and, looking in at the door, perceived there was something there that would suit his appetite. So in he walked with noiseless tread; and doubtless he would have pounced upon the tempting meal and soon made an end of it, had not the boy, half in play, seized a burning stick, the flaming end of which he thrust against the mouth of the ravenous beast. The lion instantly turned his head and bolted away. And the horrified mother, emerging from an inner chamber, was just in time to discover the retreating lion, and to rejoice in her little one's narrow escape from the jaws of death.

Just thus, Satan "as a roaring lion, walketh about seeking whom he may devour." With stealthy, noiseless tread, he is ever on the watch for prey. Let us be ever on the watch too, and we shall find that prayer, like the flaming brand, will speedily scare him away,

> For Satan trembles when he sees
> The weakest saint upon his knees.

We know the reason why. Because prayer takes hold of the Savior's heart, and immediately gathers around us the protection of His Omnipotence. Straightway the adversary hears the dreaded voice, The Lord rebuke thee! And just as the Caffre infant drove way the lion with his lighted stick, so even a little child may successfully oppose the tempter. "Resist the devil and he will flee." For our God is a WALL OF FIRE round about His people; but a CONSUMING FIRE to all their adversaries.

Of the things that we have spoken on this occasion this is the sum: God hath given us innumerable precious Gifts; but there is among them One so grand, so glorious, so amazing, that we call it, by way of eminence, the

UNSPEAKABLE GIFT. This GIFT is a Grant to the whole world so that "whosoever will" may appropriate it to himself, may have it in possession, may take freely of the

WATER OF LIFE so freely given. Again, this GIFT is given to be a

WITNESS to the people. And what this WITNESS testifies for our instruction and guidance is true and infallible, for His Name is called the

WORD OF GOD. Not true only; but of the highest importance, and mar-velously adapted to our circumstances; for He is also the

WISDOM OF GOD. He is therefore God's Medium of communication to us; and also our Medium of communication with God; for He is the

WAY TO THE FATHER. Wherefore "stand in the ways and see, and ask for the old path, where is the GOOD WAY, and walk therein, and ye shall find rest to your souls." And, once more, to all who walk in this WAY He is a

WALL OF FIRE round about, for their defense and protection.

52

Wonderful. Well-Beloved. Young Child. Zerubbabel.

IT may be few who read these pages have aught to do with pearls, and diamonds, and amethysts. But all may have seen such things. Beautiful they are and rare, and therefore very highly prized. Exquisitely beautiful each one by itself; but their appearance is even more fascinating to the eye, when different kinds of choice gems are set side by side in harmonious combination, as on a regal coronet; or, as of old, on the High Priest's breast, arranged according to the Divine plan. The diamond seems to flash more dazzling light when contrasted with the deep grass-green emerald; and the blue sapphire looks all the more charming when conjoined with the flaming ruby, or the opal with its wondrous play of many colors. The jeweler can add nothing to the intrinsic excellence of these beautiful things. He can only remove what obscures their luster, and choose from gems of varied hue such as will present striking contrasts or pleasing harmonies, and set them in a fitting framework of pure gold. Thus did those inspired workmen, Bezaleel and Aholiab, when they prepared the priestly breastplate. And as Aaron stood in the sunlight, one of the jewels sparkled like a bright flame, and another glowed like a burning coal; one flashed rainbow tints upon the eye of the beholder, while its fellow glistened like a silver star; and bright blue, and pale pink, and delicate amber, shone forth with an enchanting luster from richly chased settings of the most fine gold.

In writing the preceding pages, I have seemed to myself like the jeweler who has before him gems of priceless value, and studies to arrange them suitably, and set them fitly. And I have said, "Would I had the wondrous heaven-inspired skill of those ancient artificers, that I might fix in worthy settings of select words, these jewels more glorious far than theirs, and quite incomparable! Jewels wherewith the heavenly Bridegroom hath adorned Himself, for doth He not wear some of them emblazoned on His vesture and on His thigh? Oh if some angel would guide my faltering pen, and help me to trace lines upon this paper which shall glow, and burn, and glisten so as to arrest even the careless reader, and waken a desire to become personally acquainted with that Fairest One

"Whom eyes have seen or angels known!" But vain was the wish. While we remain on earth our eyes are still "holden." We do but darkly see spiritual truths, as through a glass discolored with the dingy smoke of sin and ignorance; and even when we think we get a glimpse of the Divine glory, we strive but ineffectually to convey the impression to others. But, as I have still added one to another, I have prayed for myself and my readers, that our eyes may be opened; and that the Holy Spirit may shed down bright beams of light upon the sacred Symbols, so that we may see the glory of God as it shines in them. But, even judging of Him by the imperfect ideas we have thus attained, is He not well called

WONDERFUL (Isa. 9:6). Wonderful is the exquisite perfection and delicate finish of the tiny gnat which, as she dances in the sunbeam, waves her gauzy wings of azure, emerald, and gold. Wonderful is the great orb of day, fountain of light and heat. Wonderful is heaven's high arch, studded with glittering worlds of light. Wonderful is your outward frame and mine: and much more Wonderful the immortal soul which resides therein. All is Wonderful, wherever we fix our gaze. "Great and marvelous are Thy works, Lord God Almighty!" But passing WONDERFUL is He to Whose Name these pages are dedicated.

> God in the Person of His Son
> Hath all His mightiest works outdone.

Here "the commonplaces of admiration fail us altogether—words are inadequate." When I was a boy, the visitor at St. Paul's Cathedral used to read on the organ-screen, an inscription in Latin to this effect: "Dost thou say, Where is the monument of the man who built this hallowed fane? *Circumspice!*—look around!" And surely this one word would suffice us for a comment on the expressive appellation now under consideration. Look around! Let the multitudinous array of sacred Symbols through which we have been passing (as through long aisles of stately pillars in a temple) speak for themselves, without further remark of ours. But yet we cannot resist the temptation to gather up some few rays of the diffused glory, as into a lens, that we may see a little way further into the wonders of this "WONDERFUL." Dwell a moment on the following points:

First. *He is* WONDERFUL *as a* MAN. As to His *Birth*, unique, unlike all others; for who, save Himself, was miraculously born of a virgin? As to His *Life*, separate from everyone else; for where shall one be found, but He, unstained with sin! As to His *Death*, alone and unapproachable; for it was a sacrificial death. Upon everyone else there rests the weight of his own sins; but upon this Man "was laid the iniquity of us all." He is indeed a *Nonsuch*. There never was such a man before Him; there never will be after Him. "He is the FIRST and He is the LAST."

Second. *He is more* WONDERFUL *still as* GOD. As Man, He was created; as God, He is the Creator. He only hath immortality. There is no searching of His nature. It is higher than heaven; it is deeper than hell. He is past finding out, and will ever remain the Infinite Unknown. "Who hath gathered the wind in His fists? Who hath established all the ends of the earth? What is His Name, and what is His Son's Name, if thou canst tell?"—But must we not stop here? What can be more WONDERFUL than God? Why this—

Third. *He is* WONDERFUL *as* GOD *and* MAN *combined in One Person.* It is and ever shall be the Wonder of wonders. Well may the Prophet call His name WON-DERFUL, who is the Mighty God and the Child Given, the Everlasting Father and the Son Born, the Equal and Fellow of God and the Brother and Companion of man!

Fourth. *And is there not something more* WONDERFUL *still?* For was He not the most WONDERFUL *Sufferer* that ever was? All that apostate angels, after long ages of experience, were capable of inflicting in their most malignant cunning and defiant hatred—all that Roman barbarity, violence, and scorn could invent—all that Jewish treachery, malice, and despite could think of—were ruthlessly emptied into the overflowing cup of suffering which He was to drink. But was this the whole of the dreadful compound? Not so. The most bitter ingredients of all, none can analyze. His heart alone knew their full bitterness.

> We may not know, we cannot tell
> What pains He had to bear.

We ponder with deepest and most reverent scrutiny the solemn words, "It hath pleased the Lord to bruise Him; He hath put Him to grief"; and the prayer extorted from Him by "exceeding sorrow" in Gethsemane, "O my Father, if it be possible, let this cup pass from Me"; and the overwhelming surprise (as it were) expressed in the remonstrance on the cross, "My God, My God, why hast Thou forsaken Me?" But in vain we try to dive into the mystery. "When I thought to know this, it was too painful for me"; too difficult to search into, too WONDER-FUL to find out. We can only gaze, and admire, and bow down before all this great mystery of Godliness required to make you truly blessed—and withal, One who is waiting to reciprocate your love, and longing to bless you forever and ever!

And now, having almost reached the termination of our Alphabet, we, for the first time, encounter a letter that affords us no contribution; unless indeed, we regard its very form, X, as suggesting the symbol of the cross. On this many might be disposed to lay some stress. But leaving to those who value them, their idolized crucifixes and symbolic forms, for ourselves, we prefer the spirit to the letter, and the living, speaking doctrine to the dumb sign. The Apostle's boast was, "We preach Christ Crucified"; we read nothing of the lifting up of crosses and consecrated wafers for adoration. Those who call themselves successors of the Apostles should surely substantiate their claims, by working in the Apostles' spirit and after their example. To us there seems some danger lest the devotees' faith should stop at the crucifix, and never reach that which it symbolizes. Yet we will not, on the other hand, forget that it is quite possible to substitute a mere belief of the doctrine of "Christ Crucified," for a living faith in Him; and that the last error is as fatal as the first; for a formal creed will avail no more than a wooden cross. May we be saved not only from false doctrines and ruinous heresies, but from a hollow profession and a lifeless faith!

Christ Crucified! A brief and well-worn phrase; but what an infinite meaning it embodies! It expresses the cardinal doctrine of the Christian religion, and the most stupendous event in the history of earth, and heaven, and the universe.

Christ Crucified! Whose heart doth not heave with unutterable emotions, whenever he tries to fasten upon and realize the amazing fact! The Co-equal Son of God, impaled on a cross! It seems a thing scarcely to be believed. Thought staggers; reason is confounded; till faith, coming to our aid, affirms the great Mystery of Godliness, and the prostrate spirit worships and adores.

Christ Crucified! What ignominy and shame were there! What anguish intolerable of bleeding wounds, and parching thirst, and burning fever! What a pressure of inconceivable mental distress from sin's appalling load, and the hiding of God's countenance! forcing from the lips of the Majestic Sufferer the bitter cry, "My God! My God! why has Thou forsaken Me?" Surely it was that deadly sorrow, that preternatural agony (and not so much the pain of crucifixion), which, after a few hours of continuance, brought Him to the dust of death; for Pilate marveled that He died so soon, and both the thieves, who suffered with Him, lived some time after He had given up the ghost.

That great sight was "seen of angels." And, says Toplady, "If ever sorrow was in heaven; if ever the harps of the blessed were suspended, silent and unstrung on the willows of dismay; if ever angels ceased to praise, and glorified souls forgot to sing; if ever the harmony of the sky was exchanged for lamentation and mourning—it must have been during the six tremendous hours, (such hours as nature never saw before, nor will ever see again), that the dying Jesus hung on the tree."

> Seraphs and saints, with drooping wings
> Cease their harmonious breath;
> No sweet celestial music rings,
> While Jesus yields to death.
>
> Their harps are mute—not one faint string
> Thrills to the strange surprise;
> But all in silence mourn their King,
> Who loves, and bleeds, and dies.

And that great sight was seen of devils—doubtless with malignant delight. For surely, if ever there was joy in hell, its gloomy caverns echoed on that occasion to the mutual congratulations of exulting fiends.

And it was seen of men also. And from the tree of shame and agony the dying Savior seemed to say, "Is it nothing to you, all ye that pass by? Behold, and see if there be any sorrow like unto My sorrow, which is done unto Me, wherewith the Lord hath afflicted Me in the day of His fierce anger." With what various impressions *they* regarded it, we must not stay to inquire. But how are *we* affected by it? Is the gospel history a familiar tale which makes no more impression upon us than a baseless myth? Or do we make it the sole foundation of our hope? And, as sinners needing the atonement then accomplished, do we commit ourselves to the Lord Jesus by "an act of total and eternal trust"? And in the spirit of entire unreserved consecration say:

> When I survey the wondrous cross
>> On which the Prince of Glory died,
> My richest gain I count but loss,
>> And pour contempt on all my pride.

> Forbid it, Lord, that I should boast,
>> Save in the death of Christ my God;
> All the vain things that charm me most,
>> I sacrifice them in His blood.

> Were the whole realm of nature mine,
>> That were a present far too small;
> Love so amazing, so divine,
>> Demands my soul, my life, my all.

The next letter furnishes, at least, one subject. It is a designation of the Infant Savior, which occurs nine times in one chapter.

YOUNG CHILD (Matt. 2:13). And this takes us to Bethlehem. We have been there before, again and again, in the course of our inquiries; and a most attractive place it is. But, referring the reader to what has already been written on Babe, Ruler, Root, etc., we will now only stay long enough just to notice an incident which took place there when our Lord was a very "Young Child," with a lesson or two drawn therefrom.

There it was in yonder dark cave, fit only for the purpose for which it was designed, the stabling of asses, and camels, and oxen, "far from home and friends, among strangers all to busy to care for her, that Mary brought forth her firstborn Son, and having swathed him with her own weak hands, laid him in a manger." But our visit is at a subsequent period. Some three or four weeks have passed away; and the stir is over, and the visitors who crowded the little village and filled the "Khan" to overflowing, have all taken their departure. A cavalcade stops at the gate. The travelers have come from a far distant country. They are Magi, most likely from Persia. Princes they are as to rank. And one camel, more carefully loaded than the rest, bears treasures on his back; gold, frankincense, and myrrh. These wise men belong to the class of priests and teachers by whom astronomy was particularly cultivated. In their nightly watches they had discovered a new star. This star, by some instruction imparted to them from heaven, they were led to connect with the birth of a great Deliverer, in Whom all the world had an interest, though He was to be born "King of the Jews."

Guided by the new star, they set out on their long journey to pay homage to this Great King. Somewhere on the road they lost sight of the star. What were they to do? Where could they get tidings of the YOUNG CHILD? Where, but in the King's palace, at Jerusalem? So to Jerusalem they come, eagerly inquiring of the crafty Herod, "Where is He that is born King of the Jews?" They cannot find Him there. But they learn from the doctors of the temple, that ancient prophecy had fixed upon Bethlehem as the place of His birth. So to Bethlehem they go. But how shall they know the house? In this difficulty, their miraculous star reappears, and, to their great joy, hovers over "the house where the YOUNG CHILD lay" (Matt. 2:9).

We know very little of their interview; one verse comprising all the particulars. They saw Him Whom they had traveled so far to behold, in His mother's arms, and, very likely, wondered much at the poverty that surrounded them. But that did not hinder them from yielding Him the profoundest homage. They fell down and worshiped Him, and, having paid their devotions, they opened their treasures, and laid their gifts at His feet. Gold, frankincense, and myrrh, are spoken of as "the rarest productions of the East, an offering such as any monarch might have had presented to him by the ambassadors of a foreign prince." This is the offering of the "wise men" to the King of the Jews. And, having finished their errand, they take their departure into their own country. Thus did "Gentiles come to His light, and kings to the brightness of His rising."

"These Magi," as Dr. Hanna observes, "in the welcome with which they greeted the Savior of the World, were the representatives of the Gentile races, as the shepherds and Simeon and Anna were of the Jewish people. Let us then," he goes on to say, "rightly follow up what they did in our name. First they worshiped, and then they gave the best and richest things they had. First, then, let us give our hearts to the Lord; and then, the heart once given, the hand will not grudge the richest thing it can hold, nor the best service it can render."

But to such as are sincerely seeking after Christ, we say, Is there not much to instruct and encourage you in the example of those travelers, who came so far to find the infant Savior? You complain of fresh difficulties ever arising in your path. No sooner is one surmounted than another presents itself, more formidable than the former. You meet with forbidding coldness in some from whom you reasonably expected helpful sympathy. When you first set out, you thought (like the burdened pilgrim in Bunyan) you could discern across the wide plain a light, which glimmered as a star, to indicate your path. But that light has become dim, or it has quite vanished, and you grope in darkness. And did not the Magi meet with similar discouragements? But they went on, still feeling their way, till at last success crowned their perseverance. Oh! be not intimidated by delays and difficulties! "The vision is yet for an appointed time; it will surely come; it will not tarry." Only follow on to know the Lord, for everyone that seeketh findeth.

There may be many who shall stand before the great white throne, who will be able to say, "Indeed, Lord, we did go a long way to find Christ. We did take great pains in religion. And it was only because we met with so many disappointments that we relinquished the search, and went back unto the world." Ah! they might have gone far, very far, but it was not far enough, and in vain they will now say, "Open to us." But among all the millions collected together at the last day, there will not be found one who will be able to say, "Lord, Thou knowest I sought Thee sorrowing all my life. I called on Thee with cries and tears constantly. Many a time I did cast my soul at Thy feet. I did even thrust it into Thy hands that it might be saved. But Thou wouldst not save me. I did come to Thee, but Thou didst cast me out." Oh no! no! none shall tell such a tale as that; for "everyone that asketh receiveth, and to him that knocketh, the door shall be opened."

But now the time is come for us to add the last stone to our building. It is a personal type of our Lord.

ZERUBBABEL (Zech. 4:7–9). This prince of the Jews was of the royal house of David. He is supposed to be the "Sheshbazzar" to whom Cyrus delivered the 5,000 gold and silver vessels that had been taken from the temple. Returning with these, and 50,000 liberated captives, he laid the foundations of the second temple, and in twenty years completed it in spite of all opposition. And herein he is a type of Jesus Christ. The church is the temple—individual believers are the stones, "lively stones,"—and Christ is the ZERUBBABEL. His hands laid the foundation, He appoints every stone to its place, and He also will complete it. The Author of our faith will be its Finisher.

The building has occupied a long time already, and it will take a great while yet to finish. Sometimes its progress has seemed at a stand, but only seemed. Faith could always "see the plummet in the hands of ZERUBBABEL and rejoice," saying, with holy scorn of every obstruction, however formidable, "Who art thou, O great mountain? Before ZERUBBABEL thou shalt become a plain." And still in our day, the temple riseth, and groweth; and doth continually shame the dark forebodings of its friends, and laugh to scorn the insolent predictions of its foes, and defy all the efforts of the gates of hell to hinder its completion. Let patience have its perfect work. For God's works, as well as man's, are for the most part progressive, and show too as men count slackness.

This work—the preparation of all these pages—has gone on towards completion, step by step. I have written here a little and there a little. I have added line to line and sentence to sentence. It has been interrupted again and again, but still as often resumed, till now, the same hand that wrote the opening sentence, is about to be employed in tracing the last. Just so is it with the spiritual temple. There will come a day when it shall be said, It is done! The wheels of time roll on towards the destined goal, and, in their mighty revolutions, they will at length bring the inevitable hour. As surely as we have come to the last of our long series, so surely, at the appointed time, the last stone "will be brought forth with shoutings of Grace! Grace!"—the number of the elect will be completed—the stupendous temple be finished, and this outward world, which is but the scaffolding set up to help forward the erection, will be taken to pieces and burned up.

Then shall the great design of the Architect stand forth before the eyes of the admiring universe in all its perfect beauty and completeness. While it is still only "growing to a holy temple in the Lord," the carved work of its delicate tracery, the exquisite finish of its moldings, the magnitude of its proportions, are shrouded in obscurity and covered with dust. But it shall then shine forth in all the luster of its surpassing grandeur and celestial beauty—"having the glory of God, its light like unto a stone most precious, even like a jasper stone clear as crystal."

In the august day of days, when the Savior shall see of the travail of His soul and be satisfied with the perfected work of His hands, and shall present the church "faultless before the presence of the Father's glory with exceeding joy," where will you and I be found? Must we wait till then to ascertain our place? Nay, it may be determined now. God refers the question to us, so that each one may answer it for himself. He says, "Why will ye die? Look unto Me! and be ye saved." This language means nothing unless it means you may choose your part, and either become a lively stone in the living temple of the church of Christ, or remain among the refuse in outer darkness forever. Yes, each one of us may either be "a pillar in the temple of God, polished after the similitude of a palace," to go no more out forever and ever; or, gathered with the reprobate, and the rejected, and all things that offend, be swept away into utter destruction. Dread alternative! Which will you choose?

Here, having arrived at the Omega of my Alphabet, I lay aside my pen. The subject is one of superlative excellence and transcendent interest. I have tried to find out acceptable words wherewith to utter something not altogether unbecoming the greatness of the Prince of Princes, something not unsuitable to the infinite love of the Friend of Sinners. It is not for want of effort, nor through neglect of prayer to the Great Father of Lights, that I have not fully attained my end, but because my powers are altogether unequal to the sublime theme. If, in my endeavor to express some great truth, which has only faintly revealed itself out of "depths of burning light," I have used expressions inappropriate or unworthy, may the error be forgiven! What man, or angel even, can worthily set forth that Name which "none knoweth but He Himself" Who weareth it? The highest thoughts and best words must ever be altogether beneath Him, Whom cherubim and seraphim do but imperfectly know and inadequately extol. O Thou indulgent Master! Whose searching eye scans our every failure, but Whose loving heart makes allowance for our every infirmity, permit me to lay at Thy feet this humble contribution to Thy praise, craving forgiveness for my imperfect words, and imploring Thy blessing on the work of my hands, notwithstanding its meanness.

A Classified List of the Names of Christ

Titles Pertaining to Deity:

All and in All, Almighty, Alpha and Omega, Ancient of Days, Beginning and End, Blessed and Upright, Creator, Everlasting Father, Faithful Creator, Former of All Things, God, Highest, Holy One, I Am That I Am (Ejah), Immortal, Incorruptible, Invisible, Jehovah-Jah, Jehovah-Jireh, Jehovah-Nissi, Jehovah-Shalom, King of Kings, Lord God Omnipotent, Lord God, Lord of All, Lord of Glory, Lord of Hosts, Lord of Lords, Lord of the Whole Earth, Maker, Mighty God, Mighty One, Most Mighty, Only Wise God, Preserver of Men, True God.

Titles Peculiar to Sonship:

Brightness of the Father's Glory, Dear Son, Delight, Elect, Express Image of the Father, Image of the Invisible God, Only Begotten, Son of God, Son of the Blessed, Son of the Highest.

Official Titles:

Amen, Angel, Anointed, Apostle, Arm of the Lord, Author and Finisher of Our Faith, Author of Eternal Salvation, Christ, Governor among the Nations, Governor of His People Israel, Head of All Principality, Head of the Body, Head over All Things, High Priest, Hope of Israel, Immanuel, King of Glory, King of Israel, King of Saints, King of the Jews, Lawgiver, Lord Both of the Dead and Living, Lord from Heaven, Lord of Peace, Lord of the Sabbath, Mediator, Merciful and Faithful High Priest, Messenger of the Covenant, Messiah, Minister of the Circumcision, My King, Our Hope, Priest, Prince and Savior, Prince of Life, Prince of Peace, Prince of Princes, Prophet, Redeemer, Ruler in Israel, Savior, Shiloh, Word.

Titles Characteristic and Descriptive:

Altogether Lovely, Anointed with the Holy Ghost, Beloved, Called, Chosen, Confidence, Consecrated, Consolation of Israel, Desire of All Nations, Despised and Rejected, End of the Law, Equal with God, Eternal Life, Fairer Than the Children of Men, Faithful and True, First-Born of Every Creature, Glory, Help, Just, Life, Lord Our Righteousness, Love, Lowly, Mighty to Save, Peace, Power of God, Precious, Quickening Spirit, Redemption, Resurrection, Rich unto All That Call upon Him, Righteousness, Salvation, Strength, Truth, Well-Beloved, Wisdom, Wonderful.

Titles Derived from Social Distinctions and Occupations:

Advocate, Carpenter, Chief Shepherd, Comforter, Counselor, Daysman, Deliverer, Example, Faithful Witness, Forerunner, Friend, Good Shepherd, Great Shepherd of the Sheep, Guest, Guide, Heir, Intercessor, Interpreter, Judge, Keeper, Leader, Master, Nazarene, Physician, Rabbi, Refiner and Purifier, Servant, Shepherd and Bishop of Souls, Sower, Surety, Teacher, Testator, Witness.

Titles Derived from Human Relationships:

Babe, Bridegroom, Brother, Child, First-Begotten, First-Born, Husband, Jesus, Man, Man of God's Right Hand, Man of Sorrows, Man That Is My Fellow, Offspring of David, Second Man, Seed of the Woman, Son of David, Son of Man, Son, Young Child.

Symbols Derived from Architecture:

Ark, Corner Stone, Dwelling-Place, Foundation, Habitation, Head of the Corner, House of Defense, Living Stone, Sanctuary, Wall of Fire.

Symbols Derived from the Firmament:

Bright and Morning Star, Day Spring, Day-Star, Dew, Light of the Morning, Light of the World, Morning Star, Star of Jacob, Star, Sun.

Symbols Derived from the Earth and Its Elements:

Covert from the Tempest, Fountain of Living Waters, Fountain Opened for Sin, Hiding-Place from the Wind, Place of Broad Rivers and Streams, Rain and Showers, Refuge from the Storm, Rivers of Water, Rock of Ages, Rock of Offense, Shade Upon Thy Right Hand, Shadow from the Heat, Shadow of a Great Rock, Stone of Stumbling, Water of Life.

Symbols Derived from the Plant World:

Apple-Tree, Branch, Bread, First-Fruits, Fruit of the Earth, Goodly Cedar, Lily of the Valley, Lord of the Harvest, Manna, Myrrh and Camphire, Plant of Renown, Rod Out of the Stem of Jesse, Root of David, Root Out of a Dry Ground, Rose of Sharon, Tender Plant, Tree of Life, Vine.

Symbols Derived from the Animal World:

Horn of Salvation, Lamb of God, Lion of Judah, Lamb in the Midst of the Throne, Lamb Slain.

Symbols Derived from Military Terms:

Breaker, Captain of Salvation, Captain of the Lord's Host, Chief Among Ten Thousand (Standard Bearer), Commander, Defense, Ensign, Fortress, Man of War, Michael, Polished Shaft, Shield, Stronghold, Sword.

Typical Persons:

Aaron, Adam, David, Eliakim, Joseph, Joshua the Captain, Joshua the High Priest, Melchizedek, Moses, Solomon, Zerubbabel.

Symbolical Things:

Anchor, Covenant, Crown and Diadem, Door, Exceeding Great Reward, Pearl of Great Price, Portion, Ransom, Scepter, Treasure, Unspeakable Gift, Way.

Types Connected with Hebrew Institutions and Rituals:

Altar, Brazen Serpent, City of Refuge, Mercy Seat, Minister of the Sanctuary, Offering for Sin, Passover, Peace Offering, Propitiation, Sacrifice, Scapegoat, Tabernacle, Temple.